Footprint

Alan Murphy, Julius Honnor and
Fourth edition

Next morning we were up at dawn to see the magnificent view of the main Cordillera of the Andes sharply defined in the crackling frosty atmosphere, a chain of jagged snow-covered peaks dominated by the white masses of Sorata, Huayapotosi, Murarata and Illimani – seventy miles of unbroken snow.

Col PH Fawcett, Exploration Fawcett (Century, 1988)

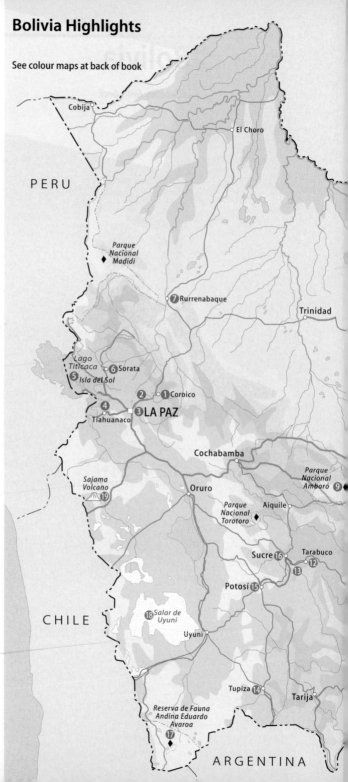

1 Coroico
Town of swimming pools and relaxation in the Yungas, between the mountains and the jungle

2 World's most dangerous road
Downhill adrenaline rush on two wheels

3 La Paz markets
Shop in the multicoloured indigenous areas of La Paz

4 Tiahuanaco
Remnants and artefacts of a giant ancient civilization

5 Lake Titicaca
Crystal clear waters and skies and the stunning holy island of Isla del Sol

6 Sorata
Beautiful centre for trekking and biking in the Cordillera Real

7 Rurrenabaque
Catch a tour upriver to Madidi or downriver to the pampas

8 Noel Kempff Mercado
Remote wilderness that inspired Conan Doyle's *Lost World*

9 Amboró
At the convergence of the Amazon, the Andes and the plains

10 Samaipata
Eastern outpost of the Inca Empire with ruins, waterfalls and the Che Guevara trail nearby

Bolivia Highlights

See colour maps at back of book

PERU

Cobija

El Choro

Parque Nacional Madidi

7 Rurrenabaque

Trinidad

Lago Titicaca

6 Sorata

5 *Isla del Sol*

2 **1** Coroico

4
Tiahuanaco

3 LA PAZ

Cochabamba

Sajama Volcano **19**

Oruro

Parque Nacional Amboró **9**

Aiquile

Parque Nacional Torotoro

Sucre **16** Tarabuco

13

12

CHILE

18 *Salar de Uyuni*

Uyuni

Potosí **15**

Tupiza **14**

Tarija

Reserva de Fauna Andina Eduardo Avaroa

17

ARGENTINA

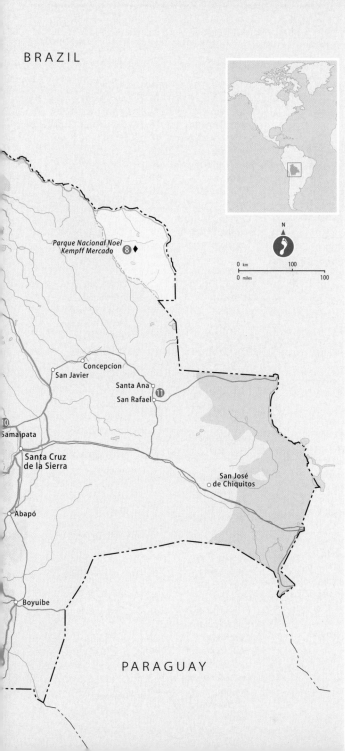

BRAZIL

Parque Nacional Noel
Kempff Mercado **⑧** ◆

Concepción
San Javier
Santa Ana **⑪**
San Rafael

⑩
Samaipata

Santa Cruz
de la Sierra

Abapó

San José
de Chiquitos

Boyuibe

PARAGUAY

N

0 km   100
0 miles   100

⑪ Jesuit Missions
Six surviving Jesuit
Mission churches in
UNESCO world
heritage villages

⑫ Tarabuco
Colourful Sunday
market with
helmets and
traditional clothes

⑬ Cal Orcko
Take the Dino
Truck to see some
of the 5,000
paleontological
footprints

⑭ Tupiza
Fertile southern
town near Butch
Cassidy and the
Sundance Kid
territory

⑮ Potosí
Poverty and silver
mines in the
highest city in
the world

⑯ Sucre
Attractive
whitewashed
colonial city
with a lively
student culture

**⑰ Eduardo
Avaroa**
Weirdly coloured
lakes, flamingoes,
volcanoes and
surreal rocky
landscapes

⑱ Salar de Uyuni
Vast white salt plain
with stunning
views and cactus-
covered islands

⑲ Sajama
Bolivia's highest
peak has a park
with thermal
springs, geysers
and glaciers

4

Contents

5

On the sacred waters of Lake Titicaca life has barely changed since the days of the Incas.

The Amazon

Background

Footnotes

Inside covers

Bright lights, big city
The lights of La Paz rise up the edges of its bowl-shaped valley so that, at a certain point of evening, it's hard to tell where the houses end and the stars begin.

A foot in the door

Bolivia is weird. Everything about this land-locked country in the heart of the continent is out of the ordinary – like the surreal inventions of Gabriel García Márquez. It's the kind of place where you start taking the strangest things for granted. Like sitting next to an alligator on a bus or waiting behind a group of piglets at the check-in desk. In Bolivia, it seems, pigs really do fly.

The minute you arrive in La Paz, you realize this is no ordinary place. The airport, at 4,000 m above sea level, is the highest in the world. So high, in fact, that incoming flights almost have to ascend to land. The capital is one giant street market, where indigenous women in bowler hats and voluminous skirts will sell you everything you could possibly need – from a pair of black market designer jeans to a dried llama foetus. These grotesque objects are burned and used along with incense, bits of wool, grease and coca leaves in white magic ceremonies and to rid houses of evil spirits.

Bolivia's strange curiosities are not confined to La Paz. Only a few hours north is Lake Titicaca, the highest navigable lake in the world, which gave birth to the Inca empire. In the southwest of the country, near a train graveyard, is the Salar de Uyuni, the world's highest and largest salt lake – 12,000 sq km of blinding white nothingness. South of the salt lake is a Salvador Dalí landscape of deserts, volcanoes, bizarre rock formations, bubbling geysers, peculiar green plants and a blood-red lake filled with flamingoes. East from here is a hollow silver mountain, dinosaur footprints, villages where annual festivities revolve around ritualized fights and national parks that are so isolated they're almost impossible to get to.

10 Trouble brewing

Just over a century ago a diplomatic crisis was brewing in La Paz over a glass of chicha, a fermented wheat beer. The new British ambassador to Bolivia had made the mistake of sneering at the local drink when served by the incumbent dictator. As punishment, he was led through the streets of the capital strapped naked to a donkey. When news reached London, Queen Victoria was not amused. She demanded a map of South America, drew a cross through the country and declared "Bolivia does not exist!" Though relations between Bolivia and the outside world have improved since then, on a global economic level, Bolivia might as well not exist. It remains the second poorest country in Latin America (after Haiti). On the bleak Altiplano, where the vast majority of the rural population live, infant mortality rates are disgracefully high, most people die before the age of 50 and the average family income is a little over US$10 a month.

A sight for snore eyes
From lush and green to barren and red, Bolivia's landscapes are almost always interesting, though less often comfortable places to sleep.

Popular uprising

It's a situation that is only exacerbated by the fact that Bolivia's main export earner gets right up the noses of its First World counterparts. Once the world's third largest grower of coca (which is used to produce cocaine), Bolivia has been forced to destroy 90% of the plant, leading to increased unemployment, even higher levels of poverty and frequent and violent clashes between angry coca farmers and the military. Adding fuel to the fire of resistance are proposals to export the country's huge natural gas resources – via Bolivia's neighbour and nemesis, Chile. The massive uprising that the original plans provoked drove the US-backed president, Gonzalo Sánchez de Lozada, from power and into exile. His successor, Carlos Mesa, has faced further road-blocks and protests. In 2004 he narrowly won a referendum on watered-down proposals by offering many concessions to the country's large indigenous population.

Yungas at heart
Clouds shift across the fertile hillsides of the sub-tropical Yungas, one of Bolivia's main coca-growing areas.

1	*Two wheels are often better than four in the rutted roads in the Amazon basin.* ▸▸ *See page 356.*

2	*Spongy in appearance, but rock hard, yareta is a form of green lichen, strangely out of place amidst the brown terrain of the far southwest.* ▸▸ *See page 199.*

3	*La Paz's Sagárnaga is a multicoloured bazaar of bags, hats, scarves and pieces of material.* ▸▸ *See page 104.*

4	*Despite being one of the most biodiverse places on the planet, Bolivia also has plenty of areas where very little grows except cacti.* ▸▸ *See page 202.*

5	*Four thousand feet up, Bolivia's many-hued lakes are home to an enormous population of flamingoes.* ▸▸ *See page 210.*

6	*In the waters of the country's low-lying wetlands, anaconda could be anywhere.* ▸▸ *See page 358.*

7	*Bolivia's ancient civilizations, such as the Tiahuanacans and the Incas ruled much of the country in pre-Columbian times.* ▸▸ *See page 140.*

8	*Potosí's silver is long gone, leaving most of the city's colonial buildings as a fading testament.* ▸▸ *See page 236.*

9	*A pampas tour from Rurrenabaque gives you the opportunity to come face-to-face with large numbers of small monkeys.* ▸▸ *See page 358.*

10	*The waters and islands of Lake Titicaca are still considered sacred by those that live around its shores.* ▸▸ *See page 146.*

11	*Bowler-hatted and colourfully skirted, the altiplano women are an iconic image of Bolivia.* ▸▸ *See page 104.*

12	*The so-called Arbol de Piedra (Rock Tree) is just one of many weird and wonderful wind-whipped shapes in the otherworldly landscapes of the desert near Laguna Colorada.* ▸▸ *See page 207.*

13

14 **Going downhill fast**

With close to a thousand peaks over 5,000m, Bolivia is often referred to as the Tibet of South America, but most of the country is tropical lowlands – a vast green carpet stretching east to the Brazilian border. Threading their way down from the high Andes to the steaming jungles is a series of twisting, tortuous roads. One of these, from La Paz down to sub-tropical Coroico, is officially the world's most dangerous road. Barrelling down this 70-km dirt track is like sliding down a giant helter-skelter – without the safety barrier. Those of a nervous disposition can opt for the less scary route to the lovely Yungas town of Chulumani, where the ancestors of African slaves work in the surrounding coca plantations, and where your tour guide, hotel-keeper or waiter is likely to be a descendent of Nazi war criminals who fled here to escape justice after the Second World War.

Jungle spells

Down in the Bolivian Amazon and Eastern Lowlands, the romantic image of the jungle found on the glossy pages of National Geographic is alive and well. Only three hours from the city of Santa Cruz is Parque Nacional Amboró, a beautiful wilderness encompassing three distinct major ecosystems – the Amazon River Basin, the foothills of the Andes and the Chaco Plain – and 11 life zones. The park is home to thousands of animal, bird, plant and insect species, and is reputed to contain more butterflies than anywhere else on earth.

Just outside Uyuni, on the edge of a vast salt lake, is a very strange graveyard, where the country's clapped out rolling stock rests in pieces.

The little town of Coroico, in the sub-tropical Yungas at the end of the death-defying road from La Paz, is a popular weekend retreat for those needing to escape the Andean chill.

Andes to Amazon

In the remote eastern corner of the country is Parque Nacional Noel Kempff Mercado, with virgin rainforest, spectacular waterfalls and strange, eerie-looking mountains. One of these, the vast Huanchaco Plateau, is said to have been the inspiration for Conan Doyle's 'Lost World'. In the far north of the country, near the popular gringo tour town of Rurrenabaque, is Madidi, possibly the most biodiverse place on the planet. Within its borders is a vast range of habitats, from the freezing Andean peaks of the Cordillera Apolobamba, through cold, elfin and dry forest, to steaming tropical jungle. This primary Amazonian watershed contains a pristine ecosystem that is home to nearly half of all the mammals known in the Western Hemisphere and provides shelter for more than a third of the known amphibian and bird species in the New World. Here also are the wonderful Chalalán and Mapajo eco-lodges, arguably the finest examples of community/indigenous ecotourism in all of Latin America.

Nature calls

From ancient Tihuanaco and the Incas, through colonial times to the 21st century, people have made some impressive scratches on the surface of Bolivia but they may begin to seem relatively insignificant as you trek through the world's highest forest on the slopes of the Sajama volcano, trek amongst wild vicuñas in the Cordillera Apolobamba, or glide in silence down the Beni river with only fireflies for company.

Park and hide
Noel Kempff Mercado National Park attracts few visitors and those who do make it here have all the wonders of nature to themselves.

Essentials

○ Footprint features

Planning your trip

Where to go

Bolívia's major attraction for tourists is its wild natural beauty. Much of the country lies off the beaten track; a vast wilderness waiting to be explored and appreciated. This isolation, of course, brings its own problems as many parts of the country are remote and can be reached only with a lot of time and effort.

Seeing a lot of Bolivia by bus in the space of a few weeks is a forlorn hope. If time is limited, then you'll need to fly in order to see more than the capital and its immediate surroundings. In saying that, however, many of the country's most popular tourist sights are within a few hours' drive from La Paz.

One week

If you have only a week in the country, your best bet is probably to stay within reach of the capital. The centre of **La Paz** is fairly small and manageable and easy to explore on foot in a couple of days. There are several worthwhile museums to visit and the warren of streets running west uphill off the Prado – the city's main thoroughfare – lead you into a strange and fascinating world.

Several interesting trips can be made from La Paz, including the ruins of the great pre-Incan city of **Tiahuanaco**. Further north you reach the shores of **Lake Titicaca**. From the attractive little town of **Copacabana** you can visit the beautiful **Isla del Sol** (Island of the Sun), site of the Inca creation legend. Three hours away on a spectacular and terrifying road is the little town of **Coroico**, a popular resort in the sub-tropical valleys of the **Yungas** and the perfect place to escape the Andean chill. Northeast of the lake, four hours from La Paz is the much-loved town of **Sorata**, surrounded by beautiful mountain scenery, and a major climbing and trekking centre. La Paz is also the jumping-off point for some of Bolivia's best **treks**, over the cordillera and down to the warm Yungas valleys.

Two weeks

A fortnight gives you the possibility of getting further away from La Paz. Two of the most popular trips are to the **Amazon Basin** and the **Southern Altiplano**, one of the most remote corners of Bolivia and also one of the most fascinating. Old colonial **Potosí** is probably the most interesting of all Bolivia's cities and a visit to its former silver mines is a must. Nearby is the country's official capital, **Sucre**, a real gem of colonial architecture. Southwest from Potosí is Uyuni, the starting point for a three- to four-day tour to the **Salar de Uyuni**, a vast, blindingly white salt lake and one of the most spectacular sights in the entire country. South of the Salar, near the Chilean border, are deserts, volcanoes and multi-coloured soda lakes teeming with flamingoes.

Those visiting Bolivia during the dry season – April to October – would be strongly advised not to miss a trip to **Rurrenabaque**, from where you can take a jungle or pampas tour and experience the country's amazing diversity of wildlife. Rurrenabaque is a gruelling 18-hour bus journey from La Paz, or a short flight. Those braving the bus trip can break the journey at Coroico in the Yungas. Rurre is also the starting point for the fantastic **Chalalán Eco-lodge**. Ecotourism with a capital 'E', it stands in the **Madidi National Park**, one of Bolivia's newest protected areas, and one which boasts a greater biodiversity than anywhere else on earth.

For those with more time, there are many other attractions in the south. You could visit the vineyards of **Tarija**, the footprints of dinosaurs or the graves of Wild West outlaws Butch Cassidy and The Sundance Kid amid the stunning eroded landscape of **Tupiza**. You could easily spend a week just exploring the many weaving villages around Sucre and Potosí. Climbers have the added attraction of the **Sajama National Park**, near the Chilean border, which includes Bolivia's highest peak.

Essentials Planning your trip

The eastern part of Bolivia is probably the least visited, except by those heading to or from Brazil. **Cochabamba**, seven hours east of La Paz by bus, is one of the country's less interesting cities but offers a pleasant respite from the cold Altiplano nights and hot, humid lowland days. The nearby national park of **Torotoro** is stunning, full of fossils, dinosaur footprints, canyons, caves and waterfalls – a real must for those who like to get off the beaten track. Further east, around 10 hours by bus, the relatively prosperous city of **Santa Cruz** serves as a base for one of Bolivia's most beautiful national parks, **Amboró**, the archaeological site of **Samaipata**, or a tour of the **Jesuit mission towns**. You would need 10 days at the very least to do justice to all of these. Further east, on the border with Brazil, the **Bolivian Pantanal** is now opening up to tourism and offers great wildlife-watching, as does the stunning but difficult to reach **Noel Kempff Mercado National Park** further north. Both of these would require at least another two weeks to visit.

When to go

The main consideration for travellers regarding the weather is how it affects the condition of Bolivia's notoriously poor roads. The rainy season is November to March and some roads into the tropical lowlands may be impassable at this time. These are also the months when mosquitos and other biting insects are at their worst, so this is not a good time to visit the jungle.

As for the rest of the country, the Altiplano does not receive much rain, so timing is not so crucial here, although hiking trails can get very muddy during the wet season. During the winter months of June and July, nights tend to be clearer but even colder than at other times. These are the best months to visit the Salar de Uyuni, as the salt lake is even more impressive under clear blue skies.

June to August, while offering the best weather conditions, are also the busiest months. At this time some of the better hotels will be full and tour prices will be higher. Furthermore, many of the best festivals happen during the rainy season, such as Carnival and Holy Week.

Trekkers and climbers should, of course, pay closer attention to local weather conditions. General guidelines can be found under climbing, in the Sports and activities section on page 49 and also in the Hiking, biking and climbing chapter.

Tour operators

In the UK and Ireland

Condor Journeys and Adventures, 2 Ferry Bank, Colintraive, Argyll, PA22 3AR, T01700-841318, www.condorjourneys-adventures.com.
Cox & Kings Travel, Gordon House, 10 Greencoat Pl, London, T0207-873 5001, cox.kings@coxandkings. co.uk.
Dragoman, Camp Green, Kenton Rd, Debenham, Suffolk, IP14 6LA, T01728-861133, www.dragoman.co.uk.
Hayes & Jarvis, 152 King St, London, W6 0QU, T0870-898 9890.
Journey Latin America, 12-13 Heathfield Terr, Chiswick, London, W4 4JE, T0208-747 8315;

and 2nd floor, Barton Arcade, Deansgate, Manchester M3 2BH, T0161-8321441, www.journeylatinamerica.co.uk.
Last Frontiers, Fleet Marston Farm, Aylesbury, Bucks, HP18 0PZ, T01296-653000, F01296-658651, www.lastfrontiers.com.
Magic of Bolivia, 182 Westbourne Grove, London W11 2RH, T0207-221 7310, F0207-727 8756, www.bolivia.co.uk.
Passage to South America, Fovant Mews, 12 Noyna Rd, London, SW17 7PH, T0208-767 8989.
South American Experience, 47 Causton St, Pimlico, London, SW1P 4AT, T0207-976 5511, F020-7976 6908, www.southamerican experience.co.uk.

Steppes Latin Adventure, 51 Castle St, Cirencester, Glos, T01285-885333, www.steppeslatinamerica.co.uk.
Travelbag Adventures, 15 Turk St, Alton, GU34 1AG, T01420-541007, www.travelbag-adventures.com.

In Europe

South American Tours, Hanauer Landstrasse 208-216, D-60314, Germany, T+4969405897-0, sat.fre@t-online.de.

In North America

eXito, 5699 Miles Av, Oakland, CA 94618, T1-800-655 4053, (worldwide) T510-655 4566, www.wonderlink.com/exito.
Explore Bolivia, Colorado, T877-708 8810, F303-545 6239, www.explorebolivia.com. One of the very best ecotourism outfits, based in the US.
GAP Adventures, 19 Duncan St, Toronto, Ontario, M5H 3H1, T1-800-465 5600 (in the UK: T01373-858956), www.gap.ca.
Ladatco Tours, T1-800-327 6162, www.ladatco.com.
South American Explorers, www.SAexplorers.org, T800-274 0568.

In South America

America Tours, Edif Av, P.B No 9, Av 16 de Julio 1490, La Paz, T02-237 4204, www.america-ecotours.com. Run by a local ecotourism specialist.
Bala Tours, Av Santa Cruz, Rurrenabaque, T591-3892 2527, www.balatours.com. Jungle and pampas tours.
Asociación Hombre y Naturaleza, T03-762 8699, www.hombreynaturaleza. com. Non-profitmaking association working for sustainable development.
Boliviajes, Samaipata, T03-944 6082, www.lavispera.org. Perhaps Bolivia's best tour operator, offering dozens of customizable tours and treks and familiar with every region.

Essentials Planning your trip

Crillon Tours Bolivia, La Paz, T02-233 7533, F02-211 6482, www.titicaca.com. The country's largest and oldest operator, they are especially good for group tours to the Altiplano, Yungas, and Lake Titicaca.
Fremen Tours, La Paz, T02-2417062, F02-2417327, www.andes-amazonia.com. Experts in the Andes and the Amazon basin, as well as central Bolivia.

Queen Travel, La Paz, T02-277 3609, www.boliviatravel-queen.com. Cultural tourism, nature and adventure trips.
Southtrip, head office in Buenos Aires, www.southtrip.com. Bespoke travel.
Vicuñita Tours, Cochabamba, T04-452 0194, F04-452 0196, vicunitatours@ yahoo.com. Tours around Cochabamba, the Beni, the Chapare, and Santa Cruz.

Finding out more

For **national parks information** contact: Sistema Nacional de Areas Protegidas (SERNAP), Edif El Cóndor, piso 13-15, C Batallón, Colorados 24, La Paz, T02-231 6077, F02-231 6230.
For a list of **useful books** on Bolivia, see p426.
Amerispan Unlimited, PO Box 40007, Philadelphia, PA 19106-0007, T1-800-879 6640 (USA & Canada), worldwide T215-751-1100, www.amerispan.com. Information on travel and language schools is available from Amerispan, one of several language school brokers in the USA.
South American Explorers (SAE), offices in Lima and Quito and also in Cusco – the most convenient for Bolivia, cuscoclub@ saexplorers.org. An excellent source of information. Books, maps and travel-planning services are available at the US office: 126 Indian Creek Rd, Ithaca, NY 14850, USA T800-274 0568, www.saexplorers.org.
The Latin American Travel Advisor, T1-888-215 9511 (toll free), www.amerispan.com/lata. Complete travel information service offering up-to-date, detailed and reliable information on 17 South and Central American countries.

Useful websites

www.bolivia-tourism.com Has inform-ation on Bolivian cities, pre-Columbian cultures, folk dances, festivals and more. It is in Spanish, English and German.
www.boliviaweb.com A comprehensive site with many links.
www.bolivian.com Another comprehensive tourist guide to the country.
www.boliviangeographic.com Magazine about Bolivia on adventure sports and tourism off the beaten track.
www.gorp.com/gorp/location/latamer/ bolivia/basic_b.htm Overview of the coun-try, with detailed information on Amboró, Las Yungas, Choro Trail and jungle trips.
www.omnimap.com Pay to get 50:000 topographical maps and many more.
www.planeta.com Guide to eco-travel and ecology in South America.

Language → *For a list of useful words and phrases, see page 430.*

The official language in Bolivia is Spanish, though many in the countryside may only speak their native Aymara and Quechua languages, or a confusing mix of the two. Outside La Paz and the main tourist centres, travelling with some knowledge of Spanish is a major help. **Amerispan** ① *PO Box 58129, Philadelphia, PA 19102, T1-800-879 6640, www.amerispan.com*, run language courses throughout Latin America.

Disabled travellers

As in most Latin American countries, facilities for disabled travellers are severely lacking. Wheelchair ramps are a rare luxury and getting a wheelchair into a bathroom or toilet is practically impossible except for at some of the more modern hotels. Pavements are often in a poor state of repair or crowded with street vendors requiring passers-by to brave the passing traffic. Disabled Bolivians obviously have to cope with these problems, mainly having to rely on the help of others to get around.

But of course only a minority of disabled people are wheelchair-bound and it is now widely acknowledged that disabilities do not stop you from enjoying a great holiday. Some travel companies are beginning to specialize in exciting holidays, tailor-made for individuals depending on their level of disability. General holiday and travel information for disabled people in the UK is provided by the **Holiday Care Service** ① *T01293-774535*, and **Tripscope** ① *T08457-585641*. For those with access to the internet, a Global Access – Disabled Travel Network Site is www.geocities.com /Paris/1502. It is dedicated to providing travel information for 'disabled adventurers' and includes a number of reviews and tips from members of the public. You might also want to read *Nothing Ventured*, edited by Alison Walsh (Harper Collins), which gives personal accounts of journeys by disabled travellers, plus advice and listings.

Gay and lesbian travellers

Bolivia, as is the case in most of Latin America, is not particularly liberal in its attitudes to gays and lesbians. Even in La Paz, people are fairly conservative, and more so in rural areas. It is therefore wise to adapt to this and avoid provoking a reaction. For more information on tours for gay and lesbian travellers, check out the website of the **International Gay and Lesbian Travel Association** ① *T1-800-448-8556 (toll free), www.iglta.org*. Also helpful are **www.outtraveller.com** and **www.travelgay.net**.

Student travellers

If you are in full-time education you will be entitled to an **International Student Identity Card (ISIC)**, which is distributed by student travel offices and travel agencies. The ISIC gives you special prices on all forms of transport and access to a variety of other concessions and services. Student cards must carry a photograph if they are to be of any use for discounts. To find the location of your nearest ISIC office check www.aboutistc.org. If you're planning to study in Bolivia for a long period, make every effort to get a student visa in advance.

Travelling with children

People contemplating overland travel in Bolivia with children should remember that a lot of time can be spent waiting for buses, trains, and especially for aeroplanes. You should take reading material with you. Food can be a problem if the children are not adaptable. It is easier to take biscuits, drinks, bread etc with you on longer trips than to rely on meal stops. Make sure you pack that favourite toy. Nothing beats a GameBoy – unless it's two GameBoys and a link cable.

Travel with children can bring you into closer contact with Bolivian families and, generally, presents no special problems – in fact the path is often smoother for families. Officials tend to be more amenable where children are concerned and pleased if your child knows a little Spanish. Even thieves and pickpockets may have some of the traditional respect for families, and leave you alone because of it.

On all long-distance buses you pay for each seat, and there are no reduced fares if the children occupy a seat each. For shorter trips it is cheaper, if less comfortable, to seat small children on your knee. Often there are spare seats which children can occupy after tickets have been collected. On city and local excursion buses, small children generally do not pay a fare, but are not entitled to a seat when paying customers are standing. On sightseeing tours you should always bargain for a family rate – often children can go free. All civil airlines charge half for children under 12, but some military services don't, or have younger age limits.

In all hotels try to negotiate family rates. If charges are per person, insist that two children will occupy one bed. You can almost always get a reduction at cheaper hotels. Occasionally you will be refused a room in a hotel that is "unsuitable".

Women travellers

You should be aware that unaccompanied Western women will be subject to close scrutiny and exceptional curiosity. Don't be unduly scared – or flattered. Unless actively avoiding foreigners like yourself, don't go too far from the beaten track; there is a very definite 'gringo trail' which you can join, or follow, if seeking company. Avoid arriving anywhere after dark. Remember that for a single woman a taxi at night can be as dangerous as wandering around alone. If you accept a social invitation, make sure that someone knows the address and the time you left. Ask if you can bring a friend (even if you do not). A good rule is always to act with confidence, as though you know where you are going, even if you do not. Someone who looks lost is more likely to attract unwanted attention. Do not tell strangers where you are staying.

Working in Bolivia

Getting a work visa is easy – just marry a Bolivian. Alternatively, you can get stuck in a bureaucratic maze. But be patient: it does actually work and there is far less bribery involved than you probably imagine. You will need to start a couple of weeks before your tourist visa runs out. There is a US$1.50 per day fine for exceeding your stay. For more information on arranging work permits, visas and immigration in South America, contact **Jobs Abroad** ⓘ *Worldwide House, Broad St, Port Ramsgate, Kent, CT11 8NQ*. For information on voluntary work projects worldwide, visit www.voluntarywork.org.

Before you travel

Visas and immigration

Few nationalities require more than a valid passport to visit Bolivia. Citizens of almost all Western European, North and South American countries, Australia and New Zealand only need a passport to enter. Irish nationals have had problems entering the country and should enquire with the Bolivian embassy before departure. On entry, you will be given a tourist card entitling you to a 30-day stay in the country but ask for a 90-day stamp which avoids the hassle of having to extend later. Immigration officers are becoming less inclined to give these out but you never know your luck.

Among those countries whose nationals require a visa and must gain authorization from the Bolivian Ministry of Foreign Affairs (which can take three to five weeks) are: Bangladesh, China, Egypt, Haiti, India, Indonesia, Iran, Iraq, Ireland, Jordan, Kuwait, Laos, Lebanon, Libya, Malaysia, North Korea, Oman, Pakistan, Palestine, Saudi Arabia, Singapore, Syria, Taiwan, Thailand, Tunisia, Vietnam and Yemen. Those countries which require a visa but not authorization are: Croatia, the Czech Republic, Cuba, Hungary, South Korea, Malta, Mexico, Panama, Romania, Slovenia and Venezuela. This takes one to two working days. Nationals of African countries, the rest of Asia, former Yugoslavia and former Soviet Union countries should make special enquiries as the Bolivian government had yet to decide if they needed visas at the time of going to press. The cost of a visa varies from nationality to nationality.

Visas (or permit to stay) can be renewed at any Migración office for up to 90 days; you should not pay any money to extend your visas. If an immigration office refuses to stamp your passport without payment you may be better off waiting until you arrive at the next town with an immigration office. Although you will have to pay a fine for overstaying your visa, it could be cheaper than the amount requested. After three months, further renewal is at the discretion of the immigration officer. If refused, leave the country and return. On arrival ensure that visas and passports are stamped with the correct date of entry or this can lead to 'fines' later. If you outstay your visa the current fine is US$1.50 per day. Business visitors (unless passing through as tourists) are required to obtain a visa from a Bolivian consulate. This costs £35 (or equivalent); applicants should check all requirements and regulations on length of stay and extensions in advance.

It is your responsibility to ensure that your passport is stamped in and out when you cross frontiers. The absence of entry and exit stamps can cause serious difficulties. Seek out the proper migration offices if the stamping process is not carried out as you cross. Also, do not lose your entry card, as replacing one causes a lot of trouble, and possibly expense. Citizens of countries which oblige visitors to have a visa can expect more delays and problems at border crossings.

Embassies

Australia 74 Pitt St, Level 6, Sydney N.S.W. 2000, T02-923 51858.
Austria Waaggasse 10/4 A-1040 Wien, T43-1-587 4675 or 586 6800, F43-1- 586 6880.
Belgium & Luxembourg 176 Av Louise, Bte 6 1050 Brussels, T32-2-647 2718, F32-2-647 4782.

Canada 130 Albert St, Suite 416 Ottawa, Ontario, KIP SG4, T1-613-236 5730, F1-613-236 8237.
Denmark Amaliegade 16 C 1256 Copenhagen, T45-33-124900, F45-33-124903.
France 12 Av du President Kennedy 75016 Paris, T01-452 78435, F01-452 58623.
Germany Konstantinstrasse 16, D5300, Bonn 2, T0228-362 038.

Israel P.O. Box 2823 90805 Mevasseret Zion, T972-2-533 5195, F972-2-533 5196.
Italy Vía Brenta 2A Int. 18, 2o piso 00198 Rome, T39-6-884 1001, F39-6-884 0740.
Japan Kowa No 38 Building, Room 804 4-12-24, Nishi Azabu Minato-Ku, Tokyo 106, T81-3-349 95441, F81-3-349 95443.
Netherlands Nassaulaan 5 2514 JS, The Hague, T31-70-361 6707, F31-70-362 0039.
New Zealand 74 Pitt St. Level 6, Sydney N.S.W. 2000, T02-923 51858.
Spain C Velázquez No. 20 - 7o piso 28001 Madrid, T34-1-578-0835, F34-1-577 3946; Av. República Argentina 22-A, 3º 41011, Seville, T34-954-27 7788, F34-954-27 5928.

Sweden Sodra Kungsvagen 60 181 32 Lidingo, Stockholm, T46-8-731 5830, F46-8-767 6311.
Switzerland c/o United Nations and other international organizations in Geneva, T41-22-731 2725, F41-22-738 0022.
UK 106 Eaton Sq, London SW1W 9AD, T0207-235 4248, F0207-235 1286.
USA 3014 Massachusetts Av, NW Washington DC 20008, T1-202-483 4410, F1-202-328 3712; 211 East 43 Rd St - Suite 702, New York, NY 10017, T1-212-499 7401 , F1-212-687 0532.

Customs

Duty-free imports 200 cigarettes, 50 cigars and 450 g of tobacco. Also one opened bottle of alcoholic drink.

Vaccinations

You should be inoculated against typhoid, and you'll need a yellow fever vaccination when visiting Santa Cruz or the Eastern Lowlands. Two British tourists who had lost their yellow fever certificates were involved in a random bus check en route to Villa Tunari. Their options were to turn back or to be re-inoculated with the same needle used on their fellow passengers. Needless to say they spent several hours on the roadside waiting for a bus going back to Cochabamba. A yellow fever certificate, at least 10 days old, is officially required for leaving and entering the country from Brazil. Hepatitis is widespread so vaccination against Hepatitis A is a very good idea. See Health, page 51.

What to take

Everybody has their own preferences, but listed here are those most often mentioned. These include an inflatable travel pillow for neck support and strong shoes (remember that footwear over 9½ English size, or 42 European size, is difficult to find in Bolivia). You should also take waterproof clothing and waterproof treatment for leather footwear and wax earplugs, which are vital for long bus trips or noisy hotels. Also important are flip-flops or similar, which can be worn in showers to avoid athlete's foot, and a sheet sleeping-bag to avoid sleeping on filthy sheets in cheap hotels. Always take more money and fewer clothes than you think you'll need on your trip.

Other useful things to take with you include: a clothes line, a nailbrush, a vacuum flask, a water bottle, a universal bath- and basin-plug of the flanged type that will fit any waste-pipe (or improvise one from a sheet of thick rubber), string, electrical insulating tape, a Swiss Army knife, an alarm clock for those early-morning bus departures, candles (for frequent power cuts), a torch/flashlight, pocket mirror, pocket calculator, an adaptor, a padlock for the doors of the cheapest hotels (or for tent zip if camping).

A list of useful medicines and health-related items is given at the end of the Health section. To these might be added some lip salve with sun protection, and pre-moistened wipes (such as 'Wet Ones'). Always carry toilet paper, which is especially important on long bus trips. Contact lens wearers should note that lens solution can be difficult to find in Bolivia. Ask for it in a chemist/pharmacy, rather than an optician's.

Insurance

Always take out travel insurance before you set off and read the small print carefully. Check that the policy covers the activities you intend or may end up doing. Also check exactly what your medical cover includes (for example, ambulance, helicopter rescue or emergency flights back home). Also check the payment protocol. You may have to cough up first (literally) before the insurance company reimburses you. It is always best to dig out all the receipts for expensive personal effects like jewellery or cameras. Take photos of these items and note down all serial numbers.

You are advised to shop around. STA Travel and other reputable student travel organisations offer good value policies. Young travellers from North America can try the **International Student Insurance Service (ISIS)**, which is available through **STA Travel** ① *T1-800-777 0112, www.sta-travel.com*. Other recommended travel insurance companies in North America include: **Travel Guard** ① *T1-800-826 1300, www.noelgroup.com*; **Access America** ① *T1-800-284 8300*; **Travel Insurance Services** ① *T1-800-937 1387*, and **Travel Assistance International** ① *T1-800-821 2828*. Older travellers should note that some companies will not cover people over 65 years old, or may charge higher premiums. The best policies for older travellers (UK) are offered by **Age Concern** ① *T01883-346964*.

Money

Currency
The unit of currency is the **boliviano** (Bs), and the exchange rate has been relatively stable in recent years at around 8 Bs to the US$. The boliviano is divided into 100 centavos. There are notes for 200, 100, 50, 20, 10, and 5 bolivianos, coins of 2 and 1 boliviano and 50, 20 and 10 centavos. Expensive items, including hotel rooms, are often quoted in US dollars. Note that it is almost impossible to buy dollars at points of exit when leaving or to change bolivianos in other countries.

Make sure you always have small change as changing high denomination notes can be very difficult. Small change is often given in forms other than money: for example cigarettes or sweets.

Exchange
Changing dollars presents no problems. Sterling and other currencies are not recommended. Better rates and lower commissions can usually be obtained for dollars. As in many other South American countries, notes are only accepted if they are in excellent, if not perfect condition. It is very difficult to change 100-dollar bills; even some banks will not accept them. If you are travelling on the cheap it is essential to keep in funds; watch weekends and public holidays carefully and never run out of local currency, especially when making trips into the interior.

Traveller's cheques are not widely accepted outside of La Paz and a few other main cities (where rates are generally not as good as in the capital). The better hotels will normally change traveller's cheques for their guests (often at a rather poor rate).

The easiest way to stay in funds while travelling is by using a **credit/debit card** to withdraw money at ATMs. La Paz airport is blessed with one *Enlace* dispenser which accepts all major credit and debit cards. Check expiry dates on all your cards before you leave. If travelling for a long time, consider a direct debit to clear your account regularly. Do not rely on one card, in case of loss. If you do lose a card, immediately contact the 24-hour helpline of the issuer in your home country (keep this number safe).

For purchases, credit cards of the Visa and Mastercard (Eurocard, Access) groups, American Express (Amex), Carte Blanche and Diners Club can be used. Visa is most widely accepted. For the location of Visa ATMs check www.visalatam.com; for Mastercard www.mastercard.com; for American Express www.americanexpress.com; for Western Union agents www.westernunion.com.

Cost of living and travelling

Tourists from Europe and North America, and indeed from many other South American countries, will find Bolivia a cheap country to visit. Food, accommodation and transport are not expensive. Budget travellers can get by on US$30 a day (especially if you are a pair travelling together), without enduring any hardship. For a basic hotel expect to pay US$3-5 per person, while breakfast can cost as little as US$1-2 and a cheap lunch, or *almuerzo*, costs from US$1-2.50. Although Bolivia is cheaper than most South American countries for visitors, it can be expensive for its inhabitants, many of whom have to scrape a living on as little as US$60 per month. Rents, electrical appliances, some clothing, and especially toiletries and medicines, are highly priced.

Getting there

Air

The busiest times of year are from 7 December to 15 January and 10 July to 10 September. If you intend travelling during these times, book as far ahead as possible. From February to May and September to November special offers may be available. Those flying with **Lloyd Aero Boliviano (LAB)** can buy a 30-day air pass. If you're delayed at an airport or have a transfer wait, you can pay around US$10-25 to enter the first-class lounge, and in exchange you get free coffee, croissants, juice, papers, a shower and some peace.

From UK, Ireland and Europe There are no direct flights from Europe to La Paz. Those wishing to fly to Bolivia from Europe have to go to Lima, São Paulo, Rio de Janeiro, Buenos Aires or Miami for connections to La Paz. Flights from Miami also go to Santa Cruz. It is generally cheaper to fly from London rather than a point in Europe to Latin American destinations. Fares vary between airlines, destinations and according to time of year. Check with an agency for the best deal for when you wish to travel. For a return flight London-La Paz during the high season, expect to pay around US$1,100-1,200, and during the low season around US$900-1,000.

From North America American Airlines ① T1-800-433 7300, *www.american air.com*, and **LAB** fly from Miami daily to La Paz and Santa Cruz. **Continental Airlines** ① T1-800-231 0856, *www.flycontinental.com*, fly from Miami to Santa Cruz three times weekly.

From Australia and New Zealand There are no direct flights from down under. You will have to get an onward flight from London or the USA to reach the country. **Aerolíneas Argentinas**, *www.aerolineas.com.ar*, offer flights from London to Sydney via Buenos Aires for around US$900 and from Buenos Aires to Auckland and Sydney for around US$650.

From South America There are flights to Bolivia from the capitals of all South American countries, as well as Rio de Janeiro and São Paolo, Brazil. There are also six flights a week from Cusco to La Paz with **LAB** and **Aero Continente**, and regular flights from Arica and Iquique in Chile, besides those from Santiago. Many international flights call at Santa Cruz and/or Cochabamba as well as, or instead of, La Paz. **LAB** flies from Manaus in Brazil to Santa Cruz.

Circle fares and open jaws With open jaws you fly into one point and return from another, having travelled by other means at your expense between the two 'jaws'. These can work out as great value for money.

Discount travel agents

UK and Ireland
STA Travel, 86 Old Brompton Rd, London SW7 3LQ, T0870-160 0599, www.statravel.co.uk. Have 65 other branches in the UK, including many university campuses. Specialists in low-cost student/youth flights and tours, also good for student IDs and insurance.
Trailfinders, 194 Kensington High St, London, W8 7RG, T0207-938 3939. They also have other branches in London, as well as in Birmingham, Bristol, Cambridge, Glasgow, Manchester, Newcastle, Dublin and Belfast.

North America
Air Brokers International, 685 Market St, Suite 400, San Francisco, CA94105, T01-800-883 3273, www.airbrokers.com. Consolidator and specialist on RTW and Circle Pacific tickets.
Discount Airfares Worldwide On-Line, www.etn.nl/discount.htm. A hub of consolidator and discount agent links.

Essentials Getting there

STA Travel, 5900 Wiltshire Blvd, Suite 2110, Los Angeles, CA 90036, 1-800-781 4040, www.sta-travel.com. Also branches in New York, San Francisco, Boston, Miami, Chicago, Seattle and Washington DC.

Travel CUTS, in all major Canadian cities and on university and college campuses, T1-866-246 9762, www.travelcuts.com. Specialist in student discount fares, IDs and other travel services. Also in California, USA.

Travelocity, www.travelocity.com. Online consolidator.

Australia and New Zealand
Flight Centre, with offices throughout Australia and other countries. In Australia call T133 133 or www.flightcentre.com.au.
STA Travel, T1300-360960, www.statravel. com.au; 208 Swanston St, Melbourne, VIC 3000, T03-9639 0599. In NZ: 130 Cuba St,

PO Box 6604, Wellington, T04-385 0561, cuba@statravel.co.nz. Also in major towns and university campuses.
Travel.com.au T02-9249 6000, outside Sydney, T1300-130482.
NB Using the web for booking flights, hotels and other services directly is becoming an increasingly popular way of making holiday reservations. You can make some good deals this way. Be aware, though, that cutting out the travel agents is denying yourself the experience that they can give, not just in terms of the best flights to suit your itinerary, but also advice on documents, insurance and other matters before you set out, safety, routes, lodging and times of year to travel. A reputable agent will also be bonded to give you some protection if arrangements collapse while you are travelling.

Touching down

Airport information

The main arrival point is El Alto (sometimes known as JFK) airport in La Paz. It's at over 4,000 m, so visitors will have to take precautions against altitude sickness (see page 53). For details of airport facilities and transport to the city centre, see the La Paz chapter. Some flights also arrive at Santa Cruz. Departure tax on all international flights is US$25, payable in dollars or bolivianos. You will not be allowed to go through to departures without this.

Tourist information

Tourism is under the control of the Dirección Nacional De Turismo, Edificio Ballivián, piso 18, Calle Mercado, La Paz, T02-236 7463. Details of tourist information offices within Bolivia are given under Ins and outs sections under the respective towns and cities, though services vary from place to place and can be described as adequate at best.

Local customs and laws

People in the highlands may not be the friendliest and most open people in the world, but they are polite and courteous. A smile, a greeting and a few friendly words in Spanish will go a long way to endearing you to the local people, and generally making your trip easier and more enjoyable.

Remember that politeness – even a little ceremoniousness – is much appreciated. You should be prepared to shake hands, as this is much more common in Latin

! Touching down

→ **Emergency services** T911 (police T110, ambulance T118, fire T119).
→ **IDD code** +591.
→ **Directory enquiries** T104.
→ **Official time** GMT-4 hours.
→ **Official languages** Spanish, Quechua, Aymara.
→ **Business hours** Normally 0900-1200 (sometimes 1230 in La Paz), and 1400-1800 (sometimes 1900 in La Paz). Saturday is a half day. Opening and closing in the afternoon are several hours later in the provinces. Government offices are closed on Saturday. Banks open 0900-1200, 1400-1630, but are closed on Saturday.
→ **Voltage and plugs** 110 or 220 voltage. Sockets usually accept both continental European (round) and American (flat) 2-pin plugs.
→ **Weights and measures** Metric.

America than in Europe or North America. Always say "Buenos días" (until midday) or "Buenas tardes" and wait for a reply before proceeding further. Always remember that the traveller from abroad has enjoyed greater advantages in life than most Bolivian minor officials, and should be friendly and courteous. Never be impatient, and try to maintain a sense of humour when confronted with mind-numbing bureaucracy.

Most Bolivians are disorderly queuers. In commercial transactions (buying a meal, goods in a shop, etc) politeness should be accompanied by firmness, and always ask the price first. Politeness should also be extended to street traders; saying "No, gracias" with a smile is better than an arrogant dismissal.

Also note that Latin Americans, especially officials, are very document-minded, and Bolivians are no exception. You should always carry your passport in a safe place about your person or, if not going far, leave it in the hotel safe. Keeping photocopies of essential documents, including your flight ticket, and some additional passport-sized photographs, is recommended.

Never give children money or sweets. Their parents often spend the whole day working for less than their kids earn begging. This only encourages more begging, and helps create a generation of kids with no education, no way of making a living and a belief that gringos are nothing more than a dollar piggy bank to be dipped into at will. It's a better idea to give books, pens, toothbrushes, soap and the like to the schools and orphanages, or play a game with the kids instead.

Most Bolivians, if they can afford it, devote great care to their clothes and appearance; it is appreciated if visitors do likewise. How you dress is mostly how people will judge you. Buying clothing locally can help you to look less like a tourist. Visitors to the Altiplano and the Puna should be prepared for the cold at night. A medium-weight scarf or shawl is recommended: it can double as pillow, light blanket, bathrobe or sunscreen as required. A soft, cosy pashmina is ideal.

Up to 10% is an acceptable tip in restaurants. In all other cases a tip (an extra boliviano or two) is given in recognition of a service provided, for example to a taxi driver who has been helpful, to someone who has looked after a car or carried bags.

Responsible tourism

Much has been written about the adverse impacts of tourism on the environment and local communities. It is usually assumed that this only applies to the more excessive

⋮ How big is your footprint?

→ Where possible choose a destination, tour operator or hotel with a proven ethical and environmental commitment, and if in doubt ask.

→ Spend money on locally produced (rather than imported) goods and services and use common sense when bargaining – your few dollars saved may be a week's salary to others.

→ Consider staying in local, rather than foreign-owned, accommodation – the economic benefits for host communities are far greater – and there are far greater opportunities to learn about local culture.

→ Use water and electricity carefully – travellers may receive preferential supply while the needs of local communities are overlooked.

→ Don't give money or sweets to children – it encourages begging – instead give to a recognized project, charity or school.

→ Learn about local etiquette and culture – consider local norms and behaviour – and dress appropriately for local cultures and situations.

→ Protect wildlife and other natural resources – don't buy souvenirs or goods made from wildlife unless they are clearly sustainably produced and are not protected under CITES legislation.

→ Always ask before taking photographs or videos of people.

end of the travel industry such as the Spanish Costas and Bali. However, travellers can have an impact at almost any density and this is especially true in areas 'off the beaten track' where local people may not be used to Western conventions and lifestyles, and where natural environments may be very sensitive.

Of course, tourism can have a beneficial impact and this is something to which every traveller can contribute. Many national parks are part funded by receipts from people who travel to see exotic plants and animals. Similarly, travellers can promote patronage and protection of valuable archaeological sites and heritages through their interest and entrance fees.

However, where visitor pressure is high and/or poorly regulated, damage can occur. It is also unfortunately true that many of the most popular destinations are in ecologically sensitive areas easily disturbed by extra human pressures. This is particularly significant because the desire to visit sites and communities that are off the beaten track is a driving force for many travellers.

Fortunately, there are signs of a new awareness of the responsibilities that the travel industry and its clients need to endorse. For example, some tour operators fund local conservation projects and travellers are now more aware of the impact they may have on host cultures and environments. We can all contribute to the success of what is variously described as responsible, green or alternative tourism. All that is required is a little forethought and consideration.

It is impossible to identify all the possible impacts that could be addressed by travellers, but it is worthwhile noting the major areas in which we can all take a more responsible attitude. These include changes to natural ecosystems (air, water, land, ecology and wildlife), cultural values (beliefs and behaviour) and the built environment (sites of antiquity and archaeological significance). At an individual level, travellers can reduce their impact if greater consideration is given to their activities. Canoe trips up the headwaters of obscure rivers make for great stories, but how do local communities cope with the sudden invasive interest in their lives? Will the availability of easy tourist money and gauche behaviour affect them for the worse, possibly diluting and

implications of increased visitor pressure been considered? Where does the fresh fish that feeds the trip come from? Hand caught by line is fine, but is dynamite fishing really necessary, given the scale of damage and waste that results?

Some of these impacts are caused by factors beyond the direct control of travellers, such as the management and operation of a hotel chain. However, even here it is possible to voice concern about damaging activities and an increasing number of hotels and travel operators are taking 'green concerns' seriously, even if it is only to protect their share of the market.

Environmental legislation

Laws are increasingly being enacted to control damage to the environment, and in some cases this can have a bearing on travellers. The establishment of national parks may involve rules and guidelines for visitors and these should always be followed. In addition there may be local or national laws controlling behaviour and use of natural resources (especially wildlife) that are being increasingly enforced. If in doubt, ask. Finally, international legislation, principally the Convention on International Trade in Endangered Species of Wild Fauna and Flora (CITES), may affect travellers.

CITES aims to control the trade in live specimens of endangered plants and animals and also "recognisable parts or derivatives" of protected species. Sale of black coral, turtle shells, protected orchids and other wildlife is strictly controlled by signatories of the convention. The full list of protected wildlife varies, so if you feel the need to purchase souvenirs and trinkets derived from wildlife, it would be prudent to check whether they are protected. Bolivia is a signatory of CITES, most European countries, the USA and Canada. Importation of CITES protected species into these countries can lead to heavy fines, confiscation of goods and even imprisonment. Information on the status of legislation and protective measures can be obtained from **Traffic International** ① *UK office T01223-277427, F277237, traffic@wcmc.org.uk.*

Green travel companies and information

The increasing awareness of the environmental impact of travel and tourism has led to a range of advice and information services as well as spawning specialist travel companies who claim to provide 'responsible travel' for clients. This is an expanding field and the veracity of claims needs to be substantiated in some cases. The following organizations and publications can provide useful information for those with an interest in pursuing responsible travel opportunities.

Tourism Concern ① *Stapleton House, 277-281 Holloway Rd, London N7 8HN, UK T0207-753 3330, www.tourismconcern.org.uk,* aims to promote a greater understanding of the impact of tourism on host communities and environments. **Centre for Responsible Tourism** (CRT) ① *PO Box 827, San Anselmo, California 94979, USA,* co-ordinates a North American network and advises on North American sources of information on responsible tourism. **Centre for the Advancement of Responsive Travel** (CART) ① *UK T01732-352757,* has a range of publications available as well as information on alternative holiday destinations. **CARE International UK** ① *10-13 Rushworth St, London SE1 0RB, T0207-934 9334, www.careinternational.org.uk,* works to impove the economic conditions of people living in developing countries. They are currently involved in the development of the Che Guevara Trail (see pages 318 and 347).

Ecotourism → *Details of protected areas are given in the relevant section.*

Increasingly, visitors to Bolivia are arriving in search of the astounding – in some cases, unique – flora, fauna, and habitats found in abundance throughout the country's national parks, wildlife reserves, and other protected areas. In

: For a list of recommended tour operators, see page 20. See also page 419 for more on wildlife and vegetation.

fact, ecotourism is the fastest-growing type of tourism in Bolivia today. The best way to check the viability of a park or reserve is through an experienced, recommended in-country agent or guide, whether you intend to utilize their services or simply enquire as to the feasibility of a trip. Many are listed throughout this book under the appropriate geographical section. Most operators tend to be more knowledgeable about a specific local park or region, so if your itinerary calls for a visit to an area in particular, your best bet is to go with a local agency. On the other hand, if you are planning to see more of the country, there is now a growing number of excellent countrywide resources.

Currently, there are 29 major officially protected areas: 12 are national parks, six wildlife sanctuaries, and 11 are wildlife reserves, including the four popular biosphere reserves. There are another 30 or so smaller areas that also are considered protected lands in addition to those still under consideration. Check out www.bolivia-industry.com/sia/bolivia/datosgen/areas.html for an excellent assessment of each park's primary flora and fauna and other characteristics. The Santa Cruz-based **Instituto de Derecho Ambiental** ① *T03-334 2221*, has useful information and is particularly well-versed on park rules and regulations.

Those of primary interest to the traveller, based upon annual estimates of visitors, are, in order of popularity: **Parque Nacional Amboró** (in Santa Cruz Department); **Parque Nacional Noel Kempff Mercado** (Beni); **Parque Nacional Madidi** (La Paz); **Parque Nacional Sajama** (Potosí); **Parque Nacional Tunari** (Cochabamba); **Reserva Biosférica Pilón Lajas** (Beni); and **Reserva de Fauna Andina Eduardo Avaroa** (Potosí). Two others are rapidly gaining in popularity: **Reserva de Vida Silvestre Ríos Blanco y Negro** (Santa Cruz), and **Área Protegida Apolobamba** (La Paz). The brand-new **Parque Nacional Kaa-Iya del Gran Chaco** (Santa Cruz) also bears mentioning as perhaps the last frontier amongst Bolivia's parks.

The classification of Bolivia's protected lands, known as **Sistema Nacional de Áreas Protegidas** (or its acronym, SNAP) can be confusing to the traveller. It falls to the **Bolivian National Park Service**, or **Servicio Nacional de Áreas Protegidas** (also better known by its acronym SERNAP), a division of the Ministry of Sustainable Development and Planning, to do so. Those wishing further information can contact SERNAP directly. Their website (unfortunately in Spanish only at the moment) is www.sernap.gov.bo. A good overview of each of the protected areas (again, in Spanish) is also available on the newspaper *El Diario*'s website: www.eldiario.net/bolivia/medioamb. It should be noted that a passing ability in Spanish is a requirement for those in search of first-hand information on Bolivia's parklands. Another outstanding Spanish-language website for those interested specifically in Andean national parks is www.ciedperu.org. It features useful data on **Parque Nacional Condoriri, Área Protegida Apolobamba, Parque Nacional Torotoro, Reserva Nacional de Fauna Andina Eduardo Abaroa,** and **Parque Nacional Sajama**.

Safety → *Additional advice for women travellers is given on page 26.*

Bolivia is generally a safe country and free from many of the problems that beset its larger neighbours. However, crime is not unknown to the country and travellers should take the same precautions that they would anywhere else, especially around markets and bus terminals in the larger cities. Also be aware that Bolivia is the poorest country in South America and getting poorer because of the US-sponsored coca eradication plan (see also page 391). Impoverished campesinos, rebelling against the coca clamp-down and ethnic discrimination, frequently blockade the roads for weeks at a time. Be careful, especially when travelling around the Yungas, Altiplano and Chapare regions, where people are becoming increasingly desperate and protests are escalating.

Drugs

Users of drugs, even of soft ones, without medical prescription should be particularly careful, as heavy penalties – up to 10 years' imprisonment – are possible for even the simple possession of such substances. Travellers should note that the planting of drugs on travellers, by traffickers or the police, is not unknown. If offered drugs on the street, make no response at all and keep walking. This may be a ruse by a plain-clothes police officer.

Hotel security

It is best, if you can trust your hotel, to leave any valuables you don't need in safe-deposit there, when sightseeing locally. Always keep an inventory of what you have deposited. If you don't trust the hotel, lock everything in your pack and secure that in your room (some people take eyelet-screws for padlocking cupboards or drawers). If you lose valuables, always report to the police and note details of the report – for insurance purposes.

Police

Whereas in Europe and North America we are accustomed to law enforcement on a systematic basis, in general, enforcement in Latin America is achieved by periodic campaigns. The most typical is a round-up of criminals in the cities just before Christmas. In December, therefore, you may well be asked for identification at any time, and if you cannot produce it, you will be jailed. If a visitor is jailed his/her friends should provide food every day. This is especially important for people on a diet, such as diabetics. In the event of a vehicle accident in which anyone is injured, all drivers involved are automatically detained until blame has been established, and this does not usually take less than two weeks.

Never offer a bribe unless you are fully conversant with the customs of the country. Wait until the official makes the suggestion, or offer money in some form which is apparently not bribery, for example, 'In our country we have a system of on-the-spot fines (*multas de inmediato*). Is there a similar system here?' Do not assume that an official who accepts a bribe is prepared to do anything else that is illegal. You bribe him to persuade him to do his job, or to persuade him not to do it, or to do it more quickly, or more slowly. You do not bribe him to do something which is against the law. The mere suggestion would make him very upset. If an official suggests that a bribe must be paid before you can proceed on your way, be patient (assuming you have the time) and he may relent.

The procedure for reporting a robbery is to go to the Departamento de Criminalística, or the office for stolen property, in the town where the theft took place. Purchase official paper from the police for them to write the report, then, with patience and politeness, you may get a report costing between US$1.30 and US$5.25.

Protecting money and valuables

Keep all documents secure and hide your main cash supply in different places or under your clothes. Extra pockets sewn inside shirts and trousers, pockets closed with a zip or safety pin, neck or leg pouches, a thin chain for attaching a purse to your bag or under your clothes and elasticated support bandages for keeping money and cheques above the elbow or below the knee are safety measures that have been repeatedly recommended.

Keep cameras in bags (preferably with a chain or wire in the strap to defeat the slasher); take spare glasses (spectacles); don't wear watches or jewellery. If you wear a shoulder-bag in a market, carry it in front of you. Backpacks are vulnerable to slashers: a good idea is to cover the pack with a sack (a plastic one will also keep out rain and dust). If attacked, remember your assailants may be armed, and try not to resist.

There are several scams to watch for. A bowl of water or urine may be thrown over you from a window above or a sticky mustard-like liquid may be sprayed over your rucksack in the street. In both cases a 'helpful' passer-by will commiserate, ready to snatch your backpack as you take it off to inspect the damage. In other cases, a 'passer-by' may drop a large roll of money at your feet. An accomplice will pick it up and suggest you and he share the wad. He'll entice you down a side street and encourage you to take out your wallet before sharing out the cash, which is in fact just a couple of banknotes rolled around a piece of wood. At this point the man who 'lost' the money will return and both will go for your wallet. In the final scam, a plain-clothes 'policeman' will flash a fake ID card and demand to search your bag. Bolivian law states that police may do this only at a police station. Insist on going to the police station, or call the uniformed police if in doubt, but *do not* get into a vehicle with him or take him back to your lodgings. Identity must be checked only by immigration officials; see their identity card and verify the date. If at all possible, insist on your right not to show your passport to anyone on the street. If you can get a witness, so much the better. If someone tries to extort a bribe from you, insist on a receipt – in most cases they will give up.

Street children/shoe-shine boys have been known to spit in travellers' faces as a prelude to stealing their daypacks. This is particularly prevalent in Cochabamba.

Public transport
When you have all your luggage with you at a bus or railway station, be especially careful. Lock all the items together with a chain or cable if you are waiting for some time, or use your backpack as a seat. Take a taxi between airport/bus station/railway station and hotel if you can possibly afford it, but pay only when you and your luggage are safely out of the vehicle. Make sure the taxi has inner door handles, in case a quick exit is needed. Be extra careful on night buses, especially when everyone gets off at a meal stop. Keep an eye on your belongings whether they are stowed inside or outside the cabin and keep your valuables with you in a little daypack. Roof-top luggage racks create extra problems, which are sometimes unavoidable – make sure your bag is waterproof. Major bus companies often issue a luggage ticket when bags are stored in the hold. When getting on a bus, keep your ticket handy; someone sitting in your seat may be a distraction for an accomplice to rob you while you are sorting out the problem. Finally, never accept food, drink, sweets or cigarettes from unknown fellow-travellers on buses or trains. They may be drugged, and you would wake up hours later without your belongings. In connection with this, never accept a bar drink from an opened bottle (unless you can see that that bottle is in general use): always have it uncapped in front of you.

Rape
Sexual assault can happen anywhere in the world. If you become a victim then you are advised in the first instance to contact a doctor (this can be your home doctor if you prefer). You will need tests to determine whether you have contracted any sexually-transmitted diseases; you may also need advice on post-coital contraception. You should also contact your embassy, where consular staff are very willing to help in cases of assault.

Getting around

Many parts of Bolivia are remote and can be reached only with a lot of time, effort and patience. The trouble is the country's road network – or lack of one, especially in the wet season. With the country's rail service severely depleted, often the only real alternative to road travel is flying, a relatively cheap and efficient way to see the country. Flying is also a great way to appreciate the unique geography of this amazing country: a flight from the lowlands over the Andes to La Paz is an unforgettable experience. On election day no public transport runs whatsoever; only cars with a special permit are allowed on the road.

Air

Two companies, **Lloyd Aéreo Boliviano** (LAB) and **Aero Sur**, are the main airlines and both offer a fairly reliable service with not much to choose between them. They fly to all the main cities and also to many of the smaller lowland towns. **TAM** also fly, slightly less reliably, to many of the smaller settlements in the tropical lowlands. Note that **TAM** flights from La Paz leave from the military airport, which is situated next to the main commercial one in El Alto. **Amaszonas**, a relatively new company, now offer cheaper flights between La Paz, Rurrenabaque, San Borja, Trinidad, Guayaramerín and Riberalta.

Boarding passes are issued only at airports; after obtaining one, pay the airport tax. **LAB** offers a 45-day, five-coupon domestic airpass for US$250 for international travellers using **LAB** (or a foreign carrier with whom **LAB** may have a pooling arrangement). This allows a maximum of five flights between the main cities but you cannot visit the same city twice. Note that many flights radiate from La Paz, Santa Cruz or Cochabamba. **LAB** have 5% discounts for family members if they travel together, for example, a husband and wife, (remember to take your passport). **LAB** and **Aero Sur** also offer discounts of 5% to students under 26 and **Aero Sur** offer a 20% discount to passengers over 65. **LAB** can be contacted at 0800 3001 (toll free) and **Aero Sur** in La Paz on T02-243 0430. **Amaszonas** has 5% discounts for students, 20% off for the over-60s, 50% off for children 2-12 years old and 90% off for babies and toddlers.

Note that a 'through' flight may require a change of plane, or involve a delay while waiting for a connecting flight from elsewhere. Only on international flights is overnight lodging provided during delays. Insure your bags heavily as they tend to get left around. If your internal flight is delayed keep your baggage with you and do not check it in until the flight is definitely announced. There have been robberies of prematurely checked-in baggage. Flights into and out of the tropical regions are badly affected by weather conditions in the wet season and may be cancelled at a moment's notice.

Rail

The limited rail network in Bolivia is underfunded and its future is uncertain. The only reliable rail routes in the country are the one east from Santa Cruz to the Brazilian border at Puerto Quijarro (see page 344), and south from Oruro to the Argentine border, via Uyuni.

Road

Only 4% of the nation's roads are paved and in many cases only nominally. Furthermore, a mere 20% of roads can be used all year round. The rest are often impassable in the rainy season due to landslides or being washed away. Nearly all Bolivian road surfaces, even the paved sections, are bad, and after flooding or rough weather they are even worse. Even main roads may be closed in the rainy season.

Roadblocks allowing, the only roads that will not present any problems all year round are the ones heading north from La Paz to Lake Titicaca, west to Tiahuanaco, south to Oruro, and the stretch of road between Potosí and Sucre. Other than these routes, travelling can be difficult during the November-March wet season, especially in the tropical lowlands. During the rest of the year, you can go wherever you want, given enough time, patience and stamina.

Bicycle

At first glance a bicycle may not appear to be the most obvious vehicle for a major journey, but given ample time and reasonable energy it most certainly is the best. It can be ridden, carried by almost every form of transport from an aeroplane to a canoe, and can even be lifted across one's shoulders over short distances. Cyclists can be the envy of travellers using more orthodox transport, since they can travel at their own pace, explore more remote regions and meet people who are not normally in contact with tourists. It is now easier to find spares for mountain bikes in La Paz than before, while conversely touring bikes are harder to find spares for. A rear-view mirror is recommended to forewarn you of vehicles which are too close behind. You also need to watch out for oncoming, overtaking vehicles, unstable loads on trucks and protruding loads. Make yourself seen by wearing bright clothing and a helmet.

Inter-urban buses are called flotas and urban ones are called micros. Trufis and colectivos are shared taxis.

Bus

Going by bus in Bolivia may be the cheapest way to get around but it can also be dirty, uncomfortable, extremely time-consuming and, at times, downright scary. As a rule of thumb, the newer carriers have the best amenities. Actually catching a bus can present serious problems. La Paz and the other major cities have central bus terminals, but not all buses leave from them and finding out when and where the others leave from can take as long as the journey. On top of this, bus times are regularly changed to take account of local, regional and national festivals, elections and soccer matches. During the wet season journey times can be increased by hours, even days, as roads get washed out and vehicles get stuck in the mud.

In general, try to reserve, and pay for, a seat as far as possible in advance and arrive in good time, as buses often depart when full. Substantial savings can be made by buying tickets just before departure when there is competition to fill seats. In the wet season, bus travel is subject to long delays and detours at extra cost. In the dry season journeys can be very dusty. On all journeys, take food and toilet paper. Note that a small charge is made for use of major bus terminals; payment is before departure.

It is always possible to buy food on the roadside, as buses stop frequently, but make sure you have very small-denomination notes. Always carry your valuables with you, even when leaving the bus at a meal stop. On overnight trips, especially in the Andes, you will appreciate extra clothing or a blanket as many buses do not have any form of heating. Toilet facilities on buses are almost non-existent. Bus drivers are generally happy to stop anywhere for you to relieve yourself but be prepared to drop your pants in full view of the other passengers. If your bus breaks down and you are transferred to another line and have to pay extra, keep your original ticket for a refund

: Bus travel in the Bolivian Andes

Bolivian road warning signs take the shape of crosses, which line the side of the road to indicate where vehicles have gone over the edge. Most of the crosses appear on particularly dangerous bends and many drivers, being devout Catholics, will cross themselves on seeing one. This, of course means that many of the sharpest bends on the road are negotiated with one hand on the steering wheel.

Similarly, many of the buses do little to inspire confidence. For a start, they are usually packed to suffocation point with people, luggage and livestock. Overcrowded, it seems, is not a word familiar to Bolivian bus company employees. And secondly, they tend to break down a lot. But don't worry – seemingly anything can be repaired at the side of the road, given time. The driver and his *ayudante* (helper) will disappear under, or into, the engine, hit things, tie bits together with wire and probably pray a lot. Magically, the bus starts and the journey continues.

Probably the worst bus journey in all of Bolivia is the trip from La Paz to Pelechuco in the Cordillera Apolobamba – around 18-24 hours of dust-filled torture crossing the Altiplano in some battered old hulk that should have been consigned to the scrapheap years ago. Anyone over 172 cm tall will spend the entire trip smashing their kneecaps into the back of the seat in front and arrive in need of major surgery and a good night's rest. The pain, cold and tedium is only alleviated by the need to get out and push the bus every so often. All males of working age get off and push with all their might until it becomes obvious that the combined weight of the female passengers still on board is preventing any significant movement. So, off they get and the bus can then be pushed out of the mud/sand/hole.

But it's not all discomfort and near-death experiences. There's no better way to see the country, meet the people, sit on their chickens, sleep on their sheep, or be kept awake all night by their screaming children. Just look on it as cultural interaction.

from the original company. Avoid the back seats at all costs. On unpaved roads you will spend more time airborne than seated, and the windows will be jammed open, causing you to cough your lungs up from the exhaust fumes and clouds of choking dust, as well as freeze to death at night in the mountains. If your bus has a VCR, don't expect to see any scenery by day, and don't expect to get any sleep at night.

Car → *Petrol is sold from the drum in every small village.*
Aside from the awful condition of the roads, there are other hazards that may make you think twice. There are road tolls and for prolonged motoring over 3,000 m, you may need to fit high-altitude jets on your carburettors. At the very least you will have to advance your ignition to compensate for the lack of oxygen. Cyclists do not usually have lights, truck drivers almost never dip their headlights and it's not that uncommon for other drivers to be drunk, or fall asleep at the wheel. Day or night, watch out for people asleep at the roadside in lowland areas: they tend to lie with head and torso in the road where there are fewer mosquitoes. Bureaucracy regulations are tight and police checks frequent.

Always carry your passport, a driving licence and an International Driving Permit. You can be fined or imprisoned for not doing so. You also need the registration document in the name of the driver or, in the case of a car registered in someone else's name, a notarized letter of authorization.

The police may ask for a 'contribution' to the police force (*colaboración*). Locals seem to pay without question but it is illegal and if you ask the police for a receipt (*factura*), they will probably give up and wave you on. Two authorization certificates are required in La Paz: the first from the **Automóvil Club Boliviano** ① *on the corner of 6 de Agosto and Arce, T/F02-237 2139*, and the second from the traffic police at the **Comando Departamental** ① *Organismo Operativo de Tránsito, on the corner of Mariscal Santa Cruz and Plaza San Francisco.*

Car hire

The minimum age for renting a car is 25. Car hire companies and rates are given in the text, but they tend to be very expensive. When hiring a car, the rental company may only require your national licence but a clued-up policeman will ask for an international licence.

Check exactly what the hirer's insurance policy covers. In many cases it will only protect you against minor bumps and scrapes, not major accidents, nor 'natural' damage (for example flooding). Ask if extra cover is available. Also find out, if using a credit card, whether the card automatically includes insurance. Beware of being billed for scratches which were on the vehicle before you hired it.

Motorbike

Bolivians are generally very amicable towards motorcyclists and you can make many friends by returning friendship to those who show an interest in you. Try not to leave a fully laden bike unattended. A cheap alarm gives you peace of mind if you leave the bike outside a hotel at night. Most hotels will allow you to bring the bike inside. Look for hotels that have a courtyard or more secure parking and never leave luggage on the bike overnight or whilst unattended. Passport, International Driving Licence and bike registration document are all necessary. Riders fare much better with a *libreta* than without it. Get your licence endorsed by police in Bolivia.

Truck

Trucks congregate at all town markets, with destinations chalked on the sides. They are normally about half the cost when there is competition. Otherwise they charge what they judge the market will bear and can therefore seem expensive.

Maps

Those from the **Institutos Geográficos Militares** in La Paz are often the only good maps available. It is therefore wise to get as many as possible in your home country before leaving, especially if travelling by land. A recommended series of general maps is that published by **International Travel Maps** (ITM): South America North West includes all of Bolivia (1:4,000,000). More widely available, and at better scales is the **Nelles** Bolivia and Paraguay (1:2,500,000) and the **Berndtson & Berndtson** Bolivia (1:1,750,000).

Liam O'Brien covers the whole of the Cordillera Real at 1:135,000. Bigger-scale sheets are listed with each mountain. Another useful Liam O'Brien map is his *Travel Map of Bolivia* (1:2,200,000), which shows the road network as well as the national park areas. The **German Alpine Club** (Deutscher Alpenverien) produces two good maps of Cordillera Real North and South. Takesi, Choro and Yunga Cruz are covered by the **Walter Córdova** 1:50,000 map, which is available from bookshops in La Paz. There are also the **IGM** 1:50,000 sheets: *Takesi Chojlla 6044 IV*; *Choro Milluni 5945 II, 6045 III* and *Coroico*; *Yunga Cruz Lambate 6044 II* and *6044*.

Maps can be ordered from **Stanfords** ① www.stanfords.co.uk, from www.boliviaweb .com, or through the **South American Explorers' Club** ① www.saexplorers.org.

Sleeping → *See inside front covers for price codes.*

Away from the main cities, high-class hotels are few and far between. Getting off the beaten track usually means sacrificing creature comforts, but not necessarily standards of hygiene. Many of the hotels we recommend are not luxurious but conform to certain basic standards of cleanliness and are popular with travellers, which is often the best sign of an establishment's pedigree.

Prices are low in Bolivia, but not uniformly so. The eastern part of the country tends to be a bit more expensive, especially the city of Santa Cruz, which is geared more towards commerce than tourism and therefore has few good budget places to stay. Smaller places which see plenty of tourists, such as Coroico, Rurrenabaque, Sorata or Copacabana, on the other hand, are full of good-value budget accommodation.

Even in La Paz, it is quite easy to find a clean, comfortable hotel room, without a private bathroom, for around US$4-5 per person. For those on a tight budget, a cheaper room can be found in a *hospedaje*, *pensión*, *casa familial* or *residencial*; they are normally to be found in abundance near bus and railway stations and markets. Note that there are often great seasonal variations in hotel prices in resorts, and prices can rise substantially during public holidays and festivals.

Hotels must display prices by law. Throughout Bolivia some hotels impose their own curfews. In La Paz it tends to be midnight (check), but it can be earlier in Copacabana. These locking-up times are strictly adhered to by hotel keepers. Ask for the hot water schedule, as it changes with the season, water pressure, etc, although now even the cheapest hotels tend to have electric showers which offer hot/warm water all day. Some of these can give electric shocks so check the wiring before you jump in. Clothes washing is generally not allowed in bathrooms but many of the cheaper hotels have a hand-washing area. Many mid-range hotels will keep money and valuables in the safe if there are no safety-deposit boxes. Only the most expensive hotels tend to have heating in the rooms.

Prices given in the Sleeping listings are for two people sharing a double room with bathroom (shower and toilet). Where possible, prices are are also given per person, as some hotels charge almost as much for a single room. If travelling alone, it's usually cheaper to share with others in a room with three or more beds. If breakfast is included in the price, it will almost invariably mean continental breakfast. Prices are for the high seasons (June-August, Christmas and Holy Week). During the low season, when many places may be half-empty, it's often possible to bargain the room rate down.

All Bolivian hotels are ranked by number of stars. In most cases, these are accurate, and travellers can expect the appropriate level of service. A hotel attempting to upgrade itself can be fined. As a rule of thumb, five-, four- and three-star hotels are generally safe and have the mod cons you'd expect.

Many hotels, restaurants and bars have inadequate water supplies. Almost without exception used toilet paper should not be flushed down the pan, but placed in the receptacle provided. This applies even in quite expensive hotels. Failing to observe this custom will block the pan or drain, a considerable health risk.

Hotel price codes explained

LL to AL Hotels in these categories are usually only found in La Paz and the main tourist centres. They should offer pool, sauna, gym, jacuzzi, all business facilities (including email), several restaurants, bars and often a casino. Most will provide a safe box in each room.

A and B The better-value hotels in these categories provide more than the standard facilities and a fair degree of comfort. Most will include breakfast and many offer 'extras' such as cable TV, minibar, and tea and coffee making facilities. They may also provide tourist information and their own transport. Service is generally good and most accept credit cards. At the top end of the range, some may have a swimming pool, sauna and jacuzzi.

C to E Hotels in these categories range from very comfortable to functional, but there are some real bargains to be had. At these prices you should expect your own bathroom, constant hot water, a towel, soap and toilet paper, TV, a restaurant, communal sitting area and a reasonably sized, comfortable room with air conditioning (in tropical regions).

F In the better hotels in this range you can expect some degree of comfort and cleanliness, a private bathroom with hot water and perhaps continental breakfast included. The best value hotels in this price range will be recommended in the travelling text. Many of those catering for foreign tourists in the more popular regions offer excellent value for money in this range and many have their own restaurant and offer services such as laundry, safe-deposit box, money exchange and luggage store.

G A room in this price range usually consists of little more than a bed and four walls, with barely enough room to swing a cockroach. If you're lucky you may have a window, a table and chair, and even your own bathroom, though this tends to be the exception rather than the rule. Anywhere that provides these facilities, as well as being clean and providing hot water, will normally be recommended in our hotel listings.

Cheaper places don't always supply soap, towels and toilet paper. In colder (higher) regions they may not supply enough blankets, so ask for more, take your own or use a sleeping bag. Some places include a meagre breakfast in their price.

Camping

This presents no problem in Bolivia. There can, however, be problems with robbery when camping close to a small village. Avoid such a location, or ask permission to camp in someone's backyard. Most Bolivians are used to campers, but in more remote places, people have never seen a tent and you may find yourself the centre of attention. Be casual about it, do not unpack all your gear, leave it inside your tent (especially at night) and never leave your tent unattended.

Obey the following rules for 'wild' camping: arrive in daylight and pitch your tent as it gets dark; ask permission to camp from the parish priest, or the fire chief, or the police, or a farmer regarding his own property; never ask a group of people – especially young people. If you can't get information from anyone, camp in a spot where you can't be seen from the nearest inhabited place, or road, and ensure that no one saw you go there.

Eating → *See inside front covers for price codes.*

Though few would come to Bolivia for the cuisine, there are interesting local specialities worth trying and with a bit of effort you can manage to vary your diet away from the meat and potato orthodoxy.

Food

Bolivian cuisine can be divided into three distinct regional varieties: the Altiplano; the Valleys; and the Tropics.

The Altiplano

The high plateau produces mostly grains and potatoes. *Quinoa* is a grain unique to this area. It has an exceptionally high protein content and is the basis of the Altiplano diet.

There are hundreds, perhaps thousands, of varieties of potatoes. The use of many types is highly localized. Some of the most commonly used in cooking are the *oca*, which is sweet, and *chuño*, which is a kind of freeze-dried potato (rumoured to be used by Bolivian women to suppress their husbands' sexual desires).

Bolivian highland cooking is usually very tasty and often cooked in *ají*, a very piquant chilli-like plant. You won't fail to notice the *salteña*, a meat or chicken pastry which is sold absolutely everywhere. These originate from Salta in Argentina, but are popular throughout the Andean countries. *Salteñas* are eaten regularly by Bolivians, especially in the morning, and accompanied by a cold drink. The trick is to eat them without spilling copious quantities of gravy all over yourself (not very easy, particularly on buses). Some are *muy picante* (very hot), but for lesser mortals (wimps, in other words) *medio picante* and *poco picante* are available.

Near to Lake Titicaca fish becomes an increasingly important part of the local diet and freshly caught trout, though not native, is usually delicious.

Other local specialities include *chairo*, a soup from La Paz made of meat, vegetables, and *chuño* and *ají* (hot pepper), to which the locals like to add *llajua* or *halpahuayca* (hot sauces always set on restaurant tables) to make it even more *picante*. *Fricasé* is a traditional hangover cure, which we would not recommend. It is another soup made with pork, *chuño*, *ají* and God knows what else. *Anticuchos* are small slices of beef heart and a boiled potato on a skewer cooked over an open grill, and simply delicious. *Thimpu* is a popular lamb dish served as a kind of soup and usually found on more native restaurant menus. *Plato paceño*, as the name suggests, is a native La Paz dish, made from cheese fried and served with potato, broad beans, corn on the cob and the very piquant sauce called *llajua*.

A *picante* is a meat cooked in an *ají* sauce and served with boiled potato and *chuño*. Among the most popular *picante* dishes are: *sajta de pollo*, hot spicy chicken with onion, fresh potatoes and *chuño*; *saice* (chopped beef); *ají de lengua*, ox-tongue with chillis, potatoes and *chuño* or *tunta* (another kind of dehydrated potato); and *ranga ranga* (tripe). Those with strong stomachs could try a local Oruro favourite, *rostro asado*, which is baked lamb's head. A speciality in Potosí is *fritanga*, which is *fricasé* without the broth, made with red *ají*.

The Valleys

The departments of Cochabamba, Chuquisaca and Tarija produce some of Bolivia's finest cooking. Tarija is the wine and *singani* capital, while Cochabamba is the agricultural and dairy centre.

Among the typical dishes from Cochabamba, two stand out: *silpancho* is fried, breaded meat with eggs, rice and bananas; and *pique a lo macho* is a delicious, and massive, dish of roast meat, sausage, chips, onion and pepper. *Chicharrón* is pork cooked in its own fat and is an ingredient in other dishes, such as *chairo*. In Cochabamba it is served with *quesillo*, or fresh cheese. Sucre is famous for its *chorizos* and also claims to have the best *salteñas* in the country. Tarija, being so close to Argentina, is, of course, a carnivore's paradise. Restaurant menus here basically consist of meat, meat and more meat. *Parrillada* is a Bolivian kind of mixed grill.

The Tropics

The staple foods produced in the tropics are yucca, rice, bananas, tropical fruits, soy and beef and dishes here tend to feature these heavily.

A favourite dish in the tropics is *locro*, a rice soup made with beef jerky or chicken, bananas, potato and egg. Another is *masaco*, fried jerky and banana. *Pollo broaster* is chicken with rice, chips, yucca and fried banana.

Note that many types of wild meat are served in tourist restaurants and on jungle tours. Bear in mind that turtles whose eggs are eaten are endangered and that other species not endangered soon will be if they stay on the tourist menu.

The bread in this region is often sweet with cheese on top, and the rice bread is also unusual. Among the pastries produced are *cuñapes*, made with yucca flour and cheese; *biscochos*, which are corn biscuits; and also *empanadas* (cheese pasties) and *humitas* (maize pies). The latter two are also popular throughout the country. Before trying some of these pastries it should be noted that a method of preserving them in the humid climate is to dry them in the oven until they become very hard.

Drink

The several makes of local beer (lager-type), are recommendable, though trying to pour a beer at altitude without ending up with a glass of froth is an art in itself. *El Inca* is a dark beer, and sweet like a stout. *Singani*, a brandy distilled from grapes, is quite cheap and drinkable. *Chuflay* is *Singani* with *7 Up* or *Canada Dry* (or whatever carbonated drink is available). The best wines are produced in Tarija and many of them are very recommendable, for example *La Concepción* (see Tarija, page 251).

Chicha is a traditional Andean drink made from fermented corn in the valleys around Cochabamba, where it is sold in *chicherías*, which are small places without a sign or a name. They can be found by looking out for a little white flag on a pole in front of the house. *Chicha* is also served in *chicharronerías*, where it is drunk to accompany a dish of *chicharrón* cooked in huge vats.

The hot maize drink, *api* (with cloves, cinnamon, lemon and sugar), is good for breakfast, especially on the freezing cold Altiplano. *Tostada* is a cold drink made by boiling toasted corn and barley with honey, cinnamon, cloves and fennel. In Tarija it is called *aloja*. In the tropics fruit juices are delicious; *tamarindo*, *carambola* and *guapurú* are particularly good.

Bottled water, *viscachani*, is readily available but make sure the seal is unbroken (rain water is sometimes offered as an alternative). There are also several brands of flavoured mineral water, *Cayacayani*, *La Cabaña* and *Mineragua*. *Naturagua* is purified water and should also be fine. The local tap water should not be drunk without first being sterilized. Local water purifier is *lugol fuerte solución*, an iodine-based product, US$1.75 for a small bottle; also *iodo* from *farmacias*, US$0.50. For milk, try sachets of *Leche Pil* (plain, chocolate or strawberry-flavoured), at US$0.25 each.

Eating out

Eating out in Bolivia can be hazardous, and this is one area where travellers should not over-economise. The satisfaction accrued from saving the odd dollar here and there by eating in the markets will be soon be heavily outweighed by the trauma of spending your entire trip on the toilet. That's not to say that market food is unhygienic, just that you need to be careful, especially until your stomach has had time to adjust. La Paz and most other major cities offer a wide variety of eating places, some of which are of a very high standard. Away from the main centres, however, your chances of suffering from 'Atahuallpa's revenge' are increased. Eating live yoghurt two weeks before you leave may help build up 'friendly' bacteria in your system, so that you can cope with more Bolivian cuisine.

In the *pensiones* and cheaper restaurants a basic lunch (*almuerzo* – usually finished by 1300) and dinner (*cena*) are normally available for around US$1-1.50. The *comida del día* is the best value, in any class of restaurant and costs only around US$1.50-3.00. Good cheap and clean breakfasts are served in the markets in most towns (most restaurants do not open very early in the morning). Lunch can also be obtained in many of the modern market buildings in the main towns, but eat only contains parasites (similar to those in pork), so make sure it has been cooked for a long time and is hot when you eat it. Be very careful of salads; they may carry a multitude of amoebic life as well as vile green bacteria.

Big cities and popular travellers' destinations have an increasing number of cafés and restaurants catering mainly to the gringo market and offering decent international cuisine at reasonable prices. Cooked breakfasts, toasted sandwiches, omelettes, muesli, beer, milkshakes and travelling tales proliferate. Good coffee (often Bolivian) is usually possible to find too, though it's much less common than its usually vile instant counterpart.

Entertainment

Bolivians like to have a good time all year round, not just during the frequent fiestas. Go into any bar in La Paz at the weekend and you'll experience a level of drinking that is almost nihilistic in its fervency. You should have no trouble experiencing a decent night out. In the main cities and tourist destinations there is a wide variety of entertainment available – from more highbrow pursuits such as theatre and classical music to the rather more visceral art of competitive drinking. In La Paz and Santa Cruz you can see all the latest Hollywood movies and there's also an arthouse cinema in La Paz for independent films. The one thing, above all, you can be sure of is being able to dance to your little legs' content. Bolivians are tireless dancers and once they hit the dancefloor there is no stopping them. The most popular music is salsa and merengue and you will hear this blasting out on buses, in bars and in nightclubs. There are good clubs in La Paz and Santa Cruz, and you'll also be able to strut your funky stuff in other major cities such as Sucre and Cochabamba, as well as in popular gringo hangouts such as Coroico, Potosí and Samaipata.

More traditional types of Andean music can be heard in *peñas*, which are sort of Bolivian supper-clubs where you eat a meal and watch some people in costume dance around to panpipe music. These can be rather staid affairs. The best place to hear folk music and watch dancing is during a local fiesta, when everyone really lets their hair down.

Festivals and events

Below is a list of Bolivia's main festival dates. For a more detailed list of each region's festivals and a description of the activities, see under the relevant section in the main travelling text. Note that dates may change slightly from year to year.

1 Jan Año Nuevo: rural communities on the Altiplano, in Cochabamba and in the Chiquitano area of Santa Cruz hold a celebration to thank the outgoing civil authorities and welcome the incoming officials.

6 Jan Reyes Magos: a celebration of the arrival of the Three Kings in various provinces of the Beni, also in Oruro, Sucre and Tarija. In the rural communities of Cochabamba and Potosí there are traditional ceremonies for the changing authorities.

24 Jan Alasitas: festival of **Ekeko**, (God of Plenty), celebrated over 6 days in La Paz.

2 Feb Virgen de la Candelaria: one of the most important festivals, celebrated in Copacabana, Samaipata, Aiquile and Colomi in Cochabamba, Tarija and Challapampa near Oruro.

Feb/Mar Many of the towns and rural communities have their **Carnival** at this time, though there are no fixed dates. The most elaborate is at Oruro, though there are worthwhile celebrations in Sucre, Tarija and Santa Cruz and the outlying villages.

8 Mar San Juan de Dios: in Tarija; also around this time is the Celebration of the Grape.

2nd Sun in Mar Phujllay: in Tarabuco near Sucre. One of the largest fiestas in Bolivia.

19 Mar San José: the patron saint of carpenters is honoured in Cochabamba and Potosí.

Mar/Apr Semana Santa: Easter is celebrated nationally but varies according to location. In the Jesuit missions near Santa Cruz festivities are solemn, while in Tarija celebrations are more enthusiastic. On 15-16 Apr Tarija also goes wild during its anniversary celebrations.

3 May Fiesta de la Cruz: celebrated throughout the country. In the Andean rural communities they are more pre-Columbian than Christian. In Potosí the ritual Tinkus are carried out (see p245).

Jun Santísima Trinidad: is the most important festival in the Beni; there's no fixed date but it's usually around the start of the month. Similarly Corpus Cristi in Potosí, Sucre and Copacabana. Gran Poder is La Paz's biggest party, held also at the beginning of Jun.

13 Jun San Antonio de Padua: celebrated in small towns in the departments of La Paz, Santa Cruz, Cochabamba and Tarija.

24 Jun San Juan: celebrations take place in rural provinces throughout Bolivia and in Tarija and Santa Cruz. Also at this time is the traditional burning of woods and fields.

29 Jun San Pedro and San Pablo: fiestas are held throughout the country.

1st Sun in Jul Pentecost: in the Cochabamba countryside offerings are made to Pachamama.

16 Jul Virgen del Carmen: takes place in La Paz, Oruro, Cochabamba, the Yungas and Sucre.

25 Jul Apostle Santiago: held throughout the Andes and in Tarija, which has Santiago as its patron saint.

31 Jul San Ignacio de Moxos: one of the most important festivals in the Beni.

2 Aug Dia del Indio: in Iturralde province in La Paz.

5 Aug La Virgen de las Nieves: in Italque and Copacabana.

6 Aug San Salvador in Oruro.

10 Aug San Lorenzo: in Tarija and Santa Cruz.

15 Aug Virgen de Urkupiña: the greatest religious celebration in Cochabamba department is held in Quillacollo. Hundreds of other festivals are held across the country on the same day, for example in Tarija, La Paz, Sucre and Oruro.

24 Aug San Bartolomé de Huayco: also known as the festival of the Chutillos, held in Potosí.

28 Aug San Agustín: an 8-day festival in Toledo, 40 km from Oruro.

1st Sun in Sep San Roque: a major 8-day party in Tarija.

8 Sep Virgen de Guadalupe: in Santa Cruz and Sucre. Also the Fiesta of Viacha near La Paz.

14 Sep Lord of the Exhaltation: celebrated in Potosí, Cochabamba and over a marathon 15 days in Oruro. There is also a festival in Sorata.

21 Sep Spring Equinox: celebrated at Tiahuanaco.

29 Sep San Miguel: held in Potosí and featuring *Tinkus*.

1-2 Oct Virgen de La Merced and Virgen del Rosario: a sacred procession in Potosí.

7 Oct Virgen del Rosario: held in Oruro (where it is known as *Huayllas*), Warnes in Santa Cruz, Sucre and Cochabamba. Also in Cochabamba is the Luzmilla Patiño Folklore Festival, held every 2 years (next in 2006).

1st Sun in Oct Virgen de Guadalupe: held in Entre Ríos in Tarija. On the 2nd Sun it is held in the city of Tarija.

24 Oct San Rafael: a popular 4-day festival in Santa Fe, near Oruro.

1-2 Nov Todos Santos and Difuntos: All Saints and Day of the Dead, celebrated in cemeteries throughout the Andean world; particularly interesting in Potosí.

1st Sun in Nov Virgen de Socavón: the first training parade for the Oruro Carnival 3 months later. Also in Oruro, on 10 Nov, is Santo Domingo.

18 Nov Anniversary of the foundation of Beni Department: festivities in Trinidad are recommended.

30 Nov San Andrés: celebrations in Santa Cruz and Taquiri in Cochabamba.

3 Dec San Francisco Javier: celebrated in the various Jesuit mission towns in Santa Cruz.

8 Dec Dia de la Inmaculada Concepción: held in towns in Santa Cruz and Cochabamba departments.

14 Dec Santa Bárbara: 7-day festival in Oruro. On 21 December in Oruro is the **Virgin of Lourdes.**

24 Dec Navidad: celebrated throughout Bolivia. Some of the best are Villa Serrano (Chuquisaca), Vallegrande (Santa Cruz), San Ignacio de Moxos (Beni) and Tarija where celebrations continue until the end of Jan.

Public holidays

1 Jan, New Year's Day. Carnival Week: **Mon, Shrove Tue, Ash Wed.** Holy Week: **Thu, Fri** and **Sat. 1 May**, Labour Day. Corpus Christi (moveable). **16 Jul**, La Paz Municipal Holiday. **5-7 Aug**, Independence Day. **12 Oct**, Columbus Day. **2 Nov**, Day of the Dead. **25 Dec**, Christmas Day.

Shopping

All but the most hardened anti-shopping visitors to Bolivia should arrive with plenty of space in their rucksacks.

What to buy

Llama- and alpaca-wool knitted and woven items are at least as good as those from Peru and much cheaper. Among the many items you can buy are *mantas* (ponchos), bags, *chullos* (bonnets), gold and silverware and musical instruments such as the *charango* (a mandolin traditionally with armadillo-shell sound-box, now usually of wood) and the *quena* (Inca flute), and other assorted wooden items. Rurrenabaque is a good place to buy well made (and colourful) hammocks for around US$5; around the Salar de Uyuni locals sell handicrafts made of salt. Clothes are good value but large sizes are hard to find, and remember that many things will shrink when washed.

Tips Bartering seems to be the general rule in most street markets, but don't make a fool of yourself by bargaining over what, to you, is a small amount of money.

Sport and activities

Adventure tourism in Bolivia may be at a relatively primitive stage of development, but the potential for eager thrill-seekers is limitless. Not for nothing is Bolivia known as the Nepal of South America. It certainly matches anything the Himalayas have to offer in the way of climbing and trekking and has the added benefit of not appearing like Piccadilly Circus on a hot summer weekend. Those prepared to 'rough it' a bit will pretty much have the place to themselves, for much of Bolivia remains pioneer country. ➤➤ *See also the hiking, biking & climbing chapter for detailed information, p61.*

Climbing

Bolivia has getting on for 1,000 peaks over 5,000 m (12 at or above 6,000 m) in four cordilleras: the Real (the main area for mountaineering), Apolobamba to the northwest, Quimza Cruz to the southeast and the volcanic Occidental near the border with Chile. The Bolivian climbing season runs from May to September. In June-August the weather is better and more stable than in any other major mountaineering area in the world. This is just as well as there is no rescue service in the country. Access is easy from the Altiplano, but public transport is not always possible. Proper technical equipment, experience and/or a competent guide are essential to cross glaciers and climb snow and ice safely. A number of summits are achievable by acclimatized beginners with a competent guide and the correct high-altitude climbing equipment. ➤➤ *For further information, see page 89.*

Bolivia is blessed with some of the most dramatic mountain-biking terrain in the world, and a fantastic dry season just perfect for mountain biking – seven months of nearly daily crystal-clear skies and perfect weather. ▸▸ *Detailed information on mountain biking is given in the hiking, biking & climbing chapter, page 61.*

Skiing

Ninety minutes by car from La Paz (36 km) is Chacaltaya, the highest ski run in the world at 5,345 m and incorporating the first ski lift in South America, opened in 1940. Unfortunately there has been little development in the last 50 years and the lift is no longer working. Furthermore, ski equipment is very limited and of poor quality (equipment-hire costs US$10). Another major problem with Chacaltaya is that the glacier is receding at 6-10 m a year. If this continues there will be nothing left in 30 years. A sad state of affairs, especially when you remember that the first president of the Club Andino was killed in an avalanche at Chacaltaya in 1943. The only time you can really ski now is immediately following a fresh snowfall. However, it's still fun to visit and take plastic bags for a spot of poly-bag tobogganing. The Club Andino Boliviano are converting the old clubhouse into a plush *refugio*, complete with all mod cons. This will appeal to serious hikers and also mountain bikers, as the ride down from the top is wonderful. Laguna de Milluni, near Chacaltaya, is a beautiful lake to visit, but do not drink its heavily contaminated water.

NB Do not go to Chacaltaya without first spending at least a week at the height of La Paz or equivalent due to the danger of potentially fatal altitude sickness. When

you get there, move slowly and drink plenty of clear liquids. Take 100%
ultraviolet-proof sunglasses. Note also that emergency services here are
non-existent. ▸▸ *See also page 123.*

Trekking
Bolivia is endowed with many excellent treks, some of them on existing Inca roads.
Most of the popular treks begin around La Paz and cross the Cordillera Real, finishing
in the sub-tropical Yungas, but many other parts of the country also offer excellent
possibilities. Intrepid hikers could find themselves in glorious isolation for days on
end with only the occasional llama for company, passing through campesino villages,
where the inhabitants may never have set eyes on a fleece jacket or pair of hiking
boots. ▸▸ *For further information see the hiking, biking & climbing chapter, p61.*

Other sports
Football (soccer) is the main sport and is played in all the major cities. Rivalry between
the two teams in La Paz is particularly fierce. If you don't catch one of these games
you'll see Bolivians (including voluminous skirted women) kicking a ball around on
any reasonably flat piece of ground. Volleyball (or a Bolivian version, 'Wallyball') and
basketball are popular.

Health

Local populations in Bolivia are exposed to a range of health risks not encountered
in the western world. Many of the diseases are major problems for the local poor
and destitute and though the risk to travellers is more remote, they cannot be
ignored. Obviously five-star travel is going to carry less risk than backpacking on a
minimal budget.

The health care in the region is varied. There are many excellent private and
government clinics/hospitals. As with all medical care, first impressions count. If a
facility is grubby then be wary of the general standard of medicine and hygiene. It's
worth contacting your embassy or consulate on arrival and asking where the
recommended (ie those used by diplomats) clinics are. Providing embassies with
information of your whereabouts can be also useful if a friend/relative gets ill at
home and there is a desperate search for you around the globe. You can also ask
them about locally recommended medical do's and don'ts. If you do get ill, and you
have the opportunity, you should also ask your medical insurer whether they are
satisfied that the medical centre or hospital that you have been referred to is of a
suitable standard.

Before you go

Ideally, you should see your GP or travel clinic at least six weeks before your departure
for general advice on travel risks, malaria and vaccinations. Make sure you have travel
insurance, get a dental check (especially if you are going to be away for more than a
month), know your own blood group and if you suffer a long-term condition such as
diabetes or epilepsy make sure someone knows or that you have a Medic Alert
bracelet/necklace with this information on it.

Basic vaccinations recommended for almost anywhere other than Western Europe,
North America, Australia and New Zealand include Polio if none in last 10 years;
Tetanus again if you haven't had one last 10 years (after five doses you have had

enough for life); Diphtheria if none in last 10 yearsTyphoid if nil in last three years; Hepatitis A as the disease can be caught easily from food/water.

Special vaccines for Bolivia include Yellow Fever and Rabies if staying more than one month or visiting rural areas. All adventure travelers, hikers, cave explorers, and backpackers would be wise to have a rabies vaccination. Dog and bat bites or scratches while in this country should be taken seriously and post-exposure prophylaxis sought even in those already immunised. A new cholera vaccine is available (Dukoral). Discuss the possible need for this vaccine with your travel health advisor.

Malaria

Risk (predominantly P. vivax) exists throughout the year in rural areas below 8,200 ft (2,500 m) in the departments of: Beni, La Paz, Pando, Santa Cruz, and Tarija. Lower risk exists in rural Chuquisaca and Cochabamba departments. P. falciparum malaria is most likely to occur in Beni and Pando (northeastern areas bordering Brazil), especially in the localities of Guayaramerin, Puerto Rico, and Riberalta. There is no risk on many typical itineraries including all urban areas and high altitude destinations such as Lake Titicaca.

Symptoms Malaria can cause death within 24 hours. It can start as something just resembling an attack of flu. You may feel tired, lethargic, headachy, feverish; or more seriously, develop fits, followed by coma and then death. Have a low index of suspicion because it is very easy to write off vague symptoms, which may actually be malaria. If you have a temperature, go to a doctor as soon as you can and ask for a malaria test. On your return home if you suffer any of these symptoms, get tested as soon as possible, even if any previous test proved negative, the test could save your life.

Cures Treatment is with drugs and may be oral or into a vein depending on the seriousness of the infection. Remember ABCD: Awareness (of whether the disease is present in the area you are travelling in), Bite avoidance, Chemoprohylaxis, Diagnosis.

Prevention This is best summarized by the B and C: bite avoidance and chemo-prophylaxis. Wear clothes that cover arms and legs and use effective insect repellents in areas with known risks of insect-spread disease. Use a mosquito net dipped in permethrin as both a physical and chemical barrier at night in the same areas. Guard against the contraction of malaria with the correct anti-malarials (see above). Some would prefer to take test kits for malaria with them and have standby treatment available. However, the field tests of the blood kits have had poor results: when you have malaria you are usually too ill to be able to do the tests correctly enough to make the right diagnosis. Standby treatment (treatment that you carry and take yourself for malaria) should still ideally be supervised by a doctor since the drugs themselves can be toxic if taken incorrectly. Note that the Royal Homeopathic Hospital in the UK does not advocate homeopathic options for malaria prevention or treatment.

Mosquito repellents (you may need these anywhere from Scotland to South America). Remember that DEET (Di-ethyltoluamide) is the gold standard. Apply the repellent every four to six hours but more often if you are sweating heavily. If a non-DEET product is used check who tested it. Validated products (tested at the London School of Hygiene and Tropical Medicine) include Mosiguard, Non-DEET Jungle formula and non-DEET Autan. If you want to use citronella remember that it must be applied very frequently (ie hourly) to be effective. If you are popular target for insect bites or develop lumps quite soon after being bitten, carry an Aspivenin kit. This syringe suction device is available from many chemists and draws out some of the allergic materials and provides quick relief.

What to take

Pain killers. Paracetamol or a suitable painkiller can have multiple uses for symptoms but remember that more than eight paracetamol a day can lead to liver failure.

Ciproxin (Ciprofloaxcin). A useful antibiotic for some forms of travellers diarrhoea.

Immodium. A great standby for those diarrhoeas that occur at awkward times (ie before a long coach/train journey or on a trek). It helps stop the flow of diarrhoea and in my view is of more benefit than harm. (It was believed that letting the bacteria or viruses flow out had to be more beneficial. However, with Immodium they still come out, just in a more solid form.)

Pepto-Bismol. Used a lot by Americans for diarrhoea. It certainly relieves symptoms but like Immodium it is not a cure for underlying disease. Be aware that it turns the stool black as well as making it more solid.

MedicAlert. These simple bracelets, or an equivalent, should be carried or worn by anyone with a significant medical condition.

For longer trips involving jungle treks taking a clean needle pack, clean dental pack and water filtration devices are common-sense measures.

An A-Z of health risks

Altitude sickness

Symptoms Acute mountain sickness can strike from about 3,000 m upwards and in general is more likely to affect those who ascend rapidly (for example by plane) and those who over-exert themselves. Teenagers are particularly prone. On reaching heights above 3,000 m, heart pounding and shortness of breath, especially on exertion, are almost universal and a normal response to the lack of oxygen in the air. Acute mountain sickness takes a few hours or days to come on and presents with heachache, lassitude, dizziness, loss of appetite, nausea and vomiting. Insomnia is common and often associated with a suffocating feeling when lying down in bed. You may notice that your breathing tends to wax and wane at night and your face is puffy in the mornings – this is all part of the syndrome.

Prevention With appropriate medical advice the following regime will be useful to some people but common sense measures should still prevail:
Diamox (Acetazolamide) 250 mg twice a day (this is prescription only) dDay before ascent, day of ascent, day after ascent, total of six tablets per person.

Cures If the symptoms are mild, the treatment is rest, painkillers (preferably not aspirin-based) for the headaches and anti-sickness pills for vomiting. Should the symptoms be severe and prolonged it is best to descend to a lower altitude immediately and reascend, if necessary, slowly and in stages. The symptoms disappear very quickly with even a few 100 m of descent.

Prevention The best way of preventing acute mountain sickness is a relatively slow ascent. When trekking to high altitude, some time spent walking at medium altitude, getting fit and getting adapted, is beneficial. On arrival at places over 3,000 m a few hours' rest and the avoidance of alcohol, cigarettes and heavy food will go a long way towards preventing acute mountain sickness.

Other problems experienced at high altitude are sunburn, excessively dry air causing skin cracking, sore eyes (it may be wise to leave your contact lenses out) and sore nostrils. Treat the latter with Vaseline. Do not ascend to high altitude if you are suffering from a bad cold or chest infection.

Bites and stings

It is a very rare event indeed for travellers, but if you are unlucky (or careless) enough to be bitten by a venomous snake, spider, scorpion or sea creature, try to identify the creature, without putting yourself in further danger (do not try to catch a live snake). Snake bites in particular are very frightening, but in fact rarely poisonous – even venomous snakes bite without injecting venom. Victims should be taken to a hospital or a doctor without delay. Commercial snake bite and scorpion kits are available, but are usually only useful for the specific types of snake or scorpion. Most serum has to be given intravenously so it is not much good equipping yourself with it unless you are used to making injections into veins. It is best to rely on local practice in these cases, because the particular creatures will be known about locally and appropriate treatment can be given.

Certain tropical sea fish when trodden upon inject venom into bathers' feet. This can be exceptionally painful. Wear plastic shoes if such creatures are reported. The pain can be relieved by immersing the foot in hot water (as hot as you can bear) for as long as the pain persists or citric acid juices in fruits such as lemon is reported as useful.

Remember that it is risky to buy medicinal tablets abroad because the doses may differ and there may be a trade in false

Symptoms Fright, swelling, pain and bruising around the bite and soreness of the regional lymph glands, perhaps nausea, vomiting and a fever. Symptoms of serious poisoning would be: numbness and tingling of the face, muscular spasms, convulsions, shortness of breath or a failure of the blood to clot, causing generalized bleeding.

Treatment of snake bite Reassure and comfort the victim frequently. Immobilize the limb by a bandage or a splint and get the person to lie still. Do not slash the bite area and try to suck out the poison because this sort of heroism does more harm than good. If you know how to use a tourniquet in these circumstances, you will not need this advice. If you are not experienced, do not apply a tourniquet.

Precautions Do not walk in snake territory in bare feet or sandals – wear proper shoes or boots. If you encounter a snake stay put until it slithers away and do not investigate a wounded snake. Spiders and scorpions may be found in the more basic hotels, especially in the Andean countries. If stung, rest and take plenty of fluids and call a doctor. The best precaution is to keep beds away from the walls and look inside your shoes and under the toilet seat every morning.

Chagas disease

Symptoms The disease occurs throughout Bolivia, and affects locals more than travellers, but travellers can be exposed by sleeping in mud-constructed huts where the bug that carries the parasite bites and defacates on an exposed part of skin. You may notice nothing at all or a local swelling, with fever, tiredness and enlargement of lymph glands, spleen and liver. The seriousness of the parasite infection is caused by the long-term effects which include gross enlargement of the heart and/or guts.

Cures Early treatment is required with toxic drugs. Prevention: Sleep under a permethrin treated bed net and use insect repellents.

Dengue fever

Unfortunately there is no vaccine against this and the mosquitoes that carry it bite during the day. You will feel like a mule has kicked you for two to three days, you will then get better for a few days and then feel that the mule has kicked you again. It should all be over in seven to 10 days. Heed all the anti-mosquito measures that you can.

Diarrhoea and intestinal upset

→ *One study showed that up to 70% of all travellers may suffer during their trip.*

Symptoms Diarrhoea can refer either to loose stools or an increased frequency; both of these can be a nuisance. It should be short lasting but persistence beyond two weeks, with blood or pain, require specialist medical attention.

Cures Ciproxin (Ciprofloaxcin) is a useful antibiotic for bacterial traveller's diarrhoea. It can be obtained by private prescription in the UK. You need to take one 500 mg tablet when the diarrhoea starts and if you do not feel better in 24 hours, the diarrhoea is likely to have a non-bacterial cause and may be viral (in which case there is little you can do apart from keep yourself rehydrated and wait for it to settle on its own). The key treatment with all diarrhoeas is rehydration. Try to keep hydrated by taking the right mixture of salt and water. This is available as Oral Rehydration Salts (ORS) in ready-made sachets or can be made up by adding a teaspoon of sugar and a half teaspoon of salt to a litre of clean water. Drink at least one large cup of this drink for each loose stool. You can also use flat carbonated drinks as an alternative. Immodium and Pepto-Bismol provide symptomatic relief.

Prevention The standard advice is to be careful with water and ice for drinking. Ask yourself where the water came from. If you have any doubts then boil it or filter and treat it. There are many filter/treatment devices now available on the market. Food can also transmit disease. Be wary of salads (what were they washed in, who handled them), re-heated foods or food that has been left out in the sun having been cooked earlier in the day. There is a simple adage that says wash it, peel it, boil it or forget it. Also be wary of unpasteurised dairy products, these can transmit a range of diseases from brucellosis (fevers and constipation), to listeria (meningitis) and tuberculosis of the gut (obstruction, constipation, fevers and weight loss).

Hepatitis

Symptoms Hepatitis means inflammation of the liver. Viral causes of the disease can be acquired anywhere in the world. The most obvious symptom is a yellowing of your skin or the whites of your eyes. However, prior to this all that you may notice is itching and tiredness.

Cures Early on, depending on the type of hepatitis, a vaccine or immunoglobulin may reduce the duration of the illness.

Prevention Pre-travel hepatitis A vaccine is the best bet. Hepatitis B (for which there is a vaccine) is spread through blood and unprotected sexual intercourse, both of these can be avoided. Unfortunately there is no vaccine for hepatitis C or the increasing alphabetical list of other Hepatitis viruses.

Leishmaniasis

Symptoms If infected, you may notice a raised lump, which leads to a purplish discoloration on white skin and a possible ulcer. The parasite is transmitted by the bite of a sandfly. Sandflies do not fly very far and the greatest risk is at ground levels, so if you can avoid sleeping on the jungle floor do so. Seek advice for any persistent skin lesion or nasal symptom.

Cures Several weeks treatment is required under specialist supervision. The drugs themselves are toxic but if not taken in sufficient amounts recurrence is more likely.

Prevention Sleep above ground, under a permethrin treated net, use insect repellent and get a specialist opinion on any unusual skin lesions soon after return.

Leptospirosis

Various forms of leptospirosis occur throughout the world, transmitted by a bacterium which is excreted in rodent urine. Fresh water and moist soil harbour the organisms, which enter the body through cuts and scratches. If you suffer from any form of prolonged fever consult a doctor.

Prickly heat

A very common intensely itchy rash is avoided by frequent washing and by wearing loose clothing. It is cured by allowing skin to dry off (through use of powder and spending two nights in an air-conditioned hotel!).

Rabies

Remember that rabies is endemic throughout certain parts of the world, so avoid dogs that are behaving strangely and cover your toes at night from the vampire bats, which also carry the disease. If you are bitten by a domestic or wild animal, do not leave things to chance: scrub the wound with soap and water and/or disinfectant, try to at least determine the animal's ownership, where possible, and seek medical assistance at once. The course of treatment depends on whether you have already been satisfactorily vaccinated against rabies. If you have (this is worthwhile if you are spending lengths of time in developing countries) then some further doses of vaccine are all that is required.. If not already vaccinated then anti rabies serum (immunoglobulin) may be required in addition. It is important to finish the course of treatment.

Schistosomiasis (bilharzia)
Symptoms The mansoni form of this flat worm occurs in Suriname and Venezuela. The form that penetrates the skin after you have swum or waded through snail infested water can cause a local itch soon after, fever after a few weeks and much later diarrhoea, abdominal pain and spleen or liver enlargement.
Cures A single drug cures this disease.
Prevention Avoid infected waters, check the CDC, WHO websites and a travel clinic specialist for up to date information.

Sexual health
The range of visible and invisible diseases is awesome. Unprotected sex can spread HIV, Hepatitis B and C, Gonorrhea (green discharge), chlamydia (nothing to see but may cause painful urination and later female infertility), painful recurrent herpes, syphilis and warts, just to name a few. You can cut down the risk by using condoms, a femidom or avoiding sex altogether.

Sun protection
The Australians have a great campaign, which has reduced skin cancer. It is called Slip, Slap, Slop. Slip on a shirt, Slap on a hat, Slop on sun screen.
Symptoms White Britons are notorious for becoming red in hot countries because they like to stay out longer than everyone else and do not use adequate sun protection. This can lead to sunburn, which is painful and followed by flaking of skin. Aloe vera gel is a good pain reliever for sunburn. Long-term sun damage leads to a loss of elasticity of skin and the development of pre-cancerous lesions. Years later a mild or a very malignant form of cancer may develop. The milder basal cell carcinoma, if detected early, can be treated by cutting it out or freezing it. The much nastier malignant melanoma may have already spread to bone and brain at the time that it is first noticed.
Prevention Sun screen. SPF stands for Sun Protection Factor. It is measured by determining how long a given person takes to 'burn' with and without the sunscreen product on. So, if it takes 10 times longer to burn with the sunscreen product applied, then that product has an SPF of 10. If it only takes twice as long then the SPF is 2. The higher the SPF the greater the protection. However, do not just use higher factors just to stay out in the sun longer. 'Flash frying' (desperate bursts of excessive exposure), as it is called, is known to increase the risks of skin cancer. Follow the Australians' with their Slip, Slap, Slop campaign referred to earlier

Ticks and fly larvae
Ticks usually attach themselves to the lower parts of the body often after walking in areas where cattle have grazed. They take a while to attach themselves strongly, but swell up as they start to suck blood. The important thing is to remove them gently, so that they do not leave their head parts in your skin because this can cause a nasty allergic reaction some days later. Do not use petrol, vaseline, lighted cigarettes etc to remove the tick, but, with a pair of tweezers remove the beast gently by gripping it at the attached (head) end and rock it out in very much the same way that a tooth is extracted. Certain tropical flies which lay their eggs under the skin of sheep and cattle also occasionally do the same thing to humans with the unpleasant result that a

maggot grows under the skin and pops up as a boil or pimple. The best way to remove
these is to cover the boil with oil, vaseline or nail varnish so as to stop the maggot
breathing, then to squeeze it out gently the next day.

Water

There are a number of ways of purifying water. Dirty water should first be strained
through a filter bag and then boiled or treated. Bringing water to a rolling boil at sea
level is sufficient to make the water safe for drinking, but at higher altitudes you have to
boil the water for a few minutes longer to ensure all microbes are killed. There are
sterilising methods that can be used and there are proprietary preparations containing
chlorine (eg Puritabs) or iodine (eg Pota Aqua) compounds. Chlorine compounds
generally do not kill protozoa (eg Giardia). There are a number of water filters now on
the market available in personal and expedition size. They work either on mechanical
or chemical principles, or may do both. Make sure you take the spare parts or spare
chemicals with you and do not believe everything the manufacturers say.

Other tropical diseases and problems found in jungle areas

These are usually transmitted by biting insects. **Onchocerciasis** (river blindness)
carried by blackflies is found in parts of the world by fast flowing streams. Wearing
long trousers and a long sleeved shirt in infected areas protects against these flies.
DEET is also effective. Epidemics of **meningitis** occur from time-to-time. Be careful
about swimming in piranha or caribe infested rivers. It is a good idea not to swim
naked: the Candiru fish can follow urine currents and become lodged in body orifices.
Swimwear offers some protection.

Further information

Websites

**Blood Care Foundation (UK),
www.bloodcare.org.uk** The Blood Care
Foundation is a Kent-based charity
"dedicated to the provision of screened
blood and resuscitation fluids in countries
where these are not readily available". They
will dispatch certified non-infected blood of
the right type to your hospital/clinic. The
blood is flown in from various centres
around the world.
**British Travel Health Association (UK),
www.btha.org** This is the official
website of an organization of travel
health professionals.
**Department of Health Travel Advice (UK),
www.doh.gov.uk/traveladvice** This
excellent site is also available as a free booklet,
the T6, from Post Offices. It lists the vaccine
advice requirements for each country.
**Fit for Travel (UK),
www.fitfortravel.scot.nhs.uk** This site
from Scotland provides a quick A-Z of
vaccine and travel health advice
requirements for each country.

**Foreign and Commonwealth Office
(FCO) www.fco.gov.uk** This is a key
travel advice site, with useful information
on the country, people, climate and lists
the UK embassies/ consulates. The site
also promotes the concept of 'Know Before
You Go'. And encourages travel insurance
and appropriate travel health advice. It
has links to the Department of Health
travel advice site.
**The Health Protection Agency
www.hpa.org.uk** This site has up to date
malaria advice guidelines for travel around
the world. It gives specific advice about the
right drugs for each location. It also has
useful information for those who are
pregnant, suffering from epilepsy or
planning to travel with children.
**Medic Alert (UK),
www.medicalalert.co.uk** This is the
website of the foundation that produces
bracelets and necklaces for those with
existing medical problems. Once you
have ordered your bracelet/necklace
you write your key medical details on
paper inside it, so that if you collapse,

a medical person can identify you as someone with epilepsy or allergy to peanuts etc.

Travel Screening Services (UK), www.travelscreening.co.uk A private clinic dedicated to integrated travel health. The clinic gives vaccine, travel health advice, email and SMS text vaccine reminders and screens returned travellers for tropical diseases.

World Health Organisation, www.who.int The WHO site has links to the WHO Blue Book on travel advice. This lists the diseases in different regions of the world. It describes vaccination schedules and makes clear which countries have Yellow Fever Vaccination certificate requirements and malarial risk.

Books

The Travellers Good Health Guide by Dr Ted Lankester, ISBN 0-85969-827-0.
Expedition Medicine (The Royal Geographic Society) Editors David Warrell and Sarah Anderson ISBN 1 86197 040-4.
International Travel and Health World Health Organisation Geneva ISBN 92 4 158026 7.
The World's Most Dangerous Places by Robert Young Pelton, Coskun Aral and Wink Dulles ISBN 1-566952-140-9.

Keeping in touch

Communications

Internet

As in many places popular with travellers nowadays, internet access in Bolivia is extensive and often easier and more reliable than the phone (especially in view of the new changes outlined in the box below). Every major town now has at least one internet café, with more springing up daily. Outside La Paz connections can still be slow and frustrating, but persevere and you'll get through. Though prices vary widely, it works out much cheaper than phoning home. It is also useful for booking hotels and tours and for checking out information on the web.

Post

Post offices use the post box (*casilla*) system. Items sent by post should therefore bear, not the street address, but the casilla number and town. Hours are Monday-Saturday 0800-2000, Sunday 0800-1200. For security, send mail 'certificado'. There is a national and international express post system; special counters and envelopes provided. Airmail letters to and from Europe take between five and ten days. Letters/postcards up to 20 g to Europe cost US$0.90, to North America US$0.75 and to the rest of the world US$1. Letters over 30 g to Europe cost US$2.20, to North America US$1.50. Parcels up to 2 kg can be sent airmail after inspection by customs; to Europe a 2 kg parcel costs US$30, to North America US$20.30 and to the rest of the world US$42. There is a choice of airmail (which takes one week) and APR/SAL, surface mail, (which takes anything up to three months). Surface mail parcels up to 2 kg cost US$16 to North America, to Europe US$19 and to the rest of the world US$21. Parcels are checked by customs officers before being sealed. We have received reports of customs officers trying to charge for inspecting parcels: politely refuse to pay. After inspection and repacking parcels are wrapped in cloth and sewn up for security reasons, there is a small fee for this service. Two correspondents sent four parcels by surface mail over a five-month period and all of them arrived intact within the time scale. The postal service appears to be improving.

⋮ Ringing the changes

Since an overhaul of the national telephone system, standard Bolivian phone numbers have seven digits. To call long distance from a public phone to towns and cities in the departments of La Paz, Oruro and Potosí – the 'Occidente' – add the prefix '02' before the number. Those in Santa Cruz, Beni and Pando – the 'Oriente' – take an initial '03'. Communities in Cochabamba, Chuquisaca and Tarija – the 'Centro' – pick up a '04'.

Calling from a private phone is more complicated – you'll need to add a two–digit telephone company code (Entel's is 10) after the initial '0'.

Bolivian mobile phone numbers have eight digits, unless the reciever is out of the area, in which case you need to add an initial '0'.

It is much cheaper to send your parcels to the USA by **American Airlines** (T02-281 0215). They have a desk at El Alto airport, to the right of the main terminal.

NB Check before leaving home if your Embassy will hold mail, and for how long, in preference to the Poste Restante/General Delivery (*Lista de Correos*) department of the Post Office. Although, again, this service seems to have improved. (Cardholders can use American Express agencies.) If there seems to be no mail at the Lista under the initial letter of your surname, ask them to look under the initial of your forename or your middle name. Remember that there is no 'W' in Spanish; look under 'V', or ask. For the smallest risk of misunderstanding, use title, initial and surname only. If having items sent to you by courier (eg DHL), do not use Poste Restante, but an address such as a hotel: a signature is required on receipt.

Telephone

The national telecommunications company is **Entel,** which handles all phone, telex and fax services, although at the end of 2001 the government deregulated the industry, opening up the market to other companies. In the Department of La Paz, **Cotel** operates local services, alongside **Entel**. There is now direct satellite communication with Bolivia. Direct calls are possible from major cities to Europe, USA, Australia and elsewhere, with clear lines and minimal delays. Costs are: US$2.10 per minute to Europe and Mexico, US$1.79 to USA and South America, US$2.25 to Australia. This is peak rate; 2100-2300 and all day Sunday, calls are US$0.31 cheaper. From 2300-0730 weekdays and Saturday they are US$0.62 cheaper. At the La Paz exchange you can pay by cash and the phone shows the cost as you speak. Outside La Paz there are no problems either. Phone calls within city limits are free for private calls from a private phone; for public phones, coins/*fichas* or phone cards are necessary.

Direct collect-call numbers: US AT&T, T0800-1111; **MCI** T0800-2222, **Sprint** T0800-3333, **IDB (TRT)** T0800-4444; **UK BT** T0800-0044; **Spain Telefónica** T0800-0034; **Brazil** T0800-0055; **Chile Entel** T0800-0056; **Canada Teleglobe** T0800-0101; **Japan KDD** T0800-0081.

In La Paz: morning papers – *Presencia*, daily, the largest circulation, largely Catholic; *La Razón*, *Primera Plana*, *Hoy* and *El Diario* (sensationalist). *Meridiano* (midday): *Ultima Hora*, and *Jornada* (evenings). **In Cochabamba**: *Los Tiempos, Extra.* **In Oruro**: *La Patria*, mornings (except Monday). *El Día, La Estrella del Oriente, El Mundo* and *El Deber* are the **Santa Cruz** daily papers; *Deber* also appears in La Paz and Trinidad. **In Sucre**: *El Correo. Presencia, El Diario, El Mundo, La Razón* all have good foreign coverage. Weekly: *Nueva Economía*.

La Paz papers are on sale in other cities. The English language monthly *The Llama Express* ① *Pasaje Muñoz Cornejo 15, Sopocachi, T02-241 3704, thellamaexpress@hotmail.com*, free, is available in major cities and tourist destinations, with many travel and cultural features and local news reports. Some international papers are available in La Paz. Also, there are about 85 radio stations, a commercial government TV station and a university TV service. More expensive hotels have satellite television, though reception is often bad and English language stations limited.

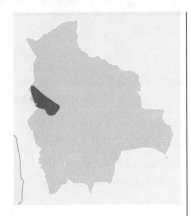

Hiking, biking & climbing

Introduction

Near La Paz, the so-called 'Inca' trails (Takesi, Choro, Reconquistada and Yunga Cruz) have excellent sections of stonework that may or may not have been built by the Incas. Predominantly downhill, they link the cold, bleak Altiplano with the verdant sub-tropical Yungas. Also reachable from La Paz are are some excellent shorter one-day walks among herds of alpaca and ice-tipped mountains, or down to cloudforest, banana trees and waterfalls.

Near Sorata, in the Cordillera Real, you can climb to see Lakes with icebergs and glaciers, hummingbirds and pre-Columbian ruins, or head downhill, from the Andes to the Amazon.

Further north, in the Cordillera Apolobamba, there are more archeological sites, mysterious medicine men, isolated villages and beautiful hills with plenty of pretty vicuñas but no humans for miles.

Bolivia also has great possibilities for climbing and cycling – there are several mountains over 6,000 m that can be climbed, including the impressive Huayna Potosí and the five-peaked Illimani. Beginners and less experienced climbers are also well catered for, with nearly 1,000 mountains reaching heights over 5,000 m.

Similarly, there are cycle routes to please even the most demanding of mountain bikers – not just the infamous 'world's most dangerous road', but also great routes to and from Sorata, in the Zongo valley and even down from the world's highest ski slope at Chacaltaya.

Trekking near La Paz

Finding the route on the Takesi and Choro trails is easy and only marginally more difficult on the Yunga Cruz. La Reconquistada trek is unusual in that it passes through a 200-m abandoned mining tunnel (take a torch). The differences in weather, temperature, and vegetation from the start to the finish of all these treks are extreme, taking you from the high Andes to the sub-tropics; so be prepared. ▶▶ *For Sleeping, Eating and Transport, see pages 110-132.*

Maps Walter Guzmán's *Los Caminos de los Incas* covers all four treks described at a scale of about 1:166,666 as does Liam O'Brien at 1:135,000 in his *A New Map of the Cordillera Real*. IGM sheets are listed with each trek.

Takesi trail

Due to accessibility, beauty, and shortness (a little over 30 km), the Takesi Trail is popular with gringos and Bolivians. As a result there is a lot of litter along the trail (by Bolivian standards). The trail is especially popular with Bolivians on holiday weekends. At Easter up to 2,000 people have been known to do the trek. From Mina San Francisco to Yanakachi takes between one and two days.

Ins and outs
Maps IGM Chojlla 6044 IV (and if you want the section from Ventilla to Mina San Francisco, Palca 6044 III).
Transport To Ventilla and Palca: there are regular buses leaving from outside the Comedor Popular in C Max Paredes above the junction with C Rodríguez at 0530 every day, cost US$1. Alternatively, get any bus going to Bolsa Negra, Tres Ríos, or Pariguaya (see Yunga Cruz below). Or get a micro or minibus to Chasquipampa or Ovejuyo and try hitching a lift with anything heading out of La Paz. If there isn't any transport, haggle with drivers of empty minibuses in Ovejuyo; you should be able to get one to go to Ventilla for about US$10. To Mina San Francisco: there is no public or regular transport, it is necessary to hire a jeep from La Paz for US$60, less than two hours.

> ● *If you need a trekking (or climbing) partner, put a notice up in the popular backpacking hostels and/or Club Andino. These are also the best places to advertise buying or selling kit.*

The trek
From Ventilla (3,200 m) head up the valley taking the left-hand road just outside the village. After 1½ hours following the road gently uphill on the left-hand side of the valley you will reach the traditional village of Choquekhota where it is necessary to ford the ankle-deep Río Quela Jahuira. Above Choquekhota on the right-hand side of the road is a cemetery. Higher up a track goes off to the right. Do not follow it unless you want to get really close to Mururata.

● *The best-known Bolivian treks are: **Choro** (see page 67); **Takesi** (see page 63); **Yunga Cruz** (see page 69); **Mapiri** (see page 80); **Camino de Oro** or **Gold Diggers Trail** (see page 83); **Illampu Circuit** (see page 76); and **Apolobamba** (see page 84).*

Shortly after a river crossing about three hours out of Ventilla, you will reach a crumbling wall with a map of the trail on it. The road continues left to Mina San Francisco and the start of the Reconquistada trail. Do not follow it. Instead follow the path on the right for an hour over the prehispanic paving up to the large *apacheta* (cairn – or pile of stones) at the 4,630 m pass.

The excellent stonework continues below the *apacheta* down to Estancia Takesi which is reached in another hour. Camping is possible above Estancia Takesi and also near the small lakes just below the pass.

Below Estancia Takesi the vegetation becomes ever-more dense and the path rises right and above the Río Takesi (fill water bottles before leaving the river). You will reach the rather incongruous 'CGI' café in two hours (where the path up from Estancia Chima joins the Takesi trail) and 'Don Pepe's' café in the village of Kakapi in another 30 minutes where it is possible to sleep at the G Kakapi Tourist Lodge, a white building with a green roof. There are 10 beds with good matresses, solar shower and toilet. It is run by the local community and sponsored by Fundación Pueblo. It is also possible to camp here. Ask for Señor Genaro Mamani, a very helpful local expert and guide.

Better camping is found 15 minutes below Kakapi after crossing the Río Quimsa Chata where the Alto Takesi rejoins the Takesi trail. While half the built bridge has long since been washed away, there is a dodgy-looking and flexible-feeling three-log bridge over the river. If you don't like the look of that it is quite easy to boulder hop slightly higher up.

From here it is uphill for 20 minutes along a clear-cut and paved path to another café in Chojila. After 40 minutes of descent over mainly paved path you reach a bridge back over the Río Takesi. Cross the bridge and follow the path right to reach the start of an aqueduct in 40 minutes. There are a couple of clearings between the path and the river where it is possible to camp if you don't feel like finishing the trek in the dark. When you feel concrete under foot and can see telephone wires overhead you are close to the rather unpleasant mining village of Chojlla, where you can sleep at the schoolhouse for US$0.80, and eat at the rather grandly named but basic Sheraton. A Veloz del Norte colectivo leaves Chojlla for La Paz twice daily at around 0530 and 1230, US$1.60.

At the point where the aqueduct ends, follow the road around and at the junction head up and left and go through some mine workings. Stick with the road as it rises up to the right of Chojlla and then starts the descent to Yanakachi which is reached in two hours from the end of the aqueduct. Just before Yanakachi there is a 4-m-high gate across the road to control access to the mining settlement of Chojlla. The gate keeper often asks tourists to register. Do not pay anything for this privilege. At night the gate is locked and it is necessary to wake up the armed gatekeeper and ask him politely to open the gate.

Back to La Paz

There are a number of hotels and *alojamientos* in **Yanakachi** around the end of the trail at the top of the village (see the Yungas, page 173). The centre and lower parts of the village are completely colonial in style and very attractive. There are a number of shops, a Cotel telephone office, and places to eat which are sometimes open and sometimes have food.

From Yanakachi there are regular minibuses to La Paz at 0600 but they are often full. Buy your ticket the day before departure; US$2.85, four hours. It is possible to continue down to the Chulumani road in one hour from Yanakachi and hitch a lift. To get to the Chulumani road do not follow the road out of Yanakachi at the top of the village but walk down to the plaza. With your back to the Cotel office, leave the plaza by the downhill left hand cobbled street. A track wide enough for vehicles zigzags down but takes forever. There is a direct path which cuts off the zigzags, repeatedly crossing the track which will get you down from Yanakachi to the Chulumani road in under one hour passing through citrus orchards. Head up and left to go to La Paz. Alternatively, jump a bus or truck going down and right to Chulumani (see page 179).

Takesi Alto

This trail is higher and harder than the Takesi – it takes two to three days – but is rarely done so it is litter-free and you can enjoy complete solitude. (For maps and transport, see Takesi above).

The trek

Follow the Takesi route until 35 minutes below the *apacheta* when you reach the abandoned camp of Mina David. At Mina David do not follow the good paving down but continue along the broad but unpaved path that starts climbing right. After one hour there is a lake and camping possibilities among more derelict miners' houses.

Follow the path up to the *apacheta* in 1¾ hours. Cross the valley to reach the right-hand side and follow the path down to the abandoned mining camp of Mina Inca, which takes 1½ hours. Camping is possible here or you can continue down the valley for another 35 minutes to reach some more derelict houses and your first views of Chojlla, more than 1,700 m below.

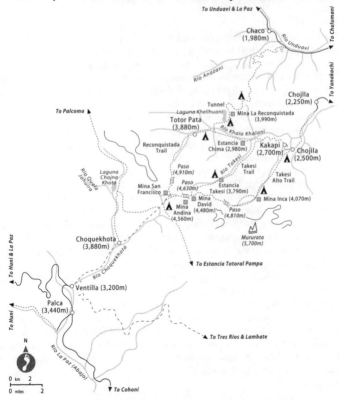

Takesi, Takesi Alto & La Reconquistada Trails

Unfortunately, the path is missing for the next section. The páramo grass has retaken what is its own since the mine was abandoned. It is necessary to descend steeply on the left hand side of the valley and then work a way back to the stream. The effort is compensated for by a beautiful waterfall from where it is basically flat and the path magically reappears at the other side of the flat section to the right of the stream. To reach this path can take up to two hours depending on the line you follow and your grass-descending abilities.

The difficulty of path-following then varies from easy to virtually impossible when it goes through a series of abandoned terraces, but stay on the right-hand side of the valley, gradually moving farther and farther away from the stream. After two hours you arrive at some houses to the side of a group of mature trees. Relax – path finding is straightforward from now on and you can in fact see the next section below.

Follow the path right, cross the pipe-fed stream to arrive at a fence across the path designed to stop animals attempting the airy descent on the other side. Climb over the fence and do not slip off the path. About 25 minutes below the houses you arrive at an ideal camping spot near the stream. At this point the Alto Takesi finishes, rejoining the Takesi trail (see above).

La Reconquistada

Mina San Francisco to El Castillo takes two to three days. For maps and transport to the start see Takesi above. The path from Mina San Francisco to Totor Pata was rebuilt in 1995 with money from Conservation International showing what is possible with regards to path regeneration in Bolivia.

The trek
The first three hours from Ventilla are the same as for the Takesi Trail above. When you reach the disintegrating plastered wall with the map, stay on the road and follow it to its end 30 minutes later among abandoned mining buildings.

The newly rebuilt path continues from where the road stops. After one hour there is a lake where it is possible to camp and where it is advisable to fill water bottles. It takes another 40 minutes to reach the narrow pass, or *apacheta*.

Camping is possible from 20 minutes below the *apacheta* and it takes another hour to reach the bridge at Totor Pata and the end of the rebuilt path. Stay close to the stream on its right-hand side to reach a *pampa* with good camping at the far end 45 minutes from the village.

From the end of the *pampa*, pick up the increasingly clear path to descend towards the Río Khala Khalani. As you descend, check out the path rising up in zigzags on the other side of the valley. While it looks very clear it is difficult to find the start so remember where it is. After 45 minutes of descent there is a wood and mud bridge. Cross it and then leave the path and make your way down left to the river. It is possible to find the remains of the bridge and boulder hop to the other side. However, early in the season or after heavy rain, crossing the Río Khala Khalani can be a serious business involving fast flowing waist-deep water.

With the remains of the bridge behind you, head up right, aiming roughly northwest, to meet up with the path which is very unclear near the river but becomes clearer and clearer the higher you get, being cut and paved.

From the bridge remains it is one hour and 45 minutes to reach an *apacheta* and then some deserted mine buildings on the side of Laguna Khellhuani, where camping is possible with great views of Mururata. Follow the path along the right-hand side of the lake to reach the abandoned Mina La Reconquistada buildings in 45 minutes. The area is perfectly flat for camping but there is very little, if any, water.

It takes 20 minutes to head directly up from the mine on a zigzag path that takes you to the tunnel entrance. The tunnel is 200 m long but it is not possible to see the other end because of bends and a 15 m descent. Immediately before the descent there is a shaft on the left dropping steeply down. The descent is very roughly stepped but extreme caution should be exercised while descending. From the bottom of the descent you can see the light at the end of the tunnel.

It is possible but extremely dangerous to avoid the tunnel by going around the mountain. This cannot be recommended as it involves scrambling followed by a narrow path along a very steep hillside with a very large drop and then scrambling up steep loose scree. The tunnel is the safer, and by far the quicker, option.

From the tunnel exit, follow the broad road to reach an excellent wide path skirting around the valley head before arriving at a narrow pass (*apacheta*), and deserted mining buildings in 1¼ hours.

The descent is easy but long and takes you from the mountains at 4,080 m to the heart of the Yungas at 1,950 m. From scrubby high-altitude grass, the vegetation rapidly increases to dense sub-tropical forest. After 35 minutes you can see the Chulumani-La Paz road way down to the right, five minutes later you can see the Coroico-La Paz road way off to the left at about the same height. It is possible to camp here, near a lake. Another 15 minutes later on is another lake with the last camping and water options.

From the lake it is three hours down to the Sud Yungas road. The path becomes narrow as the vegetation has grown back. You can feel below your feet that the road is level and gravel-covered but you are still pushing your way through vegetation. There is water only one and a half hours below the last lake and 30 minutes below that from small streams flowing across the path.

Come out on the road and flag down anything going up and left towards La Paz, which is reached in about three hours, or flag down anything going down and right if you want to visit Chulumani which is reached in two hours (see page 179). While the La Paz-Chulumani road is statistically a lot safer than the La Paz-Coroico road, it is just as impressive and drivers avoid driving it at night. There is little transport in the afternoons and none once it gets dark.

If you can't get a lift or just want to relax, walk up to the striking stone-towered **El Castillo Hotel** in the village of Chaco. The distinctive, round-towered stone building was built by prisoners of the 1932-1935 Chaco War with Paraguay and is now a relaxing hotel with its own swimming pool, river, and waterfall (see also page 177).

Choro trail

Prehispanic paving and a spectacular but savage descent plus easy route finding – once you've found the start – make the Choro trail a popular choice for trekkers. La Cumbre to Coroico takes around three to four days.

Ins and outs
Maps IGM Milluni 5945 II and Unduavi 6045 III.
Transport To La Cumbre: take a bus or camión from Villa Fátima in La Paz, US$1. It takes less than one hour to climb the 22 km, but make sure the driver knows you want to get off at La Cumbre. Alternatively, get a radio taxi from central La Paz for about US$12 or hire a jeep for US$40.

The trek
Immediately before the paved Yungas road drops down from La Cumbre there is a crumbling, plastered brick-wall on the left which marks the start of the trail. However, there is nothing to help get you across the 3 km of featureless moonscape to the Apacheta Chucura (one hour) where the trail starts properly.

Follow the jeep track. When you reach a lake, look out for a path that rises up right to the *apacheta*. Cloud and bad weather are normal at the 4,660 m La Cumbre. Follow the left hand of the statue of Christ, take a map and compass to get you to the start of the trail which is then well (and pointlessly) marked with lots of paint splashed around.

The descent is spectacular following a well-built prehispanic road down the left-hand side of the valley. The gradient slackens off once you hit Samaña Pampa, 4 km farther on and 1,300 m farther down. It takes four hours to get to Achura (also known as Chucura) and then another 1¼ hours to get to Challapampa (also known as Achapalla Pampa) where it is possible to camp, though the locals will ask for money or food. Doña Juana lets rooms. It is possible to camp in Achura but this would just extend what is a long second day. There is little to buy in Achura and nothing in Challapampa.

The sub-tropical vegetation begins and in two hours and 8 km below Challapampa you will reach the Choro bridge. Fill your water bottles as the next two hours and 7 km are dry until you cross the Río Jacu-Manini which is a nice spot for lunch with limited camping space. It is another dry three hours to Sandillani where it is possible to camp in the garden of Tamiji Hanamura, a Japanese immigrant who has lived in Bolivia for many years. He keeps a book with the names of every passing traveller and he likes to see postcards and pictures from other countries. Another family in the village sells food and drinks.

From Sandillani there is good prehispanic paving down to Villa Esmeralda and then continue for two hours to Chairo, where there are limited supplies for sale, such as bread and tinned food. If you've got the money, stay at the five-star Hotel Río Selva. There is also cheaper accommodation, or sleep under the eaves of the schoolhouse. The friendly Paredes de la Tienda family will provide food.

From Chairo it is 17 km and four hours to Yolosa; 'an awful walk'. The trudge along the road is alleviated by the views of orange, grapefruit, lemon, banana, and coffee plantations, but it is hot. Early in the season the river-crossing can be tricky; take care. Allegedly, there is a truck at 0600, but you are unlikely to get there on time. A truck will run if there are enough people willing to pay US$2.25 each, which makes it one of the most expensive truck trips in Bolivia given the distance, but it is well worth it. From Yolosa it is 8 km uphill to Coroico with regular transport for US$0.60 per person.

Choro Trail

Yunga Cruz

This is the best but hardest of the three so-called 'Inca' trails, and therefore less popular. A major advantage of this is that there is less litter and begging than on the other treks and more wildlife, such as condors, hawks, and hummingbirds. Water is a major consideration. Once you get below Cerro Khala Ciudad fill water bottles where you can. Everyone should have containers to carry at least two litres each and preferably more. Lambate or Chuñavi to Chulumani is three to seven days of hard walking, depending on your level of fitness.

Ins and outs

Maps IGM Lambate 6044 II and Chulumani 6044 1.

Transport Take the bus going to Pariguaya at 0900, Monday-Saturday, from the corner of Calle General Luis Lara and Venacio Burgoa, San Pedro, US$2, six hours to Chuñavi, US$2.25; six hours and 45 minutes to Lambate which is 3 km farther on. Buses to Tres Ríos and Bolsa Negra also leave at the same time but stop well before Chuñavi or Lambate. It is not possible to buy tickets in advance as there is no ticket office, so send someone up at 0700-0800 on the day to ensure you get a ticket. The bus stops at 1000 for an hour in the outskirts of La Paz for lunch.

The trek

From Chuñavi: follow the path left (east) from the La Paz road, which follows the contour gently up the hill. You pass some small lakes after 50 minutes and reach the deserted shell of a building after another 30 minutes. Camping is possible down to the right. Continue staying on the left-hand side of the ridge to reach a stream and camping after one and a half hours, below Cerro Khala Ciudad (literally, 'Stone City Mountain' – you will see why). A good paved stone-path continues along and up. After 50 minutes you reach a junction where the path from Quircoma comes up from the right to join the Chuñavi path. Camping is possible down to the right. There is also accommodation in Chuñavi at the school or in the garden, but ask for permission.

From Lambate: from the village, drop down almost 1,000 m to the Río Kheluluni and follow the path alongside the right-hand side of the river. The river changes its name to Río Chunga Mayu and just before the confluence with the Río Colani, cross the Río Chunga Mayu, then the Río Colani and start the climb to Quircoma. In Quircoma, start the unrelenting five-hour climb towards Cerro Khala Ciudad, staying at first to the left of the Río Kasiri and then swinging right to join it. Camp near Laguna Kasiri and then go around it to the right and up and over a 4,200 m pass to the right (east) of the mountain and descend to join the path from Chuñavi. This option normally takes two days from Lambate, involving a hot and sweaty haul up from the Río Chunga Mayu.

From the junction, continue north to Cerro Cuchillatuca and then on to Cerro Yunga Cruz in 1½ hours, where there is water and it is possible to camp. The next water and camping is possible in 30 minutes just before the start of the descent to the Yungas.

The path deteriorates as it descends before going left around a ridge and dropping further, improving before making two stream crossings, the first in cloud forest, the second in the open, in 15 minutes. The quality of the path then deteriorates again. There are three streams (the last water on the trek) within the next 30 minutes with camping possible just before the third stream. Camp or fill up at least two litres as there is no more water for a very long time. There are a number of clearances on the way down, but no place for camping with water until you reach Chulumani.

The whole way down from this point is tiring. The vegetation increases often obstructing the way, forcing you to duck under bamboo and other plants which form tunnels. This is tremendous fun with a full rucksack. A machete is useful, especially early in the season when not many other people have passed through.

After 1½ hours the track forks amid dense vegetation. Take the right-hand fork and come out into the open on the side of a ridge five minutes later. After another 30 minutes you come to what was a clearing, where Bolivians regularly camp and leave their litter.

At the end of the clearing the trail goes to the right of Cerro Duraznuni in front. Go up and then drop down. From the shoulder of Cerro Duraznuni descend on the other side to reach a road which is followed into the village of Sikilini. Just before a tennis court on the right, there is a good path leading off to the left to a viewpoint giving a good view to the left of Huancane. Follow the path down which soon turns into a track which leads down to Chulumani in one hour and 45 minutes.

Yunga Cruz

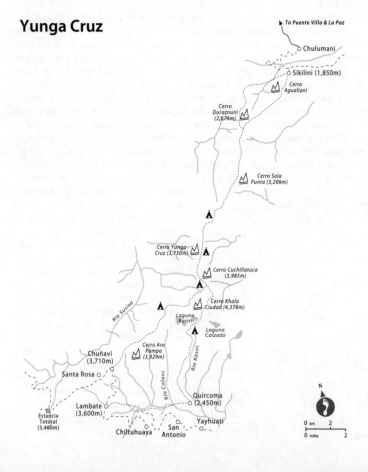

66 99 Their jagged vertical rock formations, with brilliant patches of snow, announce to the most intrepid human beings: "Here no one will ever climb."

From Chulumani there are buses and minibuses to La Paz every couple of hours during the morning, US$2.50, 4-5 hours. For further details on Chulumani, see page 179.

It is possible to do this hike in reverse from Chulumani as far as Chuñavi then back again with a guide from Country House bed and breakfast. See Chulumani section for contact details.

One-day hikes near La Paz

Fundamentalist trekking guides recommend many great hikes that 'seem' near La Paz. But access to the trail-heads is complicated and may rob you of a whole day, plus a long-distance taxi fare.

Without diminishing the virtues of the oft-touted treks, some travellers to La Paz would love the challenge of a spirited hike through rough wilderness but do not wish to spend the night in a crumbling hut with deadly *vinchuca* bugs lurking between the adobes. Others who love the stars as their roof may simply not have the time to invest in pre- and post-hike travel.

Other would-be hikers remain in La Paz, fearing that nearby trails would simply offer more of the same dusty, chalky foothills. Or they yearn for the healthy pleasure of a back-country hike, but would much prefer to return to a comfortable bed in La Paz.

Hidden in the hills, are a number of splendid hikes with easy access, challenging terrain, aesthetic surroundings, and an uncomplicated return. Fundamentalist trekking Calvinists might be scornful of such soft-core adventure, but given the physical stamina requirements and the total lack of comfort facilities along the way, these hikes can hardly be considered hedonistic.

Many of the same materials for longer hikes are required: protective dark glasses (especially in blinding snows), sunscreen, a hooded windbreaker, a plastic bag for picnic refuse, bottled water, and of course, comfortable shoes with good grip. You'll be returning the same day, so you'll have a lighter backpack and won't be mistaken for one of the beasts of burden on the trail.

Ins and outs
The dry season, June-August, is the safest period. One of these hikes, Palca Canyon, is excluded from these pages since it is already covered on page 109. What remains are four very different hikes, all accessible via La Cumbre, at the beginning of the road to Las Yungas. Transportation to trailheads begins from Villa Fátima. Hail a bus (slowest option), a minibus (labeled either 'Coroico/Caranavi' or 'Chulumani'), or hitch a ride (fastest option but not necessarily the safest). If you hitch, always offer to pay a fare. Some drivers will accept your offer. Others will decline. To La Cumbre, the fare in bolivianos is roughly US$1.

Hike 1
This hike begins at La Cumbre, at around 4,600 m (30 minutes by mini-bus from Villa Fátima).

But for the altitude, this is the easiest of the four hikes. Get out of the minibus at La Cumbre and, to your right, spot a rutted jeep track that will wind up nearly 400 m via hairpin turns to a telephone station at the top of Mont Valeriani, 5,000 m above sea level. It should take 1¼ hours to reach the top. The climb is relatively gradual. You will see no other human being along the way, unless one of the occasional jeeps is bumping up to or down from the telephone relay station. What you will see are untended herds of alpaca, and to your right, near the top, a fresh lake. You're well above the tree line, so there's no shade. Patches of rough grass and diminutive yellow and purple butterflies break up the stony decor. Once at the level of the telephone relay station (a small whitewashed structure with a signal tower), there is a rock formation that will take you to the peak. Scaling these rocks in five or ten minutes is the only difficult part of this hike.

When you arrive at the top of Mont Valeriani, from either the stony ledge at the level of the telephone station, or from the outcrop above, you'll behold an awesome view, straight down to the highway (a distant ribbon winding its way to Unduavi 1,200 m below) and brilliant glaciers on the craggy face of several imposing mountains, staring you in the face. To say these mountains were towering above the highway would be an understatement. Their jagged vertical rock formations, with brilliant patches of snow, announce to the most intrepid human beings: "Here no one will ever climb."

Mont Valeriani is a magnificent place to have a picnic, and even a dry piece of bread with a stale slab of cheese acquires banquet status.

Hike 2

Mont Valeriani is to the right of the Cumbre highway coming from La Paz. This hike begins at the same place but at the left of the highway. You'll usually find only patches of snow on the path up Valeriani, but on the twin-teeth side, you should have good shoes with a grip that keep out moisture from snow patches that widen as you ascend. Begin at the Cumbre lake. The trail winds to the right of the lake, then switches back left and uphill. You'll hear what sounds like a waterfall (about 20 minutes into the hike), simultaneous to a fork in the trail. Keep left at the fork, with the creek running below to your left. In another 10 minutes you'll reach a pair of lakes with a natural causeway in between. You should be able to spot two jagged "teeth" looming above. These are the twin peaks. These peaks do not appear in any hiking book. One local claims they're called Khala Huyo, at 5,200 m, but we're still seeking a second opinion. From here you are about one hour and ten minutes from either one of these peaks. (A conservative estimate is to allow two hours from La Cumbre to the top of either of these peaks.)

Still resting at the causeway between the two lakes, you can hear the brook water slurping into the lake. Ten minutes to the left of the lake, not on the route of this hike, there is a geyser.

Enjoy the total silence. Follow the footprints in the snow that are heading for Abra Chacura, the trailhead of the Cumbre-Coroico trek. Soon, the trail reaches a fork. Up and right on a rounded hill is Abra Chacura. To the left, you dip down slightly over some (usually firm) bogs by a small stream. Be tentative with each step. After you cross the trickling stream, the footpath divides (a) left and lateral, or (b) right and up. You want right and up. The two jagged teeth now become more striking. The one to the right is a slightly easier climb. Both are above and to the left of Abra Chacura. If you choose the left of the two "teeth", you should be especially careful of slippery ledges with unstable snow.

For either of the two peaks, the climb becomes steeper as you near the top. Under the snow patches are shavings of shale with good traction. But approaching the top, every step must be measured.

From either of the two peaks you have three views. Behind and below is where you just came from. Forward and to your left is the shiny glacier of the most attractive

mountains in the Cordillera, Wila Mankilisani. Straight down, is the plunging
Cumbre-Coroico trail. It's a deep gash in the earth, at first walled with glaciers but
progressively greener as it descends.

Sitting on the rocky point of either of the twin teeth, with Wila to the left and the
plunging olive green gash in the earth straight below, the view is memorable.
Rumours have it that several atheists arriving at this point on the tip of the world
suddenly became believers in a supreme being. But don't expect the Gods to help
you on the way down. In the early part of the descent, it can be treacherous if you
don't contemplate each and every step.

Hike 3

This hike begins at Unduavi, beyond and down from La Cumbre 3,800 m (45 minutes
from Villa Fátima).

Lovers of green may not be satisfied with the blue-and-white above the Cumbre.
A mainly downward hike of about four hours will get you into the Yungas cloudforest
and the caressing warm ambience of banana trees and waterfalls. Once more you take
a minibus up to La Cumbre. But remain aboard until you've wound down a spectacular
road to the *tranca* (police checkpoint) at Unduavi. The fare is less than US$2.

A few metres beyond some dubious public toilets, there's a right turning down
where the pavement ends. The sign says Sud-Yungas. This winding dirt path is
technically a road but the tropical solitude is only occasionally interrupted (by a
dust-kicking bus or a truck transporting legal coca). You begin at 3,800 m dressed in
four layers, gradually stripping down; as the road descends, the temperature rises,
typically from less than 10° C at Unduavi to nearly 30°C at Velo de la Novia.

Set your timer at 0:00 at Unduavi. The fern-lined road will lead you down past an
old ghost town at 0:30. Keep left. By 1:15 you'll be walking parallel to a cold-clear river
just below (an ideal picnic spot with a choice of shade trees). Along the way you'll be
staring into lush green mountain walls with exposed stone ribs. At 1:30 you'll reach
some rapids where two rivers are perpetually clashing. At 2:15, with the combined
river now far below and slender waterfalls leaping from 500-m cliffs, the dirt road
rises. Once at the top of the brief rise, the downward hairpin turns accentuate as the
vegetation continues to thicken. At 3:15 there's an outcrop to the right for a welcome
rest and view of the river below and the luxuriant green wall above. At 3:40, the river
once more rises close enough to enjoy. Several paths take you down to the flowing
turquoise water and you discover a sculptured canyon. At 4:00 you've reached *Velo
de la Novia* (the Bride's Veil), a slender waterfall plunging from a towering green ridge.
Four hours represents a moderately fast pace with no stops.

At Velo de la Novia there are two basic and unassuming restaurants: the first sign
of civilization since Unduavi. If you don't feel like taking a chance with the food, they
sell crackers, cookies and beverages. You may find a couple of stray pigs hanging out
in the dirt at the side of the road, waiting to become fricassee. The banana trees
decorating the immediate foothills loudly announce that this is *tierra caliente*.

For the return to La Paz, flag down a bus or minibus. If you start out too late,
there's the choice of either hiking down another 20 minutes to the pleasant El Castillo
hotel (see page 177), or flagging down a coca truck. An overnight stay at El Castillo is a
seductive alternative to returning to La Paz. It looks like a real castle and in the vicinity
you can explore the clean rivers.

Hike 4

This hike begins at Cotapata, another 15 minutes past Unduavi, where the
pavement ends.

Everyone knows about the "road of death", the hairpin dirt road to Coroico that
hangs on a winding ledge, with 1,000-m, 88° plunges never more than a few
centimetres from the car window. One of these days, when someone finally pays for

tunnel construction, the new Cotapara-Santa Barbara road will replace this legendary road to Coroico. When that happens, the road of death will become a popular path for hikers.

As with the previous three hikes, take a mini-bus at Villa Fátima. Make sure the bus says 'Coroico' or 'Caranavi'. Do not get off at La Cumbre, and remain on the bus past Unduavi until the paving stops at the exit to the new road to Nor-Yungas. Get off the bus and walk straight ahead on the old dirt road.

You are seven walking hours from Yolosa, where you will have descended from 3,400 to 1,150 m. Where else in the world is there such easy access to a descent of nearly 2,500 m and a change of several climate zones along the way?

For the first hour of the hike, you will view the luxuriant Sud-Yungas paradise to your right, 1,000 m below. On a clear day, you will also see the flat-topped snow-covered Mururata above.

You'll reach Chuspipata, the ruins of an historic railroad station with a row of food stalls. With the planned opening of a new road, Chuspipata has been relegated to purgatory and may be a ghost town by the time you read these pages.

Past Chuspipata, the green gorge shifts to the left. Here the (future) trail becomes a ledge carved into the side of the deep ravine. On the other side of the ravine, you'll make out the new Yungas road. A third of the way down, the path veers around a secondary gorge. Below are the scattered remains of trucks that failed to navigate the turn.

About two-thirds of the way to Yolosa, after having passed by numerous crosses that pay homage to this road's victims, you'll walk beneath a rocky overhang and get showered with refreshing spring-water.

If you have chosen to do this hike before the new highway across the ravine has been opened, then allow at least another hour, for you will have to step out and wait on precarious ledges each time a vehicle passes. A wet towel on the face acts as protection from the dust that has been kicked up by the passing vehicle.

At sultry Yolosa you can bathe in the Río San Juan, or catch a specially designated pick-up truck for about US$0.50 that will take you the 600 m up to Coroico. At least an overnight stay is recommended in the charming hillside town of Coroico (see page 175). Theoretically, if you've begun this hike in the early morning, you will be able catch a minibus back to La Paz the same day. But most people who see Coroico for the first time do not want to leave.

Trekking near Sorata

All routes out of Sorata are difficult to follow, owing to the number of paths in the area, which makes it difficult to pick the right one. Another downer is that all routes climb very steeply out. To overcome these two problems it makes sense to hire mules for the first day – ask at the Residencial Sorata or Hotel Copacabana. Sorata Guides and Porters (see also page 167) rent out mules and porters for US$12 per day, and also trekking equipment. Note that you have to feed your guide/porter. When trekking in this area avoid glacier melt-water for drinking and treat all other water with iodine.
▸▸ For Sleeping, Eating and Transport, see pages 165-168.

Ins and outs

Maps and guidebooks DAV Cordillera Real Nord (Illampu) or IGM Sorata 5846 I and Warizata 5846 II, Liam O'Brien. Nearly the whole of the Mapiri Trail and the middle of the Camino del Oro are unmapped at any useful scale. Tacacoma 5847 II covers the start of the Mapiri Trail and Tipuani 5947 I covers the end of the Camino del Oro. *Trekking in Bolivia* by Yossi Brain (The Mountaineers, 1997) covers all the treks

Brain (The Mountaineers, 1997), or *The Andes: A guide for climbers*, by John Biggar (Andes, 1999).

Lagunas Glaciar and Chillata

This trek is short, steep and beautiful, especially on the way up. Guides from Sorata will take donkeys to carry bags and food but you'll need to be fit. Laguna Glaciar is high – 5,038 m – and has small icebergs floating around in it, but there are also ducks and hummingbirds, amazing sunsets and fantastic views of Illampu and across the San Cristóbal valley. Laguna Chillata is a sacred lake shrouded in legend and mystery, tales of gold and the deaths of those who have tried to extract it. Local witches (*brujos*) communicate with the lake to cure people of diseases. There are also the ruins of Inca Marka, dating back to the pre-Columbian Mollu culture. This is a burial place, and therefore a sensitive area. Do not touch anything, not even bits of paper or old bottles, which may be offerings.

The trek

It's a four-day trek. **Day 1**: To Titisani. **Day 2**: To Laguna Glaciar. **Day 3**: To Laguna Chillata. **Day 4**: Down to Sorata. To give yourself a good idea of the route, wander up to Plaza Obispo Bosque in Sorata from where you can see Illampu, Ancohuma and the ground joining them. Laguna Glaciar is immediately below the lowest point between the two massifs.

From the main plaza in Sorata head up and aim to leave the village heading southeast and into the left-hand (northern) side of the Río Lakathiya valley. After 45 minutes, head down right towards the Río Tucsa Jahuira which is crossed to the right 1¼ hours out of Sorata. Follow paths up and over the ridge above in another hour. Cross the fairly flat section but do not follow the road because it takes too long to get to where you are going. Follow a gently rising southerly traverse and then turn left and up following the first decent stream to reach an excellent spot for lunch in 30 minutes with full-on views of Illampu on the left and Ancohuma on the right.

Continue southwards and upwards following any of the numerous paths heading for the gap between Illampu and Ancahuma. A notch at 4,400 m is reached in 1½ hours overlooking the moraine, rock, and glacier below Pico Schulze. Mules cannot make the short, steep descent so you will have to carry your packs down, and then up, to reach the abandoned mine and camping at **Titisani** in 25 minutes.

From the camp, head up the right-hand side of the stream that runs through the camp and then follow a rising traverse with views of Sorata 1,700m below, Titicaca and, way to the north, the glaciated peaks of the Cordillera Apolobamba. The path is normally clear and there are spray-paint marks on the rocks which sometimes help when needed. Two hours later cross a series of streams flowing from the glacial tongue and then head up on to the right-hand side moraine ridge to arrive at **Laguna Glaciar**, and camping in another hour. The main stream from the lake is full of sediment, but there are a number of clear ponds within a few minutes of the camping area.

The descent is the same to the notch above the abandoned Titisani mine. Fifteen minutes from the notch at about 4,300 m head off right following a series of faint paths to reach **Laguna Chillata** (4,204 m) in 45 minutes, where it is possible to camp. The ruins are to the north of the lake.

From Laguna Chillata you can head straight down until you meet up with the path again or head off cross country following animal paths to reach the valley of Río Tucsa Jahuira above the confluence with the Río Lakathiya. Descend to the river, cross to the right and follow the good path back to Sorata in four hours.

Illampu circuit

This is a tour around the entire Illampu-Ancohuma massif. It's hard work, with three passes over 4,000 m and one over 5,000 m. However, the effort is worth it with stunning mountain views and the chance to see condors, viscachas, and Andean geese amongst others. The Illampu Circuit is normally done in seven days, camping above Lakathiya, at Ancoma, before Cocoyo, above Chajolpaya, at Lago Kacha and at the top of the Millipaya valley. Due to a number of armed robberies at Laguna San Francisco this trek has become much less popular and guides may be unwilling to go. Check at Pete's Place in Sorata for the current situation.

The trek

The trek starts with a solid ascent from Sorata to **Abra Illampu** at 4,741 m. This normally takes a day and a half but it is highly recommended to organize mules to **Lakathiya** at 4,000 m. Hiring mules neatly solves the route-finding problems of getting out of Sorata and onto the right path. There are myriad paths as the area is densely populated, by Bolivian standards, and intensively cultivated – mainly maize and other cereals lower down and potatoes higher up. For the first section of the trek see map.

From the main plaza in Sorata head up and aim to leave the village heading southeast and into the left-hand (northern) side of the Río Lakathiya valley. There are many paths, if you're not sure keep asking for **Quilambaya** (3,200m) which is reached in 1¾ hours.

Illampu Circuit north

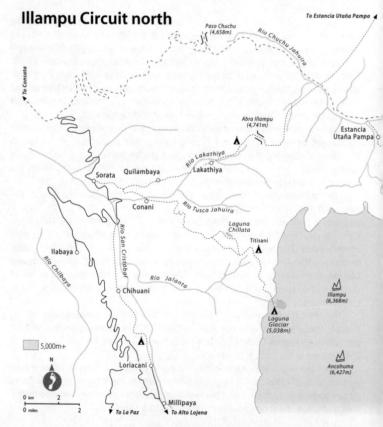

In Quilambaya go around the back of the church, up through a cactus-lined avenue and continue. Cross the aqueduct and carry on up before turning right (east) to follow the contour along to a bridge across the Río Lakathiya in 1¼ hours. From the bridge stay on the path on the right-hand (eastern) side of the stream for 15 minutes and then head up right through once-cultivated terraces and reach the village of **Lakathiya** (4,000 m) in another 35 minutes.

Locals (if they are not carrying a load) can get to Lakathiya from Sorata in 2½ hours; it takes a mule four to five hours depending on how obstinate the beasts are and how many rests are taken. Gringos carrying their own packs take six hours or more.

In Lakathiya the bigger path drops down left to a stream crossing. Do not take it. Instead, continue along the narrow path following the contour and continue right through the village before dropping down to cross the stream at a small bridge below the soccer pitch. Do not follow the path up the broad valley of the soccer pitch but take the smaller valley to the left above the bridge. There is excellent camping 45 minutes after the bridge. If you have time and energy continue for an hour up the path on the left-hand (northern then western) side of the valley until immediately before the stream crossing at 4,200 m for camping .

Fill water bottles for the dry ascent to **Abra Illampu** which takes 1¼ hours. The pass gives fantastic views of Illampu and is marked by an *apacheta* (small pile of rocks).

The descent through Quebrada Illampu to the Sorata-Ancoma-Cocoyo road takes 1½ hours and passes plenty of camping possibilities. Join the road and turn right (southeast) and follow it down for 40 minutes to **Estancia Utaña Pampa** (3,877 m). The Estancia, now a small village rather than a single farm, is also home to a trout farming co-operative.

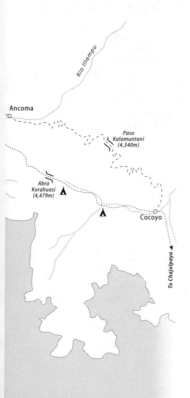

From Estancia Utaña Pampa take the track down to the right immediately before the road bridges the Río Chuchu Jahuria to reach a one-stone bridge across Quebrada Ancohuma Jahutra, and then head along the left-hand side of the stream keeping a look out for a path heading up left (southeast). Camping is possible around Estancia Utaña Pampa but not recommended owing to the close proximity of the village. If you want to camp here, head up the Quebrada Ancohuma Jahutra valley as far as possible – but not as far as the climbers who use this valley to Aguas Calientes as one of the approaches for Illampu – and then retrace your steps the next morning.

Head up and into the hanging valley and continue to **Abra Korahuasi** (4,479 m) arriving after two hours of ascent. The descent passes plenty of camping possibilities before the path swings right and out of the valley giving impressive views down to the Cocoyo plain – wide, long and flat with steep sides. The path follows a series of zigzags to reach the head of the plain 1¾ hours after the pass, where excellent camping is possible.

It is 35 minutes to the village of **Cocoyo** (3,512 m) staying on the left-hand (northern) side of the valley. There are two shops close to the bridge – one before and one after – where bread, tuna, tinned tomatoes and some other basics are normally available (though Sunday mornings and the mornings after a fiesta are not good times for shopping here as elsewhere). Cocoyo is mainly peopled by inquisitive children and dogs and their mining and llama-herding parents and owners.

Cross the Cocoyo bridge and follow the track up and right (southeast) and out of the village. Go around the corner where there is a bridge across the Río Sarani. Do not cross the bridge. Continue up the right-hand (western) side of the valley. Camping is possible 15 minutes above Cocoyo and then in many places the whole way up the Sarani valley.

After 1½ hours a huge, flat boulder forms a bridge across the Río Sarani taking the path onto the left-hand (eastern) side of the valley. A couple of minutes later there is a group of houses on the left. Go towards the houses and then follow the path that rises up left immediately after them. There is camping on the flat and sometimes boggy valley floor, but better camping 15 minutes along the path up the left hand side of the valley near a couple of derelict houses. It takes another hour to Paso Sarani (4,600 m).

Camping is possible 10 minutes below Paso Sarani; 15 minutes below the pass cross the stream to the right. Five minutes after the stream there is a good path going off right (south) which reaches the valley bottom in 30 minutes.

The Illampu circuit continues up the right-hand (northwest) side of the Río Chajolpaya. Initially the path is not clear as it crosses and goes around a boggy section, but after that it becomes a wide, roughly paved path – the Calzada road.

Illampu Circuit south

It takes five hours to reach the **Paso Calzada** at 5,045 m (see map below). It is a long way so it's best to try and get as far up the valley as possible before camping. There is excellent camping 35 minutes up the Calzada road and then 1½ hours farther up with views of Calzada to the left and Kasiri to the right. The last good camping before the pass is immediately before the path climbs up left (southwest) from the valley floor, 4¼ hours after you join the Calzada road. The Río Chajolpaya is full of sediment; the side streams are clear but spread out. The Paso Calzada is broad and barren but camping is possible near the numerous small lakes if you want to try sleeping at over 5,000 m.

From the pass follow the broad path down to the right (west) of **Laguna Carizal** and on down to **Laguna Chojña Khota** in 1¼ hours. Camping is possible at the southern end of the lake. The path then crosses Quebrada de Kote to the left (east)

Illampu Circuit south

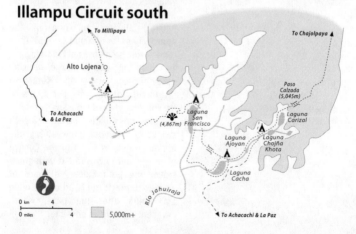

and rises up on the other side. Either follow the path and then drop back down to **Laguna Cacha** or go cross country staying on the right-hand side of the valley to Laguna Cacha. Either way, you should be at Laguna Cacha in another 1¼ hours.

From the northern end of Laguna Cacha there are two options: 1) follow the path down and around to the right (west) and then up to **Laguna San Francisco**; 2) or better, head straight up to the ridge to the northwest. The climb takes 50 minutes but is worth it for the views of Lake Titicaca, Ancohuma, Kasiri, Calzada, Chearoco, and Chachacomani. From the ridge, descend right (northwest) to the top (north) end of **Laguna San Francisco** in 1¼ hours, where there is excellent camping. **Note**: at Laguna San Francisco a family have been extracting a 'tourist tax' from trekkers. They are armed and may ask for as much as US$30, less if you're with a local guide from Sorata. There have also been cases of armed robbery here.

From the lake head up to join the path which goes left (southwest) and then bears right (west) across a plain, joining and then leaving the disused road to reach a pile of stones, Point 4,867, in 1½ hours. Kasiri, Calzada, Chearoco, and Chachacomani are all visible, as is Lake Titicaca, 1,057 m below. If you think that is a long way down remember that Sorata is 1,132 m below the lake and that's where the trek is going.

Follow the disused road down for 1¼ hours from Point 4,867. As the valley flattens out to the right and you feel closer to civilization the road crosses a small disused aqueduct and a path which cuts back right (north) to a stream. Follow this path, cross the stream and then five minutes later look out for a path heading right (northwest). Head north-northwest for Laguna Hualatani and then follow the path on the right-hand (eastern) side. The path crosses an aqueduct shortly before reaching an *apacheta* an hour after the stream crossing. From this point on the rest of the trail is basically down, down, down.

Camping is possible after the trail crosses a new road 20 minutes below the *apacheta*. The new, rarely used road is not marked on any available maps. The descent joins the road shortly before **Alto Lojena** which is reached 35 minutes after the road crossing. The road has been washed away at a number of points – no one built culverts for the streams – explaining its lack of use. It takes another 40 minutes to get to **Millipaya** at 3,475 m (see Illampu Circuit north map).

Transport to Sorata
Trucks to La Paz leave irregularly from Millipaya joining the La Paz-Sorata road above Umanata. If you want a lift back to Sorata take a ride to the junction and then get a lift with anything heading right (north) to Sorata. There is irregular transport to Sorata along the road on the right-hand (northeastern) side of the valley.

Returning to Sorata on foot
If you ask any locals the way to Sorata they will tell you to take the road, which takes about four hours. Don't do this. You won't see Illampu, Ancohuma and the other snow peaks high above the right-hand side of the valley.

Instead, from Millipaya go to **Loriacani**, the end of the driveable road, 25 minutes from Millipaya. Route-finding for the next hour is difficult because of the vegetation and the numerous narrow paths linking fields, going up and over the ridge to the La Paz road and dropping down to small riverside mines. However, it is worth the effort for the views across the valley and down to Sorata. At Loriacani cross the stream and head down following the path through some houses, along a stream bed and out between some cultivated fields. Head up left to join a good but narrow path that takes you in and out of a series of *quebradas*. There is excellent camping 45 minutes after Loriacani up and left from the path.

From here the path gets clearer and broader, there are no more route finding problems and there are fantastic views across the valley of the glaciated massifs, Illampu on the left and Ancohuma on the right. From Loriacani to **Chihuani** at 3,140 m takes 1½ hours, dropping down right (north) to the village, through the village after which the path drops more steeply. There are many paths. Avoid dropping too quickly to the Río San Cristóbal or going too high. It is possible to pick paths that will bring you out exactly at the point where the La Paz-Sorata road bridges the Río San Cristóbal at 2,665 m in just over an hour. Cross the bridge to reach the right-hand side of the Río San Cristóbal and follow the road to Sorata in one hour.

Mapiri trail

This is only for hardcore trekkers owing to the fact that the trail is covered in fallen trees in many places so you have to crawl under them. There are also very many insects, and problems with over-inquisitive cows. On top of this it either rains a lot or you are in cloud and there is a lack of water for much of the route – you need capacity to carry at least four litres of water per person for the lower part of the trail which is dry; the upper part is wet. If you get into trouble you will have to get yourself out of it as there are very few, if any, people about.

Matthew Parris, author of *Inca Kola: a traveller's tale of Peru*, called Mapiri the "trail of blood and tears". He goes on: "When the Lord sent 10 plagues down on the Egyptians, he was only testing. From the slopes of the Andes to the depths of the rainforest; through snow, sun, rain, mud and jungle; through blisters, toads, flies, bees, wasps, hornets, mosquitoes and ants; through humming-birds, butterflies and parrots; through such beauty and exhaustion as I never thought to see; it was an incredible journey, a week of fury and exhaltation." You get the picture.

The history of the Mapiri Trail has been investigated by Louis Demers, the manager of the Residencial Sorata. The trail is not Inca or prehispanic – it was built to facilitate the transport of quinine out of the Mapiri area. Unfortunately, the trail was finished around 1879, just in time for quinine to be industrially cultivated in other parts of the world where it was considerably cheaper to transport and the bottom fell out of the Bolivian quinine market.

However, rubber was then found and developed in the same area and the trail was used for that trade until the 1950s. Following the decline of the rubber trade, the Mapiri Trail was used less and less and disappeared until reopened by miners looking for gold in 1989.

The trek

As long as the path has been used or cut recently, route-finding is straightforward. Mules cannot do this trek because of the sections where you have to crawl under fallen trees, but guides can be hired in Sorata. Start as early as possible each day as cloud normally rolls in around 1200-1400 and it rains most days during the afternoon.

It's an eight-day trek. **Day 1**: Sorata to Ingenio by pick-up from Sorata (four hours, US$6), and then trek to the Río Ticata. **Day 2**: to Mamurani. **Day 3**: to before or after Nasacara. **Day 4**: to ridge-top camp at 3,100 m. **Day 5**: to Altopalmar. **Day 6**: to drying lake below Pararani. **Day 7**: to San José. **Day 8**: to Mapiri. From Mapiri it is possible to continue to Guanay by boat.

From **Ingenio**, walk 50 m to the start of the trail running down the right-hand side of the village. Follow the paving down to the **Río Yani**, cross to the other side and then cross the tributary **Río San Lucas** and follow the trail, reaching camping at 3,550 m after one hour just before the **Río Ticata**.

Cross the Río Ticata and carry on up past the last two inhabited houses to a pass in 1¼ hours at 3,900 m. Drop down, cross a ridge, through **Huilapata** and cross a river which runs back to the Río Yani and camping.

Head over another ridge and up to a second ridge in 1¼ hours which marks the divide between the Río Yani and Río Chiñijo valleys. Below the **Cóndor Cuevas** at another 30 minutes to the **Apacheta 'Nacional'**.

A well-built staircase drops 120 m down. After the bottom of the zigzags a path leads off left. Do not follow it, it is probably an attempt to reopen a very old path to Chiñijo but whoever tried it, gave up. In 45 minutes from the pass there is another stream and, immediately afterwards, good camping at **Mamurani** at 3,650 m, but watch out for the over-eager cows.

From Mamurani it is 1¼ hours to a lake where it is also possible to camp. Another 1½ hours takes you through an area called **Kalapampa** to the next river and possible camping, 15 minutes below the next pass. Half an hour further on is another stream and camping. Then climb up some stone steps, cross the next stream and you will reach the top of a ridge at a point called **Nasacara** at 3,950 m. Farther on it is possible to look back to the valley of the Río Yani.

From here the trail follows the top of the ridge where the cloud comes up from the jungle and condenses on the ridge. The river down to the right is the Río Corijahuira. After two hours or so on the ridge there is a cave off to the right and camping before the next river. Half an hour further on is **Tolapampa** marked by an abandoned house (built in 1895 to shelter mule drivers), a stream and camping. Following the ridge, you drop into and rise out of bits of jungle, and after three hours reach excellent camping on top of the ridge at 3,100 m. Enjoy it – after this it's all jungle. If this area is dry and parched you should seriously consider abandoning the route and walking back to Ingenio because water will be very scarce – if you can find any at all – below this point.

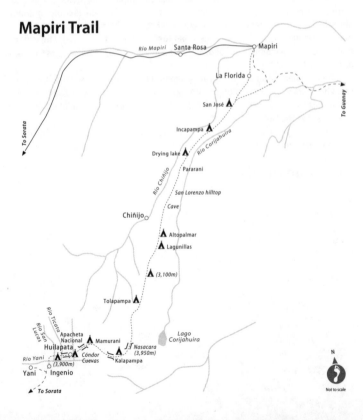

Mapiri Trail

Note that the water sources mentioned below exist during average years of rainfall. As you enter the jungle, keep a careful eye on the trail – which is visible – and keep right. Two hours later there is a small clearing with water.

Landslides are quite common on the ridge and there is a big one here. **Do not attempt to cross the landslides**. It is quite easy to slip and slide 400 m down the landslide – which is not too bad – but then be dumped 20 m into rocks. It would take anyone with you a long time to get down safely and a very long time to get you out, on the off chance that you survived.

Beyond the landslide is a hilltop at 2,800 m, 1½ hours from the clearing. Two more dry hilltops and four hours later you get to **Lagunillas** which is the last guaranteed water and a good place to camp, but leaves you with a very long and waterless next day. Fifty years ago, when the trail was in regular use, muleteers would wade waist-deep across this section through a bog which was churned up by mule trains every day. A better alternative is to fill all water containers and carry on up for one hour to **Altopalmar** at 2,700 m. This part is dry, but it is possible to camp and it shortens the dry section by one hour.

From here on it is down and dry all the way. You need to have enough water to get through the whole of the next day. After four hours, when you reach the lowest point, there is a cave to the right of the trail with a drip which would provide emergency water for a small group.

From the cave it is 45 minutes up to the dry **San Lorenzo hilltop** at 2,200 m and the bees and flies start in earnest. Three hours further down, 1½ hours below an area called **Pararani**, there is a drying lake which is the next source of water. This is eight hours from Altopalmar and nine hours from Lagunillas. Camp before the lake.

Exit the jungle and four hours later is **Incapampa** and a marsh, which can sometimes provide water in the middle if you dig a bit, and there is camping shortly afterwards. Three hours later there is better camping and water at a long-abandoned hacienda site called **San José** (watch out for cows). The water is 300 m from the hacienda site following a trail to San Carlos, a hacienda still in use, back up to the right.

This section is famed for its long grass which conceals snakes, bees, and horseflies. Cows are also a problem; they graze at night keeping you awake and they are inquisitive and will push around, knocking down tents unintentionally or intentionally. They appear to be after the sodium in your sweat.

From San José, carry on down for an hour to reach a junction. You can make a run for the road off to the right which is 1½ hours away, but unless you get a lift it is a four-

Camino del Oro

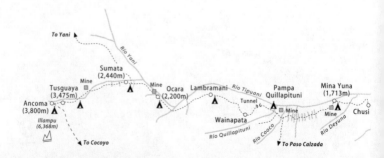

can reach Mapiri in four hours.

Mapiri is an ugly mining town on the river of the same name. There are five alojamientos in Mapiri, all **G**, of which Zuñega, in front of the Entel office, has mosquito nets.

Mapiri to Sorata

From Mapiri get a pick-up for the one-hour journey to Santa Rosa, where the **Residencial Judith** is nice, with a pool (though the water in the pool is green and mosquitos abound), the owners are friendly and the food in their restaurant is excellent. Wait here for a lift to La Paz or Sorata. From Santa Rosa it is 11 hours to Sorata (US$12 per person). The scenery is superb, but the road is 'marginal', especially in the rainy season. Try to sit in front with the driver; there is usually a carpet to protect passengers against rain but there is also a lot of dust. Have warm clothing handy as the road crosses the pass at 4,700 m before dropping to Sorata.

On the return route it takes four hours to Consata, a village with a waterfall in the middle. There's accommodation in a small hotel, the **G Hotel Don Beto**. You can also stop halfway from here back to Sorata (7 hours) in Tacacoma (alojamiento, **G**) from where, 30 minutes walk away (ask locals for directions), there are the remnants of a pueblo from the Inca period named Tuili and abandoned 150 years ago. There is a 2,250-m near-vertical drop to the river below and a tremendous view.

Alternatively, take a boat to Guanay (3 hours, US$6), from where it is possible to get a bus back to La Paz or continue down by boat to Rurrenabaque, US$20 (see the Yungas, page 173).

Camino del Oro

This very hot and strenuous five- to seven-day hike to Guanay may not be in existence for much longer. The road from Guanay has been moving up the Tipuani valley, destroying the trail from below. Mining has already badly affected the landscape on the lower parts.

Either walk to **Ancoma** in two days (see Illampu Circuit above) or hire a jeep from the main plaza in Sorata (US$55, three hours). Locals like to charge US$2 per person to camp in Ancoma. There is no legal basis for this charge and you don't get anything for your money. Similarly, people in **Lambramani** try to collect a toll, but don't pay as it will only encourage such attempts at extortion.

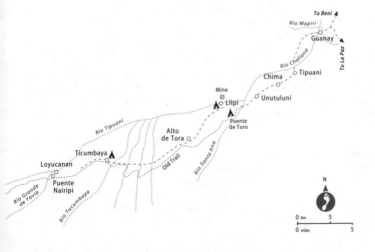

Camp in Ancoma or **Tusguaya** and then **Sumata, Pampa Quillapituni** and **Ticumbaya**, and then stay in whichever village you get to before returning to La Paz.

Follow the valley of the Río Illampu down to where it becomes the Río Tipuani. Continue downwards through the villages of **Sumata, Wainapata** and **Chusi** (18 hours from Ancoma). The Ancoma-Llipi section is the most interesting, following the Río Tipuani, climbing Inca staircases, crossing rivers on precarious plank-bridges and going through an Inca tunnel. Trail-finding is straightforward but there is not much flat ground for camping.

End the trek where the trail joins the road or continue down until you meet up with transport to **Llipi** (eight hours from Chusi), **Unutuluni** (two to three hours from Llipi), or **Tipuani**. From Tipuani there is regular transport to Guanay (US$5) and on to Caranavi and La Paz.

Trekking in the Cordillera Apolobamba

▸▸ *See also Cordillera Apolobamba, page 168. For Sleeping, Eating and Transport, see pages 172-172.*

Apolobamba South trek

This five-day trek from Charazani or Curva to Pelechuco is probably the best mountain trek in Bolivia, passing through traditional villages and then up into the mountains of the southern Cordillera Apolobamba. There are more people around than in the northern half of the range, but after Curva you are unlikely to see more than a few people a day and almost certainly no other gringos. For the few people there are, their first language is Quechua followed by Aymara and then Spanish. It's a five-day trek. **Day 1**: Charazani to beyond Curva. **Day 2**: to Incachani. **Day 3**: to Sunchuli. **Day 4**: to above Hilo Hilo. **Day 5**: to Pelechuco.

The route is covered by Bolivian IGM sheet 3041 'Pelechuco', at 1:100,000. Also the Peruvian IGM sheet 30-Y 'La Rinconada', at 1:100,000. The Bolivian map is hard to find but it does exist.

The trek

Starting in Charazani it takes four hours to walk to **Curva**. Do not follow the road to Curva – it takes forever. Instead, follow the road to Curva out of the village, drop down to the thermal baths, cross the river and follow paths up the other side to rejoin the road.

Follow the road until opposite the village and then look for a path heading up left to the church on the hill with white tower and yellow building. Down on the right you can see the village of **Niñocorin** where in 1970 the remains of a Kallawaya medicine man were found, and later carbon-dated to 800-1000 BC. From the church go down on the other side of the hill and turn left when you reach the better path which follows the contour of the hill and drops through terraced wheat-fields to a bridge. Cross the river and head up to Curva, arriving in the main plaza.

Curva is an attractive hilltop village at 3,900 m. It is the capital village of the Kallawayas, the travelling witch-doctors of the area, and is situated below their sacred mountain of Akamani. However, Curva has no accommodation or food. Its fiesta is particularly well supported by the local population for most of the week around 29 June.

From the plaza in Curva it is possible to see a cross on the hill to the north overlooking the village. Walk around the hill keeping the cross on the left and descend to a stream-crossing in one hour.

Move up towards the first valley on the right through walled fields. Stay to the right of the stream and continue upwards. There are a number of possible camping sites, but if there is time continue up until you cross the stream above some small, cultivated, walled fields and join a well-defined path coming into the valley from the left. Follow this to reach an excellent camping spot in a narrow but flat *pampa* with a stream in another 1¼ hours, called locally **Jatunpampa** (4,200 m).

Continue up the valley and across a second *pampa* to reach a col in one hour. It takes another 20 minutes to reach the pass at 4,700 m which gives fantastic views of Akamani to the left. At the col cairn, head off downhill to the right to reach a camping spot near the waterfall of **Incachani** at 4,100 m in 1¼ hours. There are plenty of places to stop for lunch on the way down. An early camp gives plenty of time to wash in the cold, fast-moving stream, to spot wild horses and *viscachas* and to examine the ascent which faces you first thing next morning.

Apolobamba south trek

Cross the stream at the bridge below the waterfall and follow the zigzag path up into a scree gully which is often frozen together and remains in the shade until 1000. It takes 1¼ hours to get to the col from where it is possible to see Ancohuma and Illampu to the south before reaching the pass at 4,800 m in another 15 minutes.

Swing left and gently up until you join the ridge in 20 minutes which gives views of Ancohuma, Illampu and the Cordillera Real to the south and Sunchuli mountain to the north. Follow the path down, past a small lake, before arriving at a second larger lake in 30 minutes which gives fantastic views of Akamani and where it is possible to camp.

From the lake, rise up to another ridge before descending left to the small mining settlement of **Viscachani** in 30 minutes where the dirt road to Hilo Hilo (Illo Illo) starts. Follow the road to the pass at 4,900 m, which takes 45 minutes, from where it is possible to see the Cordillera Real stretching away to the south and Sunchuli mountain and the other mountains surrounding the Sunchuli valley to the north and west.

As the road drops down into the valley and bears right, look out for a path that leads off to the left. The path drops quickly towards the gold-mine of **Sunchuli** – worked by up to 100 miners – then walk along the side of the valley for an hour, staying above the aqueduct, until you arrive at a camping spot at 4,600 m, below Cuchillo.

The next section is possibly the best of the trek but it is north all the way (equivalent to south in the northern hemisphere) so the sun is in your face all day. From here on there is a good path all the way used by Inca goldminers and *campesinos*.

From camp, head up to the road which reaches the pass via a series of switchbacks. The plod uphill can be shortened and made more exciting by cutting off the corners. It takes 1¼ hours to reach the pass, which is the highest of the trek at 5,100 m, and gives excellent views. It is possible to scramble up to a cairn above the road for even better views, dominated by Cololo, the highest mountain in the southern Cordillera Apolobamba at 5,915 m.

Follow the road down from the pass for a couple of minutes and then head off right, down a steep path which crosses a stream after 15 minutes, opposite the glacier lake below Sunchuli mountain. Continue down to the bottom of the valley, which takes one hour. Turn right and join the road a couple of minutes above the small, traditional, and picturesque stone and thatch village of **Piedra Grande**, which is reached in 15 minutes.

Stay on the road until a prehispanic paved path leads off downhill to the right after one hour. Cross a bridge and follow the path up to the right to reach the village of **Hilo Hilo** in one hour. There are a couple of small shops selling crackers, pasta, tuna, soft drinks, beer, candles, matches, and batteries, but not much else and rarely anything fresh.

Be careful when leaving Hilo Hilo not to follow the path up to the left which leads west to Ulla Ulla and the Altiplano. It is necessary to walk out of the village between the *baño* and the cemetery. Note that the newer and richer graves are roofed with corrugated iron.

Follow the path above the new school and then pick a route through walled fields and llama pastures before the path becomes clear again, crosses a bridge and heads up the valley with a pointed rock peak at its head. It takes two hours passing through two flat areas, called *pampas*, to reach a bend in the valley with large fallen stones where there is ideal camping. It is also possible to camp in either of the other *pampas*.

Continue up the valley to reach a bridge across the stream after 30 minutes, then climb up to the final pass at 4,900 m, which takes one hour. From here it is downhill all the way via a lake after 20 minutes, through llama and alpaca pastures and some prehispanic paving, before arriving in Pelechuco (see page 170) in 1½ hours.

Mountain biking

Bolivia offers easy access to a myriad of scenic and ecological zones (snow covered mountain peaks, highland tundra, cloud forest, and tropical rainforest), as well as mountain ranges, magnificent lakes, and prehispanic (Inca and pre-Inca) ruins and trails. The region is incredibly scenic, historic, and photogenic, and while mountain bikes would not be suitable for visiting all of Bolivia, many areas do have huge mountain-biking potential. Yet, mountain-biking is a relatively new sport to Bolivia, and an even newer tourism activity. Generally speaking, many areas have yet to be explored properly and as of now there is no mountain-biking guidebook to Bolivia. Hardcore, experienced, fit and acclimatized riders can choose from a huge range of possibilities. Either take a gamble and figure it out from a map, or find a guide and go tackle the real adventure rides, but most of these are secrets that need to be researched and discovered.These are some popular rides in the La Paz region, achievable by all levels of riders.

The most frequently recommended mountain biking company for quality bikes and expert guides and advice is **Gravity Assisted Mountain Biking** ① *La Paz, T02-231 3849, www.gravitybolivia.com*, run by Alistair and Karin.

Down the 'world's most dangerous road'. Quite deservedly this mountain bike ride is one of the most popular, made so by travellers looking to combine a great downhill ride with the arrival at a very special destination. This ride features incredible scenic variety and a spectacular descent of over 3600 m from snow-covered plains and mountain ranges down to the steaming Amazonian Jungle. Part of the ride is on the dramatic and scenic road described by the Inter-American Development Bank in 1995 as the World's Most Dangerous, and there is other vehicular traffic on the ride. After the ride relax pool-side in the quiet jungle town of Coroico. Continue from here to Rurrenabaque and the Amazon jungle, or return at your leisure by mini-bus to La Paz.

Zongo Valley ⇥ *See also page 109*

Descent into the Yungas. This ride includes a visit to the base of spectacular Huayna Potosi (6,088 m) and Zongo Dam (the access point for those climbing Huayna Potosi). From there cyclists take a dramatic and fun descent down a dirt road, downhill for over 40 km in distance and 3,600 m vertical loss of altitude. The ride finishes riverside in the steamy lush Yungas jungle. The Zongo Valley road is a dead-end and as such does not have a destination at its finish, and all cyclists are returned to La Paz at the end of the day. However this means that, there is little or no traffic during the day. Much more suitable for nervous beginners or speed demons than the ride to Coroico.

Chacaltaya to La Paz ⇥ *See also page 123*

Down from the world's highest ski-slope. Drive up to the world's highest developed ski-slope (5,345 m), and from there enjoy fantastic panoramic views of the mountains of the Cordillera Real. Begin by riding downhill along abandoned mine roads stopping for plenty of photos of mountain peaks, El Alto plains, snow-covered tracks, and distant La Paz. You can savour this fun, BMX-style, downhill mountain-bike ride as you descend the 2,000 m back into the centre of La Paz.

Hasta Sorata ⇥ *See also page 164*

A better way to a trekking paradise. Not only is Sorata the 'trekking capital' of Bolivia, but the area is also saturated with hidden mountain-biking possibilities. Mountain biking to Sorata is a matter of jeeping or busing to the main pass on the road to Sorata, and then picking one of the many road, track or trail options down. Most of them lead directly to Sorata (but watch out for those that don't!). All of the routes wind rapidly down from the pass, along dirt roads or single-track through villages and rural Bolivia. Throughout the ride you will be presented with spectacular and photogenic views of the mountains and steep valleys of this area. You should organize to deliver your backpack to Sorata and only ride with a small bag.

Bringing your own bike

Travellers wishing to bring their own mountain bikes to Bolivia will have to be willing to explore and experiment in order to find good rides, unless they can hook up with some local riders (although these have a tendency only to know rides close to cities), or an experienced and knowledgeable guide. If you are planning on bringing your own mountain bike here, and doing some hard riding, be prepared for incredibly abusive conditions (and that's in the dry season – in the December-February wet season, the conditions are often so bad as to be unsafe), and an almost complete absence of spare parts (bring spares of everything you might possibly need), and very few good bike mechanics (you will need to know how to fix most problems yourself). While some of the shops in big cities have adequate mechanics, many lack experience with more complicated equipment such as hydraulic and disk brakes, and newer suspension.

For travellers not wishing to drag a mountain bike around the world with them, there are now a number of operations offering guided mountain-biking tours in Bolivia. These are concentrated out of La Paz due to its proximity to the Andean mountain ranges just before they drop down into the jungle. With this natural geographic advantage, companies are able to offer downhill mountain bike rides involving as much as 65 km of almost continuous downhill riding, and one-day altitude losses of over 4 km.

Currently there are few agencies renting good quality, safe, mountain bikes. Furthermore, the wealth of good downhill rides has encouraged a number of companies to opt for the 'quick buck' approach with their operations, using cheap, inappropriate, and potentially dangerous bicycles, inexperienced guides, insufficient guide-to-client ratios, and little or no instruction and advice during the ride. The same company mentioned above, **Gravity Assisted Mountain Biking**, is also repeatedly recommended for this type of trip.

This would be less of a problem if these companies were running tours around the Bolivian Altiplano, or countryside near La Paz. Instead, these companies are offering tours down the current travellers' favourite, the 'World's Most Dangerous Road' – 64 km of downhill riding, 3,600 m of vertical descent, on a narrow (as little as 3.5 m wide), two-way, relatively busy, mud and gravel road. The potential for disaster on this road is high if: a bicycle fails (as has been the case for travellers on cheap bikes); a client is not being advised which side of the road to be on (as has been the case with several groups of riders); a client goes 'missing' for a few hours due to insufficient supervision (again, a real incident) or a client crashes without rapid attention from a guide (as with one group where the guide was over an hour behind the client). After all, the drop from the side of the road is over 600 m in places, and there is traffic on the road throughout the ride!

Yet when run correctly the risks are manageable, and arguably cycling this road is safer than travelling it by bus! But this requires good quality (US-made) bicycles, experienced guides (who can and do communicate instructions, advice, and coaching before and during the ride), and good supervision (a guide in front, and a guide behind when there are more than seven people in a group). Aside from the 'world's most dangerous road' ride to Coroico, the area around La Paz presents opportunity for a huge variety of one-day dirt-road rides suitable for all levels of riders (for example: Zongo Valley-Sorata-Chacaltaya-La Paz), through to extremely technical one-day rides in remote areas and multi-day rides exploring a huge variety of terrain for up to two weeks. All of these rides can be organized to take customers from high Andean passes down through mountain grasslands, past grazing llamas and alpacas, alongside various types of cloud forest, and into the Amazon Jungle. The rides are characterised by incredible scenic and ecological variety, a thrilling challenge, and a whole lot of fun.

Choosing the right operator

Ensuring that the cycle tour is fun and safe is often difficult for travellers without specific cycling knowledge. However, as a general rule, if a company is opting to run tours on cheap Chinese- or Chilean-made bicycles, then they are also unlikely to be bothering to use experienced and knowledgeable guides. Reliable giveaways to bad bikes are: front and/or rear suspension made by JST, block-shocks, or, even more revealing, without a brand-name on them, or bikes with no front suspension at all. Reliable and safe suspension forks are made by: Rock-shoxs, RST, Manitou, and Mazzochi. Note that the other companies are trying to imitate these brand names, but these cheap imitation forks are designed for children riding around cities; they are not designed for serious riding down serious roads or trails. Failures of these kinds of forks are common, and potentially fatal.

Chinese- and Chilean-made bicycle brands such as Santosa, or Bianchi, are generally of lower quality, and again, designed for children riding around cities, not serious riding. Some companies will try and hide the fact that they are using these cheap, potentially dangerous bikes by painting over the brand name, or replacing it with another name that sounds better (as a hint, Shimano is not the name of a bicycle brand – it is a name of a brand of bicycle parts!). Reliable brands currently available in Bolivia include Trek, Cannondale, Kona, Raleigh, and Specialised. If you aren't being offered one of these brands be warned that the quality standards on construction and parts selection are likely to be questionable at best. Cheap, low-end parts will often also confirm whether a bike is of poor quality, or if the bike was once of good quality, short-cuts have been taken in maintaining it. Shimano Alvio and Acera-X deraileurs (the mechanism that moves the chain from gear to gear on the cogs) are low level, cheap components that do not cope well under harsh conditions. More reliable models are Shimano STX-RC, Deore, LX, or XT.

Remember also, that if you don't speak Spanish, and your guide doesn't speak your language, it is unlikely he or she will be able to communicate important information such as braking and cornering techniques, which side of the road to be on, coaching advice, or, even more importantly information in an emergency.

Climbing

None of the following climbs should be attempted without first spending at least a week at the height of La Paz or equivalent, owing to the danger of potentially fatal altitude sickness.

Most equipment is available for hire in La Paz but if your feet are smaller than size 38 or larger than 44 it could be difficult or impossible to hire plastic boots. All mountaineering agencies have some equipment for hire, though Colibrí has the biggest selection. Remember to take 100% ultraviolet-proof glacier glasses as snowblindness is a real danger and counts as a permanent eye injury.

If you are interested in climbing, check out possibilities for **Pequeño Alpamayo** 5,370 m (three days), **Huayna Potosí** 6,088 m (two days), **Illimani** 6,439 m (four days) and Bolivia's highest mountain, **Sajama** 6,542 m (four to five days). Other peaks of 6,000 m or over are: **Ancohuma** 6,427 m, **Illampu** 6,368 m, **Chearoco** 6,104 m, **Chachacomani** 6,000 m.

Equipment

The best selections in La Paz are at **Caza y Pesca** ① *Unit 9, Edificio Handal Center, Av Mariscal Santa Cruz y Socabaya, T02-240 9209*, good English spoken; or **Andean Summits** ① *Comercio Doryan, Sagárnaga y Murillo*, which sells white gas. Another shop there, **No 18**, sells Lowe Alpine rucksacks. Kerosene for pressure stoves is available from a pump in Plaza Alexander. **Condoriri** ① *Local 8, Galería Sagárnaga, C Sagárnaga 339, opposite Hotel Alem, T/F02-231 9369, Mon-Fri 0930-1300, 1430-2000, Sat 0930-1200*, also do an excellent repair service and hire out equipment.

The cheapest way to buy kit is from climbers who are leaving the area. **Club Andino Boliviano** (see below) has a notice board where you can advertise your wares for sale. Also many adventure travel agencies, including those mentioned above, will buy second-hand kit. **NB** If you are offered builders' helmets instead of UIAA- approved climbing helmets, refuse them. They are not up to the job and don't have chin straps.

It's not worth getting involved unless you are going to be around for a few months. The national mountaineering club is **Club Andino Boliviano** ⓘ *C México 1638, La Paz, T/F02-232 4682, Sun-Fri*. It has a staffed office and is happy to give specific advice to those just looking for information. A small donation is always appreciated to their funding. They also run the Chacaltaya facilities.

Club de Excursionismo, Andinismo y Camping (CEAC to its friends) ⓘ *C Goitia 155*, contactable through **Condoriri** (see above). Friendly, organizes regular climbing, hiking and camping trips, produces a magazine about once a year.

Guides

Guides must be hired through a tour company. **Club Andino Boliviano** (see above) can provide a list of guides. **Ozono** ⓘ *Edificio Labtec, planta baja, Av Ballivián y Calle 14, Calacoto, La Paz, Casilla 5258, T02-279 1786, F02-272 2240, bolivia@ozono.bo*. Specialists in mountaineering, trekking, rock climbing and other types of adventure tourism, including skiing, can also organize radio cover. **Colibrí** (see page 124), specialists in climbing, with up-to-date information, trips arranged for all levels of experience and adventure tourism in all parts of Bolivia. They are very helpful, recommended and have a full range of equipment for hire.

Asociación de Guías de Montaña y Trekking ⓘ *C Chaco 1063, Casilla 1579, La Paz, T02-235 0334*, has been recommended. **Trek Bolivia** ⓘ *C Sagárnaga 392, T/F02-231 7106*, organizes expeditions in the Cordillera as well as trips to Peru. Also recommended are **Ricardo Albert** at **Inca Travel** ⓘ *Av Arce 2116, Edif Santa Teresa*; and **Dr Juan Pablo Ando** ⓘ *Casilla 6210, T02-278 3495*, trained in Chamonix, for mountaineering, rock climbing, trekking and ecological tours.

In Europe the following have been recommended for group tours: **Aventura Ultimos** ⓘ *Arzgruben weg 1, 8102 Mittenwald, Germany*, and **Dr Erich Galt** ⓘ *A-6020 Innsbruck, Amraser Strasse 110a, Austria*.

The **Club de Excursionismo, Andinismo y Camping** ⓘ *Casilla 8365, La Paz, T02-278 3795*, help people find the cheapest way to go climbing, trekking, etc; foreigners may join groups or ask at the University or for Catherina Ibáñez at **Plaza Tours,** *Av 16 de Julio 1789, T02-237 8322, F02-234 3301* (she has an information service for CEAC). Each week there is a meeting and slide show. See also the list of La Paz tour operators, page 123.

Huayna Potosí

This is the most popular peak, normally climbed in two days, including one night camped on a glacier at 5,600 m. Climbing Huayna Potosí requires climbing experience to tackle ice and crevasses on the way to the top. Bad weather, apart from mist, is rare.

To get to the start of the normal route take transport to the Zongo Pass (see page 109). Do not camp in the Zongo Pass area as there is a major theft problem. The **Refugio Huayna Potosí** organises regular transport plus guides and porters. The refuge has bedrooms, a kitchen, electric light, food and water and sleeps 10; it costs US$10 per night, food is extra. For information, contact the very helpful **Club Andino Boliviano** (see page 90).

Illimani

This beautiful five-peaked mountain overlooks La Paz and the normal route is not technically challenging, but is difficult because of the altitude. Public transport is difficult and irregular to Estancia Una (mules and porters are available for US$6;

Antonio Limachi is recommended) where most people start the four-hour walk-in to the first camp at Puente Roto. The only reliable way to avoid paying the US$150 jeep fare (one way) is to get a bus going to Tres Ríos or further (see Takesi trek, page 63), get off at Paso Pacuani and follow a disused mining road to Puente Roto in four to six hours (carry your kit – there are no mules or porters). Day two is spent moving up a rock ridge to high camp at Nido de Cóndores where there is no water; take extra fuel for snow-melting. A 0300 start to day three should see you to the summit, down to Nido de Cóndores and on down to Puente Roto for running water. Day four is basically a walk back to where you find transport.

Condoriri

This is a group of 13 mountains, 5,100-5,700 m, including Pequeño Alpamayo, which is beautiful and not technically difficult. Non-climbers can go up to the *Mirador* for fantastic views of the surrounding peaks and Huayna Potosí. There is no public transport; take a jeep to Tuni dam (US$70 one way) and then it's a three-hour walk-in to base camp (mules are available).

There are alternatives, but we don't recommend them: one is to take public transport to Milluni (see Zongo Valley, page 109) and then walk for 24 km to Tuni; another is to take a bus/truck/minibus heading north from La Paz (eg to Lake Titicaca, Huarina or Achacachi) to Patamanta (garage on the left) and then walk 20 km or more to Tuni. There's an established tent-guarding system at base camp which costs from US$3 per tent per day.

Quimza Cruz

This very beautiful range of mountains is still considered the future of Bolivian mountaineering because it is difficult to reach and few people make the effort to get there. The northern part, the Araca, offers good rock climbing on peaks up to 5,300 m; it's near Mocaya, 6 km after Viloco. The southern part offers easy ice climbs up to 5,700m. There are beautiful lakeside campsites and trekking possibilities, for example, Viloco to Mina Caracoles in two to three days. It takes a day to get in and another to get out. The whole region is virtually unexplored, so you pretty much have to find your own way.

Sleeping The only place to stay is in Araca at *Hacienda Teneria*, a Swiss-style chalet, US$5 per person, hot showers, sauna, spectacular views of Illimani, camping possible. The German owner, Hans Hesse, can take his jeep to Mocoya, from where it's a four-hour hike to base camp for the climbs.

Transport A jeep can do the drive in under seven hours for about US$300. Make sure the driver knows where to go. One driver who does is Vitaliano Ramos ① *La Paz T02-241 6013*.

If you have a jeep, there are two routes. The best is to go to Konani (Km 149), 20 km north of Oruro on the road to La Paz (there's a garage here – check everything and fill up tank plus extra containers with petrol). Turn left, then take the Quime road to Caxata (55 km); 3 km after Caxata turn left to Rodeo which is 30 km further on. From here the road to Viloco (50 km) is very poor but spectacular, often passing the foot of glaciers. Some of the southern peaks can be reached in a day from the road. There are buses and trucks as far as Viloco, a poor mining village with no accommodation. From there, with luck, you can catch a truck to cover the last 15 km to Araca, but it is better from Tallapata, a village 2 km away, where there is a small shop that sells gasoline and basic foodstuffs (bring anything else from La Paz). The driver will let you off at Hacienda Teneria.

The other route is shorter but difficult and there's no public transport. It's only 150 km but can take up to three days. Follow the road south past Valle del la Luna until Tawapalca. The road climbs steeply past Cohoni to Mina Uranai (4,200 m) at the foot of Illimani, then descends again to cross Río La Paz (1,700 m), then it climbs up to Araca. The road is very scenic but is prone to landslides.

For the Western Cordillera with the peaks of Sajama, Parinacota and Pomerape, see page 199. The Cordillera Apolobamba, the northern extension of the Cordillera Real, with many peaks at over 5,000 m, can be reached by public transport from La Paz. The main starting out points for this area are Charazani and Pelechuco (see page 170).

Climbing near Sorata

Sorata is dominated by views of the Illampu-Ancohuma massif which is made up of 30 or so peaks higher than 5,000 m and marks the northwestern end of the Cordillera Real. Ancohuma is the highest mountain in the area, at 6,427m, and one of the highest in South America (the highest is Aconcagua in Argentina, at 6,960 m).

The normal routes on Ancohuma are long but without technical difficulty. Access is traditionally via Cocoyo, five hours by jeep from Sorata (US$80), or a two-day walk via Abra Illampu. Once in Cocoyo arrange llamas – which only carry loads of 12 kg each – for the next day to base camp at Laguna Jacha Leche Khota, at 4,721 m, in six hours. It is cheaper to go in from the west following the route to Laguna Glaciar (see page). From the exit end of Laguna Glaciar, head up aiming for Point 5573. From here, rope up and pick a way across the heavily crevassed glacier, aiming to get as far across as possible and set up camp on the glacier at about 5,800 m.

Even the easiest route on Illampu (6,368 m) is difficult. This should not be attempted by inexperienced climbers with or without a guide. There are no mountain guides based in Sorata. If you want a mountain guide you will have to organise one in La Paz which is expensive. You have to pay the guide to get to Sorata and then go to the mountain.

⁑ Footprint features

Introduction

Few cities can boast such an impressive setting as La Paz. Architecturally, the city is no beauty. There are few surviving examples of colonial architecture. Furthermore, there is little in the way of classic tourist attractions – no great museums or art galleries. Yet La Paz is arguably the most fascinating 'capital city' in all of South America. What sets it apart are not only the sights, sounds and smells of the streets but the phenomenal views of the encircling mountains. Particularly towards dusk, you will be strolling through the centre of the city and casually look up and what you see will leave you awestruck: the sight of the triple-peaked **Illimani**, with its snow-capped peak ignited a blazing orange by the setting sun.

Lying huddled at the bottom of a huge canyon, the first view of La Paz is a sight that leaves most visitors breathless – literally – for La Paz stands at over 3,500 m, making it the highest capital city in the world. Airborne visitors touch down at the highest commercial airport in the world, and can then play golf at the highest golf course in the world, or ski (just about) on the highest ski slope in the world.

Apart from its obvious highs, the other striking feature about La Paz is that it appears to be one gigantic street market. Every square inch of street space is taken up by Aymara women in traditional bowler hats and voluminous skirts squatted on their haunches yelling at passers-by to buy their wares. There is a vast array of handicrafts, entire markets devoted to fake designer labels, food and drink, bags of coca leaves – everything under the sun, in fact. There's also a **Witches' Market**, where you can find everything you need to put a spell on that annoying hotel guest or crooked tour operator, or even buy dried llama foetuses to bury in the foundations of a new house in order to rid it of evil spirits.

★ Don't miss...

1 **The Museo Nacional de Arqueología** Mummies and Incan and Tiahuanacan remains are all ready and waiting to introduce you to ancient Bolivian history, page 99.

2 **Browsing the markets** Soak up the sights and sounds of the city's many and varied street markets where you can buy anything from imported Levi jeans to a dried llama foetus, page 105.

3 **The Valle de la Luna** Have a wander round the weird rock formations, cactus gardens and perfect picnic spots, page 108.

4 **The start of the Takesi Trail** Take a trek on the wildside on Bolivia's very own Inca highway, page 109.

5 **Sopocachi's nightclubs** Strut your funky stuff on the dancefloor or attempt to wiggle your hips, Latin-style, at a salsa club, page 119.

6 **Chacaltaya** Visit the world's highest ski resort, from where you get stupendous views of Huayna Potosí and, on a clear day, all the way to Lake Titicaca, page 123.

La Paz

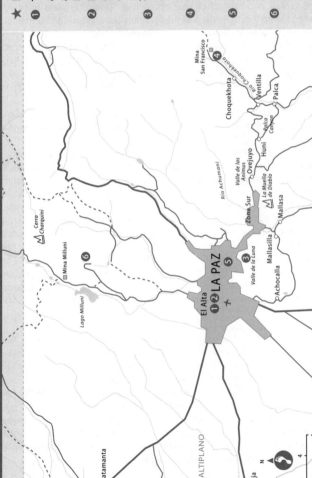

Ins and outs → *Phone code: 02. Population: 1,004,440. Altitude: 3,600 m.*

Getting there

Air The **airport** ⓘ *To2-2810122*, is at El Alto, high above the city and the highest commercial airport in the world, at 4,058 m. It is connected to the city by motorway. A taxi between the centre and airport takes about 20 minutes and costs Bs45 (US$5.70) or Bs15 (US$1.90) each for a shared taxi. Current prices, including luggage, should be on display at the airport exit. Enquire at the tourist office in town, or at the airport. **Cotranstur** minibuses, white with 'Cotranstur' and 'Aeropuerto' written on the side and back, go from Plaza Isabel La Católica or anywhere on the Prado to the airport between 0800-0830 to 1900-2000; Bs3.50 (US$0.44 per person, allow about one hour (it's best to have little luggage). They leave from the airport every five minutes or so. Colectivos from Plaza Isabel La Católica charge US$3 per person, carrying four passengers. Flight details are given on pages 30 and 128.

There is an **Enlace** ATM that accepts Cirrus, Plus, VISA and Mastercard credit/debit cards in the international departures hall for taking out local cash when you arrive as well as a bank which changes cash at reasonable rates. To change money when the bank is closed, ask at the departure tax window. The international departures hall is the main concourse, with all the check-in desks, and is also the hall for all domestic arrivals and departures. There's a small **tourist office** at the airport with some maps available, where English is spoken, and is helpful (when staffed). There's an expensive bar/restaurant and a cheaper café/comedor upstairs, as well as a duty-free shop. **Air Military** flights with TAM leave from the military airport next door to the main commercial one.

There is a US$25 exit tax payable at the airport for international flights, US$1.50 for domestic flights. You will not be able to go through to departures without paying it.

Bus Buses to Oruro, Potosí, Sucre, Cochabamba, Santa Cruz, Tarija, Villazón and all points south of La Paz leave from the raucous main terminal at Plaza Antofagasta, as do international buses (these desks are further back in the building). For information, To2-2280551. Micros 2, M, CH or 130 go there from the centre of town. The terminal (open 0700-2300) has a post office, Entel, restaurant, luggage stores (0530-2200), internet and even hot showers! There is also a **tourist information** booth outside. When arriving at the terminal, pay no more than Bs8 (US$0.90) for a taxi to hotels in the centre. Agencies to Peru, such as Turisbus, Diana and Vicuña are cheaper here than their offices in town. Touts find passengers the most convenient bus and are paid commission by the bus company. Buses for Sorata, Copacabana and Tiahuanaco leave from the cemetery district. Those for the Yungas and Rurrenabaque leave from Villa Fátima. ▸▸ *For further details, see Transport, page 128*

Getting around

Most of the centre of La Paz can be walked around, though this is often a slow process, especially as you get used to the altitude. For trips further down the valley, possibly to Sopocachi and definitely to Zona Sur, you'll want to take a bus or taxi. Taxis are cheap and plentiful – those marked 'Radio Taxi' charge per journey rather than per passenger and so are cheaper for more than one person, around US$1 for a journey, slightly more to Zona Sur. Taxis can be flagged down in the street or your hotel will order you one. Micros (shared minibuses, around US$0.15-0.25 per person depending on the journey) are worth experiencing, but not with anything more than the bare minimum of luggage. La Paz's buses are colourfully painted antiques which chug around the streets for about US$0.20 a journey.

Arriving at night

Arriving in La Paz at night presents few problems beyond the usual issues of finding a hotel in the dark. It's certainly worth booking somewhere in advance and also checking that there will be someone to let you in.

The altitude is often a shock on first arriving, and stumbling around the city's dimly lit steep streets in the middle of the night looking for a hotel would be no fun. If you're flying in get a taxi from outside the airport, insist on being taken right to the door of the hotel and politely refuse when the driver offers to show you a better hotel run by his cousin.

Tourist information

The **tourist information office** ⓘ *at the bottom end of Av 16 de Julio (Prado) on Plaza del Estudiante on the corner with C México, Mon-Fri 0830-1200, 1430-1900*, has staff who speak English but very little in the way of information to disseminate. There are a few free leaflets and a map of La Paz (US$2.25). There are smaller offices at C Linares 932, which has a good selection of guidebooks for reference, purchase or exchange, and outside the main bus terminal. **Secretaria Nacional de Turismo** (Senatur) ⓘ *Edificio Ballivián, 18th floor, C Mercado, To2-2367463/64, Fo2-2374630, Casilla 1868*. Telephone directories in La Paz have economic and tourist information in English on all the provinces.

Orientation

Orientation around the centre is relatively simple. Running along the bottom of the canyon is the broad main street called El Prado (though it has four official names, starting in the north: Av Montes, Av Mariscal Santa Cruz, Av 16 de Julio and Av Villazón). All streets go uphill from the Prado. On Sunday it is often closed to traffic while various displays and events take place. It is also the centre point for any demonstration taking place in the city, which inevitably causes traffic chaos.

El Prado runs southeast from Plaza San Francisco down to the Plaza del Estudiante. To its northeast is the grander area of the city, with government buildings and much of La Paz's remaining colonial architecture. To the southwest of the Prado the streets rise into the city's indigenous heart, teeming with markets and travellers. At the southern end of the Prado, Plaza del Estudiante is, as the name suggests, epicentre of student life, while a short distance on down the valley, the smart area of Sopocachi has many of the city's best restaurants, bars and nightclubs. Five kilometres further south, Zona Sur is another world: the modern flipside of the city centre, full of shiny office blocks, businessmen and supermarkets.

Background

La Paz was originally founded on the Altiplano in what is now Laja, a small town with an old church 30 km west of La Paz on the way to Desaguadero on the route to Lima. The Spaniards soon had enough of the cold plateau. In 1548 they moved down to the valley of the Río Choqueyapu to escape from the cold winds and the city of Nuestra Señora de La Paz was founded. Another factor was the alluvial gold in the river whose name in Aymara means 'God of Gold', though 'Lifeless God of Heavy Metal and Major Pollutants' would be more accurate today. Silver had been discovered in Potosí three years earlier and La Paz was on the route between the mines and Lima, initially the main Spanish city.

24 hours in La Paz

The ideal La Paz day is a slow one with plenty of time for appreciative wandering through its stall- and people-laden streets and with café breaks for coffee and high altitude recuperation.

Start the day with a slow and civilised breakfast in Café Pepe. Wander down Linares and check out the llama foetuses and other strange delights of the witches' market. Browse too through the shops selling handicrafts, jewellery and textiles on Linares and Sagrnaga. Further up Sagárnaga the market area becomes much less touristy and stalls sell fruit, traditional dresses, bits of engines and hats. On Eloy Salmón you can buy cheap electronic goods.

Head back down Sagárnaga to Plaza San Francisco and have a look in the church of the same name. Wander down El Prado, the city's main thoroughfare, to the Museo Nacional de Arqueología and marvel at the Incan and Tihuanacan artefacts and mummies. Alternatively, the Museo de Arte Contemporaneo, on the other side of El Prado, has a range of modern art in a beautiful colonial-era building.

Many of the best lunch places are back near Sagárnaga, so either head back the same way or take a detour via Calle Strongest and have a look at the infamous San Pedro prison on Plaza Sucre. Pot Pouri des Gourmets and Angelo Colonial are both great places for lunch, though there are plenty of other good options.

After lunch you could have a look at the fascinating history and background of the famous leaf in the Museo de Coca or head straight across to the eastern side of El Prado. Start at Plaza Murillo, where you can have a good look at the cathedral, the Palacio Presidencial (though if you linger too long here you'll get moved on by soldiers with bayonets)

and the Congreso Nacional. The plaza is also a good place to sit and people-watch. Men and women in fluorescent jackets rent out mobile phones which are chained to their waists and others sell nuts or revoltingly coloured drinks. Nearby is the Museo Nacional de Arte, with many of the country's best colonial era paintings. Calle Comercio is a pedestrianized street full of fast food joints and locals wandering up and down browsing the ubiquitous stalls.

North of here is Calle Jaén, a small street with much of the city's notable colonial architecture and several interesting little museums.

By now you'll probably need some re-energising so head to Café Alex on Socabaya for a coffee and a cake.

If it's a clear day, don't miss a quick look betweeen the buildings at the snowy peak of Illimani as it turns pink in the light of the setting sun.

After a short lie-down at the hotel, get ready for a night out in Sopocachi, La Paz's trendy eating and drinking area to the south of Plaza del Estudiante. It's a walkable distance from the centre, but you might want to take a taxi from El Prado to Plaza Avaroa. Have a look around the plaza and on and around Avenida 20 de Octubre and if you fancy an aperitif, try Art-Café La Comedie or one of the other bars in the area. Eating options are plentiful and international – there are good Italian, Japanese, Mexican, Chinese, Argentinian and French restaurants in the vicinity.

This is also a good area for evening entertainment – the Thelonius Jazz Bar is on Avenida 20 de Octubre, as is Diesel Internacional, an industrial style club. Alternatively, if you fancy your music and drink mixed with other fellow travellers, try Mongo's or the new RamJam before heading home for a well earned rest.

Unlike, the rest of Bolivia's cities, La Paz has grown steadily since its foundation and has not fluctuated with the prosperity (or lack of it) of mining. This is due to its role as the commercial centre of the northern Altiplano and its links with the Yungas to the east.

The official capital of Bolivia is technically Sucre, a pleasant colonial town in the southeast of the country, but La Paz has been the country's biggest city since the decline of Potosí in the 17th century. While the supreme court is still based in Sucre, government has been based in La Paz since a short civil war in 1899. However, La Paz's economic superiority is coming under threat from the continuing agriculture-fuelled growth of Santa Cruz.

The centre of La Paz has always been around Plaza Murillo and the cathedral. The first real suburb was Sopocachi which boasts mature trees, cobbled streets and some fine buildings. The spread down to what is now Obrajes happened during the early 20th century while the development of the Zona Sur has been going on for 30 years. During this time working-class areas have spread out farther and farther from the centre and include Villa Fátima and anything with Alto in its name; Alto Obrajes, Alto Seguencoma, Alto Sopocachi.

Apart from the airport, there was nothing on the bleak Altiplano surrounding the canyon of La Paz until the 1960s. Since then the relatively poor district of El Alto has sprung up. With a population of over 500,000, El Alto is not only now a city in its own right, but the third largest in the country. Apart from the district known as Ciudad Satelite, its inhabitants are almost entirely indigenous. El Alto currently holds the record for the fastest growing city in South America – its population growing by around 10% per year. Immigrants from the countryside seeking their fortune, or at least integration into the monetarized economy, arrive in a steady stream. They build adobe brick huts, and after a whole suburb has developed, roads are put in, followed by electricity and finally water. The flatness of the land means there are no physical obstacles to growth and the people are used to the temperatures and thin air, at over 4,000 m. However, it freezes virtually every night from the start of June to the end of August and drunks who do not make it home face the risk of hypothermia. Costs are much lower than in La Paz, but construction and infrastructure are much more basic.

East of the Prado

Plaza Murillo and around

Plaza Murillo, three blocks northeast of the Prado, is the traditional centre. Facing its formal gardens are the huge, modern, **Cathedral** and **Palacio Presidencial**. The latter, usually known as the Palacio Quemado (Burnt Palace), is in Italian renaissance style and has twice been gutted by fire in its stormy 130-year history. On the east side of Plaza Murillo is the **Congreso Nacional**.

In front of the Palacio Quemado is a statue of former President Gualberto Villarroel who was dragged into the plaza by an angry mob and hanged in 1946. Across from the Cathedral, at Calle Socabaya 432, is the **Palacio de los Condes de Arana**, dating from 1775, with a beautiful exterior and courtyard, now the **Museo Nacional del Arte** ① *T02-2408600, www.mna.org.bo, Tue-Fri 0900-1230, 1500-1900, Sat and Sun 1000-1300, US$1, students US$0.25*. The 18th-century baroque palace has a fine collection of colonial paintings including works by Melchor Pérez Holguín, one of the masters of Andean colonial art, and also exhibits the works of contemporary local artists.

The streets around Plaza Murillo are lined mostly by buildings dating from the late 19th and early 20th centuries. Running northwest to southeast across the plaza is Calle Comercio where you'll find most of the shops. Northeast of the plaza, on the corner of Calles Ingavi and Yanacocha, is the church of **Santo Domingo** (originally the cathedral),

La Paz

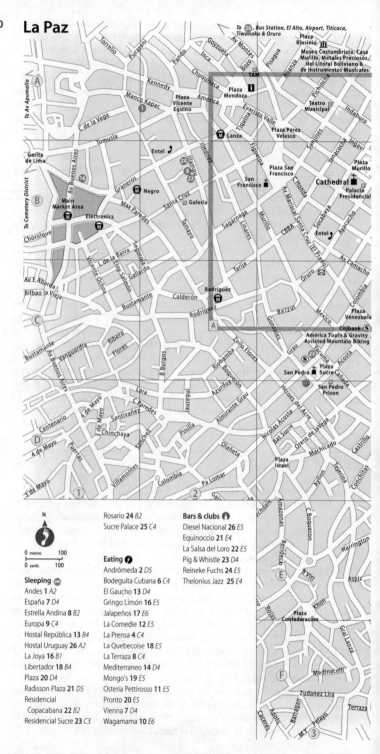

N

0 metres   100
0 yards   100

Sleeping 🛏
Andes **1** A2
España **7** D4
Estrella Andina **8** B2
Europa **9** C4
Hostal República **13** B4
Hostal Uruguay **26** A2
La Joya **16** B1
Libertador **18** B4
Plaza **20** D4
Radisson Plaza **21** D5
Residencial
  Copacabana **22** B2
Residencial Sucre **23** C3
Rosario **24** B2
Sucre Palace **25** C4

Eating 🍴
Andrómeda **2** D5
Bodeguita Cubana **6** C4
El Gaucho **13** D4
Gringo Limón **16** E5
Jalapeños **17** E6
La Comedie **12** E5
La Prensa **4** C4
La Quebecoise **18** E5
La Terraza **8** E5
Mediterraneo **14** D4
Mongo's **19** E5
Osteria Pettirosso **11** E5
Pronto **20** E5
Vienna **7** D4
Wagamama **10** E6

Bars & clubs 🍸
Diesel Nacional **26** E5
Equinoccio **21** E4
La Salsa del Loro **22** E5
Pig & Whistle **23** D4
Reineke Fuchs **24** E5
Thelonius Jazz **25** E4

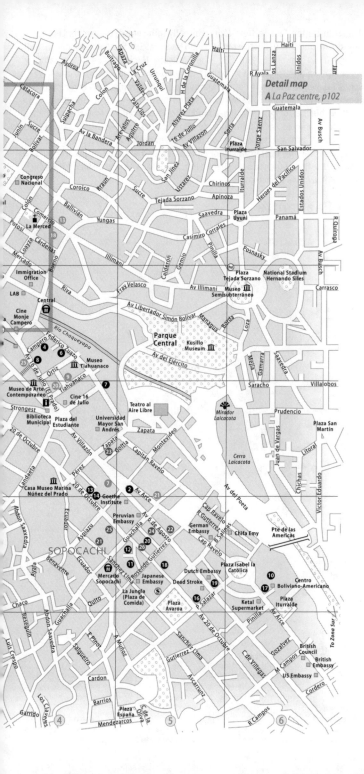

Detail map
A La Paz centre, p102

with its 18th-century façade. Next door is the early 19th-century Universidad Pacensis Divi-Andreae, and the distinctive pink Colegio Nacional San Simón de Ayacucho. Still on Ingavi, at number 916, is the **Museo Nacional de Etnografía y** Folklore ① *T02-2358559 Tue-Fri 0900-1230, 1500-1900 Sat/Sun 0900-1300, free*, which is housed in the palace of the Marqueses de Villaverde, with exhibits on the Chipaya and Ayoreo Indians. It's worth a visit and has quite a good library adjoining it.

Other churches of note near Plaza Murillo are **La Merced**, on a plazuela at Calles Colón and Comercio, and **San Juan de Dios**, on Loayza between Merced and Camacho, with a carved portico, circular paintings of the life of Christ and, above the altar, figures holding lighted (electric) candles around a statue of the Virgin. **San Sebastián**, the first church to be built in La Paz, is on Plaza Alonso de Mendoza, which is north of Plaza San Francisco.

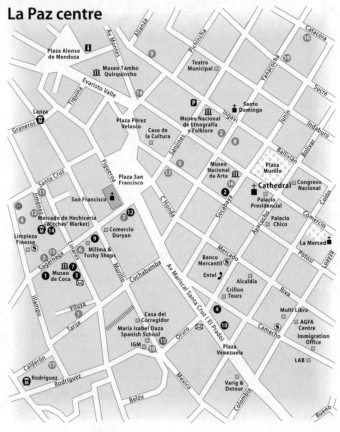

La Paz centre

0 metres 100
0 yards 100

Sleeping
Arcabucero 1
Austria 2
Cactus del Milenio 12

El Alem 3
El Lobo 4
Gloria 5
Hospedaje Millenio 19
Hostal Happy Days 6
Hostal Naira 7
Hostal Señoral 8
Ingavi 9
Julia Rojo Briseño 10
Majestic 11
Milton 17

Posada El Carretero 18
Presidente 13
Residencial Plaza 14
Sagárnaga 15
Torino 16

Eating
100% Natural 1
Angelo Colonial 3
Banais 12
Café Alexander 2

Confitería Club de la Paz 4
Laksmi, Colque Tours
 & Internet Café 9
Los Escudos 10
Pepe's 14
Pot Pourri des Gourmets
 & O Mundo 7

Bars & clubs
La Luna 15

Calle Jaén

Running parallel (northwest) to Calle Ingavi is Calle Indaburo which leads into Calle Jaén at its northern end. Calle Jaén is home to the city's finest examples of colonial architecture, as well as craft shops and four museums (one single ticket from Museo Costumbrista, US$0.50) with well-displayed items housed in attractive old buildings.

Museo Costumbrista ① *on Plaza Riosinio, at the top of C Jaén, T02-2378478*, has miniature displays depicting the history of La Paz and well-known Paceños. It also has miniature replicas of reed rafts used by Norwegian, Thor Heyerdahl and Spaniard, Kitin Muñoz, to prove their theories of ancient migrations.

Museo Casa Murillo ① *C Jaén 790, T02-2375273, Tue-Fri 0930-1230, 1500-1900; Sat and Sun 1000-1230* was originally the home of Pedro Domingo Murillo, one of the martyrs of the abortive La Paz independence movement of 16 July 1809. The colonial house has been carefully restored and has a good collection of paintings, furniture and national costumes of the period. There is also a special room dedicated to herbal medicine and magic (Kallawaya) along with two rooms of paintings.

The **Museo de Metales Preciosos** ① *C Jaén 777, T02-2371470, Tue-Fri 0930-1230, 1500-1900; Sat and Sun 1000-1230*, pretty much does what it says on the label. It's well set out with Inca gold artefacts in basement vaults, and also has ceramics and archaeological exhibits.

Museo del Litoral Boliviano ① *C Jaén 789, T02-2378478, Tue-Fri 0930-1230, 1500-1900; Sat and Sun 1000-1230*, houses artefacts of the War of the Pacific, and an interesting (to some) selection of old maps.

Also on Jaén, but not included on the combined ticket, is the **Museo de Instrumentos Musicales de Bolivia** ① *C Jaén 711, T02-2331075, Tue-Fri 0930-1230, 1500-1900; Sat and Sun 1000-1230, US$0.75, students US$0.15,* run by Ernesto Cavour and based on 30 years of research. The International Charango Association is based here and lessons are available.

Further west, on the other side of Avenida Montes, at Calle Evaristo Valle, near Plaza Mendoza, is the excellent **Museo Tambo Quirquincho** ① *Tue-Fri 0930-1230, 1500-1900, Sat and Sun, 1000-1230, US$0.15, (Sat and students free)*. It is housed in a restored colonial building, displaying modern painting and sculpture, carnival masks, silver, early-20th-century photography and city plans.

Around Plaza del Estudiante

At the southern end of the Prado is the aptly named **Plaza del Estudiante**, only a stone's throw from the Universidad Mayor San Andrés and unsurprisingly always mobbed with students going to and from lectures and photcopying booths. A few blocks north of the plaza, back from the Prado on the right by the Hotel Plaza and María Auxili church, a flight of stairs leads down to the Museo Tiahuanaco, or **Museo Nacional de Arqueología** ① *Mon-Fri 0900-1230, 1500-1900, Sat 1000-1200, 1500-1830, Sun 1000-1300, US$0.75, includes a good video show, students US$0.10*. This modern building, built in mock-Tiahuanaco style, contains good collections of the arts and crafts of ancient Tiahuanaco and items from the eastern jungles. It also has a two-room exhibition of gold statuettes and objects found in Lake Titicaca.

West of the Prado

Plaza San Francisco and around

At the upper end of Avenida Mariscal Santa Cruz is the Plaza San Francisco, with the church and monastery of **San Francisco** ① *Local indigenous weddings can be seen on Sat 1000-1200; otherwise the church opens for Mass at 0700, 0900, 1100 and 1900, Mon-Sat and also at 0800, 1000 and 1200 on Sun*, dating from 1549. This is one of the finest examples of colonial religious architecture in South America and is well

⋮ La Chola Paceña

The traveller arriving in La Paz will be struck by the distinctive dress of the *chola paceña*, a woman born in La Paz who wears full skirts and a bowler, or derby, hat.

There is some disagreement as to the origin of the term cholo, which is used to refer to Indians who have abandoned the traditional rural life and moved to the towns. One version is that the word comes from the Aymara word *chhulu*, which means mestizo in Castilian Spanish. Another is that the term derives from the Spanish word *chulo*, still used to refer to people from the lower-class areas of Madrid. At the time of the conquest, the Spaniards referred to the mestizos (children born of native and Spanish parents) as cholos.

It is said that the style of dress of the *chola paceña* was influenced by the women of 17th century Toledo. The most distinctive garment of the chola is the voluminous skirt known as the *pollera*. This comes from the Spanish word *pollo* (chicken), so pollera translates as some kind of cage for chickens. Up until 1920 polleras were made of silk, velvet, taffeta and brocade in bright colours. Today, for practical as well as economic reasons, polyester and other acrylic fabrics are used.

The long-fringed *manta* (shawl) has not changed in shape since originally worn by the cholas in the 16th century. It is similar to that worn by the women of Salamanca in Spain, the only difference being that the chola wears it folded in a rectangular shape, in keeping with the tradition of the llijlla, which was worn by the ñustas, the princesses of the Inca empire (see page 398).

The hat of the *chola paceña* has changed in shape and in the materials used since its original design. The felt hat of today appeared only after 1925. Its origin is something of a mystery, though one theory is that a merchant mistakenly imported this kind of derby hat. Not knowing what to do with them, he passed them off as ladies' hats, which turned out to be a very lucrative move. In the 1930s the Italian firm of Borsalino began to mass produce the derby hat for export to Bolivia.

The future of the distinctive style of the *chola paceña* would appear to be in some doubt. One of the reasons is that women want their daughters to adopt a European style in order to better their chances in society. Another reason is a simple economic one, since the purchase of a pollera alone represents one month's salary (about US$95), not to mention the cost of the derby hat and manta.

worth seeing. The church is richly decorated using native religious themes; the mestizo baroque façade clearly displays how the traditional baroque vine motif is transformed into an array of animals, birds and plants. The interior contains huge, square columns and gilt altars on which stand many saints. The plaza outside the church is always a hive of activity and often the focal point for the frequent political protests that are a feature of life in the 'capital' of South America's poorest country.

Behind the San Francisco church a network of narrow cobbled streets rises steeply. Much of this area is a permanent street market. The lower part of **Calle Sagárnaga**, from Plaza San Francisco to Calle Illampu, is lined with shops and stalls selling handicrafts, clothes, guitar covers, silver and leatherware. So informal is the retail trade here that stall holders go for lunch leaving their stall with a piece of plastic or blanket over it to show that it's shut.

After a few days wandering around La Paz you may come to the conclusion that it's one great street market, and you wouldn't be far wrong. Everywhere you'll find Aymara

Fiesta del Gran Poder

In 1939 one of the most important folkloric festivals of La Paz began its life. This has come to be known as Festividad de Nuestro Señor Jesús del Gran Poder. The name derives from a sacred painting of Jesus which was moved around various barios, or neighbourhoods, in the city as a symbol of Christian faith until, after a long pilgrimage, it came to rest in a house in Chijini. Years later, a temple was built and that particular barrio, came to be known as Gran Poder.

Many of the inhabitants of this part of La Paz were originally migrants from the Altiplano, working their way up the social ladder as traders, drivers or craftsmen to achieve the level of cholos, who as part of the lower middle class have reached positions which earn them respect and status. As in the rural villages, the many patronal festivals in the towns offer people an opportunity to enhance their status by means of generous financial contributions towards the huge costs involved. And Gran Poder is such a festival. The various traders and dealers make their presence felt by sponsoring groups in the procession. While the extravagantly costumed and masked dance groups compete for honour and status, los señores del Gran Poder, the rich and powerful of La Paz, compete for bigger stakes with ever larger contributions.

Over the years Gran Poder has developed into a massive carnival in which tens of thousands participate. A far cry from its humble beginnings when local people and those from further afield would come on pilgrimages to the temple of Gran Poder and burn candles as an act of devotion and to ask for celestial favours. Now, this custom has diminished and the festival has become music-based, attracting numerous groups of dancers and musicians, some even from the famed Oruro Carnival. The festival has also spread out from its own barrio and now completely takes over the centre of La Paz.

La Paz West of the Prado

women in traditional dress squatted on their haunches selling fruit and vegetables, razor blades, camera film, Vicks Vaporub, Snickers bars, dried llama foetuses – anything, in fact, you'd find in the local supermarket. The llama foetuses are used to protect a dwelling from evil spirits and you can find great piles of them, like extras from a horror movie, in the **Mercado de Hechicería** (Witches' Market), on Calle Linares between Calle Sagárnaga and Santa Cruz, where charms and herbs are also sold.

Don't miss out on the **Museo de Coca** ① *Daily 1000-1800, US$1.05,* also on Linares, at number 906. It presents a historic and scientific explanation of the production and drug effects of this controversial plant, chewed for thousands of years by indigenos Bolivians. A fantastic and provocative little museum with English, French and German written guides, that every visitor to Bolivia should see.

Western markets

Further up Sagárnaga turn right on Max Paredes, heading west, between Santa Cruz and Graneros, is the **Mercado Negro**, a bewildering labyrinth of stalls where you can pick up a cheap pair of Levi jeans, or almost anything else. Continuing west towards the cemetery district, Max Paredes meets **Avenida Buenos Aires**, one of the liveliest streets in the indigenous quarter, where small workshops turn out the costumes and masks for the Gran Poder festival (see page 105). This is the main market area and the streets are crammed with stalls selling every imaginable item – household goods, clothing, hats, food, festive goods. Do not expect to go anywhere in a hurry in this part of the city; just enjoy the atmosphere and the marvellous views of omnipresent Mount Illimani.

South off Max Paredes just below Avenida Buenos Aires, **Eloy Salmón** is a street filled with shops and stalls selling the latest technological devices, from digital cameras to motherboards, at sub-European (and often sub-American) prices. Note that you may have to pay tax on purchases when you return home.

Heading back southwards along Max Paredes, where it meets Calle Rodríguez and becomes Calle Zoilo Flores, is the **Mercado Rodríguez**, a riot of colour, fruit, vegetables and identifiable and unidentifiable parts of animals. The main market days are Saturday and Sunday mornings but there are stalls here every day.

Plaza Sucre and around

Less than 100 m south from Mercado Rodríguez, a road branches left from Zoilo Flores and leads to the pleasant Plaza Sucre. Here, at Avenida 20 de Octubre and Colombia, is **San Pedro** church, built in 1720. It boasts large paintings of the life of Christ along the nave, a huge chandelier below the dome and a gilt altar.

Also on Plaza Sucre is one of the city's less well-known tourist attractions, **San Pedro Prison**. This may not be everyone's idea of a pleasant outing, but it does offer a truly surreal, if slightly disturbing, experience. Many of the 1,500 mostly violent criminals will talk freely and openly about the bizarre goings-on in an open complex where new inmates buy their accommodation from paroled prisoners. These range from luxury penthouse apartments complete with jacuzzi costing US$5,000 to a more modest US$20 for a cramped space under the stairs. The poorest prisoners have to work in the kitchens and, worse still, eat what comes out of them. Many inmates even share their accommodation with wives and children. Visits have been officially stopped by the authorities, but it may be worthwhile trying your luck.

The eastern side of the plaza is bordered by Calle Strongest and running parallel to it, further east towards the Prado, is Calle México. Here, at number 1710, is the **Museo del Deporte Nacional** ⓘ *Mon-Fri 0830-1200, 1430-1830, US$1, T02-2320221* which tells the history of Bolivian sport with photographs, flags and a collection of trophies and past strips.

Back on the Prado is **Museo de Arte Contemporaneo** ⓘ *Av 16 de Julio 1698, T02-2335905, www.museoplaza.com, Mon-Sun 0900-2100, US$1.26.* In an amazing old colonial building, strikingly decorated with glass roofs and iron fretwork, the museum itself is a missed opportunity. In three floors of contemporary art, Bolivian and international, the occasional interesting piece is swamped by some some embarrassingly bad dross. A map and information room has some useful lists of La Paz attractions.

South of Plaza del Estudiante

Running south from Plaza del Estudiante is Avenida Villazón which then becomes Avenida Arce and heads southwards towards the suburbs of Zona Sur. Branching off to the right at the bridge is Avenida 6 de Agosto which takes you into the district of **Sopocachi** where you'll find many good bars and restaurants. Due west of Plaza del Estudiante, Calle Landaeta leads to 20 de Octubre. Turn left (south) and it soon forks, with Calle Ecuador heading off to the right towards Sopocachi Alto. A short distance after the fork is the **Casa Museo Marina Núñez del Prado** ⓘ *T02-2324906, Tue-Fri, 0930-1300, 1500-1900, Sat, Sun & Mon 0930-1300, US$0.75, students US$0.30,* at Ecuador 2034, with an excellent collection of the artist's sculptures housed in the family mansion.

Running southeast from the old centre, leading to the respectable suburb of Miraflores, is Avenida Libertador Simón Bolívar, with Mount Illimani providing a

⁝ Plenty to cheer about

One of the most intriguing items for sale in Andean markets is *Ekeko*, the god of good fortune and plenty and one of the most enduring and endearing of the Aymara gods and folk legends.

He is a cheery, avuncular little chap, with a happy face to make children laugh, a pot belly due to his predilection for food and short legs so he can't run away. His image, usually in plaster of Paris, is laden with various household items, as well as sweets, confetti and streamers, food, and with a cigarette dangling from his lower lip. Believers say that these statues only bring luck if they are received as gifts.

The *Ekeko* occupies a central position in the festival of Alasitas, the Feast of Plenty, which takes place in La Paz every January. Everything under the sun can be bought in miniature: houses, trucks, buses, tools, building materials, dollar bills, suitcases, university diplomas, you name it, you can find it here. The idea is to have your mini-purchase blessed by a *Yatiri* (an Aymara priest) and the real thing will be yours within the year.

La Paz Zona Sur

backdrop. At its beginning, on the corner with Calle Bueno, is the Central Market, called **Mercado Camacho**. It's a colourful and raucous affair with the ubiquitous cholas haranguing passers-by with their cries of "Cómprame! Cómprame!" as they preside over their stalls. Further east is the residential district of Miraflores. Libertador Simón Bolívar leads to the national stadium, the Estadio Hernan Siles. In front of the stadium is the **Museo Semisubterráneo**, or Templo del Estadio, with restored statues and other artefacts from Tiahuanaco. It's in a sunken garden and much can be seen from street level. No information is provided and the statues are being badly eroded by pollution.

Further into Miraflores are a couple of interesting sights. The **Museo de la Revolución Nacional** ⓘ *Tue-Fri 0930-1230, 1500-1900, Sat and Sun 1000-1230, US$0.15*, is on Plaza Villarroel, at the end of Avenida Busch. It has a photographic and art exhibition of the 1952 revolution (see page 388). The **Botanical Gardens** ⓘ *Mon-Sat 0800-1200, 1400-1830, Sun 1000-1300*, are on Calle Lucas Jaimes, between H Palacios and Villa Lobos, with original flora from the altiplano and Yungas valleys.

At Cerro Laicacota Hill, on Avenida del Ejército to the east of Avenida Arce , is the **Kusillo Cultural Complex** ⓘ *T02-2226371, www.quipusbolivia.org, Tue-Sun 1030-1830, Tue-Fri US$0.75, Sat and Sun US$1.50, children US$0.75*, featuring interactive exhibits on Bolivian culture and textiles, craft shops, a Museum of Science and Play and the world's highest funicular railway. From the top you get great views of the city, especially at dusk, when all the lights begin to twinkle on the surrounding hillsides.

Zona Sur

The Zona Sur district is in The Valley 15 minutes south of the city (US$0.40 by trufi or minibus – take any minibus marked Calacoto, San Miguel, Achumani or Chasquipampa from the centre). Home to the resident foreign community it has developed into an important area in its own right. It has international shopping centres, a modern church that looks like a cockroach, supermarkets stocked with imported items and some of the smartest restaurants and bars in La Paz. The area begins after the bridge at La Florida where there is an attractive park, Plaza Humboldt, which has exhibitions of local art work on Sundays and a collection of kiosks selling cheap snacks. The main road, Avenida Ballivián, begins here at Calle 8 and continues up the hill to the shopping district of San Miguel on Calle 21 (about a 20-minute walk). The place comes alive in the evenings, when La Paz's affluent youth cram the streets in their parents' flashy cars and the city's ex-pats visit national-themed cafés and bars to talk about home.

Excursions from La Paz

In addition to the trips detailed below there are some good one-day walks that can be done in the area. See page 71 for details.

Valle de la Luna

The best nearby excursion is to Río Abajo and the Mallasilla golf course. The route passes through the rich suburbs of Calacoto and La Florida, following the river road past lovely picnic spots and through some weird rock formations, known as the Valle de la Luna (Moon Valley). Just before la Luna are the Aranjuez Forest, the Aniceto Arce cactus gardens (which are badly eroded) and the Playa de Aranjuez, a bathing spot popular for lunch at weekends. About 3 km from the bridge at Calacoto the road forks; sharp right leads to the Caza y Pesca Club and Mallasilla Golf Course. Get out of the minibus at the turning and walk a few minutes east to the valley entrance, or get out at the football field which is by the entrance. Take good shoes and water. ▸▸ *For further details, see Transport, page 128.*

The **Zoo** ① *Daily 0900-1700, US$0.40,, US$0.20 children* is on the road to Río Abajo (the entrance is just past Mallasa). It has well-housed animals in a beautiful, wide open park-like setting. The climate in this valley is always much warmer than in the city, where the zoo previously was.

Achumani

Beyond Valle de la Luna is Achumani which offers good views of the valley and glimpses of the palatial mansions of the wealthy. To reach it go up Avenida Ballivián

Zona Sur

Sleeping ⬤	Eating ❶	La Campana 1	Café Montmartre 11
Camino Real Suites 1	Café Alexander 8		Reineke Fuchs 10
Casa Grande	Chalet Suisse 2	**Bars & clubs** ❶	
(Aparthotel) 2	El Arriero 9	Britannia 14	

N — Not to scale

through Calacoto and turn left at Calle 17. Further beyond Calacoto and Cota Cota is the new residential zone of Chasquipampa on the Palca road, near which is the Valle de las Animas. Here the eroded landscape is similar to, but much larger than, the Valle de la Luna and is good for walking and picnics. ▶ *For further details, see Transport, page 128*

Palca Canyon
It is possible to get there and back in one day from La Paz, the Palca Canyon is an amazing eroded mud-valley surrounded by steep mud walls and pinnacles. The canyon's river runs into the Río Abajo which cuts through the Andes to split the Cordillera Real from the Cordillera Quimza Cruz. The route follows the bed of the Quebrada Chua Kheri and should not be attempted in the wet season.

In Huni look out for a broad road leading down to the right and follow it down, past the school and onwards. The path turns into prehispanic stone paving and leads down to the canyon floor. Walk through the canyon for two hours until it opens out. Follow the path up and left to Palca which will take you another 30 minutes.

Palca is a pleasant village, often full at weekends with visiting Paceños but quiet the rest of the week with limited accommodation and many shops. There are regular buses back to La Paz especially at weekends, US$1. Or arrange to be picked up by jeep, US$35. From Palca, you could walk 30 minutes up the road to Ventilla and then up the valley of the Río Choquekhota to Choquekhota and continue up the valley to Mina San Francisco at the top of the valley for Takesi, Alto Takesi, and Reconquistada trails. Map IGM Palca 6044 III covers the trail but is not really necessary. ▶ *For further details, see Transport, page 128.*

Corazón de Jesús
A climb to Corazón de Jesús is worth it for the views over the city and the Altiplano, but is for the acclimatized only. The statue at the top of the hill is reached via the steps at the north end of Calle Washington, then left and right and follow the stations of the cross. Watch out where you put your feet. Do not go alone as there is a risk of robbery, and beware of dogs. Take a bus to Ceja El Alto (eg Número 20 or 22) to save yourself some of the walk.

Comanche
To see the stunning Puya Raimondii flowers, go to the village of Comanche, 2½ hours from La Paz.

La Muela Del Diablo
This is a huge, tooth-shaped rock which can be seen from the Valle de la Luna road. Take Micro 'Ñ' from Murillo and Sagárnaga or from the University (last stop Cota Cota), combi 213 to Rosales, or trufi 288 from Plaza Isabel La Católica to Urbanización Pedregal (ask the driver where to get off). Cross the river and climb through the village to the cemetery; then it is one-and- a-half hours climb, which is 'more impressive, especially if the wind is blowing, than Moon Valley'. The road continues to Ventilla, the start of the Takesi trail.

Zongo Valley
Global warming has completely destroyed the ice cave, which used to be the Zongo Valley's main attraction. The Valley lies at the end of a steep but scenic ride down past several of La Paz's electric power plants. From the dam, the road drops almost 3,000 m in less than 40 km and is popular with mountain bikers (see Mountain biking, page 86). It is quite safe to drive yourself (in a suitable vehicle) and to hike. The road passes a series of lakes and an aqueduct on the left. Keep left at each junction en route. About 20 minutes past the abandoned Milluni tin mine, its large roadside cemetery (which is also on the left) and the colourful but polluted Lago Milluni, you

come to the last hydroelectric dam and, on the right, a white guard house (4,750 m) where you get off. Walk up and over the small hill on the right-hand side of the road until you meet the aqueduct again. Follow it for 45 minutes, taking special care as it is cut into the side of a sheer cliff in places with some spectacular drops, then cross it and walk up to reach the base of the Charquini glacier. Do not go onto the glacier unless you have crampons and are roped. At the end of the bridge, turn right uphill to a marker of rocks piled one on top of the other. Continue over the hill, cross a stream and go straight up the next hill at a similar rock marker. From the top of the hill, it is only a few minutes down to the site of the former ice cave. It's about 1¼ hours walk in total. ▸▸ For further details, see Transport, page 128.

Urmiri

Take the asphalted road from La Paz south to Oruro to Km 75 where a sign points to Urmiri. A steep scenic descent on narrow, hair-raising hairpins (dangerous in the wet season) leads to two pools filled by mineral springs, a sauna, a hot waterfall and a pleasant though basic hotel with a restaurant. The thermal baths are completely isolated in a beautiful mountain setting and definitely worth a visit. There's a good walk down to the village of Sapahuaqui, and you can hitch back up to the hotel.

The best time to visit the thermal baths is Tuesday-Friday. At weekends it's full of locals and kids. The main pool is closed Monday for cleaning, refilling and cooling (the water comes out of the ground at 72°C; it takes two to three minutes to boil an egg). Daytrippers pay US$3.73 per person for use of the pools and sauna.

◉ Sleeping

Most of the budget accommodation is concentrated in 2 areas: in the streets which lead steeply up from behind San Francisco, especially Sagárnaga, Illampu and Santa Cruz; and around Plaza Murillo, in the triangle formed by the Prado, C Ingavi and C Loayza. Much of the upmarket accommodation can be found in Zona Sur and on the Prado, more especially south of Plaza del Estudiante, around Av Villazón and Av Arce. For real luxury though, you should go all the way down to Zona Sur.

East of the Prado *p99, map p100*

LL **Europa**, Tiahuanacu 64, T02-2315656 (0800-5656), F02-08113930, www.hoteleuropa.com.bo. Behind the Plaza, with difficult access but excellent facilities and plenty of frills.
LL **Presidente**, Potosí 920 and Sanjines, near Plaza San Francisco, T02-2406666, F02-2407240. 'The highest 5-star in the world' has great views from top floor and pool, gym and sauna all open to non-residents. Some of the Las Vegas styling (mirrored ceilings and indoor waterfalls) feels out of place but it's comfortable and service is excellent.

L **Plaza**, Av 16 de Julio 1789, T02-2378311, F02-2378318, www.plazabolivia.com.bo. A smart hotel with an excellent, good value restaurant (see Eating on page 110), peña show on Fri.
B **Gloria**, Potosí 909, T02-2407070, F02-2406622, www.boliviantravel.com. All rooms at this modern and central hotel have bathtubs and cable TV. The attached French-style Café Pierrot is good. There is also a canteen restaurant and a tour agency, Gloria Tours, on-site.
C **Hostal República**, Comercio 1455, T02-2202742, F02-2202782. With bathroom (D without). In the beautiful old colonial-era house of a former president, friendly República has attractive courtyards and a helpful travel information desk. The café, opposite reception, has free internet for hotel guests and serves good breakfasts. Book ahead. Recommended.
D **Hostal Señoral** , Yanacocha 540, T02-2406042. (E without bath) Price includes breakfast and use of kitchen. Newly decorated, comfortable beds, close to Plaza Murillo.
E **Ingavi**, Ingavi 727, T02-2323645. Nice rooms, not much hot water. Poor service but good value.

E **Julia Rojo Briseño**, Murillo 1060, 10th floor, press 1001 on bellpush outside, T02-2310236, juliarojo@hotmail.com. Friendly family house, 1 block from central post office, use of phone, fax and washing machine, includes breakfast, US$60 for 1 week.

E **Torino**, Socabaya 457, T02-2406003. An old colonial building near Plaza Murillo. Some of the older rooms are dingy, run-down and can be noisy. Newer rooms are better. There is a restaurant, a free book exchange and a good (if pricey) internet café.

F **Alojamiento Illimani**, Av Illimani 1817, T02-2202346. A fair way from the centre, Illimani is friendly, clean, quiet and safe, with laundry facilities and a cooking area but uncomfortable beds.

F **Austria**, Yanacocha 531, T02-2408540. There are no private bathrooms and it can be gloomy (make sure you get a room with a window) but rooms are clean and staff are generally friendly. The three showers (for the 22 rooms) have hot water and there is also a safe deposit, laundry and TV lounge.

F **Residencial Plaza**, Plaza Pérez Velasco 785, T02-2406099. In a pleasant old building, rooms are clean, water is hot and there are washing and luggage storage facilities. Cheaper without bathroom.

G **Hospedaje Millenio**, C Yanacocha 860, T02-2281263. Small, family run place that makes guests feel at home. Good value.

G **Posada El Carretero**, Catacora 1056 between Yanacocha and Junín, T02-2322233. Five beds to a room, helpful, hot showers, can use kitchen for breakfast, unreliable laundry service. A real travellers' hangout: run-down and with mixed reports on security.

West of the Prado *p103, map p100*

B **Galería Virgen de Rosario**, Santa Cruz 583, 4th floor, T02-2461015, F02-2461253, hgaleria@ceibo.entelnet.bo. Great rooms, all with private bathroom, cable TV and breakfast included. Slow and expensive internet access; friendly staff.

B **Hostal Naira**, C Sagárnaga 161, T02-2355645, F02-2311214, hostalnaira@entelnet.bo. Big, carpeted, fairly modern rooms are arranged around an internal courtyard with potted plants. Rooms at the front have balconies overlooking

Sagárnaga; others lack much natural light. Staff are friendly but speak little English. Price includes a decent buffet breakfast downstairs at Café Banais. Try bargaining. Recommended.

B **Rosario**, Illampu 704, T02-2451658, F02-2451991, www.hotelrosario.com. Almost on the doorstep of the Witches' Market, this very popular, attractive and modern 42-room, colonial-style hotel has a Turisbus travel agency downstairs (see below) as well as a fair trade shop. A 'Cultural Interpretation Centre' explains everything for sale in the nearby markets, from textiles to llama foetuses. All rooms have cable TV, safes and excellent showers – two have bathtubs. Price includes a huge buffet breakfast. There is also a family suite for up to six, an excellent restaurant (see Eating) and a café with free internet. Stores luggage, friendly and helpful experienced staff. Highly recommended.

C **Estrella Andina**, Av Illampu 716, T02-2456421, F02-2451401, juapame_ 2000@hotmail.com. All the rooms (most of the walls in fact) in this friendly hotel have Tolkienesque murals depicting Bolivian scenes. Continental breakfast is included and rooms all have bathrooms and safes. English is spoken and there's a roof terrace with fantastic views over the city to Illampu.

C **Sagárnaga**, Sagárnaga 326, T02-2350252, F02-2360831. With red-jacketed bell boys and a smooth mirrored lift, Sagárnaga has pretensions to grandeur. Rooms come in two levels of quality – those higher up (C) have bigger, more comfortable beds and views, while those lower down are cheaper (E) and plainer. Hot water comes from solar panels on the roof and there is a cash machine and a regular peña.

D **Arcabucero**, C Viluyo 307, Linares (close to Museo de Coca), T/F02-2313473. Facing a small park, this helpful and good value hotel has clean, pleasant new rooms with bathrooms in a converted colonial building.

D **Condeza**, Diagonal Juan XXII 190, between Illampu and Linares, T02-2311317, www.hotelcondeza.web1000.com. With private bathrooms, generously sized rooms and TV. Good value.

D **La Joya**, Max Paredes 541, near Buenos Aires, T02-2453841, F02-2453496, www.hotelajoya.com. In the heart of the

market district, a modern and comfortable hotel with breakfast, cable TV and phone. Laundry, elevator, free transport to and from city centre and airport.

D Majestic, Santa Cruz 359, T/F02-2451628. Rooms are simple and on the small side and there isn't much of a view, but there are private bathrooms, cable TV, and it's clean. Breakfast US$1 extra.

D Milton, Illampu and Calderón 1124, T02-2368003/2353511, F02-2365849 (PO Box 5118). A dated looking concrete block in the market district, Milton has private bathrooms, hot water, laundry, safe parking around the corner. Good views from roof, restaurant, friendly and clean. Rooms at the back are quieter.

D Residencial Copacabana, Illampu 734, T02-2451626, F02-2451684, combicop@ceibo.intelnet.bo. The beds are very soft but the water is hot (**E** without bath), the price includes breakfast, and travellers' cheques can be changed. Jaded but good value.

D-E Residencial Sucre, Colombia 340, on Plaza San Pedro, T02-2492038, F02-2486723. A friendly and helpful place with big rooms are set around a courtyard with a beautiful garden. There's a quiet area, warm water, it's clean and luggage is stored. Cheaper without bathroom.

D-E Tambo de Oro, Armentia 367, near the bus station, T02-2281565, F02-2282181. Hot showers, cable TV in rooms, clean, friendly, helpful and safe for luggage. Unusually for a place near the bus station this is good value.

E Hostal Happy Days, Sagárnaga 229, T02-2314759, F02-2355759. Despite being painted a bright shade of yellow, Happy Days can be a bit gloomy. There's 24-hr hot water though and it's quite popular with travellers. No English spoken.

La Paz Sleeping

F **Andes**, Av Manco Kapac 364, T02-2455327. Near the ex-railway station. With bathroom, soap and towels provided, good breakfast included, clean, hot water 24 hrs a day (**G** per person in single room without bathroom and including breakfast), discount for IYHA card holders, safe deposit box, stores luggage for US$0.20 per day, good restaurant, very good value.

F **Bamboo Hostal**, Av. Manco Kapac 451, T02-2450379. A hostal which doubles as a pub/peña. Rooms have private bathrooms, heating and cable TV. Discounts for groups. All designed and decorated with bamboo.

F **El Lobo**, Illampu, corner with Santa Cruz. (**E** without bath) Popular Israeli backpacker's haunt, basic rooms and noisy at night from both road and guests. Ask for rooms away from road. If using communal showers, try to get one of the two that are gas-powered.

F **Maya**, Sagarnaga 339, T02-2311970, mayahost@hotmail.com. Maya is gloomy in places and some of its rooms are windowless and horribly poky and mouldy, but the better ones have views over Sagarnaga and as a whole the place has more to offer than nearby El Alem. Internet US$1/hr. Money exchange, laundry, safe deposit, massage, will look after luggage. Cable TV in living room.

G per person. **Hostal Cactus del Milenio**, C Jiménez 818. In what used to be just 'Milenio', the downstairs rooms are dark; those upstairs are better though still very simple. Kitchen, limited hot water, very peaceful, excellent position.

G **Hostal Uruguay**, Av Uruguay 470. Shabby, and nearly half of the 170 rooms lack windows, but the showers are good and if you need somewhere near the bus station it's worth considering.

South of Plaza del Estudiante
p106, map p100

LL **Radisson Plaza**, Av Arce 2177, T02-2441111, F02-2440593, www.radisson.com/lapazbo. Formerly Hotel La Paz (and still referred to as the Sheraton), this 5-star hotel has 239 rooms, all modern facilities, good views and an excellent buffet in its restaurant (see Eating on page xx).

AL **Camino Real Aparthotel**, Ravelo 2123, T02-2441515, F02-2440055, www.caminoreal.com.bo. Luxury self-catering apartments, includes breakfast, sauna and fitness centre and parking. The company have now also opened an even more modern and luxurious suite hotel in Zona Sur (see below).

AL **El Rey Palace**, Av 20 de Octubre 1947, T02-2393016, F02-2367759, www.hotel-rey-palace-bolivia.com. Including breakfast, large suites, excellent restaurant, stylish and modern. Top floors have good views.

B **Sucre Palace**, Av 16 de Julio 1636, T02-2311424, sph@kolla.net. Despite the hot water and cable TV, this 1970s-style hotel is overpriced. No English spoken.

D **España**, Av 6 de Agosto 2074, T02-2442643, F02-2441329, www.hotel-espana.com. Set back from the Prado near Plaza del Estudiante, Hotel España is an unexpectedly peaceful gem. Rooms have shared bathroom, hot water and cable TV and those at the back are set around a beautiful garden. There is a restaurant as well as free internet and a travel agency just outside. Recommended.

Zona Sur *p107, map p108*

L **Camino Real Suites**, Av Ballivián 369 esq C 10, T02-2792323, F02-2791616, www.caminoreal.com.bo. One of La Paz's most strikingly modern buildings holds the sparklingly new Camino Real Suites hotel. Lots of chrome and modern art decorate a business centre and swimming pool.

L **Casa Grande**, Ballivián 100, on corner with C 17, T02-2795511, www.casa-grande.com.bo. Very smart and stylish apartment hotel with a sauna. All rooms have a kitchen and dining room, high-speed internet, cd player and cable TV. Recommended.

A **Libertador**, Obispo Cárdenas 1421, T02-2313434, F02-2318924, libertad@ceibo.entelnet.bo Good value, good cheap restaurant, helpful (baggage stored).

Excursions from La Paz

Urmiri *p110*

B-C **Hotel Gloria Urmiri**, T02-2370010. The best rooms have private pools for 2 people or a thermal bath tub; cheaper ones have a shared pool. **AL-A** for a cabin for 4 people with private pool. Breakfast included, other set meals are available lunch US$4.50, dinner US$3.70. 10% discount for groups of 5 or

more staying for 2 nights and having all meals. Reservations necessary. Shiatsu US$12.75 per hr and massage US$6 for 30 mins. Camping US$1.50.
B **Oberland**, in Mallasa, 12 km from centre, T02-274 5040, www.h-oberland.com.

A Swiss-owned, chalet-style restaurant (excellent, not cheap) and hotel resort, gardens, cabañas, sauna, pool (open to the public, $2), beach volleyball, tennis, permit camping with vehicle.

● Eating

East of the Prado p99, map p100

Around Plaza Murillo and also on the Prado itself there are numerous snack bars and cheap restaurants, though most are fairly humdrum. There are many snack bars and Chinese restaurants on C Comercio.
$ **Hotel Gloria**, Potosí 909. Good almuerzo for US$3, also buffet breakfast, and dinner (US$2.20) after 1900, Sun 0700-1000 only. International basics and a salad bar.
$ **La Casa de los Paceños**, Av Sucre 856. Near the Calle Jaen museums, this little restaurant offers very good Bolivian food, especially its *fritanga*. Also good *almuerzos*.
$ **La Kantuta**, in Hotel Presidente, Potosí 920. Excellent food and good service.
$ **La Prensa**, C Campero 52. A long restaurant going back to a pleasant garden, the limited menu is typically Bolivian (meat and fish only, in huge quantities) and the company is lively.
$ **Los Escudos**, Av Mariscal Santa Cruz 1223, Edificio Club de La Paz, T02-2322028. Munich-type bierkeller with fixed 4-course lunch, good peña on Fri and Sat nights (2100-0100), US$5 cover charge.
$ **Marbella**, Av 16 de Julio 1655, T02-2317075. Mon-Sun 0800-0000, lunch until 1430. The friendly Marbella is enshrouded in plastic foliage and flowers, and has a peculiar mock-Arabian mural. The music is heartfelt Bolivian and the place fills up with businessmen. A big menu has Bolivian, Mexican and international food and some good breakfast options, including fruit, yoghurt and cereal.

West of the Prado p103, map p100

$$ **Tambo Colonial**, in Hotel Rosario (see page), Illampu 704. Huge buffet breakfast with fruit, yoghurt, pancakes and excellent wholemeal bread (there are even toasters)

from 0700 for US$2.84. In the evenings it becomes one of La Paz's best restaurants, with excellent local and international cuisine, including good llama steaks. Recommended.
$ **Angelo Colonial**, Linares 922. Fantastic, affordable food at candelit tables in a ramshackle upstairs room overflowing with antiques. Good and plentiful vegetarian options and delicious steaks. Jazzy music with regular smatterings of The Beatles. One of the best central restaurants. Recommended.
$ **El Lobo**, Santa Cruz 441. Up the hill on the corner with Illampu, El Lobo has a huge menu, huge portions, and is fairly cheap and very popular, especially with Israeli travellers. Great falafel on Wed night.
$ **Laksmi**, Piso 1, Galeria Chuquiago, Sagárnaga. A genuinely vegetarian Indian at back of one of the courtyards off Sagárnaga. Indian hippie influenced, but with an unexpected lack of curry. Almuerzos are thali-like, with everything served together on a metal dish and the vegetarian burgers are excellent. There are some sunny tables outside overlooking the courtyard. Set lunch US$1.25, Dinner US$1.
$ **Manjabi**, Linares 277, corner of Santa Cruz. A vegetarian restaurant right amongst the llama foetuses of the witches' market. The tasty thali-style almuerzo, (typically soup, rice and veg, salad, fruit and yoghurt, drink) for under US$1 is a real bargain. Breakfast too.
$ **Pot Pourri des Gourmets**, Linares 906. In an attractive barrel-vaulted, wood and brick room, Pot Pourri offers an excellent value set lunch (US$2.20) with choice of soup, main course and dessert. Bolivian/French owners have produced a good mixture of local drinks and food combined with many international options. Exceptional value, great atmosphere and very friendly. Recommended.
$ **Restaurant Naira**, Sagárnaga 161. Hidden away below Hostal Naira and rather dark,

⠸ Cevicherías

Increasingly popular with Paceños are cevicherías which serve only spicy raw fish dishes. Don't try this until your stomach has adjusted to South America, but after that, it's great. Normally, you get a bowl of marinaded raw fish and then a very spicy soup. The nearest thing to the Indian curry effect and great for hangovers.

Try **Acuario** at the bottom of C Rodríguez, above Murillo behind the central post office. **Cevichería El Pulpo** at Galería Los Cántaros (Av Montenegro 1337, local 3, next to Automanía T02-2792563) is also good, as is the cevichería on the 4th floor of Shopping Norte, Potosí and Socabaya.

Restaurant Naira serves good-value almuerzos but will only serve 30 people before confining you to the more expensive menu. Soups, chicken dishes, pizzas and llama fondue.

$ **Yussef's**, Sagárnaga 380. Poorly signposted and well hidden on the right of Sagárnaga as you go up the hill, but well worth the effort for wonderful Lebanese food. Excellent vegetarian options as well as meaty choices. The mixed plate of mezes for US$4.50 is a real feast, or you can mix and match individual portions for US$0.75. Friendly service, relaxed atmosphere. Highly recommended.

South of Plaza del Estudiante
p106, map p100

Most of the top-class restaurants are in this part of town and Av 20 de Octubre has become the trendy place to eat and be seen eating, with new arty, funky cafés and restaurants springing up all the time. If just wandering around here whets your appetite, you can always get an excellent choripan (chorizo sausage in bread) from a seller around the edge of Plaza Avaroa. There are several great *chifas* along Av 6 de Agosto offering tasty and cheap food. Pick any one of them for a delicious lunch menu.

$$$ **El Gaucho**, Av 20 de Octubre 2041, 1100-1500, 1800-late. A good but expensive Argentinean steakhouse. Accepts credit cards.

$$ **Chifa Emy**, Av 20 de Octubre 927, Plaza Avaroa, T02-2440551. Mon-Fri 1130-1430, Sat 1130-1500, Sun 1130-1530, Mon-Wed 1800-2300, Thu 1800-0000, Fri-Sat 1800-0100, Sun 1800-2200. One of the best Chinese restaurants in town, with good service, over 170 dishes and a big screen TV.

Accepts credit cards. Shows and concerts Wed-Fri at 2130.

$$ **El Arriero**, 6 de Agosto 2535, T02-2141201. Great Argentinean barbecue with large portions. Also in Zona Sur.

$$ **Jalapeños**, Av Arce 2549, T02-2435288. Excellent Mexican food at midrange/ expensive prices (main course up to US$6.50).

$$ **La Comedie**, Pasaje Medinacelli 2234, T02-2423561. Branding itself as an 'art-café restaurant', La Comedie is a cool, terracotta-coloured, contemporary place with good salads, a predominently French menu, round windows and plenty of candles. Also good for cocktails.

$$ **La Quebecoise**, Av 20 de Octubre 2387, T02-2121682. With an interior rather like a 19th-century French living room, this French-Canadian restaurant has an open fire and top-notch service.

$$ **Madero**, T02-2432732, Av 9 Octobre 927, Mon-Sat 1130-1430, 1930-2300, Sun 1200-1430. A warm, modern international restaurant with lots of dark wood and incongruous disco music. ,

$$ **Mediterraneo**, 20 de Octubre 2453, T02-2419150. Good food in slightly bland surroundings with a seafaring theme. Buffet lunch.

$$ **Osteria Pettirosso**, Pasaje Medinacelli 2282, T02-2423700. Tue-Fri 1200-1430, Sun 1200-1530, Mon-Sat 1900-2300. A welcoming Italian restaurant, Pettirosso has live music Fri and Sat, cool jazz at other times, fig trees, terracotta walls, an open fire, proper wood-burning pizza ovens, Italian wine and even an Italian chef. Takeaway pizzas are also available and are slightly cheaper.

$$ **Pronto**, Jauregui 2248, T02-2441369, Mon-Sat 1830-2230. Opposite Reineke Fuchs, Pronto is in a basement and not easy to find. It's well worth the effort though for its upmarket Italian cuisine. There are 3 different types of pasta – regular, integral and *de quinoa*. Popular, good service.

$$ **Vienna**, Federico Zuazo 1905, T02-2441660, Mon-Fri 1200-1400, 1830-2200, Sun 1200-1430. www.restaurantvienna.com. A smart, European-style restaurant with excellent German, Austrian and local food, excellent service, antique prints, a great atmosphere and huge, juicy steaks at moderate prices.

$$ **Wagamama**, Pasaje Pinilla 2557, T02-2434911, Tue-Sat 1200-1430, 1900-2000, Sun and Mon closed. Huge plates of amazing sushi. Complimentary tea and excellent service. Popular with ex-pats – hardly a Bolivian in sight.

$ **Andromeda**, Av Arce 2116, T02-2440726. European-style and vegetarian food, with an excellent 5-course set lunch. Closed evenings.

$ **Bodeguita Cubana**, Federico Zuazo 1653. Cuban favourites such as ropa vieja and excellent mojito cocktails in an atmospheric Cuban setting. Strictly meat and fish so vegetarians will have to concentrate on the drinks.

$ **Gringo Limón**, corner of Salazar and 20 de Octubre. A smart restaurant painted in eponymous muted yellow . There's a US$3.50 buffet and a grill. Take-away also available. Accepts credit cards.

$ **Mongo's**, Hermanos Manchego 2444, near Plaza Isabela la Católica, T02-2440714. Open Mon-Thu 100-0130, Fri-Sun 1800-0300. There are plans to take Mongo's upmarket but until that happens it remains the most popular gringo spot in town. There's an open fire, cable TV for sports, US$2.90 set lunches which change every day and excellent food including fish and chips, great burgers, and Mexican dishes. Service can be slow for food but there's always the fastest and coldest beer in town to keep you going.

$ **Radisson Plaza Hotel** (see Sleeping section). Excellent buffet Mon and Wed, 2000-2300, US$5.50, friendly to backpackers.

$ **RamJam**, C Presbitero Medina 2421, T02-242-2295. Above Plaza Avaroa, RamJam, set up in 2004 by some of the team that created Mongo's, offers everything a

homesick gringo could want, from coffee to curry, Sunday roasts to cable TV. RamJam should do well by plugging a youthful, energetic gap in the La Paz market. With the world's highest micro-brewery beer, expect some late nights and wobbly walks home.

Zona Sur *p107, map p108*

$$$ **Chalet Suisse**, C23, T02-2793160. On the main avenue, up the hill between C 24 and 25, Chalet Suisse is expensive but highly recommended, with excellent fondue and steaks. Booking is essential on Fri evenings.

$$ **El Arriero**, C 17, T02-2791907. Good Argentinean food with plenty of meat but also trout and a salad bar.

$$ **El Asador**, Gutierrez 740. A popular Bolivian grill with a good salad bar. The *Parillada Completa* selection of meats, advertised as being for one or two, would happily feed three or four.

$$ **La Campana**, Av Ballivián 969, T02-2791880, daily 1200-2300. Advertising itself as 'casual cuisine', La Campana is a high class fast food joint offering pizzas, salads, soups and burgers in a friendly modern restaurant.

$ **Eli's**, Av Mariscal de Montenegro. A branch of the Bolivian chain which also sells Chilean wine, alongside the standard pizzas, burgers and sandwiches.

Cafés

Many La Paz bars and restaurants also operate as cafés during the day – Mongo's and RamJam are good examples, though both are a little out of the way. Conversely, many cafés are good places to get light meals.

100% Natural, Sagárnaga, opposite El Alem, closed Sun. Good breakfasts and fantastic fresh juices and shakes. Service, however, can be surly. More substantial sustenance is available in the form of burgers, llama, sandwiches and salads.

Banais, Sagárnaga 161. Below Hostal Naira, one of central La Paz's grovviest cafés has wooden floors, laid-back music and especially good lemon meringue pie, salads and sandwiches. Downstairs there's a room of computers with internet access for US$0.50 per hr. The buffet breakfast (US$1.50) is simple but good, with delicious crusty bread and fruit salad.

British Council, Av Arce 2730, Mon-Fri 0645-2100, closed Sat. Café serving English breakfast with a good selection of British newspapers and a book exchange,

Café Alexander, Av 16 de Julio 1832, T02-2312790, also on C Potosí 1091, T02-2406482, Mon-Fri 0800-2230, Sat and Sun 0900-2230. A modern, international-style café serving excellent coffee, smoothies and muffins. The cakes, salads and sand-wiches are also good. Usually referred to as 'Café Alex', there's also a branch in Zona Sur.

Confitería Club de la Paz, Camacho 1202, on the corner where Ayacucho joins Av Mariscal Santa Cruz. Good, if expensive, traditional tea room, a meeting place for businessmen and politicians, great coffee and cakes.

Kuchen Stube, Rosendo Gutiérrez 461, Edificio Guadalquivir, , Mon-Fri 0930-1230, 1500-1900. Excellent cakes, coffee and German specialities.

La Gaita Salteña, Potosí 1365, between Loayza and Colón. La Paz's most celebrated salteñas and empanadas come from this unassuming little café and bakery which also sells good cakes.

La Terraza, Av 6 de Agosto 2296, Av 16 de Julio (next to Burger King) and at Gutiérrez in Zona Sur. A mini chain with wooden floors and chairs and a modern US feel. Pancakes and 80s pop. You can make your own salad from a selection of ingredients on menu.

Modern – coffee beans in tables. Good range of coffee. Bs10-Bs18 for breakfast options. Wouldn't make an omlette, only scrambled or fried, excellent sandwiches and coffee.

Mokka Cafeteria, Potosí 1146, T02-2407959. In this modern café not far from Plaza Murillo there are 4 breakfasts available, including egg muffins and 'mokkachino' – espresso with milk foam and chocolate. Avoid the orange 'juice' though. An enormous coffee machine churns out good brews and a mixed bag of paintings decorates the walls. Lots of papers and an information board.

O Mundo, Linares 906, T70695788, cafeomundo@hotmail.com. Open only until 1500, café O Mundo is downstairs from Pot Pourri des Gourmets and as well as a good range of drinks, you can order food from the restaurant upstairs.

Pepe's, Pasaje Jimenez 894 (off Linares between Sagárnaga and Santa Cruz), T02-2450788, pepcoff@hotmail.com. Service can be a little slow but is invariably friendly in this chilled and welcoming little café. Great all-day breakfasts range from US$1-3 and sandwiches and omelettes are also good. You can relax at an outside table in the sun after scouring the textiles and handicraft shops nearby, play with the provided dominoes and cards, or leaf through the guidebooks and magazines. The local pottery found in many cafés in the city is also for sale here.

🍸 Bars and clubs

Fri night is Big Night Out in La Paz. Thu and Sat are quieter and the rest of the week is very quiet. For up-to-the-minute information, check out *The Llama Express* or *Quéhacer*, a free magazine with Sat's *La Razón* newspaper, or visit www.la-razon.com. The 2 most popular drinks are beer (in volume) and *Singani*, a spirit which gives you a hangover from hell. *Singani* is traditionally mixed 50-50 with Sprite or 7-Up and drunk while playing dice. The game appears to be over when one of the players falls unconscious face down on the table thereby preventing further play. If the player falls over backwards or sideways there appears to be some confusion as to whether the game

should go on. If you want to see Bolivians in action on Fri night, pop into any of the small bars on the Prado or the streets off the Prado. Note that the toilets in these establishments are usually pretty much indescribable.

Some cafés and restaurants stay open late and some have regular music. **Mongo's** **RamJam** and **La Comedie** are all good places for a drink. Check flyposters for details of gigs.

West of the Prado *p103, map p100*

Sol y Luna, Murillo and Cochabamba, 1800-late. The best bar in the centre of town, and possibly in La Paz, Sol y Luna is warm, comfy and cosy. A Dutch-run place, it has stone walls and wooden floors, a good range of bottled beers, a travel book library, candles, and laid back grooves emanating from the music system. There are also different teas and coffees on offer, bar snacks and toasted sandwiches and a wide choice of cocktails including 'Mojito Boliviano' (with coca leaves) and 'Bolivia Libre' (with Singani instead of rum).

La Luna, C Oruro 197 and Murillo, 1900-late, publalunabolivia@hotmail.com. Good value cocktails and other drinks in a friendly environment, though it can get very crowded. Cable TV and board games. Happy hour 2000-2100.

Bocaisapo, Indaburo 654, corner with Jaén. Live music in a bar whose name means 'mouth of the toad'. No cover charge.

South of Plaza del Estudiante
p106, map p100

Many of the good bars and clubs are in the area of Sopocachi. C Belisario Salinas is also full of bars, starting just below Plaza Abaroa and continuing all the way up to Av Ecuador, beyond Plaza España.

Café en Azul, Av 20 de Octubre 2371. Open Sun-Thu 1700-0200, Fri and Sat till 0300. Very friendly and good-fun café-bar with a bohemian atmosphere.

Café Montmartre, Fernando Guachalla 399, off Av 6 de Agosto; also in Zona Sur on Av Mariscal de Montenegro, T02-2442801, Mon-Sat 1200-1500, 1700-0200. Fashionable bar with live jazz some weekends, also good

French menu, set lunch US$4. Sandwiches, salads and crepes too.

Deadstroke, Av 6 de Agosto 2460, 1700-late. US-style pub, café and billiards bar serving food and good value drinks.

Diesel Nacional, Av 20 de Octubre between Gutierrez and Guachalla. A hip, modern club with an industrial theme.

Equinoccio, Sánchez Lima 2191. Live music nearly every Thu, Fri and Sat.

La Salsa del Loro, Rosendo Gutiérrez, corner of Av 6 de Agosto, Thu-Sat. A salsa club where once you hit the dancefloor there will be no respite until you're carted off on a stretcher suffering from exhaustion. It's probably a good idea to take a few lessons first; try Gym Cec, Illampu 868, 1st floor, T02-2310158, US$4 per hr.

Pig and Whistle, Goitia 155, T02-2390429. Pints of beer and a variety of whiskies in, architecturally, one of the most interesting places to drink.

Reineke Fuchs, C Jauregui 2241; also in Zona Sur on Av Mariscal de Montenegro, Mon-Sat 1800-0100. Many European beers (such as *Pilsener Urquell* and *Becks*) and food in a German-style bar.

The Forum, Sanjines 2908. La Paz's biggest nightclub and disco, open until 0600 Fri, Sat and Sun mornings, US$5 cover includes a drink. Popular with teenagers. Strict dress code, so leave that poncho in the hotel.

Thelonius Jazz Bar, Av 20 de Octubre, 2172, T02-2337806, Tue-Sat from 1700. Good jazz bar.

Underground, Pasaje Medinacelli 2234. The nightclub to be seen in on a Thu or Fri night.

La Paz Bars & clubs

Zona Sur *p107, map p108*

Over the last few years a vibrant night life has been developing along Av Ballivián and through San Miguel. C 21 appears to have been brought to Bolivia directly from some town in the US and reflects the fact that many rich Bolivians are US-educated. Many of Zona Sur's bars are nationally themed – Reineke Fuchs for Germany, Montmartre for France (both on Av Mariscal de Montenegro, see city centre branches above) and the Britannia for Britain.

The Britannia, off Av Mariscal de Montenegro, T02-2793070, Mon-Sat from 1700. Opened as an authentic English pub by an Englishman, the Britannia now has an Asian restaurant attached. Slightly peculiar theming includes a thatched roof and a vaguely Hawian green wall.Fri night is particularly popular with ex-pats and diplomats. Belgian bottled beers and a Boddington's tap which is no longer connected. Happy hour 1800-1900.

🎭 Entertainment

Cinemas
The good films are mainly in English. Some of the best cinemas are: **Cine 16 de Julio**, on the Prado by Plaza del Estudiante, T02-2441099, films at 1530, 1900 and 2130; **Monje Campero**, on the Prado, Av 16 de Julio 1495, T02-2330192, next to *Eli's Pizzeria*, films at 1000, 1530, 1900 and 2130; and **6 de Agosto** (on 6 de Agosto, would you believe), T02-2442629, films at 1545, 1930 and 2130. Expect to pay around US$2.50. Most of the rest of La Paz's cinemas are flea pits showing kick boxer movies or flesh flicks. Films are advertised in all the papers every day. For film buffs there is the excellent **Cinemateca Boliviana**, Capitán Ravelo and Rosendo Gutiérrez, 2 blocks from Puente de las Américas. This is La Paz's art film centre with festivals, courses, etc; entry is US$1.20, students US$0.60.

Galleries
Casa de la Cultura 'Franz Tamayo', almost opposite Plaza San Francisco, hosts a variety of exhibitions, paintings, sculpture, photography and videos, mostly free. The **Palacio Chico**, at Ayacucho and Potosí, in the old Correo, is operated by the *Secretaría Nacional de Cultura*, it has exhibitions, concerts and ballet, Mon-Fri 0900-1230, 1500-1900, closed at weekends, free. Listings are available in Palacio Chico.

Peñas
The best traditional entertainment for visitors are the folk shows, or *peñas*. Various restaurants also have shows worth seeing. At these, visitors will be able to listen to the wide variety of local musical instruments (for

a full description see page). Enquire at the Rumillajta shop (in the galería close to San Francisco church) about future performances by the famous folk group of that name. There's a good peña at **Casa del Corregidor**, dinner show Mon-Thu, no cover charge, Fri and Sat peña both start at 2100, US$4, colonial atmosphere, traditional music and dance. Another peña is **Marko Tambo** on C Jaén 710. US$7 all inclusive, recommended (also sells woven goods).
El Calicanto, Jenaro Sanjines 467, between Potosí and Comercio, T02-2408008, calicanto@usa.net. Enjoy grilled llama steak while listening to live local and Latin American music. **El Parnaso**, Sagárnaga 189, corner with Murillo, T02-2316827. This is a peña purely for tourists but a good way to see local costumes and dancing. Indigenous dance halls, eg on Max Paredes, should only be visited in the company of Bolivians. If you wish to learn a local instrument, contact **Academia 'Walisuma'**, Av Apumalla 512 (old Cemetery District between José M Asin and José M Aliaga): Pedro March teaches bi-lingual courses, English/Spanish, for quena, zampoña and charango.

Theatre
La Paz has a resident ballet and symphony orchestra and several theatre companies. **Teatro Municipal** has a regular schedule of plays, opera, ballet and classical concerts, at Sanjines and Indaburo. Next door is the new **Teatro Municipal de Cámara**, a small studio-theatre which shows small-scale productions of dance, drama, music and poetry.

⊛ Festivals and events

For a fuller description of festivals and a list of those outside the capital see page 47.

Jan-Feb Particularly impressive is the **Alasitas Fair** held from the last week of Jan to the first week of Feb, in Parque Central up from Av del Ejército, and Plaza Sucre/San Pedro.

May-Jun At the end of May/early Jun is the **Festividad de Nuestro Señor Jesús del Gran Poder** (generally known simply as the 'Gran Poder'), the most important festival of the year, with a huge procession of costumed dancers. Among the many dances is the *Waka Thokoris*, which derives from the disdain and reproach for the Spanish bullfight. The *Morenada* and *Diablada* are also featured. These two are more commonly associated with the Oruro carnival (see page 192). *Los Caporales* originates in the Afro-Caribbean tradition of the Yungas and is a burlesque of the African slave bosses. This dance is a recent addition to the Gran Poder and has spread to other parts of the country.

Jun Other festivals include **Corpus Christi**, at the beginning of Jun; and San Juan, on 21 Jun, which is based on the Aymara New Year. People used to mark the passing of the old year by burning all their rubbish in the streets, especially old tyres; now it is mainly an excuse to let off fireworks.

Jul Fiestas de Julio, through Jul, is a month of concerts and performances at the Teatro Municipal and offers a wide variety of music, including the **University Folkloric Festival**.

6 Aug Independence Day is marked by a very loud gun salute at 0630 which can be heard all over the centre of the city.

8 Dec A festival is held around Plaza España. It's not very large, but very colourful and noisy.

31 Dec On New Year's Eve fireworks are let off and make a spectacular sight – and din – best viewed from a high vantage point.

⭘ Shopping

You need never go into a shop in La Paz. Everything is available on the street – from computers and cellular phones to tummy trimmers, and a few useful things like food.

Bookshops

Gisbert, Comercio 1270, for books, maps, stationery, will also ship overseas (libgis@ceibo.entelnet.bo), Mon-Fri 0900-1230, 1500-1900, Sat 0930-1230.

Multi-Libro, Loayza 233, T02-2391996, small, but good for maps, politics, religion, psychology, etc, Mon-Fri 0900-1230, 1500-2000, Sat 0930- 1300.

Librería Plural, Pedro Salazar 489, on Plaza Abaroa. A good selection of hard-to-find books on culture, sociology and ecology. Historian Antonio Paredes-Candia has a kiosk selling rare historical works on Villazón, opposite San Andrés University.

Los Amigos del Libro, Mercado 1315, T02-2204321, also branches at Edificio Alameda, Av 16 de Julio (1 block from Plaza Hotel), El Alto airport and Montenegro in the Zona Sur. Large stock of English, French and German books, and US magazines here; they also sell a few tourist maps of the region from Puno to the Yungas, and walking-tour guides; and will ship books.

There are 2nd-hand stalls on Av Ismael Montes and occasional book fairs on the Prado.

Camping equipment

Andean Summits, Comercio Doryan, Sagárnaga and Murillo, sells white gas, while another shop there at No 18, sells Lowe Alpine rucksacks. Kerosene for pressure stoves is available from a pump in Plaza Alexander.

Caza y Pesca, unit 9 Edificio Handal Center, Av Mariscal Santa Cruz and Socabaya, T02-2409209, good English spoken.

Cycle spares

Bicicar (Trek Bikes), Av Montenegro and C 18, local 2.

Gravity Assisted Mountain Biking Av 16 de Julio 1490, office 9, (opposite Cinema Monje Campero), T02-2374204, F02-2310023, www.gravitybolivia.com.

Very knowledgeable and also runs tours (see page 86).

Massa (Raleigh and Nishiki), C 21 No 8341, T/F02-2797820.

Nosiglia Sport (Cannondale), Av Costanera 28, T02-2749904, nossport@ceibgo.entelnet.bo.

Handicrafts

On C Sagárnaga, by the side of San Francisco church (behind which are many handicraft stalls in the Mercado Artesanal), are booths and small stores with interesting local items of all sorts, especially textiles, leather and silverware. It's best to go on Sun morning when prices are reduced. At Sagárnaga 177 is an entire gallery of handicraft shops. There are also many shops on Linares, between Sagárnaga and Santa Cruz, as well as Sagárnaga/Linares.

Artesanía Sorata, Linares 862 and Sagárnaga 311. Open 0930-1900, Mon-Sat, and Sun 1000-1800 in high season, specialises in dolls, sweaters and weavings made using natural dyes by a women's co-operative, and handmade textiles.

AYNI, Illampu 704, www.hotelrosario. com/ayni, is a fair trade shop inside Hotel Rosario (see Sleeping) promoting handicrafts instead of coca.

Comart Tukuypai, Linares 958, T/F02-2312686, www.terranova.nu/comart. High-quality textiles produced by an artisan community association.

El Guitarrón, Sagárnaga 303 and Linares, and Marka'Wi at No 851. Shop around as prices vary greatly.

Javier Núñez de Arco, Av 6 de Agosto 2255, You'll find good antiques downstairs here; his father is upstairs; nice items, very expensive, also old photographs. Try also **La Casa de Pino**, Hermanos Manchego near Mongo's in Sopacachi; **Tradicional**, C Pinilla between Ascarrunz and Presbitero Medina; and **Da Vinci**, Salinas 345. The lower end of Sagárnaga is also good for antiques.

Joyería Cosmos, Handal Center, Local 13, Socabaya and Av Mariscal Santa Cruz, sells Inca and Bolivian designs in gold and silver, and colonial objects. There is inexpensive silver and jewellery in the little cabinets outside Lanza market on Av Santa Cruz.

Kunturi, Nicolas Acosta 832, T02-494350. Here you will find wonderful handicrafts produced by the Institute for the Handicapped including embroidered cards.

Millma, Sagárnaga 225, and in *Hotel Radisson*, for alpaca sweaters (made in their own factory) and antique and rare textiles.

Mother Earth, Linares 870. High-quality alpaca sweaters with natural dyes. Good-quality alpaca goods also at **LAM** shops on Sagárnaga.

Rumillajta, one of the Galería shops adjacent to the San Francisco church entrance. For musical instruments.

Toshy on Sagárnaga, for top quality knitwear.

Wari, in unit 12 of the Comercio Doryan shopping centre, Sagárnaga and Murillo will make-to-measure very quickly, English spoken, prices reasonable.

Markets

The markets are a good place for ponchos and local handicrafts. Many local objects are sold near Av Buenos Aires, and musical instruments can be found much cheaper than in the shops on C Granier, near the main cemetery. At Gallardo 1080, 1 block above Buenos Aires, there is the small workshop of the late master mask-maker Antonio Viscarra, now run by his daughter and son-in-law. Costume, mask and trinket shops for Gran Poder abound above Buenos Aires. Mercado Rodríguez street market is good for fresh food. Sat and Sun mornings are the main days but the market is open every day. The street of Eloy Salmón is packed with shops selling cheap electronic goods, cameras and computer components.

Shopping malls and supermarkets

Hipermaxi in Miraflores, C Cuba on the corner of C Brazil, is cheaper and good for trekking food.

Ketal in C 21, San Miguel and Av Arce, opposite *Jalapeños* restaurant, has a better range and the one on Av Ballivián at the corner with C 15 is the biggest supermarket in the city, with a vast array of western goodies, many of them at non-western prices.

Shopping Norte, Potosí and Socabaya, is a modern mall with restaurants and expensive merchandise. Also try **San Miguel** in Zona Sur.

Zatt supermarket chain is small but well-stocked. The branch closest to the centre is on C Sánchez Lima on the corner with Plaza Avaroa, Sopocachi.

▲ Activities and tours

Football

The 'great game' is popular and played on Wed and Sun at the national Hernando Siles Stadium in Miraflores (Micro A), which is shared by both main La Paz teams, Bolívar and The Strongest. Any national soccer match is marked by lots of flag-waving, driving around with horns beeping and face painting – and that's before kick-off. Most match days are de facto half holidays depending on the time the match starts. During the game all Bolivian goals are marked by fireworks and if the team wins its party, party, party. There are many sports shops on C Santa Cruz selling football strips.

Golf

Mallasilla is the world's highest golf course, and there's also one at **Pinos**. Non-members can play at Mallasilla on weekdays. Club hire, green free, balls, and caddie costs US$37, the course is empty on weekdays, so there's no need to book; it is in good condition and beautiful.

Jogging

Those who would like to go running with the world's highest branch of the **Hash House Harriers** should ask at *The Britannia* pub in Calacoto (see Bars above).

Skiing

A vehicle will get you to the car park of Chacaltaya in 1½ hours from central La Paz, leaving only 45 m of ascent for you to climb before claiming to have climbed a peak in excess of 5,000 m. When there is a lot of snow giving the best conditions the road becomes impassable. There are plans to asphalt it, but don't hold your breath.

The **Club Andino Boliviano**, organizes the cheapest regular transport to Chacaltaya; US$10 per person for the 2½-hour bus journey, leaving La Paz at 0800 on Saturday and Sunday, and returning about 1530. A taxi or minibus costs US$30 (whole car) for a half-day trip. Hiring a jeep and driver for the trip costs US$70. The trip can be hair-raising as buses carry no chains. Often the buses and tours only go half way. Many agencies do day trips for US$12.50, often combined with Valle de la Luna. ▶▶ *See also p50.*

Snooker/pool

San Luis, Edificio México, segundo Sótano, C México 1411.
Picco's, Edificio 16 de Julio, Av 16 de Julio 1566. Both are friendly and have good tables.

Sports centres

YMCA sportsground and gymnasium opposite the University of San Andrés, Av Villazón, and clubhouse open to the public, Av 20 de Octubre 1839 (table tennis, billiards, etc).

Swimming

There is an Olympic-sized swimming pool in Alto Obrajes, which sometimes has water in it.

Tour operators

Most agencies now sell airline tickets at standard rates; many agencies arrange also excursions or travel to Peru.
Akhamani Trek, Illampu 707, T/F02-2375680, tourtrek@ceibo.entelnet.bo. For trekking in Sorata and Coroico, also day trips, English spoken, safe, good porters, well-organized. Highly Recommended.
America Tours, Av 16 de Julio 1490 (opposite the Monje Campero Cinema), inside Edif Avenida, office 9, T02-2374204, F02-2310023, www.america-ecotours.com. Highly recommended for tours to all parts of the country, especially to Chalalán where they have special rates. Also now running trips to Noel Kempf Mercado and Amboro National Parks. This genuine ecotourist agent helps local communities benefit from responsible tourism.
Bolivia Adventure Planet Expeditions, C Vincenti no 850, Sopocachi, T02-2423855, www.planetaventura.com. Adventure travel service, including mountaineering, trekking and rock climbing plus 4WD tours.
Bolivan Journey, Sagárnaga 363, T/F02-2357848, bolivian@latinwide.com. For climbing, camping and mountain bike tours, also equipment rental. Fluent English and French spoken, maps for local cycling routes. Bracha, T02-2327472, has details of, and sells for, trains from Santa Cruz.

La Paz Activities & tours

Bolivian Mountains, Calle Murillo 947 (entre Sagárnaga y Cochabamba), Galeria Siglo XIX, T02-2313197, www.bolivianmountains.com. A high-quality mountaineering outfit using very experienced guides and top quality equipment, though their climbs don't come cheap. They also have an office in the UK.

Camel Travel, C Murillo 904, T02-2310070, F02-2311028, www.boliviatrek.com. Mountain biking, climbing, trekking, English and German spoken. Recommended.

Carmoar Tours, C Bueno 159, T02-2317202, F02-2340633, carmoar@zuper.net. Headed by Günther Ruttger. Information and maps for the Inca Trail to Coroico, rents trekking gear.

Colibrí, Sagárnaga 309, T02-2371936, F02-2355043, www.colibri-adventures.com. For information on and arrangement of climbing and adventure tours see Mountaineering section on page 89.

Crillon Tours, Av Camacho 1223, (PO Box 4785), T02-2337533, www.titicaca.com. For trips on Lake Titicaca see page 158.

Deep Rainforest, C Illampu 626 (in Hotel Continental), T02-2150385. Professionally run biking, trekking climbing and jungle tours with small groups. Branch in Rurrenabaque, from where they run a jungle survival tour.

Detour, Av Mariscal Santa Cruz, Edif Camara Nacional de Comercio (next door to Varig), T02-2361626. Mon-Fri 0900-1200, 1400-1900, Sat 0930-1230. Excellent for flight tickets. Very professional, English spoken.

Eco Adventure, Sagarnaga 368, T02-2310272, www.ecoadventure bolivia.com. The only real competitor for the 'world's most dangerous road' trip in terms of quality to Gravity Assisted Mountain Biking. Eco have a newer, less experienced outfit, but generally impressive levels of customer care, decent (Trek) bikes and they promise a radio-equipped guide for every 4 riders. US$39 per person.

Explore Bolivia, Sagárnaga 339, Galería Sagárnaga, office 1, T/F02-2391810, explobol@ceibo.entelnet.bo. Recommended for adventure sports, good bikes (Trek).

Fremen, C Pedro Salazar 537, Plaza Avaroa, T02-2417062, F02-2417327, Casilla 9682, vtfremen@caoba.entelnet.bo. They own *Flotel* in Trinidad for jungle cruises in the Beni and *Hotel El Puente* in the Chapare, and run tours throughout the country (eg Salar de Uyuni and Che Guevara Trail), Michel Livet is helpful and speaks English, French and Spanish, also have offices in Santa Cruz, Cochabamba and Trinidad.

Gloria Tours, see Hotel Gloria, p110.

Gravity Assisted Mountain Biking Av 16 de Julio 1490, T02-2374204, www.gravitybolivia.com. Office Mon-Fri 9-7, Sat 10-1. No rides on Mondays. Top tours with excellent bikes and guides to Coroico ('world's most dangerous road') for US$50. Also trips to Sorata, Zongo and other locations, depending on demand. More expensive than others but definitely the most highly recommended, especially for the risky but exhilarating Coroico trip. Book early as trips genuinely fill up fast. The office is well hidden on the Prado.

Magri Turismo, C Capitán Ravelo 2101, on corner with Montevideo, T02-2442727, F02-2443060, Magri_emete@megalink.com. Amex representative, gives travellers'

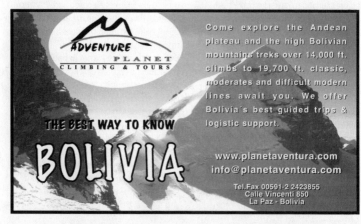
La Paz Activities & tours

cheques against American Express card, but cannot give cash or exchange TC's, offers all other Amex emergency services and handles clients' mail, recommended for tours in Bolivia, travel services.

Nuevo Continente, at Hotel Alem, Sagárnaga 344, and also next door which does not close lunchtimes, T/F02-2373423, quiquisimo@ mixmail.com. Recommended for trip to Zongo, Clemente is a good driver, cheap service to airport, very friendly and helpful.

Pachamama Tours, Sagárnaga 189 (Doryan shopping centre, 2nd floor, office 35), T/F02-2319740, www.megalink.com/ pachamama. Cheap air fares within South America, very knowledgable and professional, English spoken, also arranges cultural tours to indigenous groups, Mon-Fri 0900-1230, 1430-1830, Sat 0900-1230. Recommended for tours of La Paz, Tiwanaku, Titicaca, etc, also arranges tours throughout Bolivia.

Sun Island Tours, 6 de Agosto, on corner with Pedro Salazar (Galería Ilimani II, of 2), T02-2434202. Very helpful, tours and flights.

Tauro Tours, C Mercado 1362, Galería Paladium Mezz, local 'M', T02-2201846, F02-2201881. Top-end adventure tourism agency, jeep tours anywhere in the country,

La Paz Activities & tours

organized by the very experienced and German Mountain Guides Association-trained Carlos Aguilar.

Tawa Tours, Sagárnaga 161, T02-233 4290, F02-239 1175, www.info.tawa.com. French-run, offering jungle tours to their own camp as well as the Salt Lake areas, good guides (they can also arrange charter flights to Europe and the USA). Highly recommended.

Toñito Tours, Office 9, Comercio Doryan, Sagárnaga 189, T/F02-2336250, www.bolivianexpeditions.com. Organizes trips to Uyuni salt flats. Run by American Chris and Bolivian wife Suzy. Friendly and helpful, will take reservations by internet. Also rent sleeping bags for US$5 the whole trip.

Transturin, C Ascarrunz 2518 (off our main map), PO Box 5311, T02-2422222, www.travelbolivia.com. Full travel services, with tours ranging from La Paz to the whole country (for full details of their Lake Titicaca services see under Lake Titicaca).

Turismo Balsa, Capitán Ravelo 2104, T02-2440817, F02-2440310, turismo_balsa@ megalink.com, and Av 16 de Julio 1650, T02-2354049, F02-2371898. City and local tours are recommended (see also under Puerto Pérez, page), also great deals on international flights.

Turisbus, Illampu 704, T02-2451341, www.travelperubolivia.com. Agent for Peruvian railways (ENAFER), tickets to Puno and Cusco, also local and Bolivian tours.

⊖ Transport

La Paz *p96, maps p100, p129 and p130*

Air

LAB and Aero Sur fly to the main cities and towns and TAM (Transportes Aéreo Militar) and Amazonas fly to destinations in the eastern and northern lowlands. Fares are comparatively low for internal flights. For details, see under destinations.

Airline offices

Aerolíneas Argentinas, Edif Gundlach, 2nd floor, oficina 201, Reyes Ortiz 73, on the corner with Federico Suarez, T02-2351711, F02-2391059.

Aero Sur, Av 16 de Julio 616, T02-2430430, F02-2313957, www.aerosur.com.

Amazonas Av Saavedra 1649 (Miraflores), T/F02-2222045, www.amaszonas.com.

American Airlines, Av 16 de Julio 1440, Edificio Herman, T02-2351316, F02-2391080, www.aa.com.

British Airways and **Iberia**, C Ayacucho 378, Edif Credinform, 5th floor, T02-2203885, F02-2203950.

Continental Airlines and **Korean Air**, C Alto de la Alianza 664.

Ecuatoriana, T02-0800-3001.

LanChile, Av 16 de Julio 1566, 1st floor, T02-2358377, F02-2392051, www.lanchile.com.

Lloyd Aéreo Boliviano (LAB), Camacho 1460, T02-0800- 3001. Www.labairlines.com.

KLM, **TAM** and **SAETA**, Plaza del Estudiante 1931, T02-2441595, F02-2443487.

Swissair, Edif Gundlach Torre Oeste, 5th floor, oficina 502, Reyes Ortiz 73, on the corner with Federico Suarez, T02-2350730, F02-2391740.

Transportes Aéreo Militar (TAM), Av Montes 738, on the corner with Serrano, T02-2379286. Mon-Fri 0830-1200 and 1430-1830.

Varig, Av Mariscal Santa Cruz 1392, Edificio Cámara de Comercio, T02-2314040, F02-2391131.

Bus
Local

There are 3 types of city bus: large Fiat buses run by the city corporation, on fairly limited routes; micros (Bluebird-type buses), which charge US$0.18 in the centre, US$0.24 from outside the centre; and combis (minivans), US$0.20/0.34, which are quicker than micros. Don'texpect to get anywhere fast in the centre as micros and combis often have to stop every few metres to let passengers on and off. When you want to get off scream "¡en la esquina!", and be sure to allow a few minutes to squeeze past everyone on your way to the exit.

NB If you can't keep your backpack on your lap, you may be charged extra in combis.

Long distance

Buses to **Sorata**, **Copacabana**, **Tiahuanaco** and destinations north of La Paz leave from various streets around the Cemetery district (see Cemetery district map). Companies include **Flota Copacabana**, **Manco Kapac**, **2 de Febrero**, **Ingavi**, **Trans Perla Andina**. To get to the **Cemetery district**, take any bus or combi marked 'Cementerio' going up C Santa Cruz (US$0.17); the route is Santa Cruz, Max Paredes, Garita de Lima, Mariano Bautista, Plaza Reyes Ortiz/Tomás Katari. Look out for the cemetery arch on your left. On Plaza Reyes Ortiz are **Manco Kapac**, (recommended), T02-2350033 and 2 de Febrero, T02-2377181, for **Copacabana** and **Tiquina**. Several micros (20, J, 10) and combis (223, 252, 270, 7) go up Av Kollasuyo; look for 'Kollasuyo' on the windscreen in most, but not all, cases.

Buses to **Coroico** and the **Yungas** leave from Villa Fátima, which is 25 mins by micros B, V, X, K, 131, 135, or 136, or trufis 2 or 9, which pass Pérez Velasco on the way down from Plaza Mendoza – get off at the service station (see Villa Fátima map above). Details of bus times and fares are given under each relevant destination.

Buses to **Oruro**, **Potosí**, **Sucre**, **Cochabamba**, **Santa Cruz**, **Tarija**, **Villazón** and all points south of La Paz leave from the main terminal at Plaza Antofogasta.

To Cochabamba, 7 hrs, US$3, from 0700 with **Trans El Dorado** until 2300; **Jumbo Bus Bolívar** run throughout the day. Other companies include **Trans Copacabana MEM**, **Sind Trans Copacabana**, **Jumbo Bus Bolivia**, **Jumbo Bus Cisne**, **Jumbo Bus Cosmos**, **Flota San Francisco**.

Cemetery district

Transport	Cooperativo Transporte	Trans Soncko Sua **11**
2 de Febrero **1**	to Tiahuanaco	Trans Titicaca **12**
Buses to Cohana,	& Desaguadero **5**	Trans Tours Tiwanaku **13**
Aygachi & Iquiaca **2**	Minibuses to Achacachi **6**	Trans Unificada to Sorata **14**
Buses to Cotapampa,	Minibuses to Batallas,	Trucks to Ancoraimes
Charazani, Ancoraimes,	Pucarani & Peñas **7**	& Caranavi **15**
Ulla Ulla, Antaquilla	Trans Altiplano **8**	Trans 9 de Noviembre
& Pelechuco **3**	Trans Larecaja **9**	to Desaguadero **16**
Buses to Warisata,	Trans Manco Kapac	Unión Ingavi
Umapusa & Tacamarca **4**	to Copacabana **10**	to Desaguadero **17**

To **Oruro**, 3 hrs, US$1.80, from 0530 with Jumbo Bus Fenix, til 2030 with Jumbo Bus Nobleza and Jumbo Bus Bolivia. Other companies include Copacabana MEM.

To **Santa Cruz**, 17 hrs, US$10.50, from 1630 with Trans Copacabana MEM, until 2300 with Jumbo Bus Bolivia. Other companies include: Jumbo Bus Cosmos, Jumbo Bus Bolivia, Sind Trans Copacabana, Trans El Dorado.

To **Sucre**, 19 hrs, US$9, at 1830 with Trans Copacabana *bus cama*, arrives 0830, Trans Illimani 1900, 10 de Noviembre 1830 via Potosí.

To **Potosí**, 10 hrs, US$9, from 1830 with Trans Illimani, until 2030 with Trans Copacabana MEM. Other companies include Trans El Dorado, Trans Relampago, Trans Sucre, 10 de Noviembre. Times and prices will vary, ask in advance of booking. Times for other destinations are given in their relevant chapters.

International buses also leave from the main terminal at Plaza Antofogasta. The offices are towards the back. To **Buenos Aires**, daily at 1630 (San Roque, office 40, T02-2281959), via Yacuiba, or at 1700 with San Lorenzo, T02-2282292, both take 2½ days and cost US$110. Expresso Sur, T02-2281921 leaves at 1630 and charges U$10 more. Also **Atahualpa** via Yacuiba or La Quiaca/Villazón. Alternatively, go to Villazón and change buses in Argentina.

To **Santiago**, Chile, **Chilebus** (office 38, T02-2282168) leaves daily at 0630, reaching Arica at 1400 and Santiago at 1700 1½ days later, US$43. To **Arica** via the frontier at Tambo Quemado and Chungará, at 1300 Mon-Thu with Trans Litoral, 9 hrs on paved road, US$12 (office No 29, T02-2281920). Also with Chile Bus daily at 0630, US$12 (good service), and Trans Salvador 3 times a week, and Transportes Cali. There is no direct service to Arica via the frontier at Charaña and Visviri; the trip must be done in stages. Senobus, C Hujutri (400 m from train station in direction of the Cementerio), departs Tue, Fri and Sat evenings, US$11; also El Cariñoso, which is cheaper. In Charaña take a taxi to Visviri (US$0.65), then a bus on Tue and Fri, US$7, or colectivo taxi to Arica. It is a beautiful though exhausting trip, but doing it in stages, rather than straight through, involves extra waiting at the border. All companies involve several changes of bus; the entire trip takes 18 hrs. Military checks can be expected on both sides of the frontier.

To **Iquique**, via **Arica**, with Trans Litoral at 1300 Mon-Thu, arriving Arica 2200-2230 and Iquique at 0400, US$15 including breakfast and lunch.

To **Cusco**, direct with Trans Litoral on Wed, Fri and Sun at 0800, 12 hrs, US$17. Colectivos and agency buses leave daily to Puno with different companies and are most easily booked through travel agencies, US$12-15.50, 10 hrs.

Of the various La Paz-**Puno** services, only **Transturin** does not make you change to a Peruvian bus once over the border. **Exprinter/Cruz del Sur**, T02-2362708, go via Desaguadero Tue, Thu, Sat 0800, US$7.20. For transport to **Peru** see under Lake Titicaca (page 146).

Car hire
Imbex, Av Montes 522, T02-2455432, F02-2455433, www.imbex.com. Well-maintained Suzuki jeeps from US$60 per day, including 200 km free for 4-person 4WD. Highly recommended.
Kolla Motors, Rosendo Gutiérrez 502, T02-2419141. Well-maintained 6-seater 4WD Toyota jeeps, insurance and gasoline extra.

Villa Fátima

Buses
24 de Agosto to Chulumani & Chicaloma **1**
Agencies with buses to Caranavi, Guanay & Rurrenabaque **2**
Flota Yungueña to Coroico **3**
Flota Yungueña to Rurrenabaque, Caranavi Riberalta & Guayaramerín **4**
Veloz del Norte to Yanacachi & Chojlla **5**
Turbus Totai to Coroico **6**
Trans Totai to Coroico **7**
Flota Unificada to Beni **8**
Trans Arenas to Chulumani **9**

Petita Rent-a-car. Calle Valentin Abecia 2031, T02-2420329, www.rentacar petita.com. Swiss owners Ernesto Hug and Aldo Rezzonico, recommended for well-maintained VW beetles and 4WD jeeps, etc, they also offer recommended adventure tours, ('Jeeping Bolivia'), German, French and English spoken. Ernesto also has a garage for VW and other makes at Av Jaimes Freyre 2326, T02-2342279. Highly recommended.

Those needing a **car park** can find a safe and central one on the corner of Ingavi and Sanjines, US$1.35 for 24 hrs.

Motorcycle rental
J Landivar, Av Saavedra 1235, T02-2329774, F02-2392427. Motorcycle spares, good for Honda and other Japanese makes.
Moto Rent, Av Busch 1255, Miraflores Norte, T02-2357289. 650cc Kawasaki endurance type, US$50 per day unlimited mileage, US$250 per week.

Taxis
Normal taxis charge US$0.75 (5Bs) for short trips within city limits. Trufis are fixed-route collective taxis with a little flag on the front which charge US$0.28-0.40 per person within city limits. Taxi drivers are not tipped. Don't let the driver turn the lights out at night. Radio taxis (eg *Alfa* T02-2322427, *La Rápida* T02-2392323) charge US$1.45 in the centre and US$2.80 to the suburbs. They are also good value for tours for 3 or more people, but negotiate the price.
Adolfo Monje Palacios, in front of *Hotel El Dorado*, T02-2354384, is recommended for short or long trips.
Eduardo Figueroa, T02-2786281, taxi driver and travel agent, has been recommended.
Oscar Vera, Simón Aguirre 2158, Villa Copacabana, La Paz, T02-2230453, specialises in trips to the Salar de Uyuni and the Western Cordillera, he speaks English and is also recommended.

Excursions from La Paz

Valle de la Luna *p108*
Combi A, numbers 231 and 273 pass the **Valle de la Luna** en route to the Mallasa recreation area, a large weekend excursion area near Mallasa village. If you do not want to walk in the valley, stay on the bus to the

end of the line and take a return bus, 2 hrs in all. Alternatively, take micro 11, a small bus marked 'Aranjuez', from C Sagárnaga, near Plaza San Francisco, US$0.65, and ask the driver where to get off. Most local travel agents organize tours to the Valle de la Luna. These are generally brief, 5 min stops for photos as part of a US$15 tour of La Paz and surroundings. A taxi will cost US$6.

Achumani *p108*
To **Chasquipampa** take any combi or micro marked 'Ovejuno' or 'Chasquipampa' from the Prado. On the way back there are good views of the southern districts and the city above.

Palca Canyon *p109*
Take the bus to Palca and get off at **Huni**. The bus leaves from outside the Comedor Popular in C Max Paredes above the junction with C Rodríguez at 0530 every day, US$1. Alternatively, get the micro Ñ or minibus 385 from central La Paz to Chasquipampa or Ovejuyo and then it takes 30 mins to walk along the road to reach a pass area near a lake with great views of Illimani and Mururata. From here its 25 mins down to Huni where the trek starts.

Comanche *p109*
Micros leave from the railway station to Viacha one hour away, from where it's a rough, dusty and cold truck-ride to Comanche. Trains leave Tue 2200, and return on Wed only at 1500, US$1.50 each way. Some travel agencies arrange tours.

Zongo Valley *p109*
Either arrange a jeep through a tourist agency for US$70, or go to Plaza Ballivián in El Alto to catch a camión at midday on Mon, Wed and Fri for US$1; or haggle with the drivers of empty minibuses for around US$10. You can also hire a taxi for US$30 for the return trip. If driving, make sure you have your passport and driving documents as there is a police checkpoint immediately before the mine.

To get back from the dam if you haven't arranged transport, the truck returns passing the Zongo dam at about midday on Tue, Thu and Sat. There are La Paz-bound jeeps and minibuses at irregular intervals during the season.

Hotel Gloria (see Sleeping) runs transport every day at 0800 with a minimum of 6 people, US$6.75 per person return, 2 ½ hrs.

Return to La Paz same day at 1600. Alternatively, take any bus going to Oruro and get off at Km 75. Lifts from the crossroads are few and far between.

● Directory

Banks
Citibank, Av 16 de Julio 1434, T02-2791414, cashes its own travellers' cheques for free but will not advance cash to holders of Citibank Mastercard. Bisa, 16 de Julio 1628, open 0830-1200, 1430-1800, Sat 1000-1300, good service changes cash and Amex TCs. Cash advance (in Bolivianos) on Visa at: Banco Santa Cruz de la Sierra (branch in Shopping Norte is open Sat afternoon). Banco Mercantil, Mercado 1190, on corner with Ayacucho (good, quick service). Banco Popular; Banco Nacional and Banco Boliviano Americano, Camacho (good, quick service). Visa has an office on Av Camacho 1448, 11th and 12th floors, T02-2318585 (24hrs), F02-2816525, for cancelling lost or stolen credit cards. Automatic cash dispensers for Visa and Mastercard can be found at several sites in the city including Av Camacho 1223, the airport and Shopping Norte shopping centre. It is difficult to change travellers' cheques at the weekend, especially on Sun. Take care accepting large bills – not only are they almost impossible to change, there have been forgeries circulating.

Exchange houses (*casas de cambio*) are generally faster for money changing than the banks. Sudamer, Colón 256, good rates, also for currencies other than US dollars, no commission on TCs into bolivianos, 2% commission into dollars, frequently recommended. Unitours, Mercado 1300, 1% commission on TC's. There are several others around Mercado and Colón. Very few deal in Argentine and Chilean pesos. Money changers can be found on street corners around Plaza del Estudiante, Camacho, Colón and Prado. Always count your money immediately, in front of the money changer.

Dentists
Those recommended by the British Embassy are: Dr José Artieda, Edif Mercurio, 2nd floor of 202, Av 6 de Agosto, on corner with Cordero, San Jorge, T02-2430100; and

Dr Humberto Jauregui, Edif Columbia, 1st floor, office 8, Av Arce, T02-2432320. Dr Remy Zegarra at Hostal Austria, Yanacocha 531, T02-2212083 (home). Dr Horacio M Rosso, Av 20 de Octubre, Edificio Guadalquivir, T02-2354754, his wife speaks German. Dr Benjamín Calvo Paz, Edificio Illimani, Av Arce corner with Campos, T02-2343706, and Dra Esperanza Aid, Edificio Mercurio, 3rd floor, 6 de Agosto 2809, opposite US Embassy, T02-2431081, both speak English.

Doctors
Dr Ricardo Udler, Edificio Mariscal de Ayacucho, Calle Loayza, T02-2360393/ 2327046, speaks very good German. Dr César H Moreno, Pinilla 274, Edificio Pinilla, T02-2433805 (home). Dr Eduardo Fernández, Edificio Av, Av 16 de Julio, 9th floor, oficina 3, T02-2370385 (surgery) T02-2795164 (home), speaks English, US$30 for consultation. Dr Mauricio Gutfronjd, Terapia del Color, Av Arce 2630, consultario 207, T02-2431133, T02-2390222 (emergency) specialist in acupuncture, speaks English and Hebrew. A recommended gynaecologist is Dr Marcelo Koziner, oficina 313, 3rd floor, Edificio Mariscal Ayacucho, C Loayza corner with Camacho, T02-2377283, speaks English and German. Recommended by the British Embassy are: Cardiologist, Dr Octavio Aparacio (Unimed), Arce 2630, T02-2220303 (emergency), T02-2431133 (surgery). General Practitioners, Dr Ciro Portugal, Edif El Escorial, 2nd floor, Av Arce, on corner with Cordero, San Jorge, T02-2220303 (emergency), T02-2434781 (surgery). Paediatrician, Dr Eduardo Mazzi, CIgnacio Cordero 976, Edif Terranova office 1a, San Miguel, T02-07936600 (emergency), T02-2279215 (surgery). Gynaecologist/ Obstretrician, Dr Ovidio Suarez, Edif Illimani, 1st floor, Av Arce, on corner with C Campos, San Jorge, T02-2220303 (emergency), T02-2431501 (surgery).

Embassies and consulates

Argentina, Sánchez Casilla 64, T02-2322172, 24 hrs for visa, 0900-1330. Austria , Edif Petrolero, 1st floor, office 11, Av 16 de Julio 1616, T02-2313953, 1430-1600. Belgium, C 9, No 6, Achumani, T02-2770081, 0830-1700. Brazil , Av Arce, Edif Multicentro, T02-2440202, Mon-Fri 0900-1300, (visas take 2 days). Canada, Edif Barcelona, 2nd floor, C Victor Sanjinez 2678, Plaza España, T02-2414453, Mon-Fri, 0900-1200. Chile , H Siles 5873, on corner with C 13, Obrajes district, T02-2785275, Mon-Fri 0900-1200, 1500-1700, visa same day if requested in the morning (take microbus N, A or L from Av 16 de Julio). Denmark , Av Arce 2799 and Cordero, Edif Fortaleza, 9th floor, T02-2432070, Mon-Fri, 0800-1600. France , Av Hernando Siles 5390, on corner with C 08 Obrajes, T02-2786189 (take microbus N, A or L down Av 16 de Julio), Mon-Fri 0830-1230, 1400-1600. Germany, Av Arce 2395, T02-244006, F02-2441441, Mon-Fri 0900-1200. Israel, Av Mcal Santa Cruz, Edif Esperanza, 10th floor, T02-2374239, Casilla 1309/1320, Mon- Fri 0900-1600. El Lobo restaurant deals with mail for Israeli travellers. Italy, Av 6 de Agosto 2575, PO Box 626, T02-2434955, F02-2434975, Mon-Fri 1030-1230. Japan, Rosendo Gutiérrez 497, on corner with Sánchez Lima, PO Box 2725, T02-2373151, Mon-Fri 0830-1145. Netherlands, Av 6 de Agosto 2455, Edif Hilda, 7th floor, T02-2444040, F02-2443804, Casilla 10509, nlgovlap@unete.com, Mon-Fri 0830-1700. Norway, C René Moreno 1096 in San Miguel, T/F02-2770009, Mon-Fri 0900-1230, 1430-1700. Paraguay, Edif Illimani, 1st floor, Av 6 de Agosto and P Salazar, very good visa service, T02-2432201, F02-2433176, Mon-Fri 0800-1600. Peru, Edif Alianza office 110, Av 6 de Agosto 2190 and C F Guachalla, T02-2440631, F02-2444199, Mon-Fri 0900-1300, 1500-1700, visa costs US$10 in US dollar bills, issued same day if you go early. Spain, Av 6 de Agosto 2827 and Cordero, T02-2430118, Mon-Fri 0900-1330. Sweden, Av 14 de Septiembre 5080 and C 5 Obrajes, T/F02-2787903, Casilla 852, Mon-Fri, 0900-1200. Switzerland, Edif Petrolero, 6th floor, Av 16 de Julio 1616, T02-2315617, F02-2391462, Casilla 9356, Mon-Fri 0900-1200. UK, Av Arce 2732, T02-2433424, F02-2431073, Casilla 694, Mon-Fri 0900-1200, Mon, Tue, Thu also 1330-1630, visa section open 0900-1200 has a list of travel hints for Bolivia, doctors, etc. USA, Av Arce 2780 and Cordero, T02-2433520, F02-2433854, Casilla 425, Mon-Fri 0800-1700.

Hospitals and clinics

Clínica del Accidentado, Plaza Uyuni 1351, T02-2328632, which provides first aid; Clínica Americana, Av 14 de Septiembre 78, T02-2783509; Clínica Alemana, 6 de Agosto 2821, San Jorge, T02-243676, has English-speaking doctors; Clínica Bustillos, Héroes del Acre 1793, T02-2321553, US$20 for consultation; Clínica Rengel, T02-2390792; Clínica Santa María, Av 6 de Agosto 2487, English-speaking doctors, consultation costs US$16, simple analysis US$24, course of antibiotics US$8; Clínica del Sur, Av Hernando Siles 3539 and C Siete, Obrajes, T02-2784001. Red Cross, opposite Mercado Camacho, will give inoculations if required, T02-2323642. The Methodist Hospital, 12th block of Obrajes, (take micro 'A' from the Prado) T02-2783809 runs a clinic, US$5 for a consultation, telephone for appointment. Travellers with insurance can try Hospital Obrero. For those without insurance there is Hospital General.

Internet

There are many internet cafés in La Paz and the number is increasing almost daily. Most charge US$0.75-1.00 per hr and are open Mon-Sat 0900-2100/2300. Connections are normally faster in the mornings and at weekends. MicroNet, Av Mariscal Santa Cruz 1088, upstairs, free scanner use, coffee and cakes, 0900- 2100. ExpaNet, Av Arce 2132, Edif Illampu, open Sun. WeBolivia, Av 16 de Julio 1764. Fast machines. Meganet, Av Mcal Santa Cruz, Edif Club de la Paz, T02-0811-3872, and Av 16 de Julio 1215 esquina Colón. Meeting Point, Casa de la Cultura, good music. Chasquinet, Sagárnaga 339. VIP, Murillo y Tarija, Santa Cruz 1282, Ayacucho 208, América 446 y Unión, US$1 per hr. Ajayu, Cochabamba 163, US$0.85 per hr. Entel, Ayacucho 267. El Lobo, Santa Cruz 441, on corner with C Illampu. Computers with Hebrew keyboards.

Centro Boliviano Americano (*CBA*, address under Libraries below), US$140 for 2 months, 1 hr tuition each afternoon. **Alliance Française** (next to *Café Montmartre*, see page). **Instituto de La Lengua Española**, C 14, on corner with Aviador No 180, Achumani, T02-2796074, US$7 per hr for one-to-one tuition, recommended, will arrange accommodation with local families. **María Isabel Daza**, Murillo 1046, 3rd floor, T02-2311471, S$3 per hr, individual or group lessons for travellers as well as students wanting a certificate, speaks English and Danish and has one of the only vegetarian dogs in the world. Recommended. **ABC**, run by William Ortiz, C Pisagua 634 (bell marked 'ABC'), T02-2281175, T01262657 (mob), williamor@hotmail.com. Recommended for 21-hr, week-long courses at US$5.50 an hr. Also, **Enrique Eduardo Patzy**, T02-2415501 or 07622210, epatzy@hotmail.com. US$6 an hr one-to-one tuition. Recommended. For English-language teaching try **Pan American English Centre**, same building as Gravity Assisted Mountain Biking, Edificio Av, 7th floor, Av 16 de Julio 1490, T02-2310079, Casilla 5244, native speakers only, minimum stay 3 months; similarly **Goethe-Institut**, **Alliance Française**, **CBA** and foreign schools. Also, the **British Council** next door to the British Embassy at Av Arce 2732, employs English-language teachers but you must have a TEFL qualification.

Laundry

Wash and dry, 6-hr service, at **Lavaya Lava-Sec**, 20 de Octubre 2019, suite 9, helpful service, US$1.40 for 1 kg. **Lavandería Cinco Estrellas**, 20 de Octubre 1714, US$3 for 3 kg. **Limpieza Rosario**, Av Manco Kapac, near Hotel Andes, US$1 per kg, quick and highly recommended. **Lavandería Bandel**, Av Mariscal Santa Cruz 1032, local 10, T02-2353563. **Lavandería Select**, Av Arce 2341, 3-hr service, recommended. **Limpieza Finesse**, Illampu 865, good but closed Sun, US$0.90 per kg, same-day service.

Libraries

Centro Boliviano Americano (*CBA*), Parque Zenón Iturralde 121, T02-2351627/2342582, has public library and recent US papers, open Mon-Wed 0900-1230, 1500-1930, till 2000

Thu and Fri. **USIS** has a lending library and second-hand paperbacks. **Goethe-Institut**, Av 6 de Agosto 2118, T02-2442453, www.goethe.de. Library open Mon, Tue, Thu 1600-2000, Wed and Fri 1000-1300, 1600-2000; institute open Mon-Thu 0900-1300, 1500-1900, Fri 0900-1300. Excellent library, recent papers in German, CDs, cassettes and videos free on loan.

Maps

Instituto Geográfico Militar head office is at Estado Mayor General, Av Saavedra Final, Miraflores, open 0900-1100, 1500-1700, take your passport to purchase maps immediately; or go to Oficina 5, Juan XXIII 100, cul-de-sac off Rodríguez between Murillo and Linares, Mon-Thu 0800-1200 and 1430-1800, Fri 0800-1400. IGM map prices: 1:50,000 topographical sheet US$6.25 (photocopy US$4.70); 1:250,000 sheet US$7.00 (copy US$5.50); national communications map (roads and towns) US$7.80; 4-sheet Bolivia physical 1:1,000,000, US$14; 4 sheet political 1:1,500,000, US$14. **Senac** (the national road service) publishes a Red Vial 1989 map,which is probably the best, but is still inaccurate, for around US$4.50, from the office on 8th floor of Ministerio de Transporte and Comunicaciones, Av Mariscal Santa Cruz. It's the tall building behind the Correo, open till 1800, you have to show your passport. Also reported as inaccurate are the maps of the **Automóvil Club Boliviano**. In general maps are hard to find. They are sold at **Ichthus** bookshop on the Prado, No 1800; also at **Librería La Paz** and **Amigos del Libro** (see Bookshops above). A map and guide of La Paz, in English, is published by **Editorial Quipus**, Casilla 1696, C Jaúregui 2248, T02-2340062; also Tiwanaku, Sucre and Cochabamba guides.

Medical services

Contact your embassy or the Tourist Office for a recommended doctor who speaks your language. Check that any medical equipment used is sterilized. The following clinics have been recommended as efficient and not too expensive and doctors and dentists listed below are understood to be registered to practice and suitably qualified. Ambulance service, T02-2224452.

Pharmacies

There are lots of pharmacies and prescriptions are unnecessary. Every day the newspapers print a list of those that will be open that night and the police (Radio Patrulla T110) also have a list. Tampons may be bought at most *farmacias* and supermarkets; others say they are impossible to find, especially outside La Paz. For contact lenses, Optaluis, Comercio 1089, has a stock of 5,000 lenses, including 'semiduros'.

Photography

Alvarel offers good, friendly photo processing and will also copy digital photos to a cd for US$3. C Loayza 136, T02-2312933 or Av M Santa Cruz 1320 (corner of A Grau), T02-2311153. www.alvarel.com. Any film can be developed at a decent developer. It is normal to get a free film, album or 15 x 21 cm print. **Foto Visión**, 6 de Agosto 2044 and other branches, cheap, good prints. **Kavlin**, Potosí 1130, develop black and white. **Agfa Centre**, Loayza 250, for slide film, US$2.25. Mon-Fri 0830-2000, Sat 0830-1500. Fuji and Kodak slide film is more expensive. All slide film should be developed *'sólo revelado'*, ie without mounts, because they tend to get scratched, about US$2 per film. Cheap Fuji, Kodak or Agfa film can be bought at street stalls, US$2 for 36. Check the date on the film and take care – it may be old cinema reel taped to the leader section; pull the film out a little way to check. **Foto Color Capri**, Av Mariscal Sucre, corner with Colón, T02-2370134, open 1500-1900.

Places of worship

Protestant Community Church (inter-denominational), American Co-operative School, C 10 Calacoto (T02-2795639/2792052). Sun service in English at 1100, but there are 'lots of activities during the week'. Anglican-Episcopalian services are held at the Community Church on the 3rd Sun of each month.

Synagogues C Landaeta 330 (Sat morning services only); **Colegio Boliviano Israëlito**, Cañada Strongest 1846, for Fri service (it looks like a private house).

Post Office

Correo Central is at Av Mariscal Santa Cruz and Oruro, open Mon-Fri 0800-2000, Sat 0830-1800 and Sun 0900-1200, has a good selection of postcards at the back. There is another at Linares, next to the Coca Museum, 0830-2000, postcards, letters and parcels up to 10 kg can be sent from here and the process is quicker and easier. See Essentials chapter at the front of the book for prices. Stamps are sold only at post offices and by some hotels as a service to their guests. There are a number of shops selling good postcards, gifts and stationery. The Poste Restante keeps letters for 2 months and offers a good service at no charge. Check the letters filed under your surname and first name.

To send parcels the procedure is as follows: all is arranged downstairs at the main post office – although it is easier at the office in Linares (see above) – office hours only, Mon-Fri 0830-1200, 1230-1830); have contents inspected by customs, then seal parcel with glue, US$1 for each parcel (for mailing prices see page). To collect parcels costs US$0.15. Express postal service (top floor) is expensive. The cheapest and best way to parcel home goods is via Lufthansa for Europe (T02-2811922) and American Airlines for the USA (T02-2810215). Both have cargo offices to the right of the passenger terminal at El Alto international airport. Also, there are the usual couriers: DHL, Av Mariscal Santa Cruz 1297; FedEx, C Rosendo Gutierrez 113, on corner with Capitán, T02-2443437.

Telephone

Entel (T02-2367474) office for telephone calls and fax is at Ayacucho 267 (the only one open on Sun), and in Edificio Libertad, C Potosí. There's a long wait for incoming calls. There are also many small *Entel* offices throughout the city, with a quicker service. For international and national calls, rather than wait for a booth, buy a phonecard (5, 10, 20 or 100 Bs) and use it in the phones to the left in the main *Entel* office and in the *Entel* offices or phone boxes throughout the city. Buy a ficha (US$0.10) from the person selling them next to the booth. Or use a phone in any shop or stall with 'teléfono' sign (US$0.20), or pay one of the many people renting out mobiles.

Asociación Boliviana de Agencias de Viajes y Turismo, Edificio Litoral, Mariscal Santa Cruz 1351, Casilla 3967. Instituto Nacional de Arqueología de Bolivia, C Tiwanaku 93. To renew a visa go to Migración Bolivia, Av Camacho 1433 (opposite Banco de Santa Cruz), T02-2379385/2370475, open Mon-Fri 0900-1200, 1600-1800, fast and efficient service. Tourist Police, Plaza del Estadio, Miraflores, next to *Love City* disco, T02-2225016, for insurance claims after theft, English spoken, helpful. YMCA, 20 de Octubre 1839, Casilla 963.

Vaccinations

Unidad Sanitaria La Paz, on Ravelo behind *Hotel Radisson Plaza*, gives yellow fever shot and certificate for US$12. Ministerio de Desarrollo Humano, Sectretario Nacional de Salud, on Av Arce to the right of *Hotel Radisson Plaza*, vaccination for yellow fever plus certificate, also rabies shots and anti-malaria pills, bring your own syringe which costs US$0.20 from any pharmacy. Anti-malaria pills are available at Centro Piloto de Salva, Av Montes and Basces, T02-2369141, about a 10-min walk from Plaza San Francisco, north of the main bus station, recommended as helpful and friendly. Laboratorio Inti, Socabaya 266, has been recommended, also for vaccines (human immunoglobulin, cholera, typhoid, rabies vaccine – but make sure you know precisely how it should be administered).

⁞ Footprint features

Introduction

Within striking distance of the capital is an enormous variety of landscapes, extraordinary historical sites and potential for adventure. The most popular excursion from La Paz is the remarkable site of **Tiahuanaco**, 72 km west of the city. Rising out of the vast flatness of the altiplano are the remains of pyramids and temples of a civilization which predated the Incas.

No visit to Bolivia would be complete without witnessing the sapphire-blue expanse of mystical **Lake Titicaca** and its beautiful **islands**. This gigantic inland sea covers 8,000 sq km and is the highest navigable lake in the world, at 3,856 m above sea level.

In the mountains of the **Cordillera Real**, to the east of the Lake, **Sorata** is a neglected old colonial town enjoying one of the most beautiful settings in the whole country, nestled at the foot of **Mount Illampu** with panoramic views over lush, alpine-like valleys. To the north of here the hills and mountains of the **Cordillera Apolobamba** are fantastic trekking and wildlife territory, while to the southeast the valleys drop steeply towards the Amazon Basin through the **Yungas**, where **Coroico** and **Chulumani** are good places for walking or chilling, especially if you've just cycled down the **'world's most dangerous road'**.

★ Don't miss...

❶ Tiahuanaco ruins Step back in time and piece together the mysteries of one of South America's great ancient civilizations, page 144.

❷ Fish dishes Treat yourself to some delicious lake trout in one of Copacabana's many restaurants, page 148.

❸ Isla del Sol Take a boat trip to this charming island and spend a few days walking through tiny villages that seem to belong in another age, page 152.

❹ Exhilarating trekking Attempt the masochistic Mapiri Trail or the threatened Camino del Oro, both guaranteed to test the toughest of travellers, pages 165 and 175.

❺ Area Protegida Apolobamba Visit this remote area and see the graceful vicuñas grazing against a backdrop of spectacular snowy mountains, page 171.

❻ The world's most dangerous road Brave the helter-skelter ride to Coroico by bus, truck or mountain bike, page 174.

❼ Yanakachi Drop down a gear or three in this timeless colonial village at the end of the Takesi Trail, page 177.

North & east of La Paz

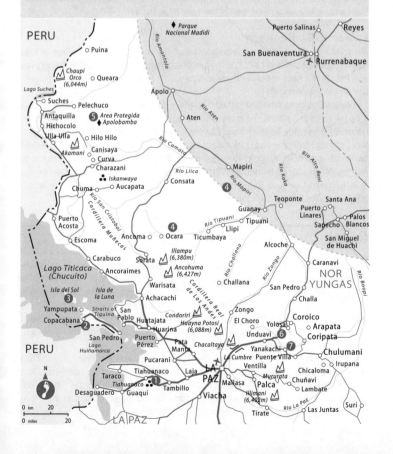

Tiahuanaco

At first sight, there's not much to recommend the Pampa Koani, a cold, bleak, windswept valley on Lake Titicaca's southeastern edge. But a few kilometres west is the site of the ruins of an ancient culture of the same name, Tiahuanaco (or Tiwanaku), one of the world's greatest and longest-running empires. ➤➤ *For Sleeping, Eating and other listings, see page 145.*

Ins and outs

Getting there Transportes Ingavi, José María Azin and Eyzaguirre (take any micro marked 'Cementerio') all go to Tiahuanaco; US$0.90, 1½ hours (see map of La Paz Cemetery district on page 129). They leave almost hourly, from 0700. The frequency may change according to demand, so the earlier you go the better. They are usually full but tickets can be bought in advance. Some buses go on from Tiahuanaco to **Desaguadero** and virtually all Desaguadero buses stop at Tiahuanaco. Return buses leave from the plaza in the village. The last one back is at around 1730-1800. A taxi for two costs about US$20 for the return trip with unlimited time at the site. A trip by taxi including the **Valle de la Luna** (see page 108) costs US$30-40. Most tours from La Paz cost US$15 return; they usually stop at Laja and the highest point on the road before Tiahuanaco, and sometimes also at the Valle de la Luna.

La Paz to Tiahuanaco

The road from El Alto is now completely paved. It passes through the village of **Laja** (Laxa), the original site of La Paz, at the junction of the roads between Potosí and Lima and Potosí and Arica. Because there was no water, La Paz was moved to its present site on the Río Choqueyapu.

Laja's church was the first cathedral of the region. On its mestizo baroque façade, note the fruits and plants, the monkey (an indigenous symbol of reconstruction), the Habsburg eagle (the Spanish king, Charles I, was also Habsburg Emperor), and the faces of King Ferdinand and Queen Isabella as natives on the left bell-tower. The right bell-tower was built in 1903. The church has a solid silver altar, but is closed to visitors. Meals can be found for US$0.80 in the village. At the highest point on the road between Laja and Tiahuanaco are views of the Cordillera and a site where offerings to Pachamama are made.

Background → *See also History, page 384.*

Archaeologists had long believed that Tiahuanaco represented a relatively unimportant era in the history of Andean civilization. Until, that is, Alan Kolata, an anthropologist from the University of Illinois in Chicago, led an archaeological expedition to the site in 1986. Kolata came up with some amazing finds, not least of which was evidence that the Pampa Koani, now barely able to sustain a population of 7,000 in dire poverty, was, 1,500 years ago a vast agricultural area that produced enough to support 125,000 people.

Kolata's expedition showed that the Pampa Koani was just one Lake Titicaca valley among many that produced great harvests every year for a 1,000 years. This was due to an immense system of raised fields (Sukakollu) built by the Tiahuanaco Empire more than 2,000 years ago. These harvests fed the equivalent of the entire population of Bolivia today and even allowed for surpluses to be stored for poor

⁝ Learning from the past

Of all the accomplishments of the Tiahuanaco culture, including its trade routes, architecture and artistry, the single greatest feat has to be its system of raised fields, or *sukakollu*. The many, many years of empirical study that went into perfecting them, the sheer effort of building them and the amazing levels of production that came out of them are all unparalleled in history, according to US anthropologist, Alan Kolata.

The ancient people of Tiahuanaco had to overcome the many problems that bedevil local farmers today – floods, droughts, soil exhaustion and salinization from Lake Titicaca's slightly salty waters. Even international aid agencies have failed to improve conditions. At such extreme altitude the climate seems too harsh and the soil too poor to succeed in making a difference.

The system of raised fields developed by the Tiahuanaco people was so carefully engineered and built that many of them remain intact today. They are massive constructions, over 1 m high, with planting surfaces sometimes as large as 15 m wide and 200 m long. Each is a carefully layered structure with a thick cobblestone base which is covered with a layer of impermeable clay. Over the clay is a layer of coarse gravel and then another layer of finer gravel. Over all that sits the topsoil.

The raised fields lie parallel to one another, separated by deep irrigation channels running in straight lines or graceful curves which form precise geometric patterns. The irrigation ditches provided water in times of drought and the elevated fields protected crops in times of flooding. These fields and ditches cover nearly 50 sq km of the Pampa Koani. To achieve this, the ancient engineers straightened the Catari river and moved it 1,500 m to the east.

The layer of clay at the base of the fields prevented the brackish water of nearby Lake Titicaca from seeping up from below ground and into the topsoil. The exact positioning of the fields and ditches was designed to take advantage of the fierce Andean sun. By efficiently exposing the ditches to the sun, the water in them gets enough heat by day to protect the fields from frost damage during the bitterly cold nights. The heated water in the ditches also promoted the rapid growth of algae that fed the fish. Furthermore, it attracted a resident population of ducks which also entered the local diet as meat and eggs. Duck droppings, decayed algae and fish remains then formed a rich sludge that was scraped off the bottom of the ditches to be used as fertilizer for the topsoil.

The idea of using this ancient, long-forgotten agricultural technology to increase output on the barren Altiplano is currently under discussion, spurred on by the efforts of Alan Kolata. If the Tiahuanaco people could grow what they needed to eat and more, using these same fields and without the benefit of tractors, water pumps and chemical fertilizers, surely it could be done again. Rural Bolivians today could yet reap what their ancestors sowed.

North & east of La Paz Tiahuanaco

years. The raised fields proved that, far from being a minor period in Andean civilization, Tiahuanaco was a great imperial capital and the inspiration for the better-known Inca Empire that followed it.

The Tiahuanaco Empire comprised nearly half of present-day Bolivia, southern parts of Peru, the northwest section of Argentina and nearly half of Chile. It was built on the vast produce of its agricultural systems. The continual surplus crops gave

⦂ Fashion victims

Physical appearance and beauty were regarded very highly in the culture of Tiahuanaco. Costume and jewellery played a very important part in daily life. But the most striking physical characteristic of the 50,000 inhabitants of the city of Tiahuanaco was the shape of their heads. One of the few things that the elite and their subjects had in common was the practice of skull deformation on their children; a popular trend in many ancient Andean cultures.

Shortly after the birth of a baby, its head was clamped between two boards to force the soft skull into a more pointed shape. The boards stayed on the child's head until the age of five, by which time the pointed shape was permanent, leaving them with no brow and a forehead that sloped back dramatically from the eyebrows to a point at the back of the skull. This pointed skull was regarded as a mark of cultural distinction. Or perhaps it was just a way of keeping 'ahead' in the fashion stakes.

Tiahuanaco the time and energy to raise armies that went on to conquer the Andes. This empire continued to expand after AD 1000, establishing huge agricultural colonies across the Andes based on its own system of raised fields. Its armies reigned supreme over many different cultures and its engineers built a vast system of paved highways over mountains and through jungles and deserts, which enabled it to maintain a constant flow of goods throughout the empire. All these roads led to one place – next to the little market town of today, and once the site of a mighty imperial capital of 50,000 inhabitants.

The ancient city of Tiahuanaco must have been an impressive sight with its skyline dominated by great pyramids, temples and palaces. The two largest edifices, the Kalasasaya Temple and the Akapana Pyramid, were 200 m long and over 20 m high. They were constructed from blocks of andesite weighing more than 150 tonnes that were ferried on reed boats from quarries across Lake Titicaca. The exterior of the buildings was decorated with intricately-carved stone friezes and bas-relief work, much of it covered with thin plates of gold or painted in hues of blue, red, gold and black.

Life in Tiahuanaco

Life in the capital city 1,500 years ago would have revolved around the comings and goings of the emperor-priest, who was both leader and god to his people. He and his family conducted both the affairs of state and the culture's most sacred religious rituals. The empire's rulers inherited their positions and were raised to lead their people in spiritual and temporal matters. They married the daughters of families of equally high status, sometimes even their own sisters.

The city was also populated by the most skilled artisans in the empire; sculptors, jewellers, weavers and potters. They were patronized by the elite in order that they might further develop their skills and produce the finest possible examples of their crafts.

Life in the royal household was sumptuous and lived on a scale of barely conceivable wealth and power. Much of their time was taken up with the observance of religious ceremonies. Powerful hallucinogenic drugs, imported from the low-lying coastal desert regions, played an integral part in these ceremonies.

All the great temples were decorated with carved sacred monoliths up to 5 m high which depicted idols in human form. They were positioned to remind the priests of the passage of important ritual days. One of these, the Bennett Stelae – named after the 1930s – shows complex markings that have been deciphered as a solar and lunar calendar more accurate than our own.

The calendar was of vital importance as an agricultural guide. It also kept track of the religious rituals, including animal and human sacrifices, that had to be observed with the arrival of the planting season. This was a time of great celebration in the imperial city when members of the nobility would congregate from all parts of the empire. The great avenues leading to the temple and the lanes running through the adobe houses of the commoners would have been full of drunken revellers and crowds gathered to watch the specially-trained young virgins offered as human sacrifices to the gods.

Life for the commoners and colonial subjects of Tiahuanaco was rather less sumptuous than that enjoyed by the ruling elite, but it was not without its benefits. For a start, the empire offered them security. It also ensured freedom from hunger. Furthermore, with its vast armies, there was protection from the hostile kingdoms and savage tribes that lurked on its frontiers.

Survival through conquest

Besides their advanced agricultural techniques, the Tiahuanaco culture also relied on the conquest of rival kingdoms as a form of insurance. This allowed access to regular supplies of foods that could be grown at the extreme altitude of the Altiplano as well as precious minerals and medicinal and psychedelic drugs.

The imperial armies were well-armed and organized. The soldiers were particularly ferocious in battle, beheading anyone who dared to oppose them. Ritual trophy head-taking was an important part of Tiahuanaco art.

The style of conquest was to lay siege to the enemy. Supplied from their base by a secured route of llama caravans, the army would surround an enemy town, wait until its people began to starve, and then move in for the deciding battle. Each time a kingdom or territory was conquered an administrative army of up to 5,000 was sent to start the business of running things. At the extreme edges of the empire, groups of traders and soldiers established frontier posts to protect the empire's interests.

The maintenance and protection of these far-flung outposts was one of the emperor-priest's biggest headaches. Taxes had to be levied, armies maintained and communications kept open with distant administrators. To this end, huge llama caravans of up to 500 beasts were used to provide transportation of goods coming in from the deserts of Chile and Peru and the tropical regions of Bolivia and to export highland products and agricultural knowledge.

By 100 BC Tiahuanaco was emerging as the most important urban centre on Lake Titicaca. The products from its raised fields fed the growing trade routes to neighbouring kingdoms and trade became the impetus for empire-building. But like most Andean cultures, the rulers of Tiahuanaco did not want to rely simply on trade to get what they needed from other regions. They wanted direct access, so they colonized the areas that produced what they needed rather than rely on uncertain trade partners.

Tiahuanaco was more successful in this respect than any predecessor. By AD 100 it ruled all of its neighbouring kingdoms at the southern end of the lake. By AD 400 it had defeated its main rivals, the Pukara people of Peru, and ruled the entire lake basin.

The fall of empire

Tiahuanaco was the longest-running empire of all the Andean civilizations. But sometime after AD 1000 it all ended. The empire collapsed and, the raised fields were abandoned, and no one really knows why.

In a 50-year period Tiahuanaco disappeared rapidly and completely. One of the earliest theories was that it was destroyed by a massive earthquake, but there is no geological or archaeological evidence of such a cataclysmic event. Another theory was that the empire was invaded. But again, there is no evidence to support this idea. Except for the looting by the Spanish invaders, Tiahuanaco's temples and religious icons have largely remained as its people left them.

Yet another theory holds that the Tiahuanaco empire was ended by a prolonged drought. This is perhaps the most credible proposal, given that a drought ended the great Pueblo civilization in the United States around the same time. Whatever the cause, the empire collapsed between AD 1150 and AD 1200 and was supplanted by smaller kingdoms made up of Tiahuanaco's former subjects. These smaller kingdoms were constantly at war with each other for more than two centuries until the armies of the newly emerged Inca empire marched down from Cusco and conquered them all around 1430.

Tiahuanaco today bears little relation to its former magnificence. The gold-crazed Spanish had a lot to do with this. It did not take them long to tear apart every one of its temples and palaces. But not only were the Spanish to blame. Indeed, until the middle of this century, vast quantities of stonework from the imperial city were used as building material for local churches and houses. Shamefully, too, a British construction company in the 1890s dynamited temple stoneworks and icons, turning them into gravel for the train tracks of a railroad from La Paz to Peru.

Fortunately, the ancient Tiahuanaco Empire was so vast in size that many of its greatest works still survive in many sites. There are other, greater sites that have never been examined closely. One of these, at Khonko Wankané, around a day's walk from the imperial city of Tiahuanaco, is believed to contain even larger temples and palaces.

The site

ⓘ *The entrance ticket to Tiahuanaco costs US$3.50 for foreigners, including entry to the museum. The site is open 0900-1700. You should allow 4 hrs to see the ruins and the village. Hiring a good guide at the site costs US$10.*

Tiahuanaco ruins

There is a good new **museum** near the entrance. It has well illustrated explanations of the raised field system of agriculture as well as ceramics, textiles and distended skulls – apparently the result of a belief that long heads were a sign of high class. Many other artefacts are in the **Museo Nacional de Arqueología** (see page 103) in La Paz, but recently many of Tiahuanaco's best pieces have been moved here, especially those (such as the **Bennett** megalith) that were previously in the *Museo Semisubterráneo*.

The main structure is the **Kalasasaya Temple**, which was the holiest part of the site and the burial place of the ruling elite. The name means 'standing stones', referring to the statues found in that part. Two of them, the Ponce monolith (in the centre of inner patio) and the Fraile monolith (in the southwest corner), have been re-erected.

In the northwest corner of the Kalasasaya is the **Puerta del Sol**, or Gateway of the Sun, which was originally at Pumapunku. The split in the top probably occurred in the move. This massive carved portal was hewn from a single block of stone 3 m high, nearly 4 m wide and weighing 10 tonnes. The central motif is a figure common throughout the empire. It displays many of the typical Tiahuanaco features: puma faces looking downwards, condor faces, two left hands and the snake with a human face. This is thought to represent the principal deity of Tiahuanaco. As mentioned above, the complex markings are thought to be part of an elaborate calendar.

In front of the Kalasasaya is a large sunken courtyard, the **Templo Semisubterráneo**. Around 1,500 years ago this was filled with the sacred monolithic icons of the kingdoms conquered by Tiahuanaco. They were positioned there for all to see that Tiahuanaco's gods were more powerful than any others. According to some theories, though, the faces on the walls depicted states of health, the temple being a house of healing.

The **Akapana**, next to the Kalasasaya, originally a pyramid, was the largest structure, but is now no more than a hill. A little way from the main site, on the other side of the railway is **Pumapunku**, a mysterious collection of massive fallen stones, some of which weigh up to 100 tonnes. The widespread confusion of fallen stones has led some to suggest a natural disaster putting a sudden end to the construction before it was finished. This part of the site is often not included on tours.

Tiahuanaco village

Tiahuanaco, the present-day village, has arches at the four corners of its plaza, dating from the time of independence. The church, built in 1580-1612, used pre-Columbian masonry. On the eighth day of carnival (Sunday) is a colourful local carnival when souvenirs are for sale. Bargain hard and do not take photographs. Market day in Tiahuanaco is Sunday.

◉ Sleeping

G **Hostal-Restaurant El Puerto del Sol** on road out of the village to La Paz. Clean, friendly, meals from around US$1, the owner is knowledgeable about the ruins.

◑ Eating

Three restaurants along the main street serve *almuerzo* and *comida familiar*.
Next to the site museum is **La Cabaña del Puma**, which serves lunch for under US$2.

Lake Titicaca

The startlingly limpid waters of Lake Titicaca straddle Bolivia and Peru only a few hours from La Paz. With the towering peaks of the Cordillera Real as a backdrop, you can wander along its shores, passing through traditional villages where Spanish is a second language and where the ancient myths and beliefs still hold true.

Lake Titicaca is officially two lakes joined by the Straits of Tiquina. The larger, northern lake – Lago Mayor, or Chucuito – contains the Islas del Sol and de la Luna at its southern end. The smaller lake – Lago Menor, or Huiñamarca – has several small islands. The waters are a beautiful blue, reflecting the hills and the distant cordillera in the shallows of Huiñamarca, mirroring the sky in the rarified air and changing colour when it is cloudy or raining. ▶ *For Sleeping, Eating and other listings, see pages 155-162.*

North & east of La Paz Lake Titicaca

La Paz to Copacabana

A paved road runs northwest from La Paz across the Altiplano for 114 km to the village of San Pablo on the eastern shore of the **Straits of Tiquina**. It then continues from San Pedro, on the opposite side of the straits, for a further 44 km to Copacabana, a convenient and worthwhile stopping-off point on the way to or from Peru. The road to Copacabana, though, is not without its own interesting diversions. If you have the time, it's worth breaking the journey somewhere along the way.

Puerto Pérez ▶ *See also listings, page 155.*

Puerto Pérez is the closest point to La Paz on Lake Titicaca; only 72 km and less than one hour by car. The views of the lake and mountains from Puerto Pérez are superb and the sunsets here are spectacular. The massive Mount Illampu provides an impressive backdrop, seeming closer than it is in the thin Altiplano air. Because of the winds off the lake, the town enjoys almost permanently clear skies. As a result it is very hot during the day, but bitterly cold at night.

The port was the original harbour for La Paz, founded in the 19th century by British navigators as a harbour for the first steam boat on the Lake. The vessel was assembled piece-by-piece in Puno.

The town has appeared to benefit from the influx of tourists who come to the **Hotel Las Balsas** (see below). The large plaza is fronted by brightly painted houses and the local people work on new water projects, building wells to irrigate what was once dry, ungiving soil. Colourful fiestas are held at New Year, Carnival (Monday and Tuesday before Ash Wednesday), 3 May and 16 July.

The road to Puerto Pérez turns off the main La Paz-Copacabana road at **Batallas**, a typical Altiplano market town so named because of the final battles between the Spanish commanders Almagro and Pizarro. It provides a fascinating insight into life on the Altiplano and makes a pleasant walk (around two to three hours). Tiny adobe houses, some with tin roofs, dot the parched brown plain. Women and children tend cattle, sheep and pigs, and the banks of streams are a blaze of colour from clothes spread out to dry.

‼ *For tours of Lake Titicaca, see page 160.*

Huarina to Chúa

At Huarina, 42 km before the Straits of Tiquina, a road turns off to Achacachi, Sorata and the road along the eastern shore of Titicaca to Puerto Acosta. The next town is **Huatajata**, which is home to the **Yacht Club Boliviano**. Its restaurant is open to non-members, but is open Saturday and Sunday for lunch only; sailing is for members only. Also here is **Crillon Tours'** International Hydroharbour and the **Inca Utama Hotel** (see page 155).

⋮ Underwater mystery

Among the many legends that abound about Lake Titicaca is the existence of an underwater city lying between the islands of Koa and Pallala, near the Isla del Sol.

This city was said to exist before there was a lake. In the city was a temple which could only be entered by women dedicated to the sun. Each day these women would go to fill their water jars at a spring located in the ruins of Chincana, near the Sacred Rock. One day two men followed the women and surprised one of them who dropped her water jar, breaking it. Due to the power of Viracocha, the Inca creator god, the water continued to flow, thus creating Lake Titicaca.

Despite numerous diving expeditions, including one led by the late Frenchman, Jacques Cousteau, no evidence of an underwater city has yet been discovered. However, investigations near the island of Koa

have uncovered many ancient artifacts lying around a natural ridge. Among the artifacts are stone boxes which are thought to have been used for ritual sacrifice offerings. It is believed, therefore, that the underwater ridge at Koa could have been a ceremonial site.

Of further significance is the name Koa, which is thought to derive from *ccoa*, the powerful feline deity that controlled the weather around Lake Titicaca. It has even been suggested that human sacrifices may have been carried out by a water or weather cult at the underwater site as offerings to the feline god. Local people today still call the ridge the 'Altar of Viracocha' and fishermen refuse to pass over it in their boats. The ridge could also appear and disappear, depending on the level of the lake waters, thus adding to the eerie reverence that surrounds it.

Beyond Huatajata is Chúa, where there is fishing, sailing and **Transturin's** catamaran dock (see below). The public telephone office, *Cotel*, is on the plaza just off the main road.

Islands of Lake Huiñamarca

On **Suriqui**, 1½ hours from Huatajata, you can visit the museum/craft shops of the Limachi brothers – who now live at the **Inca Utama** cultural complex – and Paulino Esteban, who helped in the construction, out of totora reeds, of Thor Heyerdahl's *Ra II*, which sailed from Morocco to Barbados in 1970. Heyerdahl's *Tigris* reed boat, and the balloon gondola for the Nasca flight experiment in Peru (see Footprint *Peru* or *South Amercian Handbook*), were also constructed by the craftsmen of Suriqui. Reed boats are still made on Suriqui, probably the last place where the art survives. On **Kalahuta** there are *chullpas* (burial towers), old buildings and the uninhabited town of Kewaya. On **Pariti** there is Inca terracing and very good examples of weaving. ➤ *For boat trips to the islands, see page 160.*

Straits of Tiquina → *Passports will be checked at the crossing.*

From Chúa the main road reaches the east side of the straits at **San Pablo**, which has a clean restaurant in a blue building, with good toilets. On the west side of the straits is **San Pedro**, the main Bolivian naval base (yes, that's right) , from where a paved road goes to Copacabana. Vehicles are transported across on barges, US$4. Passengers on buses to or from Copacabana get off here and pay US$0.20 to ride in a launch to the other side, all the while watching nervously as your bus is taken across by pontoon with your precious backpack on top. Expect delays during rough weather, when it can get very cold. Coming back from Copacabana, while waiting for your bus

🏮 An answer to your prayers

In Copacabana all your dreams will come true. At least that's what the local people believe. And when you see them fervently blessing all manner of material goods on the Cerro Calvario perhaps you will start to believe it too.

On Sunday, a procession of the faithful makes its way up the steps to the summit of the Calvario to perform this ritual – a strange mix of the spiritual and the material. The many believers, old and young alike, climb the steep stairs past the 14 stations of the cross, pausing at each station to bless themselves and to enjoy a brief respite from the lung-bursting ascent. Once at the top, they find an array of stalls offering a veritable multitude of miniature items to pray for: cars, trucks, minibuses, houses (for the more optimistic), bricks and sacks of cement, cookers, wheelbarrows, tiny bags of pasta, suitcases stuffed with dollar bills, even mini certificates to ensure a successful graduation from university.

The devout take their pick before descending to a series of little altars where, for a small fee, they get a bag of incense to burn during the blessing of their desired object. Cars and money seem to be the favourite choices. These are carefully arranged before a miniature version of Copacabana's famous Virgen de la Candelaria.

The ceremony then begins, in either Latin or Aymara. Those electing the latter definitely get more value for money, with much chanting, dancing, histrionics and even flames emitting from a large cup. The alternative ceremony is an altogether more sedate affair. Only smoke instead of flames, a few lines of Latin, a song and some sprinkled flower petals. At a signal from the priest a cholita then dutifully rushes over with a few bottles of beer which are shaken up and sprayed over the altar.

The ceremony over, the priest and his small congregation drink a toast to good fortune before the weekend pilgrims depart, happy in the belief that their heavenly benefactor will deliver the goods before the year is out.

to arrive off the ferry in San Pablo, admire the monument to Don Eduardo Avaroa, hero of the Pacific War. Gore should be its real title in recognition of the bright-red blood spouting from the soldier's nose and the bayonet thrust into his throat.

Copacabana → *Phone code: 02. Colour map 2, grid B1.*

This attractive little town with red-tiled roofs is nestled between two hills on the shores on Lake Titicaca, 158 km from La Paz. Copacabana, capital of the province of Manco Kapac, is a popular stopping-off point on the way to or from Peru and definitely worth a brief visit. Its main plaza is dominated by the impressive and heavily restored Moorish-style cathedral. Every Sunday in front of the cathedral a line of cars, trucks, buses and minibuses, all decorated with garlands of flowers, waits to be blessed, as a spiritual form of accident insurance, see box, page 148.

Ins and outs

By car from La Paz to Copacabana takes about four hours. Take the exit to 'Río Seco' in El Alto. The road is paved all the way. There are several agency buses that go from La Paz to Puno in Peru and vice-versa, all stopping at Copacabana for lunch, as well as public transport (see page). New arrivals may be pressurized into paying for 'entry' to the town; the fee is in fact for the sanctuary (see below). The **Tourist Information** kiosk ① *Plaza 2 de Febrero,* is helpful when open.

Sights

The cathedral, ① *Mon-Fri, 1100-1200, 1400-1800, Sat and Sun, 0800-1200, 1400-1800, only groups of 8 or more can visit, US$0.60,* was built between 1610 and 1620 to accommodate the huge numbers of pilgrims who flocked to the town when miracles began happening in the Sanctuary of Copacabana after the presentation of a black wooden statue of the Virgin Mary, carved in the late 1570s by Francisco Yupanqui, grandson of the Inca Tupac Yupanqui. The Virgin is known both as the Dark Virgin of the Lake, or the *Virgen de la Candelaria*, the patron saint of Bolivia. It is encased in glass and the only time it is ever moved from the cathedral is during the festival (see below) as the townsfolk believe that its disturbance would cause a devastating flood from Lake Titicaca.

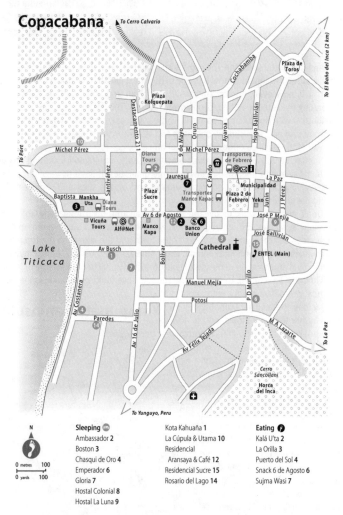

North & east of La Paz Lake Titicaca

Sleeping
Ambassador 2
Boston 3
Chasqui de Oro 4
Emperador 6
Gloria 7
Hostal Colonial 8
Hostal La Luna 9

Kota Kahuaña 1
La Cúpula & Utama 10
Residencial
  Aransaya & Café 12
Residencial Sucre 15
Rosario del Lago 14

Eating
Kalá U'ta 2
La Orilla 3
Puerto del Sol 4
Snack 6 de Agosto 6
Sujma Wasi 7

☃ Titicata titbits

→ Periodically the water level rises, inundating low-lying land, but its volume is much reduced from prehispanic times.

→ The trout fished in the lake and served in many restaurants is not native, but delicious nevertheless. The local catch is pejerrey and karachi. Also beginning to be farmed are the Lake's giant frogs, whose legs are served, fried, with chips, in several places.

→ The traditional totora-reed boats are still around but just for the tourists. A reed boat takes three days to build and last seven to eight months, while a wooden boat takes longer to build but lasts seven to eight years.

→ If someone falls into the lake, like a fisherman, it is traditional not to rescue them, but to let them drown as an offering to the Earth Goddess Pachamama. Storms do blow up on the lake, which is the size of a sea, so Pachamama is given offerings every year, averaging four fishermen normally. But don't let that put you off taking a trip on the lake. It really is a must if you're in the area.

Architecturally speaking, the cathedral is notable for its spacious atrium with four small chapels. The main chapel has one of the finest gilt altars in Bolivia. Restored in 2003, it is now even shinier. The basilica is clean and white, with coloured tiles decorating the exterior arches, cupolas and chapels. The *hospicio* (serving now as an almshouse) with two arcaded patios is worth a visit; ask permission before entering. There are 17th and 18th century paintings and statues in the sanctuary. Entrance is by the side of the Basilica opposite the **Entel** office.

Sunday vehicle blessings (which are supposed to bring good luck, and prevent accidents) outside the cathedral involve large quantities of fresh flowers and petals, garlands, firecrackers, beer scattered around and on the tires and money tucked behind the steering wheel.

Don't miss the walk to the top of **Cerro Calvario**, up a long series of steps, especially at sunset, though you're unlikely to be alone. It's a steep climb up some rough steps but there are great views of the town and the lake from the top and on Sundays you can buy miniature items (cars, suitcases and money, plus a myriad of other things) and have them blessed. Head north and uphill from the centre of town.

On **Cerro Sancollani**, the hill behind the town overlooking the lake, is the **Horca del Inca**, two pillars of rock with another laid across them. It is probably a sun clock rather than a gallows, and is now covered in graffiti. The hill is roughly southeast of the Basilica. With the church entrance behind you, turn right up Calle Murillo towards the green house at the end of the street. At the green house turn right and immediately left up a rocky hill. There is a path marked by white stones. Boys will offer to guide you, but fix a price in advance if you want their help. Above the Horca, on the other side of the ridge, is the **Flecha del Inca**, an arrow-shaped hole in a rock.

A few kilometres to the north is **Cusijata** with its **El Baño del Inca**,

Yampupata Peninsula

⁝ The sacred lake

Lake Titicaca has played a dominant role in Andean beliefs for over two millennia. This, the highest navigable body of water in the world, is the most sacred lake in the Andes.

Near Titicaca arose the population and ceremonial centre of Tiahuanaco, capital of one of the most important civilizations of South America. Tiahuanaco ceremonial sites were built along its shores, indicating that the lake was considered sacred at least 2,000 years ago.

At the time of the Spanish conquest, one of the most important religious sites of the Inca empire was located on the Isla del Sol. From its profound, icy depths emerged the Inca creator deity, Viracocha. Legend has it that the sun god had his children, Manco Capac and his sister, Mama Ocllo, spring from the lake's azure waters to found Cusco and the Inca dynasty. Legends about the lake abound. Among them are several which describe underwater cities, roads and treasures.

Titicaca was perceived by its ancient cultures to be an island sea connected to the ocean, mother of all waters. Today, people still believe that the lake is involved in bringing rain and that, closely associated with mountain deities, it distributes the water sent by them. The people who utilize the lake's resources still make offerings to her, to ensure sufficient totora reeds for the boats, for successful fishing, for safe passage across its waters and for a mild climate.

ⓘ *US$0.60.* There is also a small archaeological museum. To get there, follow Calle Junín out of town for 1½ km, then head for a large group of eucalyptus trees on a hillside 500 m away.

Trekking near Copacabana

This is a beautiful location for some easy trekking. The most worthwhile walk is to the end of the peninsula, to the fishing village of **Yampupata**. It's a bizarre experience stopping to fill your water bottle from the lake (the water is fresh) while walking along a sandy beach.

You can start this trek from the Straits of Tiquina and follow a prehispanic road through Parquipujio, Chisi (which has some ancient ruins), the stone village of Sampaya and other villages to reach Yampupata. This particular version of the trek gives fantastic views of the Cordillera Real across the lake.

Most people, though, set out from Copacabana. It is 17 km along the side of the peninsula from Copacabana to Yampupata and takes about four hours.

From Copacabana head down and northeast out of the back of town to the little-used lakeside road. After about 45 minutes the road climbs around the first headland. Half an hour later the road rises again, around a second headland. An hour and a half from Copacabana, the road forks – take the lower (left) fork, which crosses a concrete bridge over a stream. Either head immediately right, which follows the left bank of the stream and soon becomes a paved Inca road running uphill, or take the steps up to a cave and shrine (the *Gruta de Lourdes*)then head right along an unclear path through eucalyptus trees to join the Inca road.

⁝ *A map which covers the trek described here is IGM Copacabana 5745 I.*

After a 20-25 minute climb the steep Inca road rejoins the main road. Bear left here to head down to the lake again. The road continues beside the lake, through **Titicachi** to **Sicuani**, where you can buy refreshments at *Hostal Yampu*. Also here, signs advertise reed boat trips, though the boats around the sign appear too rotten to go far.

Three hours from Copacabana you go around another headland, a long slow climb of half an hour or so, before descending again around a beautiful small bay with a patchwork of fields and a few dotted houses.

❖ Begging (especially by children) on the Isla del Sol is widespread and persistent.

About 3¾ hours from Copacabana, you arrive at **Yampupata**. From the end of the road a path heads left across the beach to where you should find someone to take you across the straits, either in a rowing or motor boat. There is also an infrequent *micro* back from Yampupata to Copacabana. Rowing boats can take about an hour to the opposite point, depending on the wind and waves. Ask if you want to go further, to Pilka Kaina or the Escaliera del Inca, though it might be quicker to get off and walk. Rowing boats cost US$3.50, though after sitting through the effort of the journey you may feel obliged to offer more. Motor boats cost more but are quicker.

From the tip of Isla del Sol, Escaliera del Inca (the main boat terminal) is about half an hour's walk away. The last boats leave the island at 1600, so leave plenty of time if you plan to return to Copacabana the same day. It's a good idea to set off before 1000.

Isla del Sol and around

Though only a short distance by boat from Copacabana, Isla del Sol has an altogether different feel to it. It has a quiet, almost serene beauty and makes the perfect place to relax for a few days. It is worthwhile staying overnight on the island for the many beautiful walks through villages and Inca terraces, some of which are still in use. This is the site of the Inca creation legend. A sacred rock at its northwestern end is worshipped as the birthplace of Manco Kapac and Mama Ocllo, son and daughter of Viracocha and the first Incas.

Ins and outs Isla del Sol is, by Bolivian standards, intensively inhabited (an estimated 5,000 people live there) and cultivated, and so is covered in trails. The west side is far less cultivated and inhabited and has the highest point on the island. The most impressive ruins are at the far north at Chincana and the Labyrinth. It is possible to arrange a motor launch to take you there and then walk back across the island to be picked up at the Inca Steps at the other end, where there are a second set of ruins

❖ Beware of sunburn on the lake, even when it does not feel hot.

(much more visited) at Pilcocaina and the Inca Spring. Walking from one end of the island to the other takes five hours, so it's not really possible to see all the sites on the island and return to Copacabana in one day.

Around the island

Starting at the north end of the island is the village of **Challapampa** near the sacred rock of titicaca (after which the lake is named) and the ruins of **Chincana**, an Inca temple and nunnery which have been restored by the National Institute of Culture. It is a charming place by the water's edge with pigs running free across the fine sandy beaches. There is a good little museum, **Museo de Oro** ① *0800-1230, 1400-1800. US$1.45 on the same ticket to visit the museum*, as well as the ruins and sacred rock, which are a 25-minute walk away, in Challapampa, containing artefacts from archaeological excavations at the nearby island of Koa, plus maps and pictures with excellent explanations in English. You will see hollow stones in which offerings were placed and dropped into the lake. These were retrieved by two American and Bolivian archaeologists working together.

Next to the sacred rock is a table said to be the original sacrificial spot where llamas met their end (it is also here that the mountain path from the south end of the island finishes). Both Spanish-speaking Lucio and his father (see Sleeping on next (cheaper if staying in one of their hostels).

About 1½ hours from Challapampa, in the middle of the island, is the friendly village of **Challa**, which is very nice and worth a stay. To get there from Challapampa walk past the northern beach (about an hour), then up a hill (20 minutes) to the open area where you'll see the village church. From here head down into the valley of southern Challa (another 20 minutes) and you'll reach the excellent little museum dedicated to the Aymara culture, named the **Museo Comunitario de Etnografía** (although over the door it also bears the name Museo Templo del Sol) ① *Daily 0900-1200, 1300-1800. If it looks closed just wait for a few minutes and someone will show you around. Entry is by voluntary contribution.* The interior is nothing to shout about, with bare concrete floors, but there are some fascinating displays of traditional Aymara costumes worn for dances and in daily life, as well as artefacts from around the island. There are also excellent explanations in flawless English. The museum is run by members of the community to commemorate and preserve their traditions.

From Challa it's about two hours southeast to **Yumani**, where there are a number of places to stay. Below Yumani is the jetty for Crillon Tours' hydrofoils and other boats. A series of steep **Inca steps** leads up from the jetty to the **Fuente del Inca**, three natural springs said to aid in matters of love, health and eternal youth. A 2-km walk from the spring takes you to the main ruins of **Pilcocaina** ① *US$1.20*, a two-storey building with false domes and superb views. The Sun Gate from the ruins is now kept in the main plaza in Copacabana. There is accommodation by the ruins.

Isla de la Luna

Southeast of the Isla del Sol is the Isla de la Luna (or Coati), which can also be visited as part of a day tour, though this doesn't leave you enough time on Isla del Sol. The best ruins on Isla de la Luna are an Inca temple and nunnery, both sadly neglected.

Isla del Sol

Border with Peru

There are two main routes into Peru from La Paz, both of which skirt the shores of Lake Titicaca. The less-used one takes the road to Tiahuanaco and goes along the west side of the lake to Guaqui, then onto Desaguadero on the border. The more common route goes via Copacabana and on to Yunguyo and then Puno.

Along the west side of Lake Titicaca

The road heads west from La Paz 91 km to **Guaqui**, formerly the port for Titicaca passenger boats.The road crosses the border at **Desaguadero**, a dusty and dreary (and freezing cold at night) place 22 km further west, and runs along the shore of the lake to Puno.

Bolivian immigration ① *0830-1230 and 1400-2030*, is just before the bridge in Desaguadero. A 30-day visa is normally given on entering Bolivia, so ask for more if

❣ *Peruvian time is 1 hr behind Bolivian time.*

you need it. Get your exit stamp, walk 100 m across the bridge, then get an entrance stamp on the other side. Both offices may also close for dinner around 1830-1900. Get a visa in La Paz if you need one. **Peruvian immigration** opens same hours (Peruvian time) and has been known to give 90-day visas. Money changers just over the bridge on the Peruvian side give reasonable rates for bolivianos or dollars.

The road is paved all the way to Peru. Minibuses from La Paz to Guaqui and Desaguadero depart from *Transportes Ingavi* office in the Cementerio district in La Paz (see La Paz, page 129) every half hour, US$1.55, 2½ hours. They are usually full but tickets can be bought in advance. If entering Bolivia here, the last bus from Desaguadero to La Paz departs at 1700 though buses may leave later if there enough passengers, but will charge a lot more. The bus terminal is three blocks up from Migraciones, then three blocks on the right; ask for *Entel* which is nearby. There are frequent buses from the Peruvian side to Puno until 1930, US$1.50, 2¼ hours.

Via Copacabana

The most popular route into Peru is from Copacabana. An unpaved road leads to the Bolivian frontier at Kasani, 20 minutes away, then on to Yunguyo.

Although **Peruvian immigration** is open 24 hours, the Bolivian side, and therefore the border, is only open 0830-1930 (Bolivian time). Buses/*colectivos* stop at **Kasani** and on the Peruvian side; or you can walk (400 m), between the two posts. There should be a statutory 72-hour period spent outside Bolivia before renewing a visa but 24 hours is usually acceptable. Ask for a 90-day visa on return: 30 days is often given on entering Bolivia, but there are no problems extending it in La Paz; 90 days is normally given on entering Peru. If crossing into Bolivia with a motorcycle, do not be fooled into paying any unnecessary charges to police or immigration.

Crossing into Peru, **money** can be changed in Yunguyo at better rates than at the border. Coming into Bolivia, the best rates are had at the border, on the Bolivian side. Peruvian soles can be changed in Copacabana (see page 148).

Transport to **Puno** does not start till **Yunguyo**, a further 600 m from Peruvian immigration. A *colectivo* from Copacabana to Kasani costs US$0.50 per person; from Kasani to Yunguyo US$0.60 per person. *Colectivos* leave from Plaza Sucre in Copacabana. Agency buses will take you from La Paz or Copacabana to Puno and stop for border formalities and to change money in Yunguyo. For details of these buses see under Copacabana Transport (see page), La Paz International buses (page 128) or La Paz Tour operators (page 123). Note the common complaint that through services between La Paz and Puno (or vice versa) deteriorate once the border has been crossed – smaller buses are used, extra passengers taken on, passengers left stranded if the onward bus is already full or drivers won't drop you where the company says they will. Generally, though these services are fine.

Puerto Pérez *p146*

A Hotel Las Balsas, owned and operated by Turismo Balsa, locally T/F02-813226. In a beautiful lakeside setting with views of the Cordillera, all rooms have a balcony overlooking the lake, it's advertised as a 5-star, they are willing to negotiate out of season; fitness facilities include massage, jacuzzi, sauna and racket ball, and there's a swimming pool; the restaurant is expensive, but the set-price lunch or dinner is good value at US$12, they use a very good camembert cheese produced locally by a German priest.

D Hostería Las Islas, on the plaza, also owned by **Hotel Las Balsas'** Jacques Valletón and his wife Hortensia. Shared bath, hot water, comfortable heated rooms, **Blue Note** jazz bar is next door, also seminar rooms and there are plans to open a small cinema showing art-house movies. **Turismo Balsa** operate boat trips to Suriqui and Kalahuta as well as services to Puno and Cusco. There are some small restaurants in town which serve trout.

Huatajata *p146*

AL Inca Utama Hotel, T02-2337533 (La Paz) www.titicaca.com. Reservations through Crillon Tours. The 63 rooms in this 5-star hotel are comfortable, with heating, electric blankets and good service; there is a bar, and the restaurant serves good food. Part of the complex is the Bolivian History Museum which includes a 20-min recorded commentary in all languages; a 15-min video precedes the evening visit to the fascinating Kallawaya museum, where you can have your fortune told by a Kallawaya using coca leaves.

The Inca Utama also has a health spa based on natural remedies. Also at Inca Utama is an observatory (**Alajpacha**) with retractable thatched roof for viewing the night sky, a floating restaurant and bar on the lake (**La Choza Náutica**), a new colonial-style tower with 15 deluxe suites, panoramic elevator and 2 conference rooms. Health, astronomical, mystic and ecological programmes are offered.

B Hotel Titicaca, T02-374877, F02-391225. Address in La Paz: Potosí y Ayacucho 1220, 2nd floor. Between Huatajata and Huarina, at Km 80 from La Paz, Titicaca has beautiful views of the lake, as well as a sauna, pool and a good restaurant, it's very quiet in the week.

F Inti Karka, T02-8115058. On the waterfront, a basic, 3-storey hotel run by Máximo Catari. Breakfast is extra, rooms with shower, water is unreliable, some rooms have a lake view, ask for extra blankets, the restaurant is on the main road with a full menu, open daily, cheap-moderate prices, good fish.

Copacabana *p148, map p149*

A Hotel Rosario del Lago, Rigoberto Paredes, between Av Costanera and Av 16 de Julio, T02-8622141, www.hotelrosario. com/lago. Same ownership as **Rosario** in La Paz (see page 111) and a similar modern colonial-style building. Excellent shared spaces with internet (US$0.60 per hr), views and free tea. Rooms all have good lake views but are small and lack much character. Bathrooms are good though, with powerful, hot showers. The restaurant – *Kota Kauhaña* – has good fish specialities and the price includes a generous buffet breakfast. **Turisbus** office.

B Hotel Gloria, 16 de Julio, T/F02-8622094, www.gloria-tours-bolivia.com May look like a comprehensive school from the outside but inside is pleasing and warm, reminiscent of a seaside dance hall. Spacious, basic bedrooms have views over the lake. Restaurant.

C Hotel Chasqui de Oro, Av. Costanera 55, T02-8622343. 3-star, includes buffet breakfast and parking. Lakeside hotel, new in 2001, 50 rooms all with comfy beds, bathrooms and even some bathtubs. Café/breakfast room has great views. Also has video room.

C-D La Cúpula, C Michel Pérez 1-3, T02-8622029, www.hotelcupula.com. A short and steep walk from the centre of town, La Cúpula is one of Bolivia's best hotels. There are fantastic views, the design (incorporating the eponymous white domes) is imaginative and innovative, and the attention to the needs of travellers is exceptional. The price depends on the room: of 17 bright and comfortable rooms 7 have private bathrooms and 1 has a kitchen. The honeymoon suite is so spectacular it might just make you propose. There's also a sitting room with DVD showings, a library, a garden with hammocks, a book exchange and a great restaurant (see Eating, below). Run by German Martin Strätker. Very highly recommended.

E Hotel Utama, Michel Peréz and San Antonio (50 m from La Cúpula), T02-8622013. Spotless rooms are arranged around an orange coloured covered courtyard. Free oranges and maté no arrival. Good evening set meal. Book exchange. Price includes a good breakfast.

E-F Ambassador, Calle Jauregiu s/n, on Plaza Sucre, T02-8622216. This pink colonial building has big sunny shared spaces, rooms with balcony, a rooftop restaurant, great beds and a shrine. US$2 discount with an ISIC or YHA card. Heaters available, US$2 per day. Recommended.

F Boston, Conde de Lemos, near the Basilica, T02-8622231. With bathroom, cheaper without, clean, helpful, quiet.

F Hostal Colonial, Av 6 de Agosto, T02-8622270. A big hotel on the plaza, Colonial is under the same ownership as Copacabana's lakeside monstrosity, the Mirador. Large comfortable rooms, good value. Restaurant (see eating below). Books boats to the islands. Includes continental breakfast.

F Residencial Sucre, Murillo 228, T02-8622080. All rooms have private bathrooms with 24-hr hot water. Quiet and near the cathedral, there's a big courtyard and it's clean and friendly with good beds, parking, a good cheap breakfast and laundry.

G Emperador, C Murillo 235, T02-8622083, behind the Basílica. Very popular, breakfast served in room for US$2 if ordered the previous night, laundry service and facilities, shared hot showers 24 hrs, free clean kitchen, helpful for trips to Isla del Sol, cheap and friendly. Repeatedly recommended as great value, though it may miss the influence of the famous Sonia, who has now opened her own place (Hostal de Sonia, see below) up the road.

G Hostal La Luna, C José P Mejía 260, T02-8622051. 28 rooms around a quiet

courtyard at the back of town. Bathrooms can be dirty. Very basic but absurdly cheap.

G Hostal La Sonia, Calle Murillo s/n, T71968441 (mobile). After 12 years of working at Emperador, the inimitable Sonia's own *hostal* opens in late 2004. Most rooms have private bathrooms and big, light windows overlooking the town, though a couple of smaller rooms are a bit dark. There's a great roof terrace, a sink for laundry, a kitchen, and breakfast can be served in bed on request. Exceptionally friendly and helpful, and, at less than US$2 for a double room, the best value around.

G Kota Kahuaña, Av Busch 15. Hot showers 24 hrs, cheap, quiet and with kitchen facilities. Upstairs rooms have lake views, downstairs it's more poky.

G Residencial Aransaya, Av 6 de Agosto 121, T02-8622229. Simple, basic but clean. Comfortable and turquiose. Good restaurant and café (see Eating, below).

Isla del Sol *p152, map p153*

Apart from places to stay in Challapampa, Challa and Yumani (see below) there are plenty of places to camp, especially on the western side of the island where it is possible to camp in a secluded bay. As dusk falls the lake stops lapping and you can take in the silence. If camping take all food and water (or water sterilisers).

Yumani

Most of the accommodation is at Yumani. There are hostels opening all the time and plenty of options. With no real streets or signs on this rambling hillside community, the best thing to do is to agree a tip with one of the children at the jetty and ask them to take you to the hostel of your choice. It is worth hiking to the top of the hill where there are superb views for no extra money. By far the nicest place to stay is **Crillon Tour's La Posada del Inca**, a restored colonial hacienda which was once home to the renowned Bolivian writer Franz Tamayo. Quaint and rustic but very comfortable, it is perched on the spur of a hill overlooking this southern part of the island, it has solar-powered electricity and hot water, the rooms are heated, 1 room has private bathroom, the others have shared bathrooms, the dining room serves good food. However, you can only stay here as part of a tour (see La Paz Tour operators, page 123).

D Puerta del Sol, At the peak of the hill. Rooms with bath (**G** without).

F El Imperio del Solis. A peach-coloured building with no running water but very comfortable and friendly, breakfast US$0.60, other meals US$1.50-2. Recommended.

G Inti Huayra, up the hill from La Posada del Inca, basic but clean, no electricity or hot water, meals provided for US$1-2.

G Mirador del Inca. Further up the hill, slightly cheaper and more comfortable, clean, friendly, no shower, breakfast US$0.75, meals US$1.50-2.00.

G Posada de las Ñustas. At the top of the hill with great views all around, has 9 rooms, solar-heated shower, breakfast US$1, also snacks and meals for US$1.50-2.

G Templo del Sol, near to Puerta del Sol (see above) and owned by the same family. Clean rooms, electric showers and a restaurant.

Pilcocaina

G Albergue Inca Sama, Next to the Pilcocaina ruins. Sleeps 20 on mattresses on the floor, continental breakfast US$1.50, lunch and dinner US$4, good food, also camping in typical tents called chujlla. To arrange transport and accommodation contact Hotel Playa Azul in Copacabana, or La Paz T02-2356566, or the Entel office in Yumani (T02-0811-5006). Sr Gonzalo Pusari, who runs the place and looks after the ruins, also offers boat tours to the north of the island for US$20 per boat (6-8 people) and to Isla de la Luna, and from there to Kalaka on the other side of the lake, from where you can take a truck to Achacachi and then a bus to Sorata.

Challapampa

There are several *alojamientos* around the plaza straight up from the landing jetty, near the church. Ask for Lucio Arias or his father, Franciso, who have opened 2 basic hostels:

G Posada Manco Kapac has rooms for 35 people and a garden for camping, hot showers and views of Illampu; the second hostel has the same name but is further up the beach. Friendly Lucio is planning to build a reed boat for guests to use and can provide guides, all of whom speak Spanish and very basic English. If you need any help at all while on the island contact Lucio.

Challa

G Posada del Inca, situated right on the beach. Has 8 double rooms, very basic outside toilets, no showers, owned by Juan Mamani Ramos, contact through *Entel* office (T02-013-5006), food is provided and beer or *refrescos* are for sale.

🍴 Eating

Huatajata p146

Restaurants are of varying standards. Most are lively at weekends and in the high season.

$$ Sumaj Untavi, in Inca Utama complex, highly recommended, trout specialities and cultural visits.

$$ Inti Raymi, which has fresh fish and offers boat trips to Isla Suriqui where reed boats are still made, and Khalauta which has ruins of Aymara funerary towers, for US$22 .

$ La Posada del Inca, About 2 km before Chúa is a turning to the right for this place. A restaurant in a beautiful colonial hacienda which is open Sat, Sun and holidays for lunch only, good trout.

$ Sol Andes, next door to Inti Raymi, another restaurant with decent food.

Copacabana p148, map p149

Fantastic fresh fish is served from lots of beach shacks. In some you can choose your own fish before they're cooked and in all the food is cheap. It's hard to choose between them – pick by popularity or smell. There are many other restaurants offering decent cheap meals and good trout. Good breakfasts and other meals, especially fish, can be found in the market on C Abaroa. Very few places open before 0800.

$$ La Cúpola, C Michel Pérez 1-3, T02-8622029, 0730-1500, 1800-2130, closed Tue am. Attached to the hotel of the same name (see above), La Cúpola serves up fantastic food, including a range of fondues, a mouth-wateringly good moussaka and a memorable 'aubergine baked in the oven'. Portions are generous, you can also select the music from a 'music menu' (there's also live music) and even the Bolivian wine is excellent. Highly recommended.

$$ La Orilla, Av 6 de Agosto, close to lake, T8622267. 1000-1430. 1700-2130, miguelzamorano@hotmail.com. Open 7 days a week, generally 1000-2200 but depends on demand. One of the warmest, tastiest, most atmospheric places in town. Owners Lucas and Miguel are excellent hosts and have created a menu with great local and international combinations. The peppered steak is to die for and the stuffed trout superb. There's a terrace, an open fire, Cuban jazz, masks and dreamcatchers. Arachnaphobics should avoid looking up at the stuffed creatures in the ceiling. Main dishes cost around US$3. Highly recommended.

$ Aransaya, Av 6 de Agosto 121, T02-8622229. Good trout as well as sandwiches, omelettes, tacos and a US$1 menu del día.

$ Colonial, Plaza Sucre. A garden restaurant attached to the Colonial hotel. Decent lunch, good trout and a good place for a beer in the sun. Peñas with dinner.

$ Kalá U'ta, Av 6 de Agosto, T02-01573852. Run by same people as Sujma Wasi, warm atmosphere and good vegetarian food, organic coffee and chocolate and good music and fabrics. Recommended.

$ Pacha Café, Av 6 de Agosto. A café, restaurant and pizzeria, Pacha has good veggie options as well as pancakes, salads, ice-creams, coffee etc. Inca designs and a quiet cobbled courtyard at the back.

$ Puerta del Sol, 6 de Agosto. Good, excellent trout for around US$4. Very similar to several others along 6 de Agosto. Eat in or out.

$ Restaurant Brisas, Av Costanera s/n, T02-8622033. On the seafront, with tables outside with good views of the pedalo-hawkers, Brisas has excellent grilled trout and big portions. Set lunches and suppers US$1.25 and US$1 respectively.

$ Snack 6 de Agosto, 6 de Agosto, T02-8622114. Good trout, big portions, some vegetarian dishes including range of omelettes, serves breakfast and has outside tables.

$ Sujma Wasi, C Jauregui 127, T02-8622091. Open 0730-2300 every day from breakfast to dinner, excellent food and atmosphere (lovely and warm) in the café/restaurant plus a very good collection of books on Bolivia in their sala cultural. Breakfasts are themed on a health/mountaineer/worldwide basis. A vegetarian lunch changes daily and there's a cobbled square courtyard with stone benches, plants and flowers. Recommended.

⊙ Entertainment

Copacabana p148, map p149
Restaurant Mankha Uta, Av 6 de Agosto, towards the lake, is warm and has a Play Station and movies, although the set meals (US$1.25) are not up to much. Also has movies, video games and a big sound system and offers a selection of lunch boxes.
Yeko, Plaza 2 de Febrero, has a darts board, a floor-to-ceiling spider's web, a good music system and occasional gigs.

⊙ Festivals

Copacabana p148, map p149
Festivals in Copacabana are frequent and frantic and to be heartily recommended, especially to those who like drinking, dancing, eating and more drinking. See also page 47.
24 Jan, Alacitas, held on Cerro Calvario and Plaza Kolquepata, is when miniature houses, cars and the like are sold and blessed.
1-3 Feb, Virgen de la Candelaria a massive procession of the Dark Virgin takes place, this is a real highlight with much music, dancing, fireworks and bullfights.
End Feb/beginning Mar, Carnival.
Easter, during Semana Santa, there is a huge pilgrimage to the town.
2-5 May, Fiesta del Señor de la Cruz, this is very colourful with dances in typical costumes.
5 Jun, anniversary of Manco Kapac.
12-13 Jun, San Antonio.
23 Jun, San Juan, this is also celebrated throughout the region and on Isla del Sol.
15-17 Jul, anniversary of La Paz department, a chance to share drinks and coca leaves with the locals, also marches and bullfights.
24-25 Jul, Fiesta del Señor Santiago, dancing in typical costumes.
4-6 Aug, La Virgen de Copacabana, the town fills with people, the plaza becomes a huge market and there are dancing and fireworks. During La Virgen de Copacabana and Semana Santa, petty crime rises massively. Otherwise the town is very safe.

▲ Activities and tours

Lake Titicaca p146
Crillon Tours (address in La Paz Tour operators, page 124), run a hydrofoil service on Lake Titicaca with excellent bilingual

North & east of La Paz Lake Titicaca Listings

guides. **Crillon's** tours stop at the Andean Roots cultural complex at the **Inca Utama Hotel** (see page 155). The hydrofoil trips visit the Andean Roots complex, Copacabana, Isla del Sol and Isla de la Luna, the Straits of Tiquina and totora-reed fishing boats. You can stay on Isla del Sol at **La Posada del Inca** (see page 156). Trips can be arranged to/from Cusco and Machu Picchu: hydrofoil and train one-way and flight the other.

Other combinations of hydrofoil and land-based excursions can be arranged (also jungle and adventure tours). All facilities and modes of transport are connected by radio. **Transturin** (see also La Paz Tour operators, page 128) run catamarans on Lake Titicaca, either for sightseeing or on the La Paz-Puno route. From their dock at Chúa, 3-hr trips go to Copacabana, with a bar, video, sun deck and music on board. One-night tours to Copacabana are also available. The catamarans are slower than the hydrofoils of **Crillon** so there is more room and time for on-board entertainment. **Transturin** runs through services to Puno without a change of bus, and without many of the usual formalities at the border.

Islands of Lake Huani
Máximo Catari arranges boat trips to the islands in Lago Huiñamarca (the southeastern park of Lake Titicaca): Pariti, Kalahuta and Suriqui. Prices range from around US$25 up to US$40. Also a 1-hr boat trip for US$7-8, and sailing boat for around US$16-20 for a day. The boat trips are recommended.
Paulino Esteban is also recommended; contact through **Servitur**, PO Box 8045,

La Paz, T02-340060. Boats can also be hired from San Pablo or San Pedro (see below) for trips to Suriqui; they cost around US$3 per person in a group.

⊙ Transport

Puerto Pérez *p146*
There is a regular minibus service from La Paz's Cementerio district (see page 129) to Batallas; US$0.75. There is no public transport from Batallas to Puerto Pérez.

Huatajata *p146*
La Paz to Huatajata/Tiquina, US$0.85, with Transportes Titikaka, daily from 0400, returning between 0700 and 1800.

Copacabana *p148, map p149*
Bus
Several **agency buses** go from **La Paz** to **Puno** in Peru and vice-versa, stopping at Copacabana for lunch. They charge US$12-15 and leave La Paz at 0800. They leave Copacabana after lunch around 1300-1400. The journey from La Paz to Copacabana takes 4 hrs. These agencies continue to the Peruvian border at Yunguyo and on to Puno, stopping for immigration formalities and to change money in Yunguyo. It takes around 3½ hrs to from Copacabana to Puno and costs US$2.50-US$4, depending on the season. **Diana Tours**, have been recommended.

It is also possible to catch a tour bus to **Cusco**, usually departing around 1400; tickets cost US$17-20. You change bus in Puno; the tour company arranges the

connection. The agencies running this service are: **Diana Tours**, at Hotel Ambassador, Plaza Sucre, and on Av 6 de Agosto close to the lake; **Vicuña Tours**, 6 de Agosto, just down from Plaza Sucre, T02-8622155, open 0900-1400, 1630-1900; **Turisbus**, Rigoberto Paredes, in Hotel Rosario del Lago. For public transport to **Peru**, see page 167.

Regular bus travel to/from **La Paz** costs US$2 plus US$0.20 for the Tiquina crossing. There are several departures daily between 0700-1800 with **Manco Kapac**, T02-8622234 (or T02-2453035 in La Paz) and **2 de Febrero**, T02-8622233 (or T02-2377181, La Paz) Mon and Wed 0800-1700, Tue and Thu 0800-1730, Fri and Sat 0800-1830, Sun 0800-1800. Both have offices on Copacabana's main plaza and Plaza Sucre, and in La Paz at Plaza Reyes Ortíz, opposite the entrance to the cemetery (see La Paz buses, page 128). If you travel to Copacabana on Fri buy a ticket in advance as buses fill up quickly, similarly if coming back to La Paz on a Sun. Conversely, during the week, buses are often cancelled because there are not enough passengers. 1-day trips from La Paz are not recommended as they allow only 1½-2 hrs in Copacabana.

A bus to **Huatajata** is US$2.10 and to Huarina, US$2.50. Some hotels will offer minibus transport to **Copacabana** for US$5. This has the advantage that you are picked up at your door.

Rental
Motorcycles and bicycles can be hired on the beach, but bargain. You can also hire a kayak or rowing boat on the beachfront for US$2.50 per hr. Pedalos, complete with sunshades and life jackets, are US$2/hr. You can even rent a donkey.

Isla del Sol p152, map p153
Inca Tours and **Titicaca Tours** run motor boats to **Isla del Sol** and **Isla de la Luna**; both have offices on 6 de Agosto in Copacabana. **Andes Amazonia** run smaller boats – for maximum 10 people – which are more pleasant, but less good with waves. A full-day tour leaves Copacabana at 0815 and returns from the island at 1600, arriving back at 1730. A half-day tour returns at 1030, arriving back at 1200. With the same ticket

you can stay on the island and return another day. Half-day tours, or full-day tours which include the north and south of Isla del Sol and Isla de La Luna, are not recommended as too much time is spent on the water and not enough on dry land.

A half-day tour which goes to the southern part costs US$3 per person and is described as a waste of time as you only get 1 hr on the island. A full-day tour drops you off at Challapampa at around 1000, gives you enough time to visit the ruins, then takes you to the ruins at the southern end. Or you can be dropped off at Challapampa and picked up at Yumani at 1600, leaving you just enough time to visit the ruins in the north and hike south to Yumani.

Alternatively, you can stay on the boat and visit **Isla de la Luna** instead. A full-day tour costs US$4-5 per person, depending on the season. Tickets can be bought at the agency offices, or through your hotel.

Note that boats stop only briefly at the jetty by the Fuente del Inca, leaving punctually at 1600. Make sure the boat is equipped with life-jackets; some are not. Conditions on the lake can change very quickly and you don't want to end up as the next offering to the gods.

You can also take a boat to the island from **Yampupata** (see page 151). Motor launches from Yampupata to Fuente del Inca on the southern end of the Isla del Sol cost US$8. A rowing boat costs US$3 (or US$1 per person) and takes 40 mins. Arrange the time and day of your return beforehand.

● Directory

Copacabana p148, map p149
Banks Banco Unión, 6 de Agosto, 0830-1230, 1430-1800 closed on Mon. Reasonable rates, changes travellers' cheques for US$2 commission, cash advance on Visa and Mastercard at 3% commission. Several *artesanías* on 6 de Agosto buy and sell US dollar bills and Peruvian soles. It is also possible to get cash advances on Visa and Mastercard but check the commission; some charge up to 15%.
Internet Alf@Net, Av 6 de Agosto, next to Hostal Colonial, 0830-2200, US$2 but sliding scale, very fast connection. Also a

⁞ That swimming feline

The name Titicaca derives from the word *titi*, an Aymara mountain cat and the Quechua word caca, meaning rock. The rock refers to the Sacred Rock at Chincana on the Isla del Sol which was worshipped by the pre-Incan people on the island. The mountain cat inhabited the shores of the lake and is said to have visited the Isla del Sol occasionally. Presumably this cat was able to swim, as there is no record of tourist boats leaving Copacabana in pre-Columbian times.

The link between the rock and the cat comes from the legend that the ancient indigenous people saw the eyes of a mountain cat gleaming in the Sacred Rock and so named it Titicaca, or Rock of the Mountain Cat.

The titi has characteristics – such as its swimming ability and the brilliance of its eyes – that conceptually link it with a mythological flying feline called *ccoa*. The role of the ccoa was (and in some parts still is) important throughout the Andes. It is believed to have thrown lightning from its eyes, urinated rain (hence the expression), spit hail and roared thunder. It was generally associated with the gods that controlled the weather.

Among the Quechua people today the ccoa is believed to be one of the mountain god's servants and lives in the mountains. It is closely involved in the daily life of the Quechuas and is considered the most feared of the spirits as it uses lightning and hail.

pool bar. On Plaza 2 de Febrero the Municipal building has internet access for US$2.95. **Laundry** At Restaurant Mankha Uta, Av 6 de Agosto, towards lake, US$ 1.50 per kg. Make sure you give them plenty of time if you have to catch a bus. **Medical services Hospital**: see map of town for location. Offers medical and dental treatment and a 24-hr pharmacy, but if you're seriously ill you should go to La Paz.

Pharmacy: opposite Entel (open Tue-Sun 0900-1200, 1400-1800). **Police** On Plaza 2 de Febrero, next to the post office. **Post Office** Plaza 2 de Febrero, open Tue-Sat 0900-1200, 1300-1800, Sun 0900-1500, but they are very flexible about opening. Also Poste Restante service. **Telephone** Entel open 0800-1230, 1330-2000 every day for national and international phone and fax. They also accept dollars at a good rate.

Sorata and around → *Phone code: 02. Colour map 2, grid B1.*

Northeast of Lake Titicaca and four hours from La Paz is the gorgeous little mountain town of Sorata. Locals believe that this was the original Garden of Eden and though that claim may be stretching the bounds of credibility somewhat, it would certainly be a sin to miss out on a visit. Sorata is the starting point for some of Bolivia's most spectacular treks, from the strenuous Illampu Circuit to the masochistic Mapiri Trail, the ultimate hardcore trekking challenge, which takes you from the slopes of the Andes to the depths of the rainforest.

The popularity of the town with travellers has suffered since trouble there involving the owner of ex-hotel Landhaus Copacabana and angry locals who forced him out of town and burnt down his hotel in 2003. However the background to this incident is

● The Area Protegida Apolobamba and the Parque Nacional Madidi together, along with Pilón
● Lajas form the largest protected territory in the western hemisphere.

complex and stories about travellers being unwelcome here are untrue. The risk of getting stuck there due to road blockades is also often exaggerated though it's certainly worth checking the current situation before leaving La Paz.

Farther north, near the Peruvian border, is the remote and beautiful Cordillera Apolobamba, a wild, remote and untamed land of incomparable beauty, home to the famed Kallawayas, Bolivia's ancient and wise medicine men. This part of Bolivia is so off-the-beaten-track it makes the middle of nowhere look busy. Here you'll hardly see another soul, and the few that you do will not speak Spanish as their first language. This is a vast wilderness where condors soar over the mountains, herds of rare vicuñas run free and even the perilously endangered spectacled bear occasionally makes an appearance. ▸▸ For Sleeping, Eating and other listings, see pages 165-168.

La Paz to Sorata

The road from La Paz heads northwest to the shores of Lake Titicaca before branching off at Huarina towards the village of **Achacachi**, where there is a military checkpoint.

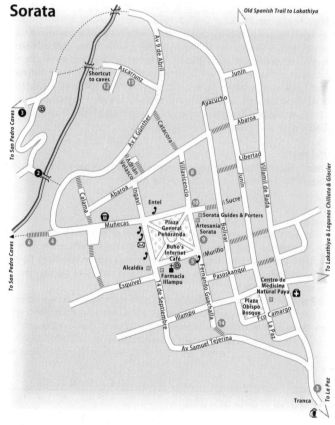

Sorata

N

0 metres   100
0 yards   100

Sleeping	Hostal Panchita **5**	Eating
Casa Reggae **6**	Paraíso **8**	Altai Oasis **2**
Gran Hotel Sorata **3**	Residencial Sorata **10**	Café Illampu **3**
Hostal Italia **9**	Santa Lucia **13**	
Hostal Las Piedras **12**	Villa Sorata **14**	
Hostal Mirador **4**		

Sometimes, all foreigners are required to get off the bus and register here, so remember your passport, and don't leave anything on the bus while registering. It's not easy to think of another good reason to linger here, although there are good views of Lake Titicaca from the church up the hill from the left side of the plaza. It is possible to walk to the lake in 1½ hours from here. There's a market behind the main plaza on Sundays and a local fiesta is celebrated on 14 September.

From Achacachi the road continues north to **Warisata**, passing through a vast marsh of water and dykes, with farms worked by people in the field, huge numbers of birds, and snow-capped peaks in the distance. It then reaches the wide open spaces of the Altiplano and climbs to a pass before beginning its descent through a series of tight bends. It continues its descent down the side of a valley then crosses a bridge and climbs up from the river to Sorata.

Sorata → *Phone code: 02. Population: 2,500. Altitude: 2,695 m. Bring insect repellent.*

The town has long been a centre for coca, quinine, and rubber growing, but more recently has been a popular tourist destination. This is not surprising as it offers superb hiking and trekking as well as being a great place to wander around and relax in. It has a lovely atmosphere, with chickens and children playing in the narrow cobbled streets, and boasts an extremely comfortable climate. It's lower and noticeably warmer than La Paz, and higher and cooler than the Yungas towns. But though it has fewer swimming pools than Coroico, the setting is more spectacular, and the road is a lot less scary.

Sorata was not always so laid back. In 1781 during the great Peru-Bolivia Indian revolt of 1780-82, Andrés, nephew of the Peruvian rebel leader Túpac Amaru, killed all the Spanish in the town following a three month siege.

Ins and outs
Buses from La Paz leave daily from the Cemetery district. Buses to La Paz leave from the main plaza in Sorata every hour or so through the day. ▸▸ *See also Transport, page 167.*

Sights
The **main plaza** is named after General Enrique Peñaranda who was born in the nearby village of Chuchulaya in 1892 and was president of the country 1940-43. On a clear day, through the giant palms, you can see Illampu (on the left) and Ancohuma (on the right). The view of the mountains is better from the smaller **Plaza Obispo Bosque**, named after the bishop who lived 1829-90 and also has a village on the Consata road named after him.

The **Residencial Sorata** (see below) on the main plaza was built by a series of 19th-century German quinine and rubber barons. It has been a hotel since only 1968 when the then mayor threatened to expropriate the buildings due to under-use.

There is a one-room museum upstairs at the **Alcaldía** ⓘ *Mon-Fri 0800-1200 and 1400-1700, Sat 0800-1300,* with a collection of locally-found ceramics from the Tiahuanaco and Mollu cultures.

Excursions from Sorata

For more serious walks from Sorata, see the trekking chapter, page 74. For mountain biking, including an innovative route all the way to Rurrenabaque, see **Hoodoo Bike Tours**, in Tour operators, page 167.

One of the most popular walks near Sorata is to the **San Pedro Caves** ⓘ *Daily 0800-1700,* beyond the village of San Pedro. The caves, although inhabited by nectar-sipping bats, are not much in themselves but the walk there and back (2½ hours each way) is worth it. The lake inside the caves is warm (21° C) and you could in theory take a swim but you probably won't fancy it. Where the road splits after San Pedro take the lower road (signed to the caves) and look for the white building above. It is also possible to walk to the cave along the Río Cristóbal, but either way get clear directions and take at least one litre of water per person before setting out. For your US$1 entry fee the guardian will fire up a generator to light your eerie path into the depths; but take a torch in case the power fails. Continue past the cave for 30 minutes to reach a point on the ridge which gives great views over the surrounding valleys. You can camp here, too. Plans have been approved to spend enormous amounts of money on the caves. Expect picnic areas, lighting and tarmac sometime soon.

A good one-day walk is to **Cerro Istipata**. Either take a La Paz-bound bus to below the cross on Cerro Ulluni Tijja (US$0.40), and follow the ridge up and over Cerro Lorockasini and on to Cerro Istipata, or walk the whole way from Sorata. Follow the La Paz road until just before the YPFB garage opposite the Gran Hotel. Drop down right, cross the Río San Cristóbal and head up through the spread-out village of Atahuallani and then up to join the ridge between Cerro Lorockasini (on the right) and Cerro Istipata.

There is another one-day walk to **Lakathiya**. Follow the old Spanish stone trail up, starting at the cemetery and following the ridge, and then descend the broad and well-used path back to Sorata. It takes four to six hours to get to Lakathiya which stands at a height of 4,000 m, and two to three hours to descend to Sorata.

Yani

Yani is a 400-year-old stone-built village in a beautiful setting. Below Yani is Ingenio which has two *alojamientos*: US$1 (with bed) and US$0.60 (floorspace only). On the other side of the Río Yani is a set of ruins called **Pueblo Antiguo**. You can also walk along a road to Tacacoma which has a hotel. It is also worthwhile exploring the **Tuili ruins** half an hour's walk away. Ask locals for directions. Ingenio is the start of the **Mapiri Trail** (see page 80). A truck to Yani leaves from the main plaza in Sorata almost every day (US$6). To walk there from Sorata takes two days. **Sorata Guides and Porters** (see page 167) can arrange guides for a four to five day trip to Tacacoma and Yani.

● Sleeping

Sorata *p164, map p163*

E **Residencial Sorata**, on the corner of the main plaza and Villavicencio, T/F02-8135218, resorata@ceibo.entelnet.bo. A huge, fascinating and ramblingly antique old place with original fixtures, fittings and drawing room (see description above), and massive 18-20 ft long snake skins on the walls. The more expensive rooms overlook the beautiful internal garden. These have sepia prints and antique furniture but the beds are either saggy or lumpy and hard. Those in the modern section are not much better. Unless you're after flies in your coffee, dirty crockery, soggy pancakes and surly service, breakfast is best avoided. Run by French-Canadian Louis Demers, who is helpful and has lots of good trekking information.

F **Altai Oasis**, T02-71519856, resaltai@ hotmail.com. At the bottom of the valley, Altai's beautiful setting has a camping area by the river and cabins and rooms higher up. It's very quiet except for the sounds of the river, and the pet parrot shouting 'ola'. The cabins are thoughtfully designed and constructed, with fireplaces, kitchens and lots of wood and tiles. There are also outside areas for barbecues and fires. A bridge crosses straight over the river to the bottom of town but the path is steep and not recommended with heavy rucksacks or after a drink or two. The long way around, via one of the bridges further upstream, is easier. There is a good restaurant on site, see page 166. Transport is available to town, US$3 for 5 people. Camping US$1.25 per person, with showers and a basic kitchen. Double rooms with private bathrooms are US$5pp, with shared bathrooms US$2.50pp. Cabins cost US$37.50 for 5 people, US$19 for a couple.

F **Gran Hotel Sorata**, T02-2817378, call from Plaza for free pick-up. Good value but marred

North & east of La Paz Sorata & around Listings

by uncomfortable beds and its location on the outskirts of town. Built in the 1940s, it is spacious, though the bathrooms are a a bit tired looking, large garden with great views and a swimming pool (open to non-residents for US$0.50), games room, restaurant. Accepts Visa, Mastercard, AmEx.

F **Hostal Las Piedras**, just off Ascarrunz, T02-71916341. There's a very good mellow feel to this new hotel, just off to the left on the way down to the cave. It's well designed, European run, very friendly, and gets its breakfast bread from Café Illampu (see Eating below) across the river. Highly recommended.

F **Hostal Mirador**, at the bottom of C Muñecas. Friendly, quiet and with great views down over the valley below. Hot showers, comfy beds and a terrace. Breakfast available.

F **Paraíso**, C Villavicencio, T02-8135043. Clean, pleasant, modern, all rooms with private bathroom, restaurant, American breakfast US$1.80, but noisy.

F **Villa Sorata**, Fernando Guachalla, T02-22135241. A small and homely place with a good eating area. New rooms with smart en-suite bathrooms are set around a ramshackle courtyard.

G **Café Illampu** has camping with great views of Illampu, US$0.90 per person with own tent, US$1.50 using owner's. Ask here too for details of 2 basic rooms (G) at the home of a nearby family.

G **Casa Reggae**, Villa Rosa. Complete with hammocks and an outdoor café bar, Casa Reggae is as laid back as you'd expect. Rooms are simple but there are also kitchen facilities. Emilio has horses and can organize rides.

G **Hostal Italia**, Plaza General Peñaranda, T2895009. Behind one of the plaza's many Italian restaurants, this is a simple but comfortable place around a square courtyard decorated with flowers and animal skins. Rooms are a generous size, some with desks and chairs. Shared bathrooms are good.

G **Hostal Panchita**, on the corner of the Plaza with Guachalla, T02-8135038. All the rooms are large and have shared bathrooms. Clean and modern, there's a sunny courtyard with flowers and a sitting room. Hot water, good restaurant, has Entel office in the entrance. Very friendly, very good value. Recommended.

G **Santa Lucia**, Ascarrunz, T02-2136686. New and modern, Santa Lucia has carpet, friendly owners and of pictures of horses and fast cars.

⑦ Eating

Sorata p164, map p163
Several **Italian restaurants** have opened up further round the square. These are much of a muchness and heavy on the cheese. Typical large pizza US$7.50, wine US$4.50 a bottle. The cheapest place to eat is the *Comedor Popular* in the market.

$ **Altai Oasis**, T02-71519856, 0830-2200. Over the river and down in the valley (see Sleeping, above) Altai Oasis does good breakfasts including porridge pancakes and fruit salad, great goulash and T-bone steaks, soy burgers and good coffee. Fresh vegetables are home-grown and honey comes from beehives in the garden.

$ **Café Illampu**, a 20-min walk from town via the short-cut, on the way to Gruta San Pedro. Run by Swiss masterbaker Stefan, it's the best in Sorata for views of Illampu. Breakfasts include home-baked raspberry and strawberry cakes and yoghurts. Also sandwiches, hammocks and camping. There are basic mountain bikes for hire (US$4.50 per half day) which eases a trip to the caves. Open 0930-1830 daily except Tue when Stefan walks his pet llamas around town. Closed Feb and Mar.

$ **Pete's Place**, Plaza General Peñaranda, T02-2895005, 0830-2200. On the corner of plaza, Pete's is the epicentre of gringo life in Sorata. Fantastic veggie and non-veggie food, great value breakfasts, set lunches and dinners. Very friendly and gets copies of the *Guardian Weekly* delivered weekly. Will change TCs for 3% commission if there is enough cash in the till. East Londoner Pete Good himself is a great source of local info (especially on trekking) and there's a good selection of books on Bolivia and maps to browse through. You may find it hard to leave.

⊛ Festivals

Sorata *p164, map p163*
7 days after Easter Another major event is the Fiesta Pascua or San Pedro.
14 Sep Sorata's biggest bash is the Fiesta Patronal del Señor de la Exaltación.

◯ Shopping

Sorata *p164, map p163*
There are small shops all over the town. The stalls and shops in C Ingavi and Muñecas cover just about everything available in Sorata - from packaged food, films and photocopying to machetes.

The **market** is just off the plaza, ½ a block down Muñecas on the right. There are stalls selling fresh fruit and vegetables every day but market days are Thu, Sat and Sun, the latter being the biggest.
Artesanía Sorata, Mon-Sat 0900-2000, Sun 0900-1600, on the main plaza near the Transportes Unificado office, sells postcards, handicrafts, jumpers, gloves and wall hangings. It also cashes travellers' cheques and accepts them as payment.
The Centro de Medicina Natural Paya, Plaza Obispo Bosque, sells natural foods and medicines.

▲ Activities and tours

Sorata *p164, map p163*
Tour operators
Associacion de Guias y Porteadores Sorata, Calle Sucre 302, T02-22136698, guiasorata@hotmail.com. Opposite Residencial Sorata, Sorata's guides and porters can arrange all kinds of trips, though most of their guides speak only Spanish and have no glacier-climbing experience. They charge US$12 per day for groups of 1-3, US$16-17 per day for 4-6 and US$22-23 per day for up to 10; food not included. They also rent out mules, porters and equipment and can organize transport to/from the beginning and end of treks.
Club Sorata (see Hotel Copacabana for contact details) organizes 7-, 9- and 24-day treks as well as the 3-day Mapiri Trail with mules and guides. These cost US$20 per person per day, all-inclusive (food,

❸ Directory

Sorata *p164, map p163*
Banks There are no banks or official money-changing outlets. Try **Artesanía Sorata** or Residencial Sorata. **Internet** Buho's internet café. US$2.50/hr. A cosy little café on the plaza but a painfully slow and expensive dial-up connection. **Medical services** There is a **hospital** on Villamil de Rada and Illampu which has both oxygen and X-ray. There is also a poorly equipped **pharmacy** on the corner of the Plaza and 14 de Septiembre, Mon-Fri 0830-1230 and

1400-2100, Sat-Sun 0830-2230. **Post Office** On the main plaza next to Cotel. Daily 0830-1230, 1500-1800.
Telephone All the phone places are on the main plaza. **Cotel** for local calls including to La Paz, same opening hours as post ofice. **Entel** for local, long-distance and international calls 0700-2130 every day. The Entel booth is underneath **Hostal Panchita** 0730-2200 every day. Calls to La Paz cost the same, whichever office you use.
There are also a number of card phones, including in the **Residencial Sorata** which sells phonecards.

Cordillera Apolobamba → *See Trekking, page 61.*

The remote and beautiful Cordillera Apolobamba stretches from Charazani north to Pelechuco and then on into Peru. There is only one other sizeable village in the area, Ulla Ulla on the Altiplano, so the area is one of the best for spotting condors and vicuñas, while on the eastern slopes of Cordillera the extremely rare spectacled bear has been seen. The area has its own park, the Area Protegida Apolobamba.
▶▶ *For Sleeping, Eating and other listings, see page 172.*

Achacachi to Charazani

The road to the Cordillera Apolobamba leaves Achacachi (see page 163) and follows the eastern shore of Lake Titicaca north and then west, passing through **Ancoraimes** (which has a small Sunday market), **Carabuco** and **Escoma**, which has a large Aymara market every Sunday morning. At Escoma the road branches: northwest to Puerto Acosta; and north to Charazani (see page 169). The road is very scenic, climbing to 4,500 m. It ends at **Apolo**.

On the road north from Escoma to Charazani is a turning to the right. The road crosses a 5,000-m pass before descending to **Aucapata**. Continue down a very poor jeep-track then hike one hour down a cactus-filled canyon to the ruins of **Iskanwaya**, a major archaeological site on the eastern Andean slopes, at about 1,500 m, where you can camp, but note, there is a small risk of malaria here. Also beware of the ants: the red ones bite and those that are brown cut your tent! The city stands on two built-up platforms, with delicate walls, plazas, narrow streets, store rooms, niches and pot shards scattered around. Admission to the museum in Aucapata is by donation. Great care is needed not to damage this site. A recommended guidebook is *Iskanwaya: la ciudadela que sólo vivía de noche*, by Hugo Boero Rojo (Los Amigos del Libro, 1992). There is a truck (and rumours of a bus) to Aucapata from the Cementerio district in La Paz. It leaves on Friday at 0600 and takes at least 24 hours. Or hire a jeep for US$550 round trip. One driver who knows the way is Oscar Vera in La Paz, T02-223 0453.

⁞ Wool meet again

The vicuña is the smallest representative of the South American camelids. It resembles the guanaco but is smaller and more slender and has a relatively long neck. They are strictly territorial, living in small herds of 8-12, led by a single male. Young males are expelled from the breeding herd by their mothers when 8-10 months old and live together in groups often 100 strong. Their territorial boundaries are aggressively defended by the dominant male, which attacks intruders by biting or by spitting regurgitated food.

Vicuña wool is probably the finest and lightest in the world. During Inca times only royalty were allowed to wear vicuña robes. Vicuña refuse to breed in captivity and so have never been domesticated. As a result, they are hunted. Estimates suggest there were more than one million vicuñas in Bolivia during pre-Inca times. The first laws to protect vicuñas in Bolivia were passed in 1918, but by the 1950s numbers were down to 400,000 and in 1965 just 6,000 were left. In 1965 there were 97 vicuñas in the area now covered by the reserve. There are now more than 5,700. It is illegal to kill vicuñas but illicit hunting still goes on. Hunters using rifles with silencers have even killed vicuñas in sight of the Ulla Ulla reserve headquarters.

Escoma to Puerto Acosta

From Escoma a road runs northwest to **Puerto Acosta** just before the border with Peru. The Peruvian authorities do not officially recognize the road as being a border crossing. Officially, you must get your entry stamp in the Department of Puno, but as this is next to impossible on this route, you will run into difficulties later on. There is an immigration office in Puerto Acosta, but it is advisable to get an exit stamp in La Paz first.

The area around Puerto Acosta is good walking country and the locals are friendly. From La Paz to Puerto Acosta the road is fine during the dry season (approximately May to October). North of Puerto Acosta towards Peru the road deteriorates rapidly and should not be attempted except in the dry season.

Sleeping and transport There is accommodation at the **G Alojamiento Espinosa**, basic but friendly. There are no restaurants. Beware of camping in this border region – there are thieves about. **Buses** leave from La Paz (Cementerio district) to Puerto Acosta (US$3.25) on Friday at 1130, Saturday and Sunday at 0630. Many trucks travel from La Paz to Puerto Acosta on Tuesday and Friday afternoons. The only transport beyond Acosta towards the Peruvian border is early on Wednesday and Saturday mornings when a couple of trucks go to the markets, some 25 km from Puerto Acosta on the border.

Charazani → See also Transport, page .

Charazani (official name **Villa Juan J Pérez**) is the biggest village in the region. At 3,200 m it is noticeably warmer than La Paz and there are **thermal baths** ① *US$1*, 10 minutes below the village in which to cool off. Another local attraction is a three-day fiesta around 16 July which is famous for having some of the best highland music and non-stop dancing (and drinking). The road to Apolo follows the left-hand side of the valley dropping below Charazani. There are some small shops and eateries (which often serve trout for dinner) around the plaza and a number of *alojamientos* (see sleeping, below). There is a medical post but no telephone and no electricity.

North & east of La Paz Cordillera Apolobamba

⦂ A taste of their own medicine

When a Bolivian is ill, he or she is more likely to pay a visit to the local *curandero* (healer) than arrange an appointment with a doctor. In rural areas in particular, Western medicine is seen only as a last resort. Every village or community in Bolivia has its own *curandero* who knows about the medicinal properties of plants and herbs.

Traditional medicine is an integral part of Andean culture and, unlike Western practices, takes into account the patient's own perceptions of his or her illness and emotional condition. Healers believe that physical illnesses originate from the soul and are caused by the ajaya (life force) leaving the body. The healer's job is to coax the ajaya back into the body and restore the mind/body equilibrium. In this way, the healer instills confidence in the patient and lowers psychological resistance to the purification process.

The pop stars of Bolivian traditional medicine are the Kallawayas, the famous travelling healers of the Andes. With their bag of herbs, roots, ointments and amulets, the Kallawayas travel the length and breadth of the Andes from Ecuador to Argentina, dispensing spiritual wisdom and natural remedies.

Curiously, the Kallawayas all hail from the same region, a group of six small villages in the Apolobamba Mountains. Why this should be the case is something of a mystery, though one theory is that they are descendants of the Tiahuanaco culture. Something like a quarter of the residents of these villages are believed to possess considerable knowledge and healing powers. The Kallawayas' travels have given them access to and knowledge of as many as 1,000 plants and herbs.

The Kallawayas pass their knowledge on to their sons, or occasionally apprentices. Women are traditionally not allowed to become Kallawayas, though they play an essential role as midwives and as healers of the female reproductive system.

Renewed interest in natural medicine has helped preserve the Kallawaya tradition, which was in danger of disappearing. Perhaps Western doctors will finally learn to accept herbal medicine as a valuable and well-researched science instead of dismissing it as some form of witchcraft.

Pelechuco → *see also Transport, page 172.*

Pelechuco is at 3,600 m, set in the steep valley of the river of the same name on the eastern side of the Cordillera Apolobamba, bordered to the north by the snow-capped peaks of the Katantica and Matchu Suchi Cuchu groups. The village's name comes from the Quechua *puyu kuchu* which means 'cloudy corner'. While the main economic activity of the area is gold mining, Pelechuco is old enough to have many fine stone and colonial buildings. It was founded in 1560.

The village is basic, but there is a phone and electricity, at least some of the time, and a medical post which is often manned. Shops and cafés selling and serving the basics are found on all four sides of the plaza. The single-table Pelechuco pool hall is a few balls short of a rack.

The biggest fiesta is held on the week around **25 July** to celebrate the founding of the village, but there are fiestas every month. The locals are proud of this and support each one with enthusiasm and a lot of drinking.

Buses to and from Pelechuco pass through the **Area Protegida Apolobamba**. The journey through the Río Pelechuco valley is well-worth doing in daylight. Those who choose to travel by night should note that overnight journeys across the Altiplano in less than state-of-the-art transport are extremely cold, so take your sleeping bag onto the bus with you. If you're returning from Pelechuco by jeep, a visit to the Putina thermal baths, two hours by jeep from Pelechuco near **Antaquilla** is a must, followed by a daylight trip through the vicuña reserve of the Area Protegida Apolobamba. If you have time on the way out or back, try and visit some of the first colonial churches built in Bolivia in the villages of Carabuco and Escoma.

Area Protegida Apolobamba

One of Bolivia's many 'must see' parks, the Area Protegida Apolobamba, is next door to the western edge of Parque Nacional Madidi. Now at 483,744 ha, it is one of the few parks that has expanded in size in recent years. Created in 1972, it was named by UNESCO as a 'unique habitat' in 1977 and changed to a biosphere, then re-named Reserva Nacional de Fauna de Ulla Ulla in 1983, before assuming its current designation in 1999. Established specifically to help preserve dwindling herds of vicuña, the reserve is also home to the more domesticated alpaca and llama.

Ins and outs

Reaching the Area Protegida Apolobamba is not difficult. 180 km northwest of La Paz, it is on the road from La Paz to Pelechuco, and for much of the way follows the well-marked and well-known Curva-Pelechuco trail. There are full-fledged communities within the region's borders: Illo Illo, Ulla Ulla, and Pelechuco are the most prominent. The official entrance, which is still free, is at **La Cabaña** (where there is also a small hostel run by IBTA), just north of Ulla Ulla. Alternatively, you can simply get off the daily buses that pass between Pelechuco and La Paz (they run through the southwest sector of the park), although there are no entry trails outside of Pelechuco itself except at Soropata and Agua Blanca. The park's western border is the national boundary with Peru, which, in addition to being a key ecological transition zone, makes it a politically strategic area as well. It is possible (but inadvisable) to cross the border from Peru into the park: if a valid entry stamp is not on your passport, you can be asked to leave the country once you reach civilization. The nearest official entry points are at Puno or Copacabana on the western shore of Lake Titicaca, or at Puerto Heath, a good 400 km north of Pelechuco by riverboat.

Around the park

Apolobamba is well known for its scenic beauty, owing to its impressive array of snow-capped mountains, crystal clear lakes, and even glaciers (the impressive Chaupi Orcko is one of the largest intact glaciers on earth). The area is made up of several mini ecological zones, ranging from the mountainous and cold Cordillera Real to humid grasslands and finally to the jungle-like Yungas. It also boasts the Cela rain forest, now one of the most intact anywhere in South America. Apolobamba is increasingly popular with day- or short-term trippers because of its thermal springs and well-defined network of trails, which often parallel the park's rivers.

There is much to see and do in the park. If you have your own transport, the wild vicuña herds can be observed at close range and followed cross country. During the day, especially in the dry season, the vicuñas graze in the marshy areas, in amongst the alpacas, but towards evening, when their domesticated cousins return home to

● *Apolobamba's mountains Akamani, Presidente, and Katantika are the highest in the*
● *Cordillera Nor Yungas range.*

their stone-walled corrals, the vicuñas wander off to more isolated pastures. It's a particularly beautiful sight to see these graceful animals grazing on the plains at dawn against a backdrop of snowy peaks.

It is also a primary habitat for literally millions of flamingoes, and a few thousand condors, the national bird. The terrain and altitude make it a trekker's paradise (see page 84 for treks in the area), although its primary purpose remains to preserve wildlife, as evidenced by the government's choice of the Instituto Boliviano de Technología Agropecuaria (IBTA) to manage the premises.

There is strong government support to make Apolobamba a showcase park. In the last two years, several ranger stations have been added (with adjacent campgrounds), and many nearby communities have cabañas for rent. Trails within (but not to) the park have been widened, and a modicum of supplies are now available in Ulla Ulla and other perimeter towns. The best source of information on Apolobamba is **SERNAP** itself (see page 23).

The reserve headquarters are at **La Cabaña**, 5 km outside the village of Ulla Ulla. There is basic but clean accommodation and food and visitors are very welcome. Orphaned vicuñas which would otherwise die are reared at La Cabaña. This allows you to get closer to them than anywhere else. For more information contact the **Centro Canadiense de Estudios y Cooperación Internacional** ① *C Jaimes Freyre 2907, La Paz, T02-2411767.*

◎ Sleeping

Charazani *p169*
G **Hotel Kallawaya** is the best option in the village.

Pelechuco *p170*
There are a number of basic alojamientos.
G **Rumillajta**, behind the church.
G **Pensión México**, on the main plaza.
G **Chujlla Wasi**, on the main plaza.

◎ Transport

Charazani *p169*
Buses from La Paz to **Charazani** leave from C Reyes Cardona, on the corner Av Kollasuyo above the Cementerio, Fri, Sat, Sun, and Mon at 0600; US$4.40, 10 hrs (see La Paz buses, page 128).

The bus sometimes goes up to **Curva** to pick up passengers for the return trip to **La Paz** (1½ hrs, US$1.40). Buses return to La Paz from Charazani, Fri, Sun, Mon, and Wed at 0400, and Mon at 1900. A La Paz-Charazani jeep costs US$250 and takes 6½ hrs.

For the **Apolobamba South Trek** (see page 84) it is possible to continue by jeep to Curva in another 1½ hrs. Arrive early enough to trek to the first camping at or just below Jatunpampa.

Pelechuco *p170*
La Paz-Pelechuco buses leave from C Reyes Cardona, on the corner of Av Kollasuyo, 3 blocks up from the Cementerio, on Wed at 1100; US$6, 18-24 hrs. They return from Pelechuco on Fri at 2000 and Sat at 1600. Outward tickets from La Paz can and should be bought in advance from the small office in C Reyes Cardona, on the corner of Av Kollasuyo, or from the buses themselves which park in the afternoon before departure in C Reyes Cardona. Return tickets should be organized when you get to Pelechuco. To or from **Pelechuco** by jeep costs US$300 and takes 10 hrs or more.

The Yungas

Only a few hours from La Paz are the subtropical valleys known as the Yungas. These steep, forested slopes are squeezed in between the high Cordillera and the vast green carpet of jungle that stretches east, providing a welcome escape from the breathless chill of the capital as well as a convenient stopping point for those hardy souls travelling overland to the jungle.

The comfortably warm climate of the Yungas is ideal for growing citrus fruit, bananas, coffee and coca leaves for the capital and also makes this area one of Bolivia's most desirable tourist attractions. The town of Coroico, in the Nor Yungas, is a firm favourite and the road which winds its tortuous way down from the high mountains has achieved near-legendary status in South American travelling lore as the most dangerous in the world. Many tourists now opt for the relative safety of two wheels rather than four for the terrifying and spectacular 70-km downhill ride.

The lovely little town of Chulumani, in the Sud Yungas, offers a less nerve-wracking but equally attractive alternative. Tipped to become a major tourist destination in its own right, today it's still a quiet backwater, where people quietly go about their business and where the secrets and rumours of Nazi war criminals lie buried in the local cemetery. There are great routes to be hiked from other old colonial Sud Yungas villages and the warm subtropical valleys are ideal for growing fruit, such as bananas, mangoes, papayas and strawberries, as well as the excellent local coffee.
▸▸ *For Sleeping, Eating and other listings, see pages 181-186.*

Towards Coroico

La Paz to Coroico

The most commonly used route to the Yungas goes via **La Cumbre**, northeast of La Paz. The road heads out of La Paz and climbs up and over La Cumbre pass at 4,725 m, reaching its highest point an hour out of La Paz, with towering snow-capped peaks all around (see page 69 for treks in this area). The roads to Chulumani (see page 177) and Coroico divide just after **Unduavi**, where there is a *garita* (checkpoint), a petrol station (the only one until Coroico or Chulumani) and dozens of food stalls.

Soon after Unduavi the road becomes 'all-weather' and drops over 3,400 m in only 70 km to the green semi-tropical forest. From Unduavi the steep, twisting road winds it way down to **Yolosa**, the junction 7 km from Coroico, where another road branches off to the village of **Chairo**, which marks the end of the **Choro Trail** (see page 67).

If you're adventurous (or crazy) enough to make this journey by truck, the best views can be seen in May and June, when there is less chance of fog and rain on the heights. Also note that it's very cold at La Cumbre and, further down, there are waterfalls at San Juan that 'baptize' those travelling in open vehicles.

At Yolosa, trucks wait by the bridge to shuttle passengers up to Coroico, including those who have taken a mountain-bike tour from La Paz. Also note that buses from jungle towns such as Rurrenabaque do not enter Coroico, but drop passengers off here. Yolosa has a couple of simple accommodation options, see page 181, and a restaurant, **Espagetti**, which doesn't serve what the name suggests.

The new road from Chuspipata to Yolosa

Many visitors to Coroico hire mountain bikes and get there under their own steam, or go as part of a mountain-bike tour, complete with an experienced guide and back-up. It is 70 km down to Yolosa, mostly on a rough road, and choosing an expensive,

⦂ The most exhilarating road in the world

The journey from La Paz to Coroico must be the most impressive in all Bolivia. It's an absolute must for adrenalin junkies but a definite no-no for those of a more nervous disposition. Beginning at La Cumbre, a mountain pass above La Paz at 4,700 m where there is often snow the bike ride drops more than 3,600 m in around four hours and 64 km to the sub-tropical jungle of Yolosa, below Coroico. For most of this route the road is little more than a bumpy, rocky ledge carved into the rockface of the mountains, through streams and under waterfalls and often with a sheer drop of as much as 1,000 m on the left hand side. Almost every turn of the road seems to be punctuated with crosses for those that have died there. Into this mix should be added Bolivian drivers who think nothing of the odd tipple or two before they set out and trucks who stop for nobody.

The claim that this counts as the most dangerous road in the world originally came from Inter-American Development Bank in 1995 - a source which gave the idea enough credence for what seems to be a large part of Bolivia's tourist industry to have built up around it. Whether or not it still has genuine claim to the statistic, the biggest single road accident in history apparently happened here in the 1980s, when a lorry packed with almost one hundred campesinos plunged over the edge.

The worrying accident rate can't be helped by the fact that, according to Bolivian road law, the vehicle going downhill should keep to the outside of the road, closest to the drop.

If you're travelling by bus, bear this in mind when you board in La Paz, and insist on a seat on the left for the best views. A few hours later you will regret this foolish act of bravado. The scenario is this: your driver rounds yet another bend to come face to face with yet another massive timber truck. He reverses back uphill, getting ever closer to the edge of the precipice until you look out the window and can see no part of the road, only the tops of the trees hundreds of metres below. This gets to you after a while.

Similarly, while hurtling downhill on two wheels trying not to look at the view, all your instincts will scream at you to keep away from the edge as a mammoth truck trundles up the road toward you. To date, six people have died cycling down this road and it's worth picking a good tour company from among the 30 or so that now offer the trip.

But the dangers of the road to Coroico are far outweighed by the thrill of the journey. The views are magnificent as you descend from the snows of the Cordillera to the humid sub-tropics. Not forgetting the considerable delights of Coroico itself, of course. After a couple of days relaxing by the pool, enjoying a cold beer and the magnificent scenery, this trip won't seem so bad. Until of course, it's time to go back.

well-maintained bike with good suspension is better than renting a cheap bike and going it alone. It is dangerous – six cyclists have died on the ride – you are strongly advised to use a reputable firm with good bikes and guides. A recommended bike-hire agency is **Gravity Assisted Mountain Biking,** see page 86.

A new road being built from Chuspipata to Yolosa is damaging the **Choro Trail,** as the new road is being cut along the ridgetop and down in a series of switchbacks facing Coroico. Check locally before attempting this route as falling rocks could make it dangerous. Much of the road is finished but at the time of writing it is only open for uphill traffic. Once completely finished, the old road to Yolosa will probably become a bikers-only route, though there may still be some local traffic which uses it. From Chuspipata there is 4WD track which connects to the lower road, 5 km uphill from **El Castillo** at Chaco (see page 177).

The Mine Railroad which turns off at Chuspipata takes two very full, or three to four comfortable, days to hike to Yolosa and is excellent for birdwatching. Access is easy: take any Coroico bus and asked to be dropped off at Chuspipata. The route gets very overgrown in the rainy season, so it's best to take a machete at this time. The new Cotapata Park (see below) runs from the old road across the Choro valley and is supposed to be protecting both the cloud forest and the Choro Trail. However, the construction of the new road has already left a deep scar on the forest and falling material from the road construction has made a mess of the trail in parts.

Alternative routes to Coroico

An alternative route to Coroico is from Sorata via Guanay. There are various ways to get to Guanay. You can take a truck from Sorata to the mining town of **Mapiri** via Santa Rosa (see Sorata Transport, page 167), or hike the tortuous **Mapiri Trail** to Mapiri (see page 80) and get a boat from there to Guanay (see below). Alternatively, you can hike the **Camino del Oro** to Tipuani and catch a bus from there to Guanay. From Guanay the road goes to Caranavi and from there to Yolosa (see previous page).

Cotapata National Park and Integrated Use Nature Area

This tiny (583 km2)) park is located just 20 km northeast of La Paz on a paved road. Part of the famous **El Choro Trek** (La Cumbre-Coroico, see page 67) passes through the park, as does the **Takesi Trail** (see page 63), making it a popular destination for day-trippers.

The park is not quite within the Cordillera Oriental, but shares much of that altitude's flora and fauna. It is especially well known for its wealth of medicinal plants and vegetation. For such a small area, it has amazing biological diversity (as do nearly all of Bolivia's protected areas), with more than 1,800 identified species and still others as yet unclassified.

As popular as it is, even given its proximity to La Paz, Cotapata is still largely unregulated and has no infrastructure, or accommodation. For further information contact **SERNAP** ① *La Paz, T02-2434420, elias_mamaniyanez@hotmail.com.*

Coroico → *Phone code: 02. Colour map 2, grid B2. Altitude: 1,760 m.*

The little town of Coroico has long been a favourite with visitors to Bolivia and residents of La Paz. It clings to the flanks of a steep, forested mountain amid orange and banana groves and coffee plantations, with stupendous views, particularly to the southwest, where you can see the distant snowy peaks of the Cordillera Real. Coroico isn't a place for the hyperactive. There's not a huge amount to do here, except lay by the hotel pool soaking up the sun and sipping ice-cold beer as you enjoy the views, swap travelling tales with your equally chilled-out fellow travellers and recover from that harrowing bus trip or thrilling bike ride.

Ins and outs

Buses leave La Paz several times daily, all from the Villa Fátima district for the three hour trip to Coroico. There are also daily buses from Coroico to La Paz. Buses, trucks and pick-ups run from Yolosa to Caranavi, Guanay and Rurrenabaque. **Tourist information** ① *Cámera Hotelera on the plaza.* ▸▸ *See Transport, page 185 for more details.*

There are a number of good walks around Coroico. One is down to the pools at the **Río Vagante**, 7 km away, off the road to Coripata. It takes about three hours to get there. Ask Fernando at **Hotel Esmeralda** for directions.

Another good walk is up to the waterfalls, starting from **El Calvario**. Follow the Stations of the Cross by the cemetery, off Calle Julio Zuazo Cuenca, which leads steeply uphill from the plaza. Facing the chapel at El Calvario, with your back to the town, look for a path on the left, which soon becomes well-defined. It leads in one hour to the **Cascada y Toma de Agua de Coroico**, the source of the town's water supply. Walk beyond this to a couple of waterfalls further on which are better for swimming.

Possibly the best walk is up **Cerro Uchumachi**, the mountain behind El Calvario. The mountain is considered sacred and witchcraft is practised at various sites here. Once again, follow the stations of the cross but this time look for the (now faded) red and white antenna behind the chapel. From there it's about 1½ hours' very steep uphill walk. At the top of the mountain another trail continues to the right for about one hour to a campsite. The views from Uchumachi in the morning are spectacular but in the afternoon there can be fog. There's no water en route, so take your own and watch out for biting insects. Cerro Uchumachi is also good for birdwatching, in the elfin forest at the summit. There is horse riding with **El Relincho** ① *T02-71923814*, 100 m past **Hotel Esmeralda** (see below for location). We have received reports of several incidents of assault on the trail. Women should definitely not go alone.

Coroico to other Yungas towns

It is possible to visit the other Yungas towns from Coroico. There are daily buses from La Paz with **Flota Yungueña** (from 1000-1230, but check times in advance) and

Coroico

Sleeping
Bella Vista 1
Cerro Verde 3
Don Quijote 14
El Cafetel 16
El Viejo Molino 13
Esmeralda 15

Gloria 4
Hostal Kory 5
Hostal Uchumachi 6
La Residencial Coroico 8
Residencial de la Torre 12
San Carlo 17
Sol y Luna 7

Eating
Bamboo 1
Café de la Senda
Verde 5
Back-Stube 2
Pizzeria Italia 4
Snack Hawaii 6

0 metres 100
0 yards 100

Transportes Totai (at 1100) to **Arapata** (five hours) which pass through Coroico about three hours after leaving La Paz, stopping briefly in the plaza. You can stay the night in Arapata in one of the two *alojamientos* and continue to **Coripata** the next morning.

It's a 15-km or three-hour hike to Coripata, which is about halfway between Coroico and Chulumani. **Tours Yungeña** micros leave from 15 de Abril 400 y San Borja, T02-2212252, at 0800, 1000, 1200, 1300 and 1400 in the dry season. These roads are normally still passable in the rainy season, but journey times can take as much as three times longer. From Coripata there are several buses daily to **Puente Villa**, where you have to change for buses to Chulumani (see page 179).

From the road junction at Yolosa the lower fork follows the river northeast to **Caranavi**, an uninspiring town 156 km from La Paz and 75 km from Yolosa. From here the road continues towards the settled area of the Alto Beni, at times following a picturesque gorge. Market days in Caranavi are Friday and Saturday.

Some 70 km northwest of Caranavi is the gold-mining town of **Guanay**, an interesting, friendly place at the junction of the Tipuani and Mapiri rivers. You can change cash with shopkeepers or gold dealers. Electricity is intermittent and water is available before 1200 only.

The road to Chulumani

The road to the Sud Yungas branches east just beyond Unduavi. Though less nerve-wracking than the road to Coroico, this is nevertheless a scenically rewarding trip as the road follows the steep-sided valley of the Río Unduavi. It also passes under a waterfall.

Further along you will pass by (not under) another waterfall. This one is beautiful, named Velo de la Novia, or The Bride's Veil. Only those on the left of the bus will see it. Next is the first settlement after Unduavi, **Chaco**, which is 1 km before the end of **La Reconquistada trek** (see page 66) and home to Hotel El Castillo, which is sadly closed and falling into disrepair. A few kilometres further on is Florida, where a dirt road turns off to the right to the attractive colonial village of Yanakachi (see below), where the Takesi Trail ends (see Trekking, page 63). The main road continues to Chulumani, passing through **Puente Villa**, 25 km before Chulumani.

An alternative and rarely travelled route to Chulumani is possible if your have your own transport. The road starts 10 km before **Panduro** on the La Paz-Oruro road. From the turn-off, it's 88 km to **Quime** along a good gravel road. There is basic and clean accommodation, **F**, in Quime. From Quime it's a seven-hour drive to Chulumani (200 km) passing through pristine cloud forest before reaching the village of **Irupana** (see page 181). There is no public transport on this route between Inquisivi and Circuata.

Yanakachi

This tiny colonial village is the ideal place to really get away from it all and relax. It lies at the end of the Takesi Trail, or can be reached by turning off the road to Chulumani at Florida and following the rough track (signposted). Yanakachi stands in a commanding position overlooking two major river valleys and there are great views over the village and surrounding areas from the bell-tower of the village church, one of the oldest in the Yungas, dating from the 16th century. A more recent addition to the village is a major hydroelectric scheme.

Yanakachi also offers various activities and several small hiking trails. You can hike the three-hour trail down to the river and swim in one of the delightful pools below the waterfall. Or you can help out in the local **orphanage** for the day, which

⁞ From Africa to the Yungas

One of the more incongruous sights in the tropical Yungas are the black cholas, women of African origin wearing the traditional Aymara bowler hat and voluminous skirts.

Some 17,000 blacks, descendants of African slaves, were brought from Peru and Argentina to work in the silver mines of Potosí, 4,000 m up on the Altiplano. But they could not adapt to the harsh climate and were moved to the Yungas to work on coca plantations. Slaves that spoke the same language were separated to prevent them conspiring against their owners. But they learned Spanish and developed a dialect based on Spanish that could not be understood by the colonial rulers or the indigenous people. Bolivian

blacks still speak these dialects, which include African words. Many of them also speak Aymara.

Africans were first brought to South America in the 16th century by European slave traders. By the 17th century half a million blacks lived on the continent. The vast majority live in rural areas with little or no access to economic or political power, but their influence has been felt in the music and dance of the country. In La Morenada, one of the most famous of Bolivia's folkloric dances, performed at the Oruro Carnival, figures wearing masks to represent black slaves and to caricature their bosses play a prominent role (see Oruro Carnival, page 192).

cares for 80-120 children. To find out where this is, ask at the office of **Fundación Pueblo** ⓘ *on the plaza, daily 0800-1230, 1430-1830*, which also has maps and local information. The foundation itself is interesting for its work to prevent people migrating to the cities in search of better jobs. Programmes include boosting local services to tourism to create more jobs (they've rebuilt a refuge on the Takesi Trail), environmental education, better farming techniques and adult literacy classes. After chatting with the volunteers, you could go for a swim in the pool at **Alojamiento San Miguel**, 15 minutes' walk out of town on the road towards Florida.

Around Yanakachi

There are some lovely walks in the area surrounding Yanakachi, with several out-of-the-way places to stay, making it the ideal alternative for those who want a little hiking but don't want to camp. From the northeast side of the village walk the one-hour pre-Hispanic trail down to Sakha Waya, and from there catch a passing bus up to La Paz or down to Chulumani, or Coripata. You can also hike the often-ignored final day of the Takesi Trail. From the bottom of the village, this pre-Hispanic trail continues on the south side of the ridge, past several small ruins and communities, and Villa Aspiazu, to the tiny settlement of **Puente Villa**. See Sleeping, page 183, for details on a recommended hotel 30 minutes walk upstream from here. You can wait in town beside the Río Takesi for buses onwards to Chulumani, which leave 0900-2100. From the Unduavi bridge you can also take transport back to La Paz 0500-1000 and to Coripata at 1100 and 1200, from where are two daily buses to Arapata and on to Coroico (see page 175).

Chaco (see also Sleeping, page 183) is a kilometre up from the end of the **La Reconquistada Trail** (see page 66). There are several hiking trails to waterfalls and a suspension bridge over the river.

Chulumani and around → *Phone code: 02. Colour map 2, grid B2.*

Chulumani is the capital of Sud Yungas. It's an attractive, relaxed and friendly little town, perched on the slopes of a hill with magnificent views across the valley to the forest of Apa Apa and the villages of Chicaloma and Irupana.

Ins and outs Buses from La Paz all leave from Villa Fátima district. Buses to La Paz leave from the San Bartolomé office on the plaza. Micros to other Yungas villages leave from the *tranca* 0500-1900 when full. Petrol station is at the entrance to the town, by the *tranca*.
Tourist office ⓘ *in the centre of the main plaza, allegedly open Mon-Fri 0900-1330, 1500-2200, Sat and Sun 0700-2200*, sells locally-grown coffee, teas, jams and honey.

Chulumani's neat little streets are a mix of colonial-style houses and modern buildings. Running off the lovely plaza is Calle Lanza, lined with stalls selling fruit and vegetables, piles of green bananas and several cheap eating places. Saturdays and Sundays are market days when Afro-Bolivians come dressed in traditional costume.

Chulumani

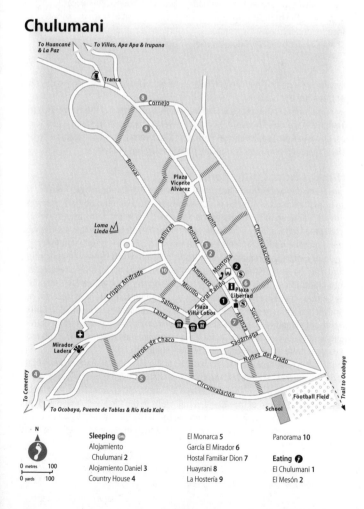

N

0 metres 100
0 yards 100

Sleeping 🛌
Alojamiento
　Chulumani **2**
Alojamiento Daniel **3**
Country House **4**

El Monarca **5**
García El Mirador **6**
Hostal Familiar Dion **7**
Huayrani **8**
La Hostería **9**

Panorama **10**

Eating 🍴
El Chulumani **1**
El Mesón **2**

North & east of La Paz The Yungas

⁞ Chulumani's dark secrets

In the late 1930s Chulumani was the very end of the road, a remote sub-tropical refuge surrounded by impenetrable forests. After the Second World War, this quiet, out-of-the-way town was home to Klaus Barbie, Adolf Eichmann and several other Nazi top-brass who had come here to escape justice. Stories abound of how the Nazis settled in Chulumani and locals recall with irony how they arrived to discover a group of Jews had beaten them to it by 12 years. Escaping the growing Nazi menace in Europe, the Jews had populated the mercado area. "The locals wondered why the gringos spat at each other," says guesthouse owner Xavier Sarabia. Barbie lived in relative tranquility in a house below the town, at Puente de Tablas (it is still in good repair), occasionally visiting La Paz to act as military consultant for the various Bolivian dictatorships. The whole subject of Chulumani's Nazis is shrounded in secrecy and still spoken of in hushed tones, especially as many top Bolivian industries are said to have been founded with Nazi money. The truth may lie buried in the cemetery (which has many German names on the gravestones). Even local carpenter, Hitler Mamani, knows little of the origin of his rather unusual name.

The town throws a party, Fiesta de San Bartolomé on 24 August. It lasts for 10 days but the first three are the best.

Near Chulumani is the village of **Sikilini**, which is at the end of the Yunga Cruz trek (see Trekking, page 69). There are plenty of interesting walks in the area – to ancient villages, down to **Apa Apa Ecological Park**, up to **Inca terraces** at Pastogrande, to one of 12 clean rivers or simply by taking any path leading out of town.

Short hikes from Chulumani

There are many day walks from Chulumani. **El Paraíso** is a one-hour trek. Take the left road up from the hospital. After 30 minutes you come to a tennis club (left) and water tanks (right). Climb up to the right here on any one of the many paths for a 20-minute detour to **Loma Linda**, a large cross with 180-degree views over the valleys. Otherwise continue along the path 20 minutes more through a pine forest until you fork right, about 300 m before La Granja, a former Jesuit mission which is now an agricultural school run by the army. After 5-10 minutes the road ends at El Paraíso where trails lead into cloud forest. Call in on the last house on the right where Don Rojelio, a friendly German-speaking Belgian, will show you his dairy farm. He sells milk, yoghurt and sandwiches. From here it's a three-hour hike (it is best to have a guide) to **Chirca**, a 500-year-old village with a Spanish feel, a sanctuary church and a setting high on the ridge with great views. From Chirca it's a half-hour walk down to the main road, where you can take an afternoon bus back to Chulumani.

To get to **Río Kala Kala**, take the lower road at the Mirador Ladera and down to the Puente de Tablas, downstream from here there are natural swimming pools and forest.

Another hike is to the village of **Ocabaya** to visit its old church. From the football field at the southeast end of the village, a trail leads to the Río Misquimayo and then up to Hacienda Tiquimpaya, just 1 km from Ocabaya. The hike takes 2½ hours. For all these trips carry plenty of water, a packed lunch and start early as it gets pretty hot and dry in the valleys.

● *Price codes for Sleeping and Eating are given inside the front cover. Further information on*
● *hotel and restaurant grading can be found in Essentials, pages 43-44.*

Irupana and Chicaloma

From Chulumani it is 1½ hours by bus to the old colonial village of **Irupana**, which hosts a fiesta on 5 August. Three hours beyond Irupana by truck (one leaves twice a week – check in advance for times) are the seldom-visited Inca ruins and terraces of **Pastogrande** with a beautiful river flowing below.

Another road to Irupana goes via the ancient village of **Ocabaya** (2½ hours away), where the 1952 revolution began, also passing through the Afro-Bolivian community of **Chicaloma**, where the Saya, a traditional world-famous African dance, was born. This village hosts its Santísima Trinidad festival on 16 July and you can see the dancing at its Corpus Christi celebrations in late May. This road is less direct and used less often, and transport from the tranca in Chulumani is infrequent, so ask around.

Apa Apa Ecological Park

The main road to Irupana passes the turn-off to Apa Apa, a protected forest area of 800 ha, 8 km from Chulumani. This is the last area of original subtropical Yungas forest with plenty of interesting wildlife, such as small deer, agoutis, hoachi, nocturnal monkeys and many birds including parrots and hummingbirds. Even porcupines, pumas and the rare Andean spectacled bear are seen here and there are many tree orchids.

The flora includes the giant *leche-leche* trees which have a small 'cave' in the trunk. A recent study revealed seven new types of tree and many new ferns in the park. At the time of writing only two trails are open for tourists – a three-hour hike through the lower part of the forest and a 4½-hour trip to the tip of the mountain.

The park is managed by Ramiro Portugal and his US-born wife, Tildi. Ramiro was born locally and knows the area well; he also speaks English. Their home is an 18th-century hacienda which runs as a working dairy farm and has accommodation for two or three people. Near the house is a campsite with bathrooms and campers can buy food from the farm.

Day trips can be arranged for groups of up to five for a US$25 flat fee, which includes transport and a guide ① T02-8136106, or T02-2790381 (La Paz). You can also take a bus or truck to Huancane and from there follow the high trail to the right which leads around the hillside to the upper parts of the Apa Apa cloud forest. For details of tour operators in Chulumani, see page 185.

⊜ Sleeping

Towards Corioco *p173*
Yolosa
G **Alojamiento El Conquistador**, basic accommodation. Upstream is a small resort which offers bathing in the river.

Coroico *p175, map p176*
For such a small town, Coroico has a large variety of accommodation. Due to its popularity, however, the best hotels are booked up during holiday weekends when prices rise. See also Language classes in Directory, below, for details of a private room available for rent.

North & east of La Paz The Yungas

L **Hotel Río Selva Resort**, in Huarinillas, on the road which branches off at Yolosa and heads to the village of Chairo. Reservations in La Paz at C Romecín Campos 696, Sopocachi, T02-2327561, or generico@rioselva.com. The most expensive accommodation in or around Coroico is this 5-star place with all meals included, cabins as well as bedrooms, pools, gym, sports complex and sauna.

B **El Viejo Molino**, a 20-min walk out of town on the road to Caranavi, T02-8136004, valmar@waranet.com, or book through Valmar Tours, T02-2361076, F02-2352279 (La Paz). Expensive option with a sauna, jacuzzi and pool.

B **San Carlo**, 1 km out of town on the road to Yolosa, T02-2813266, F02-2372380 (La Paz). Includes breakfast, restaurant, pool and sports facilities. Recommended.

C **Gloria**, near the football pitch at the bottom of C Chacopata, T02-8136020, or in La Paz T02-2370010. Part of the Hotel Gloria chain, this huge red and white hotel includes breakfast, changes travellers' cheques for a small charge, has 2 large pools, a terrace, good views, a restaurant, parking, free pick-up from plaza and internet facilities. Gloomy but friendly.

D **Bella Vista**, C Heroes Chaco (2 blocks from the main square), T02-71569237 (mob). (E without bath but much smaller). Modern, smart and clean rooms with beautiful views. 2 racquetball courts (15Bs per hr) but no pool. Terrace, bikes for rent. Recommended.

D **Don Quijote**, a 10-min walk out of town on the road to Coripata, T02-8136007 (T02-2721254 in La Paz), quijote@mpoint.com.bo. Discounts in low season, pick-up from plaza, restaurant, pool, gardens, TV in rooms, private bathrooms, quiet, English spoken.

D **Esmeralda**, 10-15 mins steep walk uphill from the plaza, T/F010-22136017, www.hotelesmeralda.com. This large hotel is worth the walk up the hill. There's a great pool, a fantastic sauna and a lovely garden and around 200 videos which can be played on demand from your room. Rooms at the front have great views and good hot showers; those at the back are cheaper. The owner Fernando speaks English, German and Spanish and is a good source of local information. There's a free pick-up service (ring from **Totai Tours**) from the plaza and Visa and Mastercard are taken with no commission. The excellent restaurant has a buffet, there's a terrace, a laundry service, free internet access for 2hrs each night, the possibility of burning cds of digital images and satellite TV. The only downside might be that sweaty bikers arrive en masse every day from 2 'world's most dangerous road' groups and hog the showers. Recommended.

D-F **Sol y Luna**, a 15-min walk beyond Hotel Esmeralda, T02-2362099 (La Paz), www.solyluna-bolivia.com. A dreamily rustic set-up among verdant woods and flowery gardens, Sol y Luna is a sprawling fairy tale place with winding paths connecting well designed wooden 'cottages', a swimming pool and hammocks with stunning views across the valley to the distant mountains. Meals are also available, try their superb Indonesian banquet. 7 rooms, US$3.50-6 per person; 5 cottages USUS$14-20; camping US$2.50 by prior booking. For US$12 you can even have a 50-min shiatsu massage. Highly recommended.

E **Cerro Verde**, C Ayacucho 5037. A colonial building with a slightly run-down feel. 20 rooms all with private bath. Good views and a pool but a steep walk down from the plaza. Breakfast extra US$1.25.

E **Hostal Kory**, at the top of the steps leading down from the plaza. (F without bathroom), T02-2431311. Bang in the middle of town, Kory offers discounts for stays any longer than a couple of days. There's a big pool, a lovely terrace good views, a video room and comfy beds in the smallish rooms. Recommended.

F **El Cafetal**, Miranda, T02-719-33979 (mob). Hammocks, great views, clean rooms, friendly, though a fair walk from the centre of town. Also a fantastic restaurant. See eating, below, for directions.

G **Hostal Uchumachi**, on the plaza. A smart exterior belies a grotty interior cluttered with junk. It's cheap though and rooms with bathroom overlooking the plaza are lighter.

G **La Residencial Coroico**, C F Reyos Ortiz. Cheap but worth bargaining further. All rooms share bathrooms. Dark rooms, sagging beds and no great views.

G **Residencial de la Torre**, on Julio Zuazo Cuenca. Friendly and with a flowery courtyard but the clean sparse rooms could do with a lick of paint. No alcoholic drinks.

Coripata
F **Hotel Florida** is not a bad option.

Caranavi
C **Caturra Inn**, C Batallon de Ingenieros, T02-8232209, jmiranda@mail.entelnet.bo. 3 blocks from the plaza, includes continental breakfast, pool, gardens.
F **Landiva**, Av Mariscal Santa Cruz. On the main street. Nice pool, unhelpful staff.

Guanay
F **Panamericana.** Helpful, popular with tour groups.
F **Perla Andina**. Cold water, rooms on the street are less hot than those on the courtyard, there are fans in the rooms but electricity 1800-2400 only.
G **Alojamiento Los Pinos**, opposite the football pitch. Cold water, basic, may arrange exchange of TCs with commission.
G **Hotel Ritzy**, on the main plaza. With mosquito nets.
G **Pahuichi**, nice restaurant. Camping is possible next to the football field.

Puente Villa
C **Tamampaya**, T02-2706099 (La Paz). At Puente Villa, cross the Río Unduavi and 30 mins walk upstream, in a beautiful setting, is the recommended Hotel Tamampaya. It has attractive gardens and pool and birdwatching trails, good rooms with shower, good set meals and à la carte. The price includes breakfast. Camping is possible midweek.

The road to Chulumani p177
Chaco
At Santa Rosa, between Sakha Waya and Chaco, there's a tourist complex and cabins (**C**).
E **Hotel Romulo y Remo**, set on a promontory below the road (T02-2232621, La Paz, for reservations). From the end of the Reconquistada Trail, it's a short walk down to this hotel.
Rancho Eco, above Chaco, in the scrub forest valley at the end of the Asiru Marka Trail, offers accommodation and horse riding.

Yanakachi p177
F **Hotel San Carlos**, at the junction entering the village (no sign), T02-2230088 (La Paz). Rooms 5, 6 and 7 have great views across

the valley, clean, hot showers, also offers full board in its restaurant - the best place to eat in town.
G **Alojamiento Don Tomas**, ask at the shop on the left before the plaza (look for the Fanta sign). Clean.

Chulumani and around p179, map p179
B per person **San Antonio**, 7 km out of town back along the road to La Paz, T02-2341809, F02-2377896 (La Paz). Pleasant cabins with pool.
B-C **San Bartolomé Plaza Resort**, 2 km from the *tranca* down the road to Irupana, www.sanbartolome@usa.net. Arrange hotel transport beforehand if arriving by bus - there are no taxis. Alternatively, if it's open, call from the tourist information centre in the middle of the plaza. Pleasant cabins in a superb setting with fabulous views of the surrounding valleys, swimming pool. Can be booked through the **Hotel Plaza** in La Paz, T02-2378311, Ext 1221 (or **Plaza Tours** in La Paz).
D **El Monarca**, on the outskirts of town below C Lanza (see map). Price includes breakfast, negotiable in low season, somewhat run down, overpriced, gardens and pool (open to non-residents for US$1.50).
D **Huayrani**, near the *tranca* just off C Junín, T02-8136351. Cabins for 1-8 people, includes breakfast, nice garden, pool, TV, and there are even plans for private saunas.
E **Country House**, 10 mins walk southwest from the plaza towards the cemetery. The best backpackers' retreat, price includes breakfast. Real home-from-home place to relax in the rustic charm of a family house, swimming pool fed by natural source, stock of 200 videos for hire (US$4.50), restaurant (tasty home cooking, home-grown coffee, jams), pool table and cold beer, good views, owner Xavier Sarabia has information on all hikes, arranges trips (see Tours below) and is great for a Nazi yarn or two. No double beds otherwise highly recommended.
E **Hostal Familiar Dion**, C Alianza, just off the plaza, T02-8136070. Spotless, modern and new rooms, roof terrace, includes breakfast, laundry facilities and use of kitchen. (**F** without bathroom and breakfast).
E **Hotel Panorama**, at top of the hill on C Murillo, T02-8136109. Overpriced for basic

rooms although some have views, garden, restaurant and small pool, friendly.
E La Hostería, C Junín, close to the *tranca*, basic, styleless rooms but a good restaurant (see below), cheaper options available.
G Alojamiento Chulumani, Bolívar. Up a steep hill from the plaza. Basic, clean with shared bathroom.
G Alojamiento Daniel, Next door to is Alojamiento Chulumani and similar but more modern.
G García El Mirador, on Plaza Libertad, T02-8136117. Basic but clean, the restaurant has a nice terrace with great views across to Apa Apa, noisy at weekends from disco, rooms at back without bathroom are cheaper.

Irupana
E Hotel La Bougainvillaea, with a small pool. There are also 4 cheap, basic *alojamientos*.

⑦ Eating

Coroico *p175, map p176*
Cheap meals can be found at the market, near the plaza on the street beside the post office. Honey is sold in various places throughout the town.
$$ Bamboo, Iturralde. Good Mexican food in an atmospheric little restaurant. Live music some nights with a small cover charge; otherwise usually recorded reggae. Happy hour 1800-1900.

$$ El Cafetal, Miranda, T02-719-33979 (mob). A 10-min walk from town, some of which is poorly lit, some of which is not lit at all. Soon after the road starts going downhill there is a turning off on the right, down steps. French-run, with excellent French cuisine. Laid back jazz, roof, stone tables, good caipirinhas, menu includes pastas, savoury souffles, steak, llama and trout. *Copa cafetal* – ice cream of the house, with fruit, chocolate, cream and nuts. Good value. Recommended.
$ Back-Stube, next to Hostal Kory, T02-71935594 (mob), closed Tue. Excellent cakes and German breads, delicious vegetarian lasagne, lots of breakfast options and a friendly atmosphere. They also have a fully equipped house for rent, for up to 5 people for 3 or more days.

$ Pizzeria Italia, on the plaza. Possibly the best of an unexpected glut of mediocre Italian restaurants.
$ Snack Hawaii, Plaza Manuel Victorio Garcia Lanza. This basic snack bar on the plaza next to Incaland Tours is open all day, serving breakfasts, sandwiches, burgers, steaks and juices etc. It also changes money.

Cafés
Café de la Senda Verde, Plazuela Julio Zuzo Cuenca, T02-71532703, Mon-Sun 0630-1900. The home-roasted Yungas coffee is the highlight in this friendly café on the corner of Hostal Kory. Healthy breakfasts, oven-toasted sandwiches and cinnamon rolls are also available.

Caranavi
$ Paradiso, cheap meals. Tropical, good set menu and cheap.

Guanay
Restaurant La Bamba, opposite Panamericana. Good value, English spoken. There are many other eating places on the main street which have fixed-price meals.

Yanakachi *p177*
Don Edgar, on the plaza facing the church, has good food and its owner unsurpassed knowledge of local history and hiking trails.
Pension Candelaria on the plaza also does food. See also **Hotel San Carlos**, above.

Chulumani and around *p179, map p179*
El Mesón, just off the Plaza, open 1200-1330 only. Good cheap lunches and great views.
El Chulumani, overlooking the plaza is the very friendly, with a pleasant, breezy balcony and good almuerzo.
La Hostería on Junin close to the *tranca*, Texan-run, serves good pizzas and hamburgers. There are many cheap restaurants near the plaza and lots of street food at weekends.

⑨ Bars and clubs

Coroico *p175, map p176*
Barpension Los Jasmies, Iturralde, just up from Bamboo. Bar and disco, popular with locals.
Wiskería Taurus, C Julio Zuazo Cuenca. Good for a beer.

☼ Festivals

Coroico *p175, map p176*
15 Aug Virgen de Asunta festival in Tocana, a village 20 km from Coroico, lower down the valley.
19-22 Oct Colourful 4-day **festival**, accommodation is hard to find. It is great fun, but it might be an idea to wait a day or two before returning to La Paz, in order to give your driver time to recover.
2 Nov All Souls' Day. The local cemetery is festooned with black ribbons.

▲ Activities and tours

Corioco *p175, map p176*
Horse riding Ask Dany at El Cafetal for information. Also T02-8136015; US$6 per 2 hrs, group rates and organized trips.

Tour operators
Eco Adventuras and Inca Land Tours, both on the main plaza.

Chulumani and around *p179, map p179*
Tour operators
Xavier Sarabia of **Country House** (see Sleeping above) is pushing hard to develop tourism in Chulumani and offers a number of good value guided hiking tours including: 2-day **Chulumani-Ocabaya-Chicaloma- Irupana**, US$8 per day per person including breakfast and lunch but not dinner or accommodation;
Pastogrande US$5 per day per person plus US$50-60 transport between group; half day/1 day to **cloudforest and on to Chirca**, US$5 per person including lunch; Apa Apa, upper path, US$5 per day including lunch and 1-day El Chajcro photographic trail 500 m above river.
Also 5-10 day **Amazon Basin** hiking/camping trip along the very clean Rio Bopi, US$8 per day for guide and boat, described as 'no picnic', and the **Yunga Cruz Trail** in reverse (see page 69 for details) as far as Cerro Khala Ciudad then back again, 5-6 days, US$8 per day.

☼ Transport

Coroico *p175, map p176*
From La Paz all bus companies serving **Coroico** (3 hrs, US$2) are in Villa Fátima. **Turbus Totai**, Yanacachi y América, have big buses which leave several times daily from 0730-1630 as does **Trans Totai** further up Yanacachi. **Flota Yungueña**, C Yanacachi y Alcoche (T02-2213513), have micros from 0730-1630.
To La Paz buses leave daily from Coroico, 0730-1630, although **Turbus Totai** claims to start at 0300. Extra services run on Sun. It's worth booking in advance, and note that it can be difficult to book journeys to La Paz on holidays and on Sun evenings/Mon mornings, though these are good times for hitching. Trucks and pick-ups from La Paz may drop you at Yolosa, from where trucks shuttle people up to Coroico; or you can walk for 2 hrs uphill. Trucks in Coroico leave from the market. 13 de Mayo, on Virgen del Carmen in Villa Fátima, run 4-6 day jeep tours of the Yungas. The Yungueña office is in the plaza, T02-2895513.
Buses, trucks and pick-ups run from Yolosa to **Caranavi**, 3-4 hrs, US$3.25 (see below), **Guanay**, 7-8 hrs, US$5.20 (see below), and **Rurrenabaque**, 13-15 hrs, US$8.75 (see page 357).

Caranavi
To **Caranavi** leave from Villa Fátima in La Paz. **Flota Yungueña**, Av América next to the petrol station, T02-2213513; daily at 0830, US$2.25, 6 hrs, returning between 2000-2200. **Veloz del Norte**, Av las Américas; several daily from 0730-1800, US$2.25, returning between 0730-1400 and 2030-2100, US$3.75. **Turbus Totai**, C Yanacachi, T02-2210392; daily 0700-1700, US$2.25. **Trans Tours Palmeras**, next door, leave daily from 0700-1500 when full. There are several other companies around América y Virgen del Carmen in Villa Fátima.
Buses to **Rurrenabaque** (10-12 hrs) pass through Caranavi and Guanay (see below), but buy your ticket in La Paz if you want to break the journey here as no transport into the jungle originates here.
A direct bus from Coroico to **Caranavi** leaves on Sun, or you can take a truck, US$2.15.

Bus There are direct buses from La Paz. Turbus Totaí leaves Villa Fátima at 0900 and returns at 1700 (9 hrs, US$4.50). This company also has buses to **Caranavi**. Buses to **Rurrenabaque** pass through Guanay, but it's best to buy your ticket in La Paz.

River To Mapiri from **Guanay** dock, 3 blocks from the plaza daily at 0700, or when full, US$5. Do not rely on cargo boats at other times. En route mines can be seen among the tropical vegetation. Boats go down the Río Beni to **Rurrenabaque** (see page 357), 8-12 hrs; it will cost US$10-20 depending on how successfully you negotiate and the availability of vessels. Cargo is now carried by road so you have to wait till the boat is full, which can take several days. 'Expreso' boats can be hired from **Flota Fluvial**, opposite Perla Andina, for about US$400, depending on size and your ability to bargain. The journey goes past gold-mining settlements, then alongside narrow, fertile river banks.

Yanakachi p177

There are 2 daily buses to **Yanakachi** from La Paz. Veloz del Norte (T02-2218279) leaves from Ocabaya and Av Las Americas in Villa Fátima, at 0900 and 1400; 3 ½ hrs. These continue to **Chojlla**, a distinctly unappealing mining town a few kilometres further on.

Buses to **La Paz** (US$1.65) leave from Yanakachi at 0545 and 1245-1300 or 1400 daily – readers must check. There may also be a bus leaving Yanakachi on Fri and Sun at 1430; buy tickets from Doña Yola on the plaza.

Chulumani and around p179, map p179

From La Paz Trans San Bartolomé buses leave from C Virgen del Carmen 1750, T02-2211674; daily 0800-1600 or when full, 4 hrs, US$2.50. **Trans Arenas** leave 0730-1800, US$2.25. **Transportes 24 de Agosto** micros leave from C 15 de Abril 408 y San Borja, T02-2210607; daily from 0600-1600 when full.

To La Paz Cost US$2.25, US$0.30 more on Sun and leave from the San Bartolomé office on the plaza at 0530 and 1230. On Sun there are extra buses at 1300, 1400 and 1500.

Chicaloma

There are direct buses from La Paz to **Chicaloma**, via Chulumani on Tue and Fri at 0800 with **Transportes 24 de Agosto** (5 hrs). There's also a bus from La Paz to **Ocabaya** on Tue and Fri at 0800 (6 hrs) with San Bartolomé. These buses leave Chulumani at around 1200/1300 from the tranca (US$0.75). It can be difficult finding transport back to Chulumani.

● Directory

Coroico p175, map p176

Banks Banco Mercantil on central plaza, Mon-Fri 0830-1230, 1430-1830, Sat 0900-1230, cash advances (no commission) on Mastercard, VISA and Maestro. You can change TCs at Turbus Totai, but the rates are poor. Better rates at Hostal Kory or Hotel Esmeralda. **Internet** Carlos has a small internet café on C Caja de Agua, T/F02-8136041. He will also exchange Spanish for English lessons. **Language classes** Siria Leon Dominguez, Julio Zuazo Cuenca 062, T71955431, siria_leon@ yahoo.com, gives Spanish Lessons, US$3.60/hr and also has a single room to rent. She also makes silver jewellery and has plans to offer natural juices for sale. **Laundry** Lavanderia Express, Calle Hurralde 4009, past the *comedor municipal* and right. **Medical services** Hospital, T02-8136002. The best in the Yungas, good malaria advice. **Police** East side of main plaza. **Post office** on the plaza. **Telephone** Entel is on Sagárnaga, next to Flota Yungueña, for international and local calls. Cotel is next to the church; it also has a public TV.

Chulumani and around p179, map p179

Banks Banco Union, on the main plaza, changes sums of US$100 or more only in cash and TCs (5% commission), Mon-Fri 0830-1200, 1430-1800; **Co-Operativa San Bartolomé**, left of the plaza church, will change US dollars cash only, no minimum amount, Mon-Fri 0800-1200, 1400-1700, Sat and Sun 0700-1200. **Internet** in the tourist office, US$1.05 per hr. **Post office** beside the Prefectura building just off the main plaza. Cotel and Entel telephone offices are both on the plaza, Entel open 0700-2230 daily, has fax.

Southwest Bolivia

⦂ Footprint features

Introduction

The remote southwestern corner of Bolivia stretches from the mining centre of Oruro, south to the borders of Chile and Argentina. There would appear to be little to attract the tourist to this barren plateau sitting on the roof of the world. It's a bleak, windswept terrain of parched scrub, with the occasional tiny adobe settlement blending into the uniform brown landscape. The main settlement, **Oruro**, is nothing to write home about, unless you happen to be there during **Carnival** when it explodes into action during one of Latin America's great celebrations.

But tourists do come to this starkly beautiful corner of Bolivia and are rewarded with some of the greatest visual delights that this country has to offer. In the far south is the **Salar de Uyuni**, the largest and highest salt lake in the world. You can take a tour and drive across this inconceivably vast expanse of blinding-white salt flats. Further south is a Salvador Dalí landscape of bizarre rock formations, white-capped volcanoes, and sparkling soda lakes of jade and scarlet, filled with pink flamingoes and steaming geysers.

★ Don't miss...

1 **Museo Etnográfico Minero** Head down some of the oldest mining tunnels in Oruro to reach the god of the underworld, El Tío, page 190.

2 **Dancing with the devil** ...and everyone else too at the Oruro Carnival, one of Latin America's greatest celebrations, page 192.

3 **Sajama National Park** For unmissable views of the volcano, the world's highest forest and herd of vicuñas, page 199.

4 **Lago Poopó** The birdlife around this lake, south of Oruro, will have even casual bird-lovers twitching, page 202.

5 **The largest and highest salt lake in the world** Drive across the Salar de Uyuni on your way to kaleidoscopic soda lakes, erupting geysers and weird rock formations, page 204.

6 **Laguna Colorada** The coloured lake shimmers in the sun and wind and is home to 80 species of bird, including pink flamingoes, page 210.

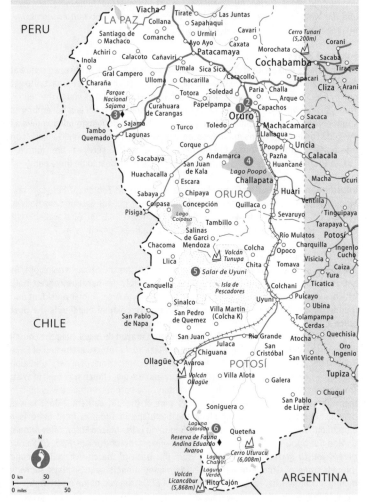

Southwest Bolivia

Oruro → *Phone code: 02. Colour map 3, grid B2. Population: 188,422. Altitude: 3,706 m.*

Oruro is the biggest settlement on the Altiplano. Arriving at the bus terminal, you are faced with a 10-block journey up the broad, windy and desolate Avenida 6 de Agosto to reach the city centre. This is not a good introduction to the city, however, as the centre has many fine buildings and churches revealing its former wealth. The other immediately obvious feeling is the cold: in the heat of the midday sun the temperature can reach 18°C, but at night it can plummet to minus 10°C. The biting cold, though, is forgotten in time for Carnival in February when Oruro explodes with colour and life in the country's biggest and best celebration. Carnival has made Oruro the official folklore capital of Bolivia.

Oruro began life in the 16th century as a mining community extracting silver, tin, antimony and lead from the hills to the west of the city and was formally founded in 1606 as the Villa Real de San Felipe de Austria de Oruro. It became the second largest city in the Americas after Potosí and later the centre of the Bolivian rail network. It is now the commercial and administrative centre of the southern Altiplano though nearby gold mines, such as Inti Raymi (the largest and most profitable mine in Bolivia) and the Vinto tin smelter (the biggest in the country) are important economically.

>> *For Sleeping, Eating and other listings, see pages 196-199.*

Ins and outs

Getting there and around The bus terminal is 10 blocks north of the town centre at Avenida Raika Bakovic and Avenida Aroma, T02-5253535. US$0.20 terminal tax to get on any bus. Micro 2, or any one marked 'Plaza 10 de Febrero', takes you to the centre. Those saying 'Mercado' take you close to the train station, which is a dozen blocks south of the bus terminal, at the south end of Avenida 6 de Agosto (also known as 'Avenida Folklórico'). Trains run only south from Oruro to Uyuni and on to Villazón on the border with Argentina. Check in advance which services are running, T02-5260605. The ticket office is open 0700-1700, but it's best to be there early.

Information Tourist office ⓘ *Montes 6072, Plaza 10 de Febrero, T/F02-5250144, Mon-Fri 0800-1200 and 1400-1800.* There's also a kiosk outside Entel in Calle Bolívar, same hours. They have a colour map and guide (Spanish only) US$1. Also available is a colour guide to Parque Nacional Sajama US$1, and a free Oruro city map.

Around the centre

The central square, **Plaza 10 de Febrero**, is named after the anti-Spanish revolt of 1781 and is surrounded by grand colonial buildings, notably the **baroque concert hall**, which is now a cinema. There is also a statue of Aniceto Arce, former president and founder of the Bolivian railways. Another impressive colonial building is the **post office** at Calle Montes, half a block from the main plaza.

There is a good view of the city from the **Cerro Corazón de Jesus**, near the church of the **Virgen del Socavón**, five blocks west of Plaza 10 de Febrero at the end of Calle Adolfo Mier. Worship of the Virgen del Socavón – the central point of miners' Christian worship – began at this site in the 16th century and the first church was built in 1781. The present church was built in the 19th century. The baroque entrance was built in the 16th century by the Jesuits and was part of the old cathedral until it was demolished in 1979. It was rebuilt at the Santuario in 1994. In front there is a monument of an armed miner. Inside the Santuario is the **Museo Etnográfico Minero** ⓘ *Mon-Sat 0900-1200 and 1500-1800, Sun 0800-1200 and 1600-1800, US$0.60; permission to take photos US$0.60.* From the back of the church you descend through some of Oruro's oldest preserved mining tunnels past displays showing mining techniques to reach a representation of *El Tío*, the god of the underworld.

The **Casa de la Cultura**, at Soria Galvarro 5755, was built by French architects in 1900-13 as a palace for the 'King of Tin', Simón Patiño, and was finished a year after he emigrated to Hamburg in Germany. It now houses the **Casa de la Cultura Museo Patiño** ① *Mon-Fri 0900-1200, 1400-1830, US$0.30*, and contains colonial art, French furniture in the style of Louis XV and XVI, and other displays.

Iglesia de San Miguel, presently hidden inside the Penny Children's Home in Calle Soria Galvarro, is the oldest church in the city. Built to convert the local people, it contains much original colonial art; ask at the tourist office for details of how to visit.

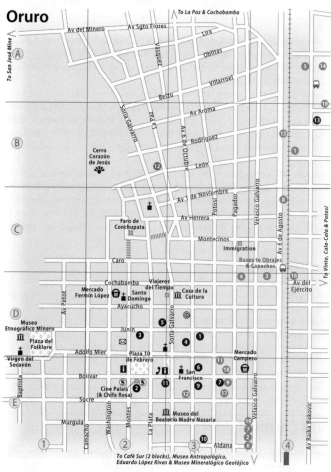

Oruro

N

| 0 metres | 200 |
| 0 yards | 200 |

Sleeping 🛏

Alojamiento
 15 de Octubre **8** *C4*
Alojamiento
 Concordia **1** *B4*
Alojamiento

Copacabana **2** *E4*
Alojamiento La Paz **3** *D4*
Alojamiento La Paz II **4** *D3*
Alojamiento
 Los Angeles **5** *A4*
Alojamiento
 San Gerardo **6** *E4*
Alojamiento
 San Juan de Dios **7** *E4*
América **9** *E3*
Bernal **10** *B4*
Gloria **11** *E3*
Gran Sucre **12** *E3*

International Park **14** *A4*
Lipton **15** *B4*
Monarca **16** *D4*
Repostero **17** *E3*
Residencial Ideal **18** *E3*
Residencial
 San Salvador **19** *E4*

Eating 🍴

Bravo's Pizza **1** *D3*
Chifa Rosa **2** *E2*
Club Social Arabe **3** *D2*
El Nochero **4** *D3*

Gaviota **5** *D2*
Govinda **6** *E3*
Hotel Gutiérrez **13** *B4*
Libertador &
 El Huerto **7** *E3*
Mateos **9** *E3*
Nayjama **10** *E3*
UM Confitería **11** *E3*

Bars & clubs 🍸

Pub Alpaca **12** *B2*

Respect to the Gods

The *cha'lla* is not only an important part of carnival but of Andean customs and beliefs in general. It consists of sprinkling alcohol on all things, fixed or moving, and in adorning them with confetti and streamers so that abundance will come, or that it will continue or even increase. This is how the protection of the gods of plenty is invoked and respect shown to them.

Other interesting churches include **San Francisco** in Calle Bolívar near Soria Galvarro, which has an 18th-century façade, and **Santo Domingo** in Calle Ayacucho next to Mercado Fermín López. It was started in 1602 but was subsequently remodelled in the 18th and early 20th centuries.

Museo del Beaterio Madre Nazaria ① *For opening times check with the tourist office, US$0.40,* on Calle Soria Galvarro between Sucre and Murguia, has a display of masks. Nearby, in the same street, the baroque stone **Portada de Beaterio Madre Nazaria** is worth a look, as is the Colegio Nacional Simón Bolívar which was built in 1827 and is impressively grand and colonial. It's in Calle Murguia between Montes and La Plata.

The **Faro de Conchupata** at the end of Calle Montes is easily seen at night; its torch-like glass structure atop a column is illuminated. It marks the first place where the present Bolivian tricolour was raised in 1851 and gives a good view over the flat city below. The flag was not formally adopted until 1888: the red represents the courage of the Bolivian army, yellow (gold) the country's mineral wealth and green the fertility of its soil.

Beyond the centre

Museo Mineralógico y Geológico ① *Mon-Fri 0800-1200 and 1430-1700, US$0.60,.* is part of the University. There are 5,500 examples of rocks – one of the largest collections in South America. Take any micro south to the Ciudad Universitaria.

Museo Antropológico Eduardo López Rivas ① *South of the centre on Av España esquina Urquidi, T02-5260020, Mon-Fri 0900-1200, 1400-1800, Sat/Sun 1000-1200, 1500-1800, US$0.75. To get there, take micro A heading south or any trufi going south,* has a rare collection of stone llama heads, pre-Hispanic mummies, artefacts from the Uru, Wankarani and Chipaya peoples and carnival masks and costumes. It also has a good selection of postcards and an *artesanía* shop.

Oruro Carnival

The normally cold, austere city of Oruro undergoes a complete transformation during its carnival. Over the week or so of celebrations the townsfolk go wild, so you can get hopelessly drunk with the locals, dance until you drop and in the process get soaked to the skin from a million water bombs. This is a rare opportunity to get involved in some serious partying with the indigenous people and not stand out like a sore thumb. You would be well advised not to miss it. For culture vultures this is also a fascinating insight into Aymara folk legends and a chance to enjoy some of the finest Bolivian music and dance.

Carnival is a movable feast, usually held around the middle of February. When it was first held only the miners danced, but several other guilds have taken up the custom and now traders, business people and professionals take part. The working-class Oruro district known as La Ranchería is particularly famous for the excellence of its costumes.

The origins of Carnival

The origins of the Carnival go back to the late 18th century and the worship of the *Virgen del Socavón*. Legend has it that an outlaw who lived in the area was mortally wounded, but was saved at the last moment by an unknown woman of great beauty. She turned out to be the *Virgen de la Candelaria*, whom the outlaw had worshipped in the cave where he lived. A century later, the church of the Virgen del Socavón was built on the very spot where he was saved. This was how the Virgen de la Candelaria became the *Mamita del Socavón* (Beloved Mother of the Mineshaft) and her feast was changed to Carnival Saturday, as it was on that day that she saved the outlaw.

The cult of the *Virgen del Socavón* has gradually merged over the years with the worship of the devil, or *Supay Tío* as he is known in these parts. Coincidentally, it was around the end of the 18th century that a company of *Diablos* first took part in Carnival and the association of *Supay Tío* with the Carnival began.

In the early 19th century, in an attempt to counter these indigenous myths and deities, a Spanish priest introduced the *relato*, the depiction of the struggle of the Seven Deadly Sins against the Archangel Michael. Like so many expressions of Bolivian culture, therefore, the Oruro Carnival is a mix of indigenous elements and those of the Catholic Church.

The dances

The most impressive part of the Oruro Carnival is the **Entrada**, or entry procession, which starts its 5-km route through the town at 0700 on the morning of the Saturday before Ash Wednesday. Over 50 dance companies take part, not just from Oruro but from all over the country. The most important are the *Diablos* (Devils) and *Morenos* (Blacks). The size of the companies ranges from around 50 dancers up to 200-300 – so you can imagine the massive scale of the Entrada.

Leading off the procession are the *cargamentos*, a motorcade of vehicles covered with fine embroidery, jewels, gold and silverware, old coins and banknotes. These are to recall the treasures once offered up in worship of the sun on Inti Raymi (the ancient Inca feast day), or the wealth of *El Tío* (Uncle) who lives in the mineshafts.

Next comes **La Diablada**, the central part of the Entrada. The procession is led by a condor and a pack of frolicking apes and bears. Then follows a procession of masked dancers, led by two luxuriously costumed masqueraders representing Lucifer and Satan. The Archangel Michael urges on hundreds of leaping, dancers in ferocious diabolical costumes. Prancing seductively at the head of columns of demons, a band of female dancers, wearing red wigs and masks, represent China Supay, Lucifer's consort, who plays the role of carnal temptress. A mighty brass band drives on the first great team of devils.

The costumes always feature the heavy, gruesome mask modelled in plaster, with a toad or snake on top, huge glass eyes, triangular glass teeth, a horsehair wig and pointed, vibrating ears. Tied around the neck is a large, silk shawl embroidered with dragons or other figures, and the dancer also has a jewelled, fringed breastplate. Over his white shirt and tights he wears a sash trimmed with coins and from it hang the four flaps of his native skirt, embroidered in gold and silver thread and loaded with precious stones. Special boots equipped with spurs complete the elaborate outfit. Satan and Lucifer wear scarlet cloaks and carry a serpent twisted around one arm and a trident.

Behind the Diablada follow at least 50 other groups, including more Diabladas, each with its own band. Among the following groups is the company of the Incas, representing

⁑ La Diablada

The most important part of the Entrada is *La Diablada*, the Dance of the Devils. It dates back to the 12th century, and the region of Catalonia in Spain, where they performed the *Dance of the Devils* as well as the *Dance of the Seven Deadly Sins*. It has since been adopted by the miners of Oruro as part of their own faith and mythical ancestory.

La Diablada is a religious/pagan dance which incorporates the forces of evil, as represented by Lucifer, Satan and China Supay, the seven deadly sins and the forces of good, represented by the Archangel Michael. The condor and the bear, ancient Andean symbols, also take part. During Carnival the Devil fights with the Archangel Michael, who is the only celestial figure capable of overcoming the forces of evil.

The main symbol of Carnival is the Devil (*Supay* or *El Tío*), who must be honoured to avoid his wrath and to receive his protection. According to tradition, the Devil lives in the shadows and caves of the mines, only appearing on the Sunday of Temptation.

The Devil plays an important part in Andean mythology. In mining centres such as Oruro he is the lord master of the rich mineral seams running through the cordillera. He lives in the mines, giving minerals to show kindness, or hiding them at will, and causing or preventing the collapse of tunnels. The miners are careful not to invoke any other gods, so as not to offend Supay. They offer him coca, cigarettes, alcohol and light candles in his honour next to a crude image of him.

important figures from the time of the conquest, such as the Inca Huáscar, and the conquistadores Francisco Pizarro and Diego de Almagro. The jungle tribes conquered by the Inca Yupanqui during the empire's expansion are portrayed by the *Tobas*, who perform war dances with large tropical feathers on their heads and carrying lances. Other companies taking part in the Entrada are the *Llameros* (llama drivers) and the *Kallawayas*, the ancient medicine men who dance with their bags of herbs.

One of the most important of the dancing groups are the *Morenos*, or blacks, who perform the famous **Morenada**, led by the *Rey Moreno* (Black King) and the *Caporal* (chief). According to tradition this dance represents the black slaves brought to South America and led off in chains to work in the mines of Potosí. The richly decorated costumes of the participants represents the wealth of the slave owners, while the protruding eyes and tongue of the masks conveys the fatigue of the slaves and their suffering from altitude sickness. The dance of the *Caporales*, which satirises the Spanish slave bosses, has its origins in the African culture of the Yungas.

The parade ends at 0400 on Sunday when it reaches the Sanctuary of the Virgen del Socavón, where the dancers invoke her blessing and ask for pardon. The company then proceeds to the Avenida Cívica amphitheatre, where the Angel and Devils perform two masques: the first is a contest between good and evil, in which Saint Michael defeats the Devils. In the second, the *relato de los diablos*, seven devils are forced to confess to the Seven Deadly Sins. After the performance the dancers all enter the sanctuary, chant a hymn in Quechua and pray for pardon.

Before and after the Entrada

The preparations begin four months before the actual event, on the first Sunday of November, with the 'First Invitation' and a mass in honour of the Virgen del Socavón. Rehearsals are held every Sunday until one week before Carnival, when the 'Second Invitation' takes place, preceded by a communion mass for the participants.

The Friday before Entrada is the *Anata Andina*, when peasants come to the city from all over the surrounding area to celebrate the harvest in Plaza 10 de Febrero. Traditional miners' *cha'llas* are also held at mines, including the sacrifice of a llama. Visitors may only attend with a guide and permission from Comibol, via the tourist office.

The Entrada is followed the next day (Sunday) by the *Gran Corso del Carnaval*, a very spectacular display.

On Monday is *El Día del Diablo y del Moreno* in which the Diablos and Morenos, with their bands, compete against each other on Avenida Cívica in demonstrations of dancing. Every group seems to join in the wonderfully chaotic spectacle. The action usually parades out of the amphitheatre, ending up at the Plaza de Armas. In the afternoon is the *Despedida de la Virgen* (Farewell to the Virgin). At dusk dancers and musicians go their separate ways, serenading until the early hours.

By Tuesday the main touristic events have ended. *Carnaval del Sur* takes place, with *ch'alla* rituals to invoke ancestors, unite with Pachamama and bless personal possessions. This is also the *día del agua* on which everyone throws water and sprays foam at everyone else (though how they distinguish this from the other days remains a mystery).

On Wednesday, Thursday, Friday and Saturday more *cha'llas* are held, this time for the condor, the toad and the viper, followed by huge parties on Avenida Cívica. The following day is Temptation Sunday, when a ceremony is held in the southern part of the city to 'bury' the Carnival until next year. Paradoxically, while this going on, a celebration of the birth of the next Carnival takes place, ending in a week of more partying!

Carnival essentials

Seating Around the Plaza de Armas, along Avenida 6 de Agosto and on Avenida Cívica, seats range from US$5-10 a day, bought from the Alcaldía in the plaza, or whichever business has erected stands outside its building. Buy early to get a good seat; the top or bottom rows offer more space. Seats on Avenida Bolívar, etc, cost from US$2 a day from the shops who built the stands. Take a cushion, water bombs and rain ponchos even if it's sunny, as you are bound to get wet, unless you look over 50. To wander among the dancers you are officially supposed to purchase a professional photographer's ticket for US$15, but amateurs can pay only US$1.50 by showing a small camera and insisting.

Sleeping Accommodation costs two to three times more than normal during Carnival and must be booked well in advance. Hotels charge for Friday, Saturday and Sunday nights. You can stay for only one night, but you'll be charged for three. The tourist office has a list of all householders willing to let rooms. Host and guest arrange the price, but expect to pay at least US$10 per person.

Transport Prices of buses from La Paz increase by up to three times. Buses get booked up quickly, so buy tickets in advance. There's usually no transport back to La Paz on Tuesday, so travel on Monday or Wednesday. Many agencies in La Paz organize day trips from La Paz for the Saturday parade. They leave at 0430, most will pick you up from your hotel. They return at round 1600-1700, so you'll miss out on a lot of the fun. Trips cost US$30-45, and include breakfast and a snack.

Excursions from Oruro

The disused **San José mine** worked for over 450 years for silver, tin and other minerals, lies 3 km west of the city. It can be visited with a permit from Comibol, To2-5251156, the state mining company. The Intendencia of the mine will provide a guide. A 20,000 tonnes-a-year tin smelter at **Vinto** is open to visitors with a permit; apply 24 hours in advance at NAF (T02-5252320) in Oruro. To visit either of these mines it is best and easier to go through Viajeros del Tiempo (see Tour operators on page 198). Micro D does go to the mine.

There are **thermal baths** at **Capachos** ⓘ *US$0.80*, which is 12 km from Oruro, and at **Obrajes** ⓘ *US$1.65*, 25 km away. Both have long been visited for the medicinal properties of the thermal waters and have covered swimming pools, but Obrajes is the better of the two. There is a choice of private baths or swimming pool. There's also now a hotel at Obrajes (**E** per person) and a disappointing restaurant. Buses leave from Calle Caro either side of 6 de Agosto, 0700-1700, US$0.40 to Capachos, US$0.80 to Obrajes. Go early as return transport is difficult after 1600. Taxis sometimes make the run. Avoid Sunday, when it is very crowded. **Viajeros del Tiempo** run trips here (see page 198).

The **Qala Qala (Cala Cala) cave paintings** are 20 km to the southeast of Oruro. The pictures and carvings are mainly of llamas and are thought to date from the Wankarani period, 800 BC-AD 400. Find the guardian, Francisco León, and pay the US$1 entrance. Trucks and buses leave 0700-1100 from Calle Brasil esquina Ejército. A taxi there, plus wait and return is about US$16. **Viajeros del Tiempo** also runs this trip (as above).

● Sleeping

Oruro *p190, map p191*
Near the bus terminal
B **International Park**, above the bus terminal, T02-5276227, F02-5275187. Oruro's best hotel, price includes continental breakfast, every room has phone, TV and private bathroom, parking facilities.
E **Bernal**, C Brasil 701, opposite the terminal, T02-5279468. Clean, modern, good value, excellent hot showers, heaters on request. Very friendly and can help arrange tours and jeep trips.
E **Gutiérrez**, C Bakovic 580, T02-5256675, F02-5276515, open 24 hrs, cable TV, heaters on request, internet access US$0.90 per hr, good restaurant (see Eating), clean and friendly.
E **Lipton**, Av 6 de Agosto 225, T02-5276583. Secure, parking US$0.45, open 24 hrs, good value. (G per person without bathroom).
E **Residencial El Turista**, 6 de Agosto 466, T02-5241888. Good showers, cable TV, safe parking US$0.45 per day. (G without private bathroom).
G **Alojamiento Concordia**, C León 110, T02-5277376. Basic, friendly.
G **Alojamiento Los Angeles**, C Bakovic 432, opposite the terminal, T02-5276185. Basic and noisy.

Between bus terminal and centre
C **Monarca**, Av 6 de Agosto 1145 esquina Ejército, T02-5254300, F02-5279006. Cable TV, sauna, garage, money exchange, restaurant.

G **Alojamiento 15 de Octubre**, Av 6 de Agosto 890, T02-5276012. 1st floor, go up the stairs on the left, without bathroom, hot showers, safe, good value, friendly.
G **Alojamiento La Paz**, Cochabamba 180, T02-5274882. Cheap and basic.
G **Alojamiento La Paz II**, C Cochabamba 266, further up the road, from the people who brought you Alojamiento La Paz, dark, dingy and unhelpful. Only stay in either of these if you are desperate or masochistic.

In the centre
A **S M Palace**, Av Mier 392, T/F02-5255132. Not as interesting as the name suggests but modern, all rooms with phone, TV and private bathroom, price includes continental breakfast.
B **Gran Sucre**, Sucre 510 esquina 6 de Octubre, T02-5276800, F02-5254110. (**D-E** with shared bathroom). Includes buffet breakfast, the more expensive rooms have phone and cable TV,. More character than most Oruro hotels, heater on request, parking. Recommended.
D **Repostero**, Sucre 370 y Pagador, T02-5258001. (**E** for cheaper rooms, no double beds). Includes basic breakfast, ageing but clean, friendly, hot water, free parking.
E **América**, Bolívar 347 y Pagador, T02-5274707, F02-5260707. Ring the bell to get in, cheaper without bathroom, all rooms with TV, restaurant.

F **Gloria**, Potosí 6059 (ring bell),
T02-5276250. Interesting building, private
bathrooms available, basic, hot water.
F **Residencial Ideal**, Bolívar 386,
T02-5277863. (G without bathroom). Not as
good as the name suggests, basic but
central, not fantastic beds.

Near the railway station
F **Residencial San Salvador**, V Galvarro
6325, T02-5276771. (G without bath).
Hot water, the best of the group.
G **Alojamiento San Juan de Dios**, V
Galvarro 1846, T02-5277083. Shared bath
only, surrounds a large courtyard.
G **Alojamiento Copacabana**, V Galvarro
1856, T02-5254184. Shared bath only,
possibly slightly cleaner than its neighbours,
luggage storage.
G **Alojamiento San Gerardo**, V Galvarro
1886 (near the corner), T02-5256064. Shared
bath only, cheapest of the 4 hotels on this
street and bigger and older than its
neighbours. Internet café planned and
renovations by the new owner. The 3
alojamientos each have a standard and
cheap restaurant attached.

◑ Eating

Oruro *p190, map p191*
There are lots of cheap eats in Oruro
including the comedor popular in the
centre of Mercado Campero (*api* and
pasteles are the best breakfast available for
warming up, from 0800). For a fruity
number, 14 juice bars line the railway side
of the market. Unlike La Paz, Oruro is
reasonably lively on Sun until 2100 with
many restaurants and cafés open. A
traditional dish is *charquekan*, which
sounds like a well-known soul/funk singer
but is actually grilled sun-dried llama meat
served with maize, potato, egg and cheese.
$$ **La Cabaña**, Junín 609, T02-5258023.
Comfortable, smart, good international food,
TV screen, bar, reasonable prices (Visa and
Mastercard accepted), Sun and Mon
1200-1530 only.
$$ **Nayjama**, C Aldana 1880. The best
restaurant in Oruro, very popular for lunch,
huge servings, main dishes US$4-6.
$ **Bambino**, C Ayacucho 445. Good
traditional place.

$ **Bravo's Pizza**, 6 de Octubre and Junín,
bright, huge TV screen.
$ **Chifa Rosa**, Av Mier, on the south side of
the plaza. Good value Chinese.
$ **Club Social Arabe**, Junín 729 y Montes.
Good value lunches.
$ **El Huerto**, Bolívar 359, Another vegetarian,
good cheap food.
$ **Gaviota**, Junín 676, daily 0800-1600.
Good traditional place.
$ **Govinda**, 6 de Octubre 6071, Mon-Sat
0900-2130. Excellent vegetarian restaurant,
almuerzo US$1.40.
$ **Guadalquivir**, C Pagador 6320. Good
traditional place.
$ **Hotel Gutiérrez**, CBakovic 580. The best
place to eat near the bus terminal is the
restaurant here. Meat and fish main courses
US$3-4, breakfast served 0700, also internet
access. Owners are happy for travellers to
wait here for buses.
$ **La Casona**, Montes 5970, nearly opposite
the post office. Good pizzeria.
$ **Libertador**, C Bolívar 351. Traditional,
excellent set lunch for US$1.20.
$ **Mateos**, Bolívar y 6 de Octubre, good,
reasonable prices, also sells ice cream.
$ **Restaurant Pagador**, C Pagador 1440.
Good traditional place.

Cafés
El Nochero, Av 6 de Octubre 1454, open
1700-2400. Good coffee.
Heladería Alemana, opposite UM Confitería.
Good ice cream, including *chirimoya*.
M y M, C Bolívar 490. Confitería.
Tip-Top, C Bolivar 524. Good confitería.
UM Confitería, Bolívar esquina S Galvarro.
Salteñas, good coffee, cakes, popular at
lunch, Mon-Sat 0800-2300, Sun 0800-1600.

◉ Entertainment

Oruro *p190, map p191*
Café Sur, Arce 163, near the train station.
Arts café with live entertainment, seminars
and films Tue-Sat, good place to meet people.
Caramello, Junín y 6 de Octubre, café, bar,
almuerzo lunchtime, restaurant at night,
gigs (mainly rock) every 3 weeks, Fri and Sat,
0900-1430, 1900-early hrs (snacks available
even then).
Pub Alpaca, La Paz 690, Finnish-owned,
lively Fri and Sat.

Cinemas Palais, Plaza 10 de Febrero, showings 1500, 1630, 2000 and 2100, US$0.60-1.35.

Gran Rex, C Mier between 6 de Octubre and S Galvarro, showings 1445, 1630, 1830 and 2000, US$0.75-1.20. Make sure you dress warmly.

O Shopping

Oruro p190, map p191

C Bolívar is the main shopping street in Oruro. There's a musical instrument shop at Av 6 de Octubre 6187.

On Av La Paz the blocks between León and Rodríguez are largely given over to workshops producing masks and costumes for Carnival.

Artesanía Oruro, C Ayacucho 856, sells ponchos, wall-hangings, rugs, jumpers and bags.

Compañía Importadora Escandinavia, S Galvarro near Plaza 10 de Febrero, sells Swiss Army penknives.

Reguerín, 6 de Octubre 6001 esquina Mier, good Diablada dolls and masks.

Markets

Mercado Campero, Velasco Galvarro esquina Bolívar, for film, clothes, food, hardware, stationery, cosmetics, hats, cloth, junk and comedor popular. It also has an interesting brujería section where you can find curanderos' magical concoctions.

Mercado Fermín López, C Ayacucho and Montes, food and hardware with big covered comedor popular.

▲ Activities and tours

Oruro p190, map p191

Tour operators

Viajeros del Tiempo, Soria Galvarro 1220, T02-5271166, www.contactoenoruro.com. They offer trips to the nearby mines, hot pools and other attractions, open Mon-Fri 0900-1230, 1500-1930, Sat 0900-1200. A recommended driver and tour guide is **Juan Carlos Vargas**, T02-5240333, contact via the tourist office.

⊜ Transport

Oruro p190, map p191

Minibuses within the city cost US$0.15, taxi US$0.40 per person; taxi to **Ciudad Universitaria** US$0.75 per person, to **Vinto** US$1 per person.

Bus

Oruro is 230 km southeast of La Paz by an asphalted road. At Km 104 it reaches Patacamaya, the turn-off for the road west to the Chilean border (see page 200). It then passes Sica Sica and, 10 km before Panduro, a turn-off which eventually leads to Chulumani in the Sud Yungas (see page 179).

Buses leave daily to La Paz at least every hr 0400-2200; US$1.80, 3 hrs. To **Cochabamba** 0430-2230, US$2.25, 4 ½ hrs. To **Potosí** 0800-1900, US$4.50, 8 hrs. To **Sucre** 0845 and 2100, US$6, 12 hrs. To **Uyuni** 2000, US$3, 9 hrs. To **Santa Cruz** 0600-1530, US$10.45, 12 hrs. To **Pisiga** (Chilean border) at 1200, US$4.50, 5 hrs. To **Challapata** 0700-1830, US$1.20, 2 hrs. To **Llallagua** 0630-1900, US$1.95, 3 hrs.

International buses (US$2 to cross border) To **Iquique** via Pisiga, with **Trans Salvador**, T02-5270280, semi-cama, US$12, 14 hrs, Sun-Fri 1230, Wed also 2330, not on Sat. **Trans Paraiso**, T02-5270765, bus cama, toilet and video. US$12.75, 10hrs, Mon-Sun 1230 and 2230. **Arica** via Tambo Quemado, also **Trans Paraiso**, US$12.75, 14 hrs, Mon-Sun 1330. To **Buenos Aires** with Balut, bus cama, US$100, every day 2130.

Train

There are 2 companies running services from Oruro to **Uyuni** and on to **Villazón** via **Tupiza**. Nuevo Expreso del Sur leaves on Mon and Fri at 1530, arriving in Uyuni at 2156 (Premiere Class US$7.75, Salon US$5.40); Wara Wara del Sur leaves on Sun and Wed at 1900, arriving in Uyuni at 0200 (Salon US$4.20). For details of trains from Uyuni to **Villazón** and for trains from Uyuni to Oruro, see Uyuni trains (page 214). Passengers with tickets Villazón-**La Paz** are transferred to a bus at Oruro. To check train times, call T02-5274605.

Directory

Oruro p190, map p191

Banks Oruro has one of the worst exchange rates in Bolivia – up to 5 % below the official rate. If possible take enough bolivianos and **Enlace**-compatible plastic to avoid changing money or TCs. There's an **Enlace** ATM in C La Plata 6153 opposite Banco Nacional de Bolivia. If you have to change TCs try **Banco Boliviano Americano**, 5% commission; and at **Banco Santa Cruz**, C Bolívar 470 and Pagador y Caro, open Sat 0900-1200. Other banks: **Banco Mercantil**, C Bolívar, Plaza 10 de Febrero; and **Banco de Crédito**, Plaza 10 de Febrero, bolivar and Montes. If you desperately need to change dollars there are many shops in the centre and around Mercado Campero displaying signs saying 'Compro Dolares'. It is quite also easy to change dollars on the street.

Internet These are surprisingly few and far between; try **ICP** at Bolivar 469, or **Ultranet**, 6 de Octubre 5864. **Laundry** Alemania, Aldana 280. **Post office** C Montes 1456, ½ block from Plaza 10 de Febrero, Mon-Fri 0830-1930, Sat 0830-1800, Sun 0900-1200. DHL is at Edificio Santa Teresa, C Montes esquina Sucre. **Telephone** Entel at C Bolívar esquina S Galvarro. **Useful addresses** Immigration Montecinos y Pagador, 2nd floor, no sign.

South and west of Oruro

For nature lovers, Parque Nacional Sajama to the west of Oruro is unmissable: there are several rare species of Andean animals and plants in the park (and neighbouring Lauca) that exist nowhere else in South America. Likewise, Lago Poopó, south of the road from Oruro to Uyuni, is an excellent bird reserve.

Further south, however, the landscape is less fertile. There appears to be no visible means of support for the people who live on the bleak, barren southern Altiplano, but these hardy, redoubtable Aymaras manage to eke out a meagre existence, sustained by traditional customs and beliefs that have remained unchanged for centuries. They herd llamas and grow a huge variety of tubers, the only crop that will grow in such a harsh environment. These are freeze-dried and then carried by llama down to the warmer valleys where they are exchanged for crops such as maize, which can be used to complement the diet or to make chicha, the fermented corn beer which is an integral part of festivals. This vast region is rich in mineral deposits. Oruro and Llallagua are centres of tin production, while in the more remote southern parts concentrations of antimony, bismuth, copper, salt, sulphur and magnesium among others remain relatively unexploited owing to a lack of capital and expertise.
▸▸ *For Sleeping, Eating and other listings, see page 203.*

Parque Nacional Sajama

A one-day drive to the west of Oruro is the Parque Nacional Sajama. At 81,000 ha (recently enlarged more than three times from its original size of 26,636 ha), is Bolivia's oldest national park (1945), and is home to the eponymous volcano, the country's highest at 6,542 m (in 1939, Sajama became the last major peak scaled in South America). It is also home to the world's highest forest, consisting mainly of the rare Kenua tree (Polylepis tarapana) which survives up to 5,200 m. The scenery is wonderful and includes views of two other volcanoes – Parinacota and Pomerape – as well as glaciers, geysers and thermal springs, and borders Chile's famous Parque Nacional Lauca.

> ❈ *If your interest is high-altitude flora or fauna or climbing, Sajama is a must.*

Getting there Access to Sajama is mercifully easy: the road from La Paz to Arica (Chile) is paved the entire way, and actually passes through the park. Hop off at Lagunas and head north for 22 km and you're in Sajama itself. A much longer (but scenic) route from the north is along the road from Patacamaya. At Curahuara, take the old road (unpaved) that follows the Rio Tomarapi. Cross into the park at the village by the same name, and then on to Laguna Huaña Khota, the hamlet of Khala Choco, and finally Sajama.

From Patacamaya, the journey is seven hours; the distance roughly 200 km. It also can be reached from Oruro along Bolivia Highway 4, which passes through the park on its way to the border outpost of Tambo Quemado. The journey is on asphalt and takes six hours (265 km). Take the bus to Oruro and change at Patacamayo. Buses and micros leave for Tambo Quemado from Oruro in front of Restaurant Capitol from 1000-1600 when full; US$2.20. International buses on the paved La Paz to Arica highway will issue tickets to Tambo Quemado. Get off at the entrance to Sajama village and then walk. For details of buses, see under International buses in the La Paz transport section (page 128).

Information The **Centro Asistencia Turismo (CAT)** office will help with arrangements, The park entry fee is US$2. It is collected at the Park office, where you have to register. Various members of the community offer basic accommodation in their homes. These should have mattresses and blankets, but it can be very windy and cold at night, so a good sleeping bag is essential, as well as gloves, hats and warm clothing. There are four basic restaurants in the park but no fresh food, so take your own. An informative **colour leaflet-guide to the park** (in Spanish) is available from the tourist office in Oruro for US$1.

For further information, contact **SERNAP's Ing. Franz Guzmán** ⓘ *Av 20 de Octubre 2659, La Paz; T02-2434420 (in Sajama, T02-2135260); franzguzman@ yahoo.es or tblanco_mollo@hotmail.com.*

Around the park

Although primarily of interest to the high-altitude climber and scientists, several tour operators from La Paz and Oruro now offer excursions with non-mountaineering options. Independent travel to Sajama is not advised, given the extreme temperatures and altitude. If you do go, it's advisable to spend at least three days exploring the park. You can hire jeeps at Tambo Quemado or at the junction into the village to visit the various sights within the park. There's good bathing in the **hot springs** 5 km north of the village. There are **geysers** 6 km to the west of the village, several **lakes** and herds of **vicuñas**.

There are also numerous opportunities for trekking in the park, with or without mules or porters, but note that once you move away from the Río Sajama or its major tributaries, the lack of water is a serious problem. **Mules** can be hired for US$6 per day. Mules, equipment and guides can be hired in the village. Guides are not qualified but are experienced. Horses can be hired for around US$7 per day including guide. Crampons, ice axe and rope are needed for climbing the volcanoes. In Sajama village, at 4,200 m, Peter Brunnhart (Señor Pedro) and Telmo Nina have a book with descriptions of the various routes to the summit (Telmo Nina keeps the visitors' book).

Travelling to Chile

There are two routes into Chile. The shortest and most widely used is the road from La Paz to Arica via the border towns of Tambo Quemado (Bolivia) and Chungará (Chile). The majority of Bolivia's imports, including foreign cars, jeeps and large vehicles from Chile's Pacific sea-ports, Arica and Iquique, are brought to La Paz by truck via this route.

From La Paz take the main highway south towards Oruro to Patacamaya. The town is 104 km from central La Paz – about one-and-a-half hours on a good paved road with only the occasional wheel-buckling pothole – and 130 km north of Oruro. There is a Sunday market with no tourist items.

At Patacamaya turn right (west towards the Cordillera) at the green road-sign to Puerto Japonés on the Río Desaguadero – the sign is only visible coming from La Paz – and from there to Tambo Quemado. Take extra petrol as there is none available after the Chilean border until Arica, and food and water. The journey is worthwhile for the breathtaking views.

Midway between Patacamaya and Tambo Quemado is the town of **Curahuara de Carangas**. Accommodation is available on the plaza in an *alojamiento*, G, which is dirty, with no electricity. Watch for speed restrictions upon entering town past the military school. There's a possible overnight stop in Sajama village, 22 km east of Tambo Quemado at the foot of Mount Sajama. Nights here can be bitterly cold and very windy, but in the daytime there are spectacular views of nearby snowcapped Sajama.

Crossing the border

Bolivian customs Bolivian customs is at Lagunas, 12 km further on from Sajama village. It's a popular truck-stop, where petrol is available.

Bolivian immigration The Bolivian border control at Tambo Quemado, 10 km from Lagunas, consists of *tránsito* (highway police), immigration, and international police. It closes for lunch. It is worth double checking all documents including visa requirements with the Consulate of Chile in La Paz before travelling.

Crossing with a private vehicle The normal road-user fee for a 'particular' (private non-commercial vehicle) is approximately US$4.50. Check with the **Autómovil Club Boliviano** in La Paz for any special documents which may be required, depending on the registration of your vehicle. Bolivian vehicles require a Temporary Export Certificate in order to leave Bolivia. This has to be obtained in La Paz prior to travel. Temporary Import/Export Certificates are normally valid for 90 days.

Chilean immigration From Tambo Quemado there is a stretch of about 7 km of 'no-man's land' before you eventually reach the Chilean border at Chungará. Here the border crossing, which is set against the most spectacular scenic backdrop of Lake Chungará and Volcán Parinacota, is strictly controlled. The border is open 0800-2100. A Temporary Import Certificate, which will cost you US$2, must be obtained from customs at Chungará on entering Chile. Do expect to be waiting behind lines of lorries. It's best to travel midweek and especially to avoid Sun. Drivers must fill in 'Relaciones de Pasajeros', US$0.25 from the kiosk at the border, giving details of driver, vehicle and passengers. The Border control consists of immigration, Customs and Police and Ministry of Agriculture and Livestock (SAG) – the control of animals entering Chile is rigidly enforced. Do not take any fruit, vegetables, or dairy products into Chile.

> ‡ *It's best to change a small amount of currency into Chilean pesos in La Paz.*

Entering Chile From Chungará the first 50-km section to Putre goes through the spectacular Lauca National Park. There are some treacherous bends as the road descends dramatically to sea-level where it meets the Pan American Highway (Route 5) 12 km north of Arica. There are several carabinero road checks on the road to Arica as this is a major drug and contraband route. Searches are very thorough and professional.

An alternative route into Chile, on which there are no trucks, is to go by a good road from La Paz via Viacha to **Santiago de Machaco** (130 km), where petrol is available. Then it's a further 120 km on a very poor road to the border at Charaña.

A variation from Viacha is to take the roads which more-or-less follow the railway to Charaña (four-wheel drive essential). On this scenic route you pass **Comanche** and **General Campero** in the Ciudad de Piedra. Near the football field in General Campero is a house which lets a room and has water. From General Campero roads go to General Pérez, Abarao and on to Charaña. From this route treks can be made south to the mountains towards Sajama and, from Charaña, to Sajama itself.

Crossing the border

Immigration Behind the railway station. Only a 30-day permit is given on entry.

Entering Chile Chilean border formalities are in **Visviri**. There is no fuel, accommodation, bath or electricity here; ask for a restaurant and bargain a price. Immigration is open 0800-2400. There is a US$2 charge for private vehicles. From Visviri a regular road runs to Putre. There are buses and colectivos to Arica.

South of Oruro

A road and railway line run south from Oruro to Uyuni (323 km), which is the usual starting point for tours of the Salar and Lagunas Colorada and Verde (see page 208). The road is bad to Pazña (between Oruro and Challapata) and asphalt thereafter. The unpaved parts are sandy and very difficult after rain, especially south of Río Mulato. The train journey is quicker in the wet and, anyway, more scenic.

About 65 km south on the road to Uyuni is the **Santuario de Aves Lago Poopó**, an excellent bird reserve on the lake of the same name. The lake dries up completely in winter. The Sanctuary can be visited from Challapata, 120km south of Oruro on a fairly good gravel road. There is a petrol station in the village and basic lodging. There is a fiesta 15-17 July.

❧ *From Chipaya, with your own transport or an organized tour, it is possible to head south through the Salar de Coipasa and onto the Salar de Uyuni.*

Branching off the road to Uyuni, at Km 27, is a road that runs southeast to **Sucre**. About 100 km from Oruro on this road, at 3,881 m, is the mining town of **Llallagua**. Nearby is the famous **Siglo Veinte**, once the largest tin mine (ex-Patiño) in the country. It is now closed, but being worked by small co-operatives; visitors are welcome. There is an acute water shortage.

Further on at **Uncia**, Km 102, there are more former Patiño mines. There are good hot springs which can be reached by trufi. In town is a small *alojamiento* (**G**) near the prison. It is clean, safe and basic. The restaurants are poor so it's best to eat at the market.

A road also runs southwest from Oruro to the Chilean frontier at Pisiga (for transport to Pisiga, see page 198).

The first town on this road is **Toledo**, at Km 38, where there is a colonial church. Further southwest is **Escara**, a lovely village with a beautiful plaza. It is a friendly place and you can rent bikes. The road continues 30 km southwest to **Sabaya** and from there for 52 km to the Chilean frontier.

At Escara the road branches south to **Chipaya**, 25 km away and 190 km from Oruro. Chipaya is the main settlement of the most interesting indigenous people of the Altiplano. They are the living remnants of a 4,000-year-old culture, probably the most ancient surviving in the Americas. The Chipayas speak their own language unrelated to Aymara or Quechua, and are thought to be closely related to the almost extinct Uru. Their distinctive dress and unique conical houses are beginning to disappear, however, as the community changes.

The Chipayas are well aware of the value of tourism and demand US$50 per person to visit. They can get nasty if you don't pay up. Also bear in mind that there is very little for the visitor to do and it is very cold, so it's possibly a better idea just to check out the display at the anthropological museum in Oruro.

⊜ Sleeping

Travelling to Chile *p200*
Tambo Quemado
F **Hotel Elenita**, further south from the Tambo Quemado minibus stop, has good clean rooms with private bathrooms and electric showers as well as a clean restaurant. There is also other cheap accommodation and restaurants.

Lagunas
The restaurant/bar **Lagunas** offers a cheap set menu, and is helpful and friendly. The owner can usually find accommodation in the village for around US$1; you'll need your own sleeping bag, extra blankets and warm clothing. Facilities are very basic; you may well be sleeping on a straw mattress on a dirt floor. There's no water or electricity, and gas lamps or candles are usual. It may be possible for men to sleep at the Puesto Militar, beside the new road, 100 m from the village.

Charaña
G **Alojamiento Aranda**, Charaña.

South of Oruro *p202*
Lago Poopó
G per person **Hotel Potosí**, with good beds and a basic restaurant.

Llallagua
G **Hotel Llallagua**, small beds, no bathroom, seldom has water, perhaps the best, but not really recommended.

⊖ Transport

Travelling to Chile *p200*
For details of buses between La Paz and Arica see International buses (on page 128).

South of Oruro *p202*
Lago Poopó
Buses leave Oruro for Lago Poopó at 0800 and 1430 (2½ hrs, US$1), and are always full.

Llallagua
Llallagua can be reached by bus from Oruro; 7 a day with **Bustillos**, with **Enta** at 0900 and 1700 daily, 3 hrs, US$2.50. Also at 1900 from La Paz.

Chipaya
This part of the country can be difficult to explore without your own transport (4WD recommended), but there is a daily bus from Oruro to Sabaya, southwest of Escara, via Huachacalla; it departs at 2100, 5 hrs, US$4.50; there is also transport once a week in either direction from Huachacalla to Chipaya.

⊙ Directory

Travelling to Chile *p200*
Tambo Quemado
Banks Banco Unión (open Mon-Fri 0900-1600) offers a good rate for US dollars and changes Amex travellers' cheques at 2% commission (up to US$199, US$3 flat fee thereafter). There is also an **Entel** office and 2 petrol stations.

Salar de Uyuni and the far southwest

The Salar de Uyuni is the highest and largest salt lake in the world at an altitude of 3,650 m and covering 9,000-12,000 sq km (depending on who you believe), making it twice as big as the Great Salt Lake in the United States. Driving across it is one of the weirdest and most fantastic experiences anywhere on the continent, especially during June and July when the bright blue skies contrast with the blinding-white salt crust. After particularly wet rainy seasons the lake is covered in water which adds to the surreal experience. It feels a bit like being a tiny ant on a giant mirror. The depth of the salt varies from 2-20 m. During the last Ice Age most of the Altiplano was under a lake called Lago Minchín, of which the Salar was the deepest point. Until the Spanish arrived it was known as Paichichuta. A trip to this remote corner of Bolivia would not be complete without continuing to see two of Bolivia's most isolated marvels, the bright red Laguna Colorada and jade green Laguna Verde. These spectacular soda lakes lie 350 km southwest of Uyuni, across a surreal Dalí-esque desert landscape, and over unmarked, rugged truck tracks. Tours to all these places run from the town of Uyuni.

Reserva de Fauna Andina Eduardo Avaroa (REA), in Potosí Department's southwestern corner, is a 714,745-ha wildlife reserve founded in 1973 and enlarged in 1981. Its raison d'être is the protection of the vicuña, although it's also a great place to see some unusual desert scenery and bizarre landscapes. Indeed, from a geological perspective, it is Bolivia's greatest attraction. Seeing hundreds of pink flamingoes standing in the midst of a shimmering salt lake is definitely a sight worth seeing. However, nights are extremely cold here: a record low of minus 30°C was recorded in 1996. ▶ *For Sleeping, Eating and other listings, see pages 212-215.*

Uyuni → *Phone code: 02. Colour map 3, grid B2. Population: 11,320. Altitude: 3,665 m.*

Hot in the sun, cold in the shade and bitterly cold in the wind and at night, Uyuni is a railway junction founded in 1889 and starting point for trips to Bolivia's most amazing scenery – the salt lake of the same name in the far southwest. Though once described as "a diamond encrusted in the shores of the Great Salar", Uyuni is no beauty. Once important, as the Bolivian railways have declined so has Uyuni: depite the benefits of tourism, its functional architecture, wide, dust-blown streets and freezing winds, lend it a strange, post-apocalyptic feel.

The town is noted as the first place where a plane took off and landed on Bolivian soil in 1921 and possibly has the honour of being soccer's point of entry into the country, introduced by British railway engineers. The city was officially declared 'Hija Predilecta de Bolivia' ('Bolivia's favourite daughter') in 1983 for the help given to returning soldiers from the disastrous and bloody Chaco War with Paraguay 1932-1935.

Ins and outs

Getting there and around Incoming (and outgoing) buses stop in Avenida Ferroviaria, between Arce and Bolívar. It is quite possible to spend your entire time in Uyuni within 150 m of this point. The majority of tour operators, hotels and restaurants and all the bus companies are in this area, with the station just to the south.

Tourist office There is an under-funded **tourist office** in the public clocktower on Avenida Potosí with Plaza Arce ① *Mon-Fri 0900-1230, 1500-1930.* The **head office** ① *Av Potosí 13, To2-6932060 and ask for the tourist information office, open Mon-Fri 0830-1200 and 1400-1830, Sat-Sun 0830-1200,* has good 1:500,000 maps of the Salar and lagoons but, at the time of writing, these were sadly for sale only in La Paz. Go here also if you want to complain about a tour. ▸ *For tours starting from Uyuni, see page 214 and box, page 208.*

Sights

Once you've sorted out your **tour** there's not much to do in Uyuni, but if you have some time check out the **Cementerio de Trenes** (train cemetery) just over 1 km from the centre following Avenida Ferroviaria and then the railway line. Rusting steam engines and carriages decay slowly into the barren landscape. Some agencies throw in a swift visit at the end of a tour, thereby saving you the walk. There is also a small museum, the **Museo Arqueológico y Antropológico de los Andes Meridionales** ① *Mon-Fri 0830-1200 and 1400-1800, US$0.20,* which has a well- labelled collection of deformed skulls, mummies, cloth and ceramics.

A giant **statue** of an armed railway worker, erected after the 1952 Revolution, dominates Avenida Ferroviaria in front of the station, where there's also a British steam engine. **Market** days are Thursday, Friday and Sunday, and there's a Fiesta on 11 July.

Excursions

Pulcayo is a small mining village northeast of Uyuni on the road to Potosí. The train cemetery here contains the first locomotive to enter Bolivia and a train robbed by Butch Cassidy and the Sundance Kid shortly before the end of their career (see San Vicente, page 266). The name is best known in Bolivia for the 'Thesis of Pulcayo', a Trotskyist declaration made in 1946 which would have been forgotten, except that tin baron Simón Patiño had it reprinted in full in his newspaper *El Diario* as a warning. It remains important to miners and is still seen in graffiti. There is a small mining

Uyuni

To Post Office & Bus Offices
To Colchani & El Salar

Av Acre
Av Colón

Museo Arqueológico y Antropológico de los Andes Meridionales

Andes Salt Expeditions
Colque Tours

Bolívar
Sucre

Av Potosí

REA
Immigration

Plaza Arce
Pucara Tours

Universal Video Movie

Tunupa Tours

Esmeralda Tours
Toñito Tours

Toñito Tours Main Office
Transandino Tours

To Train Cemetery (1 km)

Lavarap Laundry
Av Ferroviaria

Railworker's Monument

To Tupiza

N

0 metres 20
0 yards 20

Sleeping	Kutimuy 4	Eating	Uyuni 4
Avenida 1	La Casita Toñito 5	16 de Julio 5	
Hostal Cactus 9	Mágia de Uyuni 6	Cafeteria Confiteria 6	
Hostal Europa 2	Residencial	Pizzeria Urkupiña 3	
Hostal Marith 10	Copacabana 7	Pub Pizzeria Arcoiris 2	
Kory Wasy 3	Residencial Sucre 8	San Gaetano 7	

museum which allows you to go underground. For times, call Señor Ciprian Nina at Uyuni tourist head office, T02-6932060.

Another possible day trip is to **San Cristobal**, see page 210.

Salar de Uyuni and Reserva de Fauna Andina Eduardo Avaroa

Ins and outs

A four-day tour across the Salar and down to Laguna Colorada and Laguna Verde in Reserva Eduardo Avaroa on the Chilean border is not to be missed, but note that this is a region of harsh extremes of climate. Temperatures of 30°C have been recorded at midday and minus 25°C the following midnight. Sunglasses are essential to avoid snowblindness. Many agencies will not send jeeps out when the Salar has reverted to a wet lake because the salt water destroys the engines; but shop around, someone will want your money.

There is a entry fee of Bs30 (pay in local currency, otherwise the fee is US$5) for Reserva Eduardo Avaroa, which is payable at Laguna Colorado. Make sure to write your name on the back of the ticket and keep it as a souvenir. Park guards may ask you for it back at the end of your trip. Refuse. This is an illegal scam on the part of the guards who will later resell the ticket and pocket the money at the expense of national park income.

The park is located in one of the more inhospitable areas of the country, and travellers will find little in the way of provisions after leaving Uyuni. Travellers coming here with their own transport will find the trip by road is an arduous, 20-hour one, although the scenery along the way is marvellous. **TAM** does fly into the park at two locations, although passage can be secured only by contacting the airline first. Alternatively, you can cross from the Chilean side, if the post at Hito Cajón is open and proper documentation is presented. There usually is a US$5 fee for this, and if your papers are not in order, you will probably be denied entry.

Information For further information on Reserva Eduardo Avaroa contact **Ing. Teodoro Blanco** ⓘ *Av Potosí 23 entre Arce y Bolívar, T02-6932225, teoblanco@hotmail.com*.

Crossing the Salar

Some 20 km north of Uyuni is the tiny settlement of **Colchani**. A couple of minutes out of the village and you are on the salt. Workers from the village dig out piles of the stuff, which are then loaded onto trucks and taken back to the village to be ground and iodised before being sold. Iodine deficiency leads to thyroid problems and goitre and it is now illegal to sell non-iodised salt.

Next is **Hotel Playa Blanca**, 34 km from Uyuni, which apart from the roof is completely made of salt. It is run by Teodoro Colque (T02-6932772) and you used to be able to stay the night until it was closed down at the end of 2001 as a result of protests at the pollution the effluent was said to be causing. You will be allowed to take photos if you buy a drink or snack there. Suffering a similar fate is the much posher **Palacio de Sal**, which is adjacent.

As you cross the Salar you pass *ojos de sal* (eyes of salt) which are breathing spaces for subterranean rivers flowing under the Salar. Approach these with caution as the salt near a hole might not bear your weight. In places minerals rise to the surface in a spectacular show of crystalline colour. The Salar is covered in pentagonal and hexagonal shapes which appear to have been hand-carved. Spectacular views north are dominated by the snow-capped Volcán Tunupa, 5,400 m.

It takes one to two hours from **Hotel Playa Blanca** (depending on the state of the Salar and your vehicle) to go the 80 km to **Isla de Pescadores**. The original name of

66 99 The Salar is covered in pentagonal and hexagonal shapes which appear to have been hand-carved. Spectacular views north are dominated by the snow-capped Volcán Tunupa, 5,400 m...

this 10-ha island was *Incahuasi* (Inca House) but it has taken on the name of another island, 15 minutes northwest (reputedly because of an error many years ago made in Footprint's legendary *South American Handbook*!). Agencies are now thinking of going to the true Isla de Pescadores because Incahuasi is being spoiled by development. There is even a branch of Mongo's (see La Paz page 118) bar-restaurant there now and around the middle of the day the place crawls with visitors.

Having said this, Incahuasi is the most impressive of the 60-odd islands in the Salar. From among the giant cacti (some are more than 10 m high and many hundreds of years old) there are stunning views across the huge white expanse of salt to the mountains shimmering on the horizon.

In the dry season, most tours then head south across the Salar to the Colcha K military post (also known as Villa Martín) and on to **San Juan** to spend the night in a basic but clean *alojamiento* with hot showers (electricity 1900-2100). Ask your driver to take you out on to the Salar for an unforgettable sunset. **Toñito Tours** and **Colque Tours** both have their own hotels on the edge of the salt. If the Salar is under water, tours normally head back to Uyuni and then continue south on not so much terra firma but certainly terra drier.

Llica

On the western side of the Salar, five hours from Uyuni, is Llica, capital of Daniel Campos province. Tours don't normally come here but it can be arranged. The village is good for llama and other wool handicrafts, but there are no shops or electricity. A bus leaves from Uyuni at 1200 daily, and a truck at 1100. The wet season causes delays. ⏵ *See also Sleeping, page 213.*

South of the Salar

Tours continue south from San Juan (see above), via Chiguana (a rail station and military post) and its small **Salar de Chiguana** to Laguna Hedionda. Or from Uyuni they head south, crossing the 50-cm-deep Río Grande to Villa Alota, a military checkpoint five hours away, with a number of **G** *alojamientos*. Then on through striking collections of eroded rocks surrounded by snowcapped mountains to Laguna Hedionda in another two hours. One of these mountains – **Volcán Ollagüe** – is actually an active volcano and wisps of smoke can usually be seen coming from just below its summit. It's possible to organise a five-day tour which includes a visit to the volcano.

Laguna Hedionda (literally, *Stinking Lake*, due to the sulphur) is popular with flamingoes which are mainly white as the algae which create the pink colour are not so numerous in this lake. Other beautiful lakes in this area include **Laguna Chiar Khota.**

Continuing south, the piles of light coloured gravel are *caliche*, which is heated up on yareta grass fires to extract sulphur. The route climbs up through a red-brown rock and sand landscape to reach the **Siloli Desert** at 4,600 m before dropping down to enter the REA and then the bizarre *Arbol de Piedra* (rock tree), an improbably balanced piece of wind-eroded rock (pictured on page 13). It continues downwards and south to reach Laguna Colorada in around three hours from Laguna Hedionda.

⚏ Advice on tours of the Salar

Of the two dozen or so agencies in Uyuni, very few can be recommended without reservation and even those are by no means perfect. Companies pass in and out of favour.Speak to travellers who have just returned from a tour and try the agencies listed on page 214, most of which are along Av Ferroviaria and in Plaza Arce. Most agencies are open until at least 2000 so you can arrive, organize a tour and leave the next day. It is also not difficult to arrive during the night and get on a tour in the morning. Most don't leave until 1000. All accept travellers' cheques, and some take credit cards.

Organization of tours from Uyuni is a hit-and-miss affair. Demand a written contract which states a full day-by-day itinerary, a full meal-by-meal menu (vegetarians should be prepared for an egg-based diet), what is included in the price and what is not. If the tour doesn't match the contract, go back to the operator, and demand a refund or complain to Sr Ciprian Nina at the tourism office in Uyuni and then to the **Director Regional de Turismo**, La Prefectura del Departamento de Potosí, C La Paz, Potosí, T02-6227477. The Prefectura recognises the problem with Uyuni agencies but needs specific information to be able to act.

Trip prices are based on a six-person group. Normally the agencies will form groups, otherwise you may have to find others to make up the numbers. This is easy in the high season (April-September). Outside this period, it is worth getting a group together before arriving. If there are fewer than six you each pay more. There is no discount for having seven people and it is uncomfortable.

The standard four-day trip (Salar de Uyuni, Lagunas Colorada and Verde) costs from US$65 up to US$220 per person depending on the agency and season and where it leaves from. Tours starting in La Paz cost double those from Uyuni. There is no refund for leaving to Chile after Laguna Verde. Shorter trips are possible depending on what you are prepared to miss, and so are longer trips (eg including an ascent of Volcán Tunupa), but four days in a Toyota Landcruiser is as much as most people's bottoms will stand. Take a good sleeping bag, sunglasses, sun hat, sun protection, lots of warm clothing, six litres of bottled water or water purification tablets or iodine tincture, lots of film or memory cards and your own tapes. Snacks are a good idea too and a bottle of something alcoholic may help make you popular.

If you're pressed for time, do not despair. Most companies will do a three-day trip across the Salar, doubling back at Laguna Colorada and missing out the geysers, Laguna Verde and Lincancahur volcano if you can get a group together for it. A two-day trip stays firmly in the region of the Salar and includes an ascent of the inactive Volcán Tunupa, while in one day you can see Salar and the Isla de Pescado.

If you can afford it, go with one of the reputable La Paz agencies (see page 123), for example **Colibrí** or **Trans Amazonas**. Agencies in Potosí also organize tours, but this mainly involves putting you on a bus to Uyuni where you meet up with one of the Uyuni agencies and get the same quality tour for a higher price. There can be communication problems between agencies and getting a refund out of a subcontractor is difficult. Better to go directly to Uyuni or book, pay and go with an agency from elsewhere.

It's possible to do the tour in a far more adventurous way. **Llama Mama** (www.llama-mam.com) does it on mountain bikes when the Salar is not flooded and, if you have your own jeep, **Toñito Tours** will let you follow one of their groups and promise help in the event of abreakdown.

The highlight of the Reserva de Fauna Andina Eduardo Avaroa is the Laguna Colorada (coloured lake). At 4,278 m high and 60 sq km, the lake gets its name from the effect of wind and sun on the micro-organisms that live in it. The shores of the lake are encrusted with borax, used for soap and acid, which provides an arctic-white counterpoint to the flaming red waters. Up to midday, though, the lake is pretty normal coloured. The pink algae provide food for the rare James flamingoes (the population here is the world's biggest), along with the more common Chilean and Andean flamingoes, which breed and live here and also gives them their pink colour. Some 40 other bird species can also be seen here. The lake is less than 1 m deep but the mud is very soft. Flamingoes can walk across it, but tourists – even very skinny ones – can't.

There are 80 species of bird in the area (64% of those found in the entire Altiplano). Other notables include the horned coot, Andean goose and the Andean hillstar, which lives in altitudes of up to 4,500 m. The birdlife is best seen during the southern summer which is from November to January; many birds migrate to avoid the cold winter, June-August, but some always remain. See the full-colour illustrated guide (in Spanish) Aves de la Reserva Nacional de Fauna Andina Eduardo Avaroa by Omar Rocha and Carmen Quiroga (Museo Nacional de Historia Natural, La Paz 1996). Animals (rarely seen) include pumas, Andean foxes and the strange, rabbit-like viscacha. Vegetation to look out for includes *thola* (which after the wet season has an edible tuber called sicha), *yareta* (which looks like a green pillow, but feels like a rock), *quinoa* plants (which produce the high altitude Andean grain) and the *kenua* bush/tree which grows at altitudes up to 5,000 m. ▸▸ *See also Sleeping, page 213.*

South of Laguna Colorada

An unpleasantly cold and early start on day three gets you to the Sol de Mañana, 50-m-high steam geyser, for dawn. Do not step over this – and putting your hand in may seem a good idea until there's a change in geothermal activity and you will have the flesh removed from your hand by boiling, high-pressure steam. There are boiling mud-holes and a strong stench of sulphur which, when combined with the 4,800 m altitude, can make some people feel ill. Borax processors use the heat of the geysers to make acid and there is a geothermal electricity generation project here.

You then continue to the 30°C thermal waters at the edge of **Laguna Chalviri**, 30 minutes from the geysers. It's a pleasant spot and the first (and last) chance for a wash. You continue for an hour through the barren, surreal landscape of the **Pampa de Chalviri** at 4,800 m, via a pass at 5,000 m, to the wind-lashed jade waters of **Laguna Verde** (Green Lake) at 4,400 m, the southernmost point of the tour. The stated causes of the lake's impressive colour range from magnesium, calcium carbonate, lead and arsenic. It covers 17 sq km and is at the foot of **Volcán Licancabur** (5,868 m) which is on the border between Bolivia and Chile. There is a small refugio at Laguna Verde; it costs US$2, has mattresses, running water and a view of the lake.

Returning to Uyuni

From Laguna Verde, tours start the 400-km-plus journey back to Uyuni. There are a number of options for routes back; check out what your agency is offering. It is possible to go through the village of **Queteña**, Laguna Celeste (not possible during the wet season) and the *bofedales* (wet grassy areas popular with wildlife), but most take the route through the bizarre and impressive Valle de las Rocas near **Villa Alota**. All the eastern routes give views of huge glaciated mountains including **Uturuncu**, at 6,020 m, the highest in the area and the only one to exceed 6,000 m.

An attractive option is to stop at **San Cristóbal**, which is being touted as an alternative base to Uyuni with the help of some sustainable tourism funding. The town is actually brand new, having been moved from its original location in order to build Bolivia's biggest mine. The 17th-century church and churchyard, however, are original, having been moved wholesale. With the emphasis on 'adventure' travel, San Cristóbal offers a **Mongo's Mad Max** bar and restaurant built from an enormous water tank, a hotel (**D**) and **Llama-Mama** mountain biking, www.llama-mama.com, an offshoot of La Paz's successful Gravity Assisted Mountain Biking (see page 86). There are condors in the area and lots of paths and bike tracks across the boulder fields with views across to the Salar. If you feel like getting off and not getting back in the jeep, you can buy tickets for onward travel from Uyuni here, and get the shuttle bus (US$2) to take you to the bus or train. There should be a San Cristóbal office in Uyuni by 2005.

Crossing into Chile

If you wish to continue from Laguna Verde into Chile, all agencies now offer the option of crossing at **Hito Cajón**. Here there is a Bolivian immigration post which will charge you Bs15 for an exit stamp. Agencies will organize a bus (US$10 – your jeep driver should ensure you are safely on before pushing off) both to the immigration post and on to San Pedro de Atacama in Chile, where the bus will wait for your lengthy immigration formalities to be completed. As with the train crossing, do not take any fresh fruit or coca leaves with you – one tourist even had her vitamin tablets analysed! Cracking jokes is also not advised (see also Travelling to Chile on page 200).

If you plan to enter Chile via one of the unattended border crossings in the southwest region, you must get an exit stamp at the Bolivian immigration office in Uyuni (open every day). The stamp is valid for three days, but more than 72 hours may be permitted if you state the exact date you intend to leave Bolivia. Most agencies will arrange transport from the border (where exit stamps are issued for Bs 15) to San Pedro de Atacama for US$10 per person. Buy Chilean pesos in Uyuni or do your own exchange with other travellers coming the other way. You will meet them as they get off the bus you are going to catch to San Pedro de Atacama.

Via Ollagüe From Colchani it is about 60 km across to the southwest shore of the Salar. There are two or three parallel tracks about 100 m apart and every few kilometres stones mark the way. The salt is soft and wet for about 2 km around the edges of the Salar. You can get directions from the Hotel Playa Blanca near Colchani. There is no real danger of getting lost, especially in the high season, but it is a hard trip and the road is impassable after rain. There is no petrol between Uyuni and Calama (Chile).

It is 20 km from the southwestern shore to 'Colcha K', the military checkpoint. From there a poor gravel road leads 28 km to San Juan, where many tour groups spend the night. Then the road enters the Salar de Chiguana, a mix of salt and mud which is often wet and soft with deep tracks which are easy to follow. Thirty-five kilometres away is Chiguana, another military post. It's 45 km to the end of the Salar, a few kilometres before the border. This latter part is the most dangerous; it's very slippery and there's very little traffic.

To hitch-hike to Chile via Ollagüe, trucks first go north, then across the Salar de Ollagüe. The scenery on this route is amazing and, once in Chile, you will see lakes similar to Lagunas Colorada and Verde. There is nowhere to stay in Ollagüe, but police and border officials will help find lodging and transport for hitchers. Change bolivianos into pesos at the small shop in a blue house opposite the water tower.

From Laguna Verde From Laguna Verde it is 7 km to Hito Cajón, the border post with Chile. A further 8 km is La Cruz, the junction with the east-west road between the borax and sulphur mines and San Pedro. There are reports of a daily bus from Hito Cajón to San Pedro, but it is much safer (and easier) to get a tour agency in Uyuni to arrange transport from Hito Cajón to San Pedro de Atacama, Chile (see page 214). The meteorological station at Laguna Verde will radio for a pick-up from San Pedro. This service costs US$10 per person Hito Cajón-San Pedro. The chance of finding other transport is remote. Adequate food, water and clothing is essential. You can get a good rate for Chilean pesos from the lady who runs the little shop at the Bolivian border post. Do not underestimate the dangers of getting stuck without transport or lodging at this altitude. Do not travel alone.

Entering Chile

The easiest way is to go via San Pedro de Atacama as part of your jeep trip to the Salar and lagunas. This can be arranged with your tour agent. Otherwise, there is a train service to Calama leaving between 0500 and 0800 Thursday, US$13.45. It takes one hour to change trains at Avaroa, then it's 40 minutes to Ollagüe, where Chilean customs take two to four hours. All passports are collected and stamped in the rear carriage and should be ready for collection after one to two hours; queue for your passport, no names are called out. After that it is an uncomfortable six hours to Calama. On Monday at 0800 a service runs only as far as Avaroa and you must organize your own change of trains; there is a service from there to Calama. Take blankets, or better still, a sleeping bag.

Predilecto and **Trans 11 de Julio** each operate a bus to Calama which leaves from their respective offices Monday and Thursday 0400, US$10.50, 15 hours (depending on border crossing). **Colque Tours**, as well as running Salar and lagunas tours that take you to the border town of San Pedro de Atacama, has a jeep direct there leaving their office every day at 1900, US$25 per person, 16 hours.

Whichever route you take, no exit stamp is needed in advance; the Bolivian border post charges Bs15 (about US$2.20) on exit. If you take your own food, eat fresh things first as the Chileans do not allow dairy produce, teabags (of any description), fruit or vegetables to be brought in. Do not attempt to take coca leaves across the border; it is an arrestable offence.

● Sleeping

Uyuni *p204, map p205*
It can be difficult to find a bed in the better hotels if you're arriving around 0500-0600 in the high season.

C **Kory Wasy**, Av Potosí. (D in low season), Av Potosí 350, T03-6932670, kory_wasy@hotmail.com. Pretty basic for the price but good fun, with doors made from cactus wood and decorated with carved Indian heads; the sun streams through to the lobby and owner Lucy Laime de Pérez is very friendly. Also has its own tour agency and a restaurant on-site. Private bathrooms, heating is promised soon and the price includes breakfast. Some rooms are dark.

C **La Casita Toñito**, 60 Av Ferroviaria, T02-6933186, www.bolivianexpeditions.com/hotel.htm. A modern hotel which opened in 2002 with cable TV, internet, laundry, restaurant, heating in rooms, parking and big beds. Owned by Toñito Tours (see page 214), who will try to persuade you to go on one.

D **Mágia de Uyuni**, Av Colón between Sucre and Camacho, T02-6932541, magia_uyuni@latinmail.com. All rooms with private bathroom, price includes breakfast. Recommended.

E **Hotel Kutimuy**, Avaroa esquina Av Potosí, near the market, T02-6932391. (F without bathroom). Includes continental breakfast, rooms nothing to shout about but better than many in Uyuni. Electric showers and laundry. Affiliated to Colque Tours.

F **Avenida**, Av Ferroviaria 11, opposite the train station, T02-6932078. With private bathrooms, (some cheaper rooms without), Avenida has good hot showers, washing facilities, and parking, but looks a bit like a prison.

G **Hostal Cactus**, Plaza Arce, also very cheap, small, basic, friendly and quite clean, hot shower US$0.50.

G **Hostal Europa**, Av Ferrovaria esquina C Sucre. Good gas-powered showers, good beds but you'll be woken up in the early hours by people arriving off the train, basic kitchen facilities, storage, secure, English spoken.

G Hostal Marith, Av Potosí 61, T02-6932174. A good place to stay on a budget; the shared showers are hot (though only from 0830) and rooms are grouped around a sunny patio in which there are sinks to do your washing.

G Residencial Copacabana, Plaza Arce. Cheap, small, US$0.45 for a shower and unfriendly to a fault but very central and some potted geraniums make it feel a little more homely.

G Residencial Sucre, Sucre 132, T02-6932047. Very cheap, clean and friendly, though the 3 stars on the sign is exceedingly optimistic.

Pulcayo
G Hotel Rancho, without bath, large rooms, hot water, good meals.

Salar de Uyuni *p206*
A good tip for freezing nights on the Salar or in the reserve is to fill a water bottle with hot water last thing at night, wrap it in a sock and use it as a sleeping bag warmer. If you're lucky it might still be lukewarm for washing with the next day.

Llica
G Alojamiento Municipal, Angel Quispe on the plaza also has 3 beds, and meals are available in private houses.

Laguna Colorada
There are 4 places to stay at Laguna Colorada. The REA (the park authorities) run the best, a modern, clean, comfortable, warmish 34-bed refuge with kitchen and friendly guardian, for US$4.50 per person. Reservations can be made through the REA office in Uyuni or insist that your agency books you in there (they will probably charge an extra Bs 10). There is also a dirty, waterless shack for US$3 per person, which remains popular with Uyuni agencies for some reason. Be careful with water – there's not much of it about.

❷ Eating

Uyuni *p204, map p205*
Avoid eating in the market. Although there have been no recent reports, there have in the past been incidences of cholera. Uyuni wouldn't be a good place to get ill, worse still if you fell sick on a tour.

$$ 16 de Julio, Av Ferrovaria. Opens 0700 for breakfast upstairs. Traditional dishes are overpriced but the place is warm and smart if dated. Limited options for vegetarians.

$ Arco Iris, Plaza Arce, the best pizza and huge pasta portions but, if it's busy, service takes an early exit.

$ La Loco, Av Potosí. Gringo grub plus open fires and music and drinks until late make this 'restaurant-bar-pub' a popular evening hang-out.

$ Pizzeria Urkupiña, Plaza Arce. Also open for breakfast, good standard stuff.

$ Pub Pizzeria Arcoiris, Plaza Arce, good pizza for US$1.20 a slice, US$8 for a whole pizza.

$ Restaurant Uyuni, Av Ferrovaria, next door to Hostal Europa. Seemingly ever-open, tastefully decorated with 2 armadillos nailed to the wall, don't breakfast here.

$ San Gaetano, Plaza Arce. A trendy restaurant with loud music, bare stone, seats outside, a warm fire in middle of the room and good breakfasts on sunny side of plaza.

Cafés
Cafeteria Confiteria, Plaza Arce. Decent café and breakfast place in the middle of the square. A good place from which to watch the world go by.

❻ Entertainment

Uyuni *p204, map p205*
One way of forgetting the night-time sensation of being locked in a deep-freeze is to pay **Universal 'Cinema'** a visit at Bolivar 60. For just US$0.90, squeeze into a 6-seat 'auditorium' to watch one of 1,000 English-language videos of your choice. The fee includes a hot drink. Open 1400-2200 every day.

Southwest Bolivia Salar de Uyuni & the far southwest Listings

● *Price codes for Sleeping and Eating are given inside the front cover. Further information on hotel and restaurant grading can be found in Essentials, pages 43-44.*

○ Shopping

Uyuni *p204, map p205*
The **market** at Av Arce esquina Colón sells the basics. There is also a smaller **indoor market** on C Bolívar above Av Ferroviaria and another at Avaroa. Fleece jackets, scarves, long wool socks and other warm clothes are available from a shop on C Bolívar below Potosí.

▲ Activities and tours

Uyuni *p204, map p205*
Tour operators
See also box, p208.
The tour companies listed below have been recommended, though even recommended companies have their off days.
AS Tours, Av Ferroviana 304J Eguivar 1751, T02-6932772. Also owns a hotel at the lakes.
Colque Tours, Av Potosí 54, T02-6932199, www.colquetours.com, can pay by Visa, Mastercard for a US$2 fee. The most popular agency, but not necessarily the best. As with many agencies, there have been bad reports about the way they deal with complaints. Colque specialize in tours ending up in San Pedro de Atacama, in Chile, where they have an office offering the trip in reverse. Even if you're heading back north to La Paz, the route through Chile may not be a bad idea – it's easy to find transport via Arica and the roads are substantially smoother. However, don't let Colque bully you into this – remember that it's in their interests to have empty jeeps for their return tours.
Esmeralda, Av Ferroviaria esquina Arce, T02-6932130. Good tours at the cheaper end of price bracket.
Pucara, Plaza Arce 4, T02-6932055.
Toñito, Av Ferroviaria 152, T02-6932819, www.bolivianexpeditions.com. Toñito own a hotel by the Salar and also have an office in La Paz (see page 123) which will book transport to and from Uyuni.
Transandino, Plaza Arce 2, T02-6932132.
Uyuni Andes Travel Office, Ayacucho 222, T02-6932227, good reports, run by Belgians Isabelle and Iver.
Licancabur, Sucre s/n, T02-6932667. Incorporates the usual trip with a journey to Tupiza, passing several beautiful and seldom-visited lagoons on the way.

○ Transport

Uyuni *p204, map p205*
Bus
All the bus offices are on Av Arce, on the same block as the post office. Departures are with several companies and daily unless otherwise stated.
To **La Paz** (change at Oruro) 2000 (also 1930 every day with **Belgrano** except Thu when they leave at 2100), US$7.45, 11-13 hrs. **Panasur** go direct Wed and Sun at 1800. From La Paz, **Panasur** leave the bus terminal (office 39) every day at 1730 and arrive at 0730 (change at Oruro, direct Tue and Fri). To Oruro at 2000, (also 1930 every day with **Belgrano** except Thu when they leave at 2100), US$3, 8 hrs (take a sleeping bag, or blanket).
    To **Potosí** 1000 and 1900, US$3, 5-7 hrs (spectacular journey). To **Sucre** 1000, 1900, US$3.75, 9-10 hrs. To **Tupiza** Wed and Sun 0900, US$5.25, 10 hrs (this is a very bad road – take the train if you can wait for the right day). To **Camargo** (via Potosí) 1000, US$6.70, 11-12 hrs. To **Tarija** (via Potosí) 1000, US$8.95, 14 hrs. To **Challapata** (change for buses to Oruro and La Paz or Potosí), daily at 2000 (with **Predilecto**) and Sat 0500, US$3, 6 hrs. To **Avaroa** Mon, Thu 0400 (with **Predilecto** and **Trans 11 de Julio**), US$5.25, 5 hrs. To get to **Chile** by road transport, see page 200.

Jeep
Trans Expreso Rapido, T02-6932839, office in same place as bus companies, goes to: **Atocha** daily at 0800 and 0900, US$3.75, 2 hrs, which, on Wed and Sun, continues to **Tupiza** US$7.45. To **Potosí** and **Oruro** by special charter US$150 for up to 10 people, 5 hrs each. **Colque Tours** also runs jeep trips to **Potosí**, US$200 for 6-7 people.

Train
Check train services on arrival, T02-6932153. **Nuevo Expreso del Sur** leaves for **Oruro** on Tue and Sat at 2352, arriving 0625 (Premiere US$7.75; Salon US$5.40). The **Wara Wara del Sur** service leaves on Mon and Thu at 0122, arriving 0825 (Salón US$4.20). To **Atocha**, **Tupiza** and **Villazón**: **Expreso del Sur** leaves Uyuni on Mon and Fri at 2216, arriving, respectively, at 0015, 0315 and, eventually, 0620 (Premier US$4.95, US$9.70 and

US$14.65; Salón US$1.95, US$4.20 and US$6.40). The **Wara Wara** service leaves on Sun and Wed at 0235, arriving 0430, 0800 and 1135 (Salón US$1.65, US$3,45 and US$5.10). The 2 companies return at 1530, **Expresso del Sur** (over an hr quicker) on Tue and Sat, **Wara Wara** on Mon and Thu. Ticket office opens at 0830 and 1430 each day and 1 hr before the trains leave. It closes once tickets are sold – get there early or buy through a tour agent.

❶ Directory

Uyuni *p204, map p205*

Banks Banco de Crédito, Av Potosí, between Bolivar and Arce, does not change money, though they may give cash advances from credit cards. The exchange shop to its left changes US dollars or Chilean pesos as well as travellers' cheques as does a cambio almost opposite **M@c Internet Café** on Av Potosí (see below). **Hotel Avenida** changes dollars cash. Some shops will change cash dollars for bolivianos. All agencies and some shops accept payment in travellers' cheques.

Internet all US$1.50 per hr: **M@cNet**, Av Potosí near Arce, open every day 0900-2300 or later if you ask, fast satellite connection. **Servinet Uyuni**, Potosí y Bolívar, open every day 0800-1300, 1400-2200.

Laundry Lavarap laundry, Av Ferroviaria 253. Some hotels also offer a service. **Post office** at Av Arce corner with Cabrera, Mon-Thu 0830-1200, 1400-1900, Fri 0830-1900, Sat and Sun 0900-1200.

Telephone Entel at Av Arce above Av Potosí, 0830-2200 every day. **Useful addresses** Immigration is at Av Potosí corner with Sucre, open 0800-2000 every day, for visa extensions; don't leave it to the last minute as often the officer is at the new border exit offices. **Reserva Eduardo Avaroa** (REA) office Av Potosí 23 (ring the top bell, suffers from sporadic opening hours) has an excellent full colour map and guide to the reserve for US$2 and full-colour birdguide *Aves de la Reserva Nacional de Fauna Andina Eduardo Avaroa* by Omar Rocha and Carmen Quiroga (Museo Nacional de Historia Natural, La Paz 1996 both in Spanish). This is also available from the tourist office and the REA headquarters at Laguna Colorada.

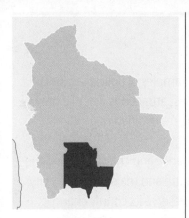

⁑ Footprint features

Introduction

Sucre and Potosí are the finest examples of Bolivia's colonial heritage and two of its main tourist attractions. They lie only three hours apart but couldn't be more different.

Sucre exudes the assured confidence and charm befitting the country's official capital, legal centre and major university city. Isolation has helped the city to preserve its courtly charm. Surrounding this sparkling white colonial masterpiece is a hinterland of traditional weaving villages which burst into life during their frequent market days and festivals. Dinosaur-hunters are also making tracks for Sucre, with the discovery of many prehistoric footprints. Ask Bolivians where in their country you should go and they will mostly answer 'Sucre'.

Potosí is not only the highest city in the world, at over 4,000 m, but was once the largest, wealthiest city in the Americas. It now has the air of a dignified, but destitute old man showing the signs of a decadent past. All around are reminders of its silver-mining heyday, from the many crumbling colonial buildings, to the massive mint, where the silver was smelted into coins for the Spanish Crown. Towering over the city is the giant pink hulk of Cerro Rico – Rich Mountain – from which the silver was extracted, at an unimaginable human cost. Visitors can burrow down into its bowels through a series of tunnels and shafts, meet the devil face to face, and experience what life was like many centuries ago for those who were forced to enter the 'Mouth of Hell'.

Further south, **Tarija** is the country's wine centre in an isolated and little-visited area with a great climate. **Tupiza** is a mining town turned popular traveller's destination, in a verdant valley surrounded by a dramatic desert landscape. Nearby **San Vincente** is where Butch Cassidy and the Sundance Kid died.

★ Don't miss...

❶ **Dinosaur footprints** Walk with dinosaurs – well, their ancient remains – in the hills around Sucre, page 225.

❷ **Textile shopping** Go in search of the best Bolivian textiles in the little weaving villages around Sucre, page 227.

❸ **The Casa Nacional de Moneda** Visit the greatest testament to colonial greed in all Latin America, the mint in Potosí, page 240.

❹ **Cerro Rico** Dig deep with the miners and explore the 16th century mineworkings here at 'Rich Mountain', which is said to have produced enough silver to pave a road all the way to Madrid, page 242.

❺ **Tarija** Sit in a pavement café on the main plaza and enjoy the sun and friendly bustle of *Chapaco* life, page 251.

❻ **Winetasting** Take a trip out to one of the famous bodegas around Tarija, where you can sample the finest Bolivian wines, page 255.

❼ **Party at the fiesta** Time your visit to coincide with Tarija's excellent *Fiesta de San Roque*, held during the first week of September, page 260.

❽ **The trail of the Wild West outlaws** Follow in the footsteps of Butch Cassidy and the Sundance Kid all the way to their final resting place, page 265.

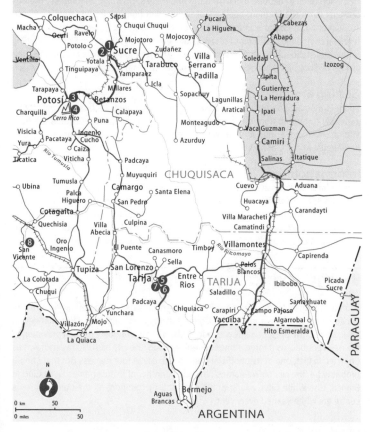

Sucre → *Phone code: 04. Colour map 3, grid B4. Population: 131,769. Altitude: 2,790 m.*

In 1992 UNESCO declared the city a 'Patrimonio Histórico y Cultural de la Humanidad' and it's easy to see why. It's an absolute must for enthusiasts of colonial religious architecture, with many beautiful churches, all painted white except San Felipe Neri which is faced in brick. Sucre is not just a colonial museum, though, but a thriving university city. It is known as the student capital of Bolivia and thousands of young students fill every street, plaza, bar and café. There are two universities, the oldest, **Universidad de San Francisco Xavier**, *dates from 1624. This was the main source of libertarian thought and gave birth to the very first demands for independence heard on the continent, on 25 May, 1809.* ➡➡ *For Sleeping, Eating and other listings, see pages 228-235.*

Ins and outs

Getting there
Juana Azurduy de Padilla **airport** is 5 km northwest of town (T04-6454445). The airport minibus goes from the entrance and will drop you off on Hernando Siles y Junín, in the centre. It returns from here, usually 1½ hours before flights leave; US$0.70, 20-30 minutes. A taxi from the centre is US$2-3. Trufis 1 and F go from the entrance to Hernando Siles y Loa, one block from the main plaza, US$0.55, 25 minutes. The **bus terminal** is on the northern outskirts of town, 3 km from centre on Ostria Gutiérrez, T04-6452029. A taxi to and from the centre is US$0.75 (5Bs) per person inside the terminal compound or US$0.45 (3Bs) outside. Alternatively take micro A or trufi 8 (going to the bus station, from Av H Siles, between Arce and Junín). Taxis around town are always US$0.45 (Bs3) per person; pay no more.➡➡ *See Transport, page 233, for further details.*

Getting around
Sucre is a small, compact city and easy to explore on foot. Its busy narrow streets generally run uphill from the plaza eastwards and downhill west towards the train station. It enjoys a mild climate with an average daytime temperature of 24°C in July-August and 7°C at night .

Information
Tourist information is available downstairs in the **bus terminal** ⓘ *Mon-Fri 1000-1230 and 1500-1730, Sat 0800-1200 (but often shut)*; and the **airport**, to coincide with incoming flights; in town and upstairs at the **Casa de la Cultura** ⓘ *Argentina 65, T04-6427102, Mon-Fri 0800-1200, 1400-1600.* For maps try **Instituto Geográfico Militar** ⓘ *Arce 172, 1st floor, T04-6455514. Mon-Fri 0830-1200, 1430-1800.*

Background

Founded in 1538 by the Spaniard Pedro de Anzúres as the city of La Plata, Sucre became capital of the audiencia of Charcas in 1559. Its name was later changed to Chuquisaca. The present name was adopted in 1825 in honour of the first president of the new republic. As if three names weren't enough, the city has also been known as Charcas. In fact, one of its unofficial titles is 'the city of four names'. But that should probably be 'the city of five names', because another of its nicknames is 'La Ciudad Blanca' (the White City), owing to the fact that, by tradition, all the buildings in its centre are whitewashed every year.

Around the centre

The city's heart is the spacious, elegant **Plaza 25 de Mayo**. Here, the local residents, or *Sucrenses* as they are called, sit and chat, shaded from the midday sun by palm and ceibo trees. The plaza is surrounded by fine buildings. Among these are the **Casa de la Libertad** ① *25 de Mayo 11, T04-6454200, Mon-Fri 0900-1115, 1430-1745, Sat 0930-1115, US$1.50, photo permit US$1.50 more, videos US$3, includes guided tours in English (Auroa is good) or Spanish*, formerly the Assembly Hall of the Jesuit University, where the country's Declaration of Independence was signed on 6 August 1825. The actual document is on display. Also among its treasures is a famous portrait of Simón Bolívar by the Peruvian artist Gil de Castro, which claims to have the greatest likeness of the man.

Also on the plaza is the beautiful 17th-century **cathedral** ① *Mon-Fri 1000-1200, 1500-1700, Sat 1000-1200, US$1.50, if the door is locked wait for the guide*. A look inside is recommended, especially to see the famous jewel-encrusted Virgen de Guadalupe (1601), as well as works by the Italian Bernardo Bitti, the first great painter of the New World, who studied under Raphael, and other church treasures. Entrance to the cathedral is through the museum, halfway down Calle Nicolás Ortiz, opposite La Vieja Bodega. If you're outside opening hours, the main door will obviously be unlocked during mass. Times change frequently, or are not observed at all.

Two blocks from the main plaza, on Calle Nicolás Ortiz, is the 17th-century **San Felipe Neri church and monastery** ① *Access to the roof is only possible for an hour between 1600 and 1800 (times change), US$1 with a free guide from Universidad de Turismo office on Plaza 25 de Mayo 22. T04-6454333 for latest details*, built in the neoclassical style with an attractive courtyard. The monastery is now used as a school and the church is closed, except for the roof which offers views over the entire city. You can ask to see inside the church.

The church of **Santa Mónica**, at the corner of Arenales y Junín, is perhaps one of the finest gems of Spanish architecture in the Americas, but has been closed to visitors since 1995. Another church, **San Francisco** ① *0700-1200, 1500-1900*, in Calle Ravelo, has altars coated in gold leaf, and 17th-century ceilings. The bell is the one that summoned the people of Sucre to fight for independence. Another one of Sucre's fine churches is the church of **San Miguel** ① *1130-1200, no shorts, short skirts or short sleeves*. Completed in 1628, it has been restored and is very beautiful with Moorish-style carved and painted ceilings, pure-white walls and a gold and silver altar. In the Sacristy some early sculpture can be seen. It was from San Miguel that Jesuit missionaries went south to convert Argentina, Uruguay and Paraguay.

San Lázaro ① *Mass daily 0630-0730, 1830-1930*, at Calvo y Padilla, built in 1538, is regarded as Sucre's first cathedral. On the nave walls are six paintings attributed to Zurbarán. It also has fine silverwork and alabaster in the Baptistery.

The **Museo Arte Indígena** ① *San Alberto 413 y Potosí, T04-6453841, www.bolivia net.com/asur Jul-Sep Mon-Sat 0830-1200, 1430-1800, Oct-Jun Mon-Fri 0830-1200, 1430-1800, Sat 0930-1200*, is housed in the Caserón de la Capellanía. It is run by **Antropológicas del Sur Andino** (ASUR). A visit is highly recommended for explanations of local indigenous groups and their distinctive textiles. Their Jalq'a exhibit is perhaps the finest display of Bolivian ethnography now available. It includes superb examples of contemporary daily dress, as well as ritual costumes, a film of dances, live weaving demonstrations, photographs of earlier weavings and clear and fulsome explanations of their history and descriptions of the iconography of the textiles. The knowledgeable and helpful staff can also arrange visits to the villages where the textile traditions have been revived. There's also a handicrafts shop downstairs which supports the project. There's a lot to see but tickets can be used again the following day.

Sucre

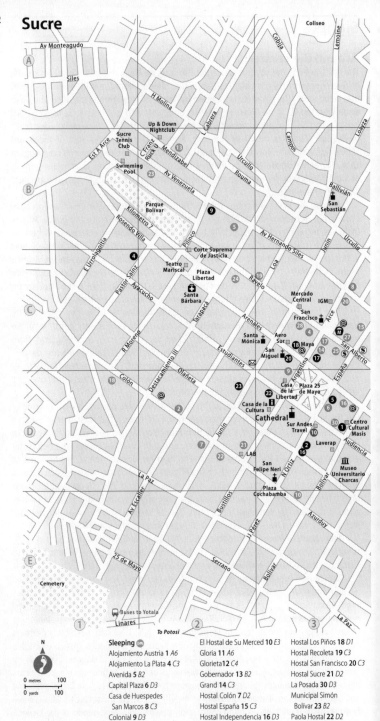

N

0 metres 100
0 yards 100

Sleeping

Alojamiento Austria **1** A6
Alojamiento La Plata **4** C3
Avenida **5** B2
Capital Plaza **6** D3
Casa de Huespedes
 San Marcos **8** C3
Colonial **9** D3
Cruz de Popoyan **2** D2

El Hostal de Su Merced **10** E3
Gloria **11** A6
Glorieta **12** C4
Gobernador **13** B2
Grand **14** C3
Hostal Colón **7** D2
Hostal España **15** C3
Hostal Independencia **16** D3
Hostal Libertad **17** C3

Hostal Los Piños **18** D1
Hostal Recoleta **19** C3
Hostal San Francisco **20** C3
Hostal Sucre **21** D2
La Posada **30** D3
Municipal Simón
 Bolívar **23** B2
Paola Hostal **22** D2
Potosí **24** C2

Premier **25** C3
Real Audiencia **26** D4
Residencial Bolivia **27** C3
Residencial Charcas **28** C3

Eating
Arco Iris **1** D3
Bibliocafé Sureña **2** D3
Café Hacheh **4** C1

Café Mirador **15** E5
La Plaza & Pizzeria
 Napolitana **5** D3
El Germen **8** D4
El Olivo **23** D2
Guardamontes **9** B2
Kultur-Café Berlin **13** D4
La Casona **14** A6
La Repizza **16** D3

La Taverne **17** C3
Maxim **18** C3
Penco
 Penquito **20** C3
Salon de Té Las
 Delicias **22** D3

Bars & clubs
Joy Ride Café **10** D3

The university's anthropological, archaeological, folkloric, and colonial collections are on view at the **Museo Universitario Charcas** ① *Bolívar 698, Mon-Fri, 0800-2000, Sat and Sun 0830-1200, 1500-1800, US$2.60, photos US$1.50,* and its presidential and modern-art galleries.

The **Museo de Santa Clara** ① *C Calvo 212, Mon-Fri 0900-1200, 1500-1800, Sat 0900-1200, US$0.75,* is next to the convent of the same name. It was founded in 1639 and amongst its displays is a valuable collection of works by Melchor Pérez Holguin, and his teacher, the Italian Bernardo Bitti. They also have exhibits of books, vestments, some silver and musical instruments (including a 1664 organ). There is a window to view the church and small items made by the nuns are on sale.

Also there's the **Museo de Historia Natural**, on the central plaza, close to the tourist information centre, containing various stuffed animals. Upstairs is **Museo Valenzuela** ① *Both museums Mon-Fri 0800-2000, Sat 0900-1200, 1500-1800, Sun 0900-1200. US$1.20,* housing works of art, sculptures and furniture collected by Sucre journalist and politician Doctor Alfredo Gutiérrez Valenzuela (1901-72). The three-tier candelabra from his home round the corner (**Hostal Independencia**) hung so low the museum could only fit in the top layer.

Four blocks northwest of Plaza 25 de Mayo is the modern **Corte Suprema de Justicia** ① *Free,* the seat of Bolivia's judiciary. You must be smartly dressed; leave your passport with the guard; a guide can be found in the library.

The nearby **Parque Bolívar** contains a monument and a miniature of the Eiffel tower in honour of Bolivia's richest 20th century tin baron, Francisco Argandoña, who created much of Sucre's latter-day splendour.

The column opposite the **Teatro Mariscal**, in the nearby **Plaza Libertad**, was erected with the money raised by fining the bakers who cheated on the size and weight of their bread. Also on this plaza is the 16th century **Hospital Santa Bárbara** (still in use).

Southeast of the city, on Plaza Pedro de Anzúres at the top of Calle Dalence, is the Franciscan monastery of **La Recoleta** with good views over the city. The monastery, which was founded in 1601 by the Franciscans, is notable for the beauty of its cloisters and gardens. An adjoining chapel still contains the intricately carved wooden choirstalls above the nave. See also the martyrs transfixed by lances. Inside the monastery is the **Museo de la Recoleta** ① *Mon-Fri 0900-1130, 1430-1630, Sat only with guides from tourist agency and minimum of 10 people. US$1.20 for entrance to all collections, guided tours only – you may have to wait; US$0.30 for use of camera.* In the grounds is the Cedro Milenario, a 1,000-year-old cedar tree.

Opposite the monastery on the far right-hand side of the plaza is **Museo de los Niños Tanga Tanga** ① *T04-6440299, Tue-Sun 0900-1200 and 1430-1800,* which has books, dance, art and workshops for children based in two exhibition halls that were once huge water tanks. Legend says Tanga-Tanga was a chieftain who had to take gold, silver and precious stones to satisfy the Spanish power and set Inca Atahuallpa free. When he heard his master had been killed, he is said to have buried the treasure close to the museum. The museum has the goal of providing the 'treasure' of education to Sucre children, hence the name. Outside is **Café Mirador** with the best view in Sucre (see Eating, page 231).

Behind the monastery a road flanked by Stations of the Cross climbs the attractive, eucalyptus-covered **Cerro Churuquella**, to a statue of Christ at the top. The **cemetery** ① *Take Calle Junín south to its end, 7 or 8 blocks from the main plaza,* is worth visiting to see the mausoleums of presidents and other famous people; boys give guided tours.

Around Sucre

Castillo de la Glorieta → *See also Transport, page 233.*
ⓘ *Daily 0830-1200, 1400-1800, US$1.05, includes a free guide but a tip is expected, you may need your passport. Take any bus bus marked 'Liceo Militiar' from the main Plaza or a bus or trufi marked 4 or E.*

Five kilometres south of Sucre on the Potosí road is the grandiose **Castillo de la Glorieta**. The former mansion of the wealthy industrialist, Don Francisco Argandoña, was built at the end of the 19th century in a miniature estate with Venetian-style canals, beautiful gardens and fountains. The residential palace is an exotic mixture of Moorish, Spanish and French architectural styles.

Don Francisco's wife became known as 'La Princesa de la Glorieta', a title bestowed on her by the Pope in recognition of her work with local orphans. Ask to see the paintings of the visit by the Pope, in a locked room. There's no extra charge, but no cameras are allowed. Today, the house and gardens are run down, but restoration is under way after years of military use and neglect. The former mansion stands in the military compound.

Cal Orcko
ⓘ *DinoTruck leaves every day at 0930, 1200 and 1430, US$3.75. The tourist office can recommend taxi drivers who have trained as guides, US$10. Untrained drivers charge US$6 per person.*

The best known and most accessible of the region's many **dinosaur tracks** are at the Fanseca cement factory, 3 km out of town. A theme park is proposed, which may take years but will eventually protect (but also move away from human touch) the footprints. There are around 5,000 footprints, making it possibly the world's largest paleontological site. The footprints are on the steep side of a rockface but it's not hard to imagine that once this was a flat muddy plain. One single set of footprints continues for 350 m. The tracks were discovered by the workers in 1994, but it took some time for them to be fully identified. There are three main types of tracks: Sauropdos, or Titanosauros, which was a giant slow-moving herbivorous quadruped which left tracks visible from the road, each about 50 cm in diameter; Anguilosaurios, which moved faster and had bony plates forming a crest on its back and walked on four legs, leaving tracks about 20-25 cm in diameter; and Teropodos, a fast-running three-toed, two-footed carnivore, with short front arms. Access is through the factory, and you should be accompanied by a company employee. Take the fantastically cheesy **DinoTruck** tour from outside the cathedral. You'll ride in the back of a red and yellow lorry with a painted stegosaurus on its side – best to go disguised but don't miss all the smiles you'll get as you drive through Sucre. Excellent explanations in good English.

Condor K'ak'a
This small farm owned by the Tango family is north of Yamparez. As many as 17 condors have been sighted at one time and at least one pair nests on the cliffs above the farm. Visits can be arranged for groups of up to 20, for US$20, and include transport from Sucre and a snack. From the end of the road there's a 2 km walk. You can also bring a tent and camp. Call Mario Tango, T/F04-6453256. He also has video shots of the condors.

Other trips from Sucre → *See also Transport, page 233.*
Another popular day trip from Sucre is the **Siete Cascadas**. Take bus D to Alto Delicias. Get off and walk for 4 km down the creek and turn left into the tributary where the falls are located. The river is full from November to April, after which the swimming holes dry up.

⦂ Reviving the past

The textile traditions of the Chuquisaca area might have vanished into obscurity had it not been for the dedication and hard work of two anthropologists, Spanish-born Gabriel Martínez and his Chilean wife Verónica Cereceda. They set out to trace the origins of a number of weavings which, years before, had been passed off as antiques in tourist shops in La Paz and other Bolivian cities.

Little was known about the creators of these textiles. Collectors and merchants referred to them as 'Potolo pieces', after the largest town (of some 600 families) in the area of their origin, 50 km northeast of Sucre. This area was inhabited by an impoverished group of nearly 25,000 people who called themselves Jalq'a.

Martínez and Cereceda, along with Bolivian ethnologist Ramiro Molina, were pleased to see most villagers still wearing traditional dress, but the women's axsus, or overskirts, were a pale reflection of the weavings that had inspired their search. Gone were the subtle colours and exotic animal motifs, replaced by repetitive rows of geometric designs.

The reason for this was economic necessity. In the 1960s and 70s a ready source of much-needed income became available. A growing market for Andean textiles among tourists and overseas dealers spawned many traders who scoured the countryside for ponchos, shawls, axsus, belts and bags to sell on. The Jalq'a motifs were particularly sought after, but the people never learned the true market value of their finest textiles.

When the boom was over the Jalq'a found the core of their weaving inheritance – their ritual costumes, wedding garments and family heirlooms – gone. With no models to inspire the next generation of weavers, the tradition seemed to have vanished for ever.

But Martínez and Cereceda were determined to revive the ancient weaving traditions in this area. They started a organization (GSO) called Antropólogos del Sur Andino (ASUR), whose centre can be visited in Sucre. ASUR encouraged the ritual life among the Jalq'a communities. They also wanted to recover traditional songs and dances which had been fading from community life and encourage the wearing of traditional costumes at festivals.

The main problem was that women still knew how to weave, but they could not recall the many strange animals, called khurus, which had been the hallmark of the Jalq'a designs. The solution was to contact the dealers and collectors in Bolivia and overseas and get them to send photographs of their weavings. Eventually enough photographs were assembled to be circulated throughout the local communities, inspiring renewed enthusiasm in their tradition and provoking a textile revival.

But that was not enough. Martínez and Cereceda wanted to let the outside world know what was going on. They collected the best of the new textiles and showcased them throughout Bolivia. This created a new respect among city dwellers not only for the neglected Jalq'a but also for other ethnic groups in the region. The effects of this were great. The price of the textiles began to rise along with the quality of weaving and women began to create their own designs, proving that the Jalq'a were at last back in touch with the same cultural sources that inspired their ancestors. This time the Jalq'a understood the value of what they were producing and could meet outside demand without selling off their inheritance. (Adapted from an article by Kevin Healy in Grassroots Development, 1992).

Quila Quila is 2½ hours away from Sucre and also has dinosaur tracks, as well as some cave paintings. An early start is needed to do it in one day and food and drink should be taken. A guide can be found in the village; ask for Epifanio, who may guide or simply help with finding a guide. Buses go from Calle La Paz near Radio Colosal from 0600-1000.

South of Sucre, 30 minutes by trufi, is the village of **Yotala**. Carnival is celebrated here a week later than everywhere else. There's one hotel on the plaza and several restaurants have pools and saunas, offering parrillada, mostly on the weekend (see Eating, page 231). There's a good two-hour hike from here to Cachimayu.

A further 5 km beyond Yotala is the village of **Kantu Nucchu**. Here, facing Cachimayu River, is a 300-year-old colonial hacienda and mill, where you can stay (see Sleeping, page 230). From here you can hike into the hills, visit campesino villages and see dinosaur tracks. Or, if you're staying, you can swim in the river or chill out in the hammocks around the garden where you can watch the hummingbirds and parrots.

Tarabuco

One of the most interesting trips from Sucre is to the village of Tarabuco, 64 km southeast on a good road. It is famous for its very colourful **market** on Sunday. The local people still wear their traditional dress of conquistador-style helmets, multi-coloured ponchos, *chuspas* (bags for carrying coca leaves) and the elaborate *axsu*, an overskirt worn by women.

The market starts around 0930-1000 and has been described as a bit of a tourist trap, but many still find it an enjoyable experience. Those in search of a bargain should have an idea about the quality on offer before buying. Many of the sellers come to Sucre through the week. The market is not held at Carnival (when all Tarabuco is dancing in Sucre), Easter Sunday or on a holiday weekend in November.

In **March** thousands of campesinos from the area join tourists and Sucrenses in the celebration of **Phujllay**, one of the best traditional festivals in the country. It is held in celebration of the Battle of Jumbate when the local people defeated the Spaniards on 12 March 1816. It is a very colourful and lively affair with great music, local food and the obligatory chicha. No one sleeps during this fiesta so there are no accommodation problems. On the first Sunday in **October** is Virgen del Rosario.

▸▸ *For Sleeping, Eating and other listings, see following pages.*

The weavers' villages

The weavers' village nearby include **Candelaria** (two hours by truck from Tarabuco), **Macha** (eight hours from Sucre), **Pocata** (one hour from Macha), or **Ravelo** (59 km northwest of Sucre). At **Punilla**, on the road to Ravelo, there is a 2½-hour walk to **Incamachay** where there are pre-Columbian drawings. Punilla is where you leave the truck for Challanaca and go on to **Potolo**, with its distinctive textile designs of red zoomorphic figures on a black or brown background. You can buy direct from the weavers – there are no stores – but it can be difficult to find them. The bus to Llalllagua passes through Ravelo, Macha, Ocuri and Uncia and much of the area where the Tinkus are held. A Sucre family runs tours to these villages. Husband and wife Lucho and Dely Lonedo (T04-6420752) both speak Quechua and their son speaks English. Can be part of a hike up to five days using transport to suit various budgets. ▸▸ *See also Transport, page 233.*

Southeast from Sucre

The main road southeast from Tarabuco continues towards ever greener valleys and mountains that signal the proximity of the tropical eastern lowlands. The road winds through Monteagudo (see below), Camiri and Boyuibe to the border with Paraguay at

Hito Villazón (see Eastern Lowlands chapter, page 6). Hito Villazón is not to be confused with the other Villazón on the border with Argentina.

At **Padilla**, a turn-off heads north 20 km to **Villa Serrano**, where the musician Mauro Núñez lived. A music festival is held on 28-29 December. It is a beautiful journey through wild mountains. This road continues towards the tiny settlement of **La Higuera**, famous as the scene of Ché Guevara's fatal last battle (see page 318). Buses leave from Sucre for Villa Serrano at 0700 and 1600 daily (six hours).

Eight hours from Sucre, at Km 323, is **Monteagudo**, lying in the sub-tropics at 1,138 m. There are several basic hotels and transport, see below.

Sucre to Potosí

The road to Potosí, 164 km southwest of Sucre, is fully paved. It goes through **Betanzos**, where there are a few *alojamientos* (**G**), and a hotel (**F**). The town holds its *Feria de Papas* within the first two weeks of May with folk dances, music and costumes. There is also a good market and 6 km away there are well-preserved rock paintings at Incahuasi. The road also passes **Don Diego** and **Chaqui**. Frequent buses leave from Plaza Uyuni and the cemetery in Potosí (US$0.70, one hour).

● Sleeping

Sucre *p220, map p222*
A **Glorieta**, Bolívar y Urcullo, T/F04-6443777, mirusta@mara.scr.entelnet.bo Modern 4-star business hotel, its disco Micerino (from 2000, free entry) is due to open after refurbishment.
A **Real Audiencia**, Potosí 142, T04-6460823, F04-6460823. 4-star, excellent restaurant, swimming pool, sauna, massages, views from lounge, all rooms have cable TV, room service, modern. Recommended.
B **Capital Plaza**, Plaza 25 de Mayo 28, T04-6422999, F04-6453588, www.capitalplazahotel.com. Beautiful colonial building, well-appointed rooms, swimming pool. Accepts credit cards.
B **El Hostal de Su Merced**, Azurduy 16, T04-6442706, F04-6912078. Converted 18th-century building, beautiful, comfortable, very helpful. Highly recommended.
B **La Posada**, Calle Audencia 92, T6460101, www.laposadahostal.com. A smart, central, colonial-style hotel with comfortable rooms with big beds and wooden beams. There's also a good courtyard restaurant (see Eating). Worth asking for a discount.
B **Premier**, San Alberto 43, T04-6452097, F04-6441232, premierhotel@hotmail.com. Includes buffet breakfast, fridge, room service and cable TV. Receptionists speak English. Modern and not the most attractive place but great beds, showers and service.

Matrimoniales and suites have bathtubs. Rooms have computers, but no internet.
B **Hostal Independencia**, Calvo 31, T04-6442256, F04-6461369, jacosta@mara.scr.entelnet.bo. Former colonial home of Dr Alfredo Gutiérrez Valenzuela, has a spectacular salón worth seeing even if you don't stay here, with gilding, chandeliers, spiral stairs and lots of velvet. The verdant courtyard is draped in greenery and towering palms and enormous rooms have oversized TVs and baths to match.
B **Paola Hostal**, Colón 138, T04-6454978, www.scr.cnb.net/~molincom. Smart, clean and helpful colonial house with modern rooms, some with bathtub, cable TV. Discount for two nights or more. Covered courtyard and small, green, sheltered garden. Buffet breakfast included. Some good views from higher rooms.
C **Colonial**, Plaza 25 de Mayo 3, T04-6440309, F04-6440311, hoscol@mara. scr.entelnet.bo. The Colonial is grander than its plain corridors and courtyard might suggest. Some rooms are noisy, the best room of all has a bathtub, an enormous bed and a great view overlooking the Plaza. Good continental breakfast included.
C **Hostal España**, España 138, T04-6440859, F04-6453388, hespana@unete.com. Cable TV and buffet breakfast included. Electric showers and foam beds but comfortable,

light and very modern. Apartments for up to 5 people for US$60.

C **Hostal Libertad**, Arce 99 y San Alberto, 1st floor, T04-6453101, F04-6460128. Clean and friendly with spacious comfortable rooms with cable TV and heating. Open stairs, well-equipped but characterless rooms, some with decent views.

C **Hostal Recoleta**, Ravelo 205, T04-6454789. Bright and friendly place, clean and kitted out in a lovely colonial style. Rooms have cable TV and phone. Price includes buffet breakfast.

C **Hostal Sucre**, Bustillos 113, T04-6451411, F04-6461928, hostalsucre@hotmail.com. A colonial place with rooms set around 2 courtyards with lots of winding stairs and corridors. Rooms have less character than the rest of the hotel but are comfortable, with TV, telephone and room service. Those at the back are quieter. Breakfast included.

C-D **Municipal Simón Bolívar**, Av Venezuela 1052, T04-6455508, F04-6451216. With restaurant, breakfast included in interior courtyard, very comfortable, helpful.

D **Alojamiento Austria**, Ostria Gutiérrez 506, T04-6454202, near the bus terminal. (F rooms also available). Modern, newly decorated, great beds and carpeted rooms, some with cable TV, cafeteria, parking (must pay if in cheaper rooms).

D **Gobernador**, Mendizabel 27, T/F04-6461505. Comfortable, friendly, quiet, includes continental breakfast, parking (US$1 per day), open 24 hrs. Recommended.

D **Grand**, Arce 61, T04-6451704, F04-6452461. Comfortable rooms with private bathrooms, hot showers and cable TV. There are lots of courtyards and plants and the price includes continental breakfast in room. Excellent central location, good value lunch in Arcos restaurant, laundry, safe, helpful. Recommended.

D **Hostal Los Piños**, Colón 502, T04-6454403, F04-6443343, H-Pinos@mara.scr.entelnet.bo. Comfortable but in need of a lick of paint. Carpets are shabby too but rooms have hot showers and cable TV, there's a great garden, a kitchen and free parking. It's also peaceful and friendly, though a bit away from the centre. Price includes breakfast.

E **Hostal Cruz de Popayan**, Calle Loa 881, T04-6440889. Comfy if rather dimly lit rooms around a sunny open courtyard with a tree.

Breakfast and internet are included but it's not as good value as they'd have you believe. Credit cards accepted. Extensive use of fake Footprint review.

E **Hostal San Francisco**, Av Arce 191 y Camargo, T04-6452117, F04-6462693, hostalsf@cotes.net.bo. A pristinely white hotel where rooms have private bathrooms, TV and phone. It's quiet and comfortable and rooms are centred around a large courtyard with a fountain. Breakfast is US$0.60 extra. Excellent value for money. Recommended.

E **Residencial Bolivia**, San Alberto 42, T04-6454346, F04-6453239. (F without private bathroom). Big hotel with spacious rooms and hot water in good bathrooms. Breakfast included, large sunny courtyard with seats, very pleasant and clean. Rooms at back lighter and quieter, downstairs rooms a bit dark. Recommended.

E **Residencial Charcas**, Ravelo 62, T04-6453972, F04-6455764, hostalcharcas@latinmail.com. (F without bathroom). Good value breakfast, sunny roof terrace, friendly and helpful but some rooms need redecoration. Reasonable but overpriced. Breakfast US$1.50-2. Runs bus to Tarabuco and back 0730 Sun, US$3.

F **Avenida**, Av Hernando Siles 942, T04-6452387. Hot showers, breakfast US$1, laundry, helpful, small, family-run, use of kitchen but good Argentine restaurant down road (see below).

F **Casa de Huespedes San Marcos**, Arce 223, T04-6462087. (G without bath). Lovely flower-filled Spanish patio, kitchen, friendly and quiet. Highly recommended.

F **Hostal Colón**, Colón 220, T04-6455823, colon220@bolivia.com. Family-run colonial house, quiet, basic but clean, laundry US$1 per kg, helpful owner speaks excellent English and German. Rooms overlook a courtyard with a flowering tree and a new coffee room opens out onto the street. Breakfast included. Small book exchange. Recommended.

G **Alojamiento El Dorado**, Loa 419. Hot showers, basic but clean and friendly.

G **Alojamiento La Plata**, Ravelo 32, T04-6452102. Popular place with no private bathrooms. Wooden floors, bathrooms a bit dingy. Beds sink, but it's set back from road and is quiet. Three hour laundry service.

G **Gloria**, Ostria Gutiérrez 438, T04-6452847. Opposite bus terminal. Clean, great value.

G **Potosí**, Ravelo 262, T/F04-6451975. castro@sucre.bo.net. Amongst the lawyers and notaries on Ravello, basic rooms are set around a courtyard with an enormous palm tree. The paint is peeling, and rooms are less than spotlessly clean but the tiled floors add character and the place is very good value.

Around Sucre p225

AL **Refugio Andino Bramadero**, near Chataquila, and Gato Diabólico 23 km from Sucre, bramader@yahoo.com or Restaurant Salamandra, Avaroa 510, T6913433. Or book through Joy Ride Café (see page 233). These fairy-tale cabins are in the middle of some beautiful countryside, with great walks from the front door. Good food, candlelight, hot water. All food and transport is included in the US$35 per person price. Family cottages or doubles and a big house too. Recommended.

A **Hacienda las Siete Cascadas**, Near Katalla, 8 km from Sucre, T04-6460603, 7cascadas@hotmail.com. Another all-inclusive rural hideaway hacienda complete with swimming pool, sports area and garden. Ask at Joy Ride Café (see page 233) for further information and bookings. US$25 per person.

Kantu Nucchu

C **Hacienda de los Molinos**. All meals are included and there are 2 more basic rooms (G per person) with 4 beds, kitchenettes and private bathrooms. Accommodation can even be had here free in exchange for light chores! The hacienda is rustic, beautiful and is being slowly restored. Reservations either T04-4380312 or drop in on Alberto Marion Argandoña at San Alberto 237, Sucre.

Tarabuco

There are at least 2 budget hotels, including G **Residencial Florida**, basic, cold and dirty, but serves a good almuerzo in the garden, with music and dancing, which is good fun.

Monteagudo

F **Fortín**, Plaza 20 de Agosto 1-2, T04-6472135, with bathroom, includes breakfast.

G **Alojamiento los Naranjos** on the road to the bus terminal, hot showers.

Eating

Sucre p220, map p222

$$ **Arco Iris**, Bolivar 567, T46423985. Swiss restaurant, good service, expensive but good, peña on Sat, excellent roesti, live music some nights.

$$ **El Huerto**, Ladislao Cabrera 86, T04-6451538. Take a taxi at night, set in a beautiful garden. Good almuerzo, international food with salad bar. Highly recommended.

$$ **Posada**, Calle Audencia 92, T04-6460101, www.laposadahostal.com, Mon-Sat 0700-2230, Sun 0700-1500. An upmarket restaurant in a courtyard with a palm tree. Quiet and laid-back, it is popular with local suits, generals and pilots. Great homemade lemonade.

$ **El Asador**, Plaza Cumaná 485. Very good steak and excellent fries.

$ **El Germen**, San Alberto 231. Open Mon-Sat 0800-2200. Very good vegetarian with good set lunches for US1.80 and excellent healthy breakfasts, US$1-1.50. Also chocolate cake, a good book exchange and German magazines. Recommended.

$ **El Olivo**, Junin, between Estudiantes and Olañeta. An eager to please little place behind a craft shop offering tofu skewers, soups, and almuerzos with a salad bar.

$ **Guardamontes**, Hernando Siles 958 block. Excellent steaks (locals say the best in town) and parrilladas.

$ **La Casona**, Ostria Guitiérrez 401, near and on same side as the bus terminal. Stylish, platos típicos, good value.

$ **La Plaza**, on the Plaza at No 33, T04-6455843, Mon-Sun 1200-0000. With a wooden balcony, good food and pisco sours, lots of fish dishes, very popular with locals, set lunch US$2.10.

$ **La Repizza**, N Ortiz 78. Very good value lunches, pizzas strangely sweet. Recommended.

$ **La Taverne**, Alliance Française, Aniceto Arce 35, ½ a block from the plaza. Mon-Sat 0800-2200. Peñas Fri and Sat. Good value French food in a setting with wooden beams and checked tablecloths, also regular films and cultural events. Good meeting place.

$ **Maxim**, Arenales 19, T04-6451798. Possibly the most chic restaurant in town, service does not live up to top quality food.

$ **Pizzería Napolitana**, on Plaza 25 de Mayo 30. Mon-Sat 1100-2300, Sun 1200-2300. Tasty if slightly doughy pizzas and good home-made ice cream. Wooden mezzanine and good lemon meringue pie. Six menu del dia options, US$2-2.50. Lunch available until 1700.

There are lots of cheap, good chicken and chips cafés on Av Hernando Siles between Arce and Loa. The best is **Pollos Claudia**. There are also many good, seriously cheap and clean food stalls in the central market.

Cafés

Amanecer, Pasaje Junín 810-B, T04-6451602. Opens 1530. Hard to find German pastelería, run by social project supporting disabled children. Excellent biscuits and cakes.

Bibliocafé Sureña, Nicolás Ortiz 50, near the plaza. Mon-Sat 1100-0200, Sun 1800-0200. Good pasta and light meals, crepes, music. Almuerzos, 1100-1600, for US$3. Atmospheric but service can be slow. And despite the name, there's a distinct shortage of books.

Café Bar Piccadilly, Ortiz, between Joy Ride and La Repizza. A little bar just off the Plaza serving beers, sandwiches, some pasta, crepes, aji and chilli con carne. There are wooden beams, a wagon wheel on the wall, and a good young mix of locals and gringos.

Café Hacheh, Pastor Sainz 233. 1000-0100. An unlikely but exceptionally good café and cultural centre, well worth the walk from the centre. The walls are adorned with lots of sexy designer nakedness, Chomsky and chess are laid out on tables, Pink Floyd plays on the stereo, and a Freddie Mercury lookalike stands behind the bar. Comfy chairs, crepes, good value juices, tasty sandwiches, real fireplace. The '70s café of your dreams. Ring the bell to be let in. Highly recommended.

Café Mirador, Plaza de la Recoleta, esq El Mirador, opposite Recoleta Monastery. T04-6440299, Tue-Sun 1000-1800. Has the best views of Sucre from its grassy terrace below the plaza. Good juices, fantastic iced cappuccino and equally good juices. Also

omelettes, crepes, pasta, cocktails. There's a book exchange too. The café is attached to the Tanga Tanga Museum (see page 224).

Kultur-Café Berlin, Avaroa 326. 0800-2400 (except Sun). A little slice of Germany. Part of a cultural centre (the Instituto Cultural Boliviano Alemán – ICBA) which includes a library and film room. Wooden tables, candles, arches, bar stools, wooden floor, black and white photos and letters, Sureña on tap, MTV on the telly. Peña every other Fri.

La Vieja Bodega, N Ortiz 38. Good food and cheapish wine in a slightly serious, barrel and ironwork filled place.

Penco Penquito, Arenales 108. Excellent coffee and cakes, in a strange fungus design interior. Be warned that many of the cakes and the lemon meringue pie can only be purchased whole.

Salon de Té Las Delicias, Estudiantes 50. Great cakes and snacks, favourite student hangout, open 1600-1900.

La Tertulia, Plaza 25 de Mayo 59, Italian and other dishes, could be great but let down by service. Good breakfasts.

Around Sucre p225
Quila Quila
Kutimuy, at Bolívar 181 (the road runs off the central plaza), T04-6480215, is good.

Tarabuco
There are 3 decent restaurants on the plaza and lots of foodstalls in the market offering tasty local dishes. See also **Residencial Florida** in Sleeping, above.

Bars and clubs

Sucre p220, map p222
Joy Ride Café, Nicolás Ortiz 14, T04-6425544 www.joyridebol.com. Mon-Sat 0730 until late (usually around 0200), weekends from 0900. Dutch-run. Good vibes and a popular night time haunt with great food and drink. Four types of Belgian beer are among the drinks from the bar and if you're lucky you might even find some Guinness. Try the nachos, pique a lo macho, chilli con carne, or the 'hangover eggs' (eggs fried with cheese, ham, onion, tomato and a splash of chilli),

which are talked about by travellers all over Bolivia. Good salads and a patio out the back with heating. A new, elegant and comfortable upstairs lounge with sofas has film showings Sun-Thu evenings. See also Tour operators, below, for details of their excellent biking and hiking trips. Highly recommended.

Julyo's Chop, Junín y Colón, T04-6452905. Popular bar, open late.

La Luna, at the back of Casa de la Cultura, Argentina 65, a popular video pub, sometimes with live music.

Mitsubanía, Av del Maestro corner with Av Venezuela, currently the most happening place, popular with a local, young, fashionable crowd, mixture of music with lots of cumbia, US$3 for men, women get in free.

Mitos, in front of Mercado Negro (ask the cabbie), smaller and slightly older crowd, US$0.75.

Up and Down, Mendizabal 222. Micerino in Hotel Glorieta (see Sleeping).

⦿ Entertainment

Sucre *p220, map p222*
Cinema
Cine Libertad, Calvo 126 y Bolívar.

Theatre
Teatro Mariscal, Plaza Libertad for music and plays.

⦿ Festivals and events

Sucre *p220, map p222*
Feb (moves dates), **Jueves de Compadres y Comadres**: held 10 days and 3 days respectively before Carnival.
Mar, **Pujllay**: in Tarabuco (see page 227).
Apr, **Domingo de Ramos**: also in Tarabuco.
25 May Celebrates the first move towards independence, most services, museums and restaurants are closed.
end May A car rally starts and finishes in the city, closing many of the surrounding roads.
16 Jul, Fiesta de la Virgen del Carmen: similar to Alasitas in La Paz (see page 118).
25 Jul, Fiesta de Santiago Apostol: Mass and processions and traditional music.
16 Aug, San Roque.
8 Sep, Virgen de Guadalupe: 2-day fiesta, followed by folkloric fiesta with dances and costumes from across Bolivia.
21 Sep, Día del Estudiante: music and dancing around the main plaza.
Oct/Nov, Festival Internacional de la Cultura, also held in Potosí, 2 weeks of cultural events.

⦿ Shopping

Sucre *p220, map p222*
Artesanías Calcha, Arce 103, opposite San Francisco Church, is recommended and the owner is very knowledgeable.
ASUR, Antropológicos del Sur Andino, in the Museo Arte Indígena, San Alberto 413, T04-6423841 (see Sights), sells weavings from around Tarabuco and from the Jalq'a; their weavings are more expensive, but of higher quality than elsewhere.
Artesanía Bolivia, Argentina 31, has a variety of arts and crafts from Tarabuco.
Chocolates Para Ti, San Alberto, just off the Plaza, T04-6454260, www.chocolates-para-ti.com. Chocaholics should note that Sucre is the chocolate capital of Bolivia, and this is one of its best chocolate shops. Service can be a little unfriendly but there's a huge selection of handmade chocolates.
Mercado Central is clean and colourful, with a wide variety of goods and many stalls selling artesanía. There are also lots of artesanía shops on the pedestrianised part of Junín between Ravelo and Hernando Siles. A bus from the central market will take you to the Mercado Campesino market on the outskirts of town, which is a vast, sprawling affair, selling local produce, second-hand clothing and some artesanía.
Camping equipment and gas is for sale at **Alfher**, San Alberto 25 (near Arce), Mon-Fri 0900-1230, 1500-2000, Sat 0900-1300, 1500-2100 and around the corner, same entrance as Hostal Libertad, at **Sport Camping**, Mon-Fri 0900-1230, 1400-1800, Sat 0900-1230 (doesn't have gas).

⦿ Activities and tours

Sucre *p220, map p222*
The **swimming pool** is on Av Venezuela, down passage before tennis courts, turn right at end, Sat and Sun only 1400-1800, US$0.75.
Sucre Tennis Club, Av Venezuela, good clay

courts, US$3 per person per hr including equipment, daily 0700-1200, 1500-1830.

Tour operators
Candelaria, Audencia 1, T04-6461661, F04-6460289. Owner Elizabeth has lots of local knowledge and was the curator of the Anthropological Museum for many years.
DinoTruck If you really fall in love with the DinoTruck you can also do a city tour in it – daily 1600, from outside the cathedral at 1630, Bs10 per person, minimum five people, book in advance, either after your dinosaur footprint tour, or by meeting the guides at 0930, 1200 or 1430 outside the cathedral.
Joy Ride Bolivia, C Mendizabal 229, T04-6425544, www.joyridebol.com, speak to Gert or Hans at Joy Ride Café (see Eating). Recommended for top-quality bike trips and guided walks among the hills of Sucre's attractive surroundings. Includes full safety gear, insurance and experienced guides. Longer trips from 2-9 days can take in Uyuni, Tupiza and Santa Cruz; contact in advance. Prices are dependent on numbers but start at around US$18 per person per day. Paragliding is also possible though they no longer run motorbike or quad trips. Put your name on the blackboard in the café if you're interested in making up a group.
Seatur, Plaza 25 de Mayo 24, T/F04-6462425, seatur@latinmail.com. Local tours, English, German, French spoken. Lucho Laredo and his son at C Panamá final 127, esquina Comarapa, Barrio Petrolero, organize treks in the surrounding area. Recommended.
Sur Andes, Nicolás Ortiz 6, T04-6453212, F04-6452632. Organizes trekking from half a day to 5 days, including to pre-Columbian sites such as Pumamachay and the Camino Prehispánico. You must take a sleeping bag and good shoes, everything else is provided.

⊖ Transport

Sucre *p220, map p222*
Air
Aero Sur and LAB fly to **La Paz** and **Santa Cruz**, LAB also flies to **Cochabamba**, **Tarija** and, like Aero Sur, to other parts of the country. Some are daily.
Airline offices Aero Sur, Arenales 31, T04-6462141, 204A, T04-6454895 (Toll free 0800 3030). **LAB**, Bustillos 127, T04-6454994,

F04-6452666 (Toll free 0800 3001), Mon-Fri 0830-1230, 1430-1830, Sat 0900-1200. **LANChile**, Arenales 209, T04-6453606.

Bus
All buses from Sucre bus terminal leave in the evening, except those to Potosí. There is an Enlace ATM outside and a post office inside (Mon-Sat 0800-1930, Sun 0900-1200).

Buses leave daily to/from: **La Paz** at 1430 (10 de Noviembre, 16 hrs via Potosí, US$6), 1730 (**Flota Copacabana**, bus cama, 15 hrs, US$7.50), 1730 (**Trans Copacabana**, buscama, 15 hrs, US$10.45).

To **Cochabamba**: several companies depart daily at 1830, arriving 0630, US$3 (bus cama, US$7.50).

To **Potosí**: 3 hrs on a good paved road. Frequently between 0630 (6 de Octubre) and 1800 (La Plata and Trans Capital), US$2.25. Silito Lindo taxis take 4 people to Potosí with door-to-door service for US$5; T04-6441014.

To **Tarija**: 0730 and 1230 (San Jorge), 1230 and 1330 (Trans Capital) 1245 (Emperador) and 0900 and 1500 (Andesbus), 16 hrs, US$8.95.

To **Uyuni**: 0700 (Emperador), 0800 (Trans Capital), 10 hrs, US$5.20. Alternatively you can catch a bus to Potosí and change; if possible book the connecting bus in advance as these fill up quickly. This can be done with **Trans Real Audencia**, Arce 99 y San Alberto (the same entrance as Hostal Libertad), T04-6443119, who also do hassle-free bus tickets reservations to: **Potosí** (0700, 1300, 1700, US$2.25), **Uyuni** (0700, 1300, US$6.70), **Villazón** and **Tupiza** (1300, US$7.45), **Tarabuco** (Sun 0700 from outside office, US$3 return).

To **Oruro**: 1700 with **Emperador** via Potosí, arrives at the ungodly hour of 0300, US$6 (bus cama, US$8.95).

To **Santa Cruz**: Many companies go between 1600 and 1730, 15 hrs, as cheap as US$4.50.

To **Villazón**: at 1300 (Transtin Dilrey, direct) and 1400 (Villa Imperial, via Potosí) both 15 hrs, US$8.20. To **Camiri**: at 1730 with Emperador, 18 hrs, US$11.95. Chaqueño leaves at 1630 and continues on to Yacuiba.

To get to **Aiquile**, take an early bus from the Parada de Camiones (see below) bound for Santa Cruz or Cochabamba, which arrives around 2200-2300. **Coop San Miguel** leaves for Aiquile on Sat and Thu at 1400. Trucks leave from the same area at around 0700.

The Parada de Camiones (truck stop) is for journeys to the north on the Santa Cruz or Cochabamba route; it's about 6 blocks north of the bus terminal, across from the gas station. Transport to the northwest leaves from Parque Mariscal Sucre, or by the first bridge on the road to the airport.

Car
Car rental Imbex, Serrano 165, T04-6461222, F04-6912687. Well-maintained jeeps.

Car mechanic at Camargo 450, recommended for Toyotas.

Motorcycle mechanic: Sr Jaime Medina, Motorservi Honda, C René Calvo Arana, T04-6425484. Will service all makes of machine. Also **Gonzalo Arce** at Hi-store Motos, Av Maestro, T/F04-64561627, speaks excellent German and some English, for Honda, Kawasaki and Yamaha, and Cannondale, Haro and Raleigh and Cannondale mountain bikes.

Taxi US$0.55 per person within the city limits.

Around Sucre p225
Yolata and Kantu Nucchu
Trufis (US$0.60) leave Sucre for **Yotala** (30 mins) and **Kantu Nucchu** (40 mins) from Mercado Campesino outside Carpintería San Juanillo, E Hochmann 231.

Tarabuco
Buses (US$1.25) and trucks leave from 0630 or when full from Plaza Huallparimachi, Av Manco Kapac and across the railway tracks (take micro B or C from opposite the Mercado); 2½-hr journey. A taxi costs US$45. On Sun at least 1 bus will wait on Ravelo by the Mercado Central for travellers, leaves at 0700, US$3 return to Tarabuco. Shared taxis can be arranged by hotels, with a pick-up service, starting at 0700, US$3.25 return. The first bus back is at 1300. **AndesBus** run a tourist service which departs at 0800, and returns at 1530, US$6. Transport is more difficult on weekdays; take an early bus and return by truck. A good guide to Tarabuco is Alberto from the Sucre tourist office, US$45 for a full day in a car for 4 people.

Buses for Tarabuco and the southeast leave from the area around Plaza Huallaparimachi, Av Manco Kapac and the train tracks.

The weavers' villages
There's regular transport to Ravelo from Parque Mariscal Sucre, or by the 1st bridge on the road to the airport. Most leave around 0700 with a few more until 1000; 3 hrs. Trucks back to Sucre are usually full. Daily buses to Potolo. A bus to Llalllagua, passing through Ravelo, Macha, Ocuri and Uncia leaves on Thu at 1700, though the road isn't always passable in the wet season.

Monteagudo
La Plata buses go to Monteagudo daily. From Monteagudo there are direct buses to Santa Cruz daily; US$8, 14 hours.

● Directory

Sucre p220, map p222
Banks Banco Nacional, España esquina San Alberto. Cash given on Visa and Mastercard, US$3 commission for whatever amount. Turn right on entering bank, good rates for dollars, TCs changed, 5% commission. Diagonally opposite is **Banco Santa Cruz**, which changes cash, good rates and gives advances on Visa, Mastercard and Amex, US$10 flat fee. Most banks have ATMs for cash withdrawal and there are many Enlace ATMs around town. Travel agencies' rates are good and at **El Arca**, España 134, T04-6460189, good rates for TCs 3% commission into US$, commission-free for changing into Bolivianos. **Casa de Cambio Ambar**, San Alberto 7, T04-6451339. Good rates for TCs. The stalls at the corner of Camargo and Arce buy and sell dollars cash as well as Argentine, Chilean and Brazilian currency at good rates. Many shops and street changers on Hernando Siles/Camargo buy and sell dollars cash. **Cultural centres** Alliance Française, Aniceto Arce 35, T04-6453599, F04-6440991. The noticeboard on Plaza 25 de Mayo (Casa de Libertad side) announces events, also offers Spanish and Quechua classes. **Casa de la Cultura**, Argentina 65, housed in a beautiful colonial building, presents art exhibitions, concerts, folk dancing etc, good breakfast in café, open Mon-Fri 0830-1230, 1400-2200, Sat and Sun 0830-1230. **Centro Boliviano**

Americano, Calvo 301, T04-6441608, F04-6912040, cba@mara.scr.entelnet.bo, library with over 5,000 books in English as well as English magazines, open Mon-Fri 0900-1200, 1500-2000, recommended for reference works, also for language courses (US$6/hr) in Spanish, Quechua and English. Also arranges accommodation with Spanish-speaking families. The **Centro Cultural Hacheh** (address under Café Hacheh, page 231) is run by Felix Arciénega, a Bolivian artist who organizes folk and jazz concerts, conferences, exhibitions and discussions, and is the editor of an art and poetry journal Hacheh. **Centro Cultural Masis**, Bolívar 561, T04-6453403, Casilla 463, promotes the traditional Yampara culture through textiles, ceramics, figurines and music. It offers instruction in Quechua, traditional Bolivian music (3 hrs a week for US$15 a month, recommended) and handicrafts. Also stages musical events and exhibitions; they will arrange peñas for groups at 24 hrs notice. Items for sale include musical instruments made to the highest professional standard and a very good CD of local traditional music. Open Mon-Sat 1430-2000 (knock if door closed); contact the director, Roberto Sahonero Gutierres at the centre Mon, Wed and Fri. **Instituto Cultural Boliviano Alemán** (ICBA – Goethe Institute), Avaroa 326, Casilla 648, T04-6452091, shows films, has German newspapers and German and Spanish books to lend (0930-1230 and 1500-2100), runs Spanish, German, and Quechua courses and it has the **Kulturcafé Berlín** (see page 231). Spanish lessons cost from US$6 for 45 mins for 1 person. The price reduces the larger the class size. The ICBA also runs a folk music peña on Fri.

Internet There are many around town (especially on Colón) charging as little as US$0.25/hr but often with slow connections. **Café Internet Maya**, Arenales, is not the cheapest, at US$0.50/hr, but it's well-equipped, well-situated just off the Plaza, and also has drinks. **Language classes** Academia Latinoamericana de Español, Dalence 109 y Nicolás Ortís, T04-646 0537, www.latinoschools.com. Also has schools in Quito and Cusco. **Margot Macias Machicado**, Olañeta 345, T04-6423567, m_macias_ machicado@hotmail.com, US$5 per hr. Recommended. **Sofia Sauma**, C Loa 779, T04-651687, sadra@mara.scr.entelnet.bo. US$5 per hr. See also cultural centres above. **Laundry** Laverap, Bolívar 617, quick, US$2.50 per full load. **Lavandería Paola**, Bolívar 543, close to Centro Cultural Masis, T04-6462477, US$1.20 per kg. **Medical services Doctor**: Dr Gaston Delgadillo Lora, Colón 33, T04-6451692, speaks English, French, German, highly recommended. **Hospital**: Hospital Gastroenterológico Boliviano-Japonés, for stomach problems. **Post office** Ayacucho 100 y Junín, open Mon-Fri 0800-2000, Sat 0830-1600, Sun 0900-1200. Poste Restante is organized separately for men and women. Branch at bus station, Mon-Sat 0800-1930, Sun 0900-1200. **Telephone** Entel at España 252 (opposite the main office), open 0730-2300 daily, fax as well. **Useful addresses Consulates** Brazil, Arenales 212, T04-5452661. **Ecuador**, Beni (no number), T04-6480205. **Germany**, Rosendo Villa 54, T04-6451369. **Italy**, Vice Consul, Dalence 9, T04-6454280. **Perú**, Avaroa 472, T04-6420356. **Spain**, Pasaje Argandoña, T04-6451435. **Immigration**: Pastor Saenz 117, T04-6453647, Mon-Fri only, 0830-1630. **Police** radio patrol: T110 if in doubt about police or security matters.

Potosí → *Phone code: 02. Colour map 3, grid B3. Population: 112,000. Altitude: 3,977 m.*

Potosí is not only the highest city in the world, but also one of the most beautiful, saddest and fascinating places you'll ever experience. Towering over the city like a giant pink headstone is the 4,824-m Cerro Rico (Rich Mountain). Silver from this mountain made Potosí the biggest city in the Americas and one of the richest in the world, rivalled only by Paris, London and Seville. But Cerro Rico also claimed the lives of countless thousands of Indian slaves. This painful history still haunts the city and is as much a part of its colonial legacy as the many magnificent old buildings which led it to be declared Patrimony of Mankind by UNESCO in 1987. The Spanish still have a saying 'vale un Potosí' ('it's worth a Potosí') for anything incredibly valuable, but though Potosí's wealth is now only a distant memory, it remains one of Bolivia's greatest attractions and is certainly well worth a visit. ▶▶ For Sleeping, Eating and other listings, see pages 246-251.

Ins and outs

Getting there
The airport is 5 km out of the city on the road to Sucre. There are flights to and from La Paz. The bus terminal, T02-6243361, is on Av Universitaria, beyond the train station (which is only for freight). It's a 20-minute downhill walk from the town – and a 30-minute lung-busting walk uphill to the town – or a short taxi or micro ride. You have to pay US$0.10 terminal tax. When you buy your ticket you check your luggage into the operator's office and it is then loaded directly onto your bus. ▶▶ *See also Transport, page 250, for further details.*

Climate
Bring warm clothes – average temperature is 9°C and there are 130 sub-zero nights a year. Also, take it easy on arrival. Remember Potosí is higher than La Paz.

Information
Tourist office ① *Plaza 6 de Agosto, ½ block above the main Plaza 10 de Noviembre, T02-6227405, gobmupoi@cedro.pts.entelnet.bo. It is supposed to be open Mon-Fri 0800-1200 and 1400-1800 but is often closed during these hours.* Town maps cost US$0.40 (English, French, German and Spanish editions) and are better than the glossy US$0.60 map (Spanish only). The colour **Spanish Guía Turística de Potosí**, published by the Plan de Rehabilitación de las Areas Históricas de Potosí, US$5. Another guide is Potosí map and guide (Quipus), US$2.50. It's possible to buy maps at **Instituto Geográfico Militar** ① *Chayanta 769, T02-6226248; Mon-Fri 0900-1200, 1400-1800.*

History

According to legend, the Inca Huayna Capac was on the point of mining silver in 1462 when a voice from above told him that he should leave it where it was because it was for someone else. The Inca then referred to the area as *Ppotojsi*, Quechua for ruin or spoil. According to another version, Huayna Capac described the voice as 'photoj nin' ('a great din'). Another story says the name comes from the Aymara-Quechua word *Ppotoj*, meaning spring, from the numerous springs in and around the city. Yet another that it is from *Potocchi* ('source of silver').

66 99 The official shield of the city carries the words, 'I am rich Potosí, the treasure of the world; the king of mountains, the envy of kings'...

Further legend says the silver was discovered in 1544 by Diego Huallpa who had lost some llamas and climbed Sumaj Orcko, as Cerro Rico was then called. It got late, he got cold and so made a fire which by morning had smelted a vein of silver. Huallpa told his mate Chalco (or Guanca) about the silver and they started mining. However, Chalco told the Spanish, who promptly arrived taking possession of the mountain and founding the city in 1545 as the 'Villa Imperial de Carlos V'. The official shield of the city carries the words "Soy el rico Potosí, del mundo soy el tesoro; soy el rey de los montes, envidia soy de los reyes" (I am rich Potosí, the treasure of the world; the king of mountains, the envy of kings).

The rise of Potosí

Within 18 months of the Spanish learning about the silver, the city had grown to 14,000. Twenty-five years later the population numbered 120,000 making it the biggest city in the Americas. Potosí became the biggest single source of silver in the world despite the fact that it was being extracted by pre-Columbian methods. Within 20 years though the surface deposits had been used up and people started going underground. The percentage of silver in the ore fell, increasing the costs of extracting it and Potosí entered the first of many crises.

The Viceroy of Lima, Francisco de Toledo, arrived in 1572 to improve mining efficiency. He introduced the use of mercury to extract the silver (and a royal monopoly on mercury supplies), set up the Casa Real de Moneda to turn all silver mined into ingots so it could be taxed (20% went direct to the Spanish Crown) and reintroduced the mita, a pre-Incan forced collective labour scheme.

The most expensive part of mining was the manual labour needed to build and maintain a gallery – equal to the cost of a cathedral. The source of power to grind the ore was water, but this required a system of artificial lakes and aqueducts for which there was simply not the capital to pay someone to build.

Toledo dealt with this by dividing up what was then Alto Perú, from Cusco to Potosí, into 16 provinces from which one-seventh of the adult male population had to work in Potosí for one year at a time, three weeks on, three weeks off. This provided 13,500 men (mitayuqkuna) a year, between a half and two thirds of the Potosí mining force. They were paid a nominal salary which did not cover living costs and so they were supported by their communities.

The boom years

Toledo's reforms turned Potosí into a boom city again. By 1585 there were 612 registered mines in Cerro Rico and a census in 1611 found there were 150,000 people living in the city including 6,000 black slaves. John Hemming, in his Conquest of the Incas, describes how, by the turn of the 16th century, Potosí had become one of the largest cities in Christendom, rivalled only by London, Paris and Seville. He states: "By the end of the 16th century the boom city of Potosí had all the trappings of a Klondike or Las Vegas: 14 dance halls, 36 gambling houses, seven or eight hundred professional gamblers, a theatre, 120 prostitutes and dozens of baroque churches.".

Between 1570 and 1650, Potosí was the source of more than half the silver produced in the Americas. This fuelled long-term inflation and growth in Europe and paid for the import of goods from Asia. The city and its surroundings could not support such a large population itself so other areas supplied the goods they needed: wheat and maize from Cochabamba; coca from the Yungas; mules, wine and sugar from northeast Argentina; cereals from Tarija; and llamas from the northern Altiplano to transport the goods.

The silver was carried out to the coast by mule train. It took 25 days to cover the 885 km to Cobija on the Pacific coast, though Toledo also studied the geography and ordered the building of Arica, further north and a mere 750 km from Potosí. When what is now Bolivia was under the control of the Viceroy of Buenos Aires the silver had to be carried for 2,500 km to reach the Atlantic, a 52-day walk.

Decline

Silver production peaked in 1650 and then went into a century-long decline – Mexico took over as the biggest source. By 1690 the mitayuqkuna were down to 2,000. An outbreak of typhoid in 1719 killed an estimated 22,000 people in less than a year and by 1750 the population of Potosí was 70,000. By the 1780s it had fallen to 35,000. All Bolivian cities except La Paz stagnated or shrank during this period as a result of Potosí's contraction.

From 1730 silver production picked up slowly, but it never reached earlier levels nor had such a great impact on the rest of the country. However, at the start of the 19th century Potosí was still a prize worth fighting for during Bolivia's 16-year long struggle for independence from the Spanish, Lima and Buenos Aries. Potosí suffered badly and by the time independence was won, the city was down to 8,000 inhabitants and 50 working mines.

The demand for tin – a metal the Spaniards ignored – saved the city from absolute poverty in the first half of the 20th century, until the price slumped due to over supply. But mining continues in the treacherous tunnels that riddle the Cerro Rico – mainly for tin, zinc, lead, antinomy and wolfram. The fabulous riches of Potosí's past have long gone. Now only the baroque churches remain to pay homage to the many hundreds of thousands who sacrificed their lives for the greed of their colonial rulers.

Sights

Just wandering around the centre of Potosí is fascinating in itself and will take you past many colonial buildings. While Viceroy Toledo tried to bring order to the city's layout in 1574, the boom had led to fast and unplanned development which has left Potosí with a less-than-gridiron plan full of small streets with unexpected twists and turns – including the **Pasaje de las Siete Vueltas** (Seven Turn Passage), off Junín – which adds to the city's charm. There are lots of beautiful and ornate religious buildings well worth seeing – during the colonial period there were 32 churches in the city. Restoration work means buildings can be closed to visitors for months, so check with the tourist office if there is anywhere you particularly want to visit.

An active restoration project is permanently going on, organized by the city council and the **Spanish Cooperation Agency,** but there is a lot of work to do – the city boasts more than 2,000 colonial buildings.

Around the centre

Most visitors would begin their city tour in the central **Plaza 10 de Noviembre**, which used to be used for bull running. It's surrounded by some of the city's best buildings, including the Alcaldía, the court, the Prefectura and the **cathedral** ① *Mon-Fri, 0930-1000, 1500-1730, Sat 0930-1000, guided tour only, US$1.*, more impressive for its size than for its internal baroque decoration.

Half a block above the plaza is the imposing façade of the **Teatro Omiste**, finished in 1753 as the Belén Church. It has since been a hospital, royalist headquarters in 1823 during the wars of independence (the royalists knocked down the twin towers of the church in order to improve their cannon emplacements), a theatre from 1862 and then a cinema in the 20th century, before returning to life as a theatre.

Opposite is **Plaza 6 de Agosto** which was occupied by a church until the aforementioned royalists decided it was in the way. The bizarre white four-arch construction is a reminder of a 44-arch construction that was demolished earlier this century. Another block up Calle Hoyos is **La Merced church**, finished in 1687, which

Potosí

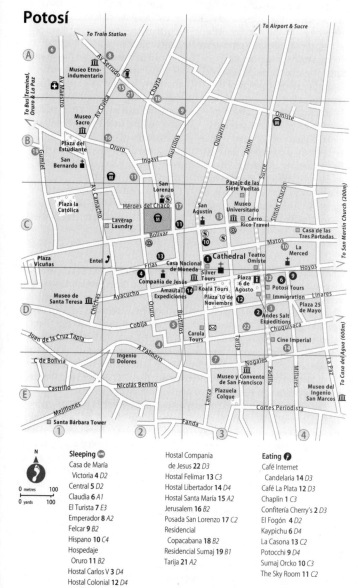

Sleeping
Casa de María
  Victoria **4** D2
Central **5** D2
Claudia **6** A1
El Turista **7** E3
Emperador **8** A2
Felcar **9** B2
Hispano **10** C4
Hospedaje
  Oruro **11** B2
Hostal Carlos V **3** D4
Hostal Colonial **12** D4
Hostal Compania
  de Jesus **22** D3
Hostal Felimar **13** C3
Hostal Libertador **14** D4
Hostal Santa María **15** A2
Jerusalem **16** B2
Posada San Lorenzo **17** C2
Residencial
  Copacabana **18** B2
Residencial Sumaj **19** B1
Tarija **21** A2

Eating
Café Internet
  Candelaria **14** D3
Café La Plata **12** D3
Chaplin **1** C3
Confitería Cherry's **2** D3
El Fogón **4** D2
Kaypichu **6** D4
La Casona **13** C2
Potocchi **9** D4
Sumaj Orcko **10** C3
The Sky Room **11** C2

0 metres 100
0 yards 100

Southern highlands Potosí

☷ The legend of Chutillos

Legends abound surrounding the origins of the festival of Chutillos, one of Potosí's greatest annual celebrations, which runs from 24 to 26 August. Chutillo is the traditional name for a miner on muleback which is now given to the main participants in the festival – the jockeys who wear white capes. On the first day of the festival, the Chutillos ride on mules or donkeys to the chapel of San Bartolomé, also known as Cueva del Diablo (the Devil's Cave), near the village of La Puerta.

According to legend, an evil spirit called Umphurruna was banished from the House of Light and sent to earth. On the way, he saw Sapallay, the sun, and instantly fell in love with her. He carried her off to La Puerta, to hide her away from the prying eyes of men. With his mysterious power, he cut into two the huge cliffs, opening up a narrow winding passage through the middle. He took her into a dark cave. This became known as the Devil's cave and Unphurruna was given the name Chutillo, or genie who harms and then escapes. If anyone threatened to discover Devil's cave, the Chutillo would cause the cliffs to close together , thereby crushing them both to death.

This finally ended when the Jesuits of the Compañía de Jesús church in the newly-founded Villa Imperial de Carlos V took an image of the Apostle San Bartolomé and put it in a smaller cave near the Devil's residence. This caused the evil spirit to rush out screaming and smash into the cliff walls, leaving a greenish black mark which is still visible today.

Ever since then the people of Potosí have celebrated San Bartolomé by visiting the site of the cave each year.

shows the Renaissance influence brought over by friars from Andalucía in Spain. Two long blocks up, just below Calle Pizarro, is the **San Martín Church** which was built by indigenous people forced to come and work in Potosí. It has an uninviting exterior, but has one of the most ornately decorated interiors of any church in Bolivia, with oil paintings and giltwork. It is normally closed for fear of theft. Ask the German Redemptorist Fathers to show you around; their office is just to the left of their church.

Those who are into colonial architecture could do worse than begin in Calle Quijarro, one of Potosí's best-preserved streets. In colonial times it was known as Calle Ollería (potmakers) and Calle de los Sombreros (hats). At Quijarro and Omiste is the **Esquina de las Cuatro Portadas** (four houses with double doors), or Balcón de Llamacancha. There is a fine stone doorway (house of the Marqués de Otavi) in Junín between Matos and Bolívar. At Lanza 8 was the house of José de Quiroz and of Antonio López de Quiroga (now a school). Turn up Chuquisaca from Lanza and after three blocks right into Millares; here on the left is a sculpted stone doorway and on the right a doorway with two rampant lions in low relief on the lintel. Turning left up Nogales you come to an old mansion in a little plaza. Turn left along La Paz and one block along there is another stone doorway with suns in relief. At La Paz y Bolívar is the **Casa del Balcón de la Horca**. Turn left here into Calle Bolívar and about 50 m down on the left is the highly-decorated **Casa de las Tres Portadas**.

Continue down Bolívar and on the right, at Calle Bolívar 698, between Sucre and Junín, is the **Museo Universitario** ① *Mon-Fri 0800-1200, 1400-1800, US$0.75.*, which has some good modern Bolivian painting, as well as sculptures, costumes, musical instruments, fossils and minerals, ceramics and colonial furniture.

Below the main plaza, on Calle Ayacucho and Quijarro, is the huge and impressive **Casa Nacional de Moneda** ① *T02-6222777, Tue-Fri 0900-1200,*

All silver mined in Potosí had to be brought to the *Casa* (or Mint) to be turned into ingots so the Spanish Crown could tax it. Founded in 1572, rebuilt 1759-73, it is one of the chief monuments of civil building in Hispanic America. It has 160 rooms and the walls are fortress-thick. You cannot fail to notice the huge, grinning Bacchus (mask) over an archway between two principal courtyards. This was put up in 1865 – according to some, the smile is said to be ironic and aimed at the departing Spanish.

The 50-odd room museum has a good collection of paintings including works by the best of the Bolivian colonial painters. One section is dedicated to the works of the acclaimed 17th-18th-century religious painter Melchor Pérez de Holguín. Also featured are Gamarra, Berrio and Cruz. Displays cover the pre-colonial, colonial and republican periods and there are fascinating examples of the overlap of politics, economics and the 'catholic' mission. There is also a collection of indigenous costumes from the Potosí Department. Elsewhere are coin dies and huge wooden presses which made the silver strip from which coins were cut. The smelting houses have carved altar pieces from Potosí's ruined churches. There are also various collections of religious architecture, swords, guns, bombs and minerals. Wear warm clothes, as it is cold inside the museum.

Further down Calle Ayacucho, below Bustillos, is the ornate mestizo style tower of the Jesuit **Compañía de Jesus Church** ① *0800-1200, 1400-1800*, finished in 1707, with an impressive bell-gable. It is possible to climb it. At the bottom of Calle Ayacucho, on the corner with Chichas, is the convent, church and **Museo de Santa Teresa** ① *T02-6223847, Daily, must take 2-hr tours (in English and Spanish). Start between 0900-1100, and 1500-1700. US$3.15, plus US$1.50 to take photos, US$25 (yes – US$25!) to video.* The building was started in 1685 and has an impressive amount of giltwork inside. There is an eye-opening collection of flagellation tools (a must for sado-masochists), colonial paintings, religious architecture and furniture. At the end of a visit you can buy *quesitos*, sweets made by the nuns according to a 300-year-old tradition.

Potosí's first church, built in 1547, is the **Museo y Convento de San Francisco**, ① *C Tarija esquina Nogales, T02-6222539, Mon-Fri 0900-1200 and 1430-1700, Sat 0900-1200, US$1.50, US1.50$ to take photos, to video US$3.* The current building, begun in 1707 has the oldest surviving cloisters in Bolivia. It contains a museum of ecclesiastical art, with more than 200 paintings including one of Melchor Pérez de Holguín's best works, *The Erection of the Cross.* Don't miss going up on the roof, which provides one of the best viewpoints over the city.

Outside the central market, on Calle Héroes del Chaco, is the ornate 18th-century mestizo-baroque façade of the **San Lorenzo Church** (1728-44), with a rich portal and fine views from the tower. The first church on this site, La Anunciación, was one of the first built in the city, but collapsed in 1557 after a heavy snowfall. You can get a good view over the whole city from **San Cristóbal Church**, at Pacheco y Cañete, but it was closed at the time of writing.

Other churches worth checking out include **Jerusalén**, on Plaza del Estudiante, which includes the **Museo Sacro** ① *Mon-Sat 1430-1830, US$0.75* with displays of gold work and painting. On the opposite side of Plaza del Estudiante is **San Bernardo** ① *Mon-Fri only, 0800-1200, 1400-1800*, which houses the Escuela Taller Potosí where you can see a display of restoration work. On Bolívar y Quijarro is **San Agustín**, with crypts and catacombs (the whole city was interconnected by tunnels in colonial times). ① *The church can only be visited by prior arrangement with the tourist office; the tour starts at 1700, US$0.10.*

Museo Etno-indumentario (also known as Fletes) ① *Av Serrudo 152, T02-6223258, Mon-Fri 0900-1200 and 1400-1800, Sat 0900-1200. US$1.10, includes tour in Spanish and basic German,* and has a thorough and very interesting display of the different dress and customs and their histories of Potosí department's 16 provinces.

Head south from the centre of the city, drop down and you cross the **Ingenios de la Rivera** area where the ore mined from Cerro Rico was processed. This was the biggest industrial area in the world at the start of the 17th century. Continue up on the other side and you enter what was the Indian part of the city during the colonial period, linked to the centre by 11 bridges. The streets are narrow and cobbled, the houses are roofed with terracota tiles. Two of the ingenios are particularly well-preserved. One is **Ingenio Dolores**, on Calle Mejillones just down from Nicolás Benino. The other, **Ingenio San Marcos**, at Calle Betazanos on the corner with La Paz, is now the **Museo del Ingenio San Marcos** ① *T02-6222781, tourist information office open Mon-Sat 1130-1230, 1430-1530; main building open every day 1000-2300; textile museum open Mon-Sat 1300-2000; restaurant/café inside 1200-2300 (speciality llama)*, the only well-preserved piece of industrial architecture in the city. It has a 6-m diameter waterwheel which was used to power the machinery for grinding down silver ore before mercury was added to extract the metal. The Ingenio had a capacity to produce 119 kg of silver a month when it was working. It also has a good restaurant (see Eating section), which has cultural activities twice a week, a tourist information office and exhibition of Calcha textiles.

Further down Calle Mejillones is the adobe tower of the long-gone **Santa Bárbara Church** which was built 1548-52 and was one of the first churches in the city. Other churches worth checking out on this side of the city include **San Pedro**, Calle San Pedro just above Vitoria, which has a wooden roof and an ornate gilded pulpit, and **San Juan Bautista**, Calle Hernández esquina Chuquisaca, which has a Collin clock from Paris. One and a half blocks further up Chuquisaca is the 1775 **Casa del Agua**.

Plaza El Minero is at the top of Calle San Pedro and has a monument of a miner with a drill in one hand and a rifle in the other, marking the role miners have played in Bolivian political history. Mine massacres are not a thing of the past: in December 1996, 12 miners, their wives and children were shot dead by the army at Amayapampa in Potosí department during a mining dispute.

Mine tours

Most people come to Potosí for the incredible experience of visiting one of the myriad mine workings of the infamous **Cerro Rico,** the pink conical mountain that towers 700 m above the city. ▸▸ *For details of Tour operators, see page 249.*

Cerro Rico was described by one Spanish chronicler in the mid-16th century as 'the mouth of hell', and visitors should be aware that descending into its bowels is both physically and emotionally draining. The tour, as Koala Tours proclaim, is 'not for wimps or woosies'. The mine entrances are above 4,000 m and you will be walking, or rather crouching, around breathing in noxious gases and seeing people working in appalling conditions in temperatures up to 40°C. You should be acclimatized, fit and not have any heart or breathing problems, such as asthma. Miners get first degree silicosis within five years of entering the mines, after 10 years it is second degree and after 15 year it becomes untreatable.

The standard price of a tour is US$10 per person – less in the low season. Make sure you are getting a helmet, lamp and protective clothing (but wear old clothes anyway). Tours follow a set itinerary. A full tour lasts four to five hours and does not give you time to join a tour of the Casa Nacional de Moneda afterwards. A trip to the thermal baths to clean up is a better option.

The size of tour groups varies – some are as large as 20 people, which is excessive. Tours last from around 0800 to mid-afternoon, with around four hours inside the mines.

● *The miners believe that the devil owns the minerals in the earth and, in order to appease*
● *him, every mine has its own statue of El Tío where the miners make offerings of cigarettes, coca or alcohol.*

▎ A man's gotta chew

Apart from the dream of striking it rich, it is coca that keeps the miners going. The only real break they get down in the bowels of the earth is El Aculli, when they chew coca.

The sacred leaves are masticated with lejía, a paste moulded from plant ashes which activates with saliva to produce the desired effect from the coca. This numbs the senses and staves off hunger pangs and exhaustion. It is only by chewing coca that the miners can work at all. "No coca, no work", as one miner put it.

They spend several hours chewing the leaves every morning before entering the mine. Not only does the coca give the miners the energy to carry on working without food, they also believe that it acts as a filter of dust and toxic gases.

Although coca is also taken in a social context, workers used to deny this because, in the eyes of the priests and bosses, an increase in labour productivity was the only permissible reason for tolerating consumption of 'the devil's leaf'.

The tour begins with a visit to **Mercado Calvario** where you are expected to buy presents for the miners such as dynamite, coca leaves, meths, ammonium nitrate and cigarettes. Then it's up to the mine where you get kitted up and enter one of the tunnels. A tour will usually go down all the way to the fourth level, meeting and talking to working miners on the way. You will see how dynamite is used and also meet **El Tío**, the god of the underworld (Friday afternoon is the main day for making offerings to El Tío). A good guide will be able to explain mining practices, customs and traditions little changed since the Spanish left and enable you to communicate with the miners. There is no problem with women visiting the mines. Women worked the mines during the Chaco War 1932-35. Many tours also include some sort of dynamite pyrotechnics.

A contribution to the miners' cooperative is appreciated as are medicines for the new health centre (Posta Sanitaria) on Cerro Rico. New projects (a radio, drinking water) have been, or will shortly be realized.

A mine often visited by tour groups is **La Candelaria**, one of over 5,000 mineshafts which snake their way into the Cerro Rico. Part of a cooperative, miners work alone or in pairs and sell what they extract to the cooperative at the market price. Conditions are, if anything, even more dangerous than in colonial times. The Spaniards introduced the use of socavones, horizontal galleries to intersect workings, allowing simpler access, ventilation and drainage and much deeper mines. But at the lowest depths of La Candelaria there is no ventilation. The cooperatives enjoy none of the privileges of the state workers such as a fixed salary, free housing and benefits; if they don't work they don't eat. But they do have one precious asset - freedom. As one miner explained: "why would I want to work for the state? They have to start on time. We can work when we like and everything we take out is ours."

Around Potosí

The thermal baths at **Tarapaya**, 25 km outside the city on the road to Oruro, are worth visiting to freshen up after crawling around in mine tunnels. There are public baths (US$0.30) and private (US$0.60); the private baths, higher up, may be cleaner. On the other side of the river from Tarapaya is a small 50-m wide volcanic crater lake, with a temperature of 30°C. It's a pleasing-enough spot but on no account swim in the lake. A tourist drowned here, and though agencies in Potosí still run trips here, it is not safe. Nearby is **Balneario Miraflores** which also has swimming pools. Camping by the lake is possible and there's accommodation at Balneario Tarapaya. North of Balneario Miraflores is **Hacienda Mondragon**, set in a beautiful canyon, which is visited by most of the tour operators. Buses to Tarapaya and Miraflores leave from outside the Chuquimia market on Av Universitaria, up from the bus terminal, and from one block higher every 30 minutes or so 0700-1700, US$0.50, 30 minutes. A taxi costs US$7.50 for a group. The last bus back from Miraflores leaves at 1800.

There are also thermal waters at **Don Diego**, 24 km from Potosí on the road to Sucre, and **Rosario**, 25 km from Potosí on the road to Uyuni. You can walk from the main road and camping is possible but avoid weekends. You can take a taxi during the dry season; US$22 per vehicle, including wait. There are more thermal baths at **Chaqui** ① *closed Wed*. Take a truck or bus from Plaza Uyuni. There are a few basic places to stay in Chaqui, which is at the end of the Kari Kari trek, 37 km from the paved road to Sucre (about 60 km from Potosí). They are pleasant and clean.

Kari Kari Lakes

Following Viceroy Toledo's reforms in the early 1570s, 32 artificial lakes were built to the east of the city to supply the *ingenios* with a steady supply of water to grind down the ore before adding mercury to extract the silver. About 20,000 Indians were used to build the dams over a 50 year period. On the afternoon of 15 March 1626 one dam wall broke sending a tidal wave through the city killing between 2,500 and 10,000 people, depending on who you believe. It was said that the ghosts of the dead inhabited the dam until the survivors said enough prayers to placate them. The lakes proved useful in the drought of 1983, having enough water to supply domestic and industrial needs in Potosí. The series of lakes makes a pleasant trekking area, though for the acclimatized only. The average altitude is 4,600 m. One and two day tours are organized by some of the tour operators in Potosí.

La Puerta

La Puerta is a village 6 km from town on the road to Oruro and site of the **Chapel of San Bartolomé** which is visited by the people of Potosí during the Festival of San Bartolomé, or Chutillos. Nearby is the legendary **Devil's Cave**. **Hacienda Cayara** is the

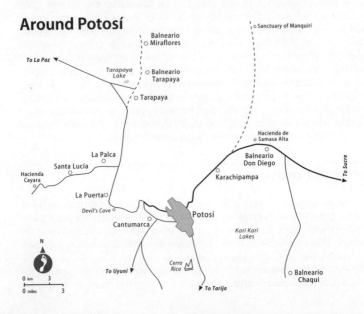

Around Potosí

Fight for the right to party

A tradition peculiar to the Potosí Department is the *tinku* ritual fight. Basically, what happens is that two neighbouring communities meet up and beat the living daylights out of one another – literally. For death, though much less common these days, is always a possibility.

The tinku may look like a drunken Saturday night pub brawl, but it is loaded with symbolism and carries a deep spiritual significance. It is a meeting of equals and is not about winning, but of recognizing your rivals, respecting them and defining your territory. It symbolizes the need to co-exist with other people. It is also a celebration of forgiveness of family or personal enemies. In the tinku any problem is solved and all debts are paid.

Before the fight, the combatants meet and drink chicha and stronger alcohol. The alcohol is to give them courage for the impending battle. The fight begins with fists; each fighter wears rings of bronze adorned with claws to ensure the opponents guts are ripped out. For protection, the pugilists wear a leather helmet,

treated so that it is hard as steel, and a leather groin protector. Fighting is hand-to-hand and reaches a fever pitch of noisy violence. The losers begin to retreat and then stones rain down on both groups.

The winner of each fight then enjoys one year of dominance over his defeated opponent. The injured are respected for standing their ground and fighting bravely. The corpses, meanwhile, are buried as an offering to Pachamama, to ensure a good harvest.

There is no sexual discrimination here. Women also fight in the tinku and it is said that they fight more cruelly and with more honour. During the tinku, bands play continuously and those who are too scared, ill, old, or sensible to fight dance around in a circle.

Tourists are a relatively new phenomenom, so be discreet. Things can get ugly after fewdays' hard drinking and fighting, so it's wise to get out before the end. Some agencies, for example Koala, organize trips to the Macha tinku on 3 May and the Uncía tinku on 2 August, among others.

best-preserved hacienda in the area, 25 km west of the city, with colonial paintings and furniture (see also Sleeping, page 210). Day trips can be arranged for US$3 per person. The hacienda is 7km from the turning off the road to Tarapaya. Buses leave from the Chuquimia market around 1430-1500; or take a taxi (US$7).

Caiza
About two hours from Potosí, on a road which forks off the Tarija road at Ingenio Cucho, is Caiza, at a much lower altitude than Potosí, so it is hotter and can provide some extra oxygen. Cooperatives produce handicrafts in tin and some silver.

South to Tarija

Camargo → *Phone code: 04. Colour map 3, grid B4. Altitude: 2,406m.*
The neat little town of Camargo is 186 km south of Potosí. The vineyards around Camargo are said to produce the country's best singani, cognac and dessert wines. To taste these renowned wines and singanis, take a taxi to **Bar La Viña** at Patapampa, set among vineyards 7 km away. Also see Sleeping below.

A driveable side road goes 45 km east from Camargo to Culpina and on to **Incahuasi,** near where a number of important fossils have been found, as well as rare varieties of cacti. Micros leave from the market area in Calle Chuquisaca.

A road runs south from Camargo, through to Villa Abecia, El Puente and on to **Iscayachi.** The road forks, southwest to the Argentine border at Villazón (see page 256), and east to the region's capital, Tarija (see page 251).

● Sleeping

Potosí *p236, map p239*

Hotels have no heating, unless stated otherwise.

B Claudia, Av Maestro 322, T02-6222242, F02-6225677. Outside the centre, tour agency on ground floor, helpful, modern.

B Hostal Colonial, Hoyos 8, near the main plaza, T02-6224809, F02-6227146. Popular and attractive colonial house, with heating. Rooms are suprisingly plain for the price but are nevertheless comfortable.

B Hostal Libertador, Millares 58 y Nogales, T02-6227877, F02-6224629, hostalib@ cedro.pts.entelnet.bo. Colonial building, central heating in comfortable, modern rooms, quiet, helpful, parking.

C El Solar, Wenceslao Alba 41 (off the map), T/F02-6227951. Quiet, clean, family-run, breakfast included.

C Hostal Cerro Rico, Ramos 123 (between La Paz and Millares, off map), T/F02-6223539, www.hostalcerrorico.8k.com. (**D** without private bathroom). Very good rooms upstairs, cable TV, friendly and helpful, parking.

C Jerusalem, Oruro 143, T/F02-6222600, hoteljer@cedro.pts.entelnet.bo. (F without bath). Includes buffet breakfast, TV, friendly, helpful, clean and comfortable, very good in the new section, comedor, garage parking a block away, US$1/day, laundry, good value, internet for US$2 per hr. Travel agency Sumaj Tours, T02-6224633, is part of the hotel.

D Emperador, Av Serrudo 167, T02-6223756, emperado@cotapnet.com.bo. Modern and bland hotel with lots of pink plastic flowers. Comfortable but a fair walk from the centre. The squash courts which were once its main pull are now used as a furniture showrooom.

E El Turista, Lanza y Nogales, T02-6222492, F02-6222517. Also LAB office, friendly, helpful, hot showers, light, breakfast for US$1, excellent view of the city from rooms 33, 34 and 35 on the top floor, good value but beds poor.

E Hispano, Matos 62, T02-6224100, F02-6222659. Clean and helpful.

E Hostal Carlos V, Linares 42, T02-6225121. (**F** without private bathroom). Breakfast, occasional hot water 0700-1200, luggage store, 2400 curfew.

E Hostal Compania de Jesus, Chuquisaca 445, T02-6223173. Very friendly, old monastery. Some rooms are dark but beds are very comfortable and it's a nice old colonial building, which was once a monastery. Hot showers once the ice in the tank melts in the morning. Price includes a basic breakfast.

E Hostal Felimar, Junín 14, T02-6224357. The price includes continental breakfast; it's US$3 cheaper to share a bathroom. 1st floor rooms have no exterior windows but are warm and quiet. There's 1 roof-top suite. Some of the ceilings were designed for people under 5 feet tall.

E Hostal Santa María, Av Serrudo 244, T02-6223255. Hot water, comfortable and friendly, though rooms have hospital beds and are on the dark side.

F Alojamiento La Plata. Directly opposite the bus station and open 24 hrs for late arrivals/early departures. All rooms shared bathroom, 9 rooms per shower.

F Casa de María Victoria, Chuquisaca 148, T02-6222132. (**G** without bathroom). Built in the 17th century as accommodation for friars from Santo Domingo, all rooms open on to a stone courtyard, clean, stores luggage, popular with backpackers, travel agency offers cheap mine tours, breakfast in courtyard, owner speaks English. Recommended.

F Central, Bustillos 1230 y Cobija, T02-6222207. Lukewarm showers, cold rooms, breakfast, basic, surrounds a courtyard which is the main source of light.

F Felcar, Serrudo 345, T02-6224966. Rebuilding in progress at the time of writing but should be a good option.

F **Tarija**, Av Serrudo 252, T02-6222711. (**G** without bath). Clean and helpful, Tarija has no obvious sign but a big cobbled courtyard with free parking. The more expensive rooms are much nicer, with wooden beds and floors and good, newly tiled private bathrooms. Recommended.

G **Alojamiento Ferrocarril**, Av E Villazón 159, T02-6224294. Basic, hot showers US$0.30, close to the railway station.

G **Hospedaje Oruro**, Oruro 292, T02-6222637. Plain and basic rooms (some of the ceilings appear to be about to cave in) but with a pleasant, sunny courtyard.

G **Koala Den**, Junin 56.. Expanded and refurbished in summer 2004, the Koala Den is heated, with TV, video, magazines and a coffee room. Rooms for 2, 3, 5 or 10. Private bathrooms and a kitchen. Look out for a Koala pub in the future.

G **Posada San Lorenzo**, Bustillos 967, in front of market. Cheapest place in the centre, colonial building, courtyard, no showers.

G **Residencial Copacabana**, Av Serrudo 319, T02-6222712. Shared bathrooms only and the showers can only be reached by a walk outside. Single or shared rooms have sagging beds but are otherwise OK. Restaurant, will change dollars, safe car park for US$0.30 per day, popular.

G **Residencial Sumaj**, Gumiel 12, T02-6223336. Small rooms all without bath, double room on top floor with good views. There's a kitchen, a laundry and a TV lounge and it's popular with travellers. It's also friendly and helpful but it's a dark place apart from the central courtyard.

Outside town

C per person **Hacienda Cayara**, 25 km west of the city. Those wishing to avoid the freezing cold nights of Potosí can stay here. This is the best-preserved *hacienda* in the area, it has space for up to 10, price includes breakfast, other meals can be prepared on request or cook your own, lunch is US$7 and dinner US$5. For reservations, T02-6226380, cayara@cedro.pts.entelnet.bo or go to the door to the right of the shop of the same name beside the main *Entel* office at Cochabamba 532.

Caiza

F **Hotel San Martín de Porres**, near the plaza, clean and with a restaurant.

South to Tarija *p245*
Camargo

E **Hostal Cruz Huasa**, on Plazuela Estudiantes, T04-6292092. With private bathroom, cheaper without, comfortable, modern, cable TV, includes breakfast, nice garden, garage, cafeteria, the owner also owns the region's main vineyards 20 km away, transport provided.

F **Hostal Las Cañitas**, near the *tránsito* up a side street, T04-6292126. Shared bathroom, **G** for single room, very friendly and comfortable, family atmosphere, TV lounge, cafeteria, nice garden, garage, owner also has an old bodega called La Compañía Baja, 3 km out of town, which produces singani and a singani and wine mixture.

G **Media Luz**, Ayacucho 282. Basic.

G **Romay**, Bolívar 101. Very basic but slightly better than nearby Okay, (**G** Chuquisaca 9), which doesn't even live up to its name.

🍴 Eating

Potosí *p236, map p239*
Some places charge 13% for credit cards. Check first. **La Casona** (see cafés, below) is also a great place to eat.

$$ **Comedor Popular in Mercado Central** between Oruro, Bustillos, Héroes del Chaco and Bolívar. Breakfast from 0700, fresh bread from 0600, api and pasteles US$0.55, possibly the best thing to warm you up in the morning.

$$ **El Fogón**, Oruro y Frías, T02-6224969. Upmarket pub-restaurant, good food and atmosphere, open 1200-1500, 1800-2400.

$$ **Museo del Ingenio San Marcos.** Attached to the museum (see page 242), diners sit among the old machinery creating a great atmosphere. Speciality is llama meat. Open 0800-2300.

$ **Belén**, 6 de Agosto, just off the plaza, 0800-2300. Belen has an impressive colonial façade, Bolivian music, good pizza and wine and ladders leading up to a mirador.

🔴 *Price codes for Sleeping and Eating are given inside the front cover. Further information on*
⚫ *hotel and restaurant grading can be found in Essentials, pages 43-44.*

$ **Chaplin**, Matos on corner with Quijarro, 0700-1200, 1600-2230, closed Sun. Friendly, good-value basic fast food such as burgers (including vegetarian). Special daily dishes: Mon, Tue spaghetti, Wed, Thu mixed plates, Fri, Sat Mexican, also great tucumanos and other breakfasts. Ineffective heating though.

$ **Kaypichu**, Millares 24. Tue-Sun 0700-1300 and 1600-2100. Good vegetarian food and an enormous selection of breakfasts. Quality of service mixed. Cultural events.

$ **Potocchi**, Millares 13, T02-6222759. Great restaurant for typical Potosí food and drink, traditional breakfast of *api* 0800-1200 as well as good muesli, excellent llama meat and natural soups also popular *peñas* at 2100 on Tue, Fri, Sat and Sun with dancing and traditional costumes, cover charge US$1.50.

$ **Sumaj Orcko**, Quijarro 46. Excellent and enormous portions and a cheap set lunch. The reasonably priced food is very popular with travellers, despite the blaring TV. Lots of meaty options on a big menu. Usually open and usually warm. Next door there's a Sumaj pub (see Bars and cafes, below).

$ **The Sky Room**, top floor, Bolívar 701, Mon-Sat 0800-2230, Sun 0800-1700. Recommended only for the fantastic view over Potosí's rooves to the mountain. Service is slow, food is very poor and the toilets are appalling. Order as little as possible, take a photo and leave quickly.

Cafés

Café Internet Calendaria, C Ayacucho 5, Mon-Sun from 0700. A part of the **Koala** mini empire, the slightly decrepit Calendaria is popular with travellers for its Bolivian food, balcony, book exchange, apple pie and travel guide library. Also has internet for US$0.40.

Café La Plata, Plaza 10 de Noviembre, corner with Linares, T02-6226085, Mon-Sat 1500-2200, also for breakfast. A great place to relax over a coffee, wine or beer. The home-baked cookies are delicious and there are games to play. Chic, warm and friendly, the owners speak English and French.

Confitería Cherry's, Padilla 8, open from 0800. Good cakes (especially the apple strudel) and breakfast but the coffee is best avoided. Good value as long as you like loud '80s pop and aren't too worried by painfully slow service.

La Casona, Frías 34, T02-6222954, Mon-Sat

1000-1230, 1800-2400. Good food (try the meat fondue, the trout or one of the good salads) and beer. The house was built in 1775 for one of the King of Spain's informers and superintendants of the **Casa de la Moneda.** There are games, a laid-back atmosphere and good service. It's warm already but the hot wine also help heat you up.

South to Tarija p245
Camargo

The best restaurant is **Media Luz** on Plaza Abaroa. Good value lunch, it's often filled with bus passengers taking their meal break. There are also 2 clean comedores populares; one is in the Mercado Central (entrance on C Litoral), the other is at the back of C Chuquisaca, both serve a good breakfast and lunch.

Bars and clubs

Potosí *p236, map p239*
Sumaj Pub, Quijarro. Next door to the restaurant of the same name, Sumaj has good heating, a TV with sport events and live music on a Friday night.
For budding Frank Sinatras there's a karaoke bar at Bolivar 789, 2nd floor, which opens at 2000.

Entertainment

Potosí *p236, map p239*
Cinema
Cine Imperial, Padilla 31, has a double matinée and a single evening showing at 1900.

Peñas
Potocchi, Millares 13, T02-6222759 at 2100 on Tue, Fri, Sat and Sun with dancing and traditional costumes, cover charge US$1.50 (see also Eating above).

Festivals and events

Potosí *p236, map p239*
Feb or Mar Carnival Minero is celebrated 2 weeks before the Oruro Carnival, on a Sat and is known locally as Tata Ckascho. The miners parade and dance down Cerro Rico from the church near the top, to Plaza El Minero, carrying their god, El Tío. This is his one and

only annual appearance outside the mine.

Another miners' festival, held 2 weeks before Carnival, is **Fiesta de los Compadres**, and 1 week later is **Fiesta de las Comadres**. During Carnival itself, Shrove Tuesday is celebrated as **Martes de Cha'lla**, when offerings to Pachamama are made at the doors of people's houses and drinks are offered to passers-by. Ash Wednesday throughout the region is **Carnival Campesina** which lasts for 5days, ending with **Domingo de Tentación** (Temptation Sunday) in many small villages.
8-10 Mar San Juan de Dios, with music, dancing and parades.
Last Sun in May Fiesta de Manquiri, a festival when vehicles and miniatures are blessed in the village of Manquiri, 26 km northeast of the city. There's transport to Manquiri from Plaza Chuquimia. Also in May there's a market on C Gumiel every Sun, with lotteries, and items for sale.

On 3 consecutive Sats at the end of **May**, beginning of **Jun**, llama sacrifices are made at the cooperative mines in honour of Pachamama.
Aug There are more llama sacrifices at the beginning of Aug: on the 1st day, **Chutillo**, people walk to the village of La Puerta, 5 km from the centre on the Oruro road, to the church of San Bartolomé to pray and then climb the nearby hill. On day 2, **Majtillo**, indigenous people in costume from all over the department make their entrance into the city. Day 3 is **Thapuquillo**, when people from the city and invited groups from other parts of the country and abroad parade through the streets.
1st and 2nd Sun in Oct is Virgen de La Merced and Virgen del Rosario, with processions through decorated streets and people throwing flower petals on passing religious images.
Oct/Nov Festival Internacional de la Cultura, when cultural events take place over 2 weeks in Potosí and Sucre.
10 Nov Fiesta Aniversario de Potosí, which celebrates the city's foundation.

Around Potosí *p243, map p244*
Caiza
4 Aug The entry of the Virgen de Copacabana is celebrated with dancing and traditional costumes.

South to Tarija *p245*

Camargo
25 May The town holds a **Feria Artesanal** when the arts and crafts of the region's rural communities are displayed.
23 Sep Feria del Vino de Singani y de la Canción Cinteña, with songs and dancing to celebrate the local wines.

Ⓞ Shopping

Potosí *p236, map p239*
Artesanías El Cisne is at Padilla 17.
The main shopping streets are Bolívar and Sucre, which is pedestrianized between Bolívar and Plaza 6 de Agosto. There are also artesanía shops along Sucre between Omiste and Bolívar.
Killay at the back of Mercado Artesanal. For musical instruments try Arnaud Gerard's workshop here, which produces beautifully-made and tuned pieces, designed to be played, will make to order, open Mon-Fri, 1700-1930.

Markets
Mercado Central, between Oruro, Bustillos, Héroes del Chaco and Bolívar, sells mainly food and produce, but silver is sold near the C Oruro entrance.
Mercado Gremial, between Av Camacho and Oruro, only sells household goods. There is an informal **swap market** every Fri night at the Plazuela, at Bolívar and Quijarro.
Mercado Artesanal, at Sucre y Omiste, sells jumpers, rugs, wall-hangings, bags, good musical instruments, some Fri the merchants organize music, food and drink (*ponche*), not to be missed.

▲ Activities and tours

Potosí *p236, map p239*
Tour operators
All guides must have an identity card issued by the Prefectura and must work through an agency. If you go with a guide who is not working through an agency and something goes wrong there is no insurance cover. If you want to book a Salar and Lagunas tour with a Potosí agency, check they operate the service themselves – many of them subcontract and just put you on a bus to Uyuni. If you pay in Potosí and then have

problems in Uyuni refunds can be difficult. It is difficult to differentiate between the agencies: they all offer (unless noted below) similar services including daily mine visits, city tours, trips to the thermal baths near Potosí, trekking to Kari-Kari or to Laguna Talacocha and trips to the Salar de Uyuni and Lagunas.

Amauta Expediciones, Ayacucho 17, T02-6225515, for trips to Uyuni, the lagoons and, of course, the mines. Like **Koala**, Amauta claims to hand 15% of its income to the miners. Geronimo Fuertes owns **Amauta** but still leads groups, of no more than 8 in size. He speaks good English and some French and Hebrew.

Andes Salt Expeditions, Plaza Alonso de Ibáñez 3 (eastern side of the plaza), T/F02-6225175, www.bolivia-travel.com.bo. English spoken, daily city tours. Also sell bus and flight tickets and run their own Uyuni tours. They have another office in Uyuni (see page 214).

Carola Tours, Lanza and Chuquisaca, opposite post office, usual trips. Santos Mamani, the owner, is an excellent guide, as is his brother Raul Braulio Mamani, who runs **Andes Expeditions**.

Cerro Rico Travel, Bolívar 853, T02-6227044, T02-71835083, jacky_gc@yahoo.com. Jaqueline knows the mines well and speaks good English. Also English and French guides for trips to village *artesanía* markets north of the city and to colonial *haciendas*, horse and mountain bike hire, treks in Kari Kari and Talacocha, trips to Toro Toro including cave visits, as well as visits to Sucre.

Hidalgo Tours, Junín y Bolívar 19, T02-6225186, F02-6229212, www.salaruyuni.com. Upmarket and specialized services within the city and to Salar de Uyuni (where they own a salt hotel).

Koala Tours, C Ayacucho 5, T02-6224708, www.koalatoursbolivia.com. Excellent mine tours, guides are former miners, speak English, frequently recommended, optional traditional breakfast or lunch including high protein, low fat llama meat, also *tinku* trips. Eduardo Garnica Fajardo, the owner, speaks English, French and some Hebrew. He rarely guides now but employs Juan Mamaní Choque who is also excellent. **Koala** offer breakfast at 0600, a *plato típico* with llama meat. They also donate 15% of their US$10

fee to support on-site health-care facilities (donations can be sent to Eduardo Garnica). Also sell bus tickets, and run the Koala Den hotel, see Sleeping.

Silver Tours Quijarro, Edif Minero 12, T02-6223600, F02-6223600, www.silver tours.8m.com. One of the cheaper firms.

⊖ Transport

Potosí *p236, map p239*
Micros within the city cost US$0.12. **Taxis** cost US$1.

Air
Aerosur, C Hoyos 10 (T02-6222088), flies to La Paz 0800 Mon-Sat, 1 hr (La Paz to Potosí 0630 Mon-Sat). **TAM** fly on Mon from La Paz at 0830, returning at 1030. **LAB** has an office in **El Turista** (see Sleeping), Mon-Fri 0900-1200, 1400-1800, Sat 0900-1200.

Bus
Potosí is 533 km southeast of La Paz. Daily services to **La Paz** at 1830 (**Trans Illimani**) to 1930, US$4.50, 11 hrs; *bus-cama* from **Flota Copacabana** costs US$7.50.

To **Oruro** at 0700, 1200, 1500, 2000, 2200 (**Trans Azul**, in front of terminal, in the street) US$3.75, 7 hrs.

To **Cochabamba** at 1830 (**Expresso Cochabamba**) and 1900 (**Flota-** and **Trans-Copacabana**), US$4.50, 12 hrs.

To **Sucre** 0700, 1200, 1700 (**Transtin Dillrey** recommended) and 1800, US$3, 3 hrs.

To **Santa Cruz** (must change in Sucre or Cochabamba) at 1900, US$12, 18 hrs.

To **Villazón** 0800 and 1900 only, US$4, 11 hrs.

To **Tarija** 1600 and 1900 only, US$6, 12 hrs.

Buses to **Uyuni** leave from either side of the railway line several blocks above the bus terminal (uphill the road is called Av Antofagasta or 9 de Abril, downhill it is Av Universitaria), daily at 1100 and 1830, US$4.75, 6-7 hrs, get there early or book in advance. **Emperador** runs to Uyuni from the terminal at 1200 (US$4.50).

Around Potosí *p243, map p244*
Caiza
Two daily buses leave from Plaza del Minero in Potosí, at 1330.

Potosí *p236, map p239*

Banks You can find Enlace ATMs outside Banco Mercantil, Sucre, 9. 1% commission on US$TCs. Almost opposite is **Casa Fernández**, which changes US$ cash. **Banco Nacional**, Junín 4-6, between Bolívar and Matos has a beautiful façade and changes dollar TCs and cash. **Banco de Crédito**, C Bolívar y Sucre. Cash withdrawals on Visa. Many shops on Plaza Alonso de Ibáñez and on Bolívar, Sucre and Padilla display signs stating they change dollars and Argentinian pesos. Dollar TCs can be changed at **Distribuidora Cultural Sud**, Matos 19, 3% commission. **Internet** All the following cost around US$0.75 per hr: **Café Candelaria**, Ayacucho 5, T02-6228050. **Tuko's Café**, Junín 9, 3rd floor, 'the highest net café in the world' (4,100 m), T02-6225489, tuco25@hotmail.com, daily 0800-2300, good lunchtime food (burgers, llama meat and vegetarian), free city maps, tourist information, helpful English-speaking owners know pretty much everything about Potosí. **Language schools** Centro Boliviano-Americano, Chuquisaca 590. Spanish and English classes, may be looking for TEFL qualified teachers.

Laundry Laverap, Camacho (next to Residencial San Andres), also at Quijarro, corner of Matos, Edificio Cademin, US$1.20 per kg, Mon-Sat 0800-1200, 1400-2000. **La Veloz**, left of Silver Tours, C Lanza. **Medical services Clinics**: Clínica Británica, on Oruro near Alojamiento La Paz, clinics mornings and afternoons, English spoken. **Post office** Lanza 3, corner with Chuquisaca. Mon-Fri 0800-2000, Sat 0800-1930, Sun 0900-1200.

Telephone Entel: on Plaza Arce at the end of Camacho between Frías and Bolívar, T02-6243496; also at Av Universitaria near the bus terminal. **Useful addresses Immigration**: at Linares, corner with Padilla, T02-6225989, open Mon-Fri 0830-1630 (though they clear off for unofficial lunch at the usual almuerzo time), allow an hr for visa extensions. Potosí immigration may try to charge 165Bs (US$24.60) for a 30-day extension. Whatever they say this is NOT the law, even if they claim it was a rule brought in the day before. A call to La Paz immigration (T02-2379385) should convince them. Otherwise wait until the next town. **Police station:** on Pl 10 de Noviembre.

Southern highlands Tarija

Tarija → *Phone code: 04. Colour map 3, grid C4. Population: 109,000. Altitude: 1,840 m.*

Situated along the banks of the Río Guadalquivir, this tranquil agricultural and wine centre is linguistically and visually reminiscent of Spanish Andalucía. It is also culturally closer to Argentina than to the rest of Bolivia, something the native Tarijeños (or 'Chapacos' as they are also known) point to with pride. Tarija is blessed with plenty of sun and a spring-like climate almost all year-round.

The city has a justly deserved reputation not only for its wonderful climate, but also for the easy-going nature of its inhabitants. Compared to the bleak Altiplano or the barren Chaco that flank it to the west and east respectively, Tarija can seem like paradise. Of all Bolivian cities, perhaps Tarija comes closest to capturing the ambience of a 'typical' post-colonial settlement, with its date and orange tree-lined plaza, wide streets and prominent churches. ▸▸ *For Sleeping, Eating and other listings, see pages 258-262.*

Ins and outs

Getting there

The **airport** is 3 km east of town along Avenida Las Américas. Airport information T04-6643135. There are flights to and from La Paz, Cochabamba, Santa Cruz and

Grape expectations

Tarijeños have been growing grapes and making wine since Franciscan missionaries brought cuttings to the region over 350 years ago. Today, the old traditions of pressing wine by foot, known as *vino patero*, or 'foot wine', still persist. But modern enterprises like Concepción, Kohlberg and Aranjuez have made the region's wine much more widely available. Nearly 2.5 million litres are now produced in the valleys that surround Bolivia's most southerly state capital, much of it very reasonable. A delicious, full-bodied Cabernet Sauvignon costs around US$3.50 a bottle, cheap but drinkable table wine about US$1 a bottle.

Sucre. A taxi to the airport from the centre of town costs US$3.75; or take a micro, linea 'A' from outside the Mercado Central which drops you one block away, US$0.25. Some hotels have free transport to town when you arrive, but you may have to call them. On arrival at Tarija, reconfirm your next flight straight away.

The **bus terminal** is in the outskirts on Avenida Las Américas, a 30-minute walk from the centre, on the way to the airport. Information T04-6636508. Trucks to all destinations depart from Barrio La Loma, 10 blocks west of the market. ▸▸ *For more information, see Transport, page 261.*

Getting around
As with most South American towns, the main Plaza Luis de Fuentes y Vargas is where most of the action is. Most of the city's restaurants, shops and offices are within easy walking distance of it, and at its centre it features the obligatory statue to the city's founder. All blocks west of Calle Colón have a small O before the number (*oeste*), and all blocks east have an E before the number (*este*); blocks are numbered from Colón outwards. All streets north of Av Las Américas (nearly all on our map) are preceded by N.

Information
The **Tourist Office** ① *on the southwest corner of the main plaza, in the Prefectura, T04-6631000, Mon-Fri only, 0800-1200, 1430-1830,* is helpful, free city map and guide. Also at Sucre y Bolívar, with 'HAM' on the window.

History

Tarija is the capital and largest city of the department of the same name. Founded on 4 July 1574 by the Spanish colonizer Luis de Fuentes y Vargas, Tarija boasts a long history of autonomous rule. Never thoroughly subjugated by the Spanish, the inhabitants declared their independence from Spain as early as 1807, in the process becoming the first region in all of Latin America to do so. A decade later, on 15 April 1817, at the Battle of La Tablada on the outskirts of the city, a local militia under José Eustaquio Méndez defeated a superior Spanish force and made good its declaration of independence. Although coveted by Argentina, Tarija and its environs opted to join the newly-declared Republic of Bolivia in 1825, ending the area's short but vibrant period of independence.

Tarija may be a pleasant enough place to hang out, but it is not exactly over-endowed with cultural and historical sites. There are four churches worth seeing, including the city cathedral, on Calle La Madrid. The **cathedral** itself ① *mornings and from 1700*, built in 1611, contains a mortuary holding the remains of many prominent Chapacos, among them the city's founding father.

Far more interesting is the **Basílica de San Francisco** ① *on the corner of Av Daniel Campos and La Madrid, open for mass Mon-Sat 0700-1000 and 1800-2000 and Sun 0630-1200, 1800-2000*. Built in 1606, this is the oldest church in the city and it is beautifully painted inside, with praying angels depicted on the ceiling. Note the four evangelists at the four corners below the dome. Besides the stunning artwork, it contains two libraries, the old one containing some 15,000 volumes, and the new one a further 5,000. A small museum boasts an outstanding collection of colonial books, including a 1501 edition of *The Iliad*, as well as numerous modern reference works and 19th-century photograph albums on Bolivia. To visit the libraries, you need permission from the Franciscan priests who maintain them. Ask for either Father Lorenzo or Maldini at the rectory, at C Ingavi O-0137.

Five blocks north of the cathedral on Avenida General Bernardo Trigo and next to a pleasant, shady square is the **Church of San Roque**, built in 1887 and dedicated to the town's patron saint. Although a minor church in ecclesiastical terms, the battleship grey building is architecturally the most interesting, and it serves as the city's most identifiable landmark.

The **Church of San Juan** ① *open only for mass on Sat evening and Sun 0700-1200*, four blocks northwest of the cathedral, at the end of Avenida Bolívar, was built in 1632 and marks the site where the Spaniards officially surrendered after the Battle of La Tablada. There are views of the city and its surroundings from the **Loma de San Juan**, a park due north of the church of San Juan. Walk to the roundabout (not very round!) and cross, bearing left, to the three benches surrounding a small pedestal and plaque (Plaza de Maestro). Walk up the road to the left, enter a gate on the right and follow the Stations of the Cross to the top. An equestrian statue of Moto Méndez is at the top (see page for details of his museum in San Lorenzo).

The **Museo de Arqueología y Paleontología** ① *on the corner of Av General Trigo and C Virginio Lema, 1 block south of the main plaza, Mon-Fri 0800-1200 and 1500-1800, Sat 0900-1200, 1500-1800, free, 2 Spanish-only videos for sale (US$10 each); one about the culture of Tarija, the other about its fossilised heritage, both 25 mins*, is part of Tarija's university. It contains, downstairs, a one-room palaeontological collection, including dinosaur bones, fossils

❧ *The best time to visit is from Jan onwards, when the fruits are in season.*

and the remains of several Andean elephants (one of which a family found under their patio following an earth tremor in 1999). Upstairs there are smaller mineralogical, ethnographic and anthropological collections. These are generally well presented and explained.

Two houses of the 19th-century merchant Moisés Navajas, one of Tarija's most prominent citizens, are also well worth a visit. The **Casa Dorada** ① *Mon-Fri 0900-1200 and 1500-1800, Sat 0900-1200, entry by voluntary contribution of a minimum US$0.30, guided tours in Spanish*, also known as **Maison d'Or**, at the intersection of Avenida General Trigo and Calle Ingavi (entrance on Ingavi), is the city's official Casa de Cultura. Begun in 1886, the house has been repainted in original colours, silver and ochre on the outside, cerise, green and dark blue, with white trim, inside. The interior has Italian murals, art nouveau copies on ceiling panels and much gold in the rooms. Don't miss the crystal table lamps in the form of bunches of grapes in the dining room or the painted roof of the private chapel. The photography room contains pictures of Tarijan history and the restoration of the house. It has been described as a superb example of Kitsch decorative art.

For those who crave more of the same, it is possible to have a guided tour from the owner of Navajas' other town house, the **Castillo de Beatriz** (also known as the **Catillo de Moisés Navajas**). It resembles a blue-and-white, square wedding cake and can be found on Calle Bolívar, just after the intersection with Calle Junín, a few blocks east of the plaza. The house is privately owned, but a knock on the front door or an enquiry around the side door to the right during office hours is usually enough to gain entry.

On the modern Avenida Las Américas (Víctor Paz Estenssoro, or Costanera), which flanks the river, is a pleasant **children's park** ① US$0.20, with open-air theatre, nice gardens, swimming pools and small zoo.

If you're in Tarija then you really should make a visit to a local **bodega** to sample some of the local wines and to see how they are produced. The easiest to see, a short walk across the river, is the **Aranjuez bodega**, at Avenida Los Sauces 1976. Their best white, which won an international silver medal, is a Chardonnay/Muscat '99

Tarija

Sleeping
Alojamiento Ocho Hermanos 1
América 2
Gran Hostal Baldiviezo 3
Gran Hotel Max 4
Gran Hotel Tarija 5
Hostal Bolívar 6
Hostal Carmen 7
Hostal Libertador 8
Hostal Loma de San Juan 9
Hostal Miraflores 10
Hostería España 11
Los Ceibos 12
Luz Palace 13
Residencial Rosario 14
Victoria Plaza 15
Zeballos 16

Eating
Cabaña Don Pepe 2

(a bargain at US$1.35). To visit, ask Señor Milton Castellanos at the Agrochemical shop at Trigo 789. If you're unlucky enough to be here at the weekend buy it at their shop which is east off Plaza Sucre, on 15 de Abril O-0241. You can also arrange a visit to the **Campos de Solana bodega** ① *Bodega Mon-Fri 1000-1200, 1500-1730, Sat 0900-1200, shop Mon-Sat 0800-1200, 1430-1800; For information on bodegas outside the city, see following pages,* through Señor Castellanos. You can also buy their wine direct from another shop, almost next door to the first, at 15 de Abril E-0259.

Around Tarija

The area around the city, and especially the banks of the river, is home to numerous fossils and dinosaur bones, several of which are on display in the university museum. About 5 km out of town, (take a micro or taxi in the direction of the airport) before the police control (*garita*), you can see lovely structures of sand looking like a small canyon (*barrancos*). Bones, teeth and even parts of spines are found here each year after the rains when they come to the surface. Amateur paleontologists can roam around to their hearts' content, but any unusual findings should be left there and reported to the university.

Four kilometres southwest of town, across the Río Guadalquivir, is the **Parque de la Tablada**, the site of Méndez's victory over the Spanish in 1817. The park is a pleasant spot to enjoy the river. During Tarija's Independence Week celebrations (see Festivals, page 260), you can see an increasingly rare gaucho rodeo (*rodeo chapaco*) here.

Twenty kilometres south of Tarija, on the road to Santa Ana (turn left off the road to Concepción), is Bolivia's first **astronomical observatory**. It has two Russian telescopes and is a good place to go at night to see the stars. It also has an atomic clock which keeps official time for Bolivia.

San Jacinto

At San Jacinto, 8 km away, is a tourist complex beside the lake formed by a dam completed in 1991. At the dam there is a café, several shacks selling food and drink and boats for hire. There is a pleasant, level lakeside walk. Cross the dam, go past the food stalls and follow the clear track to the head of the lake. It takes about an hour until climbing a shoulder and then descending to more houses. Either return the same way (in which case you miss the best part), or climb the up the hill to the left (a bit of a

Chifa New Hong
Kong **3**
Chingo's **5**
Club Social
Tarija **6**
El Solar **7**
Gringo Limón **8**
La Fontana **9**

La Taberna
Gattopardo **10**
Mateo's **11**
Pizzería Europa **12**

Bars & clubs 🎵
Bagdad Café **1**

Southern highlands Tarija

scramble to the top) for a good, all-round view. Walk back along the ridge path which descends directly back to the steep ravine which is blocked by the dam. Take care on the final descent. Don't walk over the cliff where the dam is and make sure to keep to the left, on the lake side. Take a trufi from Ingavi y Daniel Campos, by Palacio de Justicia. They leave every 30 minutes; 35-minute journey, US$0.25.

San Lorenzo

A worthwhile trip is to the village of San Lorenzo, 15 km from Tarija. The plaza is very pleasant, with palms, oranges and flowers, and the church is huge and unadorned. Just off the plaza is the **Museo Méndez** ⓘ *daily 0900-1230, 1500-1830, entry by voluntary donation (US$0.30 minimum), take a trufi from Barrio del Carmen, at the 'round'about just north of San Juan Church, they return from San Lorenzo plaza; 45 mins, US$0.45*, the house of the independence hero Eustaquio Méndez, 'El Moto'. The small museum exhibits his weapons, his bed and various bits and pieces, though not his right hand, which he lost. There are many stories as to how it happened. From the village you can walk down to the river. Head north and turn right, then ask directions in the fields for the way up the eroded cliffs. It's a 45-minute walk, with fine views.

All bodegas are closed on Sat afternoon and all day on Sun.

The road to San Lorenzo passes **Tomatitas**, 5 km from town, which is a popular swimming and picnic area. At lunchtime on Sunday, many courtyards serve very cheap meals. Further on is **Parque Nacional Los Barrancos,** an area of dramatic erosion. Beyond San Lorenzo, 22 km from Tarija, are **Los Chorros de Jurina** with natural rock pools. You need a guide to walk there. Check first if there is water in the falls.

Another local bodega is the Rugero Singani bodega at **El Valle de Concepción**, 36 km south of Tarija. To visit, an appointment must be made in Tarija with Inginiero Sergio Prudencio Navarro, Bodegas y Viñedos de la Concepción, La Madrid y Suipacha sin número. Alternatively call T04-6643763. Inginiero Prudencio will show visitors round the vineyards and the bodega. You should try their highly recommended 1994 Cabernet Sauvignon Reserve or their Muscat. To visit the bodegas outside the city, it's best to join a tour (VTB is recommended, see page 261). You can try it on your own using the directions below, but be warned, it's easy to get lost. To get to Concepción, take a trufi from Parada del Chaco every 20-30 minutes, US$0.75 (to get to Parada del Chaco catch any linea 'A' minibus from outside the Mercado Central). They return from the plaza in Concepción. The route takes the road past the airport. At the garita the road forks left to Yacuiba/Pocitos or continues straight on to Bermejo. You will take the latter and, 9 km later, turn right (the road is signposted 'Concepcion'). Then you pass the Colonial winery, the Santa Ana bridge and Santa Ana Grande vineyards and the Centro Vitivinicola, Cooperación Española, before reaching Concepción and its plaza filled with bitter orange and ceibo trees.

Travel to Argentina

There are three possible routes into Argentina from Tarija; via Villazón, Bermejo or Yacuiba. When crossing into Argentina, expect up to four hours to pass through customs and immigration. Electronic goods must be entered in your passport for later checks. Bolivia is one hour behind Argentina.

Via Villazón

A tiring 189-km dirt road to Villazón is the shortest route to Argentina and takes six hours. For full details on this border crossing see page 266.

Via Bermejo

An alternative route to Argentina via Bermejo is most easily reached from Tarija and is 210-km long. The views are spectacular (sit on the right), but it is not recommended in the rainy season or a month or so after. The road is quite rough apart from the 50 km of paved road. Do not try to cycle. Many buses leave daily, usually at night, some early in the morning (four to five hours, US$7.75). Trucks also do the trip (US$4.50). At Bermejo there are at least three hotels, and two casas de cambio on the main street. Customs searches are very thorough. Cross the river by ferry to Aguas Blancas in Argentina, then take a *colectivo* to Orán.

Via Yacuiba

From Tarija to the Yacuiba/Pocitos border is 290 km. Buses run daily morning and night to Yacuiba. From there a daily service runs to Salta and on to Buenos Aires with La Internacional. The ticket includes meals and drinks. Buses leave from Yacuiba to Santa Cruz from around 1700-1900. It can take a long time to cross here, depending on the availability of officials. During holidays and weekends the office is rarely open.
▸▸ *See also Transport, page 261.*

East from Tarija

...ija, passing through Entre Ríos to Villamontes, where it ...uz, south to Argentina and continues east to Paraguay. The ...arija is good all-weather surface, but there are a few bad ...out of Entre Ríos due to landslides and rockfalls. The last ...part of the new Tarija-Bermejo highway. The section from ...is truly spectacular (sit on the left for the best views). The ...face high above the gorge of the Río Pilcomayo as it snakes ...sely forested slopes of the Eastern Cordillera. If you are in ...st after the obvious narrow section and look for flocks of ...the river. A few kilometres further, on the inside of a hairpin bend, g...... ...ltures wheel impressively in the channelled wind above a small rubbish tip.

Entre Ríos

This charming, sub-tropical little colonial town, with cobbled streets and a pretty plaza full of roses which give off a heady scent in the midday heat, lies halfway between Tarija and Villamontes. A giant statue of Christ towers over the town from a summit on the outskirts. There are great views from the top of the steps leading up to it. Also there's good walking in the surrounding hills. Some 10 minutes' walk away, at Rio Santa Ana you can swim when there is enough water; ask directions. You can also hike to a waterfall as well as hire horses; ask Beatrice at the excellent Hotel Plaza (see below).

Some 51 km south of Entre Ríos, 6 km beyond the town of **Salinas**, is the village of **La Misión**, where the original wooden portal and porch of the Jesuit mission church survives. The road is not driveable beyond La Misión.

Villamontes → *Phone code: 04. Colour map 3, grid C5. Altitude: 383 m.*

Villamontes, 280 km east of Tarija, is a friendly town on the edge of the Gran Chaco and is on the road and rail route from Santa Cruz to the Argentine border at Yacuiba. It is hot – very hot. The local Guaraníes make fine basketwork and cane furniture which is sold in shops outside the central market. The town is renowned for fishing and holds a Fiesta del Pescado in August. The main street runs west-east with the bus terminal and train station at the west end, 1-1½ km from the main square Plaza 15 de Abril.

Two roads run east to Paraguay, both of which are only passable in the dry season in high clearance vehicles. One follows the Río Pilcomayo southeast to Hito Esmeralda. The other road runs east to **Ibibobo**. The first 80 km is an all-weather gravel surface. From Ibibobo to the Bolivian frontier at Picada Sucre is 75 km. The first 25 km is gravel; the last 50 km is still under construction and is very rough going. From Picada Sucre to the border is 15 km, and from there to the Paraguayan border at Fortín Infante Rivarola is 8 km. There are no police or immigration officials at the border. Get an exit stamp in Tarija. There are a few small shops on either side of the border but take plenty of water.

● Sleeping

Tarija *p251, map p255*

A **Grand Hotel Tarija**, Sucre N-0770, T04-6642684, F04-6644777. Modernized, comfortable, central, cable TV, free parking, accepts major credit cards for an extra 3%.

A **Los Ceibos**, Av Costañera y La Madrid, T04-6634430, F04-6642461. Includes excellent buffet breakfast, large rooms with cable TV, phone, mini-bar, good restaurant, outdoor pool and bar, accepts major credit cards, recommended.

A **Victoria Plaza**, on Plaza Luis de Fuentes, T04-6642600, F04-664- 2700. 4-star, room service, phone, cable TV, includes buffet breakfast in Café-bar La Bella Epoca, laundry service, accepts AmEx, Visa and Mastercard. Recommended.

B **Hostal Loma de San Juan**, Bolívar s/n, opposite San Juan church, T04-6644522, F04-6644206. Comfortable, 4-star, cable TV, pool, breakfast included. Can pay with Visa and Mastercard, no commission.

C **Gran Hostal Baldiviezo**, La Madrid O-0443, T/F04-6637711. New, good beds and bathrooms, cable TV and mini-bars, very central, should be able to get a discount.

C **Hotel Luz Palace**, Sucre N-0921, T04-663570, F04-6644646. 4-star close to plaza, somewhat twee with bath-tiled floors, cable TV and minibar. Tour agency attached.

D **Gran Hotel Max**, Junín N-0930, T04-6644549. (**F** without bathroom but bargain hard as it's definitely overpriced). 20-min walk from main plaza. Includes continental breakfast, characterless.

D **Hostal Bolívar**, Bolívar E-0256, T04-6642741. (**E** without cable TV). Clean, unadorned courtyards, laundry, overpriced.

D **Hostal Libertador**, Bolívar O-0649, T04-6644231, F04-6631016. Phone, electric showers, national TV, excellent breakfast extra, family-run. Recommended.

E **América**, Bolívar E-0257, T04-6642627. (**F** without bathroom). Rundown, lumpy beds, a last resort, good local restaurant attached.

E **Hostal Carmen**, Ingavi O-0784 y Ramón Rojas, T04-6643372, vtb@olivo.tja. entelnet.bo. Very good beds and bathrooms, cable TV and phone, some ground floor rooms without exterior windows, eat-all-you-can continental breakfast, transfer stand at airport, family owners have agency for tours of the area (see Tour operators, page 261), wise to book in advance. Outshines everywhere for quality in this price band. Highly recommended.

E **Hostal Miraflores**, Sucre N-0920, T04-6643365. (**G** without bath). Good position but private rooms not good value for money and cheaper rooms very basic.

E **Hostería España**, Alejandro Corrado 0-0546, T04-6641790. (**F** without bath). Hot showers, pleasant, patio, cheaper rooms musty and basic.

E **Residencial Rosario**, Ingavi O-0777, T04-6642942, residen_rosario@latinmail.com (**F** without bathroom). Great showers, quiet, clean and pleasant with basic rooms around a rose and flower garden, cable TV, laundry, good *americano* breakfast with home-made marmalade for US$1.50, parking US$0.60 per night, good value. Recommended.

E **Zeballos**, Sucre N-0966, T04-6642068. 5-min walk from main plaza. (**F** without bathroom). Includes continental breakfast, cable TV, laundry service, parking US$0.30 per day, medical service, nice atmosphere, quiet, safe, helpful. Good value, with a sunny, flower-filled courtyard in which to sit.

G **Alojamiento Familiar**, Rana S-0231 y Navajas (off map), T04-6640832. Quiet, no private bathrooms, near the bus terminal.

G **Alojamiento Ocho Hermanos**, Sucre N-0782, T04-6642111, near the main plaza. Clean, shared rooms only.

There are also several cheap alojamientos near the bus station but these are generally unpleasant.

East from Tarija *p257*
Entre Rios

F **Hotel Plaza**, on the main plaza, T04-04-6118039. (G without bathroom). The best place to stay – well decorated, spotlessly clean and spacious rooms. The friendly owner will make you want to stay even if you're only stopping to eat in its restaurant (open all day). Also has a garage and place to wash clothes. You can reserve through Viva Tours in Tarija (see page 261). There are several basic but clean residenciales, all G including: **San Jorge** and **Reyes**. The first has the best plumbing.

Villamontes

C **El Rancho**, T04-6842059, F04-6842985. Lovely rooms with bathroom, a/c, cable TV, and, best of all in this heat, a pool. Includes breakfast, restaurant, buffet lunch for US$4.50, parking in courtyard. Recommended.

C **Gran Hotel Avenida**, on the left side of the main street, 3 blocks east of the plaza, T04-6842297, F04-6842412. Very clean, a/c, comfortable, cable TV, helpful owner, parking.

F **Residencial Raldes**, 1 block back from the main street plaza, T04-6842088. (G with fan and shared bathroom). With private bathroom, poor showers, pleasant shaded patio.

🍽 Eating

Tarija *p251, map p255*

Tarija's restaurants show a strong preference for meat-based dishes, a reflection of the area's Argentine influence. The majority of the better restaurants are found around the main plaza. Many restaurants (and much else in town) close between 1400 and 1600.

$$ **La Floresta**, jump in a taxi and ask for it by name as its only address is Barrio German Busch, does great typical food, has a swimming pool, is close to the river and is very popular with locals at the weekend.

$$ **La Taberna Gattopardo**, Plaza Luis de Fuentes. One of the best, with tables on the pavement and window seats, Gattopardo

has pizza but go the whole hog (or should that be cow?) and steer your way towards the parrillada with Argentine beef. They have a great list of local wines but keep clear of the sickly house red. Sadly this is the only one served by the glass. Also has hot dogs, snacks, excellent salads, good value, lively atmosphere, opens 0700-0200 every day.

$ **Cabaña Don Pedro**, Padilla and Av Las Americas (south side), T04-6642681. Good typical, moderately-priced food, close to the river.

$ **Cabaña Don Pepe**, D Campos N-0138, near Av Las Américas, some way from the centre. Excellent steaks at moderate prices, becomes a peña at weekends, one of the few places you can hear local folk music.

$ **Chifa New Hong Kong**, Sucre O-0235. A good Chinese: smart, good service, moderate prices, excellent food, credit cards accepted.

$ **Chingo's**, Plaza Sucre. Popular – one of many places serving up cheap local food on the west and south side of the plaza.

$ **Club Social Tarija**, on east side of plaza, is pleasant, old-fashioned, and a real haunt for Tarija's business community, excellent almuerzo for US$1.80. Recommended.

$ **El Solar**, Campero y V Lema. Mon-Sat 0800-1400 only. Vegetarian, set lunch.

$ **Gringo Limón**, Gnl Trigo N-0345, off the south side of the plaza, is self-service, where you pay by weight. Good value but it's hard to have anything special when it's been kept hot for hours. The place is also like a barn with the side removed – great when it's hot outside, draughty otherwise.

$ **Mateo's**, Gnl Trigo N-0610, T04-6630797, Mon-Sat 1200-1530, 1900-1200. One of the best almuerzos in town (US$3 which includes salad bar), just off the plaza (north side). Has a sunny patio and good value evening meals with a wide selection of local and international dishes, pasta a speciality.

$ **Pizzería Europa**, Plaza Luis de Fuentes, next to the Prefectura. Good salteñas in the morning. Also has internet (US$0.90 per hr).

East from Tarija *p257*
Entre Rios

There are several restaurants around the plaza, best of which is **San Luis**. Breakfast is available in the comedores in the market as are cheap lunches. Hotel Plaza (see Sleeping, above) also has a good restaurant.

The *comedor popular* in the market serves cheap lunches and is the only place to get breakfast coffee.

$ **Churrasqueria Argentina**, half a block of the southeast side of the main street plaza. For pizzas and grilled meat.

$ **Parillada El Arriero** on the west side of the main street plaza. Good, cheap meals.

Cafés

Bar Cherenta on the southwest corner of the main street plaza.Locals favour this place.

Heladeria Noelia on the right of the main street, halfway from the plaza to the bus station. For ice cream you won't do better than this.

La Fontana, La Madrid y Campos, is good for ice cream, snacks and coffee; also Gloria, Trigo 670. For a cheap breakfast try the market.

Bars and clubs

Tarija *p251, map p255*
Bagdad Café, Plaza Sucre. On the east side of the plaza, this is where Chapacos come to relax over a beer and the ubiquitous game of dice. At night it picks up, often to live music.

Entertainment

Tarija *p251, map p255*
For **cinemas** try **Cine Avenida** on Av Potosí, between Colón and Suipacha, **Cine Eden** on V Lema, ½ a block west of Plaza Sucre, as well as **Gran Rex**, on La Madrid O-0157.

Festivals and events

Tarija *p251, map p255*
15 Apr San Lorenzo celebrates the victory of Moto Méndez over the Spanish.
Easter week Also in San Lorenzo, on the Sat of Easter week, is **La Pascua Florida**, the Sun being **Domingo de Pascua**. The town 'dresses up' to receive visitors from Tarija and elsewhere and there is a colourful procession.
15 Aug **La Virgen de Chaguaya**. People walk all the way from the city to the Santuario Chaguaya, south of El Valle, beyond Padcaya by road, and 60 km south of Tarija. The pilgrimage route is 45 km. To get to Padcaya take a *Línea P* trufi from Plaza Sucre in Tarija, US$1.05, leave all day.

From there you can catch a trufi/micro or bus to Chaguaya.
16 Aug Named after the town's patron saint, the festival of San Roque also takes place on his feast day, when the townsfolk decorate their dogs with ribbons for the day.
Sep The most famous *fiesta* in Tarija is the **Fiesta de San Roque**, held during the first week in Sep. A procession on the first Sun takes the richly dressed saint's statue around the various churches, ending in the church of San Roque. People dance before it, wearing lively colours, feather turbans and transparent veils, and women throw flowers from the balconies. The festivities last all week, with lots of music and dancing.
On the 2nd Sun in Oct is the **Fiesta de las Flores**, which commemorates the Virgen del Rosario. The procession sets out from the church of San Juan and winds its way through the town as onlookers shower the participants with flowers. The celebrations in San Lorenzo and Padcaya are particularly recommended, with colourful costumes, dancing and good food, carrying on till the next day.

Also in Oct, for 2 weekends in the middle of the month, there is a **beer festival** on Av de las Américas.

Shopping

Tarija *p251, map p255*
The **market** is in the block between Domingo Paz, Sucre, Bolívar and Trigo. You can find good basketwork here.

Artesanía Juan Gabriel, Av Domingo Paz y Suipacha, Mon-Sat 0800-1900, has a good selection of hand-woven bags, painted wooden toys, hand-embroidered garments, guitars and other musical instruments.

Wine

To buy Singani from the **San Vicente** bodega, drop into their shop at the junction of Padilla and Av Las Américas (T04-6648100).
Tarija is also the headquarters of Bolivia's wineries, the two best known of which are **Kohlberg** and **Aranjuez** (see page 252). Others worth trying are **La Concepción** (see page 256) and **Santa Ana de Casa Real** These bodegas produce both whites and reds, as well as Singani, the local grape-based brandy (San Pedro de Oro and

Rugero are recommended labels). Naturally, all Tarijeño restaurants stock these wines, which can also be bought at their respective bodegas and shops in town (see above). Wine is cheapest when bought directly from the bodegas' outlets.

▲ Activities and tours

Tarija *p251, map p255*
Tour operators
As Tarija is a compact city and most tours are 1 day affairs, travellers may find it more economical to hire a taxi or walk.
Internacional Tarija, Sucre N-O721, T04-6644446, F04-6645017. Book flights, national and international, and all the local tours, helpful.
Mara Tours, General Trigo N-739, Edif Colonial Center, ground floor, T/F04-6643490, marvin@olivo.tja. entelnet.bo, also helpful. See also under Hostal Carmen (see Sleeping section).
Viva Tours, just off Plaza Luis de Fuentes, at Sucre 0615, T/F04-6638325, vivatour@ cosett.com.bo. Vineyard tours are US$30 for a full day including lunch (per person for group of 2; US$23 for a group of 6).
VTB, in Hostal Carmen (see Sleeping section), all tours include a free city tour; a specialist 4-6 hr trip visits industrial, artesanial and Singani bodegas, US$19 (per person for group of 2; US$12 for a group of 5); comprehensive 10-hr "Tarija and surroundings in 1 Day", US$27; you can also try your hand on an excavation with their paleontological specialist.

⊕ Transport

Tarija
Air
LAB, Trigo N-0327, T04-6642195, Mon-Fri 0800-1200, 1430-1830, Sat 0900-1200, flies to **La Paz**, **Santa Cruz**, **Cochabamba** and **Sucre**. **Aero Sur**, C Ingavi between Sucre and Daniel Campos, T04-6630894, flies twice a week to **La Paz**, and other major cities. Check schedules as they change frequently. Also flights are frequently cancelled and/or delayed.

TAM fly to/from **Tarija**.
SAVE flies to **Yacuiba** and **Santa Cruz** Mon at 0910 and Fri at 1610.
Airline offices Aero Sur, C Ingavi between Sucre and Daniel Campos, T04-6630894. **LAB**, Trigo N-0327, T04-6642195, Mon-Fri 0800-1200, 1430-1830, Sat 0900-1200. **TAM**, La Madrid O-0470, T04-6642734. **SAVE**, T04-6644764.

Bus
For information, T04-6636508. There are daily departures on the 935-km route to **La Paz**, via Potosí and Oruro at 0700 and 1700 (16 hrs US$12 to Oruro, 24 hrs, US$15 to La Paz). Check which company operates the best buses – **San Lorenzo**, for example, has heating. To Potosí (386 km), daily at 1630, 12 hrs, US$6.70-7.45 with San Lorenzo, **San Jorge**, **AndesBus** and **Emperador**.
To **Sucre**, direct with **AndesBus** (recommended), **Emperador** and **Villa Imperial**; at 1600-1630, 17-18 hrs, US$5.25-6 (check if you have to change buses in Potosí).
To **Tupiza**, with Juarez at 2030, 8 hrs, US$5.20.
To **Villazón**, **Cristal** and others at 2030, 7 hrs on unpaved roads but beautiful scenery, US$3.75.
To **Santa Cruz** with San Lorenzo and **Expreso Tarija** on Mon and Thu at 0730 and Sat at 1730, 24 hrs, US$10.45-12. The route is over rough roads, though the last 140 km from Abapó is paved. The road goes via Villamontes, Boyuibe and Camiri. The section between Entre Ríos and Villamontes is truly spectacular.

Car
Car rental Barron's, Ingavi E-339, T04-6636853, www.rentacarbolivia.com.

Travel to Argentina *p256*
Yacuiba
Yacuiba can reached by train. Services leave Santa Cruz Mon, Wed and Fri at 1700, arriving 0600-0700, Pullman US$14, 1st class US$6.70, 2nd class US$5.40. Trains leave Yacuiba for the return trip Tue, Thu and Sat at 1700, arriving in Santa Cruz 0600-0700.

Entre Rios

Minibuses leave for **Tarija** daily at 0300, 0400, 1000, 1200, 1300, 1400, 1700 and 2000 with **Flota Entrerriana**, returning from Parada Chaco in Tarija (to get there catch a minibus marked linea 'A' from outside Tarija Mercado Central); 4 hrs. **San Lorenzo**, **Expreso Tarija** and **Trans Chaco** buses all pass through on their way to Tarija, Yacuiba or Villamontes. For the latter, a bus leaves every day at 2200 from outside the transport offices in Avaroa, just off the plaza.

Villamontes
Air

TAM, T04-6842135, on the main street plaza, flies to **La Paz**, **Sucre** and **Tarija** on Sun and Santa Cruz on Sat.
Airline offices TAM offices are on the south side of the main street plaza.

Bus

To **Tarija** via Entre Ríos, 10 hrs, on Thu at 0500 and 0600, Sun 0600, US$7.50. Via Yacuiba daily, 10 hrs, at 0900, 1500 and 1700, US$3.75. To **Santa Cruz** (12 hrs), **Sucre** and **La Paz** at 1030 (US$4.50), 1930 (US$7.50) and 2000 (cama, US$9). Also to **Camiri**, **Tupiza**, **Villazón**.

Trains

Leave for **Yacuiba** on Mon, Wed and Fri at 0400, US$1.20 and for **Santa Cruz** on Tue, Thu and Sat at 1930, US$11.35 (Pullman), US$5.25 (1st class), US$4.20 (2nd class).

⊙ Directory

Tarija *p251, map p255*

Banks Banco Mercantil, southeast corner of main plaza. Exchanges cash and gives cash against Visa and Mastercard (US$5 authorization charge). Banco de Crédito, Trigo N-0784 (near Casa Dorada), Bisa, east side of Plaza Luis de Fuentes, Banco

Nacional, **Trigo**, all change TCs and have ATMs which accept foreign cards. Dollars and Argentine pesos can be changed at similar rates in any of the casas de cambio on Bolívar between Campos and Sucre.
Internet Bolivia Digital, in Pizzeria Europa on the west side of main plaza, US$0.90. Café Internet Tarija On-Line, US$0.75 per hr, D Campos N-0488. Also two on the north side of Plaza Sucre. **Language classes** Julia Gutíerrez Márquez, T04-6632857, charges US$1 per hr. **Post office** at V Lema y Sucre, Mon-Fri 0800-2000, Sat 0800-1800, Sun 0900-1200 and bus terminal.
Telephone Entel: south side of main plaza, every day 0800-2230 and at V Lema O-0231 y D Campos, Mon-Sat 0730-2300, Sun 0800-2100. Also at the bus terminal.
Useful addresses Consulates Argentina, Ballivián N-0699 y Bolívar, T04-66442273, open Mon-Fri, 0830-1230. Germany, Sucre N-O665, T04-6642062, Mon-Sat 0830-1200, 1430-1830, Sat 0830-1200. **Immigration**: Ballivián esquina Bolívar, T04-6643450. If you're crossing into Argentina at the weekend the office at the border in Bermejo closed, so get your entry stamp here, or at the Argentine Consulate opposite (see above), or at the airport or bus terminal.

East from Tarija *p257*
Entre Rios

There is a branch of **Banco de Crédito**, a hospital and an **Entel** office as well as a petrol station.

Villamontes

Banks Banco de Crédito is on the main street plaza. **Internet** There is a café next to El Arriero restaurant, US$1.50 per hr, Mon-Fri 0800-1200, 1500-2200, Sun 1600-2000. **Telephone** Entel is 1 block northeast of the main street plaza, Mon-Sat 0730-2300, Sun 0800-2000.

Tupiza → *Phone code: 02. Colour map 3, grid C3. Population: 20,000. Altitude: 2,990 m.*

Tupiza is a rising star on Bolivia's 'Gringo Trail' and, if you have the time, should not be missed. It's a dramatic and very pleasant place to visit and enjoys a mild climate. Tupiza lies in the narrow, fertile valley of the Río Tupiza, a beautiful and dramatic desert landscape of red, brown, grey and violet hills. Beautiful rose-red skies can be seen at sunset over the valley from the foot of a statue of Christ on a hill behind the plaza.

Capital of Sud Chichas, a province of the Potosí Department, Tupiza is 200 km southeast of Uyuni. The town is a centre of the silver, tin, lead, and bismuth mining industries. The statue in the main plaza is to Victor Carlos Aramayo, the founding member of the Aramayo mining dynasty, which was pre-eminent in the late 19th and early 20th centuries. An Aramayo company payroll was held up by two Wild West outlaws going by the names of Butch Cassidy and the Sundance Kid (see page 265).
▶▶ *For Sleeping, Eating and other listings, see pages 268-271.*

Ins and outs
The train station is central and just two or three blocks away from most hotels; the bus station is five blocks further south. Roads out are all fairly bad: the best, still a washboard, is south to Villazón; the worst, a dry riverbed, is that to Atocha (the route to Uyuni). The second route is impassable during the wet season when (surprise) it turns into a river.

Sights
Villa **Chajra Huasi**, the palazzo-style and now abandoned home of the fantastically wealthy Aramayo mining family, lies just out of town across the Río Tupiza (see arrow on map). It was from here that the payroll set out which Butch Cassidy and the Sundance Kid eventually robbed. The place is a sad sight now but can be visited for free. The uninspiring local history museum is on the second floor of the **Museo Municipal** ① *on the south side of the plaza, Mon-Fri 0800-1200, 1400-1800, free.* Most of Tupiza's sights are actually outside the town.

Around Tupiza

The eroded desert landscape around Tupiza is the real draw of the town and offers endless hiking possibilities. Make sure to take enough water and, if camping, keep away from the dried-up river beds as flash flooding is always a danger. Only a few of the following attractions can be seen independently unless you have private transport but there are two good tour operators (see page 270), both of which offer good value trips, either by horse or by jeep.

Quebrada de Palala (*palala* means 'barren') is a tributary of the Río Tupiza in the wet season but in the dry season it is used by public transport as a route into the wilderness. It is spectacular in its own right with red fins and leads on to the stunning **Stone Forest**. If in your own transport, drive a short way just north out of town and turn left up the first riverbed you reach. Keep straight on past Palala on the left. The route will eventually take you up a steep mountain to reach, 18 km from Tupiza, **El Sillar**, a saddle between two mountains. From here you'll see, to the right and north, the 'stone forest', a breathtaking area of eroded pinnacles of rock. It is illuminated a deep red at sunset. To the left is Tupiza itself.

Further north, beyond the Quebrada Palala turn-off, is some great scenery. This is real cowboy country of glowering red rock and photogenic hills. It can be done by horse or jeep as part of an organized tour to see where Butch Cassidy and the

Sundance Kid spent the night in Salo then robbed the payroll just beyond **Huaca Huañasca**. Huaca Huañasca means 'Dead Cow Hill' although erosion may explain why no-one now can see the resemblance.

An excursion you can make on your own by foot is to **El Cañon**. Follow the road to the left of the cathedral out of town between the cemetery and the barracks. Continue as the road curves right until you reach a dry river bed. Follow this to the left towards the hills. After 200 m take the right fork in the river bed. Here are some superb rock formations – huge pinnacles of rock and soil, only a few inches thick, which seem to defy gravity. The valley narrows rapidly but the path follows a stream bed for several hundred metres to a picturesque waterfall. The whole walk takes two hours; take water and food.

Another hike possible without a tour firm is to the **Valle de los Machos** and **El Cañon del Inca**. From Plaza El Castillin walk up 26 de Agosto and then between two hills. Another 2 km later you will see the **Door of the Devil** on your right-hand side which resembles huge plates from the spine of a stegosaurus. Pass through these then turn right up a river bed. About 1½ km later take a right fork to arrive at a collection of phallic-like pinnacles, humourously named Valle de los Machos. Continue ahead to the start of El Cañon del Inca. Be prepared to climb what would be, in the rainy season, small waterfalls. You don't have to continue to the end of the canyon but if you do it is 28 km there and back. Again, take water and food.

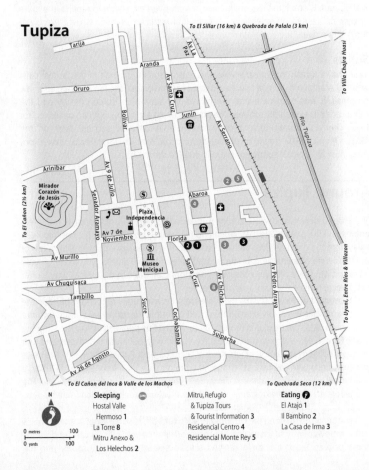

Tupiza

To El Sillar (16 km) & Quebrada de Palala (3 km)
To Villa Chajra Huasi
To El Cañon (2½ km)
To Uyuni, Entre Ríos & Villazon
To El Cañon del Inca & Valle de los Machos
To Quebrada Seca (12 km)

N

0 metres 100
0 yards 100

Sleeping
Hostal Valle
  Hermoso 1
La Torre 8
Mitru Anexo &
  Los Helechos 2

Mitru, Refugio
  & Tupiza Tours
  & Tourist Information 3
Residencial Centro 4
Residencial Monte Rey 5

Eating
El Atajo 1
Il Bambino 2
La Casa de Irma 3

A tale of two outlaws

The movie Butch Cassidy and the Sundance Kid is based on a true story. Butch Cassidy, born Robert Leroy Parker in 1866, was the eldest of 13 children in a Mormon family in Utah. A cowboy named Cassidy and a stint as a butcher inspired his nom de crime. Sundance, born Harry Alonzo Longabaugh in 1867, was the youngest of five children in a Baptist family in Pennsylvania. He got his name by serving 18 months in jail at Sundance, Wyoming, for stealing a horse.

Butch and Sundance belonged to a gang dubbed the Wild Bunch. They held up trains, banks and mine payrolls in the Rocky Mountain West. With US$1,000 rewards on their heads and the Pinkerton Detective Agency (later to become the FBI) on their tail, Butch and Sundance fled to South America in 1901, settling in Patagonia in Argentina, where they peacefully homesteaded a ranch, raising sheep, cattle and horses.

The peaceful life didn't last, however. Their names were linked to a bank robbery in Río Gallegos and the police issued an order for their arrest. In 1906, they found work at the Concordia Tin Mine in the central Bolivian Andes, but Butch still wanted to settle down as a respectable rancher. The bandits quit their jobs in 1908, soon after turning up in the mining centre of Tupiza, where they intended to rob a bank, perhaps to finance their retirement.

They soon turned their attention to the Aramayo mining company, after Butch learned that the local manager would be taking an unguarded payroll from Tupiza to Quechisla, a three-day journey to the northwest. So, on 3 November, the manager set off. As he made his way up Huaca Huañusca (Dead Cow Hill), near Salo, he was held up by two bandits.

Once the bandits had departed, the manager alerted his bosses and the alarm went out to local authorities, as well as to Argentine and Chilean border officials. With military patrols and armed miners (whose pay had been stolen) in pursuit, the pair headed north towards Uyuni. They followed the long, rugged trail to San Vicente, a tiny mining village set in an utterly barren landscape 4,000 m up in the Cordillera Occidental.

At sundown on 6 November 1908, they rode into town and were given a room for the night. There they met Cleto Bellot, with whom they discussed their plans to head north to Uyuni. Bellot went straight to the home of a neighbour, where a four-man posse from Uyuni was staying. They had galloped in that afternoon and told Bellot to be on the lookout for two Yankees.

Accompanied by Bellot, they went to the house. A gunbattle ensued, then all went quiet. At dawn they entered the house, where they found the two bandits stretched out on the floor, dead, both with bullet holes in the head. Butch had shot his partner and then turned the gun on himself.

The outlaws were buried in the local cemetery that afternoon in unmarked graves, but their deaths were not widely reported in the United States until 1930. In the meantime, wild stories of their demise circulated. Some claim that the two outlaws killed in San Vicente were not actually Butch and Sundance and sightings of them were reported after the event. An exhumation at the San Vicente cemetery in 1991 failed to settle this long-running controversy. (Adapted from *Death in the Andes: The Last Days of Butch Cassidy and The Sundance Kid* by Daniel Buck and Anne Meadows, Washington DC.)

To the south of town are five sights. **Quebrada Seca**, is a river bed so named because even when it rains it is dry again within minutes. It is said you can see nine contrasting colours in the hills, from purples to greens. To get there take a Villa Florida bus to the outskirts of town. The quebrada is immediately before the YPFB plant. You can drive or ride a horse down to **Toroyoj** on the Río San Juan de Oro, which is a good place to picnic on a sandy shore beneath weeping willows. Jeep tours can take in these two sights plus **La Torre**, a 40-m-high eroded pinnacle, **Entre Rios**, the confluence of Rio San Juan de Oro (red) and Rio Tupiza (green) and **El Angosto**, the point at which the road and train track south to Villazón head through two separate tunnels in the rock. This can be seen for free from the bus to Villazón, as can Entre Rios.

San Vicente → *Colour map 3, grid C3.*

Tupiza is a good base from which to explore Butch Cassidy and the Sundance Kid country. The outlaws were supposed to have been killed here, in the tiny settlement of San Vicente, 103 km northwest of Tupiza, at 4,500 m, on a good dirt road (it takes around four to six hours). It's a typically bleak Altiplano village, described by one correspondent as "a very sad place to die". The famous shoot-out site is off the main street – ask the locals. ➤➤ *For tours to San Vicente, see page 270.*

Villazón → *Phone code: 02. Colour map 3, grid C3. Population: 13,000. Altitude: 3,443 m.*

Villazón is a dusty frontier town tucked away at the southernmost edge of Potosí Department. It lies along the Río Villazón which separates it from the vastly more attractive Argentine town of La Quiaca. It has little of interest for the visitor other than the fact that it is one of Bolivia's most important official border crossings into and out of Argentina.

Ins and outs The bus terminal is near the plaza, 5 blocks from the border. A taxi to the border is US$0.35, or hire a porter, US$1, and walk across. The rail station is about 1 km north of the border on the main road; a taxi costs US$2.35.

Settled in the mid-19th century, the town exists primarily because of the thriving contraband trade carried on with its neighbour. Indeed, it is no exaggeration to say that fully three-quarters or more of the populace are involved in some way with illicit commercial activities, rivalling even Puerto Suárez in the Eastern Lowlands, in this *comercio de hormigas* (ant trade).

This retail smuggling endeavour is so named because at any time you will see long queues of people patiently awaiting (illegal) entry into Villazón from La Quiaca with all manner of goods bulging from overstuffed bags or strapped to their backs. The Bolivian customs officials do nothing to discourage this trafficking, and to be fair, neither do the Argentine authorities. In fact, this trade has become so institutionalised that more conventional travellers entering Villazón from (or departing to) Argentina are advised to bypass the lengthy queues and simply proceed along to the respective immigration stations.

Border with Argentina

Bolivian time is one hour behind Argentine time from October to April. From May to September Argentina loses an hour and matches Bolivian time.

Bolivian immigration The Bolivian office is on Avenida República de Argentina, immediately before the bridge over the Río Villazón. It is open from 0600 to 2000, every day. They will issue an exit stamp, but note that immigration procedures are haphazard. Visitors may or may not have to pass through customs on either or both sides. Argentine immigration is open 24 hours. Contrary to popular belief, there is no fee to cross the border either way, and any attempts to levy a surcharge or tax are illegal. This does not prevent some officials (especially on the Bolivian side) attempting to extort money from unknowing visitors. You should be on your guard at all times at this border crossing; stories of illegal practices are rife.

The Argentine consulate is situated three blocks south of the main plaza at Avenida C Saavedra 311, and is open weekdays 1000-1300.

Entering Argentina

Visitors entering Argentina from Villazón will encounter no difficulties in La Quiaca, though there are more checkpoints 20 km and 100 km further south along the road to Jujuy. The Argentine authorities do take a dim view of suspect items such as packets of coca leaves or similar derivatives of the plant. Travellers are also advised to dress reasonably smartly and not wear anything that will arouse suspicion.

Bolivian consulate: in La Quiaca is one block south and west of the plaza, at the corners of Calle República Arabe Siria and San Juan; open 0830-1100 and 1400-1700 weekdays, Saturday 0900-1200 (in theory).

Villazón

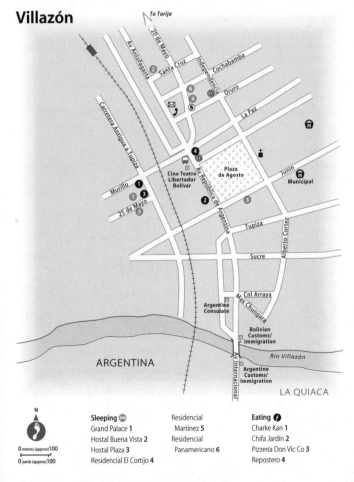

Southern highlands Tupiza

Sleeping
Grand Palace 1
Hostal Buena Vista 2
Hostal Plaza 3
Residencial El Cortijo 4
Residencial Martínez 5
Residencial Panamericano 6

Eating
Charke Kan 1
Chifa Jardín 2
Pizzería Don Vic Co 3
Repostero 4

N
0 metres (approx)100
0 yards (approx)100

● Sleeping

Tupiza *p263, map p264*

Strangely, in Tupiza it's often cheaper to have a double ('matrimonial') bed than a twin on the dubious basis that there are 4 sheets to wash, not 2.

D-E Hotel Mitru, Av Chichas 187, T02-6943001, www.tupizatours.com. Spacious and therefore still the best in town (although Valle Hermosa is giving it a good run for its money), with a wealth of tourist information. Excellent showers and cable TV, swimming pool, kitchen, washing facilities as well as a laundry service (US$1.20 per kg), book exchange, parking and a free showing of Hollywood's Butch Cassidy and the Sundance Kid and documentary. Attached to the hotel and enjoying all its shared facilities, is the excellent value **F Refugio**. (no double beds). At both you can pay by Visa, Mastercard or TCs (4 % extra). The same owners run, for the same prices as the hotel, **Mitru Anexo**, Abaroa (see map), T02-6943002, hot shower, clean, snack shop and restaurant, both open for dinner.

E Hostal Valle Hermoso, Av Pedro Arraya 478, T02-6942592, www.bolivia.freehosting.net (G with shared bathroom). The family which runs this is clearly trying to swipe Hotel Mitru's hard-earned custom with this great place (even the logos are strikingly similar). Good hot showers, pleasant TV/breakfast room (breakfast US$0.75-US$1.50 extra), book exchange and a lot of tourist advice as well as the Butch Cassidy video. No kitchen, overly-firm beds and more cramped than Mitru but cheaper in rooms with shared bath. Will let you park motorbikes. Can pay by Visa, Mastercard and TCs (5% extra).

E La Torre, Av Chichas, T02-6942633, latorrehotel@yahoo.es. In what used to be Roca Colorada, the owners have refurbished and created a well equipped place with good rooms, cable TV, a restaurant, a garden and a 'recorder tape room'. 24-hr reception, credit cards accepted.

F Residencial Centro, Av Santa Cruz 287, T02-6942705, 2 blocks from the train station. (**G** without bathroom). Clean, nice patio, electric showers.

G Residencial Monte Rey, opposite railway station. Clean, hot water, OK beds.

Around Tupiaza *p263*
San Vicente

There's a basic alojamiento on the main street marked 'Hotel'. Restaurant El Rancho is next door. Several shops sell beer, soda, canned goods, etc.

Villazón

Villazón has a surprising number of lodgings for any traveller who has to spend the weekend here before passing into Argentina. All are very cheap and offer little beyond the basic amenities. Dollars,

bolivianos or pesos are accepted, but not credit cards.

E Grand Palace, 25 de Mayo 52, 1 block southwest of the bus terminal, T02-5964693. (F without bathroom). Safety box. Recommended.

E Hostal Plaza, on the main plaza, 138 (south side), T02-5963535. (F without bathroom). Cable TV and parking.

E Residencial El Cortijo, 20 de Mayo 338, behind the post office, 1 block north of the plaza, T02-6962093. Includes continental breakfast, intermittent hot water, restaurant, parking and a pool (although this was a murky green when our correspondent visited).

F Hostal Buena Vista, Av Antofogasta 508, T02-5963055. The name belies its view but the rooms (all shared bath) are good. It's cheap, close to the train and bus stations and sits above a reasonable restaurant. Shame the owner spoils it with a US$1.05 fee to use the good gas showers.

G Hotel Bolivia, 1 block from border. Small rooms, run down, good value breakfast, hot showers extra.

G Residencial Martínez, 25 de Mayo 13, 1 block southwest of the bus station, well signed. All shared bathrooms, hot showers when town's supply is on. Recommended.

G Residencial Panamericano, 20 de Mayo 384, behind Entel, T02-5962612. Oldest place in town, all rooms without bath (saggy beds and no doubles), laundry facilities, parking (US$0.75 extra), the electric showers are also, quite literally, 'shocking'.

🍴 Eating

Tupiza *p263, map p264*

Tupiza is famed for its *tamales* – spicy dried llama meat encased in a ball of corn mash and cooked in the leaves of the plant. Unless you're vegetarian you really should try this local delicacy (no need for a strong stomach). Buy them as breakfast from outside the Mercado Negro on Av Chichas for 50 centivos each. **Sra Wala** is reputed to serve up the best.

$ Il Bambino, Florida and Santa Cruz. Recommended, especially for salteñas, closed Sat and Sun evenings.

Castro on Florida (see map). Home-cooked meat and vegetarian dishes – in fact anything using ingredients from the shop – with an hour's notice, for US$2.25.

$ Los Helechos, C Abaroa, next door to Mitru Anexo. OK for burgers and main courses, has a good salad bar, closed alternate Sun.

$ Picantería Las Brisas, the opposite side of the river, open only Nov-Mar.

$ Snack López, C Abaroa near the plaza. Good and cheap.

Cafés

El Atajo is a new café-bar with internet (US$2.10 per hr) at Florida 157. Serves sandwiches and chicharon de pollo, open Mon-Sat 0800-1200, 1500-2200.

Ice cream at **Cremelin**, on the plaza.

Around Tupiaza *p263*
Villazón

The town's culinary offerings are limited.

$ Charke Kan, round the corner from Hotel Grand Palace, on Av JM Deheza. One of the few bona fide restaurants.

$ Chifa Jardín, on the west side of the main plaza. Recommended. It appears expensive at first but the dishes feed 2.

$ Pizzería Don Vic Co, next door to Charke Kan.

$ Restaurante Repostero, Av 20 de Mayo 190, opposite the bus station. Very friendly and serves up vegetarian food. Also changes TCs.

Off the plaza, along Alberto Cortez, are many fried chicken 'joints'. There are also a handful of dubious-looking food stalls near the bus station, all of which are equally unappetizing. Many travellers suggest crossing the border in La Quiaca to eat.

🏔 Activities and tours

Tupiza *p263, map p264*

Tennis players should look in on the **Tennis Club Ferrovaria** opposite the rail station. They're very welcoming and will be glad to give you a game. Also serves good meals.

● *Price codes for Sleeping and Eating are given inside the front cover. Further information on* ● *hotel and restaurant grading can be found in Essentials, pages 43-44.*

Dr Félix Chalar Miranda, president of the local historical society, offers jeep tours to the hold-up site near Salo, the escape route and San Vicente; or contact via *Inquietud* newspaper office at Av Pedro Arraya 205.
Explore Andina Tours, Av Chichas 220, T02-6943016. This company hires out jeeps.
Potosí Tours, Galería Chuquiago, Calle Sagárnaga 213, T02-2350870, La Paz, Casilla 11034. The Butch and Sundance tour can also be booked here.
Tupiza Tours, in Hotel Mitru, Av Chichas 187, T02-6943513, Casilla 67, www.tupizatours.com. Best to use for tours following Butch and Sundance's movements in 1908 because guide Beatriz Michel Torres worked alongside investigator Daniel Buck for 3 months. Day 1 to robbery spot (great scenery). Day 2 to shoot-out scene (long, dull road – only for real Wild Bunch buffs). US$140 per person, including transport, guide, meals and lodging. Also offers horseriding/camping tours for US$2.70 per hr or US$20 per day and hikes to the local quebradas; 1-day jeep tour takes in all quebradas and the stone forest. Also offers trip to Uyuni via San Pablo de Lipez, San Antonio de Lipez, 2 rarely-seen lagunas, then up through the usual volcano, lagunas and Salar tour route, US$150 per person.
Valle Hermosa Tours, opposite Hostal Valle Hermosa, T02-6942592, offers similar tours by jeep and horse, also following in the footsteps of the outlaws. 1-day jeep ride around local quebradas and to El Sillar US$12 includes lunch, horses same price as Tupiza Tours.

⊙ Transport

Tupiza *p263, map p264*
Bus
To **Villazón** 0400, 1430 and 1900, (Thu also 1030), 2 ½ hrs, US$1.50; to **Potosí**, 1000, 1030 and 2030, 8 hrs, US$4.50 (bus cama with Boqueron 2020, same price), buses at these times also go to **Oruro** and **Sucre**, both US$7.45; to **La Paz**, 1000, 1030 (this is direct, with **Expresso Tupiza**), 2000 and 2100, 14-17 hrs, US$8.95; to **Tarija**, 1930 and 2000, 9 hrs, US$4.50; to **Uyuni**, Mon and Thu 1100, 10 hrs (a bad road – take the train if you can), US$4.50. The road from Potosí which goes on south to Villazón is bad and is often closed in

the rainy season because the road fords the Río Suipacha. Book in advance.

Train
To **Villazón**: Nuevo Expreso del Sur leaves Mon and Fri at 0325, arriving 0620; **Wara Wara** leaves on Sun and Wed at 0835, arriving 1135.

To **Atocha**, **Uyuni** and **Oruro**, Expresso del Sur leaves on Tue and Sat at 1820, arriving 2125, 2332 and 0625 respectively; **Wara Wara** leaves Mon and Thu at 1900, arriving 2224, 0042 and 0825 respectively. The ticket office is open sporadically ahead of train departures, these times do change: Mon from 0730 for that afternoon's train; Mon from 1800 for that leaving on Tue; Wed 0800 for the Thu service; Fri 1500 for the Sat train.

Around Tupiza *p263*
Quebrada de Palala
From Tupiza, in front of the Mercado Negro, take a micro (runs every 15 mins) 3 km north to Palala. From there you may be able to catch a bus to El Sillar, otherwise look for a taxi or thumb a lift. It is best (and easiest) to make this a part of an organized tour.

San Vicente
Trucks leave from Tupiza on Thu early in the morning from Av Chichas near Hotel Mitru. Alternatively hire a vehicle: Fermín Ortega at Taller Nardini, or Barrio Lourdes is recommended. Don Manuel at Hotel Mitru can suggest others. San Vicente is also accessible and a bit closer from Atocha, but there are fewer vehicles for hire there.

Villazón
An improved road goes to Tarija. The road linking Potosí with Villazón via Camargo is in poor condition and about 100 km longer than the better road via Tupiza.

Buses
To **Potosí**, several between 0800-0830 and 1800-1900, 10 hrs day, 12 hrs night, US$3-4.50 (the road is terrible in the wet and the journey can take 24 hrs); to **Tupiza**, 0645 and 0700, 1500, Sun also at 1700, US$1.50; to **Tarija**, a beautiful journey but most buses go overnight only, daily at 2000 and 2030, US$4.50, 6 hrs, it's very cold on arrival but passengers can sleep on the bus until day.

To **La Paz**, 0800 and 0830, 25 hrs, US$7.50; from La Paz at 1800 and 1900; even though the buses are called 'direct', you may have to change in Potosí, perhaps to another company. For **Sucre** and **Cochabamba** change in Potosí; for **Santa Cruz** the best route is via Tarija.

To **Buenos Aires** direct (24 hr-trip) with various firms opposite the bus station (on 20 de Mayo) at 1300 and 1430, US$76 and US$74 respectively.

Trains
To **Tupiza**, **Atocha**, **Uyuni** and **Oruro**: all leave at 1530, the faster **Nuevo Expreso del Sur** service on Tue and Sat (arrives 1810, 2125, 2332 and 0625, respectively) and **Wara Wara** on Mon and Thu (arrives 1820, 2224, 0042 and 0825, respectively). There are connecting buses at Oruro to take passengers on to La Paz. The ticket office opens at 0800; expect long queues. For details of trains from Oruro and Uyuni, see under those destinations.

⊙ Directory

Tupiza *p263, map p264*
Banks Banco Mercantil (south side of the plaza, open Mon-Fri 0830-1200, 1430-1700) and Banco de Crédito (opposite side, Mon-Fri 0830-1230, 1430-1830) will both change US$s but nothing else. For TCs, Visa and Mastercard, Hotel Mitru (see Sleeping above) charges 4%, Res Valle Hermosa 5%. Many shops will also change dollars at better rates than in Villazón. There is no ATM.
Internet Full Internet, southeast side of

Plaza Independencia, no 477, US$2.25 per hr.
Post office On Abaroa, northwest of the plaza, open Mon-Fri 0830-1800, Sat 0900-1700, Sun 0900-1200. They're supposed to go for lunch 1200-1400 but (odd for Bolivia) there's usually someone around. **Telephone** Entel is at the end of the same street as the post office, Mon-Sat 0800-2300, Sun 0800-1300 and 1500-2200.
Useful addresses Hospital Ferroviário (near Hotel Mitru), Dr Rolando Llano Navarro and staff are very helpful. The IGM office, on the 2nd floor, for maps, is in the Municipal building on the plaza, to the right of the church.

Around Tupiaza *p263*
Villazón
Banks There are 2 banks in town but only **Banco de Crédito**, at Oruro 111, (Mon-Fri 0830-1230, 1430-1830) changes money: US dollars and bolivianos but will no advance of cash on cards or exchange of TCs. For the latter, go to **Restaurante Repostero**, who charge 5% commission (also see under Eating). The easiest way to change money is at one of the many casas de cambio on Av República de Argentina approaching the border. Hotels and shops will probably not change anything other than small amounts.
Internet Cafés (US$1.50 per hr) are opposite the bus station, on 20 de Mayo, and on the corner of Oruro and Independencia.
Post office and telephone are in the same building, on Av Antofagasta across and to the left of the bus station. Both are open every day, 0730-2200 (**Entel**), post office 0800-1200, 1430-1800, Sun 0900-1130.

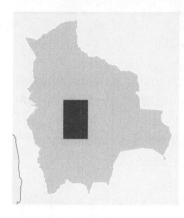

⦂ Footprint features

Introduction

The department of Cochabamba is known as the 'breadbasket of Bolivia' and the city itself is dubbed the 'City of Eternal Spring'. Set in a bowl of rolling hills at a comfortable altitude, its inhabitants enjoy a wonderfully warm, dry and sunny climate, with an average temperature of 18°C.

Economically, this region is of vital importance to Bolivia. Not only is the **Cochabamba Valley** the agricultural heart of the country, but the tropical lowlands of **Chapare** to the east produces the raw material for one of Bolivia's main export earners – cocaine.

In tourist terms, however, the area is of limited importance to the economy. It is overlooked by most visitors, who see Cochabamba and its surroundings merely as a convenient stopping-off point between the Altiplano and the tropical lowlands. Precisely because of this, it offers many effortless, off-the-beaten-track opportunities. There are crumbling, old colonial villages, ancient ruins, beautiful national parks and some of Bolivia's very best markets and festivals. This is also where you'll find the country's best **chicha**, the fermented corn beer brewed by the Incas. A visit to Cochabamba may not quite be the best thing since sliced bread, but it'll certainly 'chicha' a thing or two...

★ Don't miss...

❶ **Tarata** Take a trip to this sleepy, crumbling, colonial village and visit its fascinating convent, page 281.

❷ **The local specialities** Try a glass or two of the excellent *Taqueña* beer – or, if you're more adventurous, sample the local *chicha*, on sale from houses around Cochabamba flying a white flag outside, page 285.

❸ **Torotoro National Park** Go wild in the country and explore the deep canyons, waterfalls and dinosaur tracks in the wonderfully off-the-beaten-track reserve, page 289.

❹ **Inti Wara Yassi** Be Rolf Harris for a day at this animal rescue centre near Villa Tunari, page 292.

❺ **Carrasco National Park** Descend nearly 4,000 m through the cloud forest of the Carrasco National Park on the Caminando en las Nubes, page 293.

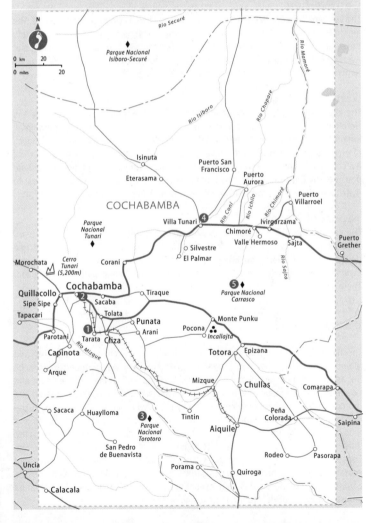

Cochabamba

Cochabamba

Though much new building is taking place throughout the city, especially in the shape of shiny new high-rise blocks of offices and apartments in the north, the centre retains much of its colonial character. There are many fine churches and streets lined with old colonial houses with overhanging eaves, balconies, wrought-iron windows and cool patios behind huge carved wooden doors. To the south of the main plaza are a wide range of colourful markets, which only add to the feeling that Cochabamba is more of an overgrown village than a modern urban centre. ▸▸ *For Sleeping, Eating and other listings, see pages 282-289.*

Ins and outs → *Colour map 2, grid B4. Population: 594,790. Altitude: 2,570 m.*

Getting there

The very small Jorge Wilstermann airport, T04-459 1820, is close to the city centre. The airport bus is micro B from Plaza 14 de Septiembre; US$0.40. A taxi from the airport to the centre costs US$1. For airline addresses, see page 287. The main bus terminal is at Avenida Aroma y Ayacucho, information T155, about 600-700 m south of Plaza 14 de Septiembre. A taxi to and from the centre costs US$0.65. ▸▸ *See also Transport, page 287.*

Getting around

The city is divided into four quadrants based on the intersection of Avenida Las Heroínas running west to east, and Avenida Ayacucho running north to south. In all longitudinal streets north of Heroínas the letter N precedes the four numbers. South of Heroínas the numbers are preceded by S. In all transversal streets west of Ayacucho the letter O (Oeste) precedes the numbers and all streets running east are preceded by E (Este). The first two numbers refer to the block, 01 being closest to Ayacucho or Heroínas; the last two refer to the building's number.

Tourist office

The **central booth** ⓘ *General Achá, next door to Entel, open Mon-Fri 0830-1230, 1430-1815, Sat 0830-1230,* are helpful and have photocopied city maps and free guides. The **administration offices** ⓘ *Colombia E-0340, between 25 de Mayo y España, T04-422 1793, open Mon-Fri 0830-1630.* The **tourist police** are here too. There's also a tourist information booth at Jorge Wilstermann airport.

Background

The name Cochabamba is derived from joining the Quechua words 'cocha' and 'pampa', which together mean swampy plain. The city was founded in 1574 by Sebastián Barba de Padilla and named Villa de Oropeza in honour of the Count and Countess of Oropeza, parents of the Viceroy Francisco de Toledo, who chartered and promoted the settlement of the place. During the heyday of Potosí's silver boom, the Cochabamba Valley developed into the primary source of food for the population of that agriculturally unproductive area. Cochabamba came to be known as the 'breadbasket of Bolivia' because of its high volume of maize and wheat production. Today, the valley is still an important agricultural centre, producing not only abundant cereal crops but also orchard and citrus fruits, as well as accounting for the bulk of the country's dairy products. This high level of economic activity has seen Cochabamba grow to become Bolivia's fourth largest city.

Cochabamba

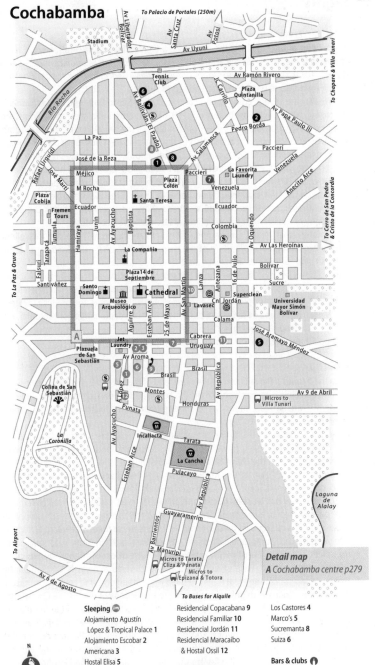

Detail map
A *Cochabamba centre p279*

Sleeping 🛏
Alojamiento Agustín
López & Tropical Palace **1**
Alojamiento Escobar **2**
Americana **3**
Hostal Elisa **5**
Hostal Gala **6**
Hostal Jordán **7**
Regina **8**

Residencial Copacabana **9**
Residencial Familiar **10**
Residencial Jordán **11**
Residencial Maracaibo
& Hostal Ossil **12**

Eating 🍴
Brazilian Coffee Bar **1**
Bufalo Rodizio **2**

Los Castores **4**
Marco's **5**
Sucremanta **8**
Suiza **6**

Bars & clubs 🍸
Wunderbar **7**

N

0 metres   100
0 yards   100

Sights

The centre

At the heart of the old city is the attractive, arcaded **Plaza 14 de Septiembre**. Facing the plaza is the neoclassical **cathedral** ① *Daily, for more information contact Alberto Butron, T04-425 0867, the president of the guides' association, he speaks English.* Dating from 1571, it has been much added to since.

Nearby are several colonial churches, including **Santo Domingo** ① *Santiváñez y Ayacucho*, where building began in 1778 but remains unfinished. **San Francisco** ① *25 de Mayo y Bolívar*, was built in 1581, making it the second oldest in the city, but was heavily modernized in 1926. Also in the centre is the **Convent of Santa Teresa**, ① *Baptista y Ecuador*, which is perhaps Cochabamba's finest religious building. Built in 1760-1790, the interior is quite beautiful and the floor is one of the most original in the Americas. Visitors are not usually allowed in but you can ask for permission to enter at the convent store nearby on Baptista. Just off the main plaza at Baptista y Achá, is the church of **La Compañía**, whose calm, whitewashed interior comes as something of a relief from the usual riot of late-Baroque decoration.

Among the city's museums, the most important is the excellent **Museo Arqueológico** ① *Mon-Sun 0800-1700. US$2, which includes a free guide (in Spanish and sometimes in French and English).* Part of the Universidad de San Simón, at Aguirre y Jordán, it is one of the most complete in the country and displays artefacts dating from 15,000 BC to the colonial period, including an interesting collection of prehistoric pieces, Amerindian hieroglyphic scripts and pre-Inca textiles.

Museo de la Casa de la Cultura puts on exhibitions of paintings both colonial and modern at **Casona Santivañez** ① *Santivañez O-0156, T04-425 9788 and ask for Casona Santivañez, Mon-Fri 0800-1200, 1430-1830, free.*

North of the centre

From the beautiful **Plaza Colón**, at the north end of the old town, the wide, palm-lined Avenida Ballivián runs northwest to the Río Rocha and beyond to the wealthy, modern residential areas. Also known as **El Prado**, Avenida Ballivián is fronted by many fashionable cafés and restaurants.

Cochabamba was the birthplace of Simón Patiño, the tin baron, who amassed one of the world's largest private fortunes. He built two houses in the city. One of these is now part of the **Universidad de San Simón** (see above). His other house, to the north of Plaza Colón at Avenida Potosí 1450, is the **Palacio de Portales** ① *Mon-Fri 1700, and 1800, and Sat at 1100 for guided tours in Spanish, 1730 in English (don't be late), US$1.50.* It has a useful **library** and an excellent **art gallery** ① *in the basement, call T04-424 3137 for latest details in English, Mon-Fri 1700-1800, Sat 1000-1200, Sun 1000-1200 just gallery and garden (hours change), to get there take micro G from Av San Martín.* This sumptuous mansion, which was built in 1925-1927 but never occupied, sits in 10 ha of extravagantly beautiful gardens designed by Japanese experts in the classic style of Versailles. The architectural style is predominantly French Renaissance. The great halls are filled with Napoleonic and Louis XV furniture. On the upper floor are chambers containing reproductions of the Sistine Chapel; the walls are covered in brocaded silk and it is decorated throughout in Carrara marble and paintings by Velásquez. There's even a copy of the Alhambra in Granada. Everything imported from Europe and no expense spared, the Palacio de Portales bears testament to inconceivable opulence. It is now an educational and cultural centre and better known as the **Centro Cultural Pedagógico Simón J Patiño**.

South of the centre

To the south of the centre, near the abandoned train station, are some of the best produce markets in Bolivia. **La Cancha** is huge and well worth a visit on Wednesdays and Saturdays, when it's packed with *campesinos*. It is also very good for souvenirs. **Mercado Incallacta** is mainly for fruit and vegetables, but also sells souvenirs.

Overlooking the bus station is the **Colina de San Sebastián**, offering great views of the city. From here you can walk to the adjoining **La Coronilla Hill**, topped by an imposing monument commemorating the defence of Cochabamba by its womenfolk from Spanish troops in 1812 (beware of robbery).

Cochabamba centre

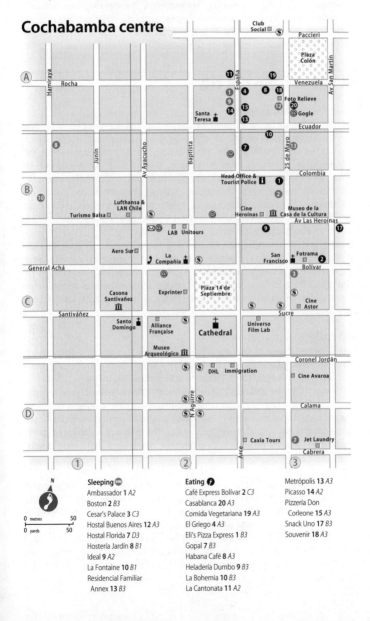

Cochabamba Cochabamba city

Sleeping
Ambassador 1 *A2*
Boston 2 *B3*
Cesar's Palace 3 *C3*
Hostal Buenos Aires 12 *A3*
Hostal Florida 7 *D3*
Hostería Jardín 8 *B1*
Ideal 9 *A2*
La Fontaine 10 *B1*
Residencial Familiar
   Annex 13 *B3*

Eating
Café Express Bolívar 2 *C3*
Casablanca 20 *A3*
Comida Vegetariana 19 *A3*
El Griego 4 *A3*
Eli's Pizza Express 1 *B3*
Gopal 7 *B3*
Habana Café 8 *A3*
Heladería Dumbo 9 *B3*
La Bohemia 10 *B3*
La Cantonata 11 *A2*

Metrópolis 13 *A3*
Picasso 14 *A2*
Pizzería Don
   Corleone 15 *A3*
Snack Uno 17 *B3*
Souvenir 18 *A3*

0 metres 50
0 yards 50

At the east end of Avenida Heroínas is another hill, the **Cerro de San Pedro**, at the top of which stands an enormous statue of **Cristo de la Concordia**. A modern **cable car** ⓘ *Mon-Sat 1000-1800, Sun 0900-1900, US$1 return,* will whizz you to the top from the east end of Heroínas. Steps which are the alternative to the cable car are reported to be unsafe. For another US$0.15 you can, if it's open, climb up 10 floors of the statue to stare out from within Christ's chest – the heart of Christianity, so to speak. Though the 34.2-m, 2,200-ton statue is claimed to be the biggest depiction of Christ in the world, it lacks any of the iconic beauty of Rio's version and the view over Cochabamba is similarly uninspiring. Nevertheless, it's cheap, gives a handy overview of the city and is the nearest the city gets to a tourist attraction. A new raised bike road starts from below Cristo de la Concordia and runs north, across the Río Rocha, through the northern part of the city, parallelling Avenida América.

Excursions from the city

Parque Nacional Tunari

Cochabamba's Parque Nacional Tunari, established just outside of the city in 1962, at 329,183 ha, is a small park by Bolivian standards, but easy to reach. Situated in what many say is the most beautiful valley in the country, Tunari's chief appeals are the magnificent vistas it affords from its summit, **Cerro Tunari** (5,035 m), and its numerous, well-marked trails. It also encompasses a number of beautiful lakes, the best of which are the Lagunas de Huarahuara and Macho, all within a day's walk from the city. However, as Cochabamba expands, its effects are being felt on Tunari, and it is inevitable that the park's southern borders will suffer unless a sustained effort is made to reign in urban encroachment.

Experienced trekkers wishing to **climb Cerro Tunari** in challenging fashion can bus or hike to the park from Quillacolla, a suburb 18 km southwest of Cochabamba, along the Liriuni Trail. You must spend the night in Liriuni, which is less than 5 km from the park. There is no accommodation other than campgrounds within Tunari itself. Information on Tunari is easily obtained by any of the major agencies or guides in Cochabamba.

Quillacollo → *Population: 20,000.*

Thirteen kilometres west of Cochabamba, Quillacollo has a good Sunday market which is completely geared towards the local *campesinos*. There are no tourist items for sale. The town is famous for its **Fiesta de la Virgen de Urkupiña** which lasts four days with much dancing and religious ceremony. Its date varies each year between June and August. The first day is the most colourful with all the groups in costumes and masks, parading and dancing in the streets till late at night. Many groups have left by the second day and dancing stops earlier. The third day is dedicated to the pilgrimage. Cochabamba gets very busy at this time. Hotels are all full throughout the festivities. Be there before 0900 to be sure of a seat, as you are not allowed to stand in the street.

El Passau, 6 km north of Quillacollo, has the oldest church in the Cochabamba Department, with gilded altars in baroque style and a choir in the Toldeo style. Take trufi 210 from Quillacollo. **Liriuni hot springs** are 15 km northwest of Quillacollo. There's no accommodation and few visitors during the week, though camping is possible. Trufi 265 goes there on weekends in the dry season. In the wet season you have to walk the last 3 km. Between Quillacollo and Cochabamba is **Colcapirhua**, which is famous for its functional ceramics, which are sold on the main street and at local markets.

Villa Albina

ⓘ *Mon-Fri 1500-1600, Sat 0900-1130, T04-426 0083.*

About 8 km beyond Quillacollo is a road to the beautiful **Pairumani hacienda**, centre of the Patiño agricultural foundation. Known also as Villa Albina, it was built in 1925-1932, furnished from Europe and inhabited by Patiño's wife, Albina. Both the house and Patiño mausoleum can be visited but be sure to ring because it sometimes closes for renovation. To get there take Bus 7 or 38, or trufi 211 from Cochabamba.

Inka-Rakay

ⓘ *It may be possible to hitch. Alternatively hire a guide. Norberto Rojas Mariscal, T04-436 0509, runs a shop on the west side of the plaza, next to O-078. He speaks English and is recommended. He charges US$7.50. Take food and plenty of water as there is none available and beware of theft on the footpath. It's also worth taking a hat and sun-block as there is no shade on the path or road.*

Some 27 km west of Cochabamba, near **Sipe-Sipe**, are the Inca ruins of Inka-Rakay. The main attraction is the fantastic view from the site of the Cochabamba Valley and the mountains ringing the ruins. From Sipe-Sipe to the ruins there is either a 6-km footpath, or a 12-km road with almost no traffic, taking three to four hours to walk. It is a beautiful trip, and reports indicate that it is slightly less terrifying on foot than in a vehicle. Start early for it is a full day. Leave the plaza in Sipe-Sipe going up the street past the church, then left at the top and then right when you come to the wider road. Follow this road out of town, and while doing so look upwards for the area of whitish rock which you should be heading for. When the road crosses the stream and makes a sharp left, continue on the path to the left for 150 m and then take the path uphill to the right, cross country, to the white rock. (At the stream do not take the obvious trail to the right; it leads to the mountains on the right of the valley). At the rock, turn about 45 degrees to the right as you climb, then you need to stay close to the valley to pick up a distinct trail to the ruins. These will appear first as a rough outcrop of rocks. If you hit the road, then you have gone too far left; turn right and climb the road to an obvious sign, from where it's five minutes on a wide path downhill. It may, of course, be easier to walk there all the way by road and return on the path, which can be found from the road a few hundred metres from the ruins.

The church in Sipe-Sipe is attractive and there are several other interesting buildings. ▸▸ *For further details, see Activities and tours, page 286.*

Tarata

Southeast of Cochabamba is an area known as **Valle Alto** with some interesting little towns, all easily reached from the city. The sleepy village of Tarata, 33 km southeast of Cochabamba, is worth visiting for its crumbling, colonial architecture. It has a lovely, old arcaded plaza on which stand the **church** ⓘ *open 0800-1300 daily,* containing an 18th-century organ and other colonial artefacts , the Casa Consistorial and the Municipalidad. Inside the **Franciscan Convent** overlooking the town are the remains of the martyr, San Severino, patron saint of the town, more commonly known as the 'Saint of Rain'. A lively and colourful festival is held in his honour on the last Sunday of November, attracting many thousands of people. The convent dates from 1808 and it would be a crime to miss. To one side of its peaceful brick courtyard is the old store for wine made by the nuns and, judging by the size of the massive urns, this was a merry place indeed! You can also see a nun's bedroom barely changed in nearly 200 years, tiny, stark and bare with the remains of a horrible bed. Three Fathers live here now who allow tourists to stay in the **convent** ⓘ *Mon-Sat 0800-1200, 1400-1800, Sun 1400-1800*. If you ask politely they may also show you the collection of antique books. The church next door has an interesting modern-day outdoor chapel.

Doña Prima Fernández Prado, who lives opposite the convent at E-0115 Arze, sells alpaca sweaters, bags and textiles at 'amazing' prices. Knock loudly on her door. The town also has a large procession on 3 May, day of *La Santa Cruz,* with fireworks and a brass band. Market day is Thursday.

Cliza and around

At Cliza, 6 km further southeast from Tarata, there is a large, colourful Sunday market. From Calle Francisco del Rivero there are trucks to **Toco,** to see its large church and Byzantine cupola, a favourite subject of many artists. About 1 km from Cliza is **Huayculi,** known for its ceramics, and you can watch the artisans at work. Take a taxi from Tarata or walk.

Punata

Punata, 48 km east of Cochabamba, is an important agricultural centre and is famous for its festival of *Señor de los Milagros* on 24 September, as well as its many baroque/mestizo works of art in the church. Behind the church, villagers line up their new vehicles for the priest to bless them. Punata also has something of a reputation for the production of the region's delicious *chicha* – the local speciality is *garapiña,* a mixture of *chicha* and ice cream. It also has a very lively and colourful market on Tuesday.

Change bus at Punata for **Villa Rivera,** a major centre for preparing wool, dyeing and weaving. The village is famous for its woven wall hangings. At **Arani,** 7 km east of Punata, there is a good *artesanía* market on Thursday. About 5 km beyond is **Collpa Ciaca,** where there's another attractive church and hills to walk in.

● Sleeping

Cochabamba *p276, maps p277 and p279*
The centre
A **Ambassador**, España N-0349, T04-425 9001, F425 7855. Includes buffet breakfast. A modern, central and reasonable hotel with a good restaurant.
A **Cesar's Palace**, 25 de Mayo S-0210, T04-425 4032, F425 0324 cph@pinocbb. entelnet.bo. Part of a chain, Cesar's is flashy and stylish with a beauty salon, travel agency and sauna as well as business facilities and conference rooms. Includes buffet breakfast (US$3.25 for non-guests).
C **Boston**, 25 de Mayo N-0167, T04-422 8530. A good, clean hotel with a restaurant, luggage deposit and safe parking. Rooms at the back are quieter. Recommended.
C **Ideal**, España N-0329, T04-425 9430, T/F04-425 7930. Includes breakfast, restaurant, comfortable, good value.
C **La Fontaine**, Hamiraya N-0181, T04-425 2838, F425 2838. Includes breakfast, with private bathroom, cable TV, phone, parking, bar and restaurant, café open at 0700 for breakfast, reasonable value.
C **Regina**, J de la Reza O-0359, T04-425 7382, F411 7231. Spacious, restaurant,

stylish, modern, helpful, breakfast costs extra. Recommended.
E **Hostal Buenos Aires**, 25 de Mayo N-0329, T04-425 3911. (F with shared bathroom.) Far from welcoming, but pleasant nonetheless, with clean communal bathrooms. Some balconies overlook the street and there's an attractive courtyard. American breakfast costs US$1.35.
E **Hostal Florida**, 25 de Mayo S-0583, T04-425 7911, floridah@elsito.com (F without private bathroom). A very good value hostal with a slightly flaking sense of chintz. Walls are painted peach, there are plastic flowers and, in the courtyard downstairs, plastic storks. It's not always too welcoming but the showers are very hot and rooms have cable TV and phones. Recommended.
E **Hostal Jordán**, 25 de Mayo S-0651, T04-422 5010. Also affiliated to ABAJ.
E **Hostería Jardín**, Hamiraya N-0248 (entre Colombia y Ecuador), T04-424 7844. (F without private bathroom). With a garden and a safe car park, Jardín is comfortable. Breakfast available for US$1 extra.

E **Residencial Jordán**, C Antezana S-0671, T04-422 9294. ABAJ affiliate (Bolivian Youth Hostel Association). Modern, clean, basic with cable TV, and a small swimming pool.
F **Residencial Familiar**, Sucre E-0554, T04-422 7988. Cheaper with shared bathroom. Pleasant, secure, good showers. Has annex at 25 de Mayo S-0234, T04-422 7986.

Near the bus station
There is lots of cheap and basic accommodation near the bus station, but much of it is of the short-term variety and it is not a safe area to wander around alone after dark. Most of the dubious places are on Junín and Aroma. Those listed below are popular with backpackers and considered relatively safe. Only some have private bathrooms.
B **Americana**, Esteban Arce S-788 y Av Aroma, T04-425 0554, F425 0484, americana@mail.infornetcbba.com.bo. A helpful 3-star option with fans, an elevator, laundry, and parking. Accepts Visa. *Rodizio* grill next door.
D-E **Tropical Palace**, N Aguirre S-0880, T04-422 8256. Modern, TV (not cable) and basic breakfast included. Recommended.
E **Hostal Elisa**, Agustín López, S-0834, 2 blocks from the bus station, T04-423 5102. (F without private bathroom.) Cable TV and good showers, good breakfast for US$2.25, modern, garden, very popular with travellers and probably the best value. Laundry service expensive – use Jet instead just around corner. Highly recommended.
E **Hostal Gala**, Estaban Arce S-0852, T04-425 2054. Modern hotel close to Av Aroma. Cable TV and good beds, electric showers. Continental breakfast included.
F **Hostal Ossil**, Agusti Lopez S-0915, close to bus terminal, T04-425 4476. A reasonably new hostal with clean rooms. Good value.
F **Residencial Maracaibo**, Agustín López S-0925, T04-422 7110. (G without bathroom). Popular with travellers, clean, basic, safe, best rooms around bright patio (40-42, 54-56).
G **Alojamiento Agustín López** Agustín López S-0853, T04-425 6926. Basic, hot water, some recent improvements.
G **Alojamiento Escobar**, N Aguirre S-0749, T04-422 5812. No private bathrooms, good value, but not to be confused with *Residencial Escobar* at Uruguay E-0213, which is not recommended.

G **Residencial Copacabana**, Av Arce S-0875 y Brasil, T04-422 7929. Only shared bathrooms. hot showers, lovely peaceful courtyard, motorcycle parking, as well as (nearby) garage for cars – US$0.50, good breakfast US$0.75, clean and very friendly. Recommended.

North of the centre
L-AL **Portales**, Av Pando 1271, T04-428 5444, F424 2071, www.portaleshotel.com. A friendly but rather utilitarian 5-star hotel with a swimming pool in the smart residential area of Recoleta, a long way from the centre.
AL **Aranjuez**, Av Buenos Aires E-0563, T04-428 0076, F424 0158, Casilla 3056. Two blocks from Los Portales, 4-star, with a small pool which is open to the public for US$1, colonial style, good restaurant, jazz in the bar on weekends. Recommended.
A **Gran Hotel Cochabamba**, Pl Ubaldo Anze, 2 blocks from Los Portales at La Recoleta, T04-428 2551, F428 2558. In a beautiful setting with a garden, swimming pool (guests only) and tennis courts, popular with tour groups. Recommended.

Excursions from the city *p280*
Quillacollo
AL **Eco Hotel Spa Planeta de Luz**, at Marquina (US$0.65 by bus from Quillacollo, trufi marked *'Bellavista'* or US$10-11 for a taxi from Cochabamba), PO Box 318, Cochabamba, T04-426 1234, F429 1031, www.planetadeluz.com. Eco-spa resort, part of the *Comunidad Janajpacha*, with kitchen, games, reading and dance rooms, vegetarian restaurant, solar heating, gardens, pool and sauna (US$5 per day for visitors), and natural medicine clinic; also camping. The main activities are meditation and tai chi. Sleeping in suites, rooms and cabañas.
C (per person) **La Cabaña de la Torre**, further along the road past Quillacollo and the turn-off to Sipe-Sipe, not far beyond the police checkpoint, T04-436 3238. This is a weekend retreat for the more affluent of Cochabamba. You can swim in a thermal pool, play tennis and volleyball or enjoy a massage. All food is included. Alternatively you can pay US$7.50 for food and facilities but no bed for the night. Take trufi 261 from 6 de Agosto and República.

F **Los Molles**, T04-426 3415 is a campsite with swimming pool, sauna, volleyball court and restaurant on the right-hand side before you enter Sipe-Sipe, US$1.50 per person.

⊙ Eating

Cochabamba *p276, maps p277 and p279*
The restaurant and nightlife district centres around España, Ecuador, Colombia, Pl Colón and north of Río Rocha near Av Santa Cruz. There are many places to eat and drink at streetside tables on Ballivián, just off Plaza Colón. Stroll up the central avenue and see which is flavour of the month. Popular places there include: Los Castores, Ballivián and Oruro, frequented by 20-25 year old locals for juices, shakes and food. Those on very tight budgets can find edible food in the Incallacta market for under US$1.

$$$ **La Cantonata**, España y Mayor Rocha, T04-425 9222, open daily, 1200-1430, 1830-2330. Upmarket Italian food – possibly the best in Bolivia. Excellent service. Highly recommended. Credit cards accepted.
$$$ **Sole Mio**, Av America 826 y Pando. T04-428 3379, www.solemioimport.com.bo. A smart Neapolitan pizza restaurant with good beer on tap. Delicious and fairly authentic pizzas and exceptionally good desserts. Attentive service.
$$$ **Suiza**, Av Ballivián 820, T04-425 7103. Popular place for international cuisine.
$$ **Bufalo Rodizio**, Torres Sofer, 2nd floor, Av Oquendo N-0654. Brazilian grill, superb all-you-can-eat buffet for US$7.50, great service, an absolute must for all self-respecting carnivores, also salads for US$4. Recommended.
$$ **Comida Vegetariana**, M Rocha E-0375. A slightly worthy atmosphere but good, filling food. There's a 4-course buffet lunch for $1.50 and a buffet breakfast for US$1. Most of the food is soya-protein based but Bolivian chickens, as in many 'vegetarian' restaurants, seem to count as vegetables. Ask for details of their country retreat if you want to discover your inner silence.
$$ **El Gran Asador**, Junín 0942, T04-428 5653. Good barbecued meats served up in a stylish restaurant.

$$ **El Griego**, España N-0386. An otherwise trendy restaurant with truly awful background music. Good kebabs and lots of pasta dishes. Colourful walls, modern art and wooden floors.
$$ **Habana Café**, M Rocha E-0348. Genuine Cuban food and drinks, delicious smells will tell you when you get there, can get lively at night, open 1200-last person leaves.
$$ **La Bohemia**, España y Ecuador. Trendy café serving meat and vegetarian meals as well as salads and snacks. Open 1600-late.
$$ **La Estancia** Anecito Padilla block 7, in a side street off Plaza Recoleta, T04-424 9262, best steak in town, also grilled fish and chicken and salad bar. Recommended.
$$ **Lai-Lai**, Recoleta E-0729, T04-424 0469. Excellent Chinese with a takeaway service.
$$ **Marco's**, Av Oquenda, between Cabrera y Uruguay. For lovers of Peruvian *ceviche*. Sat and Sun 1200-1500.
$$ **Metrópolis**, España N-0299. Good pasta dishes, huge portions, great salads, good value. Fills up with students in late afternoon.
$$ **Picasso**, España N-0327. Good Mexican food, popular. Part of **Hotel Ideal**, rather plain interior.
$$ **Pizzería Don Corleone**, España N-0350, T04-425 5255. Great pizzas in a centrally-located restaurant.
$$ **Souvenir**, 25 de Mayo N-0391. *Salteñería* and *confitería*, good place to try a variety of salteñas in a clean, modern environment. Also serves crêpes, popular early evening.
$$ **Sucremanta**, Av Ballivián. Popular with better-off locals for weekend lunches.
$ **Eli's Pizza Express**, 25 de Mayo N-0254, T04-4259249. Part of the La Paz chain of restaurants with pizzas and Mexican fast food.
$ **Gopal**, C España N-0250, Galeria Olimpia. Closed Sat and Sun night. Excellent vegetarian buffet lunch 1200-1500, US$1.50, and vegetarian restaurant in the evenings, pleasant garden.
$ **Snack Uno**, Av Heroínas E-0562. Good lunches and dinners, including vegetarian.

Cafés
There are several good **ice-cream parlours** and fast-food places on Av Heroínas, between Ayacucho y San Martín, including Heladería Dumbo (also on Ballivián just off Plaza Colón) and Unicornio.

Brazilian Coffee Bar, Av Ballivián just off
Pl Colón. An upmarket European-style café
with a TV showing international sport.
Tables outside on the pavement are a good
spot for people-watching.

Café Dor@dita, 329N 25 de Mayo y Ecuador,
T04-452 9125. A small, central, wood-clad
café which does good breakfasts including
pancakes, cappuccinos, waffles, croissants,
omelettes etc.

Café Express Bolívar, on Bolívar between
San Martín y 25 de Mayo. A long way from
Starbucks, this little café hasn't changed in
years and is very friendly. Wooden tables
with benches, black and white tiled floor,
flickering lights, antique till, excellent coffee,
limited cake selection.

Café Francés, España 140, between Heroínas
y Colombia. A laid-back café serving savoury
crêpes, a variety of different types of drinking
chocolate, ice-cream cups and teas. Parisian
photos line the colourful walls.

Casablanca 25 de Mayo between Venezuela
y Ecuador. An attractive and usually buzzing
café next to the excellent Google internet
café. Wooden chairs, art deco touches, a
jazzy soundtrack and Casablanca quotes and
misquotes add to the atmosphere. Good
food options include pasta, pizzas and salads
as well as a fine range of (19 different)
coffees. In the evenings it fills up with the
young people of Cochabamba drinking wine
and cocktails. Wicked tequila slammers.

Sipe-Sipe
$$ **El Recuerdo**, beyond Los Molles
(see sleeping) on the same side of the road.
A good place to eat.

ⓝ Bars and clubs

Cochabamba *p276, maps p277 and p279*
The main area for bars and live music is
around España, Ecuador, Colombia and
Plaza Colón, and north of Río Rocha near
Av Santa Cruz. For discos and nightclubs
head for the east side of Ballivián between
Pl Colón and La Paz.
Alcatraz, Blvd Recoleta. Opens at 2300. A
trendy nightclub playing mostly US and
European music, entry US$4, includes 1 drink.

Café Casablanca (see also cafés), 25 Mayo, is
a bar with an upstairs balcony.
Chilimania, M Rocha E-0333, is also good for
drinking and dancing but definitely not as
lively as *Panchos*.
D'Mons, Tarija y América. Opens at 2300.
Entry US$3.25, includes 1 drink, mix of Latin,
contemporary and classic rock.
El 18 Brumario, Ecuador between España y
25 de Mayo, has live music every Thu, Fri and
Sat, cover charge US$1.05.
Las Brujas, Circunvalación y Santa
Cruz. Opens at 2200. Entry US$1.65,
includes 1 drink.
Lujos, at Beni E-0330. Opens at 2300.
Entry US$3.25, includes 1 drink.
Panchos, on M Rocha E-0311, just off España,
is a lively dancing and drinking place.
Wunderbar, Venezuela E-0635. Open 1930.
A popular bar with good music, serves wings,
ribs and subs and has cable TV sports on Mon.

ⓔ Entertainment

Cochabamba *p276, maps p277 and p279*
Cinemas
Astor, Sucre E-0419, T04-422 4045.
Good sound.
Avaroa, 25 de Mayo S-0435, T04-422 1285.
Cine Heroínas, Av Las Heroínas E-0347,
shows national and international films.

Peñas
Show Folklórico is a *Fiesta Boliviana* on
Saturdays at *Aparthotel Santa Rita,* Buenos
Aires 886, T04-4280305.
Show Las Américas, weekends at Temporal
in Cala Cala.
Totos, M Rocha y Ayacucho, T04-452 2460.
Peñas Friday nights only, maybe Saturdays,
2000-0300. A locals' place. Free.

Theatre
There are frequent **concerts** and **plays** at
the elegant Teatro Achá, España y Heroínas,
T04-422 1166. More popular stage
productions (comedy, music and dance) can
be seen at **Tra La La**, Plazuela 4 de Noviembre,
opposite the Chilean Consulate, T04-428
5030, or **Champagne**, Ballivián 0658.

✪ Festivals and events

Cochabamba *p276, maps p277 and p279*
See also Festival calendar, on p118.

15 days before Lent Carnival. Rival groups
(*comparsas*) compete in music, dancing and
fancy dress, culminating in El Corso on the
last Sat of the Carnival. *Mascaritas* balls also
take place in the carnival season, when the
young women wear long hooded satin
masks. Every year, on the first Sun of Sep, a
large section of the town centre is closed to
all but man-powered traffic. Bicycles and
Shanks' Pony rule the day, 0900-1700.
On 14 Sep is the Day of Cochabamba.
The Luzmilla Patiño Festival of music takes
place every 2 years, usually around Sep/Oct.
For details, T04-424 3137.

⭘ Shopping

Cochabamba *p276, maps p277 and p279*
Fotrama is a co-operative for alpaca
sweaters, blankets, gloves, scarves, etc,
run by Maryknoll Mission. Their factory
outlet is at Bolívar 0439, T04-422 5468.
Open Mon-Fri 0900-1200, 1430-1900,
Sat 0900-1200, Sun closed.
Gamboa, Av Manco Kapac 541. Good quality
musical instruments.
IC Norte Supermarket, Av América E-0817
(take micro 10 or 35), has everything you
need for trekking.
There are several **antique shops** along
España, close to Ecuador.

Markets

Cochabamba has some great markets which
are worth visiting for the experience alone
(see also p278). The biggest and most
famous of these is **La Cancha**, which
occupies a vast area between San Martín,
Punata, República and Pulucayo. It sells
everything under the sun but is not safe late
at night. Also watch out for pickpockets
during the day. Woollen items are expensive
but high quality, around US$35-50 for an
alpaca sweater. There is also a **Saturday
market** at Av América y Libertador, which
is best before 0900.

Bookshops

Los Amigos del Libro, Av Ayacucho
S-0156 (in front of the post office), in
Hotel Portales and *Gran Hotel Cochabamba*,
and in the Torres Sofer shopping centre.
A very good bookshop, it stocks US
and English magazines as well as
Footprint Handbooks, and good city
maps and guides in colour for US$2.50
(published by Quipus).

Camping equipment

Ans Em Ex, Heroínas O-0255, has a limited
range. Camping gas is available at several
shops on Av San Martín.

Photography

Foto Relieve, 25 de Mayo N-0345. For film
developing; develops slides in an hour.

▲ Activities and tours

Cochabamba *p276, maps p277 and p279*
Most pools are open only at weekends in the
summer; check before going.
Club Social, C Méjico E-0359 (US$1.50),
swimming pool open to the public.
El Carmen, on the road to Quillacollo;
US$2, catch a micro on Junín. popular
tourist complex.
Estancia El Rosedal at Tiquipaya (take bus
12 from Antezana y Cabrera to the end of
line). Pool and restaurant.

Tour operators

Fremen, Tumusla N-0245, T04-425
9392, F411 7790. Run city and local
tours, including to Torotoro, Samaipata
and the 'Ruta del Ché' (see Eastern
Lowlands chapter), they specialize in
travel in the Bolivian Amazonia, using
the *Reina de Enin* floating hotel out of
Puerto Varador near Trinidad and run
the *Hotel El Puente* in Villa Tunari (see p294),
also have offices in Santa Cruz, Trinidad
and La Paz.
Turismo Balsa, Av Heroínas O-0184, T04-422
7610. Daily city tours, excursions to
Quillacollo, Inca-Rakay, Samaipata, Torotoro,
etc, plus airline reservations. Also have an
office in La Paz.
Unitours, Av Las Heroínas. Next door to LAB,
good for flights.

⊖ Transport

Cochabamba *p276, maps p277 and p279*
Air
Several flights daily to/from **La Paz** (35 mins) and **Santa Cruz** (40 mins) with **LAB** and **Aero Sur** (book early for morning flights). LAB also fly to **Sucre**, **Trinidad** and **Tarija**. Reconfirm all flights (and obtain reconfirmation number), and arrive early for international flights.

Airline offices
Aero Sur is at Av Villarroel 105, esquina Av Oblitas (Pando), T04-440 0909.
Aerolíneas Argentinas is at *Interfly* offices, Av Ayacucho, corner of M Rocha 409, Edif Crystal, oficina 3, T04-452 6079.
Air France, in the same building as AA, 1st floor, oficina 2, is T04-422 1864.
American Airlines is at 25 de Mayo 262, oficina 8, T04-422 6337.
British Airways/Iberia, Av Salamanca 675, 3rd floor, T04-425 8671.
LAB is at Heroínas, between Pasaje Fidelia Sánchez y Baptista, open 0800, and at the airport, opens 0500, T04-425 0750.
LAN Chile is at Av Heroínas 0-130, Edif Barna, 2nd floor, oficina 202, T04-425 3335.
Varig is in the same building, 1st floor, T04-425 5298.

Bus
Micros and colectivos around town cost US$0.20; trufis cost US$0.30. Those marked 'San Antonio' go to the market area. Trufis 'C' and 10 go from the bus terminal to the city centre. For information call T155.

Buses leave early morning and evening to **Santa Cruz**, from 0530-2200, US$3-4.50 (*bus cama* at 2200 with **Flota Copacabana** and **Trans Copacabana** US$7.50), 10 hrs. Minibuses take the mountain road via Epizana, from Av 9 de April and Av Oquendo, all day.

To/from **La Paz**, 0600-2300, US$2.25-3.75, 7 hrs. Many companies do this route, night or day, so look for best times, services and price. *Bus camas* leave from 2030 and cost US$4.50-6.

To **Oruro**, 0500-2300, US$2.25-3, 4 hrs, buses leave at least every hour.

To **Potosí**, 1830-2000 only, US$4.50-5.25, via Oruro, several companies.

Daily to **Sucre**, 1930-2030 only, US$4.50-5.25, 13 hrs on a rough but beautiful road, several companies (Flota Copacabana and Trans Copacabana recommended; the latter's *bus-cama* leaves at 2000 and costs US$8.90). To go to Sucre by day take bus to **Aiquile** (see p233), then one at 2400-0100 passing en route to Sucre. To take a truck in daylight, wait until the next day.

To **Iquique** in Chile, via Oruro, **Paraiso** takes 18 hrs and leaves from the terminal on Sun, Mon, Wed and Thu at 0845, US$16.40. **Trans Bernal** claims to take just 16 hrs, leaves daily except Fri and Sat at 0830 and costs US$15. Bus prices depend on the quality of the buses and how many spaces there are left at the time of departure, so you may save some money by turning up at the last minute.

Micros leave from Av Barrientos y Av 6 de Agosto for **Tarata**, **Punata** and **Cliza** and from Av República y Av 6 de Agosto to **Epizna** and **Totora**. Micros leave from Av Oquendo y 9 de Abril (be careful around this area) to: **Villa Tunari**, US$4.50, 4 hrs, several daily; **Chimoré**, US$5.75; **Eterazama**, US$5.75; **Puerto Villarroel**, US$7.75, 6 hrs (daily from 0800 when full); **Puerto San Francisco**, US$6.50.

Car rental
Barron's, Sucre E-0727, T04-422 2774, www.rentacarbolivia.com.

Taxis
Taxis cost US$0.50 around the centre, more if they cross the river, and charge double after dark.

Excursions from the city *p280*
Parque Nacional Tunari
Access to the park is about as easy as it gets. From Cochabamba, take micro F2 or trufi 35 (both lines run along Av San Martín and Barrientos), which will drop you roughly 500 m from the park's entrance. In theory, all guests are required to provide identification and sign in (although there is no fee), but this is not always enforced. By car or jeep drive west to Quillacolla (see below) and turn right on the road to Morochota. The road is cobbled and a nightmare for cyclists; there is also a police checkpoint.

There's plenty of transport from Cochabamba. Micros and trufis leave from Heroínas y Ayacucho (20 mins, US$0.30). Many of the excursions around Cochabamba involve changing buses in Quillacollo. Also bus companies travelling from Cochabamba to Oruro and La Paz have an office here.

Tarata

Frequent buses, micros and trufis leave for Tarata (US$0.65, 1 hr), Cliza and Punata from Barrientos y 6 de Agosto in Cochabamba. The last bus from Tarata returns at 1900

Sipe-Sipe

Bus 245 goes direct from Cochabamba to Sipe-Sipe; also trufi 145 – more frequent than the bus. From Quillacollo, buses for Sipe-Sipe wait until there are enough passengers.

⊙ Directory

Cochabamba *p276, maps p277 and p279*

Banks You can get cash advances on Cirrus, Visa or Mastercard from many banks, with no commission on bolivianos. You can also use Visa and Mastercard at 'Enlace' cash dispensers all over the town (especially on Ballivián) and next to the bus terminal. **Banco Boliviano Americano**, Aguirre y Jordán; **Banco Santa Cruz**, 25 de Mayo S-0265; **Banco de La Paz**, Baptista y General Achá, on the main plaza; **Banco Mercantil**, at N Aguirre and Calamo; **Bidesa**, Jordán E-0224, offers best rates for TCs; **Exprint-Bol**, Pl 14 de Septiembre O-0252, T04-425 4413. Will change TCs into dollars at 2% commission; **Ultramar**, 25 de Mayo between Heroínas y Colombia. Also changes TCs. **Street changers** offer good rates and are found at most major intersections, especially at Ayacucho y Achá (outside *Entel*), around Pl 14 de Septiembre, and at Heroínas y 25 de Mayo. **Cultural centres** Alliance Française, Santiváñez O-0187; **Institut Cultural Boliviano-Alemán**, Sucre E-0693. **Embassies and consulates** Argentina, F Blanco E-0929, T04-425 5859, visa applications 0830-1300; **Brazil**, Edif Los Tiempos Dos, 9th floor, Av Oquendo, T04-425 5860, open 0830-1130, 1430-1730; **Germany**, Edif La Promotora, 6th floor,

oficina 602, T04-425 4024, F425 4023, open Mon and Fri 1000-1200; **Italy**, C Ayacucho, Gal Cochabamba, 1st floor, T04-423 8650, Mon-Fri 1800-1930; **Netherlands**, Av Oquendo 654, Torres Sofer, 7th floor, T04-425 7362, Mon-Fri 0830-1200, 1400-1630; **Norway**, Av Guillermo Urquidi E-2279, T/F04-423 1951. Mon-Wed and Fri 0800-0900; **Paraguay**, Edif El Solar, 16 de Julio 211, T04-425 0183, Mon-Fri 0830-1230, 1430-1830; **Peru**, Av Pando 1325, T04-424 0296, Mon-Fri 0800-1200, 1400-1800; **Spain**, C Los Molles y esquina Paraiso Urb. Irlandes, T04-425 5733, Mon-Fri 1100-1200; **Sweden**, Barquisimeto, Villa La Glorieta, T/F04-424 5358, Mon-Fri 0900-1200; **USA**, Torres Sofer, block A, of 601, T04-425 6714, 0900-1200 (will also attend to Britons and Canadians). **Internet** There are many internet cafés around town, all charging US$0.60 per hr. **Gogle**, next to Casablanca on 25 de Mayo just off Pl Colón, is fast and has a few large flat screens. Usually a fastish connection can be had at **Full Internet** above the post office. **Cybernet**, Heroínas E-0267; **Black Cat**, Gnrl Achá, opposite *Entel* central office, open Mon-Sat 0700-2200. Also many on Cnl Jordan, between Lanza and 16 de Julio. **Language classes** There has been an explosion in the number of qualified language teachers. The following have all been recommended: **Sra Blanca de La Rosa Villareal**, Av Libertador Simón Bolívar 1108, esquina Oblitas, Casilla 2007 (T04-424 4298) US$5 per hr; **Runawasi**, J Hinojosa, Barrio Juan XXIII s/n, Casilla 4034, T/F04-424 8923, Spanish and Quechua, also arranges accommodation; **Sra Alicia Ferrufino**, JQ Mendoza N-0349, T04-4281006, US$10 per hr; **Patricia Jiménez**, Casilla 3968, T04-429 2455; **Elizabeth Siles Salas**, Av Guillermo Urquidi esq Armando Méndez 1190, T04-423 2278, silessalas@latinmail.com, Casilla 4659, US$6 per hr; **Professor Reginaldo Rojo**, T04-424 2322, frojo@supernet.com.bo, US$5 per hr; **Maria Pardo**, Pasaje El Rosal 20, Zona Queru Queru, behind Burger King on Av America, T04-428 4615, US$5 per hr, also teaches Quechua; **Carmen Galinda Benavides**, Parque Lincoln N-0272, Casilla 222, T04-424 7072; **Marycruz Almanza Bedoya**, T04-428 7201; **Haydee Lobo**, T04-424 1447. **Laundry** Super Clean, 16 de Julio y Jordán, US$0.90 per kg, Mon-Fri

0800-1230, 1400-1730, Sat 0800-1700; **Jet**, Cabrera 485, T04-4250581, US$1.05 per kg, Mon-Fri 0800-1200, 1400-1900, Sat 0800-1700. Also has branch at Av Aroma E-0127, near Ayacucho, US$0.90 per kg; **Lavasec**, Jordan E-0546, Mon-Fri 0800-2000, Sat 0800-1500; **La Favorita**, 16 de Julio N-0515, entre Venezuela y Paccieri, fast service; also at Women's Prison, Plazuela San Sebastián, good and cheap (visits possible if you ask the guards). **Medical services** A doctor recommended by the Tourist Office is James Koller, C Baptista N-0386, T04-422 4191, call between 1700-1800. **Clínica Belga**, Antezana N0455, T04-423 1404, is recommended by the Peace Corps. **Post office** Av Heroínas y Ayacucho, next to LAB office, main entrance on Ayacucho. Open Mon-Fri 0800-2000, Sat 0800-1800, Sun 0800-1200. **DHL** Jordan E-0254,

T04-425 3457, Mon-Fri 0700-2030, Sat 0700-1500; **FedEx**, Paccieri 662 (between Lanza and Antenaza), T04-422 5900; **UPS**, Edif Bolívar, Av España y Ecuador 280, 2nd floor, T04-425 8948. **Entel**: Achá y Ayacucho, international phone and fax (not possible to make AT&T credit card calls), Mon-Sat 0730-2300, Sun 0800-2300, T04-422 5210. Also at Aroma and Arce, 0730-2200 (Sun 0730-1400). **Useful addresses** Immigration Office: Corner of Junin and Arce, open Mon-Fri 0830-1630, T04-422 5553. **Tourist police** T120. Directory enquiries T104. Voluntary organizations: **Ministerio de Lustrabotas** (Shoeshine Kids Ministry), feeds 37 boys and girls every day and provides them with health care. To make a donation or get involved, email James Seaborn at ejamesseaborn@ hotmail.com.

Beyond Cochabamba

With three national parks in its vicinity, Cochabamba is an epicentre for ecotourism in a relatively unexplored area. Torotoro National Park, one of Bolivia's best, has dinosaur tracks and canyons; at Inkallajta there's a ruined Inca fortress; Villa Tunari has a nearby animal refuge where you can volunteer your services to look after monkeys and other mammals; Carrasco National Park has great birdwatching and Isiboro-Sécure, in the Chapare region, has interesting indigenous cultures.
▶▶ *For Sleeping, Eating and other listings, see pages 294-296.*

Parque Nacional Torotoro → *Colour map 2, grid C4.*

Along with the Salar de Uyuni and Lake Titicaca, Torotoro National Park is one of the natural wonders of Bolivia. Set in a beautiful, arid rocky landscape, it is an isolated and relatively unexplored area, riddled with dinosaur tracks and punctuated by dizzying drop-offs into deep canyons. You can easily climb down into one of the canyons and clamber over boulders along the river until a sunny swimming hole appears next to a shimmering waterfall. Torotoro straddles the departments of Cochabamba and Potosí but is best reached from Cochabamba (130 km). It is highly recommended for the adventurous traveller. Torotoro covers an area of 16,570 ha and was declared a national park in 1989.

Ins and outs
Although the park is just 130 km from Cochabamba, the road is so horrendous it takes 10 hours and there's sometimes no access to Torotoro by road in the rainy season. By far the best way in is to fly. A park entry fee of US$2.50 per person is charged.
▶▶ *For further details, see Transport, page 295.*

⁝ Torotoro tomorrow

Campaigning efforts of a lawyer led to the foundation of Torotoro National Park on 26 July 1989. Born in the village, Rodolfo Becerra de la Roca left when he was 10 years old, but he kept in touch and would never forget the beauty of the place. Gradually, as he witnessed the village's economy deteriorate and the population of his birthplace fall from 1,500 to 500, he realized something needed to be done.

At the same time tourists were destroying what they came to see – scores of stalactites were snapped off Umajalanta Cave as souvenirs.

The opportunity arose to rejuvenate the village economy through tourism and at the same time protect the environment. "I love this place and admire it," says Rodolfo. "I had to protect it." Through determination and political contacts, Rodolfo won national park status for the 16,570 ha around his home village. There are now six wardens and plans to create specialized programmes to protect such species as the red-headed parrot. Meanwhile, urban programmes have been introduced and a new school has been built. Rodolfo was also due to open a three-star hotel in Torotoro and there is a small airstrip for flights into the park (see page 295).

But tourism is still far from developed; the only other places to stay are very basic and to describe the road to Cochabamba as appalling would be generous. Consequently, Torotoro may be one of Bolivia's top attractions but it is still rarely visited – just seven tourists dropped by in March 2001! But get there soon, for that could all soon be changing, with Rodolfo's help.

The park

Torotoro is actually a huge hanging valley at 2,700 m surrounded by 3,500 m high mountains and criss-crossed by deep ravines. This is definitely an area of great scientific interest. Geologists, palaeontologists, archaeologists and botanists have all carried out studies here to investigate the discovery of dinosaur bones, fossils of turtles and sea shells, as well as archaeological ruins and pictographs. Other attractions include caves, canyons, waterfalls, and 80-million year-old dinosaur tracks, which can be seen by the stream just outside the village and practically everywhere you walk, if there is a guide to show you.

The area also has its living attractions. Condors and red-fronted macaws can be seen quite easily and scattered throughout the valley are small traditional communities whose people are friendly and welcoming. The climate is temperate all year round and in winter nights are fresh and the days are not too hot. Ideal in fact for walking or camping.

The village of **Torotoro** lies at the head of the valley and is actually in the province of Potosí. It serves as a convenient starting point for all the hikes in the area and its people are very hospitable. There is no electricity, only a generator which runs in the evening until the village's one video cinema ends its screening, around 2130-2200.

A good one-day trip is to **Umajalanta Cave**, a cavern with many stalactites and a lake full of blind fish, about 8 km northwest of the village. Wearing a gas-powered headlamp, it's a tight crawl in places and definitely not for the claustrophobic. Many stalactites were taken by day-trippers before the area was declared a national park. A two-hour walk away are the **Pozas Bateas**, passing 1,000 year-old rock paintings. Three hours away is **El Vergel** or 'Nariz de Vaca' (Cow's Nose), where two waterfalls pour out from the rockface and where you can swim in crystal clear water. A three-day trip from the village is to **Llamachaqui**, which are untouched pre-Columbian ruins in beautiful sub-tropical surroundings. It's 20 km each way to the ruins and a guide costs US$15 per person (with a minimum of two).

Siete Vueltas is an area of extensive fossils, 5 km from the village. There are also extensive areas of **dinosaur tracks**, and many rock paintings, close to the Torotoro river and on the many nearby walks. You can grab a clump of dead grass and be prepared to sweep out the dirt from tracks left 60-90 million years ago by meat-eating velociraptors and eight-tonne vegetarian sauropods. Look very closely and you may even see where the mud splurged up between their toes.

Cochabamba to Santa Cruz

There are two routes east from Cochabamba to the thriving city of Santa Cruz in the eastern lowlands of Bolivia (see page300). A 500-km mostly paved road goes via the mountains and Epizana to Santa Cruz. The new lowland route further north, which goes via Villa Tunari in the Chapare region, is preferred by most transport.

The mountain road

The mountain road to Santa Cruz heads for 119 km to **Monte Punku**, a renowned 'village of clay', lying in an attractive setting with tiny houses lining stone-paved colonial, or pre-Coloumbian, streets. **Sehuencas** is 13 km north of Monte Punku and is a favourite camping and fishing area for *Cochabambinos*. It's at a much lower altitude and is an excellent site for birdwatching. Three kilometres further on is the turn-off for the road to **Pocona**. Some 15 km down this road is **Collpa**, which is the turn-off for the Inca ruins of Inkallajta. About 1 km uphill from Pocona is **Tambo del Inka**, where produce and grains from this fertile valley were stored by the Incas.

Inkallajta, a ruined fortress standing on a flat spur of land at the mouth of a steep valley, is the most important archaeological site in the Cochabamba Department. The ruins are extensive and the main building of the fortress is said to have been the largest roofed Inca building. There's also an area called Inkarrakana which was an astronomical observatory.

A few decades before the Spanish conquest, the Inca Empire had expanded to cover most of the Cochabamba Valley, in an attempt to benefit from its enormous agricultural potential. To this end, the Incas built an extensive system of roads, market centres and forts. The Inca Tupac Yupanqui ordered the construction of Inkallajta in 1463-1472 to protect the advancing Imperial Army from the attacks of the fearsome local Chirihuano tribes, but after the fort was attacked it was badly damaged and abandoned. Such was the strategic importance of the site that Hauyna Kapac had it rebuilt in 1525. It was abandoned once more in the aftermath of the internal strife that marked the beginning of the end of the Inca Empire. ▸▸ *See also Transport, page 295.*

Some 13 km beyond Montepunco, at Km 128, is **Epizana**, at the junction for the 237-km road south to Sucre (see page 220), a scenic drive of six to seven hours. All but the last hour of this road is very rough, and narrow in parts. Epizana has the dubious distinction of being home to some of Bolivia's worst accommodation. There are four buildings in the village which describe themselves as 'hotels', but only the *España* actually has any 'rooms' – two filthy, airless, windowless cubicles with sagging beds which would make the average Bolivian prison cell seem appealing. There are also several restaurants and gas stations. From Epizana the road continues east to Santa Cruz, via Samaipata (see page 314).

Fourteen kilometres south of Epizana on the Sucre road, the beautiful, unspoiled little colonial town of **Totora** was badly damaged in the 1998 Aiquile earthquakes but it is still an attractive place. There are pleasant walks in the wooded hills above the town from where you get good views of the jumble of red-tiled roofs below. Days are hot and the nights are cool.

South of Totora (around 50 km south off the mountain road, towards Sucre) is **Aiquile**, 149 km from Sucre and 217 km from Cochabamba. It is famous for its fine hand-made *charango* guitars. The town hosts the annual *Feria del charango* at the end of October or in early November. Totora was badly damaged by two earthquakes on 22 May,1998. The Museo Arqueológico Regional was damaged along with many of its artefacts. Those that survived are rehoused in a new museum, **Museo del Charango**, which has been built two blocks east of the post office, in the shape of a guitar (with no strings attached). It is possible to visit some of the *charango* workshops. Perhaps the most famous is that of Don Hernán Escalera Castro, on Calle Avaroa and Barrientos.

The town's other main festival is on 2 February in honour of the patron saint, *La Virgen de la Candelaria*, and involves seven days of bull-running through the streets. There's also a busy Sunday market, which brings many *campesinos* from neighbouring villages.

The lowland road

The lowland road from Cochabamba to Santa Cruz runs through Villa Tunari (166 km, see below). The 465-km road is fully paved except for a 25-km stretch before Villa Tunari, almost at the end of the winding descent from the mountains, known as El Sillar. It's a beautiful trip, dropping from over 2,500 m down to the lush, tropical lowland forests. Travellers should note that the road passes through the Chapare, Bolivia's prime cocaine-producing region. While it's safe in the main towns, you should not stray too far off the beaten track.

The little town of **Villa Tunari**, four hours from Cochabamba, is a relaxing place. Nestled between the San Mateo and Espíritu Santo rivers, it is Cochabamba's gateway to the tropics and the main tourist centre of the Chapare region. The two rivers are excellent for white-water rafting and kayaking. Trips can be arranged for groups only; contact **Fremen Tours** in Cochabamba (see page 286). There's also good fishing and the town holds an annual **Fish Fair** on 5 and 6 August, with music, dancing and food.

Villa Tunari enjoys a warm, humid climate and nights are comfortable. Average temperature is 24°C, reaching 40°C in the summer (December-February) and as low as 10°C with the arrival of the *surazos* in the winter. The heaviest rainfall comes in from November to April.

Parque Ecoturístico Machía is just outside town, on the left-hand side of the road after crossing the bridge towards Santa Cruz. The 36-ha park includes a well-signposted 3-km interpretive trail which explains the park's ecology and other good trails through semi-tropical forest. There are also panoramic lookouts and picturesque waterfalls as well as a wide variety of wildlife.

Beside Parque Machía, by the riverside, 300 m outside Villa Tunari, heading for Santa Cruz (take the same entrance and then keep left), is the **Inti Wara Yassi**, ① *T04-413 4621, ciwy99@yahoo.com, daily 0900-1700, there is no entrance fee for the park and animal centre, but visitors are asked to make a donation, US$2.25 for cameras; US$3.75 for videos*, an animal rescue centre started by Juan Carlos Antezana and run by Nene Baltazar. In the centre are free-roaming monkeys and other mammals which are totally unafraid of humans. The centre uses money from donations to rehabilitate wild animals which have been kept in unsuitable conditions. They run programmes with schools, educating children in the rights of animals and inviting groups to help with the release of badly-treated animals back into the wild. As soon as animals arrive at the centre, they're allowed to roam free around the park and many return to the centre for extra food until they become totally self-sufficient. This is also a popular place to work as a volunteer, staying in one of three places run as part of the refuge (see also page 295 for further information). The minimum placement length is two weeks but check whether you are really needed first – travellers have shown up after a long journey only to find the centre struggling with too many volunteers.

Eight kilometres west of town, on the road to Cochabamba, is **Tres Arroyos**, a
large, natural swimming hole in the river.

Carrasco National Park

South of Villa Tunari lies the **Carrasco National Park**, covering 622,600 ha. One of
the country's largest, best-known and most accessible parks, it lies between 300
and 4,500 m and has 11 ecological life zones and superb birdwatching
opportunities. Until now it has seen mainly Bolivian visitors but it is increasingly
visited by foreign tourists.

Situated at the eastern foothills of the Cordillera Real, the terrain moves from
mountainous in the west to flat in the east. The scenery, while not as lush as that of
the Amazonian parks, is stunning nonetheless. Rainfall is heavy – rare for the
otherwise dry Cochabamba Department – especially in the north, and there are
several rivers and waterfalls that criss-cross the region; canyons and pools abound,
as do the flora and fauna associated with this landscape. The park also boasts a bird
sanctuary that is haven to some of the continent's rarest species, especially night
birds. Sitting at a higher altitude than most of the surrounding region, Carrasco is
surprisingly cool, making it a refreshing respite for the trekker, especially those
accustomed to the more tropical eastern lowlands or the Beni.

Access to the park is from any one of several nearby towns, including Chimoré,
Puerto Villaroel, Totora (the easiest route), and Villa Tunari. From Villa Tunari trufis can
be hired to drive to the park entrance. From there you cross the river on a cable pulley
and then it's a 15-minute walk to the **Cavernas de Repechón** wildlife sanctuary. This
consists of several caves inhabited by the rare *guácharo*, or oilbird. These are
nocturnal, fruit-eating birds that venture out of their cave only at night, in the process
emitting a strange clicking sound that they use for navigation by echo location.

The access road to the park is a turning off the old road to Cochabamba. From
Cochabamba this road is no longer driveable even with four-wheel drive, but it can be
hiked in four to six days. The route cuts through Carrasco, but there are no services
except at the beginning and the last 20 km. It begins in the mountains near Colomi and
follows the road to Aguirre. Ask for directions. The route ends a few kilometres west of
Villa Tunari. Trekking this spectacular route requires warm clothing for the high
mountain passes, as well as tropical clothing, insect repellent and sun protection.

Easier to arrange, but no less striking is the *Caminando en las Nubes* – a three-day
trek through the cloudforest run and guided by **Kausay Wasi**, a community ecotourism
group. The 42-km route descends from 4,100 m to just 300 m, taking in a variety of
ecosystems. Further information from **Fremen Tours** or ecoturismo_bolivia@
conservation.org.bo.

Isiboro-Sécure National Park

This 1,300,000-ha protected area lies in the northwest corner of the Chapare region.
In the heart of coca-growing territory, much of the park is considered dangerous,
particularly for independent travellers. Ranging from 200 m to 1,600 m, the park
includes vast expanses of tropical rainforest and savannah lands and is home to the
Trinitario and Yuracaré indigenous groups. Road access is difficult and there are no
tourist facilities as yet. The park can be visited by river via the Río Chipiriri from **Puerto
San Francisco**, which is about one hour from Villa Tunari. The park can also be visited
from Trinidad (see page 371). Puerto San Francisco is a popular day trip from Villa
Tunari. Micros and trufis leave from the turning just past the bridge. The trip takes one
hour. Then you can take a canoe into the forest, or just walk to one of the riverside

beaches. Several small *cabañas* sell fresh fish for lunch. You can also take a canoe to San Rosa de Isiboro (eight hours) and visit the indigenous communities.

A handful of tour companies (notably **Fremen Tours**) continue to operate in sections of the park but much of it is best avoided until security measures have been put into operation. North Americans in particular have been advised to avoid the eastern Chapare area due to resentment against their government's anti-narcotics force (the DEA), which operates in the area's coca plantations. Those looking for further information should contact SERNAP in either Trinidad, through Ing. Vladimir Orsolini ① *C Julio Céspedes No. 139, T03-462 0087*, or at regional headquarters in Cochabamba ① *C Emiliano Luján N° 2882, esq. C Joaquín Rodrigo, T04-448 6452; tipnis@pino.entelnet.bo*.

The Santa Cruz road continues east from Villa Tunari to Chimoré. Before Chimoré is the turn-off for the river port of **Puerto Aurora**, 90 minutes from Villa Tunari. From here it's possible to arrange visits to the Yurakare Indian communities, but it's best to go in a group and arrange a guide in Villa Tunari. In Chimoré water cuts are common from June to September. Restaurants *El Tamarindo*, on the right entering the village from Cochabamba, and *El Curichi*, on the left, are both mainly for bus passengers, with a token payment system and limited menu, but are OK. Beyond Chimoré is **Ivirgarzama**, which is the turn-off for the major river port of **Puerto Villaroel** (see page 379).

◉ Sleeping

Parque Nacional Torotoro *p289*
There are a few *alojamientos* in Torotoro, all G.
G Charcas will arrange basic food and is where most stay.
G Trinidad is another. The family Becerra also have a hotel being built and there are plans for cabins.

Cochabamba to Santa Cruz *p291*
Totora
G Residencial Colonial, 1 block behind the main plaza church, basic but OK, hot water mornings only, also has restaurant.

Aiquile
Hotels get booked up on Sat night, so arrive early if you want a room.
G Escudo, near Hostal San Pablo. Serves simple food.
G Hostal San Pablo, on the right as you drive into town towards Sucre. New, the best option. Shared hot showers and hoping to open a restaurant soon.
G Italia. Also serves simple but hygienic food.

Villa Tunari
A Country Club Los Tucanes, opposite the turn-off for *El Puente*. Includes breakfast, a/c, 2 swimming pools.

B El Puente, Av de la Integración, 3 km from town, T04-425 0302 (Cochabamba). Double to family-size cabins with private bathroom, including breakfast, tours to Carrasco National Park, a small tributary of the river by the hotel has 14 lovely natural pools in the forest where you can swim (US$2 per person for non-guests). Book in advance. To get there, continue on the highway through town, cross the 2nd bridge, turn right on the 1st road to the right, then go 2 km, the turn for the cabins is clearly marked.
B Los Araras, across the bridge on the main road to Santa Cruz. (**C** in midweek). Large rooms, nice gardens, good breakfast. Recommended.
D Cabañas Tío Pol, 1 km west of town, T04-424 4396 (Cochabamba). Quiet spot, pool and gardens.
D Las Palmas, 1 km out of town, T04-413 4103. Tropical breakfast included, clean, friendly, helpful, with pool and good, if relatively expensive, restaurant. The hotel grounds, next to the river, abound in birds and bats.
G Cuqui, 1 km west of town, T04-0149 6076 (mob). Has tents for camping and a pool, as well as having the best restaurant in town which serves excellent fish. Try their freshly-caught *surubí* or *pacú* served with fried cassava.

G La Querencia, pleasant terrace on river front, avoid noisy rooms at the front, good cheap food, plus clothes washing facilities.

If volunteering at the **refuge** you'll have a choice of 3 places in which to stay: **Casa de Voluntarios** is a part of the centre itself but is not too clean. You also run the risk of monkeys breaking into the rooms. **Alojamento Las Vegas** is a lively option, and **Copacabana** is quieter and you get your own bathroom, but at the extra cost of US$10 for the 2 weeks. Water in all of Villa Tunari is somewhat unreliable as pipes get blocked with mud after rain.

Tres Arroyos
There are a couple of places to stay, including an *alojamiento* and the fancy **Complejo Turístico Tres Arroyos**.

🍴 Eating

Parque Nacional Torotoro *p289*
There are also 3 pensions providing 3 meals a day. **Lydia Garcia** runs a *salon de te* with home-baked cakes, etc. There are 3 *tiendas* in the village, though the range of food sold is limited and many basic ingredients run out in between the twice-weekly truck runs.

Cochabamba to Santa Cruz *p291*
Villa Tunari
Eating upstairs at the **market** (breakfast and lunch only) is a very cheap option. Hotels **Las Palmas** and **La Querencia** also have restaurants.
$$-$ **Baveria**, close to the bridge, does good steak and fish, and tasty fruit drinks.
$$-$ **El Jazmin**, on the main road, opposite Las Palmas, is a gringo hangout which does good pizza.

🎉 Festivals and events

Parque Nacional Torotoro *p289*
25 Jun Tinku, a kind of organized street brawl, see box p245.
24-27 Jul Fiesta de Santiago, when people from surrounding communities congregate to sing, dance and drink.

⛰️ Activities and tours

Parque Nacional Torotoro *p289*
Information on the various tours available around the park is available at the national park office in Torotoro village. The park is only as good as your guide and the best around is **Mario Jaldin**, who lives 2 doors to the right of *Alojamiento Charcas* (see Sleeping). He speaks only Spanish but knows the best places to go, charges just US$1.50 per person per day and brings the landscape alive with his descriptions.

As well as the trips detailed below, he can take you to the precipitous edge of the nearby canyon and down to its river to swim in a sunny spot by a waterfall. Highly recommended. He also runs 4-day treks for US$80-100 per person with the hope of seeing cock-of-the-rocks, the Andean Bear, pumas, wolves and orchids.

🚌 Transport

Parque Nacional Torotoro *p289*
Air
Swiss pilot Eugenio Arbinsona has made his home in Cochabamba and owns a Cesna light aircraft. He does the trip from Jorge Wilstermann airport in just 30 mins for US$120 one-way. Up to 5 people can share the cost so call him to find if he has other bookings or get a group together of your own. The best thing about the trip with Eugenio is that he can be persuaded to fly through the canyons on the way there. Call him at home (T04-424 6289), at his hangar (T04-422 7042) or on his mobile (T017-23779).

Road
To check if the roads are open, call Gonzalo Milan in Cochabamba, T04-422 0207, or drop by his store, **Comercial El Dorado**, at Honduras 646.

When the roads are open buses and trucks go in convoy, leaving Cochabamba on Thu and Sun at 0600 from the corner of Av República y 6 de Agosto. The trip takes 10 hrs in the dry season. It costs US$3.25 by bus, or in the cab of the truck, or US$2.45 in the back of a truck. Buses and trucks return on Mon and Fri at 0600. If you're going in a group, make arrangements with Gonzalo the

Cochabamba Beyond Cochabamba Listings

day before and you can be picked up from your hotel. Alternatively, pay your ticket in advance and arrange to be picked up at Cliza (see above), where the trucks and buses stop for breakfast at 0800. This will allow you a few hours' shopping at Cliza's colourful Sunday market. For groups of 20 or more a tour bus can be arranged any day for around US$5 per person.

Cochabamba to Santa Cruz p291
Inkallajta
Take a micro from 6 de Agosto y República in Cochabamba (Thu and Sat only). These leave when full from 0700 onwards. Getting to Inkallajta is easier on these days as you can get off at the sign, from where it's only a 12-km walk to the ruins. Otherwise, take a micro to the checkpoint 10 km from Cochabamba, then a truck to Km 119. From there walk towards Pocona or take a truck for 15 km, to where a large, yellow sign indicates the trail. After approximately 10 km the trail divides – take the downhill path and the ruins are a further 2 km. Take food and camping gear. There are several good camping sites. The Cochabamba Archaeological Museum has some huts where visitors can stay for free, but take sleeping bag and food. Water is available at a nearby waterfall.

Totora
There are daily buses from Av 6 de Agosto y República in Cochabamba at 1600; also at 1430 on Sat. They return at 0500 Mon-Sat and at 1100 on Sun.

Aiquile
Unificado has an office on the main road in Aiquile beneath the shabby *Alojamiento Turista* with buses leaving every day for Sucre (0100), Cochabamba (1100) and Santa Cruz (2130). Other companies have fairly regular buses from Cochabamba (5 hrs): **Trans Campero** leave daily, except Sun, at 1300 (1400 on Sat), from Av Barrientos,

100 m past the junction with Av 6 de Agosto (trufis 1, 10, 14, 16, 20 pass in front); and **Flota Aiquile** leave daily except Sun at 1300 from 1 block further south on Av Barrientos.

Transportes Campero run buses to **Cochabamba** on Tue, Thu and Sat at 1700 and **Flota Aiquile** daily at 1700. All night buses from Sucre to Santa Cruz and Cochabamba pass through Aiquile between 2300 and 0130. Few companies will sell tickets only to Aiquile but one which does is **Expresso Cochabamba** to Santa Cruz, if they have seats available. **Transportes San Miguel** have buses to Aiquile (6 hrs) from Sucre at 1400 on Thu and Sat from the Parada de Camiones (truck stop), opposite the gas station on Av Marcelo Quiroga, on the way out of town to the north. They leave Aiquile for **Sucre** on Fri and Sun at 1900. To travel during the day, look for a truck leaving from this area at around 0700. For more details of transport from Sucre, see p233). There are buses from Aiquile to Mizque at 0700, 0830 and 1100.

Villa Tunari
There are direct buses to **Cochabamba** with Transporte 7 de Junio from opposite the petrol station at the west end of the village at 0830, 1100 and 1800, Sun 1300 and 1600; US$2.70, 4 hrs.

Several buses daily from Cochabamba leave from Oquendo and 9 de Abril. To head for **Santa Cruz** you will have to flag down a bus heading that way at 0600. Wait at the police checkpoint at the west end of town.

⊕ Directory

Cochabamba to Santa Cruz p291
Villa Tunari
Banks There's no ATM but cash dollars can be changed at **Las Palmas**. **Union Commercial** (a shop) exchanges travellers' cheques. **Telephone** There's an **Entel** office (T04-413 4101), which takes messages for hotels and local guides without phones.

:black_small_square: Footprint features

Introduction

The vast eastern lowlands of Bolivia are the area of the country richest in natural resources. Bordered by Brazil to the east and Paraguay to the south, this region comprises most of the enormous Santa Cruz Department, which makes up almost 34% of Bolivia's territory and at 370,621 sq km (144,542 sq miles) is larger than Germany.

The capital of the region, **Santa Cruz** (officially Santa Cruz de la Sierra, but more often than not shortened to plain Santa Cruz), is a booming modern city, more in tune with neighbouring Brazil and a world away from most people's image of Bolivia. The city is often ignored by tourists, or passed through quickly by travellers heading to or from Brazil, but that's their loss, for it stands on the threshold of one of the least-explored and most fascinating parts of Bolivia. To the northeast are the **Jesuit Missions**, a string of seven dusty cattle towns, each boasting a Jesuit church more beautiful than the next. Only three hours away is **Amboró National Park**, one of the country's truly great natural experiences and an area containing a greater variety of plants and wildlife than almost anywhere else on earth.

One of the very few places which surpass Amboró is the remote and stunningly beautiful **Noel Kempff Mercado National Park**, in the far northeast of Santa Cruz Department. This is a place so beautiful and mysterious that it is thought to have been the inspiration for Sir Arthur Conan Doyle's famous Lost World.

★ Don't miss...

① **El Fuerte** Bolivia's second most important archaeological sight is at El Fuerte, near the lovely little town of Samaipata, page 315.

② **The Che Guevara Trail** Be a rebel with a cause and follow in the footsteps of the world's most famous revolutionary on the Che Guevara Trail, page 318.

③ **Amboró National Park** Go for the full Indiana Jones experience in this National Park, one the most bio-diverse places on this planet, page 319.

④ **The Jesuit churches** Your mission, should you accept it... to visit the magnificent Jesuit churches in the remote and dusty frontier towns north of Santa Cruz, page 328.

⑤ **Noel Kempff Mercado National Park** Discover a Lost World here, home to more rare wild beasts than you could shake a zoom lens at, page 341.

Eastern Lowlands

Santa Cruz → *Colour map 4, grid B1. Population: 1,284,000. Altitude: 416 m.*

Santa Cruz has now taken over from La Paz as Bolivia's largest city, with a population of roughly 1.3 million. This vast, swelteringly hot place, grown rich on oil and agriculture, is far removed from most travellers' perceptions of Bolivia. Formerly a haven for narcotraficantes, it has largely returned to its less-opulent roots these days, although "agribusiness" is an important economic concern. The city now marks the jumping-off point for travels to the Jesuit Missions, several national parks, and the eastward journey to the magnificent Pantanal ecosystem and ultimately Brazil.

Although Santa Cruz's economic downturn has brought about a noticeable downsizing of its once many wealthy barrios, the city centre, which has retained much of its colonial air, remains the heartbeat of the city. Its narrow, congested streets are lined with low, red-tiled roofs with overhanging eaves, giving pedestrians much-needed shade from the fierce sun. It can get very hot and sticky – the temperature rarely drops below 21°C even in winter, and the mean annual temperature is 27.5°C – particularly around midday when the locals go home for lunch and their siesta, leaving the streets free from traffic and people, save for the occasional mad dog or Englishman. This is a good time to frequent one of the city's many air-conditioned ice-cream parlours or sit in the shaded plaza and watch the world go by – a local pastime. The people of Santa Cruz like to call themselves cambas and are generally more open and laid-back than their Andean (or colla) counterparts. Their relaxed, fun-loving attitude is most in evidence during Carnival, when proceedings can reach near-Brazilian levels of hedonism. ►► *For Sleeping, Eating and other listings, see pages 305-313.*

Background

The original settlement of Santa Cruz, founded in 1561 by the Spaniard Ñuflo de Chávez, was some 250 km east (in the present-day town of San José de Chiquitos). It was moved in 1590 and again in 1595 to its present location, in response to attacks from indigenous tribes. As little as 40 years ago, the city was nothing more than a remote backwater, where horses were the usual mode of transport along streets of red earth. New rail and road links, along with Viru Viru International Airport, ended this isolation. Now there is an ever-increasing flow of immigrants from the highlands, in addition to the Mennonites, who came from the USA and Canada, and Japanese settlers (such as the inhabitants of three Okinawa colonies 50 km from Montero), who came to grow soya, maize, sugar, rice, coffee and other crops. As well as agriculture, cattle breeding and timber, the exploitation of oil and gas in the Department of Santa Cruz greatly contributed to the city's rapid development.

Ins and outs

Getting there

Air The international airport is at Viru Viru, about 13 km from town (T181 for information). The airport bus runs every 20 minutes to and from the terminal to the city centre (25 minutes, US$0.70, operates 0530-2030). Taxis to town costs US$8.50. The airport has an emigration/immigration office, **Entel** office, luggage lockers, three duty-free shops, two coffee shops and a **Subway** sandwich shop. The bank is open 0830-1830 and changes cash and traveller's cheques, cash can be withdrawn using Visa and Mastercard. When the bank is closed try the **AASANA** desk, where you pay airport tax (US$25 for international departures). There's a **Tourist Information kiosk** in the check-in hall, where English is spoken (free maps available). El Trompillo airport in the southern part of the city has closed for all but a few military flights. There are rare flights with TAM (T03-353 1993) and private air taxis for oil workers.

Bus The huge new bus terminal, the *Terminal Bimodal*, for long-distance arrivals, is in the same place as the train station, on Avenida Montes between Avenida Brasil and Tres Pasos al Frente, between the second and third ring, T03-348 8382. There's also a bank, infirmary, luggage store and restaurants. Take a number 12 bus to/from the centre, or a taxi (US$1.50 – catch it from outside the terminal, it's cheaper). Local buses also use the new terminal.

Train The train station for east-bound trains to Puerto Suárez/Quijarro, for crossing into Brazil (see page 346), is in the same place as the long-distance bus terminal (see above), T03-346 3900, extension 307/303. They depart every day

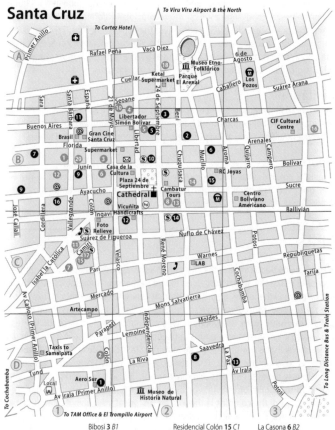

Santa Cruz

Eastern Lowlands Santa Cruz

0 metres   200
0 yards   200

Sleeping
Alojamiento Santa
  Bárbara **1** *B1*
Apart House Inn **2** *D1*

Bibosi **3** *B1*
Bolivia **4** *B2*
Colonial **5** *B2*
Copacabana **6** *B1*
Dallas **7** *C1*
Excelsior **8** *B2*
Las Américas **10** *B2*
Mediterráneo **11** *C1*
Posada El Turista **12** *B1*
Residencial
  Ballivián **13** *B2*
Residencial Bolívar **14** *B2*

Residencial Colón **15** *C1*
Residential Sands **16** *B3*
Residential 26 de
  Enero **17** *C1*
Roma **18** *A2*
Viru-Viru **20** *B1*

Eating
Capri **1** *D1*
Crêperie El Boliche **2** *B2*
El Patito Pekín **3** *B2*
Il Gatto **5** *B2*

La Casona **6** *B2*
La Esquina del
  Pescado **7** *B1*
Las Palmeras **9** *B1*
Michelangelo **8** *D2*
Pizzeria Marguerita **10** *B2*
Sabor Brasil **11** *B1*
Santa Ana **12** *C2*
Tacos Mexicanos **13** *D3*
Tapera Grill **14** *C2*
Tia Lia **15** *B2*
Vegetariano **16** *B1*

except Sunday. There are also south-bound trains departing for the Argentine border from the same station. » For further transport information, see page 311.

Information

Tourist office ⓘ *in the Prefectura del Departamento, on the north side of the main plaza, T03-332770, extension 144, 0800-1600 daily.* Along with some top-notch cultural and historical videos and exhibits, they have a free and very useful city map, as do many hotels and tour agents; the map in this chapter shows the roads only in the very heart of the city. Ask if they have a spare copy of *Bitácora Cruzeña* if you're planning trips out of the city. There's also an information kiosk at the airport. The *Handbook of Santa Cruz* (English) and *Guía Turística Metropolitana de Santa Cruz* (English/Spanish) are two of many local guidebooks. Both cost US$4 and are available in most *librerías* (stationers). *Editora Exclusiva*, who publish both guides, are themselves a good source of off-the-record local information, but should be contacted in advance with specific enquiries (they speak English), T/F03-336 8665, www.scbbs.net/exclusiva, rbirt@scbbs.com.bo. Another excellent guide (Spanish) is Santa Cruz Turístico, published by APAC and available for US$5 in most *librerías*, also at APAC's offices in Calle Beni 228 (T03-332287, 03-372526).

Orientation

The city has 10 ring roads, referred to as *anillos* 1, 2, 3, 4, and so on. Equipetrol suburb, where many of the better hotels and bars are situated, is northwest of the heart of the city, between Anillos 2 and 3; Avenida San Martin is one of its principal streets.

Climate

It is usually hot and windswept from May to August. But when the cold *surazo* wind blows from the Argentine *pampas* during these months the temperature drops sharply. The rainy season is December-February.

Sights

The **Plaza 24 de Septiembre** is the city's main square, where people are so unhurried they would make the sloths who used to live in the trees here look uptight. Facing onto the plaza is the imposing brick-fronted **St Lawrence Cathedral** ⓘ *Tue, Thu, Sun 1000-1200, 1600-1800, Bs5* ,(now technically a minor basilica after Pope John Paul II's visit in 1988), with its wonderfully cool interior featuring some interesting hand-wrought colonial silver and a museum containing what is considered the smallest book in the world, at only 7 sq mm. The city's **Casa de la Cultura "Raúl Otero Reiche"** is also on the plaza. It hosts occasional exhibitions, an archaeological display, plays, recitals, concerts and folk dancing. It also has a wonderful free gallery devoted to the works of Bolivia's beloved painter Armando Jordan on the second floor. Also part of the complex is the **Museo Historical y Archivo Regional de Santa Cruz de la Sierra** ⓘ *T03-336 5533, Mon-Fri 0830-1200, 1500-1800, occasionally Sat as well*, which has several displays ranging from ceramics to explorers' routes to native handicrafts. Perhaps its finest attribute, however, is a small shop run by the non-profit group **La Mancomunidad**, where handcrafted and signed carvings, hammocks, fabrics, and jewellery can be had. These are made by indigenous peoples, from non-threatened woods, and all proceeds are returned to the craftsmen. The **Museo de Historia Natural Noel Kempff Mercado** ⓘ *Av Irala 565, between Velasco y Independencia, T/F03-337 1216, www.museonoelkempff.org, Mon-Fri 0800-1200,*

● *The last sloth was removed from Plaza 24 de Septiembre in 2001 because of pollution and*
● *tree disease. There are no plans to introduce any new ones.*

Five blocks north of the Plaza is **Parque El Arenal**. At the lakeside is *Artesanías Salón de Exposición y Ventas*, a building housing various shops selling regional arts and crafts. Nearby, at Beni y Caballero, is the **Museo Etnofolklórico** ① *To3-335 2078, Mon-Fri 0800-1200, 1430-1830, Bs5*. It contains a small but interesting collection of musical instruments, masks, weapons, weavings and a number of other handicrafts of the various ethnic groups of the Eastern Lowlands.

An interesting area is the **Mercado Los Pozos**, which encompasses almost all of calles Quijarro, Campero, Suárez Arana, and 6 de Agosto. Here you'll see large numbers of Mennonites in their traditional clothing – the men in their high-crowned cowboy hats, check shirts and denim dungarees, the women in dark, full-length dresses, shawls and full-brimmed hats. As in all busy markets, you need to be alert to the threat of bag-snatchers. Another popular market is **Siete Calles**, which has all manner of goods and takes up all of calles Isabel La Católica, Suárez de Figueroa, and Vallegrande.

Excursions

Las Lomas de Arena del Palmar are huge sand dunes, 18 km to the south of the city, off of the road to Palmasola. In some parts are small lagoons where you can swim, but note that you shouldn't swim in the stagnant water in the nearest and most popular of the lagoons. Head to the farthest ones, where there's less chance of yeast infections. To get there take a four-wheel drive from the bus terminal, especially in the wet season when the river crossing can be difficult. It may also be possible to hitch at weekends. Windsurfing is popular here with the natives, but no rental facilities exist.

❖ Warning: do not leave anything unguarded: there have been reports of thefts along the river's banks.

Los Espejillos (small mirrors) are a series of many small waterfalls, 41 km to the southwest, en route to Samaipata on the old Cochabamba highway. They're very popular at weekends and can be accessed by *micros* in the dry season. There is a charming hotel here, aptly named **Los Espejillos** (US$20/night, including dinner), and camping may also be available on the premises. To the west, at the end of Avenida Roca Coronado, 10 minutes by bus from the town centre, you can swim in the **Río Piraí** during the wet season, though at weekends it gets very crowded. Some huts on the beach sell local delicacies.

Twenty kilometres east of the city is **Cotoca** (the journey takes around 20 minutes), where the church has a statue of the Virgin Mary thought to perform miracles, associated with which is a religious handicraft tradition. The town holds a fiesta on 8 December, where several hundred *cruzeños* making the trip on foot (with the more penitential on knees). Try the local *sonzos* in the market. At 12 km out of town on the road to Cotoca are the new**Botanical Gardens**. Take a *micro* or *colectivo* from Calle Suárez Arana (15 minutes).

Porongo is a typical *cruzeño* town (albeit one with a Brit for a mayor until recently!), about 18 km west from the city after crossing the Urubó Bridge. It has a wonderful old church in the colonial style and is a nice spot to pass an afternoon.

West of Santa Cruz towards Samaipata

Two roads run west from Santa Cruz to **Cochabamba** (see page 276). The newer lowland route is the one used most frequently by buses to and from Santa Cruz. The other route, the old mountain road, heads southwest to Samaipata and the southern (and more accessible) entrance to Amboró and then across the mountains via Samaipata and Comarapa.

Japanese settlers

Only three hours northeast from Santa Cruz you arrive in the heart of Japan – or so it seems – for the community of Okinawa is made up of Japanese immigrants who settled here in the aftermath of the Second World War.

One million Japanese left for South America, with financial assistance from the Japanese and US governments. Most settled in Brazil, Peru and Argentina but several thousand made their way to the eastern tropics of Bolivia.

The Bolivian government gave each family 50 ha of land and the US provided machinery and equipment such as tractors, but life was very tough for the pioneer settlers of the community, which is now named after their original home. They literally carved an existence out of the inhospitable jungles. Wells had to be dug for drinking water and Santa Cruz was reachable only by a two-day horseback ride over difficult terrain. But thanks to many years of hard work, and help from the Japanese government, Okinawa is now a rich agricultural area producing poultry, eggs, wheat, soya beans and rice.

The lowland road to Cochabamba

The new road route to Cochabamba passes through the fertile lowlands to the northwest of Santa Cruz. It should be noted that although touted as a faster route between Santa Cruz and Cochabamba, the bridge after Comarapa was destroyed by rains in late 2003, and the new one replacing it is less than ideal. The route goes north through **Warnes**, where there is a statue of a man leading an ox-cart-load of bananas at the town entrance, then a further 37 km north to the little town of **Montero**, named after the Independence hero, Marceliano Montero. The statue to him in the plaza is in the same style as the statue of Bolívar in Santa Cruz, the horse supported by broken cannon.

Just north of Montero the road branches west through Buena Vista and past the northern edge of Amboró National Park (see page 319) towards Villa Tunari (see page 292). Another branch runs east to the incongruously named town of **Okinawa I**, located 80 kms northeast from Santa Cruz. The name is not so strange when you realise that this is the main centre of the first of Bolivia's three Japanese immigrant communities (see box). The road then continues north to the first of the Jesuit Mission settlements at San Javier (see page 331), though this is not the route used by buses to Cochabamba.

The old mountain road to Cochabamba

Travelling west on the old mountain from Santa Cruz to Cochabamba is a journey of contrasts, and one which is well worth making. There are friendly, sleepy little towns with basic, clean accommodation, lots to see en route, and few tourists. There's excellent birdwatching and archaeological ruins, and the road passes through the southern buffer zone of the Amboró and Carrasco National Parks (see page 293). The first section of road, as far as Samaipata, is paved and it's a spectacular trip leaving Santa Cruz along the Piraí gorge and up into the highlands.

Santa Cruz *p300, map p301*

Accommodation is relatively expensive here and good value mid-and lower-range hotels are hard to find, but several of the 4- and 5-star hotels now offer excellent package deals in light of the recent economic downturn. Most of the budget hotels are to be found near the old bus terminal.

LL Camino Real, C K, in the upmarket Barrio Equipetrol Norte in 3rd ring, T03-342 3535, F343 1515, www.caminoreal.com.bo. Has everything you'd expect from a luxury hotel, and more besides.

LL Las Buganvillas, Av Roca y Coronado 901, T03-355 1212, F336 2883, www.buganvillas.com.bo. Has everything, including a sports complex, bar, pool, restaurants, gym and shops, in addition to 250 apartments. Located between the Río Piraí and Feria Exposición complex.

LL Los Tajibos, Av San Martín 455, in Barrio Equipetrol, T03-342 1000, F03-3426994, www.lostajiboshotel.com. Set in 15 acres of lush vegetation, 5-star, a/c, *El Papagayo* restaurant is good (their *ceviche* is particularly recommended), business centre, art gallery, Viva Club Spa has sauna etc, pool for residents only. Also the setting for most of the city's high-end social events.

L Apart House Inn, Colón 643, T03-336 2323, F337 1113, www.houseinn.com.bo. Modern, 5-star suites, 2 pools, restaurant, a/c, parking. Recommended.

AL Cortez, Av Cristóbal de Mendoza 280, on Segundo Anillo near the Cristo, T03-333 1234, F335 1186, www.hotelcortez.com. Pool, a/c. Recommended for medium or long stays.

AL La Quinta, C Arumá, Barrio Urbarí, T03-352 2244, F352 2667, laquinta@ cotas.com.bo Business-oriented, gym, restaurant, conference rooms, English and German spoken, 4 pools (1 for children).

A Las Américas, 21 de Mayo esquina Seoane, T03-336 8778, F333 6083. A/c , discount for longer stay, parking, arranges tours and car rental, restaurant, bar, 4-star hotel, 5-star service. Excellent value in this price bracket. Recommended.

A Urbari Apartment Resort Hotel, C Igmiri 506, Barrio Urbarí, T03-352 2288, F352 2255, www.urbariresort.com. A/c, cable TV, restaurant, bar, swimming pool, gym, tennis courts, English spoken.

B Arenal, C Beni 340, T03-334 6910, www.hotelarenal.com. A/c, cable tv, restaurant, bar, sauna, gym, pool, conference rooms, business centee, English spoken.

B California, C Charagua 23, T03-334 6295, F335 4434, hotel_ca@cotas.com.bo. Has room service, private parking, cable TV.

B Colonial, Buenos Aires 57, T03-333 3156, F333 9223. A/c, cable TV, includes continental breakfast, restaurant, comfortable. Recommended.

B Libertador Simón Bolívar, C Buenos Aires 119 esq. Libertad, T03-335 1235, F334 2696. Centrally located, clean, a/c.

B Mediterráneo, Vallegrande y Camiri 71, T03-333 8804, F336 1344. Fridge, cable TV, includes breakfast, a/c, cheaper rooms with fan.

B Viru-Viru, Junín 338, T03-333 5298, F336 7500. Includes breakfast, a/c, cheaper rooms with fan, pool, pleasant and central. Tour agency next door. Recommended.

B-C Copacabana, Junín 217, T03-332 1843, F333 0757. Fairly comfortable (3-star), a bit overpriced but often has promotions. More expensive with a/c. Cable TV, laundry service, includes continental breakfast, restaurant.

C Bolivia, Libertad 365, T03-333 6292, F333 2147. Includes buffet breakfast, a/c, cable TV, modern and comfortable.

C Dallas, has 2 entrances, one at Pari 457, the other at Camiri 168, T03-337 1011, F337 1331. Suites with private bathroom, colour TV, a/c, elevator, includes breakfast, laundry, restaurant, comfortable. Staff unprofessional and unhelpful.

C Excelsior, René Moreno 70 (1 block from plaza), T03-332 5924, excelsior@cotas.net. 2-star, includes *americano* breakfast, good rooms, good lunches.

C Roma, 24 de Septiembre 530, T03-332 3299, F333 8388. Pleasant, a/c, cable TV, good value, helpful.

⬤ *Price codes for Sleeping and Eating are given inside the front cover. Further information on*
● *hotel and restaurant grading can be found in Essentials, pages 43-44.*

C-D **Bibosi**, Junín 218, T03-334 8548, F334 8887, cheaper with shared bathroom. Cable TV, electric showers, although the bedrooms need a revamp, internet, continental buffet breakfast included. Recommended.

D **Brasil**, Santa Bárbara 244, T03-332 3530. Rooms with bathroom, includes breakfast, and is friendly.

D **Cataluña Balneario**, halfway between the city centre and the airport at 7.5 km Carretera al Norte, T03-334 26588. Private bathroom, pool, clean, very friendly and helpful, quiet. Recommended.

D-E **Residencial Colón**, Camiri 48, T03-336 8510. Cheaper without a/c, includes breakfast, very smart, clean, great beds, also friendly.

E **Residencial Sands**, Arenales 749, 7 blocks east of the main square, T03-337 7776. Unbelievable value, better than some in higher price brackets – stylish 3-star standard rooms have cable TV, ceiling fans, telephone and very comfortable beds. There's even a pool.

E-F **Residencial 26 de Enero**, Camiri 32, T03-332 1818. Cheaper without bathroom. Very clean.

E-F **Residencial Bolívar**, Sucre 131, T03-334 2500. (Cheaper with shared bathroom). Hot showers, courtyard with hammocks and toucan, excellent breakfast for US$2.10. Recommended.

F **Residencial Ballivián**, Ballivián 71, T03-332 1960. Basic, shared hot showers, nice patio. Recommended.

F-G **Alojamiento San José**, Cañada 136 (near the local bus terminal, off our map), T03-332 8024. Hot showers, but not great value.

F-G **Residencial Cañada**, Cañada 145, T03-334 5541. Near the local bus terminal. Cheaper without bathroom, good.

G **Alojamiento Santa Bárbara**, Santa Bárbara 151, T03-332 1817. All shared bathrooms, no fans, hot showers, helpful, will store luggage, very popular. Recommended.

G **Doña Felipa**, Omar Chávez 1025, T03-334 6238. Excellent value. Recommended.

G **Posada El Turista**, Junín 455, T03-336 2870. Shared bathrooms, rabbit hutch-like basic rooms with smelly mattresses, but cheap, central, quiet and friendly.

West of Santa Cruz *p303*

C **Hostal Pinocho**, Warnes 288, Montero, T03-922 0305. With a/c, the best place to stay in the area.

E **Central**, near the plaza, Montero.

🍽 Eating

Santa Cruz *p300, map p301*

There are many cheap restaurants near the old bus station on Av Cañoto, serving fried chicken. Also on the extension of C 6 de Agosto behind Los Pozos market (daytime). Excellent *empanadas* are sold in the food section of Los Pozos market. The bakeries on Junín, Los Manzanos and España sell the local specialities: *empanadas de queso* (cheese pies), *cuñapés* (yucca buns), rice bread and *humitas* (maize pies). Try the local speciality *arroz con leche* in the markets, though it's only available before 1100.

$$$ **Creperie El Boliche**, Arenales 135, open from1930. Serves the city's best salads, crêpes and fondues in a beautiful old mansion.

$$$ **El Candelabro**, C 6 Oeste 11, T03-332 1085, Mon-Sat 1130-1400, 1930-2330, closed Sat lunch. Smart eaterie in the Equipetrol suburb.

$$$ **Il Gatto**, 24 de Septiembre 285, T03-332 6159. Bright and clean, good pizzas, US$2.25 buffet 1200-1500.

$$$ **La Bella Napoli**, Independencia 635, T03-332 5402, open until 2330. Excellent Italian fare.

$$$ **La Castañuela**, 3rd Anillo Externo, Barrio Sirari, T03-343 6516. Outstanding Spanish and French cuisine.

$$$ **La Pastora**, C 5 Oeste 115, T03-332 8687. Smart restaurant in the Equipetrol suburb.

$$$ **La Sierra**, a bit out of town at Km 23 on the old road to Cochabamba, T03-384 0009. In an idyllic setting on the banks of the Río Paraí. Open only at weekends and during holidays. This is genuine Bolivian cooking at its best, both regional and national. The emphasis is on meat (roast duck, pork, steaks). Considered by the locals to be the best Bolivian restaurant around.

$$$ **Las Castañuelas**, Velasco 308 esquina Pari, T03-336 4035. In a beautifully restored colonial house, Spanish cuisine, good wine list, good seafood. Open for lunch (till 1500) and dinner.

$$$ **Michelangelo**, Chuquisaca 502, T03-336 8550, Mon-Fri 1200-1400, Sat evenings only 1900-2330. Excellent Italian fare.

$$$ **Tacos Mexicanos**, La Paz near junction with Irala, Mon-Sat,1800-2300. A recommended Mexican restaurant.

$$$ **Yorimichi**, Busch 548, T03-334 7717, Mon-Sat 1130-1430, 1900-2330. Recommended for good Japanese food.

$$ **Capri**, Av Irala 634, next to *AeroSur*. Said to serve the best pizzas in town.

$$ **Churrasquería El Palenque**, Av El Trompillo y Santos Dumont, T03-352 6022 (open Wed-Mon1200-1400,1830-2330), excellent for barbecued steak.

$$ **Churrasquería Los Lomitos**, Av Uruguay 758, T03-332 8696. A culinary highlight. Outstanding Argentine cuisine, real *parrillada* and *churrasco*; open round the clock. Also has branch on Av Mons Rivero 201, T03-334 3229.

$$ **La Buena Mesa**, Av Cristóbal de Mendoza 1401, T03-342 1284. Great for barbecued steak.

$$ **La Casa Típica de Camba**, Cristóbal de Mendoza 539, T03-342 7864. One of many barbecue restaurants around the Segundo Anillo. One long-time resident described it as "a must for the total *camba* experience. A rather hokey place where you sit outside, entertained by live music and enjoy monster portions of typical *camba* food. This place is famous by *camba* standards."

$$ **La Casona**, Arenales 222 between Murillo and Aroma, T03-337 8495. German restaurant. Open Mon 1600-2000, Tue-Fri 1030-1430, 1600-2000, Sat 1000-1400.

$$ **Mandarin** 2, Av Potosí 793, T03-334 8388. Great Chinese restaurant.

$$ **Pizzeria Marguerita**, on the plaza at corner of C Libertad and Junín, T03-337 0285. Serves pizzas and burgers and a superb filet mignon. It's a big hit with gringos and the staff are very friendly and helpful. Bar, a/c. Also recommended for breakfast and liqueurs (not necessarily at the same time!), credit cards accepted, no commission, open Mon-Fri 0900-2400, Sat/Sun 1600-2400.

$$ **Shanghai**, Av 26 de Febrero 27, T03-352 3939. Excellent Chinese restaurant.

$$-S **Vegetariano**, Ayacucho 444. Good set veggie lunch.

$ **Confetti**, on René Moreno 184, T03-332 6704. For something really sweet, this place offers what are unquestionably the finest hand-dipped chocolates and cheeses in the city. Take away only, but well worth hunting down if you're in the centre and have a craving for chocolate.

$ **El Patito Pekín**, 24 de Septiembre 307, T03-332 2344, has basic Chinese food, 1100-1400, 1800-2000 Mon-Sun.

$ **Gloriamar 2**, to the right of Tapera Grill on Ballivián, T03-337 5855, a good café for *salteñas*.

$ **La Esquina del Pescado**, at the corner of Sara and Florida. If you're angling for a taste of fish you may find yourself hooked here. They serve *pejerrey*, *pacú*, *saballo*, *surubí* and *dorado*. Sit outside on the pavement and eat for US$1.60 a plate.

$ **Las Cazuelas**, Av. San Martín 154, T03-336 2903, for inexpensive typical fare. Sundays and holidays it offers an excellent buffet for Bs 20.

$ **Las Palmeras**, Junín 381 and (bigger place) nearby at Ayacucho 590 and José Callau. Popular, good vegetarian meals, 0700-2200 (Sun 0700-1600).

$ **Rincon Brasil**, Libertad 358, T03-333 1237, every day 1130-1500, also (à la carte only) Tue-Sat from 1800. In the mould of Brazilian-style *por kilo* places.

$ **Sabor Brasil**, off Buenos Aires, between Santa Bárbara y España 20. Again, follows the popular Brazilian-style *por kilo* trend.

$ **Santa Ana**, on Ingavi 164, does eat-all-you-can for US$1.50.

$ **Tapera Grill**, Ballivián 80, T03-332 7044. Small place, plastic chairs, does breakfast.

$ **Tia Lia**, Murillo 40, T03-336 8183. One of the best places to eat in town. For just US$1.50 (US$2.25 weekends) you can eat all the beef, chorizos, pork and chicken you want from a *parillada* as well as choose from a huge selection of salads, pasta and bean dishes. Open Mon-Fri 1100-1500, Sat-Sun 1100-1600, it also has *feijoada* (the famous Brazilian stew) on Sat with *caipirosca* (Brazil's lethal sugar cane spirit-based drink).

$ **Vegetariano Buffet**, Pari 228, between Colón y Velasco, T03-337 1733. *Por kilo* vegetarian buffet.

Cafés and sandwich bars

There are lots of very pleasant air-conditioned cafés and ice cream parlours, where you can get coffee, ice cream, drinks, snacks and reasonably-priced meals.

Alexander Coffee at Av Monseñor Rivero 400 in Zona El Cristo, T03-3378653. Good coffee and people-watching.

Fridolin has 2 central locations: one at Av Cañoto esq. Florida, T3340274; the other at Pari 254, T3323768. Excellent coffee and pastry spot.

Kivón, Ayacucho 267, which is highly recommended for ice cream (also at Quijarro 409 in Mercado Los Pozos).

Subway Av Las Americas 125, near C Irala; at the Hipermaxi on the corner of Av Cristo Redentor and the 3rd Anillo; and Av San Martín, all of which have TCBY yoghurt stands attached.

☾ Bars and clubs

Santa Cruz *p300, map p301*

See also listings in the local press for nightclubs and bars. Most of the most happening clubs are in the Equipetrol suburb (to the north of the maps featured above).

Automaía, paseo San Martín, 1st floor, T03-337 7265. Ever popular club.

Bar Irlandes, on the east side of the main plaza and on 3rd Anillo, near the Cristo Redentor statue, T03-343 0671, open late. Irish theme pub. Probably the city's best-known watering hole for gringos, it boasts an owner from the Emerald Isle. Clean and fairly low volume, so some may find it a bit tame. Reasonable priced drinks, snacks and light meals. Most of the staff speak English and it even has a dartboard. A pleasant and central place to drink and have a late bite of food.

MAD, Av San Martín 155, T03-336 0333. One of the best known and most popular clubs.

Moosehead Bar Restaurant, next door to Bar Irlandes, T03-343 4757. Canadian-run bar/restaurant.

New Palladium, C Boqueron 83, T03-334 0034. One of the best-known clubs.

⏵ Entertainment

Santa Cruz *p300, map p301*

Cinemas

El Arenal, Beni 520, T03-335 0123, showings at 1630, 1930 and 2130.

Gran Cine Santa Cruz, 21 de Mayo 247, T03-332 4503, showings at 1530, 1730, 1930 and 2130.

Palace, Pl 24 de Septiembre, T03-332 2617, showings at 1700, 1930 and 2200.

René Moreno, C René Moreno 448, T03-334 7448, showings at 1630, 1930 and 2100.

Folkloric shows

Rincón Salteño, Antenor Vásquez 257, T03-333 4443. Best to call ahead as it is open on sporadic Fri and Sat only.

Tapekua, Ballivían and La Paz, T03-334 5905, shows Wed-Sat 1930-0100.

Galleries

In addition to the 2 galleries in the **Casa de la Cultura "Raúl Otero Reiche"**, you can visit **AECI**, C Arenales 538. Private gallery.

Arte Urbano, Av Cristobal de Mendoza esq. Jaime Freire, T03-33376667. This new art gallery is drawing interest. Hours are sporadic, so call ahead.

Galeria del Banco de Credito, C 24 de Septiembre 158. Private gallery.

Also check out the art on display at the **Hotel Los Tajibos** (see above).

Theatre

Visitors can take in some first-rate theatre in Santa Cruz.

Casa de la Cultura "Raúl Otero Reiche" (see p302),

Casateaotro, located in the Museo de Historia, C Junín, has occasional performances.

The Chaplin Show, Av Mercelos Terceros 202 in Barrio Sirari, T03-3420060. Usually a comedy club, occasional theatrical performances.

Paraninfo Univeritario, on C Junín esq. Libertad, parainfo@uagrm.edu.bo.

✱ Festivals and events

Santa Cruz *p300, map p301*

Cruceños are famous as fun-lovers and their music, the *carnavalitos*, can be heard all over South America.

15 days before Lent Carnival Of the various festivals, this is the best. It's a wild and raucous time with music and dancing in the streets, fancy dress and the coronation of a carnival queen. As with all Bolivian festivals at this time, you're almost certainly going to get very wet, and we're not going to gloss over the fact that people also throw paint at passers by. Well-dressed foreigners are not shown any mercy. The *mascaritas* balls also take place during the pre-Lent season, when girls wear satin masks covering their heads completely, thus ensuring anonymity. It's a good time to be in town, especially if you're male, but be aware that some Bolivian men and women take a dim view of such lewd behaviour.
6 Aug Bolivian Independence Day.
Sep International Trade Fair Rather more sedate affair.
24 Sep Departmental holiday.

○ Shopping

Santa Cruz *p300, map p301*
Books
International magazines and newspapers are often on sale in kiosks on the main Plaza, eg the *Miami Herald*, after the arrival of the Miami flight.
El Ateno, Canoto y 21 de Mayo (off our map), T03-333 3338. Has lots of books in English.
Los Amigos del Libro, Ingavi 14, T03-332 7937. Sells foreign language books and magazines, with some in English.

Film processing
ABC, Junín 467 (also Casco Viejo local 5 and Colón with Ingavi). Top quality, 36 prints, plus new film, US$9.50.
Foto Relieve, Ingavi 256. Excellent processing, English spoken.

General
There are many expensive boutiques throughout town, especially along 21 de Mayo, 2nd block, and on Ingavi, between Independencia and Chuquisaca.

There's a good *hipermarket* at 24 de Septiembre 480 and a supermarket on Florida 193 between 21 de Mayo and Libertad, also on Monseñor Salvatierra 174.

Others (called **Slan**) are found on Av Piraí 350 (T03-352 0626), Av San Martin 1000 (T03-342 0623), and Av Santa Cruz esq.

Paragua (T03-347 7745). These last 3 carry a fair selection of imported items.

Handicrafts and jewellery
Santa Cruz is a good place to buy precious and semi-precious stones, which are mined near the Brazilian border and then polished and set here in the city. Best to take someone who knows the difference between a true stone and an easily passed-off fake, however, as some merchants hawk the plentiful (and relatively cheap) bolivianite as the much more valuable amythest. There are *artesanía* shops on Libertad and on Pl 24 de Septiembre y Bolívar.

Also see the small store in the **Museo** (see above) for beautiful native carvings and fabrics. All profits go to supporting the local Chiquitano communities, and the offerings here are simply the very best: all authentic, all hand-carved or –woven, and all reasonably priced, and your money goes directly into the hands of the people who produce these beautiful pieces!
Artecampo, Salvatierra, corner with Vallegrande, T03-334 1843. Open Mon-Fri 0900-1230, 1530-1900, Sat 0900-1230. Run by a local NGO, sells handicrafts made in rural communities in the department, high quality, excellent value.
Carrasco, with showrooms at Velasco 23, T03-336 2841, and branches at the corner of Independencia and Ingavi, T03-336 2331, www.carrascojoyeros.com. For gemstones.
Gemas de Bolivia, Casco Viejo, 2nd floor, T03-357 3623, rbirt@scbbs.com. Probably your best bet before buying anywhere is to check with Bob Birt here. A trained jeweller (very rare in Bolivia), he has an impressive selection of original designs and offers custom faceting, and has been in the business longer than anyone.
Manos Indígenas, on Cuéllar 16, T03-337 2042, is a hidden jewel of a store that has great fabrics and weavings straight from native Guarayo, Chiquitano, Ayoreo, and Guaraní peoples.
RC Joyas, Bolívar 262, T03-333 2725, www.rc_limitada.com. Local gemstones including Bolivia's own beautiful, 2-tone *Bolivianita*, can be designed to order. Also has a small Inca, Tiahuanaco and

antiques collection. The German-born manager produces and sells good maps of Santa Cruz City and Department.

Richardin, 24 de septiembre 185, T03-333 7032, is also reported as fair for buying gemstones.

Vicuñita Handicrafts, corner of C Independencia and Ingavi, 1 block west of the main plaza, T03-334 0591, F03-336 8432, www.santacruz virtual.com. The best *artesanía* in town. The owners are fair and honest and can ship goods to anywhere in the world. There are 4 shops in a row (plus another at C René Moreno 150) selling everything from sweaters to jewellery and pottery, and much more. It's an excellent place for advice on what to buy and what to pay for it. Some English and French spoken (ask for Zulema).

Markets

Mercado Los Pozos takes up the whole block between 6 de Agosto, Suárez Arana, Quijarro and Campero. It is clean and good for midday meals – the food aisles serve local and Chinese food, and is worth visiting in the summer for its exotic fruits. The market is open daily. Beware of bag-snatching, especially during the build-up to Christmas and Carnival when there are lots of pickpockets at work.

Bazar Siete Calles sells mainly clothing, but food and fruit is sold outside. The main entrance is in 100 block of Isabel La Católica and there's another entrance on Camiri and Vallegrande, past Ingavi.

There is also a **fruit and vegetable market** at Sucre y Cochabamba.

Outdoors

El Aventurero Caza y Pesca, Florida 126-130, has absolutely everything you need for fishing, climbing, trekking, or arctic and tropical regions.

Jara Caza y Pesca, Bolívar 458.

Safari Camping, 21 de Mayo and Seoane, T03-337 0185.

▲ Activities and tours

Santa Cruz *p300, map p301*

Club Las Palmas, 2.5 km on the road to Cochabamba. Has an 18-hole championship golf course and olympic-length pool. Private, must be accompanied by a member.

Club de Caza y Pesca, Av Argentina 317. Gives advice on fishing, hunting and safaris.

Tour operators

Amazonas Adventure Tours, Centro Comercial Cañoto, Av Coñoto, local 122, T03-333 8350, F03-333 7587, PO Box 2527. Operates tours to Perseverancia, a centre for ecotourism and scientific research, in the Ríos Blanco y Negro Wildlife Reserve, in the far northwestern corner of Santa Cruz Department (see p335).

Bracha, at the train station, T03-346 7795. Open Mon, Wed and Fri 0800-1800, otherwise 0830-1230, 1430-1830, Sun closed. For rail tickets to Quijarro and Yacuiba and Empresa Yacyretá buses to Asunción.

Exprinter, 21 de Mayo 327, T03-333 5133, F03-332 4876, xprintur@bibosi.scz.entelnet.bo.

Fremen, Beni 79, T03-333 8535, F336 0265. Run city and local tours to Amboró, Samaipata etc, also tours of the Jesuit Missions, jungle river cruises on the Flotel Reina del Enin, all-inclusive packages covering the Che Guevara Trail and they run the Hotel El Puente in Villa Tunari (see also Tour operators in Trinidad, Cochabamba and La Paz for the addresses of other offices).

Kayara Tours, Casilla 3132, home address Tapiosí 113 (near the zoo), T03-342 0340. Mario Berndt is highly recommended for tours in the high Andes and the lowlands, he is a professional photographer, is know-ledgeable about culture, flora and fauna, and speaks English, German and Spanish.

Magri Turismo (address under Casas de cambio in Directory), helpful, recommended.

Rosario Tours, Arenales 193, T03-336 9977, rosario_tours@cotas.com.bo. Highly regarded, with English-speaking staff.

Universal Tours, in the Centro Comercial Cañoto, No. 138, T03-334 9777, www.universaltours.com.bo. Highly regarded; English-speaking staff.

⊖ Transport

Santa Cruz *p300, map p301*
Air
LAB (Lloyd Aéreo Boliviano), T03-337 1459, flies at least twice daily to **La Paz** and **Cochabamba**, also daily to **Trinidad** (book 48 hrs in advance), and to **Sucre**, **Tarija** and **Puerto Suárez**.
Aero Sur, T03-336 7400, flies to **La Paz** (several times daily), and daily to **Cochabamba**, **Trinidad** and **Puerto Suárez**. SAVE (Servicio Aero Vargas España), T03-352 1247, flies to **Trinidad**, **San Borja**, **Magdalena**, **Cobija**, **Puerto Suárez**, **Riberalta** and **La Paz**.

Airline offices
AeroPerú, Beni/Bolívar, T03-336 5385.
Aero Sur, Irala 616/Valle Grande, T03-336 7400, Mon-Fri 0800-1230, 1430-1830, Sat 0830-1230.
Aerolíneas Argentinas, Edificio Banco de la Nación Argentina, on main plaza, T03-333 9776.
Air France, Independencia, Galería Paititi, T03-334 7661.
American Airlines, Arenales/Beni 167, T03-334 1314.
Iberia, Casco Viejo Junín, corner of 21 de Mayo, 2nd floor, office 109, T03-332 7448.
LAB, Warnes y Chuquisaca, T03-334 4159.
Lan Chile, 24 de Septiembre y Florída, Glaería Martel, office 15, T03-334 1010.
SAVE, Aeropuerto El Trompillo, office 6, T03-352 1247.
TAM, T03-337 1999.
Varig, Celso Castedo 39, Edif Nago, T03-333 1105.

Buses
Local/regional Micros that serve the first few anillos and don't venture out beyond the 4th ring use the new bus terminal but also pick up passengers anywhere along their appointed routes instead. Look out for the destination posted in the windscreen and flag the bus down if it's going in the right direction, but always double-check with the driver that it's going where it says it is. Buses and micros to **Viru-Viru International Airport**, **Cotoca**, **Montero** and **Warnes** can be hailed from anywhere along their route or can be boarded at the new terminal. A colectivo taxi service runs to **Samaipata**

from C Tundy 70, near the old bus terminal.
Long distance There are daily direct buses to **La Paz**, via Oruro, between 1700 and 1930 (851 km, 16 hrs, US$10.45), some of which are *bus-cama*. There are daily buses every ½ hr to **Cochabamba** 0600-0900 and 1630-2100 (US$3.75, 10 hrs), sit on the left for best views. The only Santa Cruz-Cochabamba bus not to take the lowland route is Cinta de Plata, via Epizana, leaving on Sun at 1700. There are direct buses to **Sucre** daily between 1700 and 1800 (14 hrs, US$6-7.50). To **San Ignacio de Velasco**, see p338. To **Trinidad**, several buses daily between 1700 and 1900, (12 hrs, US$4.50). To **Camiri** (7-8 hrs, US$3.75), **Yacuiba** and **Tarija** (26-32 hrs) several companies run daily between 1730 and 1900.
International Trans Suarez buses, T03- 333 7532, all leave the terminal daily at 1830 to **Asunción** (up to 2 days, US$60-75), **Mon- tevideo**, **Buenos Aires**, **São Paulo** (24 hrs via Quijarro, US$60), and **Iguazo** (32 hrs, US$60).

Car hire
Aby's, Anillo 3, corner with Pasaje Muralto 1038 (opposite the zoo), T03-345 1560, www.abys@khainata.com.
Across, 4th Anillo, corner with radial 27 (400 m from Av Banzer Oeste), T03-344 1617, US$70 per day for basic Suzuki 4WD (200 km per day) with insurance.
A. Barron's, Av Alemana 50 esq. Tajibos, T03-342 0160, F342 3439, www.rentacar bolivia.com. Best in town, honest and reasonable rates, English spoken. Several models, US$60 per day for Suzuki 4WD with insurance, tax extra.
Localiza, Carretera Al Norte Km 3 ½, T03-343 3939, US$65 per day for basic Suzuki 4WD (150 km per day) with insurance, tax extra.

Taxis
Expect to pay 8 Bs (about US$1.15) inside the 1st ring (US$1.50 at night) and US$1.30 up to the 3rd ring. Fix the fare before getting in.

Trains
Trains to **Quijarro** for **Brazil** leave from Santa Cruz rail station (see also page 351). All trains go via San José de Chiquitos to Quijarro, from where travellers must go by

colectivo to the border post, then by bus to **Corumbá**, in Brazil.

Expreso del Oriente Pullman trains leave Santa Cruz Mon-Sat at 1530, arriving in **Quijarro** at 1000. Coming back, they leave Quijarro Mon-Sat at 1500, arriving 0900-1000; 1st class is US$16, 2nd class is US$6.30. There is also the faster (by 6½ hrs) and plusher **Ferrobus** which leaves on Tue, Thu and Sun at 1900, returning on Mon, Wed and Fri at 1900. It has a/c , meals and videos, US$35.40 for *cama*, US$30.60 for *semi-cama*.

If you are desperate, the **Tren Mixto** leaves on Tue and Fri at 1940. It is a cargo train with only 10 or so seats and can take up to 26 hrs yet is no cheaper than the basic fare of US$6.30. Take food, drinking water, insect repellent and a torch, whichever class you are travelling in. From Mar-Aug take a sleeping bag for the cold and be prepared for delays. It is a monotonous journey through jungle, except for the frequent stops at towns (where the train's arrival is a major event) and for the company of your fellow passengers.

Tickets can be bought the day prior to travel. The ticket counter opens at 0800, but go early because queues form hours before and tickets sell fast. Take your passport. Some tickets can be bought in advance at travel agencies (who can also advise on transporting vehicles by rail). There are also travel agency offices in Quijarro (T03-976 2325) and in La Paz (T02-232 7472).

To **Yacuiba**, for travelling to **Argentina**, there are 3 trains a week, see p266.

West of Santa Cruz *p303*
A non-stop shuttle **minibus** service leaves from the new bus terminal in Santa Cruz to **Montero** every 30 mins (US$1, 50 mins).

● Directory

Santa Cruz *p300, map p301*
Banks are open 0830-1130, 1430-1730. Note that they won't change TCs on Sat afternoon. **Banco de La Paz**, René Moreno y Ballivián. *Enlace* cash dispenser; **Banco Mercantil**, René Moreno y Suárez de **Figueroa**. Gives cash advance on Visa and

changes cash and TCs; **Banco de Santa Cruz**, Junín 154. *Enlace* cash dispenser, bolivianos on Visa and Mastercard, no commission; **Banco Boliviano-Americano**, René Moreno 366 and Colón y Camiri (Siete Calles). *Enlace* cash dispenser for Visa and Mastercard. **Casas de cambio Medicambio** on Plaza 24 de Septiembre. Will change TCs into dollars at 3% commission. Cambios can also be found on Libertad, esq Latina and Oriente on the 1st block, and Roberto, at 114, T03-332 3766; **Magri Turismo**, Warnes with Potosí, T03-334 5663, is the American Express agent. It doesn't change American Express TCs but you may have to go there to have cheques certified before a *casa de cambio* will accept them. An excellent *cambio* is **Menno Credit Unión**, at 10 de Agosto 15, T03-332 8800. It's a tiny, out-of-the-way office in the Mennonite part of town, they speak fluent English, German and Dutch, and change TCs quickly with no fuss and 1% commission, Mon-Fri 0900-1700. Street money changers are to be found on the northwest corner of Plaza 24 de Septiembre. **Consulates** Sometimes consulates are open on Sat mornings. Almost all have English-speaking staff. **Argentina**, in Edificio Banco de la Nación Argentina, Pl 24 de Septiembre, Junín 22, T03-332 4153, Mon-Fri 0800-1300; **Belgium**, Av Cristo Redentor, T03-342 0662; **Brazil**, Av Busch 330, near Plaza Estudiantes, T03-334 4400, Mon-Fri 0900-1500, it takes 24 hrs to process visa applications, reported as unhelpful; **Canada**, contact Centro Meno, C Puerto Suárez 28, T03-334 3773; **Chile**, Av San Martín, Torre Equipetrol, Equipetrol, T03-343 4272, Mon-Fri 0800-1245; **Denmark**, Landivar 401, T03-352 5200. Open Mon-Fri, 0830-1230, 1430-1830; **France**, Alemania y Mutualista, off the 3rd ring, T03-343 3434, Mon-Fri 1630-1800; **Germany**, C Ñuflo de Chavez 241, T03-336 7585, Mon-Fri 0830-1200; **Israel**, Bailón Mercado 171, T03-342 4777, Mon-Fri 1000-1200, 1600-1830; **Italy**, C Chaco, Edif Honnen, 1st floor, T03-353 1796, Mon-Fri 0830-1230; **Netherlands**, Av Roque Aguilera 300, Anillo 3, between Grigotá y Paraí Casilla 139, T03-358 1805, Mon-Fri

● *Price codes for Sleeping and Eating are given inside the front cover. Further information on*
● *hotel and restaurant grading can be found in Essentials, pages 43-44.*

0900-1230;

Paraguay, Manuel Ignacio Salvatierra 99, Edif Victoria, office 1A, T03-336 6113; Colour photo required for visa, Mon-Fri 0730-1400; **Peru**, Av La Salle 2327, T03-332 4197, Mon-Fri 0830-1430; **Spain**, Monseñor Santiesteban 237, T03-332 8921, Mon-Fri 0900-1200; **UK**, Parapetí 28, 2nd floor, T03-334 5682; USA, Guemes Este 6, Equipetrol, T03-333 0725, Mon-Fri 0900-1130. **Cultural centres** Centro Boliviano Americano, Cochabamba 66, T03-334 2299. Has a library with US papers and magazines, also English classes and some cultural events (art exhibits, ballet, painting classes). Open Mon-Sat, 0900-1200, 1500-2000; **Instituto Cultural Boliviano Alemán**, 24 de Septiembre 266, T03-332 9906. German library, films, language courses, etc; **Centro Iberoamericano de Formación**, Arenales 583, T03-335 1311, F03-332 8820, Casilla 875, www.aeci.org.bo. Concerts, films, art exhibitions, lectures, etc, worth a visit; **Centro Cultural Frances-Aleman**, Av Velarde 200, T03-333 3392, 0900-1200, 1500-2000. Exhibits, conferences, French and German films and classes (also in Portuguese). **Internet** There are plenty of places in town (marked with an @ symbol on the map). Also **Santa Cruz BBS**, Moldes 543, T03-336 5475, and **KF@in@.com**, Velasco 75. Standard charge is US$0.60-0.90 per hr. **Language teachers** Thomas Wallis and Denise Ruiz, C Tembéta 110, Barrio Villa Mercedes, T/F03-352 4819, tom.wallis@ scbbs-bo.com Specialists in diplomatic and corporate translations, but also handle smaller orders. Denise is considered to be one of the best language teachers in the city. **Laundry** Lavaseco Universal, at Bolívar and Quijarro, T03-332 7715, and Beni 747, T03-332 7252, same-day

service; **Lave Rápido**, Pasaje Callejas 70, side street on Republiquetas, Plaza Callejas. Self-service. **Medical services** There are 2 hospitals northwest of the city centre, Hospital San Juan de Dios and Hospital Petrolero CNSS. Nearby, around España and Cuellar, doctors of every speciality practise. The place is also packed with pharmacies. Centro de Medicina Alternativa, Charcas 170, T03-336 2213; **Clínica Lourdes**, René Moreno 352, T03-3325518; **Dr Pepe Arzabe Quiroga**, Clinica San José, Ingavi 720, T03-333 2970. He is a specialist in tropical diseases; **Dr Eliodoro Anglarill**, España 550 #5, T03-333 6929, Mon-Fri 0900-1100, 1500-1830; US-trained. **Dr Ronald Lee Firestone**, Rene Moreno 552, oficina C1, T03-332 3091. Chiropractor, very helpful and speaks English; **Hospital Japones**, 3rd Anillo a Conavi, T03-346 2031. **Dentists** The best dentist for foreigners is **Dra Carolina Ibañez de Hanley**, Av Ibérica 403, Barrio Las Palmas, T03-353 0700, F353 0686, carolinai@ cotas.com.bo. She speaks English, Portuguese and Spanish, has first-rate facilities, and reasonable prices. Her partner, is a specialist in pediatric dentisty; **Katia Saucedo**, Antonio Vaca Diez 63, T03-337 2589. Speaks English; **Unident**, Av. San Martín 1000, T03-343 2040, high-end clinic offering implants, periodontics and orthodontics. **Post office** C Junín 146, open 0800-2000 every day. **Telephone** Entel at Warnes 83 (between Moreno y Chuquisaca), T03-332 5526. Local and international calls and fax, open Mon-Sat 0730-2330, Sun and holidays 0730-2200. There's also a small Entel office at Quijarro 267. **Useful addresses Immigration** Opposite the zoo, T03-333 6442. Mon-Fri 0830-1200, 1430-1800, reported as friendly and efficient for extensions.

Samaipata and Amboró

Samaipata is set to be one of the next big destinations but is still far enough off the beaten track to attract the more adventurous traveller. This is no sleepy, laid-back little town, however. At the weekend it bursts into life when crowds of visitors from Santa Cruz come to escape the oppressive heat and party with a vengeance. Close by is El Fuerte, the easternmost capital of the Inca empire with the largest sculpted sacred rock in the whole of South America. If that doesn't turn you on, then what about waterfalls, a vast cactus desert or – best of all – comfortable, cheap Swiss-style cabañas?

Roughly equidistant from Santa Cruz, Bolivia's best-known protected area is Parque Nacional Amboró, a 637,600-ha territory only three hours west of Santa Cruz, situated at the extreme northwest edge of Santa Cruz's Ichilo province. 442,500 ha (or roughly 70%) is set aside as exclusive parkland, whilst the remaining 195,100 ha is now an integrated use area. This is one of the last untouched wildernesses on earth and a place of special beauty. ›› *For Sleeping, Eating and other listings, see pages 324-328.*

Samaipata → *Altitude: 1,650 m.*

Weekends in Samaipata are busy with visitors coming to party and escape Santa Cruz's heat; midweek, prices tend to be lower, and this is the time to relax, enjoy the comfortably warm climate and explore the area's jewels, including pre-Inca El Fuerte.

Ins and outs

There's no tourist office but all the tour operators offer free information. **Roadrunners** are particularly helpful. They will arrange the purchase of bus tickets for buses heading to Sucre so you don't have to return to Santa Cruz; give them 24 hours notice. They'll also take bookings for colectivos to Santa Cruz. ›› *For full transport details, see page 327.*

Samaipata

To Cochabamba (350 km)

Panadería Gerlinde

Centro de Investigaciones Arqueológicos y Antropolo

Bolívar

Taxis

Don Gilberto Tours

Michael Blendinger Nature Tours

Plaza

El Tambo

To Valleabajo

To El Fuerte (9km), Santa Cruz (120km) & Baden Restaurant & Cabañas

N

0 metres 100
0 yards 100

Sleeping
Achira Sierra Resort 13
Alojamiento Vargas 1
Aranjuez 2
Cabañas de Traudi 3
Campeche 4
Don Jorge 5

Fridolín 6
Hostal Saldías 7
Hostería Mi Casa 8
Landhaus 9
La Víspera 10
Quinta Piray 11
Residencial Kim 12

Eating
Café Amboró & Tours 1
Café Hamburg &
 Roadrunner Tours 2
Chakana 3
El Descanso en
 Los Alturas 4

Landhaus 5
Media Vuelta 6

Bars & clubs
Mosquito 7

Knight in shining armour

Try to plonk a child in front of a chess board in the affluent west and it will probably turn to a Nintendo in disgust, let alone master the Queen's Gambit opening move. So you may faint in shock to discover that tiny Samaipata has a chess club built to international standards with 125 young members. It is already producing teenage nationwide champions. Wolfgang Paulin was one of five foreign teachers who came to Samaipata, began building cabañas and changed the village for tourists. He realised there was little for the town's youth to do so he invested a pile of money in building a modern centre devoted to chess. Check it out, next to the museum. As well as the chequered boards there is a snack bar. You may even want to give one of the youngsters a game. But be prepared for a thrashing.

Sights

The museum **Centro de Investigaciones Arqueológicos y Antropológicas Samaipata** ① *2 blocks east and 1 block north of the plaza, daily 0930-1230, 1430-1830, US$0.75; US$3 for museum and El Fuerte*, provides a valuable introduction to the nearby pre-Inca ceremonial site known as **El Fuerte**. The carved rock can no longer be walked upon at the ancient site so it is vital to see the museum's model. There is also a collection of pre-Inca lowland ceramics with anthropomorphic designs dating from around AD 300 and a good mock-up of the cave near Mataral. English-speaking Olaf Liebhart of **Roadrunners** gives an enthusiastic tour of the museum included in his El Fuerte trip which really brings it to life.

The layout of Samaipata's **central plaza** mirrors parts of El Fuerte. In the centre is a representation of the central temple with nine seats and triangles. There are three steps up to the bandstand representing the temple of the jaguar; look out for the circular picture of the big cat on the floor nearby. You will also see three lines of rhombuses, similar to the rattlesnake patterns on the sacred rock. Walk to the south side of the square, just opposite the shop **El Tambo**. Stand in the middle of a circle on the edge, facing into the plaza and a sculpture, and speak out loud. You will find yourself in the centre of a cleverly planned echo. Some tour operators will tell you about this as part of a trip to El Fuerte.

Along with Buena Vista (see page 323), Samaipata is a major gateway into **Amboró National Park** which has more species of insect, bird, flora and fauna per hectare than anywhere else on earth – including giant tree ferns 10-m high, which can be seen from Samaipata. A day's trekking will take you to Devil's Tooth Mountain and another day right into the park, down the Río San Rafael. Note that there is no public transport into the park (see page 327). The park is managed by **Fundacíon Amigos de la Naturaleza (FAN)** ① *office at the intersection of C Sucre and Murillo, T03-944 6017, www.fan-bo.org.*

El Fuerte → *The numbers in the text relate to those on the map.*

The site is 3 km along the highway, then 6 km up a signposted road. It's a 2-hr walk one-way but you really need at least 1 ½ hrs to explore the sight so it's better to take a colectivo taxi there (US$4.50 one-way for 1-4 people) and walk back. A round trip to the ruins by taxi from Santa Cruz will cost around US$40. Daily 0900-1700 (don't cut it fine – visitors must be out of the restricted zone by 1700 and this is 2 km from the ruins). US$3; ticket also valid for the museum in town which you should see first.

‼ *A raised walkway is being built which will give better views.*

Nine kilometres east of Samaipata, and often besieged by ferocious winds, is El Fuerte, Bolivia's second-most visited pre-Columbian site after Tiahuanaco, and named 'Patrimonia de la Humanidad' in 1998. Its chief attraction is a vast carved rock, a sacred structure which consists of a complex system of channels, basins and high-relief sculptures. Behind this are the poorly excavated remains of a city. There is convincing evidence this was the easternmost fortress of the Incas' Bolivian Empire and the original Samaipata. The Spanish first took this site over then abandoned it to resettle in the valley below from where, it is said, they could control the passing silver convoys.

The carved rock will be your first stop (1). It is no longer permitted to walk on it due to the erosion this causes and the vandalism of previous visitors, so a trip to see its model in the museum (see page 315) is essential. The rock is 240 m by 40 m and 10-m high, the biggest in South America. Some suggest Amazonian people created it around 1500 BC, but the sandstone is soft and erodes quickly, so it could be a lot younger.

The main carvings are Inca. In front is a circular relief of a puma and alongside two others, badly eroded. The wall further back forms the remains of the temple of the jaguar. Also further back are the beautiful, 24 m-long patterned channels (which will be easier to see from the new viewpoint). These are thought to symbolise rattlesnakes and sacrificial blood and, during Inca rituals, *chicha* (corn beer) released from the central temple would wriggle its way down the criss-cross rhombus carvings like a moving snake.

Walking around you'll first see what may have been carved seating (2) for people to watch the ceremonies. Below (3) are a series of niches (the first of which has been re-roofed in traditional style) which would have held mummies and gold offerings. The last eight or so were still being carved when the Spanish arrived and are incomplete. A wall at the eastern end (4) may have been originally painted red with niches.

The route will take you past Inca agriculture terracing to Chinkana (5), a hole which may have been a well or an entrance to a labyrinth containing lost Inca treasure. The Spanish found nothing and the word Chinkana means 'lost'.

The rest of the site, sadly, is poorly restored. You'll pass the ruins of two Inca houses (6) before passing into what was once the central plaza of a grand town (and now looks little better than a football pitch). Imagination is needed to conjure up the image of the large, 68 m by 16 m, 12 m-high *Kallanka* (7) which flanked the southern side. This had eight doors opening onto the plaza and was used for religious and military ceremonies.

There is really very little else to see as the *Akkllawasi* (8) for Virgins of the Sun is mainly overgrown. Finish by climbing to the viewpoint (9) from where the rock can be best appreciated. As this spot is the highest it is thought there may be another, even more important, carved rock below.

El Fuerte

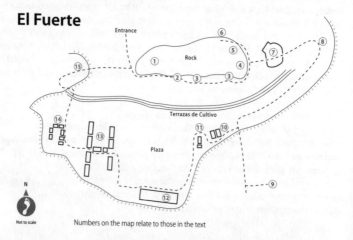

Numbers on the map relate to those in the text

East of Samaipata

Twenty kilometres east of town, beyond El Fuerte, is the pleasant **Cuevas** ① *To get there, hitch or take a taxi from Samaipata, entry US$0.80*, marked by a wooden sign on the right-hand side of the road. Head up a small stream along a path. After 15 minutes the path opens onto two waterfalls and pools, one of which has a small sandy 'beach'. It's a great spot for a swim but watch out for ticks! A third, more beautiful waterfall, can be found at the end of a short, steep path. There are some cabañas by the roadside at the entrance, or you can camp. Behind the car park opposite you can follow the river to a 10 km-long canyon. Seek advice from a tour operator first – there is dangerous sinking sand here.

Further east towards Santa Cruz, just before **Bermejo**, is the turning to **Laguna Volcán**. About 4 km uphill from the main road there's accommodation at the **B Refugio Volcán** (reservation at Calle Bolívar in Santa Cruz, T03-333 2725). Price includes all meals and transport (for a minimum of two).

For views of this fantastic volcanic landscape, turn left just after Bermejo, at the blue and white sign. It's a 12 km drive up a very steep track to El Sillar and Serranías Volcanes, best done in a jeep, but the scenery is worth it, even just 4 km up the track.

South of Samaipata, 40 km away, is **La Pajcha** ① *Taxi (often difficult in rainy season) US$30 from Samaipata, takes you to within 50 m of the falls,* an impressive 40 m-high waterfall. You can swim and hike, but beware of snakes. Another 20 km south is to **Postrervalle**, around which are many interesting walks and mountain bike trails. There's a small hostel and camping is possible.

West of Samaipata

The road from Santa Cruz west to Cochabamba (see page 276) is paved as far as **Mairana**, about 20 km west of Samaipata, and from there the paving is intermittent to a point about 90 km beyond Comarapa, where it runs out totally until Pojo Cruz. From there to Cochabamba it's more paved than unpaved, and even the unpaved sections are pretty good. From Mairana there are buses three times a week (at 1400) to Cochabamba via the old road.

At **Mataral**, there is a gas station and restaurants, and a dirt and gravel road heads south of the main Santa Cruz-Cochabamba road 55 km to **Vallegrande** (see next page). The road is terrible in the wet and it can take up to six hours. Mataral is also an access point for Amboró (see page 319) and is famous for its cactus desert and *pinturas rupestres* (4,000-year-old cave paintings made using coloured earth) which are a few kilometres from town. You can hitchhike here then recruit a guide in the village for around US$4-5. The cacti are great and the cave is 1½ hours away through them by foot. Please don't take pictures using flash as it fades the pigment. Further west, between Mataral and Comarapa is **Tambo**, 2 km from **San Isidro**, where there's accommodation in the **Hotel San Isidro**. There's excellent birdwatching around here with lots of macaws.

Saipina

At San Isidro a road branches west towards **Aiquile** (see page 292), on the main bus route between Sucre and Santa Cruz. Soon after the turn-off is the lovely, friendly old village of Saipina, with colonial houses around its plaza. Saipina sits in the valley of the Río Grande, an agricultural centre where they say "the only thing that doesn't grow is that which isn't planted." Buses often get stuck here in the rainy season as the river is subject to flash flooding.

There's a new museum in the village (entry US$0.80) which displays local archaeological finds. Three hours away by horse is the well-preserved hilltop Inca fortress of **Pukara**, where you can camp. Trips to Pukara, and other interesting local sites, can be arranged with Rolando Villaroel at the museum. He rents out horses for US$15 per day.

Comarapa and beyond

The warm, sleepy little town of Comarapa, 115 km west of Samaipata, makes a pleasant stop and a good base for birdwatching in the area. Its old, colonial cobbled streets lead up to the hill above the plaza and there are also *pinturas rupestres* (see above) nearby. A few kilometres from town are the pre-Inca ruins of **Pukara de Tuquipaya**. Ask for directions in town, or take a *cooperativa* taxi. West of town is **Khara Huasi**, which is one of the southern entrances to Amboró national park (see page 319). There's also a small park office for Amboró in Comarapa itself.

From Comarapa the road west begins to leave the cactus and desert scrub and climbs up into spectacular cloud forests bordering the Amboró and Carrasco national parks. There are few settlers in this area and some camping spots close to the road, and though there are very few trails into the forests, the traffic is so light that birdwatching can be done from the road. The mornings tend to be the clearest of traffic.

At the western end of the forest is **Pojo Cruz**, which has a hotel and a few roadside restaurants. A few kilometres off the main road, down in the valley, is **Pojo**, which has a couple of hotels. These are the last decent places to stay until you are almost in Cochabamba.

Vallegrande → *Colour map 3, grid A5. Altitude: 2,030 m.*

Vallegrande is a charming, unspoiled little colonial town in cattle-farming country. It has a Sunday handicraft market and several pleasant, basic places to stay. The town's claim to fame is its proximity to **La Higuera**, where Che Guevara was captured and executed. Here, in the hospital laundry, Che's bullet-ridden body was laid out on public view for two days after his execution, and dozens of journalists, as well as curious soldiers and civilians filed in to see it. You can still visit the hospital laundry, now an abandoned shed behind the main building. It's an evocative place, the walls covered in signatures and slogans scratched into the peeling plaster. One of the most poignant is actually on the adobe wall of the public telephone office. It reads: "Che – alive as they never wanted you to be".

On the plaza, in the Casa de Cultura, there is an **archaeological museum** ① *US$0.75*. Upstairs is the **Che Guevara Room** ① *Free entry; ask for Don Calixto Cárdenas, head of the civic committee. He saw Che's body in 1967 and is very helpful*, which has many photographs and an hour-long video in Spanish which is fascinating for its original black and white footage.

La Higuera and the Che Guevara Trail

Forty-five kilometres south from Vallegrande is the attractive, traditional mud-built village of **Pucará**, which has one basic *alojamiento* and a market on Wednesday. From Pucará there is transport to **La Higuera**, described by one commenator as a 'miserable little hamlet', where the Cuban revolutionary hero Che Guevara met his end on 9 October 1967. La Higuera is 15 km from Pucará (costing US$20-30 by taxi from Vallegrande).

Che's universal appeal lives on, but the ultimate tribute is a new **'Che Guevara Trail'** (www.rutedelche.com), which follows the last movements of Che and his band as they tried to flee the pursuing Bolivian Army. The entire 815-km circuit can be covered in three to six days. It winds its way along dirt roads in the sub-tropical area bordering the Santa Cruz and Chuquisaca departments. Tourists will travel by mule or on foot to the battlegrounds where the Cuban-backed revolutionary brigade clashed with Bolivian forces. The trail includes the crossing by boat of the Río Grande at the Vado del Yeso, scene of the ambush that killed part of Che Guevara's group. It ends near the airstrip at Vallegrande, where Che's body was dumped in a secret grave. Nervous readers should rest assured, though, that the climax of the trail will not result in execution by firing squad. Accommodation along the route will consist of basic lodges, cabins or campsites in order to keep the whole experience authentic.

Developed under the aegis of a new community tourism project, financed and supported by a number of foreign aid organizations, including CARE International, as well as the Bolivian government, local authorities and businesses, the trail was officially opened in October 2004. Over the next three years selected tours will be developed, giving visitors the chance to travel as Che and his comrades did, by mule or on foot. This region is one of the poorest in Bolivia. The Guaraní people who live here mostly rely on subsistence farming to survive. The projected influx of tourists is expected to benefit some 3,000 directly and 12,000 indirectly. Locals will be trained as guides, or in new guesthouses and restaurants, and will also have the opportunity to sell their handicrafts. For details of the southern part of the trail, around Camiri, see page 347.

Parque Nacional Amboró

The park encompasses three distinct major ecosystems – those of the Amazon River basin, the foothills of the Andes mountains, and the Chaco plain – and 11 life zones. Nowhere else in the world do three such vast environments converge, and nowhere else can you see so many diverse ecological systems. The park is home to thousands of animal, bird, plant, and insect species, and is reputed to contain more butterflies than anywhere else on earth. Several of these species, including the spectacled bear and panther, and the curassow and quetzal birds, are endangered. It is staggering to think that less than half of the area has been extensively researched. The park also contains some recently discovered Inca and pre-Inca sites, not all of which have been excavated.

Ins and outs

Getting there Access to the area is strictly by road, preferably in a sturdy 4WD jeep or similar model, although the routes to the main entrance are quite good. The best entry to Amboró is via Buena Vista (see below), to the northeast of the park along the new paved Santa Cruz-Cochabamba highway. Note that all points of access into Amboró involve crossing the Río Surutú, which can be greatly swollen in the rainy season, so plan your trip for the dry season. The crossing may be made on foot, in a vehicle, or by raft, depending on the time of year.

Amboró has several comparatively easy access routes; those from **Buena Vista**, **Comarapa**, **Samaipata**, and **Mairana** are the best known. The easiest way is to go by bus from Santa Cruz to Buena Vista, and then by *camioneta* to El Terminal; from here, you can walk to Río Surutu, the park's eastern boundary. You also can take a daily bus southward to Santa Fe from Buena Vista, and then a motorcycle taxi to the river (US$6). There are several access trails from **Río Surutu**: you can cross at San Juan del Colorado, Palestina, Las Cruces, Espejitos, or Huaytú, all south of Buena Vista; or north of Buena Vista at San Carlos or Yapacani on the old road (Antigua Carretera) to Cochabamba. Access from the west and north is possible, although currently by trail only.

Band on the run

One of the most enduring images of youthful rebellion is that of Che Guevara staring proud, implacable and defiant under that trademark black beret. It is an image that has graced many a student's wall. But how did this great 20th century icon come to die in a miserable little hamlet in the Bolivian wilderness?

Ernesto Guevara de la Serna, or Che as he became known, was born in Argentina on 14 June 1928 to wealthy middle-class parents. However, his eyes were soon opened to the plight of South America's poor during a journey around the continent on a beat-up old motorcycle, chronicled in 'The Motorcycle Diaries'.

He met Fidel Castro in Mexico in 1956 and together they planned the overthrow of the harshly repressive dictatorship of Fulgencio Batista in Cuba. This was achieved in January 1959, after an extraordinary and heroic three-year campaign with a guerrilla force reduced at one point to 12 men.

Che worked tirelessly to create the ideal socialist model in Cuba as well as establish links with other, sympathetic nations, but his overriding ambition had always been to spread the revolutionary word and take the armed struggle to other parts. Bolivia seemed the obvious choice.

He left Cuba for Bolivia in November 1966, and, after a brief stay in La Paz, at the Hotel Copacabana, Che travelled to the guerrilla base at Ñancahuazú, a farm 250 km south of Santa Cruz where together they began their preparations. But their constant movements aroused suspicion and Che and his group were on the run from April 1967 when the army began looking for them. There was little sympathy from the Bolivian peasantry, as the government had successfully played on their patriotism in the face of this `foreign invasion'.

Che and his his band were now very much on their own and worse was to come. One of his men had been captured and, under interrogation, confirmed Che's presence in the country, contrary to the CIA belief that he had been killed a few years earlier in the Congo. The USA immediately despatched a group of Special Forces to create a counterinsurgency battalion, the Bolivian Army Rangers, and stop Che gaining a foothold.

By August, Che was sick and exhausted, as were many of his dwindling force. On 31 August he lost one-third of them in an army ambush. The army had enlisted the help of local peasants to inform them of the guerrillas' movements, so they were ready and waiting when Che and his men made their way slowly north towards Vallegrande, the Argentine now crippled by his chronic asthma and travelling by mule.

They reached the tiny village of La Higuera, where these faced the US-trained Army Rangers in what would be their final battle. On 8 October the surviving guerrilla's were trapped in a ravine. A prolonged gun battle ensued during which a wounded Che was caught while trying to escape. He was held prisoner overnight in the village schoolhouse, under the supervision of a Cuban-American CIA agent, and executed the following day, 9 October, aged 39. Che's body was dumped in a secret grave, the precise whereabouts of which had remained a mystery, until it was finally discovered in July 1997. He now lies in peace in his beloved Cuba.

From Buena Vista There are three possible entrances to the park. There is a daily morning bus out of Buena Vista, which runs alongside the river for several kilometres (departure time varies so check in advance). The bus stops at all the entrances, but let the driver know at which one you want to get off at, if there are no other people going to the same place. The stops, in descending order going south from Buena Vista, are: Santa Bárbara, Huantu, San Rafael de Amboró, Espejitos (28 km from Buena Vista), Santa Rosa de Amboró and Las Cruces (35 km from Buena Vista). The third and fifth stops do not have entrances to the park. The most popular staging point is from Las Cruces, as the trail leads directly to the settlement of Villa Amboró, in the park's buffer zone.

> ♪ There is as yet no fee to enter the park itself.

Buses to Buena Vista and Yapacani (see below) leave hourly from beside the bus terminal in Santa Cruz, or sooner if they're full. The first one leaves at 0500 and the last at around 1500 (later on Friday). There are also minibuses from Montero.

There is an alternative entrance to Amboró from the north, via Yapacani, a town on the highway to Cochabamba (see above). This entrance first crosses the Río Yapacani, then the Río Surutú and has a rough track that can be negotiated by 4WD vehicle for most of the year. It leads to one of the park's cabañas, Mataracu (see Sleeping, page 325). Buses leave from Buena Vista to Yapacani at 0800; from here you can take a motorcycle taxi to the river (US$5, 1 hour). To return ask the park guard to radio for a motorcycle taxi.

From Samaipata The park can also be approached from the south, via Samaipata off the old Santa Cruz-Cochabamba road (see page 303). There are various entrances from the south and no entry fees, but there are few trails and the going is rough, so a guide is recommended. If going on your own, it's advisable to contact the FAN office in Samaipata (see park information below) first. They offer accurate up-to-date information and will allow trekkers to use their radio telephone to contact the few park rangers in the area, although it is annoyingly difficult to find a time when anyone is in the office. You can enter via Achira and Barrientos, which are 15 km away and accessed by jeep; direct from Samaipata (9 km from park boundary) for which 4WD is essential in rainy season; or from Mataral where there's a guest hut. A popular route in is via La Yunga – drive to Mairana (17 km), then it's 13-15 km by jeep. There's also an entrance at Comarapa (see page 317).

Parque Nacional Amboró: access routes

Yapacani
San Carlos
Buena Vista
Mataracu
Parque Nacional Amboró
Huantu
Río Surutú
Espejitos
La Chonta
Santa Rosa de Amboró
Macuñucú
N
Not to scale

Advice and suggestions

Amboró has the best local infrastructure to support overnight and long-term visitors. Its location in the west of Santa Cruz Department, between two major highways and not far from the city of Santa Cruz or the resort community of Samaipata (an excellent starting point for treks to Amboró), also makes it the most accessible (behind only Cochabamba's Parque Nacional Tunari). Its size can be misleading, however, and a week to 10 days are needed to cross the park from one end to the other.

Those wishing to visit Amboró should bear in mind that although access is relatively easy, penetration into the park's more remote areas should always be undertaken with an

⦂ Paradise under threat

Parque Nacional de Amboró is potentially both Bolivia's greatest ecotourist attraction and its greatest ecological tragedy. Initially only covering 180,000 ha, in 1984 the reserve was proclaimed a national park, and six years later was expanded to 630,000 ha. However, intense settlement along its eastern borders led the government to establish the park's total area at its current size of 430,000 ha in 1995.

The government's action was seen by many observers as a concession to the illegal settlers, and led to vociferous opposition by conservation groups worldwide. Nonetheless, the 200,000 hectares abandoned to the colonists was designated a 'multiple use area', ostensibly free from rampant development and theoretically to be opened up only under strict guidelines.

The reality is far different, however, and each year unchecked agricutural and mineral pursuits threaten the park's unique ecosystem. To make matters worse, Amboró lies between two of Bolivia's most heavily travelled roads, the old and the new Santa Cruz-Cochabamba highways, and is scarcely 25 km west of Santa Cruz itself. If encroachment is not halted soon, the entire area may one day fall prey to 'slash and burn' farming, its fragile ecosystem permanently damaged.

experienced guide or as part of an organized tour. Much of the park is wet all year round and many of the routes are riverine or along poorly (if at all) marked trails. A good supply of food and water, insect repellent, a machete, good boots and long-sleeved shirts and long trousers are a must.

The park's infrastructure is minimal: there are no hospitals, stores, telephones or any public facilities. Notwithstanding, a well-prepared two to three day trip into one or more of Amboró's ecosystems is an incredible experience. Keep in mind that most tours do not stretch beyond a week's stay and that great patience is needed actually to spot some of the more exotic creatures in the park. Particularly in the case of the larger game, nocturnal sightings are invariably more common than daylight ones. The best time of year to visit the park is during the May-October dry season. Note that neither the recently opened **Amboró Eco-Resort** nor the wonderful **Amboró Butterfly Farm**, although nice enough on their own, is part of the park.

Park information

There is a lot of information on both Amboró and Parque Nacional Noel Kempff Mercado. As well as a slew of websites, sources of extensive inside knowledge are Pieter and Margarita de Radd, who operate the wonderful **Cabañas La Víspera** and tour agency **Boliviajes** in Samaipata (see page 327). There's also Saira Duque, who works with the acclaimed Santa Cruz-based non-profit preservation group, **Fundacíon Amigos de la Naturaleza (FAN)** ⓘ *www.fan-bo.org*. Saira herself can be contacted at sduque@fan-bo.org.

Around the park

The park is Bolivia's second-oldest, having been officially opened in 1973 as the *Silvestre Germán Busch Wildlife Preserve*. It is also perhaps the best-managed (albeit woefully understaffed) park in Bolivia, and should be at the top of every visitor's list. Whatever a traveller's appetite, it is likely to be sated by a trip to the park. Whether you want to see large game or whether your tastes run to rare tropical or Andean birds, Amboró has it all. Only patience and, if possible, an experienced guide is needed.

The park is home to a huge number of birds, including the nearly extinct blue-horned currasow, southern-horned currasows the very rare quetzal and cock-of-the-rock, blue-throated macaws, red and chestnut-fronted macaws, hoatzin and cuvier toucans. In total, 712 species of bird have been discovered. Most mammals native to Amazonia are also here. They include capybaras, peccaries, tapirs, several species of monkey such as howlers and capuchins, jungle cats like the jaguar, ocelot and margay, and the increasingly rare spectacled bear, the only bear found in South America.

Amboró will appeal most of all to those hardy souls who are at home in the great outdoors. There are numerous tributaries of the Yapacani and Surutú rivers to explore, as well as numerous waterfalls and cool green swimming pools, moss-ridden caves and the fragile yet awe-inspiring virgin rainforest.

Buena Vista → *Colour map 2, grid B6.*

There are two places to base yourself for a trip into the park: Samaipata (see page 314) and little Buena Vista, a sleepy, friendly old place that's more mild west than wild west. The mission church dates from 1767 and was built to hold more than 700 Chiraguano Indians who had been converted to Christianity. The town hosts a *fiesta* on 26 October.There are motorbike taxis for getting around town. The only *Entel* phone is at the petrol station out by the road. Note that cell phones can't be called from the *Cotel* office.

In Buena Vista you can stock up on supplies and hire guides, or join an organized tour group. There are many tour operators in the village (see page 327). Some of the hotels also organize trips around the park. There is a **park information office**, just over a block away from the plaza. They have information and advice on the park and some maps. They can also help with guides and suggestions and will issue a permit.

Beyond Buena Vista

There are *cabañas* and interpretive trails on the other side of the Río Surutú, just past Villa Aguiles on the road from Buena Vista to the river. They are in the multiple-use area of the park, with lots of interesting flora and fauna. The trails are well set out and so you can have a pleasant meal by the river after your hike.

Perhaps the prettiest place in the park, where there are water pools just five minutes' walk away, is **Mataracu**. Explore deeper with a guide (see page 327) and you will be rewarded, 2 ½ hours in, with a 20 m-high waterfall as well as canyons, cliffs and lots of wildlife. To get there take the main road towards Cochabamba and, after 20 km, turn left just over the Yapacani bridge. From there it is another 18 km to a ford across a river and then another 5 km to the park ranger's office. By taxi it will cost US$12 – make

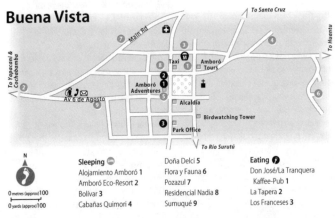

Buena Vista

To Santa Cruz

To Yapacani & Cochabamba

To Huantu

Main Rd

Taxi

Amboró Tours

Amboró Adventures

AV 6 de Agosto

Alcaldía

Birdwatching Tower

Park Office

To Río Surutú

N

0 metres (approx)100
0 yards (approx)100

Sleeping
Alojamiento Amboró **1**
Amboró Eco-Resort **2**
Bolívar **3**
Cabañas Quimori **4**

Doña Delci **5**
Flora y Fauna **6**
Pozazul **7**
Residencial Nadia **8**
Sumuqué **9**

Eating
Don José/La Tranquera
Kaffee-Pub **1**
La Tapera **2**
Los Franceses **3**

Eastern Lowlands Samaipata & Amboró

sure you book your return trip. The community should now have finished building *cabañas* and *Eco-Resort* was building 20 upmarket *cabañas* at the time of writing, otherwise ask at the park ranger's office if you can stay there for the night.

The other major destination is **Macañucú** although the waterfalls here dry up from July to September. Take the road south past Huaytu and Espejitos to Santa Rosa, a very small community. From here you can hire horses for the last 12 km trek southwest off the road (effectively a right turn). This route can be done in a jeep. The community of Macañucú has a decent infrastructure, and can offer three meals a day, a guide, hiking trails, kitchen facilities, an area for camping and showers for US$20 per person per day (confirm this in Buena Vista before setting out). Also popular is **La Chonta** which is good for a day's exploration.

● Sleeping

Samaipata *p314, map p314*
Accommodation in and around the town may be difficult to find at weekends in the high season but midweek the better hotels and resorts are willing to negotiate and there are some good discounts available. Most of the *cabañas*, or cabins, listed below are fully equipped with kitchens, bathrooms and barbecues and if you turn up unannounced and there's space they'll let you sleep in a hammock outside (**E**).

C **Achira Sierra Resort**, 5km east of town and 1 km from the road, T03-386 2101 (Santa Cruz). Cabins for up to 4, 6, 7, 9 or 19 from US$18, horse riding, pool and sports facilities, restaurant.

C **Fridolín**, To the west of town, T03-944 6168. Cabins for up to 8.

C **Landhaus**, T03-944 6033. Most central of all the *cabañas*. Beautiful place with a small pool, sun loungers, garden, hammocks, parking, internet and sauna (US$20 for up to 8 people). A group of 7 can rent a house here for US$70, also has rooms only with shared bathroom (**F**).

C **La Víspera**, 1.2 km south of town, T03-944 6082, vispera@entelnet.bo. Dutch-owned organic farm with accommodation in 4 cosy cabins, 2 of which sleep up to 2, another up to 7 and another up to 12. Can provide delicious local produce for breakfast, US$3 per person. It's a very peaceful place to stay. Margarita and Pieter know plenty about the local area and can arrange all excursions. They also sell medicinal and seasoning herbs and spices. Highly recommmended.

C-E **Campeche**, T03-944 6046, campeche@scbbs-bo.com. Cabins for 2-6 people, all self-catering, D midweek, E without kitchen.

C-F **Cabañas de Traudi**, T03-944 6094, traudiar@cotas.com.bo Has individually designed and decorated large cabins for 2-8, also (**E**) lovely rooms (F with shared bathroom), heated pool US$1.50 for non residents, sitting area with open fire, TV and music system, ceramics shop and lessons, a great place.

D **Quinta Piray**, T03-944 6136, quinta-piray@cotas.com.bo. 21 large cabins for 2-6, some with wheelchair access.

E-F **Hostería Mi Casa**, Bolívar, T03-944 6292. Some rooms are nicely decorated but not as nice as those at *La Víspera*, pretty flower patio, snack bar, (F with shared bathroom), 1 cabaña (**D**).

F **Aranjuez**, on the main road at the entrance to town, T03-944 6223. Upstairs terrace, handwashing area, food available, includes breakfast, good value.

F **Don Jorge**, Bolívar, T03-944 6086. US$1.50 cheaper with shared bathrooms, clean, hot showers, good beds, large shaded patio, good set lunch.

F-G **Residencial Kim**, near the plaza, T03-944 6161. Clean and friendly, use of kitchen, dining room, (G with shared bathroom), very good value.

G **Alojamiento Vargas**, around corner from museum. Clean rooms, some musty, narrow patio, handwashing facilities, use of kitchen, includes breakfast, owner Teresa kind and friendly. Recommended.

G **Hostal Saldías**, Bolívar, T03-944 6023. Basic, use of kitchen and handwashing facilities, run by noisy teenagers.

Camping La Víspera (see above) has excellent facilities for US$3 per person (US$4 including tent hire); Achira Sierra Resort (also above) for US$1.50 per person.

West of Samaipata *p317*

Saipina

G **14 de Septiembre**, which has 5 triple rooms.

Comarapa

Hotels on the main road are, Central, 11 de Junio and Santa Cruz. All are G and have restaurants.

Vallegrande *p318*

F **La Sede de los Ganaderos**, 1 block from the plaza, T03-942 2176. Hot water all day, large rooms around a patio, tables and chairs, comfortable beds, parking, includes breakfast, great value.

G **Residencia Vallegrande** on the plaza.

Parque Nacional Amboró *p319*

In or near the park Accommodation on the border of the park (in the multiple use area) is practically non-existent. There are a handful of *cabañas*, only one of which, **Mataracú**, can be reached by vehicle, from Yapacani, see above. All others cost US$2 per person per night and are basically no more than rooms to sleep in, but they do offer privacy and relief from insects. Take your own food. These open and close so *always* enquire in advance at the information office in Buena Vista if they are available.

Cabañas Saguayo, Agua Blanca, Macuñucú (reportedly the most popular) and **Semayo** are reached via trails from El Carmen, Huaytu and Las Cruces respectively. They are situated at various points along the park; none of the *cabañas* are actually in the park, except **Mataracú**. There is also a park rangers' campsite along the Río Isama which is usually open (US$2 per night) to campers. It has cooking facilities as well as rudimentary beds.

There are small settlements along the park's fringe in the area for development. These include **Villa Imperial** in the north, **El Carmen** in the northeast, and **Villa Amboró** and **San Juan del Colorado** in the southeast. No formal accommodation exists in these tiny settlements, but villagers often rent travellers a room for the night. Most of these settlers are at odds with conservationists and naturalists, so it is a good idea not to discuss the merits of the park's development.

Within the park itself, there is very little accommodation, even at the level of a campground. There are combination ranger stations/*cabañas* along the Ríos Saguayo, Isama, Macuñucú and Semayo, and another at Villa Amboró, all in the northeast of the region. Only **Matacurú** and **Agua Blanca** (also in the northeast quadrant) are well within the park. All the above accommodation is basic and should be secured before entry. This is done by registering in person at the Amboró National Park Headquarters in Buena Vista. Expect to pay about US$2 per person.

The best option for accommodation is in Buena Vista, where there are quite a few places to choose from.

Buena Vista

L **Flora y Fauna**, out of town (motorbike taxi costs US$1.50), Casilla 2097, T03-333 8118 (mob). Has a viewing platform for bird-watchers, extensive areas of forest and scrub with some well-planned trails. Now run by Martin Maughn, an Irishman who also runs the ever-popular **Café Irlandes** in Santa Cruz.

A **Amboró Eco-Resort**, 2 km out of town towards Cochabamba, T/F03-932 2048, www.amboro.com Centred around a luxurious pool with swim-up bar, sauna and steam rooms, this posh hotel is let down by its tiny rooms and poor restaurant service. Cable TV promised, has a/c, includes hot buffet breakfast. Oh – and there's nothing 'eco' about it.

B **Pozazul**, out on the bypass, T03-932 2091. A/c, clean, kitchen, pool, restaurant, friendly and helpful owners, also A *cabañas* and camping for US$14 per person night with use of showers and pool.

D **Cabañas Quimori**. Prices negotiable in low season, includes buffet breakfast, shared kitchen and hammocks, building a pool, offer guide service with 4WD transport into the park and horse riding to its boundary (US$10 per day). Recommended.

D **Sumuqué**, 3 blocks from plaza, Av 6 de Agosto 250, T03-932 2080. Cabins (shared kitchen) in pleasant gardens with interpretive trails, tropical fruit trees and 5 ha of preserved land.

G **Alojamiento Amboró**, facing the church. Basic.

G **Bolívar**, facing the market. Basic.

G **Doña Delci**, on the corner of the plaza (no sign), basic, has food at weekends.
G **Residencial Nadia**, T03-932 2049. Small, family-run and central.
Camping José, a neighbour of Robin Clarke was at one time running a campsite and also offers guided tours in German.

🍴 Eating

Samaipata *p314, map p314*
There are several restaurants on and around the plaza, most of which are cheap. One of the best for *almuerzo* (US$1.05) with a clean kitchen is **Media Vuelta**.
$$$ **El Descanso en Los Alturas**, wide choice including excellent steaks and pizzas.
$$$ **Landhaus Restaurant**, German-run, good for steaks and salad buffet, open only Thu-Sat 0800-2200.
$$ **Café Hamburg**, on Bolívar, is a great place to hang out. The atmosphere is laid back, there's a bar, food (curry, chorizo, spaghetti and vegetarian), well-stocked book exchange as well as internet US$2.25 per hr (only after 1900). They are also recommended for their *Roadrunners* tour agency (see next page), they have very good tourist advice and private rooms are available too.
$$ **Chakana**. Dutch-owned bar/restaurant/café open every day 0900-late, a relaxing place with *almuerzos* for US$2.25, good snacks and salads, seats outside, book exchange, and ice cream.

Cafés
Café Amboró on Bolívar. Fast-food snack bar, open 0800-2200.
Café Baden, 1 km towards Santa Cruz. Good for ice cream and torts as well as steak and schweizer *würstsalat* (by now you'll be wondering if you've gone to sleep and woken up in Bavaria).
Landhaus Café, pure German cuisine with lovely decor and delicious apple and banana pie, Mon-Thu 1400-1900, Sat and Sun 0800-1900.
Panadería Gerlinde, open daily 0700-2200. For superb value and tasting biscuits, bread, homemade pastas, herbs, cheese, yoghurts and cold meats, try this Swiss-run café which also has a weekend stall in the market.

Parque Nacional Amboró *p319*
Buena Vista
$ **Don José** does very good, cheap, Argentine steaks but is often closed.
$ **La Tapera** on the plaza is good for burgers.
$ **La Tranquera Kaffee Pub** on the plaza, pizza, hamburgers.
$ **Los Franceses**, 1½ blocks from the plaza. Good, cheap French home cooking, limited menu, friendly and helpful, open daily.
You could also try the **market**, and down the hill from the plaza, under the trees, where there is a roast chicken place.

🍸 Pubs, bars and clubs

Samaipata *p314, map p314*
Café Hamburg (see Eating above), popular.
Landhaus has a disco on Sat from 2200.
Mosquito Bar (look for the yellow VW on the roof next to El Descanso en Los Alturas!) German-run, popular. Open daily from 1800, serves soups, lasagne and chilli.

🛍 Shopping

Samaipata *p314, map p314*
There's a **market** in town every weekend, which is mostly produce but occasionally you'll find colourful handwoven woollen horse blankets from Mairana and other nearby communities for around US$10 each.
There is an amazing array of homemade food and drink in Samaipata which will satisfy many a traveller. Particularly good is Argentinian **Don Alex** who sells hand-made wines and liqueurs from a stall on the plaza Sat 1500-2000, Sun 0900-2000, and holidays 1000-2200. His wine is expensive (US$15) but he offers free tasting and sells truffles, brownies, homemade jam, cakes and biscuits which are all excellent in taste and value. You can also pick up a safe hot dog there.
Also in the market at weekends, is the delicious German cold meat kiosk which sells mustards and bread to go with the cold cuts.
Amboró Tours office. Selection of local crafts, may soon be making full-size hammocks.
Cabañas Traudi. For locally-made ceramics; you can arrange to have ceramics lessons too.
El Tambo, on the Plaza, 1000-2100, closed Mon. Sells a range of local crafts and has a good selection of books.

Landhaus Café not only sells homemade biscuits and cakes but crafts and ceramics made in their own workshops.
Michael Blendinger tour office. Selection of local crafts.
Taller de Patchwork, T03-944 6061. Run by Lisa Lösel and sells a range of hand-made household crafts, ask in Roadrunners for directions.

▲▲ Activities and tours

Samaipata *p314, map p314*
Carmen Luz runs 2-hr outdoor art classes for US$5 including materials, T03-944 6036.

Tour operators
Samaipata is blessed with good tour operators. All those listed below come highly recommended and offer trips to El Fuerte and other attractions around Samaipata . Their offices are marked on the map. Expect to pay around US$15-US$20 per person in a group of 4.
Don Gilberto Aguilera, T03-944 6050, is considered by many in Samaipata to be the most knowledgable guide around simply because he was brought up here. He speaks only Spanish, is very affordable and seems to get everywhere in his car.
Michael Blendinger, T03-944 6186, mblendinger@cotas.com.bo. For avid birdwatchers and nature lovers. Michael is a biologist and very knowledgeable but the most expensive. A German raised in Argentina, he speaks excellent English. His free horse- riding promotion is monthly only, on Thu mornings, limited to 4 beasts.
Roadrunners, T03-944 6193. Olaf and Frank here also speak excellent English. Olaf is an enthusiastic authority on many sights but especially El Fuerte which he brings alive with informed description. Frank has a great sense of humour and is fun as well as knowledgeable for trips to Amboró and other sights. They would be a good first port of call for free tourist information.
La Víspera, T03-944 6082, www.lavispera.org. Margarita and Pieter (who run **Boliviajes**) are Dutch and helped forge the tourist service of Samaipata and can arrange any trip. Their knowledge of the area is perhaps the best of all operators, which is saying quite a bit. They also run

'eco' horse and cart trips and a tour along the beautiful old trade route to Sucre, arriving in Tarabuco in time for the market.
Amboró Tours, T/F03-944 6293, erickamboro@cotas.com.bo is run by local Erick Prado who speaks only Spanish but may be able to organise trips to **Refugio Volcan** if given enough warning.

Parque Nacional Amboró *p319*
Tours
Amboró Adventures, on the plaza, Buena Vista, T03-9322090. They charge US$30 per person per day for guide and transport to and from the park; meals not included.
Amboró Tours, on the corner of the plaza, Buena Vista, T03-9322093, T71633990 (mob), amborotours@yahoo.com Open 0730-2000 daily. Marcos Velasco is highly recommended. His English is excellent and he can book Laura Gutierrez, an English-speaking biologist, for trips to all the destinations, US$27 per person in a group of 4 for 1 day, US$33 per person for 2 days, including transport, guide and tent but not food (US$10 extra). Also has keys to a birding tower 1 km from the town centre, US$6 per person for early morning trip, 20 species promised in 2 hrs.
Quimori Tours, on the plaza, Buena Vista, Often closed.

◎ Transport

Samaipata *p314, map p314*
Buses All buses leave Santa Cruz from the new bus terminal, Mon-Sat 1600. A *colectivo* taxi service runs to Samaipata from **Santa Cruz**, from C Tundy 70, near the old bus terminal (2 hrs, US$15 per taxi for up to 4 people). They leave when full, or as soon as everyone agrees to pay the full fare. Earlier departures are more frequent as fewer people travel later in the day. You can return to Santa Cruz by *colectivo* , which will pick you up from your hotel. Otherwise, a taxi will cost about US$15 from outside the petrol station. Buses and *micros* leaving Santa Cruz for Sucre and other towns pass through Samaipata between 1800 and 2000; tickets can be booked with 2 days' notice through **Roadrunners** tour agency. There are also buses to Santa Cruz at 0430, 0445 and 0545 Mon-Sat from the plaza outside **El Tambo**,

US$2.25 (ask at **Roadrunners**), returning at 1600, and sometimes an afternoon bus. Sun is easier as buses leave from 1100-1530.

You can get to Samaipata by bus from **Sucre**; these leave at night and arrive soon after dawn, stopping in Mairana or Mataral for breakfast, about ½ hr before Samaipata. Buses to **Vallegrande** pass through Samaipata at 0800 and 1300; 3-4 hrs.

East of Samaipata *p317*
Saipina
Buses to **Santa Cruz** with Trans Saipina, leave daily at 0600 and 1900; 6 hrs. They return from Santa Cruz at 1330 and 1600 from Anillo 3 y Grigota, T03-352 5287. There are buses to **Cochabamba** with Transportes Surumi on Tue, Thu and Sun at 1600; 10 hrs. They return the following day from Av República entre 6 de Agosto y Vallegrande.

Comarapa
There's a daily bus to **Santa Cruz** at 0700 which returns in the evening, and buses to **Cochabamba** on Tue, Thu and Sun at 1500.

Vallegrande *p318*
Flota Bolívar has daily buses from Santa Cruz via Samaipata at 1730 (5 hrs) and 3 others – check for times as these were in a state of flux at the time of writing. Return most days at 0730 and/or 1300 – again check. There's a direct bus from **Sucre** on Thu at 1830. Also, to **Villa Serrano**, there are trucks (with luck) at the weekend, and transport daily from there to Sucre. A daily bus leaves at 0800 from the market to **Pucará** (see below).

● Directory

Samaipata *p314, map p314*
Banks There are no banks in town, but you can change US dollars cash at **Alamacen Alba** on the plaza, or the **Cooperativo**, 1 block east of the plaza.
Internet Café Hamburg, Bolívar, from 1900; El Tambo (see Shopping above), both US$2.25 per hr. **Laundry** Michael Blendinger Nature Tours, opposite the museum, charges US$3.75 for up to 5 kg.

The Jesuit Missions

Northeast of Santa Cruz is the region called la Gran Chiquitanía, which covers the provinces of Chiquitos, Ñuflo de Chaves, Velasco, Angel Sandoval, and German Busch. This is a vast, sprawling, sparsely populated area, mainly given over to cattle ranching and seemingly of little interest to the traveller, except perhaps those with a bovine fixation. But this is a part of Bolivia with a fascinating history and a precious heritage.

Here lie the seven surviving Jesuit Mission churches of San Javier, Concepción, San Ignacio de Velasco, Santa Ana, San Rafael, San Miguel and San José de Chiquitos, all of which became UNESCO World Heritage sites in 1990. These are perhaps the finest examples of colonial religious art and craftsmanship in the country and will impress even those travellers who would not normally set foot inside a church. ➤➤ *For Sleeping, Eating and other listings, see pages 335-339.*

Ins and outs

Getting there

There are two routes to the Jesuit missions. The first is by road from Santa Cruz east through Cotoca to Puerto Pailas (41 km out of Santa Cruz) where it crosses the Río Grande and continues to Pailon (another 7 km). From there the road heads north, to San Ramón, 179 km from Santa Cruz, where the road branches northwest to Trinidad and northeast for 43 km to San Javier. All of the road is paved, but some of it is bumpy, because of the number of timber trucks and – believe it or not – a bizarre taste for asphalt on the part of some lichen-like creatures that live on the roadside!

The road then heads east, for 63 km to Concepción and then on to San Ignacio de Velasco, 171 km and four hours from Concepción. Three km out of Concepción the pavement gives way to packed earth for the rest of the way. Two roads head south to San Rafael; one via San Miguel and the other via Santa Ana (these three mission settlements are best visited as day trips from San Ignacio; otherwise, if in private transport doing the circuit, the shortest route is from San Ignacio to San Miguel and San Rafael – a good, fast road – then up to Santa Ana and back down again). One road continues east from San Rafael to San Matías – a hellishly taxing trip of 323 km along barely passable roads — and the Brazilian border. A second road from San Ignacio heads south to San José de Chiquitos. From here you can complete the circuit by catching the Quijarro-Santa Cruz train back to Santa Cruz. If you're in private transport heading for Santa Cruz, this is one stretch where you'll be pleased you had a jeep – the road is mostly terrible and, on the last stretch leading up to Tres Cruces and from there to Pailon, simply appalling.

Alternatively, you could do the tour in reverse. Take the Santa Cruz-Quijarro train to San José (266 km, 12-16 hours) and from there travel north by road to visit the other mission towns. There is an airstrip at San Ignacio, and there are flights once a week with TAM (see page 338).

You should spend at least five days on the Jesuit missions route. The most interesting time to visit is Holy Week or at the end of July when many of the settlements celebrate their patron saint festivals. As rich as the region is in cultural heritage, it is still very much a frontier. This is one of the best regions outside of the Altiplano to sample true Bolivian culture before the inevitable onslaught of mass tourism operators take over (as is already happening further to the east in the Pantanal). Tours can also be organized from Santa Cruz (see page 310).

History

The Jesuits first arrived in Lima, Peru, in 1569 and were assigned to the religious instruction of the Aymaras on Lake Titicaca. They moved to Paraguay where they set up an autonomous religious state. It was from there that they expanded northwards to the vast unexplored region of the eastern lowlands of Bolivia, reaching Santa Cruz only in 1587.

The Jesuits then set about the seemingly impossible task of converting the various indigenous communities to Christianity and persuading them to first build and then live together in self-sufficient settlements. These settlements of 2,000-4,000 inhabitants, known as *reducciones*, were organised into productive units, headed by two or three Jesuit priests. Architects, sculptors and musicians were enlisted to help construct the churches and communities. They also formed military units which, for a time, were the strongest and best trained on the continent. These armies provided a defence against the slave-hunting Portuguese in Brazil and the more aggressive native tribes.

Politically, the settlements were ruled by the Audiencia de Charcas and ecclesiastically by the Bishop of Santa Cruz, but in reality, due to their isolation, they enjoyed a considerable degree of independence. The internal administration was the responsibility of a council of eight Indians, each of whom represented an ethnic group, and who met each day to receive the orders of the priests.

In 18th-century terms the *reducciones* were run on remarkably democratic principles. The land and the workshops were the property of the community and work was obligatory for all able-bodied members. Nevertheless, the Jesuits' prime concern was to save the Indians' souls, therefore the indigenous customs and beliefs were largely suppressed. So effectively were Christian values imposed on the people, that little is known about the indigenous cultures of this region except what symbolism the natives were sometimes able to express in their ingenious carvings, replicas of which still decorate the mission churches today.

In saying that, however, the establishment of the *reducciones* brought economic advantages to this previously barren corner of Bolivia. Such was the success of the Jesuits' commercial network with the Quechuas and Aymaras of the highlands that a surplus was sent in the form of money to Europe as well as being used to enhance the splendour of the churches. These massive temples were the biggest and most beautiful in the Americas, each one built by hand by the Indians under the supervision of the priests. Because of the distances between the mission settlements, each church is distinctive from the others.

The Jesuits also trained the Indians to become great craftsmen in wood and precious metals. They even taught them to make and play unfamiliar musical instruments such as the violin and the harp. Each settlement had its own orchestra, which performed concerts and even Italian baroque operas. The orchestral music fascinated the indigenous peoples and was a factor in persuading them to partake in the Jesuit experiment. More important than that, though, in ensuring their full co-operation was the fact that those who formed part of the *reducciones* remained free from the system of *encomiendas*, whereby groups of labourers were sent to the mines of Potosí.

The Expulsion of the Jesuits

Despite the economic and religious success of the Jesuit settlements and the fact that they played a large part in limiting the territorial ambitions of Portuguese Brazil, in 1767 the missions were dismantled by royal and papal decree and the Jesuits expelled from the continent.

There were various reasons given for the Jesuits' expulsion, some of them less than credible. Basically, the Spanish Crown became aware of their influence and success in this part of South America and believed they had usurped too much power from the state. Furthermore, this was the age of enlightenment and the militant Jesuits were seen as a major obstacle to the progress of reason. Finally, the success of the Jesuits caused considerable jealously amongst some of the older religious orders, many of whom wanted to establish inroads themselves in the new continent.

Whatever the real motivation, many of the settlements were abandoned and the inhabitants suffered the consequences. The priests who replaced the Jesuits treated the indigenous peoples badly, fomenting war and hatred among the disparate groups while prospering from the livestock that had been introduced to the region. Even after independence the exploitation of the local people continued during the years of the rubber boom. Scarcely fifty years after the expulsion of the Jesuits, the missions had become decrepit shantytowns.

Amazingly, the mission buildings survived this upheaval and the more than a century of isolation that followed. But their survival was precarious at best, and the tropical climate had deteriorated them badly. By the 1950s, all of them were well on the way to ruin, although each continued to function as a church. Their salvation came in the form of a Swiss architect, Hans Roth, who dedicated 27 years to the restoration of the churches built by his fellow countryman, Father Martin Schmidt, more than two centuries before. Sadly, he developed lung cancer and died in 1999 in Austria, aged 65, before he could see the end of the restoration of the last church to be restored, Santa Ana de Velasco. At the time, he was still looking for an expert to translate the missionaries' baroque music.

Fortunately, in the past few years, much has been done to carefully promote the heritage of these Jesuit mission churches and their towns. Musical and dramatic festivals are held every two years in each community, their astonishing sacred art is displayed in museums all over the world, and a Hans Roth Museum has recently opened in Concepción. Along with Noel Kempff Mercado and Amboró National Parks, one could argue that the Jesuit missions are the best-preserved and most 'authentic' patrimonies to be found in Bolivia.

San Javier → *Colour map 4, grid A2.*

The small town of San Javier was the first Jesuit mission in Chiquitos, founded in 1692 by the Spaniards Fray José de Arce and Fray Antonio Ribas. Its **church**, one of the most striking in the region, was designed and built by Father Schmidt between 1749 and 1752. The original wooden structure had survived more or less intact until restoration was undertaken between 1987 and 1993 by Hans Roth. Subtle designs and floral patterns cover the ceiling, walls and carved columns. One of the bas-relief paintings on the high altar depicts Martin Schmidt playing the piano for his Indian choir. If the main door is closed, enter through the cloister to the right. The modern town prospers from extensive cattle ranching.

There are many fine walks in the surrounding countryside, which is also good for mountain biking. A local *fiesta* is held on 3 December. Enquire at the town's **Casa de Cultura** ① *T03-963 5149*, in front of the plaza for what may be happening in and around town. With help from the Swiss government, San Javier has just inaugurated a number of local *rutas turísticas*, which the town hopes will draw visitors.

Concepción → *Colour map 4, grid A2. Altitude: 497 m.*

The hot, sleepy colonial town of Concepción, founded by the Jesuit priest Lucas Caballero in 1708, is one of the loveliest and friendliest of the mission settlements. It boasts one of the region's most beautiful plazas, surrounded by covered sidewalks and buildings with red-tiled roofs.

The buildings are ornately painted in the style of the beautiful **church** ① *0700-2000, free but donation invited, guided tours at 1000 and 1500*, which was completed by Martin Schmidt in 1756. It was totally restored between 1975 and 1982 by Hans Roth, whose team of European experts had to recreate the building from the crumbling original. The interior of this architectural gem is mightily impressive with an altar of laminated silver. In front of the church is a bell-cum-clock tower housing the original bells and behind it are well-restored cloisters. Hans Roth used to live here and work with local artisans in the restoration of local churches. In the workshops near the church you can see the remains of the original church (guided tours at 1030 and 1530). There is a tourist office to the right of the church.

> ☀ *At sunset there are beautiful skies over the church, which is suddenly floodlit at this time.*

On the plaza, **Museo Misional** ① *Mon-Sat 0830-1200, 1400-1730, Sun 1000-1200, US$0.50*, has photographs of the appalling condition into which the church fell. It also shows a photograph of a central tower, added in 1911 and taken down as part of the restoration, together with its actual clock, which was a gift from Spain. Restoration work is also carried out here and it is possible to talk with the craftsmen and admire their workmanship. Don't miss the new **Hans Roth Museum**, which has tools, blueprints and dioramas used for the rebuilding of the churches and models of their framework.

Concepción

Mission Church ①

31 del Este & La Veloz del Norte micros to Santa Cruz

Almacén Moñita

Plaza

Museo Misional

N

0 metres 50
0 yards 50

Sleeping ⊙
Apart Hotel Los Misiones 1
Colonial 2

Ganadero 3
Gran Hotel Concepción 4
Residencial Westfalia 5

Eating ⊙
Club Social Ñuflo de Chávez 1
El Buen Gusto 2
Heladería Alpina 3

Eastern Lowlands The Jesuit Missions

There is a **lake** nearby where you can swim and fish. Ask at the **Gran Hotel Concepción** for horse riding to one of the local *estancias*.

San Ignacio de Velasco → *Colour map 4, grid B3.*

San Ignacio is a hot and dusty commercial centre lying on the main transport route going east to Brazil. A series of wide streets made of red earth run from the busy market area down to a large plaza fronted by the church, which is now nearly completely restored.

It was, in fact, a lack of funds for restoration which led to the demolition of San Ignacio's **Jesuit church** in 1948, exactly two hundred years after it was built. Hans Roth's replacement is again painted beautifully on the outside with a simple design and is an exact replica of the original, apart from the incongruous concrete bell-tower. Inside, the pillars are carved but not painted, there is an elaborate high altar and pulpit, paintings and statues of saints. If it is closed at lunch you may be able to get in through the iron gate to the right, the last door on the left. A **museum** in the Casa de la Cultura on the plaza houses a few musical instruments from the old church.

On the outskirts of town, down the road behind the church, is the artificial **Laguna Guapomó**, the source of the town's potable water. It is good for swimming, boating and fishing. The town hosts a *fiesta* on 31 July in the Casa de la Cultura, held on the plaza.

San Ignacio is the main starting off point for an overland visit to the **Noel Kempff Mercado National Park**. The park office is on the plaza. For a full description of the park and how to get there, see page 341. A paved road is still in the offing, and at the present there is only a very rough road running the 200 km north to **La Florida**, which is 25 km west of the park's only vehicular entrance at Los Fierros.

San Ignacio de Velasco

Santa Ana → *Colour map 4, grid B3.*

The tiny, timeless and peaceful village of Santa Ana has its unique original **church** on one side of a huge plaza where cattle and donkeys graze. Some of the houses still have palm thatch roofs. The church was built in 1755 and is the only one in the region which has not been fully restored. Nevertheless, this lovely wooden building is in good condition and it is fascinating to see the restoration work in progress. The walls are also interesting for they are covered in *mica*, a natural translucent silver-like substance. To see the restoration work and interior ask for Sr Luis Rocha who will also explain its history. Ask for his house at the shop on the plaza where the bus stops.

Sleeping 🛏
Alojamiento
  31 de Julio **1**
Apart Hotel
  San Ignacio **2**
Casa Suiza **7**
Guapamó **3**
La Misión **4**

Palace **5**
Plaza **6**

Eating 🍴
Barquito **1**
Pizzería Pauline **2**
Riabé **3**
Snack Marcelito **4**

0 metres 50
0 yards 50

Eastern Lowlands The Jesuit Missions

⦙ Mission impossible

The majority of the Jesuits naturally came from Spain, but one of the factors in the efficiency of their methods was that many of the priests also came from the countries of northern and central Europe. One of these was Father Martin Schmidt, a Swiss musician and architect, born in 1694.

Father Schmidt began his education with the Jesuits in Lucerne and in 1728 travelled from Cádiz to Buenos Aires. Later he travelled through Bolivia before settling in Santa Cruz. Despite having no formal training in making musical instruments, he made all kinds of instruments for the communities and even built organs for the churches. He also taught the Indians to play them and wrote music, some of which is still played today on traditional instruments.

As if that wasn't enough, Father Schmidt also built the churches of San Rafael, San Javier and Concepción and the altars of some of the others. He even published a Spanish-Idioma Chiquitano dictionary based on his knowledge of all the dialects of the region. By the time of the expulsion of the Jesuits in 1767 he was 73 years old. He died in Lucerne in 1772.

San Rafael → *Colour map 4, grid B3.*

San Rafael was founded in 1696 (also by Fr. Arce, the founder of San Javier) and its **church** was completed by Padre Schmidt between 1740 and 1748. It is beautifully restored with frescoes in beige paint over the exterior. To enter, walk up the right of the church and pull and twist the large wooden knob on the door into the sacristy at the end. Inside, look and listen for the bats nesting in the bamboo-lined roof.

San Miguel → *Colour map 4, grid B3.*

Founded in 1721 by Fr. Felipe Suárez, San Miguel is 40 minutes from San Rafael. Its **church** ① *0800-1800, free entry, donations welcome*, has been completely restored and, though it is similar in style to the other churches, its carved and gilded altar is rare. It is generally considered to be one of the most beautiful of the mission churches. The frescoes on the façade of the church, built in 1754, depict St Peter and St Paul and designs in brown and yellow cover all the interior and the exterior side walls. The pitched, red-tiled roof blends in with the village architecture. To see it, pass through the gate in the bell-tower and ring the bell of the **Oficina Parroquial**. The mission runs three schools and a workshop. The sisters are very welcoming and will gladly show tourists around. About 4 km away is the Santuario de Cotoca, beside a lake where you can swim. Ask at **La Pascana** for transport.

San José de Chiquitos → *Colour map 4, grid B3. Population: 12,000.*

San José de Chiquitos, capital of Chiquitos province, lies roughly halfway between Santa Cruz to the west and Puerto Suárez to the east. As the chief settlement between the two, the town is the area's transportation hub, cattle-raising centre and oil exploration headquarters, as well as a convenient jumping-off point for tours of the Jesuit Missions circuit.

The town is in many ways reminiscent of Santa Cruz 50 or so years ago. Although it is served by both train and bus, with a partially paved highway that connects it to the region's major towns, San José itself retains the feel of a dusty, frontier town, with its few unpaved streets and even fewer cars.

As with most South American towns, San José is centred around a main square – **Plaza 26 de Febrero** – with its statue of Ñuflo de Chávez, the founder of Santa Cruz. Scattered throughout the town are a number of concrete sculptures (some of which have to be seen to be believed), all of which appear to have been done by the same 'artist'. Clustered around the *toboroche* tree-lined plaza are the town's main enterprises and lodgings on one side and the Jesuit mission complex on the other. The other centres of activity are the town's railway depot, on the road to Santa Cruz, and the local market, a few metres up from the plaza on Avenida Monseñor Carlos Gericke. On Monday, members of the local Mennonite colony bring their produce to sell at the market and to buy provisions. The colonies are 50 km west and the Mennonites, who speak German, Plattdeutsch and Spanish, are happy to talk about their way of life.

While hardly comfortable, the climate is at least bearable, and vastly preferable to the humid lowlands to the east. The influence of nearby Brazil is obvious, in everything from the bilingual signs in shops and restaurants to the items of food found inside, the vast majority of which arrive by train from Brazil.

Sights

The town centre is dominated by the architecturally unique **mission church and compound** ⓘ *daily 0600-1200, 1430-2100, free*, which occupies the whole of one side of the plaza. Founded by the Spanish Jesuits Felipe Suárez and Dionisio de Avila on 19 May 1697, San José was the third of the seven main Jesuit missions to be established. The original church, erected in 1696, was replaced by the current one in 1748. This massive neo-baroque structure, although still incomplete at the time of the Jesuits' expulsion, was built entirely by hand by Chiquitano Indians with mostly wood and plaster. The mission compound, also built in neo-baroque style, boasts many amazing carvings. It was declared a Patrimony of Humanity by the United Nations in 1992.

San José de Chiquitos

Sleeping
Raquelita 1
San Silvestre 2

Eating
Casa é Paila 1
Enca 2

Sombrero é Sao 3

The stone buildings are connected by a wall and have a uniform façade, giving the compound an almost military appearance. The buildings consist of the restored chapel (1750), the church, with its triangular façade, the four-storey bell-tower (1748), and the mortuary (*la bóveda*), which dates from 1754, with one central window but no entrance in its severe frontage. Weather and age have taken their toll and, as a result, restoration is an ongoing concern. At any given time portions of the compound may be closed to visitors. Those wishing to find out what's open and what isn't should call the rectory, T03-972 2156, otherwise just walk in and take a look. The church office on site should also explain how to climb on to the roof of the *bóveda* which affords a good view of the surrounding hills. They will even let you up the bell-tower.

Excursions

A worthwhile trip from San José is to the **Parque Nacional Histórico Santa Cruz la Vieja** ① *daily, US$2*, 4 km south of town on the old Santa Cruz highway. The park's heavily forested hills contain much animal and bird life and interesting vegetation, including the aromatic guayacan and palo santo trees, as well as the ruins of the original site of Santa Cruz, dating from about 1540. It also contains several billion insects, so you are strongly urged to carry repellent. There's a *mirador* giving views over the jungle and, 5 km into the park, a sanctuary. Guides are available from the small village in the park to show you around the various trails.

Some 2 km further down the old Santa Cruz highway, past the park entrance (so continue straight ahead when the road bears right), at the foot of high hills, is a mountain stream – reputedly the source of much of the town's drinking water – that feeds a **municipal swimming pool** ① *US$0.75, the park and pool are best visited by car or taxi because it is a very hot, dusty walk there.*

Another excursion is to **Cerro Turubo**, a forested peak east of town (the highest in the province) that affords excellent views of San José and the surrounding area, with distant views all the way to the mysterious Kaa-Iya National Park, the hemisphere's largest. Access is along the road to Puerto Suárez, although a guide is recommended as the trail is unmarked in several sections.

Perhaps San José's best-kept secret is the **Cascadas del Suruquizo**, an easy 4 km south of Santa Cruz la Vieja National Park. Locals attribute invigorating and healing powers to these three waterfalls and their nearby springs.

Reserva de Vida Silvestre Ríos Blanco y Negro

Reserva de Vida Silvestre Ríos Blanco y Negro, in Santa Cruz Department, is located in the uppermost northwest quadrant of the province, between the Ríos San Pablo and San Martín. (Ríos Blanco and Negro are within the park, and do not form its borders.) Created in 1990 through the efforts of FAN, at 1,400,000 ha, it is Bolivia's fourth-largest protected area. It has since been privatized and no longer has protected status and FAN are no longer in charge.

‡ *In many respects, the park rivals Amboró and Noel Kempff Mercado for sheer abundance of species, and for plant life surpasses them*

● Sleeping

San Javier *p331*

AL Santa Rosa de la Mina Country Club, 8 km north on road to Concepción, T03-333 5352 or enquire at Santa Cruz travel agencies for details. Brand new astounding development on 1,300 ha of rolling fields and virgin forest, with 2 lakes, bicycle trails, horse trails, swimming pools, 18-hole golf course, football fields, 6 luxury-class cabins (Cabañas Colina Dorado), and even a 500-m landing strip for light planes. 5-star eco-resort hotel with all mod cons attached.

C Cabañas Totaitú, 3 km down the first road to the left as you enter town, T03-337 0880, totaitu@em.daitec-bo.com. Upmarket, with pool, tennis court, horse riding, restaurant (no kitchens in the cabañas) and, 8 km away, hot springs, includes breakfast. Also camping (US$10 per person) which includes breakfast and use of pool.

C Gran Hotel El Reposo del Guerrero, 1½ blocks from the plaza, heading from the opposite side to the church, T03-963 5022 (or T03-332 7830 in Santa Cruz). Includes breakfast; comfortable, restaurant.

C-E Cabañas Momoqui, on right of main street before plaza, T03-963 5095. Includes buffet breakfast, a/c, fridge, large pool (can be used by non-residents for US$3), parking, (E without bath). Will arrange tours with a guide to the church, along with trips to their dairy to milk a cow (try the local alcoholic milk drink *ambrosía*) then go horse riding!

E-F Alojamiento Ame Tauna, on the plaza, T03-6935 018, less character but smart and clean, no double beds, (F without bathroom where the pet parrot is noisy at dawn), parking.

E-F Alojamiento San Javier, on right of main street before plaza, T03-693 5038. Shared bathrooms, no double beds, nice sitting area where you can put on music or watch TV, hot water, garden. Recommended.

F Cabañas La Tuja, a 10-min walk down the first road to the left as you enter town. Large, have thatched roofs but are otherwise basic; US$1.50 cheaper without private bathroom.

F Posada El Tiluchi, on the plaza, T03-693 5149, rooms are rustic and some a bit musty but imaginatively painted by the owner, also hammocks and patio.

F Posada Pinto, 1 block from plaza (stand outside the church and turn right to face the right direction), T03-693 5042. Shared bathrooms, pleasant and friendly.

G Alojamiento Hermanos Añez, 1 block away from Posada Pinto (take the road on the other side away from the church). Shared bathrooms, cold showers, basic but clean.

Concepción *p331, map p331*

A Gran Hotel Concepción, on the plaza, T03-964 3031, granhotelconcepcion@ hotmail.com. US$25/night. Very comfortable, beautiful courtyard garden, excellent service, includes buffet breakfast, pool, bar. Highly recommended. Owner Sra. Martha Saucedo speaks some English and German.

C Apart Hotel Los Misiones, T03-964 3021. Very beautiful, small pool, also lovely US$15 apartment, TV, excellent value.

D Hotel Chiquitos, T03-964 3153 with excellent restaurant.

D Hotel Escondido, T03-964 3110. Reported as safe and clean.

F Hotel Colonial, ½ a block from the plaza, T03-964 3050. Large, clean rooms, hammocks and garden, good value. Buffet breakfast US$0.75.

F Ganadero, T03-964 3055. US$3 cheaper without bathroom, 1 block from the plaza. Basic, clean, pleasant patio, shared bathrooms.

F Residencial Westfalia, 2 blocks from the plaza on the same street as the Centro Médico, T03-964 3040. With private bathroom, US$1.50 cheaper without, German-owned and it shows, excellent rooms for the price, nice patio.

San Ignacio de Velasco *p332, map p332*

AL La Misión, on the plaza, T03-962 2333, F962 2460, hotel-amision@unete.com. Luxurious, colonial style with a/c, cable TV and pool, rooms of various standards and prices, includes buffet breakfast, can pay by Visa or Mastercard without commission.

B Apart Hotel San Ignacio, on 24 de Septiembre y Cochabamba, T03-962 2157 (or Santa Cruz T03-342 8613). Beautiful and stylish with pool and great garden. Rooms have fan (a/c US$10 extra), includes breakfast.

D-F Guapamó, on Sucre, 2 blocks from the market and bus offices. A/c and breakfast, (E with fan, F without bathroom), lovely garden with hammock.

E Casa Suiza, at the end of C Sucre, 5 blocks west of the plaza (taxi US$0.60). This small guesthouse run by Horst and Cristina Schultz is a real home from home, price includes breakfast, very comfortable, 12 beds, German and French spoken, for US$10 per person includes all meals (excellent food), they can arrange fishing trips, the hire of horses (US$3 per hr) and provide a packed lunch, Cristina is a former nurse and can help with medical problems. Highly recommended.

E Plaza, on the plaza. Includes breakfast, fan, comfortable, clean, good value, US$3 cheaper without bathroom.

F Palace, on the plaza. Includes breakfast, fan, no single rooms.

G Alojamiento 31 de Julio, on the plaza next to Hotel Palace. Basic, clean. There are several other cheap *alojamientos*.

Santa Ana *p332*

There are 2 *alojamientos* in town: one of them is an orange building, off the left of the plaza as you stand with your back to the church. **G Alojamiento Santa Ana**, is 1 block off the far right-hand corner. The best of the two options.

San Rafael *p333*

F Hotel Paradita, on the plaza (**G** without bathroom).

San Miguel *p333*

G Alojamiento y Restaurant La Pascana, on the plaza, which is basic with shared bathrooms and serves cheap meals.
Just up the hill, a few doors from the plaza, is **Alojamiento Pardo**. Opposite is another *alojamiento*, and a few doors up from there is the *Entel* office.

San José de Chiquitos *p333, map p334*

There is no electricity from 0400-0630 so don't be surprised if you wake up sweating with no fan or a/c.
E Denise, Monseñor C. Géricke, fan, small restaurant, clean.
E-F Raquelita, on the plaza, T03-972 2037. The best of the lot, comfortable beds, a/c, good value, **F** with fan, US$1.50 cheaper still with shared bathroom; laundry service, snack bar serves breakfast; owners know all latest bus and train times.
E-F San Silvestre, opposite the train station, (**F** with shared bathroom). Grubby and overpriced but alright for 1 night, serves good food.

🍴 Eating

San Javier *p331*

$$ Ganadero, in *Asociación de Ganaderos* on the plaza. Best restaurant in San Javier. Good steaks (the *lomo* is better value than the *medallones*).
There are others on the plaza and **El Tiluchi** has ice creams.

Concepción *p331, map p331*

$$** Guampomó (*churrasquería*) and **$$ Rincón Beniano (regional dishes from Beni Province), each a few blocks south and north of the plaza, respectively, also offer decent meals.

$ Alojamiento Tarija, 1 block from the plaza, T03-964 3020. Good *almuerzo*, popular, as well as rooms for US$2.25 per person (all shared bathrooms).
$ Club Social Ñuflo de Chávez on the plaza. Excellent huge *almuerzos* for US$3.00, and dinner, seating in a pleasant patio with views from the window seats of the church opposite, best value in the region.
$ El Buen Gusto, on the plaza. Opens early, serves delicious *empanadas*, snacks and meals.

Cafés

Heladería Alpina, on the plaza, ice-cream parlour and café.

San Ignacio de Velasco *p332, map p332*

There are several places to eat on the plaza.
$ Barquito, on 24 de Septiembre opposite *correos*, has a US$1.50 per kilo lunchtime buffet.
$ Pizzería Pauline, on the plaza. Reasonable and cheap, remarkable for the appearance of its waiting staff.
$ Renacer Princezinha. Brazilian-influenced, for drinks, chicken and chips.
$ Riabé, on Sucre, is cheap and good.
$ Snack Marcelito, on the plaza. Serving good *salteñas*.
There are plenty of cheap places to eat in the market (US$1) but think of your poor stomach. Note that none of the aforementioned restaurants are open on Sun until after siesta.

Santa Ana *p332*

$ Pension El Tacú on the corner next to the church, 0800-2200 daily.

San Rafael *p333*

There are 2 restaurants on the plaza and a public phone.

San José de Chiquitos *p333, map p334*

Restaurants around the plaza offer little but fried chicken, a shame considering the close proximity to Brazil and the cattle ranching of the region. There are several food stalls around the bus and rail terminals and a handful of dubious chicken-only spots near the plaza.
$ Casa é Paila, on Pasaje Linares, serves reasonable food.
$ Enca, along the road to San Ignacio near the bus station, is also good.
$ Sombrero é Sao, half a block off the plaza. Recommended.

🎭 Entertainment

San Ignacio de Velasco *p332, map p332*
Entertainment seems to consist of karaoke night at **Club Privado**.

🛍 Shopping

Concepción *p331, map p331*
Almacén Moñita sells print film. There is a good *artesanía* shop at the museum and several more around the plaza.

🚏 Transport

San Javier *p331*
Micro firm **31 del Este** has an office opposite **Alojamiento San Javier** with buses to **Santa Cruz** at 0800, 1100, 1400 and 1730, 4-4 ½ hrs, US$3.75 and to **Concepción** and beyond at 1100-1200, 1800-1900 and 2100-2200, 1 ½-2 hrs, US$1.50.
Expresso Jenecheru and **31 del Este** also run to/from **Santa Cruz** and other mission towns. Best to enquire in Santa Cruz first, as the mission towns are generally quick stops for these carriers and buses leave as soon as they are full.

Concepción *p331, map p331*
Many buses (including carriers **Jenechurú** and **Linea 102**) between Santa Cruz and San Ignacio pass through the town at around 2400-0100. They drop you at the main road, several blocks from the plaza. Ask around at one of the restaurants here for transport to the centre; the locals are friendly and helpful so it shouldn't be a problem.
Consequently, to leave here for **San Ignacio de Velasco** you have to wait for the passing buses at the petrol station from 2400 and buy your ticket as you board. To **San Javier** (1 ½-2 hrs, US$1.50) and **Santa Cruz** (6 hrs, US$4.50) at 0730, 1400 and 1700, go to 31 del Este which has an office opposite **Alojamiento Tarija**. In the wet season buses pass through after 0130, when there's no electricity in town; so bring a torch/flashlight, or you'll be staggering down the street in total darkness.

San Ignacio de Velasco *p332, map p332*
Air
Flights via **Aerosur** are available from here to **San Matías** on the Brazilian border; there are rare flights to **Santa Cruz**, but no schedule exists.

Buses
From Santa Cruz (US$6.70, 10 hrs): **Flota Chiquitana** leaves from the new terminal at 1900 daily; **Expreso Misiones del Oriente** (T03-337 8782), daily at 1930.
Several other companies leave from Santa Cruz for San Ignacio en route to **San Matías** for Brazil. These include **Trans Bolivia** at 2000; and **Flota Veloz del Este** at 1800.
To **Santa Cruz** (12 hrs) and all villages en route: **Flota Chiquitana** (US$4.50) and **Trans Velasco**, both are daily at 1900 and both are from near the market; **Trans Joa** at 2030 (office at *Hotel Palace* on plaza); **Expresso Jenechero** at 1930 (*cama*, US$6); **Trans Bolivia** at 1900 (US$4.50); **Trans Carreton** (T03-962 2441, see map), daily at 1800 (US$5.20); **Expreso Misiones del Oriente** (see map), Mon-Thu at 2000, Fri-Sun at 1930 (US$6).
To **San Matías** for Brazil there are buses to San Matías (10 hrs, US$7.50) and on to **Cáceres**: **Trans Joa** leaves Tue, Thu and Sat at 0830; **Trans Carreton** daily at 0800; **Trans Bolivia** daily at 0730 (the final 92 km of road from Las Petas is very poor).
To **San José de Chiquitos** via San Miguel and San Rafael (8 hrs, US$4.50): **Trans Carreton** on Tue, Thu, Sun at 0800. To **San Rafael** (1 ½ hrs, US$1.50) via Santa Ana (40 mins, US$1.05) with **Trans Bolivia** daily at 1600, return 0630.
There are *micros* to **Santa Ana** (1 hr, US$1.35) and **San Rafael** (1 ½ hrs, US$1.95) which leave from around the market area (see map) at 1430 and 1600, returning from San Rafael around 1300-1400. *Micros* to **San Miguel**, from the same place at 0930, 1500 and 1830 (1 hr, US$1), returning at 1230-1300; also **Trans Bolivia** daily at 0730 (30 mins, US$0.75), returns 1730. There are no tickets on sale for micros to San Miguel and San Rafael. Just turn up about 30 mins before departure and hope to get a seat. A day trip by taxi from San Ignacio to San Miguel, Santa Ana and San Rafael costs US$35-40, but bargain hard.

Santa Ana *p332*
Micros leave daily from outside **Alojamiento Santa Ana** for **San Ignacio** at 0700-0730 and San José at 1630-1700.

San Rafael *p333*
Buses from outside *Bar 7 Copas* to **San Ignacio** reportedly on Mon, Wed, Fri and Sat at 1000; to San José check with locals. For other times to the village, see under San José de Chiquitos and San Ignacio de Velasco.

San Miguel *p333*
For buses to San Miguel see San Ignacio de Velasco and San José de Chiquitos; buses leave for these towns at 1730 and 0900 respectively from outside **Pascana** on the plaza.

San José de Chiquitos *p333, map p334*
Buses To **San Ignacio**, Flota Universal, Mon, Wed, Fri and Sat at 0700, leaving from close to the railway track, a few yards west of the station building, next to **Pollos Curichi**. They also leave from their office opposite the petrol station where you can reserve a seat (best to take a taxi there). **Trans Carreton** leaves Tue, Thu and Sun at 1300 from their office at 24 de Septiembre, southeast of the plaza. Both go via San Rafael and San Miguel; 4 hrs.

Trains To **Santa Cruz** daily except Sun at 0200; Pullman US$7.20, 1st class US$3.15, 2nd class US$2.70. The luxurious **Ferrobus** goes Tue, Thu & Sat at 0200; *cama* US$27.80, *semi-cama* US$23.75. To **Quijarro** daily except Sun at 2130; Pullman US$13.15, 1st class US$4.20, 2nd class US$3.30. **Ferrobus** Sun, Tue, Thu at 2340; *cama* US$21.35, *semi-cama* US$18.20. It is possible to reserve seats on either service at the train station up to a week in advance. T03-972 2005 for information.

Concepción *p331, map p331*
Medical The private *Centro Médico* is 1 block away. **Telephone** On the corner of the plaza is the *Entel* office. As mentioned above, there is also a petrol station in town.

San Ignacio de Velasco *p332, map p332*
Banks There is a *casa de cambio* for changing US dollars and Brazilian reais on the north side of the plaza. **Telephone** Entel is 2 blocks from the plaza. **Post office** The post office is on 24 de Septiembre, close to Sucre, Mon-Fri 0800-1200, 1400-1800, Sat mornings only.

San José de Chiquitos *p333, map p334*
Banks The only bank in town is **Banco de Union**, on the plaza, Mon-Fri only, 0800-1200, 1430-1800. It changes US dollars cash only. Occasionally, stores or restaurants will change small amounts (US$30 or less), but it's best not to count on this. Dollars are accepted everywhere, but Brazilian *reais* less so, and other foreign currencies not at all. Do not attempt to change money with anyone at either the bus or rail station, unless you really want to end up with less than you started out with. **Internet** Aló-Aló, on the plaza, US$1.00 per hr. **Medical services** The municipal hospital **Bernardino Gil Julio** is best if you're sick, 4 blocks from the plaza, on Virrey Mendoza; **Hospital Ferrocaja** is across from the rail station, T03-972 2091. There is a **pharmacy** on Jesus Chávez, T03-972 2046. **Post office** There is no post office in town. **Telephone** National and international phone and fax at the local **Entel** office on Virrey Mendoza, located 2 blocks east of the plaza, T03-9722000.

Eastern Lowlands The Jesuit Missions Listings

● *Price codes for Sleeping and Eating are given inside the front cover. Further information on hotel and restaurant grading can be found in Essentials, pages 43-44.*

South and east of Santa Cruz

Towards Brazil and Paraguay are some of Bolivia's biggest, grandest landscapes. With the road stopping 150 km before the park, the Parque Nacional Kaa-Iya del Gran Chaco is an isolated behemoth of a park. The Diverse Parque Nacional Noel Kempff Mercado is also huge – big enough to make Conan Doyles' Lost World seem still plausible – and covers a striking range of ecosystems, from plateaus to wetlands, forest to mountains. San Matías is another monster park, but little visited. To the south is Che Guevara country – and a part of the Che Guevara trail – and everywhere there are great possibilities for seeing wildlife. » *For Sleeping, Eating and other listings, see pages 349-352.*

Parque Nacional Kaa-Iya del Gran Chaco

❧ *The park is larger than Belgium and not much smaller than Switzerland.*

The enormous Parque Nacional Kaa-Iya del Gran Chaco, in southeastern Santa Cruz Department, is, at 3,445,857 ha, the largest in the country, continent, and the entire hemisphere. This is the ultimate destination for the adventurer or ecotourist, and amongst the most difficult to access.

Ins and outs

Adding to the surreal quality of Kaa-Iya is the fact that its only feasible access route is by train or road track to San José de Chiquitos, still a good 150 km north of the park! From there, it's on foot across the Serranía San José range (or by 4WD in good weather) until the Bañados come into view. A compass is essential. Those wishing to make the journey should check with **Servico Nacional de Areas Protegidas** (SERNAP) before undertaking the trek. Plans are afoot for a road from El Tinto, just west of San José de Chiquitos, but at present nothing exists.

The park

Founded in 1996 by a consortium of local indigenous peoples in conjunction with several environmental non-profit organizations, this is about as far off the beaten track as one can get. It is also the only national park in the world whose administration is entrusted to the indigenous peoples who live within its borders. Although it is well-funded (US$4 million has been earmarked for the park annually for the last three years) and there is government support for infrastructure programmes, there still are no facilities of any kind, so carefully planning your trip is absolutely essential here. Solo travellers to Kaa-Iya too often have a nasty habit of not making it back, as it is very sparsely populated. So remote is Kaa-Iya that anthropologists speculate that areas within it have never seen even native tribes, let alone latter-day explorers. The majority of the park is uncharted and unknown except by local peoples, although amazingly parts of it were a battleground during the Chaco War between Bolivia and Paraguay! Today, there exists growing tension between its inhabitants and the cash-strapped government, who eyes Kaa-Iya for its oil potential. So far, the natives hold the upper hand, but without continual international recognition of this unique indigenous region all that can change. However, if you're well-supplied and have swotted up on the Gran Chaco, you'll find it one of the most rewarding experiences of your life.

The mysterious **Bañados del Izozog** wetlands are within the park, and it plays host to well over 1,500 species of birds and animals, including jaguar, panther, and a large number of rare desert-habitat creatures. It also contains a unique desert forest eco-system that has drawn considerable scientific interest.

Parque Nacional Noel Kempff Mercado

→ *Colour map 4, inset.*

In the remote northeast corner of Santa Cruz Department is **Parque Nacional Noel Kempff Mercado**, one of the world's most stunningly diverse natural habitats, with a range of animal and plant species unmatched almost anywhere else in the world. The park is astonishing in every way, especially for its Amazonian forests, spectacular waterfalls (the **Catarata el Encanto**, **Arco Irís**, and **Federico Ahlfeld** especially), and eerie-looking mountain ranges (*serranías*). If this isn't enough, recent studies show there may be even more diversity of wildlife here than in Amboró, along with some rare aquatic species found nowhere else. There are seven distinct ecosystems within the park, the highest number in any single protected area anywhere on earth.

Second only to Amboró in terms of popularity, Noel Kempff Mercado is Bolivia's third-largest protected area, at 1,583,809 ha (an area the size of Massachusetts in the USA). It was established in 1979 as **Parque Nacional de Huanchaca**. In 1988, its name was changed to honour Noel Kempff Mercado, a pioneer of Bolivia's conservation movement who was murdered there two years earlier.

Ins and outs

Getting there Access to Noel Kempff Mercado, given its size, remains limited. Its remoteness has not only helped to preserve this great bio-diversity, but has also placed the park out of the reach of most travellers. Services are marginal, except at Los Fierros and Flor de Oro, which is along the western reaches of the river. Several tour operators also offer three- to seven-day guided tours of the park (see page 350). With a required $15 per day fee per person per guide, this is Bolivia's most expensive park, but worth every penny.

Air The best known of the various routes into the park is by air, through **Flor de Oro**, a small border town along the Río Guapore that boasts a landing strip and has a provisions store and tourist lodge run by **Fundacion Amigos de la Naturaleza** (FAN). It can be reached by a five-hour plane ride from Santa Cruz. Alternatively, you can fly directly from Santa Cruz to **Los Fierros** (two hours). You can also fly from Santa Cruz to **Huanchaca** (about 2 ½ hours), which started life as a drug smuggler's laboratory but is well within the park's borders and sits at the base of the Serranía Negra. This is probably the most convenient alternative – although at more than US$1,000, it is certainly not the cheapest – for those wishing to get on the ground in a hurry. There are occasional flights to nearby Las Gamas as well. Note that all of the above flights are sporadic, and all are arranged by **FAN**. You should contact their Santa Cruz office to enquire further, www.fan-bo.org.

There are also an increasing number of air taxi services to the area, most of which land along the banks of the Río Guaporé, which forms the park's (and Bolivia's) eastern border with Brazil.

Road A paved road runs due north from San Ignacio de Velasco to La Florida and a bus runs this route. Otherwise it is an arduous 200-km journey in private transport on an appalling 'road'. At La Florida, 25 km west of the park's sole vehicular entrance, a dirt road veers right and enters the park at a guard station, Los Fierros, which also serves as the park's official headquarters. To get there using public transport it will be a tough and expensive business until the new road is finished. From San Ignacio de Velasco, **Trans Carreton** leaves Thursday at 1600 (US$9, 24 hours), **Trans Bolivia** leaves Friday 0800-1000, both to Piso Firme from where you have to charter a boat to Flor de Oro (see below).

You can drive – in the dry season – from Santa Cruz to Concepción (300 km) and from there north to Piso Firme (another 367 km), where you can stay overnight at any one of several *alojamientos*. The second half of this trip is along unmarked roads with no service stations, so bring extra petrol.

Alternatively, drive from Santa Cruz to Los Fierros (by 4WD only). This approach lets you enter the park by crossing its southwestern border along the Río Paraguá. Los Fierros, apart from serving as the park's 'official' headquarters, has a campground, barrack-style housing, and cabañas, and has some of the park's best birdwatching. If making the journey by jeep, the road taken is Santa Cruz to Santa Rosa de la Roca to La Florida to Los Fierros, and will take a minimum of 18 hours. The distance from La Florida to Los Fierros – the first settlement in the park's interior – is 40 km, and now can be made by local taxi.

River From Piso Firme you can travel by launch along the Río Guapore to Flor de Oro; US$250, five to nine hours, depending upon the season and the speed of the river's current. There is a second river option to the park, through Paucerna (formerly known as Puesto Boca Iténez). Fly first to Flor de Oro and from there go by launch in a westerly direction, reaching Paucerna, which also boats a few places to sleep (five to nine hours).

Information
The best information on the park is found on the **Proyecto de Acción Climática's** website (in English or Spanish) ① *www.noelkempff.com*. The **Bolivian government's** website ① *www.mcei.gov.bo/web_mcei/turismo/destinos/ noelkemp.htm*, also provides useful information. Another excellent source is **Richard Vaca at FAN**, the organization that is charged with managing the park (see page 315). You can also enquire at the **Museo de Historia Natural Noel Kempff Mercado** ① *Av Irala 565, between Velasco y Independencia in Santa Cruz, T03-337 1216, F336 6574, www.museo.sczbo.org*. Or, finally, for further information, you can also contact Ing. Gonzalo Peña Bello, **Fundación Amigos de la Naturaleza - Noel Kempff** ① *Km. 7 1/2, Carretera Antigua a Cochabamba, Santa Cruz; T03-354 7383; F03-355 6800; gpena@fan_bo.org*.

Around the park
Rising over 500 m above the surrounding plain is the 3,000 sq km **Huanchaca Plateau**, which is drained by numerous rivers and streams which merge to form the headwaters of the Verde and Paucerna rivers. Steep cliffs of 200-500 m bound the plateau, creating spectacular waterfalls. Arco Iris and the Federico Ahlfeld Falls on the Río Paucerna are two of the most impressive in the entire continent. An even more stunning waterfall is the 150-m high **Catarata el Encanto**, about 20 km in from Los Fierros.

The park fee also gives the visitor access to Bolivia's newest reserve, the breathtakingly beautiful **Reserva Biológica Laguna Bahía**, a small area of enormous biological interest and fecundity located within the park's southwest quadrant. The hiking in the park is considered Bolivia's best, and recently park rangers set up a trail that crosses the high plateau. The entire trek takes a week at least, but the scenery along the way is positively breathtaking.

Wildlife
The wildlife count in the park is staggering – so far over 620 bird species have been identified, which is approximately one-quarter of all the birds in the neotropics. These

❧ Pink river dolphins can be seen in the rivers as well as the black and spectacled caiman.

include blue and yellow, scarlet, golden-collared, and chestnut-fronted macaws; over 20 species of parrots; crimson-bellied parakeets; red-necked aracari; the Amazonian umbrella bird; the pompadour cotinga; helmeted manakin; curl-crested jays; hoatzin and harpy eagles, to name just some of the species found within the park's boundaries. Among the many large mammals frequently sighted are the tapir, grey and red brocket deer, silvery marmoset, and spider and black howler monkeys. Giant otter and capybara are relatively common along the Iténez and Paucerna rivers, as are jabiru and the maguari stork. Giant anteaters, marsh deer and the rare maned wolf inhabit the western grasslands and the endangered

⁑ Discovering the Lost World

The first to discover the Huanchaca Plateau was the legendary British explorer Colonel Percy Fawcett. He discovered the plateau in 1910 while exploring the Río Verde and demarcating the national boundaries for the Bolivian government.

Colonel Fawcett was the archetypal early 20th century explorer. Disappearing into the heart of the Amazon on his last expedition in 1925, never to be seen again, he became almost as much of a legend as the lost city for which he tirelessly searched. His life of jungle exploration was an inspiration to many. It is claimed that Arthur Conan Doyle, who was a friend of the colonel's, wrote The Lost World as a result of a conversation about the flat-topped Huanchaca when he was shown photographs of the apparently unscaleable cliffs and imagined an isolated plateau inhabited by dinosaurs. From the descriptions given in *The Lost World*, this link appears to be real, as the detail matches almost precisely the landscape of the park. Despite various other theories, Fawcett's claim is now generally accepted as the truth by most Doyle scholars. For a detailed account of Colonel Fawcett's adventures see *Exploration Fawcett* (Century, 1988).

pampas deer roam the dry twisted forest of the Huanchaca Plateau. There's also a chance of seeing jaguars where the narrow Río Paucerna winds its way through dense towering rainforest on its way to join the Río Iténez.

Otuquis National Park and Integrated Use Nature Area

Carved out of the southern Pantanal in 1979, this large (10,059 sq km) park is, along with nearby Kaa-Iya, and Manuripi at the country's other geographical extreme, Bolivia's most remote habitat. Like Kaa-Iya, Otuquis has no guides, no tours, and no infrastructure. It is virgin wilderness at every turn except for a small enclave near Puerto Suárez (the Zona Río Pimiento, which is easily reached from the city).

⁑ *Paucerna is rapidly becoming a favourite staging ground, as it is located just north of the park's two best-known waterfalls.*

However, all this is set to change in the near future. Both Bolivia and Brazil are intent on developing Otuquis as a gateway to the Pantanal, and, more insidiously, a big game hunter's paradise. Travellers who want to see the as-yet-untouched Pantanal's ecosystem, flora, and fauna are advised to visit soon. By 2006 much of Otuquis will be well on the way to resembling Amboró and Rurrenabaque. In the Arroyo Concepción region (between Puerto Suárez and Quijarro) there is already one five-star hotel, and others are opening soon. The road connecting Puerto Suárez to Puerto Busch via Mutún will soon be completed, opening Otuquis to vehicular traffic, which will have a deleterious affect on the pristine conditions that it currently enjoys.

Otuquis offers everything a trip to the Brazilian Pantanal does, only without any of its better-known counterpart's amenities. For the independent or seasoned wilderness traveller it is a true paradise, however. Wildlife abounds, especially aquatic mammals and reptiles, and the species count is said to rival that of Amboró in some areas. Caimans, tigers, jaguars, otters, egrets, even rare river dolphins have been spotted, along with some of the world's largest flocks of toucans and parrots. Perhaps less attractive but every bit as prevalent are the schools of piraña: bathers be warned!

Eastern Lowlands South & east of Santa Cruz

Access to Otuquis is via the rail terminus at Puerto Suárez, then by road to Mutún. You usually can hitch a ride to the park by truck, as several make runs between Mutún and Puerto Busch. Although the latter lies wholly within Otuquis' boundaries, it is accessible only by river (Río Paraguay) unless you can flag a truck in Puerto Suárez or Mutún. Be sure to carry gear with you: there are no amenities within the park itself and even Puerto Busch has little in the way of supplies.

For further information, contact **SERNAP**'s Otuquis representative, **Luis Marcus** ⓘ *in Santa Cruz, T03-355 1971; F355 5053, tucumarcus@hotmail.com.*

San Matías Integrated Use Nature Area

At a staggering 2,918,500 ha, San Matías is Bolivia's second-largest park, yet one of its least known, owing to its relative remoteness and infrequent visitors. Although an older park (by Bolivian standards: it was founded in 1973), San Matías is only just beginning to see a trickle of visitors lured to the northern reaches of the Pantanal region and its world-renown wildlife.

The flora and fauna of San Matías largely resemble that of Otuquis, as well as that of Noel Kempff Mercado to the north. Visitors will find the climate slightly drier than that of the southern Pantanal, but the primary attractions are definitely aquatic fowl and sub-Amazonian animals, including the increasingly rare jaguar. San Matías's three big lakes – Mandiore, Gaiba, and Liberaba – and its Río Curíche Grande are favourites for fishermen.

Ins and outs

Access to the park is problematic at best: there are no roads, and only one dirt airstrip at Santo Corazón. Tours may be arranged from Puerto Suárez (see page 345), and a few visitors have made the trip in a 4WD vehicle from Santiago de Chiquitos during the dry season, but the main attraction of visiting is to see it in the wet season when everything springs to life. An alternate route is a trackless path that heads due south from the border town of San Matías (which has regular air service from Santa Cruz) for approximately 120 km. You'll know you're in the park only if you stop to ask: there are no signs or official entrance posts. For further information, contact the park's overseer (resident in Santa Cruz), **Ing. Jorge Landivar** ⓘ *Barrio Fleig, C Los Limos Nº 300 esq. Majo; T03-355 1971, F355 5053, sanmatias@latinmail.com.*

Towards Brazil

There are three possible routes to Brazil: one is by air to Puerto Suárez, near Quijarro; the second is by rail to Quijarro from Santa Cruz; and a third by road from Santa Cruz via San Matías (see below), with road links to Cáceres, Cuiabá and the northern Pantanal in Brazil.

Getting there

The simplest way to Brazil is to **fly** to Puerto Suárez then share a taxi to the border (US$7.50 per car). See Puerto Suárez below.

The **rail** route from Santa Cruz ends at Quijarro, part of the populated area by the Brazilian border, made up of Puerto Suárez, Quijarro and Arroyo Concepción, which are gradually merging into one another. Trade here grew because of increasing prices in Brazil during 1995-1996 and a *Zona Franca* (customs-free zone) has been established in the area to encourage development. On the Brazilian side of the border from Puerto Suárez/Quijarro is Corumbá and the southern Pantanal.

66 99 Caimans, tigers, jaguars, otters, egrets, even rare river dolphins have been spotted, along with some of the world's largest flocks of toucans and parrots... every bit as prevalent are the schools of piraña: bathers be warned!

The **road** route from Santa Cruz is via San Ignacio de Velasco to San Matías, and then to Cáceres and Cuiabá. See under San Ignacio (page 338) for bus information. San Matías is a busy town with hotels, restaurants and a bank. **Aerosur** flies to/from Santa Cruz and San Ignacio once a week. Also, **Servicio Aéreo Pantanal** ① *El Trompillo airport, in the southern part of Santa Cruz, T03-353 1066*, flies daily from Santa Cruz.

Puerto Suárez → *Colour map 4, grid C6. Population: 15,000.*

Puerto Suárez on the shore of Laguna Cáceres, a large backwater of the Río Paraguay, was an important commercial port at the beginning of the 20th century, until a dam built by Brazil upriver reduced the water level of the lake and put an end to shipping and the town's prosperity. Today, it's a friendly, quiet, little town, with a shady main plaza. There is a nice view of the lake from the park at the north end of Avenida Bolívar. The area around the train station is known as Paradero.

> ❗ *Don't drink the water as it is straight from the river.*

Fishing and photo tours to the Pantanal can be arranged more cheaply than on the Brazilian side, though tourism in general is still poorly organized here. Recommended by the excellent tour agents of **La Víspera** in Samaipata (see page 327) is the **Centro Ecológico 'El Tumbador'** ① *T03-762 8699, www.hombreynaturaleza. com*, a non-profit-making organization working for sustainable development in the Bolivian Lowlands through research, education and ecotourism. It runs half-day to four-day river, trekking and four-wheel tours from its research station and lodge alongside Caceres Lake. Between October and March on the Río Paraguay, they can almost guarantee sightings of giant otters. Year-round you will see caimans, capybaras, iguanas, herons, kingfishers and storks. For four people, spending two all-inclusive nights at the lodge with tours (English spoken) and transfers expect to pay US$82 per person, for four nights the bill will be US$148.

Stewart and Sandra Williams of **Tours Aguas Tranquilas** (enquire at **Hotel Frontera Verde**) offer air-boat trips along small tributaries of the Río Paraguay, which are not accessible with other types of water craft. You'll see lots of wildlife and there's good fishing. Expect to pay US$10 per person per hour (minimum US$40) and US$150 to hire a boat for four hours (US$250 for seven hours). This includes lunch and fishing gear. There's a maximum capacity of nine, and English is spoken.

You can also contact **Sr Roberto J Rodríguez**, president of the **Fishermen's Association of Puerto Suárez** ① *Av América esq Addis Ababá, T03-976 2778*. He has his own boats and offers fishing and wildlife watching tours at reasonable prices.

Quijarro → *Colour map 4, grid C6. Population: 15,000.*

The eastern terminus of the Bolivian railway is at Quijarro. To coincide with efforts to develop tourism in the Bolivian Pantanal, the town is trying improve its infrastructure and image. There have been reports of drug trafficking and related problems in this border area, caution is recommended.

Bolivian immigration Get your exit stamp at Bolivian immigration, at the border at Arroyo Concepción. It's a blue building on the right just before the bridge. It opens at 0700. There's also an immigration office at Puerto Suárez airport. Formalities are straightforward and no money has to be paid to anyone at the border. Passports can also be stamped at Santa Cruz station if you're leaving by train, which may help avoid any 'unofficial' exit charges at Quijarro. You can leave Bolivia at Quijarro when the border post is closed, but you have to return from Brazil for a Bolivian exit stamp.

> ‡ *Entering Brazil: You don't need to have your passport stamped if you visit Corumbá for the day.*

Coming into Bolivia There are moves to open an **immigration office** at the border but until that happens you will have to obtain an exit stamp from the main office in the centre of Corumbá, in Praça da República, next door to the Nossa Senhora da Candelária church, open 0800-1130, 1400-1730, T03-5848.

It's open 0800-1130 then 1400-1730 (knock after hours). There is also an immigration office at the bus station which is usually closed. Your Bolivian entry stamp will be given at the border post, which sometimes closes for lunch. The Brazilian consulates are in Santa Cruz (see page 313) and Puerto Suárez (see page 345). Note that a Yellow Fever vaccination is compulsory to enter Brazil; have your certificate at hand when you go for your entry stamp, otherwise you will be sent to get re-vaccinated.

Corumbá → *Phone code: 00-55-231 (from Bolivia). Population: 220,000.*

The Brazilian town Corumbá stands on the south bank of Río Paraguay, 15 minutes from the border. It's hot and humid, but a pleasant place nonetheless, with beautiful views of the river, especially at sunset. The hottest months are September to January, the coolest June and July. There is a spacious shady town square, **Praça da Independência**, and the port area is worth a visit. **Avenida General Rondon** between Frei Mariano and 7 de Setembro has a pleasant palm-lined promenade that comes to life in the evenings. The **Forte Junqueira**, the city's most historic building, which may be visited, was built in 1772.

Corumbá had thrived on tourism and trade until 1994, but high prices have limited both and much business is moving to the *Zona Franca* in Quijarro across the border. The combination of economic hard times and drug-running make the city unsafe at night.

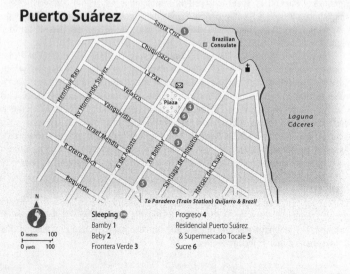

Puerto Suárez

Sleeping	
Bamby 1	Progreso 4
Beby 2	Residencial Puerto Suárez
Frontera Verde 3	& Supermercado Tocale 5
	Sucre 6

To Paradero (Train Station) Quijarro & Brazil

Laguna Cáceres

0 metres 100
0 yards 100

There is a wide range of hotels and restaurants. All services are available, including money exchange, post and telecommunications, and there are frequent air and bus links with the rest of Brazil. There is a tourist office, **Emcotur** ① *R América 969, T00-55-231 6996*, and **Bolivian consulate** ① *R Antônio Maria Coelho 852, Mon-Fri, 0700-1100, 1500-1730.*

Corumbá is the best starting point for visiting the southern part of the Brazilian Pantanal, with boat and jeep trips and access to the major hotels/farms. Many travel agencies offer tours, but visitors are advised to shop around and ask others who have been on· tours for recommendations. Footprint's *South American Handbook* and *Brazil Handbook* give full details on trips to the Pantanal.

South from Santa Cruz

A road south from Santa Cruz passes through to Abapó, Camiri and Boyuibe. From Boyuibe another road runs east to Paraguay (see below) and another heads south to Villamontes and on to Yacuiba on the border with Argentina (see page 257).

Camiri → *Colour map 4, grid A1. Population: 40,000. Altitude: 827 m.*

Camiri is a small oil town some 250 km to the south of the city of Santa Cruz and halfway to the border with Argentina. There is a paved road for part of the way but thereafter you are on a dirt track to Camiri. Camiri is the jumping-off point for the southern part of the **Che Guevara Trail** (see page 318 for the northern part). Camiri is where Che's companion, the French journalist Regis Debray, was imprisoned and tried and the Bolivian army's operational centre in hunting down Che's group. Also try to see a display of the **Chaquerera**, possibly the most energetic dance of Bolivia. Camiri is the only place in the area where there are hotels.

Che Guevara Trail → *For details of the northern part of the trail, around La Higuera, see page 318.*

One and a half hours to the north west of Camiri is the village of Lagunillas, near to which Che had his base camp and from which provisions were bought. Those visitors who have some Spanish may like to seek out Doña Hilda Blanco, the oldest inhabitant, for her story of how she met "El Che". It's worth climbing the nearby Reducto for a panoramic view of the village and surrounding countryside. More interesting is a visit to Ñancahuasu where Che's group carried out their first and most successful ambush of the Bolivian Army. After about one hour's walk from the end of the road, you reach the river canyon where the attack was carried out, a beautiful but sad place if you remember the people who died there. Señor Lucidio Aldunati, the owner of most of the land thereabouts, has a stock of documents about El Che, and is also able to rent out horses and a guide for those who want to venture deeper into Che Guevara country. An independent and very knowledgeable guide with a fund of Che stories is Edgar Panoso, who may be contacted through Lagunillas town hall.

See also box on page 320.

Visitors wishing to follow the southern part of the Che Guevara Trail are advised that there is little tourist infrastructure there other than in Camiri. Much of the area where Che Guevara was active has no roads and travel is by horse or mule. It is, however, possible to bike between the southern and northern parts of the Trail, camping on the way. Allow several days for the trip and do not expect conveniences such as tap water or electric light. The local people are predominantly of the Guaraní ethnic group and their diet is predominantly based on maize. You should try the regional dish, a substantial chicken soup called *locro*. A UK government-funded project has recently started in the area to stimulate the tourist trade to benefit the impoverished Guaraní communities.

Crossing into Paraguay

It is possible to drive from Camiri into Paraguay in a truck or 4WD high-clearance vehicle. Make sure you are carrying insect repellent and enough food and water for a week. No help can be relied on in case of a breakdown. A winch is also advisable. There are some rivers to ford and although they are dry in the dry season they can be impassable if there is rain in the area.

A much easier way to get to Paraguay is to take a bus. **Empresa Yacyretá** ① *C Cordillera 485, Santa Cruz, T03-334 9315*, run twice weekly from Santa Cruz to Asunción (Tuesday and Friday at 1300). Tickets can also be booked through the **Bracha** travel agency. It is a long, bumpy ride to Asunción and much of the scenery is missed because buses travel at night. It costs US$55 one-way and takes around two days.

Boyuibe → *Colour map 3, grid B5.*

Boyuibe is the last town of any size in Bolivia before heading east to Paraguay (Km 519). It is on the regular Tarija-Entre Ríos-Villamontes-Santa Cruz bus route. Fuel and water are available here. It is also on the Yacuiba railway (see page 257).

Border with Paraguay

It is about 115 km from Boyuibe to the Bolivian border post at **Hito Villazón** (manned by a Bolivian army unit). The road is very bad; it takes three hours by bus. You can camp at Hito Villazón, but no food is available, nor is there much water. Passports are stamped at the military checkpoint here. If travelling by bus, passports are collected by the driver and returned on arrival at Mariscal Estigarribia, Paraguay, with a Bolivian exit stamp and Paraguayan entry stamp.

About a kilometre after the military checkpoint turn left past a large water tower. From then on just follow the most used road. Accurate directions can be obtained from the army before leaving Boyuibe. If hitching, be at the customs post before 0600.

The border is 12 km east of Hito Villazón at Guaraní and the Paraguayan post is 10 km further east at Fortín General Eugenio A Garay. Camping is possible here and for a small contribution the troops may give you the use of showers and a kitchen. There is a military post at Fortín Mister Long, about 15 km further on, where water is available. Here, there are long stretches where the road disappears beneath ridges of soft dust. One traveller writes: "be prepared to spend many hours digging/pushing/pulling your vehicle out of the countless dust pits in 40° heat".

Beyond Fortín Mister Long the road improves through Estancia La Patria, although even small amounts of rain can turn the highway to mud and cause long delays. Motorists should carry plenty of food and water. The airbase at Nueva Asunción, 95 km before Estancia La Patria, may give water, but your papers may be inspected. At Estancia La Patria, in Centro Urbano Rural, is a motel (**F**), supermarket and petrol station. Buses run to Filadelfia, which is the major town in the Paraguayan Chaco, via Mariscal Estigarribia, which has a large military base and where Paraguayan entry stamps are given. If you arrive after Friday 1700, you must wait until you get to Asunción, the capital, and report to immigration there. There is accommodation in Mariscal Estigarribia, but there is more in the way of services in Filadelfia, the largest of three important Mennonite colonies, 472 km from Asunción, and 304 km from the border with Bolivia.

Parque Nacional Noel Kempff Mercado *p341*

Because of its enormous environmental importance, accommodation within Noel Kempff Mercado is deliberately kept to a minimum, and should be arranged in advance through **FAN** (see page 315).

There is a lodging in the park, at **Los Fierros Camp**, where cabins cost US$20 and up per person and include 3 meals for another US$20, and a campsite, US$10 per person plus US$5 to cook.

There are also **campsites** at Ahlfeld and Flor de Oro, which also boasts an ecolodge. There are also a few (as yet unadvertised) rooms to let in the small border towns on the other side of the Río Paraguá, at La Florida, Porvenir, and Piso Firme. These run from US$4-12, but must be negotiated and located ahead of time. Note that it is no longer permitted to camp along the lower reaches of the Río Paraguá, because of ecological considerations.

Towards Brazil *p344*
Puerto Suárez

C Bamby, Santa Cruz 31 y 6 de Agosto, T03-976 2015. A/c, cheaper with with fan and shared bathroom, comfortable.

C Sucre, Bolívar 63 on the main plaza, T03-976206. Recently renovated, private bathroom, nice rooms with a/c, colour TV, includes breakfast, good restaurant.

C-D Frontera Verde, Vanguardia 24 y Simón Bolívar, T03-976 2468, F9766 2470. Best in town, a/c, (**D** with fan) breakfast included, parking, helpful, English spoken.

D-E Beby, Av Bolívar 111, T03-976 2290. A/c, less with shared bathroom and fan.

D-E Ejecutivo, at the south end of Bolívar, T03-976 2270. A/c, parking, cheaper with fan, comfortable.

D-E Roboré, 6 de Agosto 78, T03-976 2190. Fan, with shared bathroom, basic, restaurant next door.

F Progreso, Bolívar 21. Shared bathroom, basic.

F Residencial Puerto Suárez, on Bolívar, next door to **Supermercado Tocale**. Shared bathroom, fans, showers, basic.

Quijarro

The water supply in many hotels is frequently unreliable, so try the tap before checking in. Most people prefer to go on to Corumbá where hotels are better.

AL Hotel El Pantanal, Arroyo Concepción, T03-978 2020.

C Oasis, Av Argentina 4, T03-978 2159. A/c, fridge, cheaper with shared bathroom and fan, recently renovated. Business centre.

C-D Santa Cruz, Av Brasil 2 blocks east of the station, T03-978 2113, F978 2044. A/c, cheaper with fan and shared bathroom, good rooms, nice courtyard, good restaurant, parking. Highly recommended.

D La Frontera, Rómulo Gómez, 5 blocks from the station on the south side of the tracks, T03-978 2010. Fan, parking.

D-E Gran Hotel Colonial, Av Brasil y Panamá, T/F03-82037. A/c, cheaper with fan and shared bathroom, good restaurant.

D-E Yoni, Av Brasil opposite the station, T03-978 2109. A/c, fridge, cheaper with shared bathroom and fan, comfortable, mosquito netting on windows.

F-G Residencial Ariane, on Av Brasil across from the station, T03-978 2122. With bathroom and a/c, rooms with shared bathrooms cheaper and more basic.

G Alojamiento Urkupiña, on Av Brasil across from the station. Shared bathroom, basic, unfriendly.

G Residencial Paratí, Guatemala sin número. Shared bathroom, fan, laundry facilities.

Border with Brazil

L El Pantanal Hotel Resort & Casino, T03-978 2089, F978 2020. The fanciest hotel on either side of the border, in Bolivia, 1½ km from the border. A 5-star luxury resort, a/c, buffet breakfast and airport transport included, restaurants, disco, pool, modern buildings on nice grounds, horseback riding, tours to the Pantanal and to the nearby caves.

Eastern Lowlands South & east of Santa Cruz Listings

🫛 *Price codes for Sleeping and Eating are given inside the front cover. Further information on*
⚫ *hotel and restaurant grading can be found in Essentials, pages 43-44.*

Camiri

C-E **Hotel JR**, US$21 for a double room, US$14 for a single, all a/c with private bath.

D-G **Residencial Premier**, Av Busch 60 (½ block from main plaza), T03-952 2204. A/c and private bathroom, E for a room with a fan. Spacious, clean, comfortable rooms, very welcoming owners and a hammock to while away the time, internet promised. The best hotel in Camiri.

E-F **Hotel Ramirez**, with private bathroom and fan.

F **Residencial Chaqueña**, C Comercio, clean, good. They run a bus service (see next page).

G per person **Gran Hotel Londres**, Av Busch 36. With private bathroom and fan, no double rooms available, motorcycle parking. In no way does this live up to its name, dirty and best avoided.

The town has restaurants and bars, which are generally rather expensive, and a post office.

Crossing into Paraguay *p348*

Boyuibe

G **Alojamiento Boyuibe**, on the main road next to the petrol station, has hot showers, restaurant (0700-2300), parking and telephone. Also, in the village, are

G **Chaqueño**, which has one good double bed, the rest are ropey and there's a dodgy electric shower but the owners are friendly and they have parking.

G **Res El Rosedal**, basic.

🍴 Eating

Towards Brazil *p344*

Puerto Suárez

$$ **Parillada Jenecherú**, on Bolívar, near the plaza. For grilled meats.

$ **Al Paso**, Bolívar 43. Very good value set meals and à la carte, popular.

$ **Bolivia**, at Balneario Los Delfines, friendly, good regional food, also swimming pool.

$ **El Mirador**, overlooks Laguna Cáceres. It serves regional dishes including *piraña* soup and fried *jacaré*, fresh fish, very friendly owner.

$ **El Taxista**, Bolívar 100 block, with several other small inexpensive restaurants nearby.

Quijarro

The best restaurant in the area is in Arroyo Concepción. The food stalls by the station and market are best avoided unless you have a cast-iron stomach.

Border with Brazil

$$ **Pescadería Ceará**, 250 m from the border, serving excellent fish.

🛍 Shopping

Towards Brazil *p344*

Puerto Suárez

Supermercado Tocale, Bolívar next door to **Residencial Puerto Suárez**, has a wide selection of Brazilian, Bolivian and imported goods.

There are several fishing and hunting supply shops.

Quijarro

There's a duty-free zone at Puerto Aguirre, 700 m north of Quijarro. It's mostly electrical and luxury goods for Brazilian shoppers.

⛰ Activities and tours

Parque Nacional Noel Kempff Mercado *p341*

For details on organized trips into the park see Activities and tours in Santa Cruz (page 310), or contact **International Expeditions Incorporated**, One Environs Park, Helena, AL 35080, USA, F205-428 1714, intlexp@aol.com.

Amboró Tours runs trips for US$500 for 6 days all-inclusive travelling by jeep and staying in tents.

It is also possible to do 3 months' volunteer work in the park. Go to Av Irala 565, between Av Velarde and Av Ejército in Santa Cruz (or T03-336 6574) and ask for Dorys Méndez. You can also hire a guide in Flor de Oro.

It is possible to hire a jeep with **Marcello**, the husband of Suzy who runs the park office on San Ignacio de Velasco Pl. It costs US$250 for Marcello (who acts as a guide) and his jeep for 5 days. Everything else – accommodation and food – is extra; the jeep has no roof and, for one group, broke down twice. Ask at **Casa Suiza** in San Ignacio for the latest information (see page 336). When the new road is complete to Florida expect there to be a proliferation of tour agencies in San Ignacio de Velasco.

Towards Brazil *p344*
Puerto Suárez
R B Travel, Bolívar 65 by the plaza, T03-976 2014. They sell airline tickets and are helpful.

Quijarro
Santa Cruz, in the hotel of the same name. They sell *Bracha* and airline tickets, and organise tours to Pantanal.

⊖ Transport

Towards Brazil *p344*
Puerto Suárez
Air The airport is 6 km north of town, T03-976 2347. Airport tax is US$2. There are daily flights to **Santa Cruz** with Aerosur and LAB. TAM flies to Santa Cruz, and continues to **Trinidad** and **La Paz**. Do not buy tickets for flights originating in Puerto Suárez in Corumbá, as you will have to pay more. There is an airport immigration office where they will issue Bolivian exit/entry stamps.

　　Airline offices LAB, La Paz 33, T03-976 2241; AeroSur, Bolívar 69 near the Plaza, T/F03-976 2581; TAM, C del Chaco sin número, T03-976 2205.

　　Taxis From the town centre: to **Paradero** US$1.65; to the **airport** US$2; to **Quijarro** or the border, US$5 (US$6 at night), or US$0.80 per person in a *colectivo*.
Trains The station for Puerto Suárez is about 3 km from town. It is the first station west of Quijarro. For tickets contact the Bracha agent, at Bolívar 86, T/F03-976 2577.

Quijarro
Trains Trains to Quijarro leave from the station in Santa Cruz. For details of times and fares, see page 311. All trains go via San José de Chiquitos. The Quijarro ticket office sells tickets only on the day of departure. It opens 0700-1600, but queuing starts much earlier. It gets crowded, there's much pushing and shoving, and touts resell tickets at hugely inflated prices. It is well worth buying your ticket for a couple of dollars more from one of the agencies near the Bolivian side of the border post – try Luiz at Bolivia Travel Tours, Av Bolívar 483, T03-925 0870. They have an

'arrangement' with their friends at the ticket office and save you all that queuing.

　　To buy your ticket you must take your passport with you stamped with Brazilian exit and Bolivian entry stamps; it's a long wasted wait otherwise. Bracha have an office in Quijarro (T03-976 2325). Note that the times of departure from Quijarro are approximate as they depend on when trains arrive.

Border with Brazil
Taxis At Quijarro take a *colectivo* or a taxi to the border post, at Arroyo Concepción. *Colectivos* cost US$1 per person (beware of overcharging); a taxi costs US$5 (US$6 at night). From there, take a bus to Corumbá (US$0.80). For information on taxis and *colectivos* to the border from Puerto Suárez see the relevant transport section above.

South from Santa Cruz *p347*
Camiri
Bus Transportes Chaqueña to **Yacuiba** on Wed and Sat 1030, US$6; to **Sucre** Tue and Sat, US$12; to **Santa Cruz** daily, US$6 (*bus cama*), US$4.50 (normal bus). **Emperador** and **Andesbus** run from **Sucre** via **Monteagudo** daily in each direction, at least 20 hrs, US$20. Several minibuses run daily from **Santa Cruz**, 7-8 hrs, US$10-12.

Crossing into Paraguay *p348*
Boyuibe
Bus From Santa Cruz to Boyuibe costs: *Ferrobus* US$13 and US$10; *Rápido* US$5.50 and US$4.

⊕ Directory

Towards Brazil *p344*
Puerto Suárez
Banks Supermercado Tocale changes bolivianos, reais and US dollars, cash only. Banco de la Unión in Paradero is reported to change TCs. **Embassies and consulates** Brazilian Consulate, Santa Cruz entre Bolívar y 6 de Agosto. **Post Office** on La Paz opposite the main plaza. **Telephone** Entel on La Paz, 3 blocks from the plaza and in Paradero.

Quijarro
Banks Bolivianos, reais and dollars cash are traded along Av Brasil opposite the

station and close to the border crossing by changers with large purses sitting in lawn chairs. Rates are good, but beware of tricks.

Post Office in Puerto Suárez.

Telephone Entel at the south end of Av Naval, for national and international calls, Mon-Sat 0700-2300, Sun 0700-2000. There's also a small office at Guatemala y Brasil near the station.

Towards Brazil *p344*

Border with Brazil

Banks Money can be exchanged at the Quijarro border. You will probably only be able to sell bolivianos in Bolivia.

⦂ Footprint features

Introduction

The Bolivian Amazon accounts for over two-thirds of the country. This vast region, covered by steamy jungles and flat savannah lands, is bursting with all manner of wildlife. Beni Department alone has over half the country's birds and mammals. This natural paradise is also a prime target for corrupt and ruthless logging companies. But though destruction of forest and habitat is proceeding at an alarming rate, parts of the region are opening up to ecotourism and wildlife expeditions are becoming increasingly popular, most notably around **Rurrenabaque**, which can be reached from La Paz by road or air.

Two of Bolivia's newest, and most authentic, ecotourism ventures are **Mapajo**, in the Reserva Biosferica Pilon Lajas, and **Chalalán Eco-lodge**, in the neighbouring Parque Nacional Madidi. Both are owned and run by the indigenous population. Madidi, Bolivia's newest preservation area, boasts the greatest biodiversity of any protected area on earth and a visit to Chalalán is now one of the country's top attractions. There are plans to extend the protection of Bolivia's precious tropical lowlands in the next decade and it is hoped that the influx of tourists will speed up the process.

★ Don't miss...

❶ Rurrenabaque Chill by the riverside and watch the world flow by in one of Rurrenabaque's great bars and restaurants, or in its spa, page 357.

❷ Eco-tourism opportunities Go on a nocturnal search for jaguars at Chalalán or Mapajo eco-lodges, Latin America's 'greenest' tourist facilities, pages 362 and 366.

❸ Madidi National Park Experience the glossy pages of *National Geographic* first hand in the most bio-diverse region on earth, page 363.

❹ Taking a dip in the tropical rivers Swim with the dolphins and fishes near Trinidad – but check first that they're not piranhas, page 371.

❺ The best of Bolivian bus travel Push yourself to the limits by taking a bus to Riberalta, a journey that would turn most SAS recruits into gibbering wrecks, page 377.

❻ Cobija Go nuts in a town so remote it makes the back of beyond seem accessible, page 378.

The Amazon

Map

BRAZIL

PERU

LA PAZ

PANDO

BENI

Cobija

Rurrenabaque

Trinidad

Riberalta

N

0 km 50
0 miles 50

Rurrenabaque and around

→ *Phone code: 03. Colour map 2, grid A2. Population: 10,000.*

Rurrenabaque, or 'Rurre' as the locals call it, is the jumping-off point for the many Amazon jungle and pampas tours now available in this once-remote area of northwest Bolivia, approximately 200 km northeast of La Paz. Situated on the banks of the Río Beni, with San Buenaventura on the opposite bank, Rurrenabaque is an important trading centre and transportation link for Beni Department. A rapidly growing town, its status as a gateway to the Amazon has brought it some degree of prosperity, and many of its citizens are now involved in one way or another with the burgeoning ecotourist trade.>> *For Sleeping, eating and other listings, see pages 367-371.*

Ins and outs

Getting there There are flights to and from La Paz. Check flight times in advance as they change frequently, and expect delays and cancellations in the dry season and severe delays in the rainy season. On average, 8 % of flights in and out of Rurre's airport are cancelled. Buses from La Paz leave from Villa Fátima, on Calle Santa Cruz.
>> *For further information see Transport, page 370.*

Getting around Unlike most Bolivian towns, the businesses, restaurants and offices in Rurre are not centred around the plaza (2 de Febrero), but instead are clustered together a few blocks north along Calle Vaca Diez and Santa Cruz. Just north of Calle Santa Cruz a small branch of the river effectively divides the town in half. The vast majority of businesses, including the many tour operators, are south of the estuary. Both of the town's markets are above it: the main market, on Calle Avaroa, between Anecito Arce and the old tributary; and the farmer's market, two blocks north and three blocks east.

Health and safety The area has little or no malaria, with fewer the 10 cases a year – only when you get deeper into the jungle does it become a bigger problem. However, it may still be worth being prepared for the worst by taking malaria tablets before you arrive. And in any case strong insect repellent and a good mosquito net are essential. The town is generally very safe, but take care at night, especially to the north of the stream.

Caranavi to Rurrenabaque

There are two main land routes into the Beni: one is from La Paz to Rurrenabaque via the Yungas and the other is from Santa Cruz to Trinidad. From **Caranavi** in the Yungas a road runs north to **Sapecho**, where there is an interesting cocoa co-operative and a bridge over the Río Beni. Accommodation is available at F **Alojamiento Rodríguez**, which is very friendly and pleasant. Beyond Sapecho, the road passes through Palos Blancos, 7 km from the bridge, with a Saturday market day and several cheap lodgings. A good all-weather gravel road continues to Yucumo, three hours from the Sapecho tránsito. In Yucumo there are *hospedajes* (G) and restaurants. Some 550,000 ha of jungle are under cultivation in this area, with rice, sugar, corn and fruit being planted, and the local Chimane people are trying to survive the influx of settlers from the Altiplano. At Yucumo the road heads northwest to Rurrenabaque, fording rivers many times on its way. Another road heads east to San Borja, continuing to San Ignacio de Moxos and Trinidad (see page 371).

Information Rurrenabaque's **tourist information office** ① *Av Santa Cruz, between Bolivar and Avaroa, T03-03-71289664, 0800-2000, and often later,* is probably the most helpful in the whole of Bolivia. The ranking system they run for tour companies in town has been a resounding success, meticulously quantifying customers' thoughts on nearly every aspects of tours and charting the results with glee in massive displays on the wall.

Rurrenabaque

Rurre is an astonishingly beautiful place whatever your interests. Whether it is the lush Amazon jungle, the savannah-like pampas, the sub-tropical lowlands, or the wonderful eco-lodges upriver in the national parks, this is the logical starting point. In spite of the usually humid climate, the town has a charming quality, and even if your itinerary doesn't include one of the many tours around the area, just walking about

Rurrenabaque

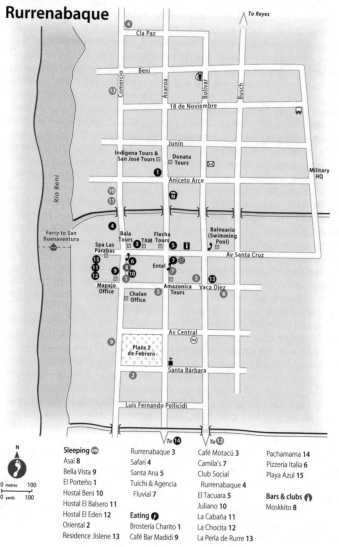

Sleeping
Asaí **8**
Bella Vista **9**
El Porteño **1**
Hostal Beni **10**
Hostal El Balsero **11**
Hostal El Eden **12**
Oriental **2**
Residence Jislene **13**
Rurrenabaque **3**
Safari **4**
Santa Ana **5**
Tuichi & Agencia Fluvial **7**

Eating
Brostería Charito **1**
Café Bar Madidi **9**
Café Motacú **3**
Camila's **7**
Club Social Rurrenabaque **4**
El Tacuara **5**
Juliano **10**
La Cabaña **11**
La Chocita **12**
La Perla de Rurre **13**
Pachamama **14**
Pizzeria Italia **6**
Playa Azul **15**

Bars & clubs
Moskkito **8**

the town itself is an unusual experience. It is with good reason that the settlement is considered the most picturesque in the Beni. The hotels almost all have hammocks, there are plenty of good bars and restaurants, an interesting **market** (see page 369), and even a **spa**, complete with sauna (see page 369). The local **swimming pool** (see page 369) is excellent and, although most come and go on tours fairly rapidly, it's also very easy to spend a few days here doing very little. The only real drawback is the occasional flooding of the Río Beni. It rarely overflows its banks, but when it does the place becomes a real mess.

Across the other side of the river is **San Buenaventura**. A passenger boat makes the short trip across throughout the day. A cultural centre here opened recently but then closed again shortly after – its future is unclear.

Tours from Rurrenabaque

Many tour agencies (see page 370) have set up recently to take advantage of Rurrenabaque's growing popularity. Anyone wanting to join a tour should investigate carefully what the various companies are offering. The state of Bolivian ecotourism has improved dramatically over the past few years, but advance preparation is still necessary. The tourist information centre is a great place to start and, if you can, speak to people returning from tours. Tour prices have been set by the government. **Jungle tours** cost US$25 per person per day, **pampas tours** US$30. Acute competition means that some companies cut their prices to be even lower than this, but quality is also often lowered. The usual minimum group size is three (four in the low season).

Pampas tours are usually four days, three nights and involve a bumpy, dusty, four-hour jeep ride at either end. They also involve boat travel in long canoes, though this is a lot smoother and more enjoyable. The pampas is wetland savannah to the northeast of Rurre and there's often little or no dry land at all – accommodation usually consists of wooden huts on stilts and most moving around is done in boats. It is an eerily beautiful and peaceful place, with watery wildlife sounds all around, fireflies at night. You can expect to see caiman, lots of monkeys, all sorts of birds and probably pink river dolphins. Anaconda are harder to see, and though you may be promised piranha-fishing, this will probably be a stop-off at a pond on the way home. Generally wildlife is easier to see in the Pampas than in the denser vegetation of the jungle. However, there are also more mosquitoes and sandflies.

Jungle trips offer the advantage of being able to leave Rurrenabaque in a boat and travel up the beautiful river Beni. Accommodation is either in special purpose-built, and relatively luxurious camps (see the wonderful Mapajo, page 362, San Miguel del Bala, page 365, or Chalalán, page 366) or tents.

Note also that not all trips offer English-speaking guides and that accommodation is usually spartan (bring insect repellent, mosquito netting, toilet paper and a torch). Always set the price in advance and make sure it includes all expenses. Most groups are of between five and ten people – either find a group before choosing a tour agency or turn up and put yourself on the list. If you arrive early in the morning you probably won't have too much problem getting on a tour straight away, if you so wish.

Two major parks are within a day's journey: **Parque Nacional Madidi** (see page 363) across the Río Beni and the **Pilón Lajas Biosphere Reserve** (see page 361), less than 100 km east on the road to San Borja. **Pilon Lajas** also offers opportunities to see wildlife in its native habitat and guides are usually available for hire in San Borja. Another day's trip south along the Beni river will bring you to the isolated **Isiboro-Securé National Park** (see Villa Tunari, page 292). This would be an ideal spot for wildlife-watching were it not for the fact that it lies in the middle of an extremely dangerous battleground between anti-narcotics squads and drug-traffickers.

Next door to the Tourist Information the **TES** office (Turismo Ecologico Social) ① *T03-03-71289664, turismoecologicosocial@hotmail.com, Mon-Sat 0730-1740*, offer excellent day-long tours of four local communities. In groups of a

Killer fish

The much-maligned piranha has a fearsome reputation as a frenzied flesh-eating monster who will tear any unsuspecting tourist to shreds within seconds of setting foot in a tropical river. But is this infamous fish really so bad? Or is it merely the victim of some bad publicity?

There are over 30 types of piranha in South America but only one or two types are flesh eaters. Some feed on other fish and some are even vegetarians. The red-bellied piranhas, though, are real flesh eaters. These 20-cm-long fish with razor-sharp teeth hunt in packs or schools in the many rivers that intersect the Beni floodplains.

They breed early in the wet season, when both sexes turn a black colour and the female is swollen with eggs. Then begins the courtship ritual, which can last several nights, as the female takes her time in deciding on her potential partner's suitability as a father. Once her mind is made up they mate and the female takes off, leaving the male to guard the eggs. Although as many as 4,000 fry come from a single batch of eggs, only a handful survive the first few months. Their greatest test comes in the dry season when there is a danger of becoming isolated from the main rivers and food becomes scarce. The weaker piranhas then become victims as they fall prey to the stronger ones in a frenzy of cannibalism. Birds also join in, feeding on the dying fish. The fabled killer now has no defence against the elements. Those that are too large to be swallowed by the storks are picked off by vultures. Caiman also feed on dying piranhas, attracted by the birds. Piranhas are their favourite snack.

But when the rains come the savannah is turned into a huge inland sea and the tables are turned. The piranhas prey on the great white egrets which nest in the trees, attracted by the young egrets' constant pleading for food. In their desperate attempts to find more food than their parents can supply the clumsy chicks leave the nest and fall into the rivers where they are grabbed by the piranhas.

maximum of ten people, minimum three, you travel around 40 km from Rurrenabaque by road to the buffer zone of Pilon Lajas Biosphere Reserve and see the ways communities in the area live and the sustainable ways in which the rainforest can be used. Tours touch on forest management, handicrafts, agroforestry and fruit. U$25 per person includes lunch, water and well-informed guides.

Around Rurrenabaque

Visitors to the vast areas of Bolivia through which the many Amazon tributaries flow, and in particular to the middle and upper reaches of the Río Beni, will encounter the broadest spectrum of wildlife the country has to offer. Whilst other regions of Bolivia are also blessed with all manner of flora and fauna, it is the area around Rurrenabaque that offers the traveller the greatest opportunity to spot exotic and rare animal life. And unlike other, more remote regions of the country, the town is no more than three hours from the jungle, with easy access by river or on horseback.

By the same token, it must be remembered that patience is a real virtue when it comes to sighting wildlife, especially in the Amazon with its elusive inhabitants. The traveller who allows only 15 minutes in the hope of seeing a jaguar or peccary in broad

The debonaire dolphin

One of the most bizarre examples of the wide diversity of flora and fauna in the Bolivian Amazon is a strange, prehistoric-looking mammal which can transform itself into a suave gentleman in a white linen suit.

Or so local legend would have it. But the Amazonian river dolphin is a strange creature indeed. Part myth, part real, this beast can change its skin colour from a pale grey to a bright, luminescent pink. The indigenous people of the Amazon rainforest have long revered what they call the bufeo, and even today, unwanted pregnancies within Indian communities are sometimes blamed on this magical animal with an impressive line in seduction techniques.

Stories about the bufeo have been passed down from generation to generation. One such tale is of an underwater city where the bufeo walk on pavements made from turtle shells and lie in hammocks strung from anacondas. While the more formal and elegant white suit is donned when in human form, underwater they prefer the casual look and lounge around in catfish shorts and stingray hats.

Another common belief serves to protect the dolphins from being hunted by local fishermen. This stems from the analogy between dolphins and witchdoctors. The bufeo can be a malevolent creature, if hunted, and will avenge the death of one of their own. To kill a dolphin, then, is the same as killing a powerful witchdoctor, with the same inevitable consequences.

These pink river dolphins were, until recently, a forgotten species, considered extinct. All that remained was the skeleton of one in Paris, brought back from South America as a gift to Napoleon, and a few vague scientific papers dating from the 19th century in the Natural History Museum in London. The bufeo was rediscovered by a British expedition in 1956, but then forgotten again. In 1987, however, Jacques Cousteau astounded TV viewers around the world with the first ever pictures of pink dolphins frolicking in the waters of the Amazon.

Now visitors to the Río Yacuma can see the bufeo in the flesh – be it grey, or pink, or even dressed in a white suit. But women travellers should beware any charming, smartly dressed gentlemen in these parts.

daylight will, inevitably, be disappointed. However, with a modicum of perseverance and luck, and a willingness to travel to the animals' natural habitat, you may be in for the experience of a lifetime.

Ins and outs

Advice and information The area around Rurrenabaque may sound like a tropical paradise, but certain precautions should always be taken. Travellers coming here should note that insect repellent is an absolute necessity at any time of year, and that the jungle during the rainy season (January-March) can be a miserable experience even under the best of conditions. Finally, patience and respect are the most valuable commodities to bring with you. Spotting elusive and rare animals takes time. Responsible ecotourism – in this case a healthy respect for the jungle and lowlands about the town, and their animal inhabitants – will ensure that future travellers have the opportunity to see one of the world's last great wilderness areas in a relatively intact state and possibly help to reverse the damaging direction in which many of Bolivia's pristine wildlife environments are headed.

Try and find out how much knowledge of natural history your guide has. Insist that your tour be conducted in an environmentally sound manner. How is waste disposed of? Does food include hunted game (not including fish)? Do guides catch wildlife for clients, for example snakes and caimans? Don't encourage this practise as incompetent guides fatally injure many animals. Even large, seemingly 'tough', animals such as anacondas are highly sensitive to damage unless handled by an expert, and expert's are few in Rurre – don't destroy what you came to see. By following these guidelines you should be making a positive contribution to the people and conservation of the area.

Best time to visit The basic rules of thumb are to avoid trips during the rainy season; the humidity and insects will conspire to annoy even the most enthusiastic adventurer, and there are far fewer opportunities to see animals. One-day trips are reportedly a waste of time as it takes three hours to reach the jungle. You see far more wildlife on a pampas tour and the weather and general conditions are far more pleasant. The best season is July-October. Take insect repellent to ward off sandflies and mosquitoes.

Wildlife

The fecundity of animal life outside Rurrenabaque is beyond belief. In addition to the better-known varieties of caiman, fish, snakes, monkeys and turtles – all of which are easily spotted here – the observant visitor will not have much difficulty spotting their rarer tropical cousins, as well as a whole plethora of bird and insect life not found elsewhere. There are a vast number of armadillos, butterflies, deer, sloths, squirrels and tapirs that roam the area, as well as many lesser-known species: river otters and dolphins, ostrich-like rheas, giant anacondas and even the nearly extinct spectacled bear.

Some of these creatures are nocturnal and are not likely to be sighted on day trips, such as the increasingly rare jaguar and many varieties of deer. However, there are also numerous animals that keep normal office hours, such as the giant anteater, capybara, jochi, peccary and tapir. Flying overhead will be macaws, parrots and toucans, while flying squirrels and monkeys flit from tree to tree. Among this dazzling array of fauna must be included the innumerable insects – over 200 species of butterfly alone – and rodents, as well as fish of every description, from the enormous Amazon sturgeon to the tiny needlefish. Outside Amboró National Park near Santa Cruz, Madidi and the Noel Kempff Mercado National Park, it is a safe bet that no other area of Bolivia harbours such a wide variety of wildlife.

Viewing wildlife around Rurrenabaque need not be a solely river-based experience. Although many trips do start by canoe and travel the Río Beni, there are also horseback expeditions and even treks on foot. The roads around Rurrenabaque, however, are not ideally suited for animal watching. A four-wheel drive is needed at all times and with the exception of the more common types of monkeys, rabbits, squirrels, snakes and the occasional badger or capybara, little wildlife will be found within eye or earshot of a road in any case.

Reserva Biosférica Pilón Lajas

The Reserva Biosférica Pilón Lajas, a 401,176-ha preserve located in Beni's Ballívian Department and La Paz's Sud Yungas and Tamayo Departments, and contiguous with Parque Nacional Madidi on its western border, was recognized by the United Nations in 1997 as being a "unique habitat". Pilón Lajas has one of the continent's most intact Amazonian rainforest ecosystems, as well as an incredible array of tropical forest animal life, including several alligator species.

Unfortunately for its inhabitants, much of the park's wood is mahogany, and there is enormous pressure to re-classify it as a multiple-use area, which would give the logging companies carte blanche to devastate the forests. As with Madidi, the high-profile conflict has been in the news enough so that the government does not dare to intervene officially on the side of the loggers. In spite of a 1998 ban on logging, illegal tree-cutting is still carried out, a situation that must change if the preserve is to survive with its purpose intact. Mapajo (see below) is a fantastic attempt to create a different, sustainable future for the reserve – one run by the local Mosetén and T'simane people.

Official park headquarters are now open, located at the park's northernmost point, immediately (less than 1 km) south of Rurrenabaque. Admission is US$6. The preserve is now administered directly by **SERNAP**. Further information from SERNAP's representative in Rurrenabaque ① *Juan Carlos Miranda, C Campero esq. C Busch s/n; T03-03-8922245; F03-03-8922246.*

Ins and outs
Getting there Reaching the reserve is a challenge unless entering from Rurrenabaque. Instead of moving westward (as you would do if heading to Madidi), you head eastward. Official entrances are few, although there is one being built just south of Rurrenabaque itself. Otherwise, for in the interim, access is through Bolivia's Highway 2, which passes through the park's northeast quadrant along the way to Yucumo (110 km, a four-hour trip from Rurrenabaque). Do not make the mistake of travelling to San Borja in hope of catching a bus back to Pilón Lajas: they leave from Yucumo (along Highway 3) as well, which is literally on the park's border.

Information Pilón Lajas, at roughly US$5 per head, is not expensive. The best information regarding Pilón Lajas is put out by the park's overseers, the French non-profit group **Vétérinaires sans Frontières** (VSF) ① *T02-2226640, F02-2227337, vsf@vsf.rds.org.bo.* The programme director is Luís Marcus, and the co-ordinator is Sophie Lewandowski, who can be reached at capidex@vsf-france.org For those wishing to deal with the indigenous groups directly, try the **Mapajo-Asociación Indígena** (MAI) ① *Rurrenabaque, at T/F03-8322524.* It also can be reached through VSF's La Paz office number (above).

Mapajo
① *Mapajo Ecotourism Indigena, Calle Commercio, Rurrenabaque. T/F03-8922317. www.mapajo.com mapajo_eco@yahoo.com.*
Candlelit walkways link beautifully built cabañas in a prime model of sustainable ecotourism. Constructed and run by the local people, Mapajo combines expertly guided trips into the jungle to see wildlife with visits to the local community. The camp itself, fully owned and operated by the indigenous people of the Quiquibey River, is about two hours upstream (less on the way back down) from Rurrenabaque. It's a rare chance to stay in the pristine jungle of the Reserva Biosférica Pilón Lajas and learn about local music, crafts and local medicine. A trip to Mapajo includes a visit to the nearby village of Asunción and a chance to meet some of its 123 inhabitants, fire their arrows, try your hand at grinding and weaving, visit the school funded by the camp and even the opportunity to play the locals at football. Towels and mosquito nets are provided and some cabañas have private bathrooms and shower. The food is good and there is a maximum of 16 visitors at any time. As with Chalalán (see page 366), the buildings have been built utilizing environmentally sound methods, with forest materials and traditional construction. Staff are courteous and friendly, though they speak no English, so some Spanish is definitely an advantage. At $55-$65/day it's relatively expensive, but well worth the outlay, especially as all profits go back into the local community.

Reserva Biosférica del Beni

The Reserva Biosférica del Beni, in the department of the same name, is a 135,000-ha preserve situated along the Río Maniqui. A truly awe-inspiring reserve, it has lost more than 60% of its original territory in the last three years, and has recently had its on-site force reduced to eight rangers, yet remains one of Bolivia's crown jewels. Even with political machinations having taken their toll, the Beni Biosphere Reserve is staggering in its diversity.

It was established in 1982 through the efforts of an international environmental organization, **Conservation International**. The reserve is home to the Chimane tribe, as well as more than 500 species of bird and 200 different mammals. There are thought to be more than 1,500 species of plant life and 900 of fauna in all. It also contains **Laguna Normandia**, which has the world's largest population of the endangered black caiman. Like other parks in the central and northern reaches of Bolivia, it also suffers from encroaching logging interests, although recent protests by the Chimane have proven effective at curtailing the felling.

Park information

Access to the park should be made at **El Porvenir** (US$5 per head), which lies at the extreme southern end of the park just off of Bolivian Highway 3. There are a few bunk beds set up in Porvenir for accommodation (run by the **Bolivian Academy of Sciences**, T03-22352071), and more exist across the road at Totaizal. There are daily buses that pass in either direction to Rurrenabaque or Trinidad, and the park rangers also operate a twice-daily *camioneta* service to San Borja, the nearest town of any size. Admission to the reserve can be telephoned in ahead of time, perhaps the only park in Bolivia to offer this service; T03-03-8953898.

Parque Nacional Madidi

Bolivia's Madidi National Park is one of the world's most important conservation areas, and is quite possibly the most biodiverse of all protected areas on the planet's surface. Quite simply, there are more plant and animal species here than any other place on Earth. Parque Nacional Madidi in the La Paz Department, is, after acquiring more territory last year, now roughly four times the size of Amboró, at 1,895,740 ha (almost half the size of Holland). A primary Amazonian watershed, like Amboró and Noel Kempff Mercado, it also contains a pristine ecosystem, one that is home to nearly one-half of all the mammals known in the Western Hemisphere. It also provides shelter for more than one-third of the known amphibian and bird species in the New World. At last count, almost 1,200 different species of bird had been identified, representing more than 90 % of all known types in Bolivia. It also has what may well be the largest number of plants anywhere in the world, with almost 6,000 classified.

Ins and outs

Madidi can be accessed from numerous different locations and the park's three major river systems provide possible arteries for river transport, but only one of these can be considered 'easy' from a tourist perspective. This shouldn't put adventurous souls off – almost any level of 'adventure' travel is possible here, and if you are prepared to rough it you'll be rewarded with an unforgettable experience.

The easiest and by far the most popular entry point is through Rurrenabaque. Boat trips with Rurre agencies will take you up the Rio Beni and into the Tuichi river system. This area is the location for the majority of jungle tours. ▶▶ For more details on tour operators, see page 370.

☷ Wildlife of the Beni

The **tapir** is a shy, nocturnal animal which confines itself to an intricate network of trails in the forests of the marshy lowlands of Bolivia, Brazil, Colombia, Venezuela, Ecuador, Peru and the north of Argentina.

Water is essential for its survival; it drinks a great deal and is an excellent swimmer. It is herbivorous, eating water plants and the leaves and twigs of trees. Its only enemies are jaguars and alligators; against which its only defence is to use its teeth.

Jaguars are the largest of the New World cats. They are great wanderers, roaming even further than pumas. Usually they haunt forests where they hunt for deer, agoutis and especially peccaries. They follow the herds of these South American swine and pounce on the stragglers. They also attack capybara. Unlike most cats, jaguars are often found beside rivers and frequently enter the water. Jaguars attack tapir that come down to the water to drink and will even scoop fish from the water with their paws. The jaguar is referred to as the *tigre* to distinguish it from the ocelot, or *tigrillo*.

The **ocelot** is the next-largest South American cat after the puma and jaguar. It inhabits forests and while its spotted buff-brown coat assists in hunting it has also made it an attractive target for man. When left undisturbed it is diurnal, but becomes nocturnal in areas where it is hunted. Though it can climb it hunts on the forest floor, making good use of its acute sight and hearing. It preys on agoutis and pacas (which are large rodents), peccaries, brocket deer, birds and some reptiles. It has even been known to kill large boas.

The **giant otter** is found along the tributaries of the Amazon. It can measure up to 2 m in length. They are active by day when they hunt for food, often in small groups. They are not rare but are rarely seen as they are shy and submerge quickly at the slightest hint of danger. They feed on fish, molluscs and crustaceans, as well as small mammals and birds. They can be tamed easily and are often raised as pets by some tribes.

The **capybara** is a large aquatic rodent that looks like a cross between a guinea pig and a hippopotamus. It is the largest of all the rodents at over 1 m long and weighing over 50 kg. They live in large groups along the river banks, where they graze on the lush grasses. They come out onto dry land to rest and bask in the sun, but at the first hint of danger the whole troop dashes into the water. Its greatest enemies are the jaguar and puma. They are rather vocal for rodents, often emitting a series of strange clicks, squeaks and grunts.

Caiman are South American alligators. They are relatively small, usually growing to no more than 2½ m in length (except for the black caiman, which can reach up to 6 m). They are found in areas of relatively still water, ranging form marshland to lakes and slow-flowing rivers. Youngsters feed mainly on aquatic invertebrates while adults also take larger prey, including wild pigs and small travellers. During the dry season when pools dry up caimans can stop feeding altogether and burrow into the mud at the bottom of a pool waiting for the rains.

Pink river dolphins are excellent at fishing and will sometimes rip fishermen's nets and steal their catch. Adults can grow to nearly 3 metres in length. The pink colouring is more marked in older dolphins, young dolphins being born a more conventional grey-blue colour. They are thought to be an ancient species and are endangered.

Wildlife and vegetation

Within Madidi's borders can be found a vast range of habitats, from the freezing Andean peaks of the Cordillera Apolobamba in the southwest (reaching nearly 6,000 m), through cloud, elfin and dry forest at mid-elevations to steaming tropical jungle and pampas (neo-tropical savannah) in the north and east. It is this, the great range of altitude and therefore habitat, that is responsible for the vast array of wildlife and vegetation to be found within the park's boundaries.

Inside the park's borders there are an estimated 1000 bird species within an area of just under 19,000 sq km – roughly the size of Wales or El Salvador. By comparison the continental United States and Canada account for some 700 species. Birdlife ranges from minute hummingbirds to the Andean Condor, with a wingspan of 3 m, and the magnificent harpy eagle, the most powerful member of the raptor family. Mammals include: 10 species of primates, including the large spider and red howler monkeys; five species of cat, with healthy populations of jaguar and puma; giant anteaters and a myriad of lesser-known species. Reptiles are represented most spectacularly by the anaconda and the black caiman, which can reach lengths of 9 and 6 m respectively. The are also several types of venomous snake, the most feared being the bushmaster and the fer de lance. Chances of encountering such snakes are very low, but caution is required!

Conservation

Madidi's significance as a protected area is amplified due to its location at the centre of a bi-national system of parks. The Heath river on the park's northwestern border forms the Bolivia/Peru border. This sector contains the renowned Tambopata Candamo Reserved Zone and newly expanded Bahuaja Sonene National Park. To the southwest the Ulla Ulla National Fauna and Biosphere Reserve protects extensive mountain ecosystems. Beyond the Beni River in the southeast runs the Pilon Lajas Biosphere and Indigenous Territory, home to several native groups. Together these areas constitute approximately 40,000 sq km, one of the largest systems of protected land in the neotropics. Plans exist to try and link this area to the Manu Biosphere Reserve in Peru (Madidi's main rival for the world biodiversity crown) further north, and to other areas in Bolivian Amazonia. Taken together this may seem to suggest a rosy picture for the area's future, yet there are numerous threats to the areas integrity. A much talked of dam project across the Bala Gorge on the Beni River lingers on as a possibility. If this project is carried through it will inundate several thousand square kilometres of pristine habitat and destroy several ecotourism enterprises, including the famed project at Lake Chalalán (see below). Road building, illegal logging and hunting also remain significant problems for the land and its wildlife. All these are familiar problems for conservationists in a country that remains one of the poorest in Latin America.

San Miguel del Bala

Especially if you don't have much time to head further up to Mapajo or Chalalán, San Miguel del Bala, built in 2004, gives an excellent taste of the jungle just an hour upstream from Rurrenabaque. In a great setting on the edge of the park it has seven ensuite wooden *cabañas* (up some steep steps) where you can stay, as well as a plunge pool and two bars. Day trips from Rurrenabaque should mean that it will become popular.

Tuichi River

The Tuichi is a beautiful, fairly fast-flowing river sandwiched between the Bala Mountains and the Andes proper. A short trip (three to four days) into this zone is a great introduction to the rainforest for first-timers although wildlife, especially mammals, can be hard to spot. Forest wildlife is always elusive, but some areas provide a greater likelihood of success. Much of this is explained by the park's recent history. Up until its creation in 1995 many larger species were hunted intensively and the area suffered at the hands of various logging operations. Only 30 years ago the river's **giant otter** population (one of Amazon's rarest and most spectacular predators) was hunted to local extinction for the fur market. For this reason many of the parks species remain timid.

There is, however, a possibility that the basin could be re-colonized by otters from nearby watersheds and wildlife viewing is improving yearly as park protection persists and the wild residents lose their fear of two-legged mammals. Many trips to the Tuichi area include a trek to the Rio Hondo on rough trails giving a great look at the forest interior and a pretty good workout!

Above San José lie areas of significant white water (Grade IV) and agencies in La Paz can arrange exciting descents of the entire Tuichi, from the mountains to the jungle, an epic white-water adventure lasting about 10 days.

Chalalán Eco-lodge

Around six hours up-river is the excellent Chalalán Eco-lodge, built by the Bolivian government in conjunction with **Conservation International**. The lodge is surrounded by primary rainforest with an amazing variety of birds and mammals. The nearby lake is home to caiman, turtles, monkeys, hoatzin, macaws and other wildlife. Chalalán is, in many people's eyes, the finest example of community/indigenous ecotourism in Latin America. It has been built utilizing environmentally sound methods, with forest materials, traditional construction and solar power for lighting. The lodge is operated exclusively by the Quechua/Tacana community of San José de Uchupiamonas, a village further upstream. Guides, food and lodging all come highly recommended. The lodge is also an invaluable source of information on the park and is worth the trip to Madidi alone. The lodge can be contacted on T/F03-02-2434058, www.ecotour.-org/destinations/chalalan.htm. You can also find some short but excellent information on Madidi produced by the Bolivian government on its website: www.snids.gov.bo/forestal/apbmp/Madidi.htm

Tours to Chalalán cost around US$100 per person per night, but vary depending on the size of group and length of tour. Prices include one night in a hotel in Rurre, airport transfers, local guides, meals and transport in Chalalán but not flights to/from Rurre, which cost and extra US$110 return. The cabins have capacity for 14, with great showers, drinking water, library, 25 km of trails, viewing stations, canoe trips and night hikes. There's a **booking office** ① *Rurrenabaque on C Comercio, near the plaza, T03-8922519*, but tours are best booked in advance for no extra commission through **América Tours** in La Paz (address under La Paz Tour operators, page 123).

Río Madidi

Harder to access is the park's namesake, the Rio Madidi in the park's centre. Various agencies in Rurrenabaque can arrange a trip up the Tuichi river to a site above San José. From there it's a hard hike across the dividing range of hills that separate the Tuichi and Madidi river basins. The third leg of the journey involves a descent of the river by means of raft or canoe and a return to Rurrenabaque via Ixiamas. The Madidi River is incredibly wild and remote and, for anyone who undertakes this two-week expedition, the ultimate wilderness experience. Several species decimated in a vast area of the Amazon Basin retain populations here, including families of giant otters.

There are lots of guides and tour agencies in Rurrenabaque offering **tours to Madidi** with widely varied and fluctuating standards. Most of these offer trips for small groups at US$25 per person per day. Beyond the usual three- to five-day jungle tour it's possible to arrange a custom itinerary for the same daily rate. It's hard to recommend agencies, other than the operation at Chalalán, as the standards vary between tours and between guides. Ask around when in Rurrenabaque; especially question travellers recently returned from trips for recommendations. There's an established companies include: **Bala Tours** ① *C Comercio s/n, T/F03-8922527*; and **Fluvial Agencia.** Ask at the **Hotel Tuichi** (see page 368).

Heath river

The last of the three major river systems in the park is the Heath river. This river lies in a frontier zone not only between countries (Peru and Bolivia) but also between lowland tropical ecosystems – the pampas savannah and the rainforest. The pampas, near the Rio Heath, support unique and varied wildlife, including the highly endangered maned wolf (imagine a wolf on stilts) and the toco toucan, largest of the toucans. Access to the Heath River is difficult and the best way to reach it is via Puerto Maldonado in Peru, from where several hours up the Madre del Dios River the Heath River joins it on the frontier. **Inkanatura**, a Peruvian tourism company, have pioneered a an ecotourism lodge on the Heath, but, at the time of writing disagreements with the Bolivian government had suspended operations (see *Footprint Peru* for details).

Highland routes

Madidi is also accessible from the southwest. Routes from Apolo and Pelechuco, provide a spectacular decent from lonely mountain passes into lush tropical forest. As with other trips in Madidi, you must be entirely self-sufficient for periods of a week or more. On all routes into the park a guide with great local knowledge is recommended. For more information about trekking to Pelechuco, see page 84.

● Sleeping

Rurrenabaque *p357, map p357*
Most hotels in Rurrenabaque are safe, good and relatively inexpensive. Most offer laundry and breakfast (usually not included in the price), although only a few take credit cards. The better ones have ceiling fans, almost none have air conditioning.
B Jatatal Hotel, Av Costanera, San Buenaventura, T03-38922054. Across the river in San Buenaventura, Jatatal is a smart, 4-star, eco hotel with a swimming pool.
B Jataumba Lodge,T03-71255763. www.jataubalodge.com heliport. Just upriver (2.5 km away) on the other side, you need to take a boat to Jataumba. Two pools. Honeymoon packages for $299, trips over the Pampas in a light aircraft $US200.
B Safari, C Comercio, T03-8922410. At the far north end of town, a 10-min walk along Calle Comercio from the centre, this relatively expensive but lovely hotel has a clean swimming pool sunk into immaculate and extensive green lawns. Palm trees create shade and all rooms have wooden floors and firm comfortable beds. Especially attractive family rooms have front doors which open onto the lawn, and double beds upstairs. The restaurant is good and the hotel accepts Visa. Prices include

breakfast. Perfect for a small dose of luxury after a long hard tour.
D Hostal Beni, Comercio (near ferry), T03-03-8922408. A big hotel on the other side of the stream, the colonial style Beni has lots of stairs and landings, a/c and good big wooden beds. Accepts credit cards.
E Asaí, C Vaca Díez, T03-8922439. A laundry area, a courtyard with chairs and tables, clean and quiet. Rooms have big bathrooms with electric showers, quiet. Breakfast is an extra US$2.50.
E Bella Vista, Plaza 2 de Febrero. On the plaza, this low pink building has a garden behind leading down to the river. Quiet rooms overlook either the square or garden. No double beds.
E Oriental, Plaza 2 de Febrero, T03-8922401. On the plaza, Oriental has a long courtyard leading into a garden strung with comfortable hammocks. Showers in private bathrooms are electric. A simple breakfast is included, but prices are higher than in other comparable hotels in town. However, it's very cheap (**G** per person) without bathroom or breakfast.
F El Porteño, C Comercio, esq. Vaca Díez, T03-8922558. This central hotel has an attractive courtyard with hammocks and a

starfruit tree, from which, if you're lucky, you'll get a welcoming glass of carambola juice on arrival. Some rooms are especially big, with TV, private bathrooms, hot water, firm comfortable beds, ceiling fans and even wardrobes. The owner speaks no English though and you may have to put up with the late night sounds of soft rock from Moskkito Bar.

F **Hostal El Eden**, at the southern end of C Bolivar, T03-8922452. All on the ground floor at the far southern end of town, El Eden is good value and has a good sandy area out the back with a few hammocks and tables. Rooms have fans, wardrobes and, mostly, private bathrooms (**G** without). Price includes breakfast.

F **Rurrenabaque**, Corner of Vaca Díez and Bolívar, T03-8922481. Painted bright yellow and turquoise, Rurrenabaque, away from the riverfront, has a good verandah and comfortable rooms with private bathrooms and hot water. No double beds though.

G **Hostal El Balsero**, Av Aniceto Arce y Av Comercio, T03-8922042. A whitewashed building near the market with balconies, private bathrooms and hammocks downstairs, Balsero has hot water, TV and fans.

G **Residence Jislene**, C Comercio (north of C Aniceto Arce), T03-8922526. Good basic cheap choice with hot water, fan, mosquito nets, free tea and coffee and a cat. An excellent US$1.50 breakfast of omelettes or pancakes with fruit, fills you up for the day and there's a great area out the back with views over river. Friendly, popular with travellers but a fair way north of the centre.

G **Santa Ana**, C Vaca Díez, 1 block north of the plaza, T03-8922399. Fairly basic but adequate rooms look out onto a colourfully verdant garden courtyard. There are no double beds and showers are usually cold, though hot ones are available for a price. Laundry and parking both available. A good value and central option.

G **Tuichi**, C Avaroa and Santa Cruz, T03-71983582. Kitchen and laundry facilities, simple rooms with electric showers and fans off a small covered courtyard. One of the best value hotels in town and the best place to make up tour groups, though the shared bathrooms are dirty. Accepts traveller's cheques and may even change them.

Reserva Biosférica Pilón Lajas *p361*
As Pilón Lajas is a reserve and home to tribal communities, there is no accommodation within the biosphere itself except for that at Mapajo. Camping permits should be obtained through VSF or MAI in advance (see above).

🍽 Eating

Rurrenabaque *p357, map p357*
For a town of its size, Rurre has a large number of places to eat. Though none are 5-star, and only the pizza restaurant next door to the **Moskkito Bar** accepts credit cards, many are excellent and almost all are good value. There are also plenty of places offering chicken and the market, of course, is fantastic for fruit juices and good *almuerzos*. For the latter expect a lot of roasted chicken and to pay US$0.75-1.20. Otherwise, from the street stalls along C Aniceto Arce on Fri and Sat nights, join the locals scoffing *salchipapas* (a kind of hot dog) with fries and far too much mayonnaise and ketchup.

$$ **Juliano**, C Comercio. Offering excellent 'French-Italian' cuisine, Juliano's opened in 2004. Blue-painted tables, a bar outside and a friendly atmosphere create a vaguely Southern Pacific feel. Some good pasta dishes, excellent fish and delicious crème brulée, but avoid the soggy gnocchi ('ñoqui').

$$ **La Perla de Rurre**, corner of Bolivar and Diez. With a big, walled courtyard under a large shady tree decked in coloured lights at night, La Perla is Rurre's smartest restaurant. Meaty and fishy menu.

$ **Brostería Charito**, Avaroa and Arce. Outside wooden tables are set down from the street next to the grill outside. Simple, meaty and predominently local.

$ **Camila's Restaurant**, C Santa Cruz. Good restaurant, next to Camilla's internet café. Lots of outside tables, plants, jungle murals and 1980s music. A big menu is good for fish dishes. Service can be slow. There's a separate heladeria just down the road towards the river.

$ **Club Social Rurrenabaque**, 1 block north of C Santa Cruz, on C Comercio. A pleasant place to sip a cold beer whilst overlooking the river but don't miss their fishburgers and jugs of fruit juice.

$ El Tacuara, C Santa Cruz. Opposite Camila's, in the middle of town. Good wide-ranging menu: soups, omlettes, pasta, meat and fish. Good for people-watching.

$ La Cabaña, just south of the ferry stop, by the river. An attractive riverside restaurant with umbrellas outside.

$ La Chocita, just south of the ferry stop by the river, next to La Cabaña. A riverside fish restaurant with a few red-clothed tables outside under awning. Simple but popular, esecially for the *almuerzo*. The special dish of *Pescado Taquara* is reportedly great here, but needs ordering a day in advance.

$ Pizzeria Italia, C Comercio, T03-8922611, Next to Moskkito, the restaurant is open to the bar next door, so you can watch games of pool as you eat. 25 types of pizza, though many seem to have the same ingredients in a different order. 3 sizes, medium is about enough for one. A young atmosphere and a creatively translated menu.

$ Playa Azul, just south of the ferry stop, by the river. 0700-2230, breakfast 0700-1100. The biggest of the three restaurants along this stretch, but not the best. Semi-open and with good views of the river, though a blaring TV does its best to spoil things. Slow service.

Cafés

Café Bar Madidi, C Comercio. Another of Rurre's new crop of cool places, Madidi has little wooden tables under an awning almost opposite Moskkito. 9 coffees, 11 juices and terrible MOR rock. Some vegetarian dishes.

Café Motacú Av Santa Cruz, next door to TAM. Mon, Wed, Thu, Fri and Sat 0830-1200 and 1730-2000. Very good and cheap veggie food: 3 types of veggie burgers, burritos, lentil dahl and quiche. Excellent breakfasts too (US0.60-1.50), good cakes and cookies, including delicious hot chocolate brownies. Run by a Scot, a Peruvian, an Argentine and a Bolivian, Motacú also has a book exchange, handicrafts and you can buy some locally produced organic products – coffee, sun-dried tea, honey, peanut butter and dried fruit.

Pachamama, C Avaroa sud, T03-03-8922620. 1200-2230. At the southern end of town, a friendly café-bar run by an English/Bolivian couple with snacks, a balcony with a view over the river, a film room, playstation, internet, table football and a book exchange.

Spa las Parabas, at the end of Av Santa Cruz, near the ferry port, T71120883. A beautifully designed dry and wet sauna with a cold plunge pool, massage, treatments, and a snack bar with great views. Even if you don't fancy the sauna itself, it's a great place to come and chill out. Use of the spa, US$5.

Last but not least, an American man drives round town in a kit car selling banana bread, cinnamon rolls and anti New World Order literature. Catch him while it's hot.

🍷 Bars and clubs

Rurrenabaque *p357, map p357*
The town's fun swings chiefly around Moskkito Bar and a myriad of karaoke bars. To find them just follow the music on Fri and Sat nights. There are also 2 dodgy discos. The one opposite Hotel Tuichi is best for gringos.

Moskkito Bar, C Comercio. With rock music and pool tables (and now an attached t-shirt shop), the Moskkito bar is a good place to drink away an evening in the company of new-found friends. Lots of beer and tales of large anacondas. You can also order in pizzas from the restaurant next door. Happy hour with half-price cocktails 1900-2100.

🔘 Shopping

Rurrenabaque *p357, map p357*
There is a good **market** on Sun and hammocks (for around US$5) are sold along the pedestrian route of the dried-up tributary, between C Commercio and C Avaroa.

There are plenty of stores selling all manner of highly priced wilderness gear and trekking equipment along the river and in the main market. However, some of the more common items can be bought more cheaply than in La Paz: head gear, mosquito nets and insect repellent.

⛰ Activities and tours

Rurrenabaque *p357, map p357*
There's a public *balneario* in C Santa Cruz, US$2 for the whole day. There's music and you can get cold drinks and beer. Grassy areas are shaded by palm trees with chairs and tables. Mon-Sun 1000-1900. No kids under 7.

Agencia Fluvial, at **Hotel Tuichi**, T03-8922372, is run by Tico Tudela. They offer jungle tours on the Río Tuichi, normally 4 days, but shorter by arrangement, including food, transport and mosquito nets. 3 nights are spent in the jungle, learning about plants, survival and the foods of the region.

Fluvial also run 3-day 'pampas tours' on a boat to Río Yacuma, US$30 per person per day. Fluvial tours can be arranged through Hotel Tuichi.

Tico has opened **Hotel de la Pampa** near Lago Bravo, 2½ hrs from Rurrenabaque. It's a base for visiting Lago Rogagua (birds) and Río Yacuma (anacondas, monkeys, caiman, capybara, pink dolphins, etc). Fully inclusive tours (including meals and accommodation) cost US$40 per person per day.

Aguila Tours, Av Avaroa, T03-8922478.
Bala Tours, next door to TAM on C Santa Cruz, T03-8922527, www.balatours.com; has a private camp for the Pampas tour well away from other groups.
Deep Rainforest (who offer a 'jungle survival' trip), C Comercio.
Donato Tours, C Aniceto Arce, T03-71795722.
Flecha Tours (who run a river trip to Guanay), C Avaroa and Santa Cruz.
Indigena Tours, T03-71979719 (mob), C Avaroa.
San José Tours, next door to Indigena on C Avaroa.

☉ Transport

Caranavi to Rurrenabaque *p356*
Yucumo is on the La Paz-Caranavi-Rurrenabaque or San Borja routes. The Rurrenabaque-La Paz bus passes through at about 1800. If travelling to Rurrenabaque by bus or truck take extra food in case of delay if waiting for river levels to fall.

Rurrenabaque *p357, map p357*
Air
TAM fly to/from **La Paz**; US$58 one-way; you'll be charged Bs3 for every kilo over 15 kg. They have an office on C Santa Cruz, T03-8922398. Check flight times in advance as they change frequently, and expect delays and cancellations in the rainy season. TAM flies 4 days a week.

Amazonas fly twice daily and are usually cheaper (US$50 return). Their office is opposite Camila's on C Santa Cruz (T03-8922472) or contact travel agents (eg **America Tours** in La Paz, T02-2374204).

Itemox Express flies from Trinidad to **Reyes**, 30 km to the north (where there's lodging and restaurants), a useful alternative to the bus ride.

Taxis and motorcycle taxis meet flights. A motorcycle taxi to or from town costs US$1, a normal taxi US$3. **Amazonas** and **TAM** also run their own minibuses to and from the airport from their offices in the centre of town, US$0.60. There is a small tourist tax and flight tax at the airport.

Road
To/from **La Paz** (you have to go to Villa Fátima to leave the capital) via Caranavi daily at 1100 with **Flota Yungueña** and **Totai**; 18-20 hrs, US$8.20. Returns at 1100. **Flota Unificada** leaves La Paz (also from Villa Fátima) on Tue, Thu, Fri and Sat at 1030, same price but, as it continues on to far-off Riberalta and Guayamerin, its return departure time depends on how well the driver copes with the road on the way back; ask in Rurre.

Flota Yungueña also has a 1030 bus which leaves Villa Fátima and continues on to **Riberalta** and **Guayamerin** from Rurre. Trucks also go to Riberalta.

To **Trinidad**, Tue, Thu, Sat, Sun at 2230 with **Trans Guaya** via Yucumo and San Borja; the road is often closed in the rainy season.

River
Boats to **Guanay** cost US$16 per person; ask at any tour agency. You'll need to take your own food. Boats may not run at times of especially low water.

❶ Directory

Rurrenabaque *p357, map p357*
Banks Getting money in Rurre is very difficult; bring plenty of it with you. There are no banks or casas de cambio. **Beni, Moskkito** and **Red Oriental** (next to Indigena Tours) all change cash for 5-10% commission. Travellers' cheques in dollars can be used to pay for tours but are difficult to cash; try **Agencia Fluvial**, who charge 5%

commission. Most if not all tour companies will accept credit cards for tours.

Internet Camila's, next to the restaurant of the same name on Santa Cruz charges US$3 per hr, minimum US$0.75 for 15 mins. **Entel:** is on C Comercio 2 blocks north of the plaza, T03-8922205, and on C Santa Cruz and C Bolívar. **Laundry** Speed Queen, Vaca Diez between Bolívar and Avaroa. US$1/kg, ready in 3½ hours.

Trinidad and southern Beni

→ *Phone code: 03. Colour map 2, grid A5. Population: 60,000. Altitude: 327 m.*

The capital of the lowland Beni Department, Trinidad, has the look and feel of Santa Cruz perhaps 30 or 40 years ago. Trinidad vies with Iquitos in Peru as the motorcycle and scooter capital of South America. The plaza resembles a race track at night. Sometimes you'll see improbable numbers on one small bike – entire families, including grandparents and distant cousins. In fact, the only people who walk here are the tourists. If you do manage to converse with the locals, on their way to or from their bikes, you'll find them open and friendly.

The city was founded in 1686 as one of the earliest Jesuit settlements in the region by Father Cipriano Barace, a revered missionary who was later martyred by an indigenous tribe he was attempting to convert. There are no buildings in Trinidad that remain from the missionary era. The impressive cathedral was built at the beginning of this century on the site of the original Jesuit church. ▶▶ *For Sleeping, Eating and all other listings, see pages 373-376.*

Ins and outs

Getting there There are daily **flights** to La Paz, and also flights to Cochabamba and Santa Cruz. A motorcycle taxi to/from the airport is US$1.20. The **bus** terminal is on Mendoza, between Beni and Pinto, 9 blocks east of the main plaza. Motorbike taxis will take people with backpacks from the bus station to the centre for US$0.45. There are 2 **ports**, Almacén and Varador, check at which one your boat is docking.

Getting around A few blocks either side of the plaza the streets are paved, but thereafter earth, turning to mud in the rainy season. The road to the bus terminal is particularly bad. Av 6 de Agosto is paved for several blocks, as is the road to the airport. Work is also under way to pave the road to Laguna Suárez (see next page).

Climate Trinidad has three types of weather: hot and sticky; very hot and sticky; and insufferably hot and sticky. So hot is the midday sun that those seen wandering the streets between 1200 and 1500 should probably be locked away as either crazy or dangerous.

Information Tourist offices ① *Prefectural building at Joaquín de Sierra y La Paz, ground floor, T03-4621305, ext 116, very helpful.*

Sights

You can hire a motorbike or jeep to go to the **river**, which offers good swimming on the opposite bank. Boat hire costs US$5. Five kilometres from town is the **Laguna Suárez**, with plenty of wildlife. The water is very warm, and near the café with the jetty, where the locals swim, the bathing is safe. Elsewhere there are stingrays and caiman. A motorbike taxi from Trinidad is US$1.30.

Seventeen kilometres north of town is **Chuchini**, a wildlife sanctuary, with an ecological and archaeological centre, the **Madriguera del Tigre**, accessible by road in the dry season and by canoe in the wet season. Contact **Efrém Hinojoso** i *C Cochabamba 232 entre Bolívar y Sucre, T03-4621811*; or **Edwin Portugal** ① *La Paz, T02-2341090, T/F02-2343930*. A trip of three days and two nights will cost US$210 per person, including accommodation and meals. Efrém will run tours with only one or two people for the same price. There is plenty of wildlife to be seen, including parrots, macaws, toucans, caiman, turtles, capybara, anacondas, monkeys and many birds. Also included in the trip is the **Museo Arqueológico del Beni**, containing human remains, ceramics and stone objects from the pre-Columbian Beni culture, said to be over 5,000 years old. Tours to Chuchini can also be booked through the tour agencies in town.

Magdalena and around

A road from Trinidad heads northeast to **San Ramón** and then turns east to **Magdalena**, a charming little town on the banks of the Río Itonama. It was founded by Jesuit missionaries in 1720, made a city in 1911 and is now the capital of the province of Iténez. Beef is the main product of the region and the river is the means of transporting cattle and other agricultural produce. Some 7 km upriver is the **Laguna La Baíqui**, which is popular for fishing. There is an abundance of wildlife and birds in the surrounding area. The city's main festival, Santa María Magdalena, is held on 22 July and attracts many groups and visitors from all over Beni and beyond.

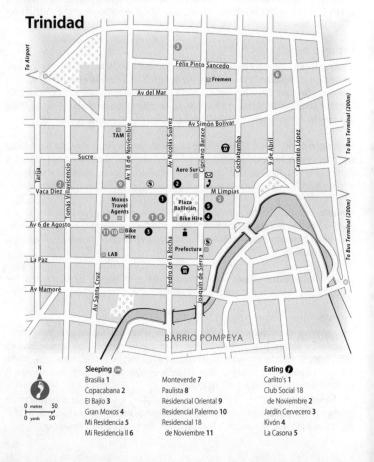

Trinidad

N

0 metres 50
0 yards 50

Sleeping 🛏
Brasilia **1**
Copacabana **2**
El Bajío **3**
Gran Moxos **4**
Mi Residencia **5**
Mi Residencia II **6**
Monteverde **7**
Paulista **8**
Residencial Oriental **9**
Residencial Palermo **10**
Residencial 18
de Noviembre **11**

Eating 🍴
Carlito's **1**
Club Social 18
de Noviembre **2**
Jardín Cervecero **3**
Kivón **4**
La Casona **5**

The Amazon Trinidad and southern Beni

East of Magdalena on the Río Blanco, **Bella Vista** is considered by many to be one of the prettiest spots in northeast Bolivia. Lovely white sandbanks line the Río San Martín, which is 10 minutes by canoe from the boat moorings below town. Local boatmen will take you there, returning later by arrangement. The sandbanks are also accessible by motorcycle. Check that the sand is not covered by water after heavy rain. Other activities are swimming and canoeing in the Río San Martín, and the countryside is good for cycling. There are three well-stocked shops on the plaza, but none sells mosquito repellent or spray/coils. Bring your own as there are many mosquitoes at the beginning of the wet season (apply repellent before leaving the plane). There is no bank or Entel office. There are flights to Bella Vista with **Itemox Express**, from Magdalena or Trinidad, but no fixed schedule.

West from Trinidad

A road heads west from Trinidad through San Ignacio de Moxos, to **San Borja** and then a further 50 km (one to two hours) to **Yucumo**, where it joins the road from the Yungas to Rurrenanbaque (see also page 356). There are five or six river crossings and, in the wetlands, flamingoes, blue heron and a multitude of waterfowl. The section of road from Trinidad to San Ignacio is good, but from San Ignacio to San Borja is poor, with long stretches rutted and pot-holed. From San Borja to Yucumo is very good. The road passes through the north part of the **Pilón Lajas Biosphere Reserve** (see page 361). Gasoline is available at San Ignacio, San Borja and Yucumo.

San Ignacio De Moxos

Lying 90 km west of Trinidad, San Ignacio de Moxos is known as the folklore capital of the Beni Department. The traditions of the Jesuit missions are still maintained, with big fiestas taking place, especially during Holy Week. The town's patron saint's day is celebrated on 31 July, and is one of the country's most famous and colourful celebrations. Over 60% of the population are Macheteros, who speak their own language.

❣ Electricity is supplied in town only from 1200 to 2400.

San Borja

West of San Ignacio, San Borja is a small, dusty cattle-raising centre with hotels and restaurants clustered near the plaza. This is a coca-growing region and it is unwise for travellers to wander alone inside the Parque Nacional Isiboro in case they are mistaken for Drug Enforcement Agency (DEA) agents by coca farmers.

◉ Sleeping

Trinidad *p371, map p372*

A **Gran Moxos**, Av 6 de Agosto y Santa Cruz, T03-4622240. Price includes breakfast, a/c, fridge bar, cable TV, phone, good restaurant, accepts Visa and Mastercard.

A **Mi Residencia**, Manuel Limpias 76, T03-4621529. A/c, includes breakfast, cable TV.

A **Mi Residencia II**, Félix Pinto Sancedo y 9 de Abril. Quieter and with pool.

B **El Bajío**, Av Nicolás Suárez 520. A/c, cheaper with fan, includes breakfast, pool (US$2 for non-residents).

C **Monteverde**, Av 6 de Agosto 76, T03-4622738. With or without a/c, fridge bar,

cable TV, breakfast US$1.50 extra, clean and comfortable, owner also speaks English. Recommended.

D **Copacabana**, Tomás Villavicencio, 3 blocks from the plaza, T03-4622811. Good value,(Fwithout bathroom).

F **Paulista**, Av 6 de Agosto 36, T03-4620018. US$1.50 cheaper with shared bathroom, comfortable, good restaurant.

F **Residencial Oriental**, 18 de Noviembre, near Vaca Díez, T03-4622534. With bathroom, good value.

G **Brasilia**, Av 6 de Agosto 46, T03-4621685. Shared bathroom, fan, basic, not very clean.

G **Residencial 18 de Noviembre**, Av 6 de Agosto 135, with private bathroom, clean, friendly, laundry facilities.

G **Residencial Palermo**, Av 6 de Agosto 123, T03-4620472. Next door to Residencial 18 de Noviembre, with shared bathroom, basic, restaurant.

Magdalena and around *p372*

B **International**, T03-8862210. A luxurious place with gardens and pool, all rooms with bathroom and hot water, fans, includes breakfast, excellent restaurant.

G **Ganadero**, modest but clean.

G **Residencial Iténez**, modest but clean.

G **San Carlos.** Private toilet, fan, shower and water bed.

Bella Vista

G **Hotel Cazador**, shared bathroom, provides meals for guests (restaurant to be built), the owner Guillermo Esero Gómez is very helpful and knowledgeable about the area.

West from Trinidad *p373*
San Ignacio De Moxos

There are a few fairly cheap *residencias* and there are other basic *alojamientos* on and around the plaza.

F **Don Joaquín**, on the main plaza. With bathroom, fan, family atmosphere.

F **Plaza**, on the main plaza. With or without bathroom, fan, good value, restaurant. Recommended.

San Borja

E **Hostal Jatata**, T03-8953103, 2 blocks from plaza. Modern, comfortable, fans, good snack bar. Highly recommended.

G **Jaropa**, clean, basic.

G **Residencial Manara**, just off the plaza. With private bathroom, clean, comfortable, some rooms with a/c.

G **Trópico**, 1 block from the main plaza, clean. Recommended.

● Eating

Trinidad *p371, map p372*

There are several good fish restaurants in Barrio Pompeya. Cheap meals, including breakfast, are served at the fruit and vegetable market. Try sugar-cane juice with lemon – delicious.

$$ **Balneario Topacare** is a restaurant and bathing resort 10 mins out of town on Laguna Suárez, it offers delicious local specialities for lunch or dinner, is set in a beautiful location, with excellent bird spotting and is a favourite spot for locals at the weekends.

$ **Brasilia**, Av 6 de Agosto, good dinner.

$ **Carlito's**, on Plaza Ballivián, recommended.

$ **Club Social**, 18 de Noviembre, N Suárez y Vaca Díez, on the plaza, good lunch for US$1.35.

$ **Jardín Cervecero**, opposite the Hotel Monteverde on Av 6 de Agosto.A good value lunch can be had for US$1.55.

$ **La Casona**, on the main plaza, for good pizzas and set lunch, closed Tue.

$ **La Estancia**, on Ibare entre Muibe y Velarde, excellent steaks.

$ **Pescadería El Moro**, Bolívar and 25 Diciembre, excellent fish.

$ **Pescadería Don Pedro**, C Manuel Maraza, Barrio Pompeya, south of the plaza across the river.

Cafés

Heladería Oriental, on the main plaza. Good coffee, ice cream, cakes, popular with locals.

Kivón, on the main plaza. Burgers, ice cream and snacks.

Magdalena and around *p372*

$ **El Gato**, on the road off the plaza beside the church, drinks and nightly dancing.

Heladería Laidi, 1 block from the plaza, simple meals and good juices. Drinking water is available in town and electricity runs from 1800-2400.

West from Trinidad *p373*
San Ignacio De Moxos

Restaurants do not stay open late.

$$ **Casa Suiza**, good European food.

$ **Donchanta**, recommended for tasty meat dishes.

$ **Isireri**, on the plaza, good and cheap set lunches and delicious fruit juices.

San Borja

$ **Club Social**, 2 blocks from the plaza, covered open-air restaurant, serves good almuerzos.

$ **Taurus**, good food, cheap.

▲ Activities and tours

Trinidad *p371, map p372*
Tour operators

Most agents offer excursions to local *estancias* and jungle tours down-river to Amazonia. Most *estancias* can also be reached independently within an hour by hiring a motorbike. Note that the more distant parts of Isiboro are at present too dangerous to visit owing to violent disputes between *cocaleros* and the authorities. Tours to Isiboro are very expensive because of the distances involved.

The tour operators are almost all located on 6 de Agosto.

Fremen, which has now moved to Cipriano Berace 332, T03-4621834, runs speed-boat trips along the Mamoré and Iboré rivers and to Isiboro-Securé National Park for US$80 per day; their Flotel Reina de Enin offers tours of more than 1 day, US$80 per person per day, US$349 for 4 days, with good food.

Jarajorechi is an ecotourism centre that offers accommodation and snacks, as well as jungle trips, and equipment and transport hire; for more information contact Graciela Neira, Av 6 de Agosto esquina 27 de Mayo, T03-4621716, Casilla 299, Trinidad.

Moxos, No 114, T03-4621141, Casilla 252, is recommended.

Paraíso Travel, No 138, T/F03-4620692, Casilla 261, does 'Conozca Trinidad' packages.

Tarope Tours, No 81, T03-4621468, Casilla 351, sells flights only.

☉ Transport

Trinidad *p371, map p372*
Air

LAB office is at Santa Cruz 234, T03-4620595; flights to **La Paz** (daily direct), **Cochabamba**, **Santa Cruz**, **Magdalena**, **San Joaquín**, **Cobija**, **Guayaramerín** and **Riberalta** (check schedules).

Aero Sur, Cipriano Barace 51, T03- 4620765; flights daily to **La Paz** and **Santa Cruz**, daily except Sun to **Cobija**, **Guayaramerin**, **San Borja**, and except Sat to **Riberalta**.

TAM, at the airport, T03-4622363, to

SAVE flies to and from **Magdalena**, **Riberalta**, **La Paz**, **Santa Cruz**; T03-4622806.

Itemox Express, at Av 6 de Agosto 281, T03-4622306, has flights to **Baures**, **Huacaraje**, **Bella Vista**, **Magdalena**, **Reyes** (near Rurrenabaque) and **Santa Rosa**.
The airport authority, **AASANA**, can be reached at T03-4620678.

Bus

Several *flotas* daily to/from La Paz via San Borja and Caranavi, 20-21 hrs, leaving at 1730, US$17.50 (see also under San Borja, Transport, page 376). A minibus goes daily to **San Borja** at 0900, US$11.50.

To **Santa Cruz**, 12 hrs in the dry season, US$5.80, and **Cochabamba**, US$11.60, with Copacabana, Mopar and Bolívar, leaving at 1700, 1730 and 1800. The Trinidad to Casarabe section of the road is paved as is Santa Cruz to El Puente, and all the sections of unpaved road have a good gravel surface.

To **Rurrenabaque** (US$15.40), **Riberalta** (US$21.15) and **Guayaramerín** (US$23), connecting with a bus to Cobija, with Guaya Tours daily at 1000. The road is often impassable in the wet season, and it can take at least 24 hrs to Rurrenabaque.

Motorcycle hire

Rental on the plaza from US$2 per hr, US$8 per half day; also at the junction of Av 6 de Agosto and 18 de Noviembre, same prices. Take passport.

River

Puerto Varador is 13 km from town on the Río Mamoré on the road between Trinidad and San Borja. Cross the river by the main bridge by the market, walk down to the service station by the police checkpoint and take a truck, US$1.70. Almacén is 8 km from the city.

Cargo boats down the Río Mamoré to **Guayaramerín** take passengers; 3-4 days, assuming no breakdowns. They are best organized from Puerto Varador (speak to the Port Captain). Argos is recommended as

The Amazon Trinidad and southern Beni *Listings*

Border with Brazil at Guayará-Mirim

Bolivian immigration Av Costanera near the port; open 0800-1100, 1400-1800. Passports must be stamped here when leaving, or entering Bolivia.
Entering Bolivia Passports must be stamped at the Bolivian consulate in Guajará-Mirim.

Brazilian consulate On 24 de Septiembre, Guayaramerín, open 1100-1300; visas for entering Brazil are issued here.
Banks Exchange money here, as it's difficult to do so in the state of Rondônia in Brazil.

friendly, US$22 per person. Take water, fresh fruit and toilet paper; ear-plugs are also a good idea as hammocks are strung over the engine on small boats. This trip is only for the hardy traveller.

Taxis
A motorcycle taxi in the city costs US$0.40; to the airport US$1.20. Motorbike taxis take people with backpacks from the bus station to the centre of town for US$0.45.

Magdalena and around *p372*
Air
SAVE flies to and from **Trinidad** on Tue and Sat (T03-8862267).
LAB flies to/from **Trinidad** on Fri and Mon (T03-8863020).
Itemox Express has daily flights to **Trinidad** (US$31, in 5-seater). There are also flights to **Bella Vista**, **Baures** and **Huacaraje**.

Road
An unpaved road goes to Trinidad via San Ramón, passable only in dry season.

West of Trinidad *p373*
San Ignacio De Moxos
The bus from Trinidad to **San Borja** stops at Restaurant Donchanta during lunch; otherwise it is difficult to find transport to San Borja. A minibus goes to Trinidad daily at 0730 from the plaza; there are also *camionetas*, but check times beforehand.

San Borja
Air
Aero Sur, C Bolívar on the plaza, T03-8953185, flies to **Trinidad** daily except Sat. SAVE also flies to/from **La Paz** and **Santa Cruz**; T03-8953785.

TAM, T03-8953272, flies to and from **La Paz**, but check schedules.

Buses
Flota Yungueña daily except Thu at 1300 to **La Paz** (19 hrs); also to **Rurrenabaque**, **Santa Rosa**, **Riberalta** and **Guayaramerín** on Thu, Sat and Sun.

Minibuses and *camionetas* run daily between San Borja and **Trinidad** throughout the year (US$15); it's about 7 hrs including the 20-min crossing of the Río Mamoré on a ferry barge. 1 de Mayo runs daily to **San Ignacio** (US$8), **Trinidad** and **Santa Cruz** at 0850. Trucks reportedly go to **Yucumo** at 0800, US$2.

❶ Directory

Trinidad *p371, map p372*
Banks Banco Mercantil, Joaquín de Sierra, near the plaza, changes cash and TCs, and gives cash advance on Visa. Street changers can be found on 6 de Agosto.
Communications Entel and the post office are both open daily till 1930; in the same building at Av Barace, just off the plaza.

Magdalena and around *p372*
Bank on the plaza, which changes TCs. Entel office also on the plaza.

West of Trinidad *p373*
San Borja
Banks Good rate for US dollars at Joyería San Borja next to the entrance to the supermarket round the corner from the central market.

Northern Beni and Pando

This northern outpost is one of the least discovered parts of the Bolivia Amazon and as such has practically no tourist infrastructure and is only for the hardiest and most experienced of travellers. The region has done little to exploit its natural draw as an ecotourism spot or its proximity to the Amazonian rivers and the borders with Brazil and Peru, but it should be remembered that it is the wettest part of Bolivia. It receives more than 1,770 mm of rain annually, a statistic which does little to endear it to tourists. The region attained temporary importance during the natural-rubber boom of the late 19th century. But this collapsed, as it did throughout South America, in the second decade of the 20th century when cheaper Asian rubber cornered the world market. It is now the centre for Brazil nut production. An area encompassed by Riberalta, Tumi-Chucua (see below), Cachuela Esperanza 98 km to the northeast, and Villa Bella a further 32 km northeast, is known as the triángulo de la goma y castaña (rubber and nut triangle). ▸▸ *For Sleeping, Eating and other listings, see pages 380-382.*

Ins and outs

Getting there From Rurrenabaque an all-weather road leads via Santa Rosa to Riberalta. In Santa Rosa there is accommodation at F **Hotel Oriental**, which changes dollars. A good place to eat is the friendly **Restaurant and Confitería El Triángulo**.

Climate The rainy season is November-March; the rest of the year is dry and hot. Temperatures average 29°C but can reach 40°C, or fall to 15°C when the cold *surazo* wind blows.

Northeastern area

Riberalta → *Phone code: 03. Colour map 1, grid A4. Population: 60,000. Altitude: 175 m.*

The charming town of Riberalta is at the confluence of the Madre de Dios and Beni rivers, which together flow into the Rio Mamoré north of Guayaramerín. It is in the very far northern reaches of the Beni and well off the beaten track. The town is also very laid back, a kind of Bolivian version of Gabriel García Márquez's **Macondo**. If you want to fit in with everyone else then you should hire a motorcycle from one of the agencies on the plaza.

Some 25 km away is **Tumi-Chucua** ① *for further information contact Dr Willy Noack, T/F03-3522497, www.bolivianet.com/tumichucua,* situated on a lovely lake where you can swim, and close to the Nature Gardens. You can also fish in the lake, and the area is good for birdwatching. There's plenty of information available on the rainforest, the rubber boom and Brazil nut production.

Guayaramerín → *Colour map 1, grid A4. Population: 35,000.*

From Riberalta the road continues east, crossing the Río Yata before reaching Guayaramerín, a cheerful, prosperous little town on the bank of the Río Mamoré, opposite the Brazilian town of Guajará-Mirim. It has an important *Zona Libre* (Free Zone). Passage between the two towns is unrestricted. The boat trip across the river costs US$1.65 (more at night).

Cobija and the northwest → *Colour map 1, grid A1. Population: 12,000.*

Altitude 252 m.

At the extreme northwest of Bolivia sits the hot, steamy and languid town of Cobija, capital of Pando, the country's newest department. Roughly 500 km northwest of La Paz, and until recently accessible only by air or river, Cobija is situated on a bend of the Río Acre which forms the border with Brazil. It is also only 40 km east of the border with Perú.

Founded in 1906 as Bahía, Cobija was settled during the rubber boom then sweeping the area. As production declined, however, so did the town's importance. Although the largest town in Pando, it remains a quiet, humid outpost whose chief importance is as a transportation centre and processor of tropical fruits and nuts. Consequently, there is little to see or do here, although it can provide a decent stop-over for Amazon-bound travellers.

In spite of its lacklustre aura, Cobija has received a disproportionate amount of national and even international aid over the past decade. In recent years, for instance, a modern Brazil nut processing plant has been built on the outskirts, an impressive hospital has been constructed and the town boasts two airports, one of which has international status (though it is used only in the rainy season).

Unlike most Bolivian towns, Cobija does not follow a standard street grid but has a number of roads that meander through the town. It does have a main plaza and most of the main buildings are located around it, such as the church which has

Cobija

BRAZIL

BRAZIL

Río Acre

To Peru

Ferry Boat Wharf

Bolivar

La Paz

Sucre

Nicolás Suárez

Immigration

Brazilian Consulate

Av Fernández Molina

11 de Octubre

C 9 de Febrero

C 4

LAB

Consejo

Ayacucho

16 de Julio

C 6

To S

BRAZIL

Río Acre

To Airport & Porvenir

Discoteca Lemon

El Curichí del Coco Karaoke

N

0 metres 100
0 yards 100

Sleeping
Prefectural Pando **1**
Residencial Cocodrilo **2**
Residencial Frontera **3**

Eating
Heladería El Tucano **1**
La Cabaina del Momo **2**
La Esquina de la Abuela **3**

Pescadería Danielita **5**
Snack Amazónico **4**

interesting primitive artwork. Scattered around the centre are a few original wooden buildings, constructed during the rubber boom. Most have long since rotted away in the intense heat and humidity, but a few interesting ones remain. Also on the plaza is the virtually redundant **tourist office**, whose city plan is hopelessly out of date as many of the streets marked on it are now non-existent due to the gradual encroachment of the surrounding jungle.

Beware of a man called Hector, who may befriend visitors and then try to cheat them out of money.

One thing Cobija does have is its **duty-free shopping** offering a huge selection of imported consumer goods at bargain prices to the Brazilians and Peruvians who flock here to stock up. Natives, however, reap no savings on prices and, in fact, pay a lot more than the rest of the country for almost everything thanks to the town's relative isolation.

Crossing to Brazil and Peru from Cobija

To Brazil
Travellers should note that there are now two official points of departure from Cobija, both of which lead to Brasileia on the opposite bank. One is by boat from the ferry boat wharf just off C Bolívar at the west end of town. The other is via the international bridge at the other end of town. The former is often quicker, and certainly cheaper (US$0.35), as taxis are expensive (US$12). Note that buses do not cross into Brazil. All visitors must carry a Yellow Fever vaccination certificate, which can be obtained at the hospital in Cobija, and go to the Policia Federal on arrival in Brasileia.

To Peru
Crossing into Peru is difficult but not impossible. But travellers should note that the Peruvian department of Madre de Dios is still considered dangerous from narco-terrorist activities. The crossing is best attempted by cargo boat from Porvenir, but only after securing all necessary papers. Travellers without the necessary documents will be turned back at the border. There is no Peruvian consulate in Cobija.

Southern Beni

Another route into the Beni Department is via the lowland road between Cochabamba and Santa Cruz. At Ivirgarzama, east of Villa Tunari, the road passes the turn-off to Puerto Villarroel, 27 km further north. Do note that, as this is coca-growing territory, the police advise against people straying from the main road, talking to strangers and guarding or carrying other people's luggage.

Puerto Villarroel
From here cargo boats ply irregularly to Trinidad taking between four and ten days. You can get information from the Port Captain's notice board, or ask at the docks.There are only a few cheap and very basic places to sleep in town, and there are very few stores.

By boat to Trinidad
Puerto Villarroel is the main port for river transport to the north of Bolivia. The road network is being extended, but many roads can only be used in the dry season. Boats sail between Puerto Villarroel, Trinidad and Guayaramerín, taking passengers. In the rainy season when the river is high it takes appoximately three to five days to Trinidad, which involves 45 hours of actual sailing, but boats do stop from

Be warned, this trip is only for the hardy traveller.

sunrise to sunset. It will cost you US$15 for three days and nights which includes meals, though prices and quality will vary. In the dry season (between May and June, and August to December), it may last eight to ten days. At this time the river is lower, cleaner and there may be more animals to see on the shore, but there may be no boats October-December. It is another five days to Guayaramerín.

If you are fussy about food in general, don't make the trip because the boat's kitchens are beyond description as are toilet facilities. Take your own drinking water, or water sterilizing tablets, as the water served is taken from the river. Supplement the diet with fruit and any other interesting food you can find beforehand. The countryside between Puerto Villarroel and Trinidad is more or less cultivated, with plantations of bananas and cattle ranches. Among the wildlife you can see are petas – small turtles basking in the sun – capybara, river dolphin, jumping fish, the occasional monkey on the beach, and many types of birds. A mosquito net is a 'must', a hammock a good idea, and binoculars for watching the wildlife a useful extra. Bathing in the river is said to be safe, but check first with the locals.

● Sleeping

Northeastern area *p377*
Riberalta
C Hostal Tahuamanu, M Hanicke 75, T03-8528006. Modern, smart, very comfortable, a/c, includes excellent breakfast. Highly recommended.
F Colonial, Plácido Méndez 1. Charming colonial casona, large, well-furnished rooms, nice gardens and courtyard, comfortable, good beds, helpful owners. Highly recommended.
F Comercial Lazo, C Salvatierra. (**D** with a/c.) Comfortable, laundry facilities, good value.
G Residencial El Pauro, Salvatierra 157. Basic, shared bathrooms, good café.
F Residencial Los Reyes, near the airport. With fan, safe, pleasant but noisy disco nearby on Sat and Sun.

Guayaramerín
B Esperanza, Casilla 171. Outside Guayaramerín in nearby Cachuela Esperanza is the eco-friendly Esperanza. You can book in La Paz through **America Tours**, T02-2374204, F02-2310023, www.america-ecotours.com Price includes breakfast.
C San Carlos, 6 de Agosto, 4 blocks from the port, with a/c (**D** without), hot showers, changes dollars cash, travellers' cheques and Brazilian reais, swimming pool, restaurant.
F Litoral, on 25 de Mayo, near the LAB office. Cold water only, free coffee. Recommended.
G Plaza Anexo, on the plaza. Good value, cold water only, ceiling fan.
F Santa Ana, 25 de Mayo, (**G** without bathroom), close to airport. Recommended.

Cobija *p378, map p378*
E Prefectural Pando, on C Ayacucho, 1 block from the Brazilian consulate (see below), T03-8422230. Includes breakfast, comedor does good lunch, poor value, manager Sr Angel Gil is helpful.
F Residencial Cocodrilo, Av Molina, T03-8422215. Comfortable, good atmosphere, rooms with fan.
G Residencial Frontera, behind the Brazilian consulate, T03-8422740. Fan rooms with private bathroom, breakfast included, basic but adequate and clean.

● Eating

Northeastern area *p377*
Riberalta
At the *comedor popular* in the **market** you can get a good lunch for US$1.50.
$ Club Social Progreso, on the plaza, good value *almuerzo*, excellent fish.
$ Club Social Riberalta, on Maldonado, good almuerzo US$3.50, smart dress only.
$ Quatro Ases, C Arce, good.
$ Tom Bowles, on the plaza, good food and a good meeting place.
$ Tucunare, M Chávez Martínez, recommended.
$ Tropical, nice atmosphere, serving good typical food.

Guayaramerín
$ Gipssy, on the plaza, good almuerzo.
$ Los Bibosis, on the plaza, popular with visiting Brazilians.

$ Only, 25 de Mayo y Beni, serves a good *almuerzo* for US$2.50, plus Chinese.

Cafés
Heladería Tutti-Frutti, on the road to the airport, is excellent.
Made in Brazil, on the plaza, good coffee. There's a great bar on C Villa Bella, a few yards from C Nicolás Suárez.

Cobija *p378, map p378*
Most food here is a delicious mixture of Brazilian and Yungas-inspired dishes.
$$ La Cabaina del Momo, just down the road a bit from the Heladería. Cobija's only true *churrasquería* offering a unique mix of Brazilian and Argentine meat dishes, all for under US$4.
$ La Esquina de la Abuela, at Av Molina and C Sucre. The overwhelmingly favourite place to eat, where you'll find excellent dishes at reasonable prices.
$ Pescadería Danielita, just outside town, on the west end of C Cornejo. Specialises in fish dishes. Good cheap meals can also be found in the comedor popular in the central market.
$ Snack Amazónico, at the far end of C Nicolás Suárez, near the ferry. Serves cheap meals, including fresh fish.

Cafés
Heladería El Tucano, opposite La Esquina, which serves ice cream and conveniently doubles as a liquor store.

⊙ Entertainment

Cobija *p378, map p378*
There are 2 good discos: **El Curichi del Coco Karaoke** and **Discoteca Lemon**, on opposite sides of C 16 de Julio on the way to the old airport. The others are best avoided.

⊛ Festivals and events

Cobija *p378, map p378*
Aug Feria de Muestras, in the last week of Aug, which showcases local crafts.
24 Sep Festival takes place.

Northeastern area *p377*
Riberalta
Air
Aero Sur, on the plaza, Acera Norte 20, T03-8522798, flies 6 times weekly to **Trinidad**. Expect delays in the wet season.
LAB fly to **Guayaramerín**, **Trinidad**, **La Paz**, **Cobija** and **Cochabamba**; office at M Chávez 77, T03-8522239. They only accept cash.
TAM flies to **Cochabamba**, **Santa Cruz** and **La Paz** (US$98 one way); their office is at Av Suárez Chuquisaca, T03-8523924.
SAVE flies to and from **La Paz**, **Santa Cruz** and **Trinidad**; T03-8522870. Check all flight details in advance.

Buses
Several companies (including **Yungueña**) go to **La Paz**, via Rurrenabaque and Caranavi Tue-Sat at 1100, also Tue, Thu and Sat at 1000; US$22.40. **Yungueña** leaves from Villa Fátima in La Paz daily at 1030, US$22.40, as does **Flota Unificada** but more pricey and not on Sun, Mon and Wed.

There are services to **Trinidad** with **8 de Deciembre** on Mon, Wed, Thu, Sat and Sun at 0830, also **Trans Guaya** daily at 0930, via Rurrenabaque.

To **Guayaramerín**, there are 12 weekly services, Tue, Thu, Sat and Sun at 0630, 1400, 1700; daily with **TransAmazonas** at 0730, 1630.

To **Cobija** on Wed, Fri and Sat at 0900 with **8 de Diciembre**; Mon and Thu at 1000 with **TransAmazonas**. Buses stop in Santa Rosa for meals.

River
Cargo boats carry passengers along the Río Madre de Dios, but they are infrequent. There are not many boats to Rurrenabaque.

Guayaramerín
Air
Aero Sur, C Macal, Santa Cruz 57, T03-8553594. Flights to **Trinidad**.
LAB, 25 de Mayo 652, T03-8553540, flies to **Trinidad**, **Riberalta**, **La Paz**, **Cobija** and **Cochabamba**.

The Amazon Northern Beni and Pando Listings

🔴 *Price codes for Sleeping and Eating are given inside the front cover. Further information on*
⚫ *hotel and restaurant grading can be found in Essentials, pages 43-44.*

TAM flies to **Cochabamba**, **Santa Cruz** and **La Paz**; office at 16 de Julio on the road to the airport.

There are also flights with **SAVE**, T03-8553882.

Bus

To **La Paz**, daily with **Flota Yungueña**, 0830, 36-38 hrs, US$22.40. From La Paz (office in Villa Fátima by petrol station), 1030. Also **Flota Unificada**, leaving La Paz Tue, Thu, Fri and Sat at 1030, US$26.90.

To **Riberalta**, 2 hrs, US$5.75, 7 departures daily 0700-1730. To **Trinidad**, on Fri, 30 hrs, US$23. To **Rurrenabaque**, US$16. To **Cobija**, 4 a week. To **Santa Cruz** via Trinidad, 1-2 a week, 2½ days.

Buses leave from General Federico Román. Roads to all destinations are very difficult in the wet season – the roads are generally appalling as it is.

River

Check the list of boats leaving port on the Port Captain's noticeboard, prominently displayed near the immigration post on the river bank. Boats up the Mamoré to **Trinidad** are fairly frequent – every 3 days at the most.

Cobija *p378, map p378*

Air

Aero Sur, Av Fernandez Molina, T03-8423132, flies daily except Sun to **Trinidad** and to **La Paz**, 3 times a week. The **LAB** office is on René Barrientos 343, T03-8422170; they fly to **Riberalta**, **Guayaramerín**, **Trinidad** and **La Paz**. **SAVE**, T03-8423090, flies to/from **La Paz**, **Santa Cruz** and **Trinidad**. **TAM** office is on 2 de Febrero, T03-8422267; check their schedule as it changes frequently.

Buses

The **Flota Yungueña** goes to **La Paz** via Riberalta and Rurrenabaque on Sat at 0700 (check the times first, T03-8422318). To **Riberalta** several bus companies and trucks, which leave from 2 de Febrero, most on Wed, Fri and Sun at 0600. The road is a good all-weather surface, the journey involves 5 river crossings on pontoon rafts and takes 10-11 hrs.

Taxi

Taxis are very expensive, charging according to time and distance – US$10 to the outskirts, US$12 over the international bridge to Brasileia. Besides regular taxis there are much cheaper motorbike taxis.

Southern Beni *p379*

Puerto Villarroel

Camionetas go from the junction on the main road at Ivirgazama to Puerto Villarroel a few times a day, 1 hr, US$1.20. From Cochabamba you can get a bus to Puerto Villarroel (see Cochabamba buses, page 287), Puerto San Francisco, or Todos Santos on the Río Chapare. Sr Arturo Linares at the Cede office organises boat trips to the jungle, but it's not cheap.

❶ Directory

Northeastern area *p377*

Riberalta

Banks No banks or ATMs, but you can change cash in shops and on the street.

Cobija *p378, map p378*

Banks There are money changers in abundance here, especially along Av 2 de Febrero. Brazilian reais are accepted by many places; Peruvian soles much less so. **Casa de Cambio Horacio** offers decent rates for dollars, bolivianos and reais; they have offices at C Cornejo and 11 de Octubre, and on Av Internacional opposite the cemetery on the east side of town. **Embassies and consulates** Brazil, on C Beni and Av Molina, 1 block east of the plaza, T8422188, open 0830-1230 weekdays. **Internet** 100 m from the main plaza, near the university. **Medical services** There is an old hospital, a recently built one (Japanese-funded), and the Red Cross. **Post Office** on the plaza. **Telephone** Entel on C Sucre, for national and international telephone calls and fax, which are much cheaper than from Brazil. **Useful addresses** Immigration: open weekdays only from 0900 to 1800, for entry or exit stamps.

Background

⁛ Footprint features

History

Pre-conquest history

The barren, windswept Altiplano, the highest plateau in Latin America, has been home to various indigenous cultures from the earliest times. Artefacts found on the Altiplano date the first human occupation at around 7000-8000 BC. Early man followed a seasonal cycle of hunting and gathering around the shores of Lake Titicaca, travelling as far as the eastern valleys and the desert coast of southern Peru and northern Chile.

One of the most important developments of life on the Altiplano was the domestication of the llama and alpaca, which centred around Lake Titicaca and developed in conjunction with arable farming. The llama was of crucial importance to the Altiplano people. It provided protein to supplement their basic diet as well as wool for weaving and was also a beast of burden. The combination of the domestication of camelids and the development of arable farming helped give rise to the great Andean civilizations.

Tiahuanaco

The greatest of the pre-Inca civilizations is at Tiahuanaco, or Tiwanaku (see page 140). Most visitors are aware of this mysterious site just south of Lake Titicaca but few people understand the extent of this culture's influence throughout the South Central Andes and the reason for its sudden demise. The remains of Tiahuanaco culture show that the inhabitants reached a high degree of development and organization. Remains of a huge ceremonial and urban centre with palaces, temples and pyramids, elaborate textiles and beautiful pottery suggest a sophisticated culture.

Sustained by forms of intensive arable farming, the Tiahuanaco region became one of the most densely populated areas of the Altiplano. The influence of the culture gradually spread to other areas, through military conquest or trade. After around AD 500 its influence was felt in almost all parts of Bolivia, southern Peru, northern Chile and northwest Argentina. Civilization reached its high point here around AD 1000, after which a period of decline set in, leading to its complete collapse around AD 1100-1200. The cause of its sudden demise remains a mystery.

After Tiahuanaco

After the fall of Tiahuanaco a proliferation of distinct political groups evolved to control the vast territory formerly under the influence of the great empire. These independent Aymara Kingdoms, which shared a common language and many cultural patterns, played a leading role on the Altiplano for 300 years until the arrival of the Spaniards. Each kingdom boasted a powerful organization based on a collective and military model.

At the centre of Aymara society were the *ayllus*, groups based on kinship which owned and worked the land collectively (see also page 413). The Aymaras cultivated potatoes and cereal crops and kept llamas and alpacas for meat, milk and wool and used them as pack-animals. Indeed, the wealth of the kingdoms was measured in the number of alpacas and llamas. Like the Tiahuanaco Empire before them, the Aymaras maintained important connections with communities in the eastern valleys and on the Pacific coast. They exchanged potatoes, meat and wool from the cold, barren plateau for fruit, vegetables, maize and coca from the subtropical valleys.

The most powerful kingdoms were the Lupaca, based at Chuquito, southwest of Lake Titicaca, and the Colla, with their capital at Huatuncolla, near present-day Puno. These two kingdoms were in constant warfare until around 1430, when the Lupaca conquered the Colla.

The Incas

While the Aymara were fighting among themselves to establish their territorial rights to lands around the Titicaca basin, the Quechua-speaking Incas from Cusco were preparing to invade the kingdoms and incorporate them into their expanding empire. Despite the fact that they were divided, the Aymaras resisted obstinately and were not finally conquered until the latter part of the 15th century in the reign of Inca Túpac Yupangi (1471-1493).

The origins of the Inca Dynasty are shrouded in mythology and shaky evidence. The best known story reported by the Spanish chroniclers talks about Manco Capac and his sister rising out of Lake Titicaca, created by the Sun as divine founders of a chosen race. This was in approximately AD 1200. Over the next 300 years the small tribe grew to supremacy as leaders of the largest empire ever known in the Americas, the four territories of Tawantinsuyo, united by Cusco as the umbilicus of the Universe. The four quarters of Tawantinsuyo, radiating out from Cusco, were: 1 – Chinchaysuyo, including northern Peru and Ecuador; 2 – Cuntisuyo, including the coastal lands; 3 – Collasuyo, southern Peru, Bolivia and Chile; 4 – Antisuyo, the eastern highlands of Peru.

At its peak, just before the Spanish Conquest, the Inca Empire stretched from the Río Maule in central Chile, north to the present Ecuador-Colombia border, containing most of Ecuador, Peru, western Bolivia, northern Chile and northwest Argentina. The area was roughly equivalent to France, Belgium, Holland, Luxembourg, Italy and Switzerland combined, a total of 980,000 square kilometres.

The first Inca ruler, Manco Capac, moved to the fertile Cusco region, and established Cusco as his capital. Successive generations of rulers were fully occupied with local conquests of rivals, such as the Colla and Lupaca to the south, and the Chanca to the northwest. At the end of Manco Capac's reign the hated Chanca were finally defeated, largely thanks to the heroism of one of his sons, Pachacuti Inca Yupangui, who was subsequently crowned as the new ruler.

From the start of Pachacuti's own reign in 1438, imperial expansion grew in earnest. With the help of his son and heir, Topa Inca, territory was conquered from the Titicaca basin south into Chile, and all the north and central coast of Peru. Typical of the Inca method of government was to assimilate the skills of their defeated enemies into their own political and administrative system.

Though the Incas respected the languages and cultures of the subjugated peoples and only insisted on imposing their religion, a certain amount of Quechuanization did occur. Around Lake Titicaca Aymara language and culture remained practically intact but the cultural and linguistic traditions of other peoples of the Altiplano were almost completely displaced, especially as groups of Quechua-speaking Incas were brought from Peru to live and work in Collasuyo. But Inca culture was tied to the highlands and they never succeeded in annexing all of the peoples of Bolivia. Their powerful armies could not defeat the semi-nomadic peoples in the lower-lying Valles (valleys) and the eastern plains, such as the Guaraníes.

Although the Incas left a great impression on the country in the shape of an extensive road system, architecture, ceramics and metal artefacts and established their own language in many parts, the duration of their stay in Bolivia was no more than 80 years.

Conquest and after

The end of the Inca Empire was signalled by the landing of Francisco Pizarro in Peru in 1532. The political capital, Cusco, fell in 1535 and soon afterwards the Spanish began the conquest of Bolivia. Diego de Almagro travelled south with an army of Spanish and native forces through Bolivia to the Chilean coast and in 1542 the entire area was annexed as the Audencia of Charcas of the Viceroyalty of Peru.

During the Spanish colonization, towns were founded and grew rapidly. In 1538 La Plata, now Sucre, was founded and, in 1559 became capital of the Audiencia of Charcas (it is still the official capital of Bolivia). Another administrative centre, La Paz, was founded in 1548. In the eastern lowlands the colonization process was rather different. Like the Incas before them, the Spaniards experienced enormous difficulties in conquering the native peoples of this region. Apart from a number of Jesuit mission settlements (see page 328), the Spanish presence here remained limited to the town of Santa Cruz.

At first the Spanish left the existing socio-economic structure more or less intact. They also adopted the system of compulsory labour (*mita*) which the Incas had imposed, though much more forcefully. Over time Spanish rule became more aggressive and motivated solely by greed. The barter economy and communal working of the land were replaced by a society based on the extraction and exportation of wealth through the ownership of large estates (*haciendas*) and mining.

Bolivia's destiny was shaped in 1545 with the discovery of silver at Cerro Rico (Rich Mountain) in Potosí (see page 236). Charcas became one of the most important centres of the Spanish colonial economy, sending a constant supply of silver to Spain. The mining town of Potosí grew rapidly and by 1610 had a population of over 160,000, making it for a long time, by far the largest city in Latin America. Potosí's opulent extravagance became legendary and for decades a favourite Spanish description for untold wealth was 'vale un Potosí' (worth a Potosí).

Together with precious metals from smaller mining centres such as Oruro, silver from Cerro Rico was crucial to the maintenance of the Spanish empire and financed their wars in Europe. Many hundreds of thousands of Indians were forced to work in the mines as miners, in the workshops of the crown mint or on the haciendas.

The Spaniards regarded the indigenous peoples as inferior and cared little for their welfare. The suppression of indigenous culture went as far as making it compulsory to wear Spanish-style dress. According to popular belief this is the origin of many of Bolivia's distinctive hats and the *chola's* skirts (see page 414). The mortality rate among the Indians was high, because of appalling working conditions in the mines and the import of European diseases, against which the indigenous population had little resistance. By the mid 17th century the Indian population had been almost halved.

During the 18th century many of Potosí's rich silver veins became exhausted and the colony of Alto Perú (as Bolivia was known), lost much of its influence.

Independence

Resistance to Spanish colonial rule had been less intense in Bolivia than neighbouring Peru. The most notable uprisings took place in the years between 1780 and 1782, led by Túpac Katari, and were eventually crushed. But inspired by the French and American revolutions at the end of the 18th century, the *criollos*, descendants of Spaniards born in Latin America, became increasingly frustrated by trade restrictions and high taxes imposed by the Spanish bureaucracy in the interests of Spain.

While Spain was occupied defending its borders against Napoleon's armies between 1808 and 1810, the University of San Francisco Xavier, at Sucre, called for the independence of all Spain's American colonies. When Spain tried to restore its rule in the following years the *criollo* commercial elites rebelled and took up arms against the Spanish authorities, under the leadership of the Venezuelan Simón Bolívar. On 9 December 1824 Simón Bolívar's general, General Antonio José de Sucre, won the decisive battle of Ayacucho in Peru and invaded Alto Perú, defeating the Spaniards finally at the battle of Tumusla on 2 April 1825.

On 9 February 1825, when he first entered La Paz, Sucre had already promulgated the decree of independence, but his second in command, Santa Cruz, was for retaining links with Peru. Bolívar was in two minds, but Sucre had his way and Bolivia was declared independent on 6 August in Sucre. In honour of its liberator, the country was named República de Bolívar, soon to be changed to Bolivia. La Plata became the capital and Sucre became the first president.

Post-independence

For most of the period since independence, three main features have dominated Bolivian history: the importance of mining; the loss of territory through disputes and wars with neighbouring countries; and chronic political instability.

The noble principles of revolution were soon forgotten as the *caudillos* (military 'strongman' leaders) revealed themselves as defenders of the political and economic status quo. Although in the 19th century the army was small, officers were key figures in power-struggles, often backing different factions of the *criollo* landowning elite, whose interests had replaced those of the former colonial rulers. At the end of the 19th century the political elite ended the existence of the *ayllus*, the Indian communal lands, which were swallowed up into the huge ranches (*latifundios*) of the landowners. The Indians, who had suffered under the *mita*, the system of compulsory labour, became serfs, as their lives and labour were owned by the estate owners.

Although silver had been so important in the colonial period, the Bolivian economy has depended for much of this century on exports of tin. The construction of railways and the demand for tin in Europe and the USA (particularly in wartime) led to a mining boom after 1900. In 1902 tin's export earnings exceeded those of silver for the first time. By the 1920s the industry was dominated by three entrepreneurs, Simón Patiño, Mauricio Hochschild and the Aramayo family, who exercised great influence over national politics.

Political instability

Bolivian politics have been even more turbulent than elsewhere in Latin America. When the governing class was not engaged in conflicts with neighbouring countries, internal power struggles consumed all its energies. Between 1825 and 1982 there were no fewer than 188 coups d'état, earning the country a place in the Guinness Book of Records. The longest lasting government of the 19th century was that of Andrés Santa Cruz (1829-1839), but when he tried to unite Bolivia with Peru in 1836, Chile and Argentina intervened to overthrow him.

After the War of the Pacific (1879-1883) there was greater stability, but opposition to the political dominance of the city of Sucre culminated in a revolt in 1899 led by business groups from La Paz and the tin-mining areas, as a result of which La Paz became the centre of government.

Since independence Bolivia has suffered continual losses of territory, partly because of communications difficulties and the central government's inability to control distant provinces. One of the most politically damaging of these losses came as a consequence of a long-running dispute with Paraguay over the Chaco which erupted into war in 1932 and ended in ignominious defeat in 1935 and the loss of three quarters of the Chaco.

The Chaco War was a turning point in Bolivian history. The political influence of the army increased and in 1936 it seized power for the first time since the War of the Pacific. Defeat in the Chaco War bred nationalist resentment among junior army officers who had served in the Chaco and among the Indians who had been used as cannon-fodder. After demobilization thousands of Indians refused to return to serfdom. Instead they settled in towns where they played a significant part in the political radicalization of the population, particularly the peasants and miners.

This growing national malaise among different sectors of society led to a group of young intellectuals setting up a nationalist party, the Movimiento Nacional Revolucionario (MNR) headed by Víctor Paz Estenssoro, Hernán Siles Zuazo, Walter Guevara Arce and Juan Lechín Oquendo. Their anger was directed against the mine owners and the leaders who had controlled Bolivian politics and they claimed to stand for the emancipation of the poor masses.

In 1944 Víctor Paz Estenssoro, a key party leader, succeeded in taking the MNR into the radical government of young army officers led by Major Gualberto Villaroel. However, in 1946 Villaroel was overthrown and publicly lynched and Paz Estenssoro had to flee to Argentina.

The 1952 revolution

The 1951 elections were won by Víctor Paz, the MNR candidate. However, the incumbent government refused to recognize the result and transferred power to a military junta. The organized and radicalized miners reacted immediately and revolution broke out on 9 April 1952, backed by sections of the police as well as the campesinos, urban factory workers and the lower middle classes. Two days later the army surrendered to the MNR's militias and the National Revolution was a fact.

Paz Estenssoro became president and his MNR government nationalized the mines, introduced universal suffrage and began the break-up and redistribution of large estates under the Agrarian Reform programme of 1953 which ended the feudal economic conditions of rural Bolivia. In the aftermath of the revolution, the COB (Bolivian Workers Central), under the leadership of Juan Lechín Oquendo, became a major political force in the country. The giant mineral barons, Simón Patiño, Hochschild and Aramayo lost their massive political and economic influence and a new leadership class developed that would dominate Bolivia's political life for almost the next 40 years.

Post revolution

As the Bolivian constitution does not permit a second successive term of office, Paz Estenssoro stood down in 1956 in favour of the more pragmatic Vice-President Siles Zuazo. Faced with a drastic fall in the price of tin, Bolivia's main source of foreign income, and galloping inflation, Siles Zuazo accepted a 'stabilization' plan designed by the International Monetary Fund (IMF). Hardest hit by the policy of freezing wages and scrapping basic food subsidies were the working class and the MNR became increasingly distanced from its original power base. The rank and file of the MNR split into peasants on the one side and miners and the urban proletariat on the other.

Víctor Paz, who had now become leader of the centre-right faction within the MNR, was re-elected president in 1960, with Juan Lechín Oquendo as Vice-President. Growing ideological divides were tearing the party apart and by 1964 it disintegrated into factional warfare. The constitution had to be changed to allow Paz Estenssoro to stand again, which he did with the support of the charismatic General René Barrientos. Shortly afterwards, however, Víctor Paz was overthrown by his Vice-President, who relied on the support of the army and the peasants to defeat the miners.

⫶ The Chaco War

In the 1920s the US Standard Oil Company was drilling for oil in the Bolivian Chaco. The company and the Bolivian government had designs on the Río Pilcomayo to transport the oil to the coast. It also seemed likely that there were further reserves in other parts of the inaccessible wilderness of the Chaco plain.

The problem was, however, that the Bolivian frontier with Paraguay had never been precisely defined. From 1928 there were border clashes with Paraguayan army patrols and in 1932 the Chaco War broke out. The Paraguayan forces knew the terrain much better than the Bolivian soldiers, who were mostly from the Andes and unused to the intense heat and humidity. By 1935 Bolivia had lost the war, practically the whole of the Chaco and 55,000 lives, but it did keep the oil-fields. Paraguay, though, won no more than a symbolic victory as no oil has ever been found in the Chaco.

Military coups

As in many other Latin American countries, the 1960s and 1970s were dominated in Bolivia by coups d'état and military governments. The many military dictatorships of this period were very different in nature. Some were authoritarian and repressive while others were more populist. Under the Barrientos régime (1964-1969) political opponents and trade union activists were brutally persecuted and miners' rebellions were put down violently, just as they had been before the Revolution. The death of Barrientos in a mysterious air crash in 1969 was followed by three brief military governments. The third, led by General Juan José Torres, pursued left-wing policies which alarmed many army officers and business leaders.

In August 1971 Torres was overthrown by the right-wing General Hugo Banzer, whose rule lasted until 1978. During those years tens of thousands of Bolivians were imprisoned or exiled for political reasons. Apart from the Bolivian Socialist Falange (FSB) and the MNR, which shared government with the military for the first three years, all political parties and trade unions were banned. The state universities were subject to military supervision and there was strict censorship. In 1974 the MNR left the government and Paz Estenssoro, who had returned in 1971, went back into exile. The new Banzer régime continued to rule in an even more authoritarian manner, though mild by comparison with contemporary régimes in Argentina and Chile. In 1978 Banzer was forced to call elections, partly as a result of the pressure which US President Jimmy Carter exerted on the military government because of its human rights abuses.

There followed another period of chronic instability, political unrest and military violence between 1978 and 1982, with three presidential elections and five coups. Civilian rule returned on 10 October 1982 when Hernán Siles Zuazo once again took office, but not before the notoriously brutal military coup led by General García Meza (1980-1981). In August 1982 the military returned to barracks and Siles Zuazo assumed the presidency in a leftist coalition government with support from the communists and trade unions. Under this régime inflation spiralled out of control.

Towards democracy

The elections of 14 July 1985 were won again by Víctor Paz Estenssoro, but only by forming a coalition with Jaime Paz Zamora of the Movimiento de la Izquierda Revolucionaria (MIR). In order to save the economy, Víctor Paz enlisted the help of Dr Jeffrey Sachs, a Harvard professor who imposed a radical programme of structural adjustment, known as the New Economic Policy (NEP).

⁝ War of the Pacific

One of the major international wars in Latin America since independence, this conflict has its roots in a long-running dispute between Chile and Bolivia over the ill-defined frontier in the Atacama desert.

There had already been one conflict, in 1836-1839, when Chile defeated Peru and Bolivia, putting an end to a confederation of the two states. The discovery of nitrates in the Atacama complicated relations. In the Bolivian Atacama province of Antofagasta nitrates were exploited by Anglo-Chilean companies.

In 1878 the Bolivian government, short of revenue, attempted to tax the Chilean-owned Antofagasta Railroad and Nitrate Company. When the company refused to pay, the Bolivians seized the company's assets. The Chilean government claimed that the Bolivian action broke an 1874 agreement between the two states. When Peru announced that it would honour a secret alliance with Bolivia by supporting her, the Chilean president, Aníbal Pinto, declared war on both states.

Despite several naval defeats and the loss of its capital, Peru did not sue for peace, although Bolivia had already signed a ceasefire as early as 1880, giving up its coastal province. Under the 1883 peace settlement

Peru gave up Tarapacá to Chile. Although the provinces of Tacna and Arica were to be occupied by Chile for 10 years, it was not until 1929 that an agreement was reached under which Tacna was returned to Peru, while Chile kept Arica. Apart from souring relations between Chile and her two northern neighbours to this day, the war gave Chile a monopoly over the world's supply of nitrates and enabled her to dominate the southern Pacific coast.

With the loss of its Litoral province, Bolivia had lost its access to the sea. Many Bolivians still blame their country's underdevelopment on this event and since 1880 it has played an important part in foreign policy. During the dictatorship of Hugo Banzer (1971-1978) the issue of Bolivia's access to the sea flared up, allowing the general to divert attention from domestic problems. In 1976 there was even talk of war.

Since then there have been continual negotiations between Chile and Peru over Bolivia's rights to the coast. In 1992 President Paz Zamora succeeded in agreeing a treaty with Peru giving Bolivia a zona franca (free zone) along the road from La Paz to the southern Peruvian port of Ilo. For the first time since 1880 goods could be transported free of duty to and from Bolivia via the Pacific coast.

No one could have predicted it would be so tough. One of its main thrusts was the radical dismantling of the state sector which Víctor Paz had himself set up 30 years before. Under Professor Sach's neo-liberal economic model the first sacrificial targets were the by-now outdated mines of the state-owned Comibol. By the end of 1985, 23,000 miners lost their jobs. Some remained to form co-operatives but most left in search of new livelihoods in the coca regions of the Oriente, or in the larger cities.

In the elections of 7 May 1989 a new character appeared on the political stage, Gonzalo Sánchez de Lozada of the MNR, chief architect of the stabilization programme. Sánchez de Lozada, or 'Goni', won most votes but the result was so close that Congress had to choose a president from the three leading contenders. Paz Zamora, who came third in the elections, was inaugurated as President on 6 August 1989 after having made an unlikely alliance with the former military dictator, the retired General Hugo Banzer of Acción Democrática Nacionalista (ADN), in return for certain cabinet posts.

The presidential election of 6 June 1993 was fought between Acuerdo Patriótico, led by Hugo Banzer, a coalition of MIR, Banzer's own ADN and two other parties, Gonzalo Sánchez de Lozada of the MNR, Unidad Cívica de Solidaridad (UCS), led by the brewery owner Max Fernández, and the populist Conciencia de Patria (Condepa) of Carlos Palenque. Gonzalo Sánchez de Lozada won the greater number of votes but failed to gain the required 51 % majority to win the presidency outright.

Shortly afterwards, however, the other candidates recognized Sánchez de Lozada's victory and withdrew from the contest. In a shrewd move to gain the support of the Indian population, Goni formed an alliance with Víctor Hugo Cárdenas, leader of the **Movimiento Revolucionario Túpac Katari de Liberación** (MRTKL), one of Bolivia's two indigenist parties which aim to promote the emancipation of the Indian population.

The 1997 presidential elections were won by former dictator General Hugo Banzer (1971-1978) with 23% of the vote. Former president Jaime Paz Zamora (1989-1993), whose US visa was withdrawn in 1996 for alleged drug money links, came second with the next three parties all polling 15-17% of the vote. Banzer's party, Acción Democrática Nacionalista (ADN), became the dominant party in a new coalition with MIR, Unidad Cívica de Solidaridad (UCS) and Conciencia de Patria (Condepa), giving the government a large majority in the Senate and the lower house of Congress. Banzer and his advisers immediately took a flight to Washington DC to secure approval from the US. Interest- ingly, it was former US president Jimmy Carter's decision to stop funding Third World régimes with human rights problems which helped lead to Banzer's downfall in 1978.

Economically, Banzer supported the previous government's privatization programme (called capitalization in Bolivia), which saw the sale of major state-owned companies. Bolivia is the largest recipient of foreign aid in South America and so major economic policies must meet with World Bank and IMF approval. Banzer's first presidential decree was one promising continued support for the neo-liberal régime that had been forced on the country since 1985 when inflation hit 24,000%.

In his first two years in office, Banzer pursued economic austerity and the US-backed policy of eradicating coca production. By early 2000, however, economic hardship in rural areas, together with unemployment and anger at a plan to raise water rates in Cochabamba to fund an expensive new reservoir project led to violent protests and road blocks in many parts of the country. Several people were killed and Banzer called a state of emergency. Amid the confusion, the police seized the moment to go on strike for higher pay (some earn only US$65 per month). This left Banzer without his specially trained riot control squads and within 48 hours the government capitulated, granting a 50% pay rise. It also backed down over the Cochabamba water scheme. But that may not be enough to end the discontent and frustration at poor economic performance and growing poverty. The coca eradication programme has had a side- effect of cutting incomes, albeit 'illegal' ones. An economic reactivation plan is seen as favouring big business, while two out of three live below the poverty line. In late April a truce was drawn up between the authorities and the radical new campesino leader, Felipe Quispe, giving the government 90 days to address the demands of the protesters.

Through 2001 and into 2002, the situation had hardly improved and demonstrations large and small against social conditions were held throughout the country. In early 2001 the Ministry of the Economy highlighted the acute hardship in a report that stated that five out of eight Bolivians live in poverty with inadequate basic food supplies, high illiteracy, and no access to transportation, irrigation or means of financial betterment. With the country's economic and social problems still severe, President Banzer was forced to resign in August 2001 because of cancer. His replacement, Vice-President Jorge Quiroga, had just a year left of Banzer's term to serve before new elections would be held.

In 2002 Gonzalo Sánchez de Lozada won the election and became president for a second time. However, Evo Morales, the leader of the coca-growers union also strengthened his position as leader of the opposition. The following year tension between the government boiled over - more than 30 people were killed in February in protests about tax, and 80 were killed and hundreds injured in October in protests about gas. Lozada was forced from office and into exile in the United States, to be succeeded by his deputy, Carlos Mesa. In 2004, at least partly in response to further protests, congress passed a measure calling for Lozada to brought to court. It seems unlikely, however, that he will return from the United States to face what he claims would be an unfair trial.

Thus far, Mesa has been cleverer than his predecessor at walking the fine line between the demands of the empowered militant left and pressure from big business and the United States. In July 2004 he called, and won, a referendum allowing Bolivia to export gas via its neighbour but long-time enemy Chile. However, the wording of the referendum was vague enough to allow congress to negate Mesa's intentions and to try to further raise taxes on foreign companies exploiting Bolivia's massive natural gas reserves. In Mesa's view, such a move would make it unlikely that foreign companies would want to invest in the country.

Though much of the focus in Bolivian politics is on the coca issue, the gas issue is an even bigger one: stocks of natural gas are estimated to be worth US$70 billion. Not only an economic issue, it's also an emotive one. Morales and his allies look back at their history, at what happened to the 62,000 tonnes of silver mined from Potosí's mountain and see a parallel – their worry is that the country's natural resources will disappear overseas and the ordinary Bolivian people will see no benefit.

Economy

Estimates from 2003 put Bolivia's GDP at US$21.01 billion, placing its economy between that of Afghanistan and Mozambique on the world and making it, apart from the Guianas, the smallest economy in South America. 70% live below the poverty line, with GDP per capita standing at around US$2,400 and the average wage around US$900. **Transparency International** rates the country as one of the world's most corrupt.

Agriculture is an important sector of the economy, contributing 15% of GDP and employing over a third of the population. Small scale farming of traditional products is in the highlands, where excess produce is sold in local markets. In the east, however, there is very fertile land. The most productive area is in the province of Santa Cruz, where the fluvial plains are extremely rich in nutrients. Here the tropical climate allows two crops a year of soya beans and farmers achieve yields of around three tonnes a hectare, compared with 1½-2 tonnes in neighbouring countries. Bolivian and foreign investors have bought large estates to grow soya and other crops, such as cotton, sunflower and sugar, and agroindustry is booming as processing plants are built.

Mining contributes only 10% to GDP, but is an area of considerable investment and growth. Bolivia is a major producer of tin, antimony, wolfram, bismuth, silver, lead, zinc and gold, while there are large reserves of iron, lithium and potassium. The state mining company, Comibol, closed most of its operations during the recession of the 1980s, forcing unemployment for 23,000 miners. In the mid-1990s all Comibol's deposits, mines, smelters and refineries were put up for sale. Comibol remained as a small operation to administer leasing and joint venture contracts. The 1991 Mining Code allows equal treatment for foreign and national companies and free remittances of profits abroad. Foreigners in joint ventures with Bolivians

The Cocaine President

In the elections of June 1980, Hernán Siles Zuazo managed to gain a decisive lead over his opponents but yet again a military *coup d'état* was to prevent the country from having its elected civilian president when the army commander Luís García Meza seized power.

A period of brutal repression began in which human rights abuses were more widespread than ever before. The régime's involvement with notorious Nazis such as Klaus Barbie and neo-fascists from Argentina and elsewhere was an open secret. Paramilitary groups made frequent night raids on political opponents, dragging them from their beds and subjecting them to torture. Following Pinochet's example in Chile, the sports stadium in La Paz was used as a prison camp. Other subversive elements were imprisoned in concentration camps in the Oriente.

García Meza's government was the most corrupt Bolivia has ever known. The dictator and his partners-in-crime amassed huge fortunes through their close involvement with the national and international drug mafia. As a result the US and most other states would not recognize the regime and Bolivia became an outcast. The end of the cocaine regime came in August 1981 when García Meza was replaced by a military junta angered that his corrupt administration had brought the armed forces into disrepute.

Despite the innumerable human rights violations and his involvement in cocaine trafficking, García Meza did not face trial until 1993, when he was sentenced to 30 years in prison. Although several of his accomplices were imprisoned at the same time on human rights charges, García Meza himself managed to escape during the much-publicized trial. He was captured in Brazil in early 1994 and held there by the military until February 1995, when he was extradited to Bolivia. He is now held in solitary confinement in a prison outside La Paz.

may now explore the previously prohibited zones within 50 kilometres of borders. Investor interest is considerable, particularly in gold. The Kori Kollo gold mine, near Oruro, is the second largest in Latin America. Total gold output is about 14 tonnes a year, making it a leading export earner. Although Bolivia is one of the largest producers of tin in the world, low prices in the 1980s and 1990s have reduced export income. The Cordillera Real is the traditional mining zone for silver and tin, but companies are now looking in the west Cordillera and east towards the Brazilian border where mineral deposits are unexploited. There are iron reserves at El Mutun in Busch province on the border with Brazil, believed to be 40,000 tonnes with 30-50% iron, making it one of the world's largest deposits.

The oil and gas industry provides the Government with its largest single source of income. The state oil and gas company, Yacimientos Petrolíferos Fiscales Bolivianos (YPFB), was the largest company in Bolivia in 1994 with a workforce of 14,900. YPFB was partly 'capitalized' in 1996. The issue of gas exports has become a highly politically charged one, with massive strikes and protests in 2003 and 2004 leading to many deaths and the resignation of President Lozada. Bolivia's natural gas reserves are estimated to be worth US$70 billion and probably hold the key to the future of the Bolivian economy.

Things go better with Coke

Coca was first cultivated in the warm valleys (Yungas) of the eastern Andes by the Aymara Indians many, many centuries ago. Awareness of coca in the First World is rather more recent, however. In 1862 German chemists had taken coca leaves brought by an Austrian scientific expedition from Peru and isolated an alkaloid, or nitrogen-based compound which they labelled *cocain*. By around 1880, it was being tried as a cure for opium addiction and alcoholism. The young Dr Sigmund Freud, reading of its effect on tired soldiers, took some himself and pronounced it a "magical substance", which was "wonderfully stimulating".

Today, there is a huge demand for this drug from the millions of North Americans and Europeans who snort, smoke or inject it. Supply on this scale is not a problem. Making cocaine hydrochloride is as easy as baking bread. The leaves go into a plastic pit with a solution of water and a little sulphuric acid where they are left to soak for a few days. Then follows a succession of mixing and stirring with more chemicals until the liquid turns milky-white and then curdles, leaving tiny, ivory-coloured granules. This cocaine base is then transported to Colombia, where it is refined into the familiar white powder, before being shipped abroad. The costs involved to produce a kilo of the stuff are around US$5,000. The return on this investment can be as much as US$50,000.

Cocaine also has its legal uses. Patent medicines containing cocaine were popular – for hay fever, sinusitis and as a general tonic. Today, it is still used in hospitals worldwide as a local anaesthetic. Another legal use of cocaine is in soft drinks. The most famous soft drink in the world doesn't actually contain cocaine, but has something from the coca plant in it. Coca leaves from Peru and Bolivia are shipped to the USA where cocaine is extracted for medical use. From what's left comes a flavouring agent which goes into Coca-Cola, enjoyed in practically every country around the globe.

Coca and cocaine production

In recent years, the production of coca and cocaine has been one of Bolivia's most important sources of employment and income. It is estimated that about 10 % of the working population are directly dependent on the coca industry for their livelihoods. Though no official statistics are available, it is a generally accepted fact that coca and cocaine production has taken over from tin as Bolivia's most important export product.

Until the 1952 revolution, coca cultivation had been concentrated in the tropical valleys of the Yungas, where the climate is warm and not too dry and the altitude ideal. Today, most of the coca grown for traditional uses and domestic consumption still comes from the Yungas. However, the huge expansion of coca production in recent decades has largely been the result of the colonization of eastern Bolivia. This coca is less suitable for chewing but international demand is high enough to ensure a market for it. Most of the coca is grown by small peasant farmers who moved from the Altiplano following the closure of the tin mines. They settled in the higher parts of the Beni and, above all, in the Chapare plain of Cochabamba and now own small parcels of land of a few hectares. Many are also attracted to these regions by the relatively high wages which they can earn as labourers: a pisador can earn US$10 a night for treading coca leaves. Coca cult-ivation provides a much higher return for the small peasant farmer than any other crop. It can continue on the same land for at least 15 years and can be harvested four times a year, whereas other crops can exhaust the soil within as little as three years. It is for these reasons that peasant farmers in the Chapare are reluctant to abandon coca cultivation in favour of the proposed crop substitution programmes.

In 1997, the US threatened a ban on aid to the country, forcing Bolivia to draw up the so-called Dignity Plan which promised 'zero coca' by 2002. Once the world's third biggest producer of coca, Bolivia has destroyed 90% of the plant thus far. In the face of mounting pressure from the *campesinos*, the government has backtracked on this promise. The US-sponsored eradication of coca being grown for export continues but it's almost impossible to see the Bolivian people accepting the illegalization of the domestic use of the coca leaf. Protests about coca have been melded to those about the gas issue, creating a powerful popular movement and a new political force in the country, the so-called 'coca politicians', led by Evo Morales.

Bolivian farmers and the new politicians state that, despite the crackdown of the last four years, cocaine consumption in Europe and the United States remains at almost the same level. They say that Colombia has simply filled the gap in the market. Bolivia, it seems, is being made to pay the price for the war on drugs.

Economic life

Bolivia has, for centuries, neglected its indigenous majority. Since 1985 successive governments have embraced the free-market model and there has been an explosion of jobs in the 'informal sector', in street trade, personal services and small workshops. Because of a shortage of real jobs, poorer families have created their own work in order to survive, often demonstrating remarkable inventiveness and making use of family networks and contacts.

Economic necessity has led to the growth in the number of working women and also the numbers of children working, which in turn has increased the level of drop-outs from school: under 40% of children of school age attend school even though it is theoretically compulsory between 7 and 14. This explosion is most obvious in the towns with the swelling ranks of shoe-shiners (*lustrabotas*), lottery ticket sellers, beggars, cigarette and sweet vendors and street musicians.

But it is the rural population which has been hit hardest by the pursuit of economic stability. Bolivia has the highest percentage of rural poverty in the world. 97% of the rural population has an income below the poverty level, according to the UN **International Fund for Agricultural Development**. This can be seen most clearly on the Altiplano, where 70% of the rural population lives. Scenes of llamas grazing on the shores of Lake Titicaca under the snow-capped Mount Illimani are misleadingly idyllic. Here, average life expectancy is 46 years, infant mortality is 172 per 1,000 live births and family incomes average US$11.50 a month. A former **World Health Organization** representative in Africa has stated that poverty in Bolivia is worse than in Ethiopia.

Migration

The departments of Bolivia show remarkable differences in patterns of population growth, caused mainly by migration from the countryside to the large towns and cities. Apart from the urban centres, the newly-colonized regions in the Llanos and in the Yungas also attracted migrants. The Department of Santa Cruz, for example, has grown twice as fast as the national average in recent decades. The Altiplano, in particular, has been rapidly depopulated since the collapse of tin mining.

As in the rest of Latin America, urbanization is increasing rapidly. In 1992, 57% of Bolivians lived in towns, compared with 42% in 1976, meaning that Bolivia has now changed from a predominantly rural society to an urban one.

A shrinking nation

By 1935, just over 100 years after its proud declaration of independence, Bolivia had lost more than half of its original territory. Between 1835 and 1841 two wars were needed to determine the border with Peru, who, along with Brazil and Argentina, were determined that Bolivia should not become too powerful.

In 1867, Brazil seized a large portion of the Bolivian Amazon region and a part of the eastern Llanos, the Mato Grosso. Argentina had already occupied the central Chaco and then proceeded to help itself to another share of Bolivian territory, acquiring the Puna de Atacama. Following its rapid defeat at the hands of Chile in the War of the Pacific Bolivia lost its coastal provinces. As compensation Chile later agreed to build the railway between Arica and La Paz.

Railways traded for valuable territory has been Bolivia's fate. A railway to Yacuiba was Argentina's return for annexing some of the Chaco. During the first decade of the 20th century Bolivia lost the greater part of its northern territories. In 1903 Bolivia recognized Brazilian sovereignty over the rich Acre region in exchange for yet another railway, which was to create a passage to the Atlantic along navigable rivers. But this Madeira-Mamoré line never reached its destination, Riberalta, and proved of little use, eventually being closed in 1972.

There was not even an unbuilt railway to compensate Bolivia for its next loss, a huge part of the Chaco, in the southeast of the country.

The political and cultural position of Bolivia's indigenous peoples has been improved significantly since the 1952 revolution, but the economic neglect of Indian communities continues. This is partly due to the fact that rural Bolivia is at a huge disadvantage in terms of education, healthcare, employment opportunity and government service. About two-thirds of the population lives in adobe huts, and medical services are few and far between outside the towns and mining camps. Epidemics are comparatively rare on the Altiplano, but malaria and yellow fever are still problems in the Oriente and Santa Cruz, and hepatitis and Chagas disease (see page 51) are endemic in the warmer parts of the country.

But not all Bolivia's Indians are 'poor'. There is a very large community of urban Indians, or *cholos*, who are, on the whole, much better off than rural Indians and who make a decent income from the wholesale or retail trade.

Regional differences

Before the arrival of the Spaniards, most of Bolivia's population lived on the Altiplano and in the higher-lying basins of the Valles. This is still the case today. The highest population densities are in the central and northern Altiplano, while the Llanos remain very thinly populated. But the rural population of the Altiplano, especially in the Departments of Oruro and Potosí, are now departing for the big towns and more economically-viable lower-lying areas.

In the Valles the population is actually growing. Most people are moving to Cochabamba and the smaller surrounding towns. This is a direct result of the process of agrarian colonization which began after the 1952 Revolution. Campesinos were encouraged to move to lower-lying regions in order to increase agricultural productivity and reduce demographic pressure on the densely-populated highlands. However, colonization has proceeded on a much larger scale than planned, creating an enormous strain on land and infrastructure.

While many migrants earn a reasonable living from coca, rice, citrus fruits and coffee, others live in rural depression.

Since 1952 successive governments have favoured the Department of Santa Cruz in terms of capital investment. This has resulted in a thriving large-scale agricultural industry. The eastern regions of Bolivia have thus become the driving force of the economy. This has led to a massive influx of people. The city of Santa Cruz has grown much more rapidly than any other Bolivian city; from well below 100,000 in 1950, the city's population has reached one million, making it larger than La Paz (not including El Alto). As a result of growing prosperity in the Oriente at the expense of the highlands, regional tensions between the *collas* (altiplano dwellers) and the *cambas* (lowlanders) have become more marked in recent decades.

Culture

Arts and crafts

The Incas inherited many centuries of skills and traditions from the peoples they incorporated into their empire. All of these played important roles in political, social and religious ceremonies. Though much of this artistic heritage was destroyed by the Spanish conquest, the traditions adapted and evolved in numerous ways, absorbing new methods, concepts and materials from Europe while maintaining ancient techniques and symbols.

Textiles and costumes

Some of the most beautifully woven and dyed textiles to be found anywhere were produced by the Aymara Indians of the Bolivian Altiplano up until the late 19th century. These reflect the incredibly rich textile tradition which flourished in the Lake Titicaca basin since ancient times.

Originally, textile production arose out of the simple need for clothing. Gradually, though, more complicated techniques and designs evolved. Far from being merely of utilitarian purpose, Andean textiles played major political, social and religious roles. Woven cloth was the most highly-prized possession and sought after trading commodity in the Andes in pre-Columbian times and was used to establish and strengthen social and political relationships. It also played a role in all phases of the life cycle.

The Incas inherited this rich weaving tradition from the Aymaras and forced them to work in *mitas* or textile workshops. The largest quantities of the finest textiles were made specifically to be burned as ritual offerings – a tradition which still survives. The Spanish, too, exploited this wealth and skill by using the *mitas* and exporting the cloth to Europe.

Spanish chroniclers reported that, upon retreating from battle, Inca soldiers sometimes left behind thousands of llamas and prisoners, and even gold and silver, but chose to burn entire warehouses filled with cloth rather than leave them for the conquistadores. Indeed, in the Quipus, the string knot recording system of the Incas, only people and camelids ranked above textiles.

It is, therefore, not surprising that ancient weaving traditions survived the conquest while other social and cultural traditions disappeared. Textiles continue to play an important part in society in many parts of Bolivia. They are still handed down from one generation to the next and used specifically for ritual ceremonies. As a result, the finest textiles have survived until today. However, the influence of modern technology has reached even remote highland areas. Rural people have begun to wear machine-made clothes and many aspects of the ancient art of weaving are now lost.

Background Culture

Prior to Inca rule Aymara men wore a tunic (*llahua*) and a mantle (*llacata*) and carried a bag for coca leaves (*huallquepo*). The women wore a wrapped dress (*urku*) and mantle (*iscayo*) and a belt (*huaka*); their coca bag was called an *istalla*. The *urku* was fastened at shoulder level with a pair of metal *tupu*, the traditional Andean dress-pins.

Probably in imitation of the Aymara, the Inca men had tunics (*unkus*) and a bag for coca leaves called a *ch'uspa*. The women wore a blouse (*huguna*), skirts (*aksu*) and belts (*chumpis*), and carried foodstuffs in large, rectangular cloths called *llicllas*, which were fastened at the chest with a single pin or a smaller clasp called a *ttipqui*.

In isolated Andean villages and communities women still wear the traditional *aksu*, a skirt over two pieces of cloth overlapping at the sides and held up by a belt. The women of Tarabuco and Potolo, near Sucre, for example, commonly wear *aksus*, while Tarabuco men wear red and orange striped ponchos, and hats similar to crash helmets, possibly inspired by the Spanish army helmets. Tarabuco women's hats are small white *monteras* decorated with sequins. One item of costume which plays a particularly important role in the lives of the native population is the belt. The Aymara devote much of their lives to making belts for different occasions.

During the post-conquest period native dress was modified to satisfy Spanish ideas of propriety. Spanish policy concerning dress demanded that the Indian population should be fully and properly dressed at all times and that each person must be dressed according to his/her class. Spanish dress was restricted to the upper-class Indian.

The last century of the colonial period was disturbed by numerous Indian uprisings. The Spanish rulers believed that by restricting the natives' traditional clothing it could diminish their identification with their ancestors and that discontent would, therefore, be reduced. Thus the native male costume became pants, jacket, vest and poncho. In the less accessible parts, people were able to preserve their customs to a certain extent. While the Spanish influence is still evident in much of the Indians' dress, indigenous garments are also worn, forming a costume that is distinctly Andean.

Textile materials and techniques

The Andean people used mainly alpaca or llama wool. The former can be spun into fine, shining yarn when woven and has a lustre similar to that of silk, though sheep's wool came to be widely used following the Spanish conquest.

A commonly used technique is the drop spindle. A stick is weighted with a wooden wheel and the raw material is fed through one hand. A sudden twist and drop in the spindle spins the yarn. This very sensitive art can be seen practised by women while herding animals in the fields.

Spinning wheels were introduced by Europeans and are now prevalent due to increased demand. Pre-Columbian looms were often portable and those in use today are generally similar. A woman will herd her animals while making a piece of costume, perhaps on a backstrap loom, or waist loom, so-called because the weaver controls the tension on one side with her waist with the other side tied to an upright or tree. These looms can't be used on the treeless Altiplano so the Aymara people use four sticks set in the ground to hold the loom in place. The pre-Columbian looms are usually used for personal costume while the treadle loom is used for more commercial pieces in textile centres such as Villa Ribera, near Cochabamba, as it provides greater efficiency and flexibility.

Most weaving occurs during the winter, after the harvest and before the next year's planting. The women spend much of their day at the loom while also looking after the children and carrying out daily chores. A complex piece of textile can take up to several months to complete and, because of the time taken, is built to last many years.

Today, there is increasing pressure on indigenous people to desert their homes and join the white and mestizo people in the cities. Furthermore, Indians in native costume are often looked down on and considered uncivilized. There is a danger of the traditional textiles of the Andes becoming museum pieces rather than articles of daily use and wear. In some areas foreign aid and leadership of experts is proving effective. In Sucre, for example, a group of anthropologists has successfully brought about the revival of traditional village weaving.

Knitting

Knitting has a relatively short history in the Andes. Fibres commonly used are alpaca, llama and sheep's wool. During the past two decades though, much of the alpaca and llama wool has been bought by larger companies for export. Today, much of the wool for knitting is bought ready-spun from factories.

Outside the towns the majority of knitting is still done by hand. Traditionally many of the *chullos*, knitted hats with ear flaps worn on the Altiplano, are knitted with four small hooked needles. In the Andes the more traditional pieces still have patterns with llamas, mountains and other scenic and geometric designs.

Dyeing

The skills of dyeing were still practised virtually unchanged even after the arrival of the Spaniards. Nowadays, the word *makhnu* refers to any natural dye, but originally was the name for cochineal, an insect which lives on the leaves of the nopal cactus. These dyes were used widely by pre-Columbian weavers. Vegetable dyes are also used, made from the leaves, fruit and seeds of shrubs and flowers and from lichen, tree bark and roots. Although the high price for cochineal in the use of food colouring has discouraged its use for textiles, it is still widely combined with man-made dyes in textile centres such as Villa Ribera and around Lake Titicaca.

Symbolism

Symbolism plays an important role in weaving. Traditionally every piece of textile from a particular community had identical symbols and colours which were a source of identity as well as carrying specific symbols and telling a story. In the Andean world the planet Venus (*Chaska*) played an important role in mythology and agricultural pattern. Its appearance was used to forecast the coming year's rainfall. This symbol and that of the Sun (*Inti*) predominated in textile decoration and were universal to the *ayllus*, the self-sufficient and self-governing communities. The Jalq'a people of Sucre weave bizarre animal motifs on their *aksus*, or overskirts. These symbols perhaps represent *chulpas*, creatures that inhabited the Earth before the birth of the Sun.

The arrival of the Spaniards in the 16th century initiated a new era of symbolism as old and new elements appeared side by side. Symbols such as *Inti* may be found together with a horse figure introduced after the conquest. Sometimes the meanings of motifs have multiplied or been superseded. The cross, for example, in pre-Hispanic times signified the constellation of Cruz del Sur, the Southern Cross, or Cruz de la Siembra, guardian of the fields. Both have been eclipsed by the Christian symbol.

Buying textiles

Bolivia is an excellent source of textiles, which vary greatly from region to region in style, technique and use. For *mantas* the best place is in the shops behind San Francisco church in La Paz (see page 122). Prices are lower if you buy direct from the Tarabuco Indians who carry their loads of textiles up and down the steep streets. Other good places to find textiles are the market in Tarabuco and at ASUR, a textile project based in Sucre which works closely with rural communities.

Background Culture

Among the many villages dotted throughout the Andes, the following produce textiles which are particularly sought after and, therefore, more expensive: Calcha, in southern Potosí; Tarabuco, near Sucre; Charazani, in the Apolobamba mountains in the north of La Paz department; Sica Sica, between La Paz and Oruro; Calamarca, south of La Paz on the road to Oruro; Challa, halfway between Oruro and Cochabamba. In the northern part of the Potosí department, southeast from Oruro and northwest of Sucre, are the villages of Llallagua, Sacaca, Bolívar and Macha. Here, traditional weaving is maintained more than in any other part of Bolivia and the textiles are the most widely sold, especially in La Paz.

If you are asked to pay US$200-300 for a *manta*, which usually takes around two months to weave, this a more realistic price than US$10-20. If a *manta* has old stains on it, it may be better to leave them, as cleaning it may damage the textile. In general, though, Andean weavings are tough and can cope with washing, though at cool temperatures. If buying a newly-woven piece, check that the dyes are properly fixed before washing. Wet a small part then wipe it on white paper to see if any of the colours appear.

Hats

Hats were an important element of much pre-Hispanic costume and Bolivia has perhaps a greater variety of styles than any other region in South America, with over 100 different styles. One reason hats are so important in Bolivia is the high altitude of the Andes, where the sun's rays are more intense, making hats a necessity. Another is the survival of traditional costume among the country's Indian majority. The hat is the most important piece of the Indian's outfit and accompanies the wearer everywhere. The reason it is so important is because it is worn on the head, the most sacred part of the body and spirit.

One of the most familiar features of La Paz are the Aymara women with their brown or grey bowler, or derby hats, locally called a *bombín*. While the vast majority of the hats are made of felt, some are still made from rabbit hair, as they all were originally. Among the many styles is the 'JR Dallas', a Stetson named after JR Ewing, a character from the hit TV show, 'Dallas'. Another style, worn by the residents of Tarija, near the Argentine border, is based on those worn by their colonial ancestors from Andalucia. In Potosí, the women's hat is like a 'stove-pipe', though these are becoming increasingly rare.

In Cochabamba, Quechua women wear a white top hat of ripolined straw, decorated with a black ribbon. According to legend, a young unmarried Quechua woman in the city was reprimanded by a Roman Catholic priest for living with her boyfriend, a practice common among Indian couples intending to marry. As a punishment, she was made to wear a black ribbon around the base of the hat. The next day at Mass, much to the priest's chagrin, all the women were wearing the black ribbon and the style stuck.

Pottery

In all their variety, the pre-Hispanic ceramics found in burial sites across the Americas have emphasized the extent to which the pre-Columbian potters were concerned with imbuing their work with religious or magical symbolism. The potter's skill was not merely required to produce utilitarian objects necessary for daily life but was evidently a specialized, sometimes sanctified, art which required more than technical expertise.

Inca ceramic decoration consists mainly of small-scale geometric and usually symmetrical designs. One distinctive form of vessel which continues to be made and used is the *arybola*. This pot is designed to carry liquid, especially *chicha*, and is secured with a rope on the bearer's back. It is believed that *arybolas* were used mainly by the governing Inca élite and became important status symbols.

With the Spanish invasion many indigenous communities lost their artistic traditions, others remained relatively untouched, while others still combined hispanic and indigenous traditions and techniques. The Spanish brought three innovations: the potter's wheel, which gave greater speed and uniformity; knowledge of the enclosed kiln; and the technique of lead glazes. The enclosed kiln made temperature regulation easier and allowed higher temperatures to be maintained, producing stronger pieces. Today, many communities continue to apply pre-Hispanic techniques, while others use more modern processes.

Jewellery and metalwork

The Incas associated gold with the Sun. However, very few examples of their fine goldwork remain as the Spaniards melted down their amassed gold and silver objects and then went on to extract more precious metals from the ground. The surviving Indians were forced to work in barbaric conditions in gold and silver mines, where the death toll was horrifically high, most notoriously at Potosí.

During the colonial period gold and silver pieces were made to decorate the altars of churches and houses of the élite. Metalworkers came from Spain and Italy to develop the industry. The Spanish preferred silver and strongly influenced the evolution of silverwork during the colonial period. A style known as Andean baroque developed embracing both indigenous and European elements. Silver bowls in this style – *cochas* – are still used in Andean ceremonies.

Part of the Inca female costume was a large silver pin with a decorative head, the *tupu*, worn at the neck of the cloak, or *lliclla*, to hold it in place. Today, it continues to be made and used by the majority of Quechua-speaking people in Bolivia, though its form has changed over the centuries. In Inca times the decorative head was usually disc or fan-shaped, thought to derive from the *tumi* knife used for surgery. During colonial times Western emblems superseded the Inca forms. When in the 19th century uprisings caused native costume to be strictly authority regulated, the *tupu* developed an oval, spoon-shaped head, sometimes incised, and had charms suspended on silver chains.

In the Amazon basin seeds, flowers and feathers continue to be used as jewellery by many peoples. The Western fashion for natural or ethnic jewellery has encouraged production, using brightly-coloured feathers, fish bones, seeds or animal teeth.

Woodcarving

Carved religious figures, usually made from hardwoods, were a central influence in the development of woodcarving. In Eastern Bolivia, as in Paraguay, the tradition of carving and painting religious figures originates with the Jesuits, whose missions, or *reducciones*, gathered the indigenous people into settlements (see also page 328). They were set to work to build churches and produce handicrafts, such as earthenware pots, paintings and woodcarvings to adorn the churches. After the Jesuits' expulsion the Indians were left to fend for themselves. They kept their techniques and traditions that had been passed on to them and from these evolved the style of woodcarving today.

In La Paz and Cochabamba good examples of indigenous woodcarving can be found. Images of Indians, mountains, condors and Tiahuanaco are carved on wooden plaques. In La Paz, carvers specialize in male and female Indian heads.

Music and dance

When people talk of Bolivian music they are almost certainly referring to the music of the Quechua- and Aymara-speaking Indians of the high Altiplano which provides the most distinctive Bolivian sound. The music of the Andes has become very well known

66 99 All you need to do is shuffle around a bit, dragging one leg behind the other, occasionally performing a clumsy spin, rather in the manner of a drunken sales rep at a Friday night disco.

throughout Europe and North America ever since the Bolivian song 'El Cóndor Pasa' was recorded with English lyrics by Simon & Garfunkel and became an international hit. Now the distinctive sound of the Andes can be heard echoing around shopping malls and pedestrian precincts from London to Los Angeles.

The origins

The music of Bolivia can be described as the very heartbeat of the country. Each region has its own distinctive music that reflects its particular lifestyle, its mood and its physical surroundings. The music of the Altiplano, for example, is played in a minor key and tends to be sad and mournful, while the music of the lowlands is more up-tempo and generally happier.

Pre-Columbian music, which is still played today in towns and villages throughout the Andes, sounds very different from the music normally associated with that region now. The original uninfluenced music can sound unusual and even unpleasant to Western ears with its shrillness and use of scales and notes to which we are unaccustomed. Pre-Columbian music consisted of a five-note (pentatonic) scale, supposedly based on the five notes ancient people discovered in the wind. With the arrival of the Spaniards Andean music changed and took on Western forms, notably the seven-note scale. As more notes became available, so more varied themes could be played and the music we understand today as being Andean began to evolve.

Musical instruments

Before the arrival of the Spaniards in Latin America, over 400 years ago, the only instruments were wind and percussion. Although it is a popular misconception that Andean music is based on the panpipes, guitar and *charango*, anyone who travels through the Andes will realize that these instruments only represent a small aspect of Andean music. Bolivian music itself has more Amerindian style and content than that of any other country in South America. It is rare to find an indigenous Bolivian who cannot play an instrument and it is these instruments, both wind and percussion, that are quintessentially Bolivian.

The *quena* is a flute, usually made of reed, characterized by not having a mouthpiece to blow through. As with all Andean instruments, there is a family of *quenas* varying in length from around 15 to 50 cm. The *siku* is the Aymara name for the **zampoña**, or panpipes. It is the most important pre-Hispanic Andean instrument, formed by several reed tubes of different sizes held together by knotted string. Traditionally they are played singly, one person having one row of pipes. *Tarkas* are a type of flute made from the wood of the taco tree, from which their name derives. They are used a lot in festivals and have a shrill sound. *Pinquillos* are bamboo flutes with three octaves manufactured in Patacamaya, between Oruro and La Paz, and *moseños* are long, thick bamboo instruments played from the side.

Phututos were pre-Hispanic trumpets originally made from seashells, wood or ceramics. Now the horn of a bull is used to produce the deep sound used by rural communities to call meetings. In Tarija, bull's horns are also used to make *erkes*, which are very similar to *phututos* but are tied to long reeds and played collectively.

Amongst the percussion instruments are the *bombo*, a drum of various sizes, originally made from a hollowed-out tree trunk with the skins of llama or goat. *Chaj'chas* are made from sheep's hooves, dried in the sun, oiled and sewn onto a wrist cloth. Virtually the only instrument of European origin is the *charango*, which is traditionally made in the village of Aiquile, near Cochabamba. When stringed instruments were first introduced by the Spanish, the indigenous people liked them but wanted something that was their own and so the *charango* was born. Originally, they were made of clay, condor skeletons and armadillo or tortoise shells. Now, though, they are almost always made from wood. One of the main production centres is Oruro. In the Chuquisaca region, a group of players of three or even four sizes of *charango* with different voices is traditional.

Where to hear music

During periods of military dictatorship many folk musicians used their performances in *peñas* to register their opposition to repression and censorship in protest songs. *Peñas* became a focus of resistance to military rule. In recent years, though, with the return to democracy and the rise of more contemporary varieties of youth culture, *peñas* have been losing their attraction. Every town in Bolivia has its own *peña*, where you can hear popular Bolivian folk music, but today *peñas* are more likely to attract tourists than native young Bolivians.

Bolivia's many festivals are also good places to hear traditional music. For example, La Fiesta del Gran Poder in La Paz (see page 105), the Carnival in Oruro, or the Luzmilla Patiño festival in Cochabamba. The Fiesta de la Cruz takes place all over the Andes on 3 May, when thousands of musicians come together to play all shapes and sizes of instruments, including the *toyos*, which are huge panpipes over one metre long and hail from the Titicaca region.

The region of Tarija near the Argentine border has a musical tradition of its own, based on religious processions that culminate with that of San Roque on the first Sunday in September. The influence is Spanish and the musical instruments are the *caña*, *erke* and violin *chapaco*. The *caña* is a long bamboo tube with a horn at the end.

There are many professional folk groups on record. The most popular, Los Kjarkas, actually wrote the original song *Llorando se fue*, but the hit version was recorded by a French group under the now-famous title Lambada. Other well-known folk groups are Wara, Los Masis, Los Quipus and Rumillajta who have built up a considerable following in Europe. The greatest exponent of the *charango* is the legendary Ernesto Cavour, who can be heard at some of the best-known *peñas* in La Paz (see page 120).

Dance

Just as music is the heartbeat of the country, so dance conveys the rich and ancient heritage that typifies much of the national spirit. Bolivians are tireless dancers and dancing is the most popular form of entertainment. Unsuspecting travellers should note that once they make that first wavering step there will be no respite until they collapse from exhaustion.

Organized group dances

Comparsas are organized groups of dancers who perform dances following a set pattern of movements to a particular musical accompaniment, wearing a specific costume. These dances have a long tradition, having mostly originated from certain contexts and circumstances and some of them still parody the ex-Spanish colonial masters. The most famous *comparsas* are those from the Oruro Carnival (see page 192).

Another notable *comparsa* is the comical *Auqui Auqui* (*auqui* is Aymara for old man). The dance satirizes the solemnity and pomposity of Spanish gentlemen from the colonial period. Because of their dignified dress and manners they could appear old, and a humped back is added to the dancers to emphasize age. These little old men have long pointed noses, flowing beards and carry crooked walking sticks. They dance stooped, regularly pausing to complain and rub aching backs, at times even stumbling and falling, to the accompaniment of *pinquillos*.

A number of dances replicate hunting scenes, the origins of which are thought to lie in the *chacu*, the great annual Inca hunt which involved 20,000-30,000 people forming a huge circle and then closing in until the animals could be caught by hand. The main protagonist in most of the hunting dances is the *K'usillu*, a mischievous character, half monkey half devil. He wears a bright costume, a horned crown and carries a whip, tambourine or *pinquillo*. The *Liphi* dance, or vicuña hunt, often involves the K'usillu carrying a stuffed vicuña while being chased by an old man representing the achachila or spirit of the mountains. When the *K'usillu* is caught, an old woman, the spirit of the earth, beheads the vicuña and the body is then carried off by a condor.

In the Wititis the *K'usillu* carries a live partridge, singing out in imitation of the bird. He is accompanied by men dressed as young women and condors. Other dancers try to lasso the fleeing partridge but often hook the young women instead. In the *Chokelas*, or fox hunt, the *K'usillu* carries a stuffed fox and chases the women relentlessly, mimicking the Spaniards' pursuit of native women.

Dances for everyone

Many dances for couples and/or groups are danced spontaneously at fiestas throughout Bolivia. These include indigenous dances which have originated in a specific region and ballroom dances that reflect the Spanish influence.

One of the most popular of the indigenous dances is the *Huayño* which originated on the Altiplano but is now danced throughout the country. It involves numerous couples, who whirl around or advance down the street, arm-in-arm, in a *'Pandilla'*. During fiestas, and especially after a few drinks, this can develop into a kind of uncontrolled frenzy.

Similar to the *Huayño* is the *Chovena* from the Beni and Santa Cruz regions. The *Chovena* originated from tribal dances, as did the *Machetero*, another folkloric dance from the lowlands. The *Chapaqueada* is a dance from Tarija which is performed at religious festivals such as Christmas and Easter. The name derives from the word *Chapaco*, a person from Tarija. The dance is accompanied by typical Tarijan instruments (see above). There are countless other indigenous dances, far too many to list here.

Of the ballroom dances, the *Cueca* is perhaps the best known. The Bolivian *Cueca* is a close relative of the Chilean national dance of the same name and they share a mutual origin in the *Zamacueca*, itself derived from the Spanish Fandango. Today the *Cueca* is very representative of Bolivia, as typical of this country as the Tango is of Argentina. Similar to the *Cueca* is the *Bailecito Chuquisaqueño*, though it is more delicate without the emphasis on provocative mannerisms. Other regional dances include the *Khaluyo Cochabambino* and *Rueda Tarijeña* from the southeast and *Carnavalito Cruceño* and *Taquirari Beniano* from the tropical lowlands.

Outside of the fiestas, the most popular dances are not of Bolivian origin: Salsa, Merengue, Caribbean *Soca*, Brazilian Samba and Columbian *Cumbia*. Salsa dancing should probably not be attempted by anyone unfamiliar with the basic steps or unable to wiggle their hips in time to the beat. If you really must attempt this, then make sure enough alcohol has been consumed to render you unaware of the fact that you are the laughing stock of the entire dance floor. Merengue, Soca and Samba are just about viable, given a crowded dance floor and very understanding partner.

Cumbia, on the other hand, is a cinch. It was originally invented by black slaves as a means of moving more easily while shackled together. All you need to do is shuffle around a bit, dragging one leg behind the other, occasionally performing a clumsy spin, rather in the manner of a drunken sales rep at a Friday night disco.

Hidden behind the mask

One of the most striking features of the Bolivian fiesta is the fantastic variety of wildly imaginative masks worn by the dancers.

The indigenous peoples of the Andes believe that masks transform individuals – not only into characters from popular folklore but also into spirits of another time and place and defenders of a sacred knowledge.

This can be explained by the legend of the *amaut'as*, or wisemen. The *amaut'as* are the keepers of the wisdom and values of the Andean civilization. They are said to personify the indigenous cultural identity and reaffirm its rebellion against foreign domination. Upon hearing of the death of the last Inca, Atahuallpa, the *amaut'as* were so horrified that, instead of rebelling, they retreated into themselves and stoically endured the injustices of a world that had ceased to be theirs.

In the same way, the Indians adapted to the oppression of daily life under a mask of submission and indifference. It is only during ceremonies of rebellion and remembrance that the Indians come back to life. Crucial to the success of such ceremonies – fiestas in other words – is the excessive consumption of alcohol, food and coca as well as repetitive, incessant dancing. This collective altered state draws the community together until the individual members are indistinguishable from one another. In this way, the community communes with itself and with its surroundings, thus affirming its will to live.

So, when the indigenous people put on their masks and costumes they cover their psychological masks of obstinate passivity, which allows them to show their true faces. Only by covering themselves up can the indigenous people uncover their repressed energies and desires and hidden resentments. These pent-up emotions overflow during the wild, excessive and colourful celebrations of the fiesta; the awakening of a sleeping culture.

Festivals

Fiestas are a fundamental part of life for most Bolivians, taking place up and down the length and breadth of the country and with such frequency that it would be hard to miss one, even during the briefest stays. This is fortunate, because arriving in any town or village during these frenetic celebrations is one of the great Bolivian experiences.

Bolivian fiestas range from the elaborately choreographed processions of Oruro to a simple llama sacrifice in a tiny rural community. Some are highly Catholicized, particularly in the more Spanish dominated towns of Tarija and Santa Cruz, while others incorporate Spanish Colonial themes into predominantly ancient pagan rituals.

Invariably, fiestas involve drinking – lots and lots of it. There's also non-stop dancing, which can sometimes verge on an organized brawl. What this means is that, at some point, you will fall over, through inebriation or exhaustion, or both. After several days of this, you will awake with a hangover the size of the Amazon rainforest and probably have no recollection of what you did with your backpack.

Fiestas also involve much throwing of water, paint, oil – anything, in fact, that people can get their hands on. The more paranoid travellers may assume that they are being picked on, but to someone from the Altiplano, a six-foot tall, blond-haired gringo makes an easier target. So, arm yourself with a waterproof jacket, plenty of water bombs, a good sense of fun and have a great time.

Eat, drink and be merry

One of the most prominent figures in Andean fiestas is the *Danzanti*, a character of Spanish origin but fully adopted by the Bolivian Indians. The dancer wears a huge, green and red mask with bulging eyes and large protruding ears, decorated with mirrors and feathers.

Traditionally, the man chosen to become the *Danzanti* would be in his prime and strong both morally and physically. For several days before the festival nothing was denied him. He gorged himself on the finest food and drink and could indulge himself on the most beautiful young virgins. The *Danzanti* was then expected to dance continually for three days and nights until exhaustion, or even death. His death was seen as a sacrifice of the best that can be offered and ensured the safety of the community from plague and drought.

The meaning of fiestas

It is only when they don their extravagant costumes and drink, eat and dance to excess that the Bolivian Indians show their true character. The rest of the time they hide behind a metaphorical mask of stony indifference as a form of protection against the alien reality in which they are forced to live. When they consume alcohol and coca and start dancing, the pride in their origins resurfaces. The incessant drinking and dancing allows them to forget the reality of poverty, unemployment and oppression and reaffirms their will to live as well as their unity with the world around them.

The object of the fiesta is a practical one, such as the success of the coming harvest or the fertility of animals. Thus the constant eating, drinking and dancing serves the purpose of giving thanks for the sun and rain that make things grow and for the fertility of the soil and livestock, gifts from Pachamama, or Mother Earth, the most sacred of all gods. So, when you see the Aymara spill a little *chicha* (maize beer) every time they refill, it's not because they're sloppy but because they're offering a *ch'alla* (sacrifice) to Pachamama.

The participants in the dances that are the central part of the fiesta are dressed in outlandish costumes and elaborate masks, each one depicting a character from popular myth. Some originate in the colonial period, others survive from the Inca Empire or even further back to the Tiahuanaco cultures. Often the costumes caricature the Spaniards. In this way, the indigenous people mock those who erased their heritage.

Over time, new details have been introduced to reflect the changing reality of Bolivian life, so that the precise origins of the dances become somewhat blurred. For example, in the most famous fiesta of them all, the Carnival of Oruro (see page 192) the traditional main characters such as monkeys, bears and condors have become peripheral players in colonial dances such as La Diablada (Devil's Dance) and La Morenada (Dance of the Black Slaves).

Who pays?

A lot a careful organization and preparation goes into a community's fiesta, and a lot of expense. The brass bands, the food, the beer, the pipe bands, the decorations, are all laid on free for the participants, and someone has to foot the bill.

Every fiesta needs a patron, or a sponsor. It's an honour to bear the *cargo* (cost) of a fiesta. So great is the prestige that it's impossible to rise in the community without sponsoring fiestas.

But how does a patron pay for it all? There are two ways: one is to save, the other is to get help from friends. They will lend the money on the understanding that when they have a *cargo* the favour will be returned. This bond of mutual assistance is known as an *ayni*. A man may spend lots of money on other people's fiestas before he can even sponsor one himself. But the more *ayni* bonds he can accrue by helping others, the more money he'll be able to raise when it's his turn. Thus, the principle of the *cargo* is that the more you do for the community, the more it'll do for you. Lay on a good fiesta and you'll rise in the hierarchy. For a list of the main festivals, see the Essentials chapter.

Literature

Pre-independence

The absence of a written language in pre-Hispanic Bolivia means that there is no recorded literature from this period, though there was an oral tradition of story-telling which still survives today. The primary function of early Spanish literature in Bolivia, then known as Alto Perú, was to spread Catholicism through the newly-conquered empire. One of the earliest known of these works was the Crónica de Perú, by Pedro Cieza de León (1518-1560). The Spaniards' fear of the unknown culture of the indigenous people meant that these early chronicles lacked much local detail, focusing more on the religion and the activities of the conquerors themselves. Even the early texts by native Bolivian authors showed the extent of their indoctrination with colonial ideas.

The only area in which the Indians were allowed to maintain their own culture was in theatre and poetry. One of the few texts to survive, La Tragedia de Atahuallpa, indicates that plays were passed orally from generation to generation. Poetry in the Quechua and Aymara languages also continued to flourish, again orally, throughout the colonial era. Not until the early 18th century does a text appear which takes the religious chronicle into the realms of literature: Bartolomé Arzán's Historia de la Villa Imperial de Potosí, written between 1700 and 1736, is an epic account of most of the colonial period. Unlike any other text produced until then, it mixes fact and fantasy, the author even immersing himself in a fictional context into phases of history hundreds of years earlier. It is a remarkable Baroque example of what later came to be known as Lo Real Maravilloso.

The transformation of Bolivia into a republic is recorded by a native of La Paz, Vicente Pazos Kauki (1779-1853) in Memorias Histórico-políticas, in which he defends the notion of Latin American independence from the Spanish. The literary qualities of this work bring the skill of fictional narrative to the sections based on historical fact.

Post-independence

The birth of Bolivia as an independent nation in 1825 coincided with the beginning of Romanticism in Latin America. European Romantic fiction was widely read and local authors developed a similar style of writing to create tales of contemporary life in Bolivia. The sentimental novel was popularized primarily by Vicente Ballivián (1816-1891) with Recreos juveniles in 1834. Julio Lucas Jaimes, a Bolivian Romantic writing in the mid-19th century, gained the admiration of the well-known Nicaraguan writer, Rubén Darío, who dedicated part of his Prosas profanas to him.

European-influenced Romanticism came to an end with the birth of Latin American Modernism at the turn of the century. Ricardo Jaimes Freyre was one of the forerunners of the movement. His La Villa Imperial de Potosí, published in 1905, examined the pervading mood in Latin America and sought inspiration from past events, such as the French Revolution of 1789, which he saw as an example of positive rational action distinctly lacking in his homeland. Jaimes Freyre went on to found an important literary review in Buenos Aires with Rubén Darío and gained an international reputation with his poetry, plays, novels and critical essays.

Nataniel Aguirre's 1885 *Juan de la Rosa* was another landmark literary work. In this highly original novel, he subverts the whole concept of the 19th century novel by placing the narrative in the hands, or voice, of one of his characters, thus relinquishing the privileged position of the author/narrator.

A major contribution to Feminism was made by the modernist poet Adela Zamudio (1854-1928). She formed a Latin American triad of Romantic-Modernist poets with José Martí in Cuba and Manuel González Prada in Peru, all of whom used their innate spirit of rebellion as an inspiration for their poetry. Zamudio dedicated her life and work to the struggle against the oppression of women.

The Bolivian Modernist movement continued to flourish with the publication of *Odas* in 1898 by Franz Tamayo (1880-1956). His analysis of post-colonial Latin America saw the huge divide between the ruling minority and the anonymous, voiceless majority. He was nominated president of the Republic in 1935, but was prevented from assuming the post by a military coup.

Early 20th century prose reflected the injustices of the *latifundista* system. Alcides Arguedas (1879-1946) began his fictional account of the inequality of Bolivian society with Wata Wara, which he later incorporated in his 1919 Raza de bronze. This is one of the major novels in Bolivian letters, examining the life of the Indian in a society dominated by a white ruling class. Jaime Mendoza's (1874-1939) novels also denounced the exploitation of the Indians, in particular their conditions in the tin mines and rubber plantations. His best known work is En las tierras de Potosí (1911). The extreme politicisation of his work has led some critics to refer to him as the Bolivian Gorky.

The literature of the Chaco War (1932-1935) was mainly by those who had fought in it, documenting a national sense of despair at having been forced to fight a protracted and futile war. Augusto Céspedes (1904-1997) was one of the key figures of this era, both in politics and literature. He had already founded the Nationalist Party of Bolivia by the time he published his account of the Chaco War, *Sangre de mestizos*, in 1936. This collection of short stories saw that for the first time whites and Indians had shared the same plight, fighting alongside each other and united in bitter disappointment at the outcome. This book is now considered a classic and Céspedes went on to become a major literary and political figure until his recent death at the age of 94.

The revolution of 1952 did not produce any significant literature, but this can be explained by the fact that a revolutionary consciousness had already been established by writers and intellectuals in the 20 years after the Chaco War. The pressing issues of exploitation of the Indians and conditions in the tin mines, criticized in fiction since the early 1930s, had finally been addressed by the revolution. Some writers also gave up their craft to work in politics. The few novels that did emerge just after the revolution, such as *Cerco de penumbras* by Oscar Cerruto (1912-1981) and *Los deshabitados* by Macelo Quiroga (1931-1980), broke with the tradition of social realism and began experimenting with a more abstract, existential kind of work, mirrored by the dark poetry of Jaime Sáenz and Gonzalo Vázquez Méndez.

The next significant change in Bolivia to be marked by literature was the guerrilla uprising led by Che Guevara, and his subsequent execution in 1967. The key novel in this new subversive literature was *Los fundadores del alba*, by Renato Prado de Oropeza, which won the coveted Cuban Casa de las Américas prize in 1969. Many poets from this period, the most important being Pedro Shimose (born 1940), denounced the violence that was then shaping society in all of Latin America.

Literature in the 1970s and 1980s continued to criticise Bolivian society, though the presence of various military dictatorships restricted the writers' freedom to chronicle the injustices around them with such blatant acrimony as before. However, an important collection of short stories Antología del terror político was published in 1979, combining the work of established figures like Raul Leyton with younger writers like René Bascope and Roberto Laserna. All the stories are concerned with the restrictions placed on all levels of life by dictatorship. Other writers of the same period avoided social realism altogether, turning to experimentation and poetic writing. The fantasies and myths of indigenous culture have also been a source of inspiration for many contemporary writers, reflecting a common trend throughout Latin American literature in general.

Painting and sculpture

Pre-independence

As a result of the discovery of the fabulously rich silver mines of Potosí in 1544 Bolivia, then part of the Viceroyalty of Peru, was one of the major commercial and cultural centres of colonial Spanish America. Artists and craftsmen followed the merchants, churchmen, colonial adminstrators and adventurers along the trade route from the Viceregal capital of Lima to Potosí via Cusco, La Paz and Sucre. The demand for paintings, sculptures and altarpieces was met first by Europeans such as the itinerant Italian Jesuit Bernardo Bitti (1548-1610?), who after a spell in Lima moved on to Lake Titicaca, La Paz, Sucre and Potosí, and the influence of his delicate mannerist style can be traced through several subsequent generations. Another mobile and important Jesuit painter but in this case of Flemish origin, was Diego de la Puente (1586-1663) who worked in towns and cities throughout the Viceroyalty. His paintings were often based on engravings after works by Rubens, an influence that was to persist in Bolivian painting until late in the 18th century. The work of Gregorio Gamarra, active 1601-1630, is typical of the first generation of Bolivian-born artists in combining elements of the Italianate style of Bitti and the Flemish tradition of Puente, as in his 'Adoration of the Kings' in the Museo Nacional de Arte in La Paz.

Colonial sculpture, however, has its stylistic roots in Spain. Andalusian sculptors were attracted by lucrative commissions for altarpieces and choirstalls. Several workshops were established in highland Bolivia by the 1570s, and Spanish-born craftsmen continued to be influential into the 17th century. The Sevillian Gaspar de la Cueva (active 1613-1640) settled in Potosí where many of his best works are still preserved in the churches for which they were made. His 'Christ at the Column' in the church of San Lorenzo, for example, is elegantly dignified despite the numerous bleeding lacerations on his white skin. This powerful colonial tradition of silent suffering in the face of physical abuse continues to reverberate in Bolivian art.

The work of painter Melchor Pérez Holguín (1660?-1733) combines Flemish, Spanish and Andean elements, and is typical of the cultural heterogeneity of later colonial painting. The composition of his 'Rest on the Flight into Egypt' in the Museo Nacional de Arte in La Paz is based on a Flemish engraving; the style, however, is reminiscent of Zurbarán, while the anecdotal detail owes much to Andean traditions. While the infant Jesus sleeps, the Virgin, dressed in a *manta* and travelling hat, washes nappies in a portable wooden basin. This 'Americanization' of subject matter owes much to the Cusco school of painting and although Holguín largely resisted the typical Cusco hallmark of applying gold to the painted surface, the next generation of Bolivian artists did not. The painting of San Francisco de Paula (Museo Nacional de Arte, La Paz) by Holguín's follower Manuel de Córdoba (active 1758-1787) is a striking example of the resulting tension between the real and the divine. The saint's hands and face are painted with close attention to every vein, tendon and wrinkle in the tradition of Caravaggio and Ribera while his habit is overlaid with a flat wallpaper pattern in gold. The effect is simultaneously to emphasize and deny the figure's corporeality. Another follower of Holguín, Gaspar Miguel de Berrio (active 1706-1762) uses gold to emphasize the divinity of the principal figures in his impressive 'Coronation of the Virgin' (Museo Nacional de Arte, La Paz). He is also remembered for his detailed documentary view of Potosí (c 1760, Museo Charcas, Sucre) which shows the distinctive triangular mountain, the colonial city below it, and in the surrounding hills the elaborate system of dams and canals which channelled water to the mine-workings.

Initially European craftsmen worked mainly for the creole elite while indigenous workshops developed to meet the needs of the newly-Christianized Indians, often with remarkable results. In 1582 Francisco Tito Yupanqui, a native of Copacabana who claimed descent from the Incas, wanted to make an image of the Virgin for his parish church and travelled to Potosí to learn to carve. The fame of the resulting sculpture derives from the tradition that after two years' work and still unable to finish the piece to his own satisfaction, Yupanqui appealed to the Virgin for help whereupon she kindly obliged. Once installed in Copacabana the miraculously-completed statue quickly became the focus of a popular cult, so perpetuating the sacred significance Lake Titicaca had had under the Incas. Native Andean beliefs include the veneration of important geographical features, and the rigid triangular representations of the Virgin can often be related to mountain peaks. The Virgin of Sabaya (Museo de la Moneda, Potosí) by the Indian Luis Niño (18th century) is associated with the Sabaya volcano in Oruro, while in the anonymous painting of the Virgin of Potosí in the same museum the Virgin's body is the mountain: her head and hands, radiating silvery light, are superimposed on the landscape making her the Christian embodiment of Pachamama, the Andean earth mother goddess. Other indigenous divinities reappeared in Christian garb in the 18th century, most famously the forces of nature. These were transformed by Andean artists into richly-dressed archangels with *arquebuses*: powerful, unpredictable intermediaries between celestial and earthly realms. Examples can be seen in many rural churches as well as in the major museums.

Post-independence

In the years following independence in 1825 itinerant artists of diverse origins played an important role, as they had in the early colonial period. The Peruvian José Gil de Castro (died 1841), the Ecuadorean Manuel Ugalde (1817-1881) and the Austrian Francisco Martín Drexel (1792-1863) helped to meet the new demand for portraits of military leaders and society hostesses. Bolivian-born Antonio Villavicencio (born 1822) trained in a conventional academic manner in Paris before returning in 1858 to head the Escuela de Dibujo in La Paz. The interest of the works of this period, including Villavicencio's monumental series of presidential portraits in the Museo Charcas, Sucre, lies less in their artistic merit than in the historical personalities they represent.

Portraiture was the dominant form of artistic expression. Nineteenth century political nationalism was not paralleled by a strong school of landscape painting although Zenón Iturralde (born 1838) and Melchor María Mercado (19th century), both self-taught, painted interesting topographical scenes. José García Mesa (1851-1905), despite extensive studies in Europe, returned to paint city views which sometimes seem closer to the colonial topographical tradition of, for example, Berrío's Potosí, than to the Impressionism of his French contemporaries (for example 'Plaza de Cochabamba', 1889, Casa de Cultura, Cochabamba).

Popular religious artistic expression was largely unaffected by the political changes. In the later colonial period many rural churches had been decorated with brightly-coloured and iconographically complex murals, a practice which persisted throughout the 19th century, and artists such as Juan de la Cruz Tapia (1830?-1892), a sculptor as well as a painter, continued to produce devotional images in the tradition of Holguín.

20th century art

Art in Bolivia during the early 20th century, dominated by figurative styles and local subject matter, is scarcely touched by developments in Europe. Cecilio Guzmán de Rojas (1900-1950) presents himself in his self-portrait of 1919 as a bohemian dandy

(Museo de la Moneda, Potosí) but although he spent the 1920s in Europe, the modern movements passed him by. In Madrid he painted sentimental visions of the Andes using naked or semi-naked Indian figures in questionable taste (for example 'The Idol's Kiss/El Beso del Idolo', 1926, Museo de la Moneda, Potosí). On his return to Bolivia in 1930 he saw his country afresh and used more sensitive if politically anodyne indigenist modes, but his real importance lies in the way in which, as Director of the Escuela de Bellas Artes of La Paz, he promoted the land, landscape and peoples of Bolivia as serious subjects for painters and sculptors. Other practitioners include Juan Rimsa (c 1898-c 1975), Gil Coimbra (1908-1976) and Jorge de la Reza (1901-1958).

The success of the revolution of 1952 inspired artists of the younger generation of '52' to add a much-needed social and political dimension to Bolivian art. As in Mexico, murals offered a way of reaching a wide audience and during the 1950s the government sponsored numerous narrative and allegorical works in schools, hospitals and the offices of nationalized companies. Two major exponents were Miguel Alandia Pantoja (1914-1975) several of whose works survive in La Paz (for example in the auditorium of the Hospital Obrera in La Paz) and Walter Solón Romero (born 1925) who executed murals and stained glass windows for the Catholic University in Sucre. The euphoria was short-lived and after the military coup of 1964 artists had to find alternative means of expression. The Indians Gil Imana (born 1933) paints in the 1970s are no longer folkloric and rural, as in the generation of Guzmán de Rojas, nor inspired by Marxist optimism, but simply hungry and oppressed. Enrique Arnal (born 1932) paints faceless Indian porters in ragged Western clothes; they inhabit not a traditional picturesque landscape but an abstract, lonely no-man's land of blank planes.

The two best-known artists of 20th century Bolivia were both women, the painter, María Luisa Pacheco (1919-1974), and the sculptor Marina Núñez del Prado (1910-1996). Both worked in a predominantly abstract mode, but with a distinctively Bolivian flavour. In her mixed-media canvases Pacheco used a cubist vocabulary and coarsely-textured surface to evoke to the peaks, crags and sharply-faceted rocks of the Andean landscape. Núñez del Prado, by contrast, carved iron-hard native wood and stone into softly curving, often feminine forms.

In recent decades Bolivia has seen the growth of numerous different artistic tendencies, dominated by a continued preoccupation with figuration. The Museo Nacional de Arte in La Paz has a very good collection of contemporary art and there are several new commercial galleries. Look out for Gaston Ugalde (born 1946), Edgar Arandia (born 1951) and particularly Roberto Valcarcel (born 1951) who produced powerful indictments of political repression in the 1970s and has gone on to explore different aspects of Bolivian iconography including a fascinating recent series in which he dissects and reworks the colonial image of the archangel.

Cinema

The Bolivian film industry has usually been known for its strength and courage in producing films against the opposing forces of repressive political regimes. However, since 1994, the industry has undergone something of a renaissance, concentrated particularly in five new feature films. Though by no means similar, the six films share a common departure from Bolivian cinema's confrontational stance, while retaining an underlying awareness of social issues.

La oscuridad radiante, based on the novel by Oscar Uzín, is about a rebel fighter who becomes a priest. He is sent by the church to a remote village near a border. When a group of rebels arrive seeking protection and help in crossing the border, the priest's former loyalties are put to a severe test.

Hair today

One of the many customs initiated by the Incas which is still practised is the hair-cutting ritual, *ruthuchiku*. The Inca custom was to hold a fiesta lasting several days when the child reached the age of two. This was accompanied by the hair-cutting ceremony in which the child's head was completely shaved. At the same time the name given to the child at birth was substituted by a new, permanent one.

Today, when a child's head is shaved, the celebration may last one day and gifts of money are given. So, if you happen to be staying with an indigenous family, you'll know what to do if you're presented with a pair of scissors and a squirming child.

Sayari, by Mela Márquez, is the first Bolivian film directed by a woman. It is about a Quechua-speaking community struggling for land rights and cultural survival. Another landmark feature of this film is the fact that the entire cast are indigenous people.

Jonas y la ballena rosada is set in Santa Cruz in the Bolivian Oriente, marking a cinematic shift in geographical emphasis. Nearly all Bolivian films have up till now been set in La Paz or the Altiplano area. Both the oil and cocaine industries have increased the political and cultural diversity of Santa Cruz and Jonas y la ballena rosada, directed by Carlos Valdivia, deals with the encroaching economic and social power of the *narcotraficantes* in the Santa Cruz area.

Director Jorge Sajinés has been a leading figure in Bolivian cinema since the 60s. His most recent film *Para recibir el canto de los pájaros*, uses the film-within-a-film format to look at the effect of the arrival of a film crew in a remote Andean village. The villagers' idea of the conquest is explored in their re-enactment of it during the film. The title refers to episodes of ritual dialogue between musicians and birds.

Cuestión de fe has broken all box-office records in Bolivia. It is the story of three marginalized urbanites trying to transport a figure of the Virgin Mary from La Paz to the Yungas in the north, an area now opening up to the drugs trade. One of the protagonists is a *santero* who performs ancient rituals before the journey. The film explores the cultural diversity of mestizos' faith through a subtle use of music and colour. Director Marcos Loayza has portrayed a society sufficiently at ease with itself to have accepted this picaresque and parodic self-portrait.

Dependencia Sexual (Sexual Dependency), 2003. Winner of the **International Critics' Prize** at the Locarno Film Festival, this verité-style drama follows five mixed-up teenagers (three in Bolivia, two in the US) as they try to understand the complex and fairly grim world around them. Featuring a gay football player and the rape of a poor Bolivian teenager, almost the whole film is shot in dual-angle split-screen.

Travellers wishing to see any of these important Bolivian films should check out the **Cinemateca Boliviana** in La Paz (see page 120).

In 2004, the lushly filmed (Cusco, Macchu Picchu, the Andes) *Diarios de Motocicleta* (Motorcycle Diaries) became a hit around the world. Made by an Argentinian team, the film is based on Che Guevara's diaries written when, as a young man, he and a friend travelled around the continent on motorbikes. It largely avoids politics and concentrates on Che-as-backpacker, as do the diaries. On this trip the young travellers by-passed Bolivia, though, if you're interested in Che-based tourism in Bolivia, it's an easy introduction to the man.

People

Bolivia is a culturally diverse country. Its population can be roughly divided into three distinct ethnic groupings: about 60% are of pure indigenous stock; about one third are *mestizos* (people of mixed European and Indian ancestry); and the remainder are of European origin. The racial composition varies from place to place: indigenous around Lake Titicaca; more than half indigenous in La Paz; three-quarters *mestizo* or European in the Yungas, Cochabamba, Santa Cruz and Tarija, the most European of all.

The Highland Indians are composed of two groups: those in the north of the Altiplano who speak the guttural Aymara (an estimated one million), and those elsewhere, who speak Quechua, the Inca tongue (three million). Both cultures were dominated by the Incas but the Aymara were allowed to keep their own language. Both have kept their languages and cultures distinct. Outside the big cities many of them speak no Spanish, but knowledge of Spanish is increasing. About 70% of Bolivians are Aymara, Quechua or Tupi-Guaraní speakers. The first two are regarded as national languages, but were not, until very recently, taught in schools, a source of some resentment.

The Aymara

The Aymaras, who populate the Titicaca region, are descendants of the ancient Tiahuanaco people. They are a squat and powerfully built race who have developed huge chests and lungs to cope with the rarefied air of the Altiplano. Since the agrarian revolution of 1952 the Aymara campesinos own the land on which they live, but still live in extreme poverty.

Though introduced to Catholicism by the Spaniards, the Aymara remain grudging converts. They are a deeply religious people who may observe Christian rituals but also continue to worship the ancient animist spirits and celebrate rituals which date from the Tiahuanaco period. Aymara culture is permeated with the idea of the sacred. They believe that God, the Supreme Being, gives them security in their daily lives and this God of Life manifests him/herself through the deities, such as those of the mountains, the water, the wind, the sun, the moon and the wa'qas (sacred places).

As a sign of gratitude, the Aymara give *wax'ta* (offerings), *wilancha* (llama sacrifices) and *ch'alla* (sprinkling alcohol on the ground) to the *achachilas* (the protecting spirits of the family and community), the *Pachamama* (Mother Earth), *Kuntur Mamani* and *Uywiri* (protecting spirits of the home).

The remote mountains of the bleak Altiplano are of particular importance for the Aymara. The most sacred places are these high mountains, far from human problems. It is here that the people have built their altars to offer worship, to communicate with their God and ask forgiveness. The community is also held important in the lives of the Aymara. The *achachila* is the great-great grandfather of the family as well as the protector of the community, and as such is God's representative on earth.

The offerings to the sacred mountains take place for the most part in August and are community celebrations. Many different rituals are celebrated: there are those within the family; in the mountains; for the planting and the harvest; rites to ask for rain or to ask for protection against hailstorms and frosts; and ceremonies for Mother Earth.

All such rituals are led by *Aymara Yatiris*, who are male or female priests. The *Yatiri* is a wise person – someone who knows – and the community's spiritual and moral guide. Through a method of divination that involves the reading of coca leaves, they guide individuals in their personal decision-making.

⁑ A way of life

Coca has always played an important role in Bolivian society. As casual as a coffee-break and as sacred as Communion, coca chewing is an ancient ritual in the Andes. Coca can be bought anywhere and most Bolivians use it regularly; from campesinos in the highlands to non-Indian urban middle classes. Coca is chewed with a piece of *cal*, or lime, which activates with the saliva to produce a slight numbing of cheek and tongue. The desired effect is to numb the senses, which helps stave off hunger pangs and exhaustion, and to help people live at high altitude with no ill-effects.

As well as being a prerequisite for manual workers, such as miners, coca is also taken in a social context. The native population used to deny this because, in the eyes of the bosses and clergy, an increase in labour productivity was the only permissible reason for tolerating consumption of 'the devil's leaf'. The only places where coca is not chewed is in church and in the marital bed. The masticated leaves are spat out at the bedside.

Coca is also used in various rituals, such as in offerings to *Pachamama*, or Mother Earth, to feed her when she gets hungry. Various items such as flowers and sweets, along with the ubiquitous coca leaves, are put together in bundles called *pagos* and burned on the mountains at midnight. In countless Andean markets different *pagos* are sold for different purposes – to put into the foundation of a new house; for help in matters of health, business or love; or for magic, white or black.

Coca also has numerous medicinal qualities and possesses healthy constituents such as protein, minerals, salts and vitamins. This was discovered in 1989 after Jaime Paz Zamora, then president of Bolivia, asked foreign researchers to make an objective analysis of the effects of coca consumption in an attempt to have coca removed from the international register of prohibited substances.

Despite the findings, coca remains a banned substance on the international market. Even *maté de coca*, an infusion of coca leaves, cannot be sold overseas, despite its outstanding curative qualities, not least of which is to limit the symptoms of altitude sickness.

The Quechua

The Quechua language was imposed by the Incas on several culturally and linguistically divergent groups and, to this day, many of these groups have maintained separate social identities.

The Quechua language, much more than the Aymara, is divided by many variations in regional dialect. Geographically, they are more varied, too. There are Quechua speakers in the fertile valleys of Cochabamba, on the high plateaus of Potosí, in Chuquisaca and parts of Oruro.

Some Quechua communities have lived free from outside influence for centuries. Others, such as those of the Cochabamba valley, have long been in close contact with *cholos*, a term used to describe indigenous people who have abandoned the traditional rural way of life and moved to the towns (see also page 104). These people have always been bilingual and have adapted easily to the *cholo* way of life, thus weakening their own ethnic distinctiveness. Their religious life lacks the specialized rituals of the

Other ethnic groups

There are other smaller ethnic groups, such as the Uru and the Chipaya of the Altiplano. The Chipaya, who inhabit the inhospitable Carangas region of the western Oruro Department and speak their own language, are now so small numerically that they are in danger of disappearing. A similar fate could befall the Uru, a fishing and herding people who live in the swamps of the Río Desaguadero on the edge of Lake Titicaca.

In the lowlands are some 150,000 people in 30 groups, including the Guaraní (numbering about 20,000), Ayoreo, Chiquitano (about 15,000), Chiriguano, Guaravo (about 15,000), Chimane and Mojo. Each group has its own language and, though the Jesuits settled missions in some of these remote areas over 300 years ago, have only recently been assimilated into Bolivian culture. There are also about 17,000 blacks, descendents of slaves brought from Peru and Buenos Aires in the 16th century, who now live in the Yungas.

Religion, customs and beliefs

Although some 97% of the population ostensibly belong to the Roman Catholic religion, in reality religious life for the majority of Bolivians is a mix of Catholic beliefs imported from Europe and indigenous traditions based on animism, the worship of deities from the natural world, such as mountains, animals and plants.

Pachamama

Ecotourism is the current buzzword on the lips of all self-respecting travellers and tour operators. But though ecology may be a relatively new concept here in the West, to the people of the bleak northern Bolivian Altiplano, this idea is absolutely fundamental to their very culture and almost as old as the land itself.

Pachamama, or Mother Earth, occupies a very privileged place in indigenous culture because she is the generative source of life. The Aymara believe that Man was created from the land, and thus he is fraternally tied to all the living beings that share the earth. According to them, the earth is our mother, and it is on the basis of this understanding that all of human society is organized, always maintaining the cosmic norms and laws.

Women's and men's relationship with nature is what the Aymara call ecology, harmony and equilibrium. The Aymara furthermore believe that private land ownership is a social sin because the land is for everyone. It is meant to be shared and not used only for the benefit of a few.

Vicenta Mamani Bernabé of the Andean Regional Superior Institute of Theological Studies explains: "Land is life because it produces all that we need to live. Water emanates from the land as if from the veins of a human body, there is also the natural wealth of minerals, and pasture grows from it to feed the animals. Therefore, for the Aymaras, the *Pachamama* is sacred and since we are her children, we are also sacred. No one can replace the earth, she is not meant to be exploited, or to be converted into merchandise. Our duty is to respect and care for the earth. This is what white people today are just beginning to realize, and it is called ecology. Respect for the *Pachamama* is respect for ourselves as she is life. Today, she is threatened with death and must be liberated for the sake of her children's liberation."

One of the most important dates in the indigenous people's calendar is the 2nd of November, the 'Day of the Dead'. This tradition has been practised since time immemorial. In the Inca calendar, November was the eighth month and meant Ayamarca, or land of the dead. The celebration of Day of the Dead, or 'All Saints' as it is also known, is just one example of religious adaptation in which the ancient beliefs of ethnic cultures are mixed with the rites of the Catholic Church.

According to Aymara belief, the spirit (*athun ajayu*) visits its relatives at this time of the year and is fed in order to continue its journey before its reincarnation. The relatives of the dead prepare for the arrival of the spirit days in advance. Among the many items necessary for these meticulous preparations are little bread dolls, each one of which has a particular significance. A ladder is needed for the spirit to descend from the other world to the terrestrial one. There are other figures which represent the grandparents, great grandparents and loved ones of the person who has 'passed into a better life'. Horse-shaped breads are prepared that will serve as a means of transport for the soul in order to avoid fatigue.

Inside the home, the relatives construct a tomb supported by boxes over which is laid a black cloth. Here they put the bread, along with sweets, flowers, onions and sugar cane. This last item is an indispensable part of the table as it symbolizes the invigorating element which prevents the spirit from becoming tired on its journey towards the Earth. The union of the flowers with the onion is called *tojoro* and is a vital part of the preparations. It ensures that the dead one does not become disoriented and arrives in the correct house.

The tomb is also adorned with the dead relative's favourite food and drink, not forgetting the all-important glass of beer as, according to popular tradition, this is the first nourishment taken by the souls when they arrive at their houses. Once the spirit has arrived and feasted with his/her living relatives, the entire ceremony is then transported to the graveside in the local cemetery, where it is carried out again, together with the many other mourning families.

This meeting of the living and their dead relatives is re-enacted the following year, though less ostentatiously, and again for the final time in the third year, the year of the farewell. It does not continue after this, which is just as well as the costs can be crippling for the family concerned.

Land and environment

Geology and landscape

Bolivia is the fifth largest of the 13 South American countries in size (just over one million square-kilometres) and the eighth largest in population (just over 8 million people in 2002). That makes it about the same size as France and Spain together but with only 7.6% of their population. This low population density – the lowest in the continent except for the Guianas – is explained by the high altitude and aridity of much of the terrain in the west and south, and the remoteness of the wetter, forested areas of the northeast.

Bolivia is bounded by Chile and Peru to the west, Brazil to the north and east, and Argentina and Paraguay to the south. It is, like Paraguay, landlocked, although the latter has access to the sea via the Paraná. Bolivia had a Pacific coastline until 1880 when it was lost to Chile in the War of the Pacific, 1879-1884. Since then its principal surface link to the rest of the world has been the railway and road to Arica built by the Chileans. The road linking the capital, La Paz, and Arica was brought up to modern standards only in 1996.

Bolivia also lost territory to Brazil (Acre was lost under the treaty of Petrópolis in 1903), and to Argentina and Paraguay, notably in the Chaco War, 1932-1935. The country lies wholly between the Tropic of Capricorn and the Equator.

Structure

The Andes are at their widest in Bolivia. They are formed of two main ranges (cordilleras), of which the most westerly is the frontier with Chile, and stretch for 250 km across Bolivia. The formation of the Andes began at the end of the Cretaceous geological period about 80 million years ago and has continued to the present day. To the east are much older structures of granite and crystalline rocks belonging to the South American Plate which comes to the surface further east in Brazil.

In Bolivia, however, these rocks are overlain with thick, geologically recent, deposits of alluvium brought down from the mountains by rivers and glaciers over millions of years of widely differing climates. During the most recent ice age (Pleistocene), a continuous ice-cap extended from the Antarctic to southern Bolivia, with a much lower snow line on the mountains to the north. With heavy precipitation and vast quantities of meltwater, the deep valleys were gouged out to the east and vast lakes were formed on the plateau, the most notable of which remains today as Lake Titicaca.

The Altiplano

The Altiplano is one of the largest interior basins in the world extending from northern Argentina some 900 km into southern Peru, and is nearly 10% of Bolivia. It is between 100 and 200 km wide throughout its length. The high Andes rise on either side of the Altiplano, the Cordillera Occidental to the west which includes the highest mountain in Bolivia, Nevado Sajama, 6,542 m, and the Cordillera Oriental to the east, whose highest point is Nevado de Illampu, 6,485 m. There are many snow capped peaks, mostly volcanic in origin, in both these ranges, between 5,000 m and 6,500 m.

The Altiplano itself lies at around 3,500-4,000 m, and being in the rain shadow from both east and west, has very little direct precipitation. It is a bleak, almost treeless area – just a few eucalyptus in sheltered spots in the north near villages – the southern part is practically uninhabited desert. The winds can be strong and are often violent, stirring up dust clouds and compounding the discomforts of the cold dry climate. Much of the time, however, the air is unbelievably clear and the whole plateau is a bowl of luminous light.

There are no passes out of the Altiplano below 4,000 m. The easiest exit, that is the least mountainous, is to the southeast, across the plateau and the salt desert to Argentina through Villazón. To the southwest is a remote area of volcanic activity which gives rise to some unusual saline lakes where specialized algae create the colourful Laguna Colorada, (bright red) and Laguna Verde (green).

In spite of this hostile environment, almost 70% of the population of the country live on the Altiplano, one of the highest inhabited areas of the world. Half are in the mining towns and the city of La Paz, and the other half live in the north on or near the shores of Lake Titicaca.

Lake Titicaca

This is the largest lake in South America (ignoring Lake Maracaibo in Venezuela which is linked to the sea) and at 3,812 m is the highest regularly navigated body of water in the world. It covers about 8,300 square-kilometres, running a maximum of 190 km from northwest to southeast and 80 km across. The average depth is over 100 m with the deepest point recorded at 281 m. The border with Peru passes north-south through the lake and about half is in each country.

Over 25 rivers, most from Peru, flow into the lake and a small outlet leaves the lake at Desaguadero on the Bolivia-Peru border. This takes no more than 5% of the inflow, the rest is lost through evaporation and hence the waters of the lake are slightly brackish, producing the *totora* reeds used to make the mats and balsa boats for which the lake dwellers are famed.

The lake level fluctuates seasonally, normally rising from December to March and receding for the rest of the year but extremes of 5m between high and low levels have been recorded. This can cause problems and high levels in the late 1980s disrupted transport links near the shoreline. The night temperature occasionally falls as low as -25°C but high daytime temperatures ensure the surface average is about 14°C which in turn modifies the extremes of winter and night temperatures of the surrounding land. One of the reasons for the relatively high population round the lake are the rich volcanic soils of which good use is made where water is available.

The outflow from the lake, called the Río Desaguadero, continues intermittently for 250 km to Lake Uru Uru, and Lake Poopó, which has no surface outlet and indeed often dries up in the summer.

Titicaca, Uru Uru, Poopó and other intermittent lakes are the remnants of a vast area of water formed in the last Ice Age known as Lake Ballivián. This extended at least 600 km south from Lake Titicaca and included Lake Poopó and the salt flats of Salar de Coipasa and Salar de Uyuni. Its surface was estimated to have been over 100 m above the present Lake Titicaca level and 225 m above Poopó.

The Yungas and the Puna

La Paz is built in several layers, starting on the Altiplano and going east down a steep, narrow valley which may have been one of the Ice Age exits of Lake Ballivián. Northeast from La Paz, the road to Coroico goes through a section of the Eastern Andes chain called the Cordillera Real. Immediately after the pass at La Cumbre (4,725 m), the descent towards the interior plains begins. This area of precipitous valleys and mountain spurs is called the Yungas, has considerable rainfall and is heavily forested.

The escarpment stretches northeast to the frontier with Peru, and in spite of the difficulty of the terrain, is the most fertile part of the country. South from this point, the escarpment, now facing east, falls less steeply towards the interior of the continent, backed by a plateau at around 4,000 m, called the Puna, whose western edge also overlooks the Antiplano between the high peaks of the Cordillera Oriental. The eastern slopes become drier to the south, but are still important crop growing areas. The name Yungas is used for all the semi-tropical mountain valleys. Most of this sector drains into the Madeira river system and thence to the Amazon, but from 20° south to the border with Argentina, the rivers flow into the Paraná basin.

The Oriente

Beyond the Yungas and the Puna are the lowlands that stretch northwards and eastwards to Brazil and Paraguay and represent more than 70 % of the territory of Bolivia. Similar to Peru and Colombia that also have extensive provinces east of the Andes, Bolivia's Oriente is remote, sparsely inhabited and poorly served by roads and other communications. In the northeast of this region there is dense tropical forest and wetlands. In the extreme east, the border runs close to the Río Paraguay and the Pantanal of Brazil. In the centre, the land is drier, more open with rough pasture and scrub, while in the south close to the Argentine frontier, there is still less rain and there is little more than arid savannah.

In the 18th century, much of this area was prosperous, guided by the Jesuit missions. However, when they were expelled the whole area fell into decay. In the recent past a revival has begun. In the 1950s, the Brazilians completed the railway from Santa Cruz crossing the Oriente to Brazil and all weather roads are being built to service this potentially productive part of the country. Santa Cruz has outstripped La Paz in terms of population (although not in economic activity).

Climate

The main factors controlling the climate of Bolivia are the trade wind systems and the Andes. The rising of the hot air in the tropical centre of the continent draws in the southeast Trade Winds from the south Atlantic, which are not significantly impeded by the eastern highlands of Brazil. As these moist winds rise up the lower slopes of the Andes, the rain falls. Humidity is high and temperatures high also, but not excessive, 27°C on the lower slopes, 19°C in the upper valleys of the Yungas. Rainfall is higher in the summer (November-March) as the Trades are less active in the winter months. Nevertheless, there is some precipitation all year round in the north of the country as far west as Titicaca.

In the Andes and the Altiplano, different conditions prevail. By the time the Trades have crossed the Cordillera Oriental, they have lost almost all their moisture. On the Pacific side, air is also drawn inwards over the Cordillera Occidental. However, because of the cold Humboldt current off the west coast, the air does not absorb moisture from the sea and is dry when it rises over the land. There is therefore no regular source of rain for this region. Violent local storms do produce snowfalls on the highest peaks and rain lower down from time to time.

Temperature in the Altiplano is a function of altitude, both in average levels and daily ranges. The average of 10°C at 4,000 m can be 20°C at midday often falling to -15°C at night. Arctic conditions prevail at 6,000 m. Although there can be considerable day to day fluctuations in climatic conditions, there are no noticeable seasonal changes apart from the tendency for rain to fall in the summer months.

There is one other factor which affects the south of the country. Winds originating in the south of the continent blow up the eastern side of the Andes across Argentina and push the southeast Trades northwards. This reduces the rainfall in the south of Bolivia particularly in the Altiplano resulting in near desert conditions. On the eastern slopes too, the land gets progressively drier to the south to become the semi arid scrubland of the Chaco.

Wildlife and vegetation

Bolivia is a land of superlatives. It contains the most extensive tropical rainforest in the world; the Amazon has by far the largest volume of any river in the world and the Andes is the longest uninterrupted mountain chain. The fauna and flora are to a large extent determined by the influence of those mountains and the great rivers, particularly the Amazon. In Bolivia there are vast forests carpeting the lowlands and ascending the slopes of the Andes. Equally spectacular are the huge expanses of open, tree-covered savannahs and dry deserts of the Altiplano. It is this immense range of habitats which makes Bolivia one of the world's greatest regions of biological diversity.

This diversity arises not only from the wide range of habitats available, but also from the history of the continent. South America has essentially been an island for some 70 million years joined only by a narrow isthmus to Central and North America. Land passage played a significant role in the gradual colonization of South America by species from the north. When the land-link closed these colonists evolved to a wide variety of forms free from the competitive pressures that prevailed elsewhere. When the land-bridge was re-established some four million years ago a new invasion of species took place from North America, adding to the diversity but also leading to numerous extinctions. Comparative stability has ensued since then and has guaranteed the survival of many primitive groups like the opossums.

Bolivia is a complex mosaic of more than 40 well defined ecological regions and the transition zones between them. Each has its own characteristic geology, soil, flora and fauna. There are seven major habitats worth considering here: descending from the Puna and the high Andes there are the narrow subtropical valleys or Yungas, the interandean valleys, the dry *chaco*, semi-humid woodlands, savannahs and lowland rainforest.

The lowland forests

Situated between latitudes 10° and 15° south and below 250 m altitude the great lowland forests of Bolivia encompass the entire department of Pando and parts of those of La Paz, Beni, Cochabamba and Santa Cruz. Bisected by the great tributary rivers of the Amazon – the Madeira, Mamoré, Madre de Dios, Manuripi and Beni – the area appears at first sight to be in pristine condition. But the past activities of timber operators extracting mahogany and South American cedar, latex tappers, Brazil nut gatherers, and present day mineral extraction have had a major impact on the larger species of mammals. These were extensively hunted and the result is an impoverished fauna in many areas.

Notable exceptions are the 1.8 million ha Manuripi-Heath National Reserve in central Pando and the Noel Kempff Mercado National Park. Here in the relatively constant climatic conditions animal and plant life has evolved to an amazing diversity over the millennia. It has been estimated that two square kilometres of lowland rainforest can harbour some 1,200 species of vascular plants, 600 species of tree, and 120 species of woody plants.

In the lowland forests, many of the trees are buttress rooted, with flanges extending three to four metres up the trunk of the tree. Among the smaller trees stilt-like prop roots are also common. Frequently flowers are not well developed, and some emerge directly from the branches and even the trunk. This is possibly an adaptation for pollination by the profusion of bats, giving easier access than if they were obscured by leaves. Lianas are plentiful, especially where there are natural clearings resulting from the death of old trees. These woody vines reach the tops of all but the tallest trees, tying them together and competing with them for space and light. Included here are the strangler figs. These start life as epiphytes, their seeds germinating after deposition by birds. Aerial roots develop which quickly grow down to the ground. These later envelop the trunk, killing the host and leaving the hollow 'trunk' of the strangler.

In the canopy epiphytes are also common and include bromeliads, orchids, ferns, mosses and lichens. Their nutrition is derived from mineral nutrients in the water and organic debris they collect often in specialized pitcher-like structures. Animals of the canopy have developed striking adaptations to enable them to exist in this green wilderness, for example, the prehensile tails of the opossums and many of the monkeys, and the peculiar development of the claws of the sloth.

Many of the bird species which creep around in the understorey are drab coloured, for example tinamou and cotingas, but have loud, clear calls. Scuttling around on the ground are the elusive armadillos, their presence marked by burrows. Pock-marked areas may be indicative of the foraging activities of pacas or peccaries, where their populations have not been exploited by over-hunting.

The forest is at its densest along the river margins; here the diffused light reduces the density of the understorey plant community. The variety of trees is amazing. The forest giants are the kapok and the Brazil nut or castanheiro. These river corridors are often the best places to observe wildlife. Caiman and turtles are commonly seen basking on the river banks. Neotropical cormorants, Roseate spoonbills and Jabiru storks are commonly observed fishing in the shallow waters. The swollen rivers of the lowland forest are home to perhaps 2,000 species of fish including piranha, sting ray and electric eel. Many species provide an important source of protein for the native communities, for example, giant catfish. River dolphins also frequent these waters.

The vast river basin of the Amazon is home to an immense variety of species. The environment has largely dictated the lifestyle. Life in or around rivers, lakes, swamps and forest depends on the ability to swim and climb; amphibious and tree-dwelling animals are common. Once the entire Amazon basin was a great inland sea and the river still contains mammals more typical of the coast, for example manatees and dolphins.

The best way to see the wildlife is to get above the canopy. Ridges provide elevated view points from which excellent views over the forest are obtained. From here, it is possible to look across the lowland flood plain to the very foothills of the Andes, possibly some 200 km away. Flocks of parrots and macaws can be seen commuting between fruiting trees and noisy troupes of squirrel monkeys and brown capuchins come tantalisingly close.

The savannah

The savannah habitat comprises grass and low shrub criss-crossed with rivers and contrasts greatly with the lowland rain forest. It is more obviously seasonal, dry in August and verdant with profuse new growth in December. Small palm groves are characteristic and provide nesting opportunities for macaws.

In the Beni region the savannahs are seasonally flooded, and the mammal fauna then has to congregate on high ground. Impressive aggregations of birds flock to feed on the fish stranded in the withering pools. Large anacondas and caiman abound and herds of russet coloured capybara and swamp deer are commonly seen from roads that intersect the area. Small isolated fragments of dry deciduous forest are found interspersed among the flooded plains, and these hold a characteristic fauna in refuges from the ingress of cattle ranching and the burning of grassland associated with it.

In the northwestern part of the Beni region and southeastern Santa Cruz there are also permanently flooded savannahs which are swampy and have characteristic floating mats of vegetation (some with trees), that are shifted around by the wind.

The well-drained soils and moderate climate of the region of Santa Cruz provide conditions for the growth of semi-humid forests from about 300 m to 1,200 m above sea level. The altitudinal and climatic range experienced provides for a wealth of flora and fauna which has been exploited by man.

The Chaco

This is a dry region with an annual precipitation of usually less than 300 mm and an average temperature of 26°C, but characterized by cold fronts that on occasion kill new growth in the forest leaving bare trunks. Somewhat surprisingly many species of larger mammals are found here including tapir, jaguar, brocket deer and peccary.

The Chaco consists of a variety of habitat types ranging from a mixture of thorny chapparal, with natural grasslands, palms and dry deciduous forests. Due to exposure to heat and intense insulation most of the animals are nocturnal, giving the impression of a low density of mammals. The Bolivian Chaco is perhaps the last refuge for the Chacoan peccary and guanacos. The saó dwarf palm used in the manufacture of the traditional straw hats from Santa Cruz is also found here.

Some of the drier valleys have a mesothermic vegetation (for example cactuses) as they are in the rain shadow of the surrounding mountains. The valleys have a very rich bird fauna, to which the military and golden macaw are unique. Rare mammals such as the spectacled bear, taruca (a deer), and the pacarana (a large rodent) are found here. At higher altitudes the cloud forests contain tree ferns and epiphyte clad trees, including birch (aliso) and podocarpus.

The Yungas

The Yungas comprise a belt of very humid forests at altitudes ranging up to 3,600 m. The headwaters of many of Bolivia's major rivers rise here and flow as clear, rapid streams through deep canyons. The vegetation ranges from that typical of lowland forest through to cloud forest and, at the tree line, elfin forest with ferns and bamboo. The great diversity of habitats has led to a great diversity of fauna, likely to be the richest in the country. The spectacled bear, and exotic birds such as the Andean cock of the rock and the horned currasow are denizens of this habitat.

The Highlands

Life is rare in the puna and high mountains. The climate is dry and cold, particularly in the Altiplano where there is little or no vegetation except for a few shrubs, cacti and dry grass. The vast climatic range, from 15°C during the day to -25°C during the night, impose severe limits on life. An exception to this concerns the Laguna Colorada where a vast lake warmed by fumaroles is home to thousands of flamingoes and other water birds. Vicuñas, vizcachas, rheas and Andean wild cats survive in a delicate balance within this fragile environment.

Protected areas

AN   Area Natural
      de Manejo Integrado
PN   Parque Nacional
RN   Reserva Nacional
RBI   Reserva Biológica
RB   Reserva de la Biósfera
RVS   Reserva Vida Silvestre
RFA   Reserva de Fauna Andina

1   RVS Amazónica Manuripi
2   AN Apolobamba
3   PN & AN Amboró

4   PN Carrasco
5   RBI Cordillera de Sama
6   PN & AN Cotapata
7   RN de Flora y Fauna Tariquia
8   RB del Beni
9   RFA Eduardo Avaroa
10 AN El Palmar
11 PN Isiboro Sécure
12 PN & AN Kaa-Iya
    del Gran Chaco

13 PN & AN Madidi
14 PN Noel Kempff Mercado
15 PN & AN Otuquis
16 RB Pilon-Lajas
17 PN Sajama
18 AN San Matías
19 PN & AN Serranía
    de Agüaragüe
20 PN Torotoro
21 PN Tunari

The Pantanal

The Bolivian pantanal is an ecologically diverse zone continuous with that in Brazil. When flooded from December to March, it creates the largest area of wetlands in the world. It also includes dry savannahs or *cerrado*, chaco scrublands as well as gallery rainforest. The area is very flat and flooded by the rising rivers leaving isolated islands (*cordilheiras*) between vast lakes (*bahais*) which become saline as the waters evaporate.

This mixed ecosystem supports a highly diverse fauna characteristic of the constituent habitat types which includes 200 species of mammal. Capybara, tapir and peccaries are common along the water's edge, as are marsh deer. Jaguar, more commonly associated with the forest, prey on these herbivores and the cattle and feral pigs which graze here. Spectacular numbers of wading birds – egrets, jabiru storks, ibises and herons – prey on the abundant invertebrate and fish fauna. Anacondas and caiman are still common, although the black caiman has been hunted out.

National parks

With nine distinct ecosystems and 42 sub-systems, Bolivia has one of the highest rates of bio-diversity on the planet. One of the top 10 countries globally for sheer diversity of animal life, it is also ranks amongst the top five for bird species, mammals, and reptiles and amphibians. The same is true for its plant life and geographic wonders: There simply is nothing like it anywhere else on earth.

The good news is that the colourful, exotic creatures and landscapes featured in the glossy brochures and websites of travel agents and tour guides are indeed out there. Better still, the traveller has a choice of seeing them independently or in a group. Better yet, the entrance fees for Bolivia's parks (not all charge fees) are far below what they are in most countries. The bad news is that getting to see things up close and personal often is not as easy as the hawkers and touts would have you believe, and once you are there, there generally isn't much choice of accommodations or provisions unless you are with an established tour company.

It must be understood that Bolivia's protected areas are similar to the country's traintables: they exist, but sometimes on paper only. When they do operate, it usually is not on the level that tourists from more developed nations expect. Doing a 'reality check' before heading out to see the wonders of the Bolivian countryside is definitely in order. The vast majority of Bolivian parks have been open for less than two decades, and infrastructure and access for most is minimal.

About 15% of Bolivia's territory – almost 18 million hectares — is classified as legally protected in one form or another (the second-highest percentage of any country in the Western Hemisphere). In reality, about 4% actually is maintained as parkland. Although there are more than two dozen areas of varying size designated as future protected habitats, how many of these 'paper parks' will make it from the drawing board to true park status is anyone's guess.

The single most important consideration for anyone making a trip to these areas should be the climate. All but two are virtually inaccessible during the rainy season, and even if they were, communication, supplies, and help are not. Apart from the few tribal groups that still inhabit some reserves, the vast majority of people associated with the operation of Bolivia's parks are not on call during the seasonal floods or inclement weather! The long treks required in some arid regions also should deter would-be visitors from trying their luck in very hot weather.

Other considerations to bear in mind are the political and social atmosphere surrounding many of the parks. In recent years, some have decreased in size (most noticeably, **Parque Nacional Amboró** and **Reserva Biosférica del Beni**) as

Bolivian National Parks

Name	Department	Size	Fee
Serranía del Aguaragüe	Tarija	108,307 ha	None
Amboró	Santa Cruz	637,600 ha	None
Apolobamba	La Paz	483,744 ha	None
Carrasco	Cochabamba	622,600 ha	None
Cordillera de Sama	Tarija	108,500 ha	US$4
Cotapata	La Paz	583 sq km	None
Eduardo Avaroa	Potosí	714,745 ha	US$5
El Palmar [Rodeo]	Chuquisaca	59,484 ha	None
Estación Biológica del Beni	Beni	135,000 ha	US$5
Isiboro-Sécure	Beni/Cochabamba	1,200,000 ha	None
Kaa-Iya del Gran Chaco	Santa Cruz	3,441,115 ha	None
Madidi	La Paz	1,895,750 ha	None
Manuripi	Pando	747,000 ha	None
Noel Kempff Mercado	Santa Cruz/Beni compulsory guides	1, 523,446 ha	None, but US$15 per day
Otuquis	Santa Cruz	1,005,950 ha	None
Pilón Lajas	Beni/La Paz	400,000 ha	US$6 per person
Sajama	Oruro	100,230 ha	US$2
[Pantanal de] San Matías	Santa Cruz	2,918,500 ha	None
Tariquía	Tarija	246,870 ha	US$3
Torotoro	Potosí	16,570 ha	US$2
Tunari	Cochabamba	300,000 ha	None

Guides/tours	Key sites	See page...
Yes/no	Cañon de Pilcomayo	
Yes/yes	Mataracú camp	page 319
	Macañucu camp	
	Cerro Amboró	
Yes/no	Cordillera Apolobamba	page 168
	Curva, Valle de Amarete	
Yes/yes	Cavernas del Repechón	page 293
	Cueva de los Pájaros Nocturnos	
	Incachaca, Todos Santos	
Yes/no	Lagos Tajzara, Coimata falls	
	Chorros de Jurina falls	
Yes/no	Valle Zongo	page 175
	Sendero La Cumbre (Coroico)	
Yes/yes	Laguna Colorada	
	Laguna Verde	
	Termes de Polques	
Yes/no		
Yes/yes	Las Torre	page 363
	Laguna Normandia	
	Sendero El Triunfo	
	Totaizal	
No/yes	Laguna Bolivia	page 293
	Río Sécure	
No/no	Bañados del Izozog	page 340
No/no	Chalalán eco-lodge	page 363
	Río Madidi	
	Río Tuichi indigenous villages	
	San José de Uchupiamonas	
Yes/yes	Chive, Río Madre de Dios	
	Río Manuripi	
Yes/yes	Arco Iris Falls, El Encanto falls	page 341
	Federico Ahlfeld Falls	
	Laguna Chaplin Reserve, Los Fierros	
	Serranía de Huanchaca	
	Sierra de Caparuch	
No/no	Banados	page 343
Yes/yes	Indigenous villages	page 361
Yes/yes	Nevado/Volcán Sajama,	page 199
	Termes de Sajama	
No/yes	El Panatal, Santo Corazón	page 344
Yes/no	Centro de la Mancomunidad	
	de Tariquí	
Yes/yes	Batea Cocha	page 289
Yes/yes	Cerro Tunari, La Pirámide	page 280

Background Land & environment

campesinos, loggers, miners, and others have pressed for more land. Although Bolivia has been extraordinarily successful in receiving international debt reductions and grants ear- marked for preserving its ecosystems, some of these areas have steadily eroded, and the government has shown little initiative in defining boundaries or enforcing encroach- ment laws. In some cases (eg **Parque Nacional Madidi**), after initial high-profile success, donor governments have withdrawn resources in the face of destruction of fragile ecosystems and commercial exploitation. In others, proximity to dangerous areas has led to a sharp decline in attendance and maintenance.

Not all the news is bad. Remote Parque Nacional Kaa-Iya del Gran Chaco presents another issue: multinational petroleum outfits seeking to explore lands granted to indigenous peoples. Both sides are in negotiations, and a settlement that allows some exploration without disturbing the natural habitat appears to be in the making. La Paz's **Area Protegida Apolobamba** (formerly **Parque Nacional de Ulla Ulla**) also has had great success integrating native interests with those of outsiders, and **Parque Nacional Noel Kempff Mercado** and **Reserva Biosférica Pilón Lajas** now have world-class habitat protection initiatives in place.

Books

Travelogues

Duguid, J, *Green Hell: A Chronicle of Travel in the Forests of Eastern Bolivia*, (Jonathan Cape, London, 1931). Entertaining account of a journey across the Bolivian Chaco in 1931. By the same author are 2 novels set in the Bolivian jungle: *A Cloak of Monkey Fur* (1936), and *Father Coldstream* (1938).

Fawcett, P, *Exploration Fawcett* (Century, 1988). Tells of the famous British explorer's quest to discover El Dorado.

Guevara, C, *The Motorcycle Diaries: A Journey Around South America* (Perennial, 2004). An account of Che's travels around South America on a beat-up old bike. This is no Pulitzer prize winner but is always engaging and offers an insight into the young Che's political development.

Jones, T, T*he Incredible Voyage* (Futura Publications, 1980). The author describes his experiences after spending over 8 months of cruising Lake Titicaca in his sailing cutter Sea Dart.

Meyer, G, *Summer at High Altitude* (Alan Ross, London, 1968). A fascinating account of a journey through Bolivia in the mid-1960s with detailed insights into various aspects of Bolivian culture and history.

Rojo, H. B, *Descubriendo Bolivia* (1989). A tour through the departments of present-day Bolivia, with photographs and road routes (the book is also available in English).

Shukman, H, *Sons of the Moon* (Fontana, 1991). An interesting insight into the lives of the Aymara.

Young, Rusty, *Marching Powder* (Sidgwick & Jackson, 2003). The true story of Thomas McFadden, a small-time English drug dealer jailed in La Paz's extraordinary San Pedro prison. He gets by giving tours of the prison to gringos.

Fiction

Cleary, J, *Mask of the Andes* (Collins, London, 1982). An entertaining novel set amidst the backdrop of post-1952 revolutionary politics.

Hutchison, R C, *Rising*, (Penguin, 1982). A gripping tale of conflict between the rich creole landowners and the Indian peasantry.

Santos, R (ed), *The Fat Man from La Paz: Contemporary Fiction from Bolivia* (2000) is an extensive collection of short stories by some of Bolivia's finest writers.

Wilson, J, *Traveller's Literary Companion, South and Central America* (Brighton, UK:

In Print, 1993). Has extracts from works by Latin American writers and by non-Latin Americans about the various countries and has very useful bibliographies in addition.

History, politics and culture

Anderson, J L, *Che Guevara: a Revolutionary Life* (Bantam Press, 1997). A must for anyone interested in the life of Guevara and his time in Bolivia.

Clawson, P and Lee, R, *The Andean Cocaine Industry* (Palgrave MacMillan, 1999). An extensive study of the economic and political impact of the drug business on Andean countries.

Cramer, M, *Culture Shock: Bolivia* (Times Editions, 1996). A wry, humorous and insightful look at Bolivia and Bolivians.

Davies, L and Fini, M, *Arts and Crafts of South America* (Tumi, 1994). Information on arts and crafts in Bolivia and the rest of South America.

Ferry, S, *I am Rich Potosí* (Monacelli Press,1999). Another fascinating read on the subject of mining.

Kolata, A, *Valley of the Spirits* (Wiley & Sons, 1996). By far the most comprehensive book on Tiahuanaco.

McFarren, P, *An Insider's Guide to Bolivia* (Fundación Cultural Quipus, 1992). Gives a good historical background and includes an interesting article by Johann Reinhard about archaeological discoveries in Lake Titicaca (see page 147). Also published by Quipus: *La fe viva: las Misiones Jesuíticas en Bolivia*, a thorough history of the Jesuit Missions with many sumptuous photographs of the churches; and *Masks of the Bolivian Andes*.

Meadows, A, *Digging Up Butch and Sundance* (New York: St Martin's Press, 1994). An account of the last days of Butch Cassidy and The Sundance Kid and the attempts to find their graves.

Nash, J, *We Eat the Mines and the Mines Eat Us* (Columbia University Press, 1972, new ed 1994). Tells the history of mining in Bolivia and gives a detailed insight into the lives of the miners.

Saldana, R and Waters, M, *Fertile Ground: Che Guevara and Bolivia* (Pathfinder, 2001). Less daunting account of Che and Bolivia than the Anderson biography.

Saunders, N J (ed), *Ancient America, Contributions to New World Archaeology* (Oxford: Oxbow Monograph 24, 1992). Includes a chapter on 'Underwater Archaeological Research in Lake Titicaca' by Reinhard.

Spitzer, L, *Hotel Bolivia* (Hill & Wang Pub.,1999), tells the fascinating story of emigré Jews who fled to Bolivia to escape Hitler's persecution, only to find themselves living with Nazi war criminals after the war had ended.

Van Lindent, P and Verkaren, O, *Bolivia in Focus* (Latin American Bureau, London 1984) A concise study of Bolivian politics, economy, culture and people.

Waters, M (ed), *The Bolivian Diary of Ernesto Che Guevara*. A detailed personal account of the abortive 1966-67 guerilla campaign.

Trekking and climbing

Biggar, J, *The Andes: A Trekking guide,* (Andes, 2001). Features some popular Bolivian treks and some lesser-known ones.

Brain, Y, *Bolivia – a climbing guide* (The Mountaineers, Seattle, 1999). Gives comprehensive coverage of Bolivia's mountains.

Brain, Y, *Trekking in Bolivia* (The Mountaineers, 1998).

Birdwatching

Krabbe, N and Fieldsa, J, *Birds of the High Andes,* (Apollo Books, Denmark, 1990).

Remsen, J V and Traylor, M A, *An Annotated List to the Birds of Bolivia* (Harrell Books, 1989).

Footnotes

Basic Spanish for travellers

Volumes of dictionaries, phrase books or word lists will not provide the same enjoyment as being able to communicate directly with the people of the country you are visiting. Learning Spanish is a useful part of the preparation for a trip to Latin America and you are encouraged to make an effort to grasp the basics before you go. As you travel you will pick up more of the language and the more you know, the more you will benefit from your stay. The following section is designed to be a simple point of departure.

General pronunciation

Whether you have been taught the 'Castilian' pronunciation (*z* and *c* followed by *i* or *e* are pronounced as the *th* in think) or the 'American' pronunciation (they are pronounced as *s*), you will encounter little difficulty in understanding either. Regional accents and usages vary, but the basic language is essentially the same everywhere.

Vowels

a as in English *cat*
e as in English *best*
i as the *ee* in English *feet*
o as in English *shop*
u as the *oo* in English *food*
ai as the *i* in English *ride*
ei as *ey* in English *they*
oi as *oy* in English *toy*

Consonants

Most consonants can be pronounced more or less as they are in English. The exceptions are:

g before *e* or *i* is the same as *j* (see below)
h is always silent (except in *ch* as in *chair*)
j as the *ch* in Scottish *loch*
ll as the *y* in *yellow*
ñ as the *ni* in English *onion*
rr trilled much more than in English
x depending on its location, pronounced *x, s, sh* or *j*

Greetings, courtesies

hello	*hola*
good morning	*buenos días*
good afternoon/evening/night	*buenas tardes/noches*
goodbye	*adiós/chao*
pleased to meet you	*mucho gusto*
see you later	*hasta luego*
how are you?	*¿cómo está?¿cómo estás?*
I'm fine, thanks	*estoy muy bien, gracias*
I'm called...	*me llamo...*
what is your name?	*¿cómo se llama? ¿cómo te llamas?*
yes/no	*sí/no*
please	*por favor*
thank you (very much)	*(muchas) gracias*
I speak Spanish	*hablo español*
I don't speak Spanish	*no hablo español*
do you speak English?	*¿habla inglés?*
I don't understand	*no entiendo/no comprendo*
please speak slowly	*hable despacio por favor*
I am very sorry	*lo siento mucho/disculpe*
what do you want?	*¿qué quiere? ¿qué quieres?*
I want	*quiero*
I don't want it	*no lo quiero*
leave me alone	*déjeme en paz/no me moleste*
good/bad	*bueno/malo*

Basic questions and requests

have you got a room for two people?	¿tiene una habitación para dos personas?
how do I get to_?	¿cómo llego a_?
how much does it cost?	¿cuánto cuesta? ¿cuánto es?
I'd like to make a long-distance phone call	quisiera hacer una llamada de larga distancia
is service included?	¿está incluido el servicio?
is tax included?	¿están incluidos los impuestos?
when does the bus leave (arrive)?	¿a qué hora sale (llega) el autobús?
when?	¿cuándo?
where is_?	¿dónde está_?
where can I buy tickets?	¿dónde puedo comprar boletos?
where is the nearest petrol station?	¿dónde está la gasolinera más cercana?
why?	¿por qué?

Basic words and phrases

bank	el banco
bathroom/toilet	el baño
to be	ser, estar
bill	la factura/la cuenta
cash	el efectivo
cheap	barato/a
credit card	la tarjeta de crédito
exchange house	la casa de cambio
exchange rate	el tipo de cambio
expensive	caro/a
to go	ir
to have	tener, haber
market	el mercado
note/coin	el billete/la moneda
police (policeman)	la policía (el policía)
post office	el correo
public telephone	el teléfono público
shop	la tienda
supermarket	el supermercado
there is/are	hay
there isn't/aren't	no hay
ticket office	la taquilla
travellers' cheques	los cheques de viajero/los travelers

Getting around

aeroplane	el avión
airport	el aeropuerto
arrival/departure	la llegada/salida
avenue	la avenida
block	la cuadra
border	la frontera
bus station	la terminal de autobuses/camiones
bus	el bus/el autobús/el camión
collective/fixed-route taxi	el colectivo
corner	la esquina
customs	la aduana
first/second class	la primera/segunda clase
left/right	izquierda/derecha
ticket	el boleto
empty/full	vacío/lleno
highway, main road	la carretera
immigration	la inmigración
insurance	el seguro
insured person	el asegurado/la asegurada

to insure yourself against	*asegurarse contra*
luggage	*el equipaje*
motorway, freeway	*el autopista/la carretera*
north, south, west, east	*el norte, el sur, el oeste (occidente), el este (oriente)*
oil	*el aceite*
to park	*estacionarse*
passport	*el pasaporte*
petrol/gasoline	*la gasolina*
puncture	*el pinchazo/la ponchadura*
street	*la calle*
that way	*por allí/por allá*
this way	*por aquí/por acá*
tourist card/visa	*la tarjeta de turista/visa*
tyre	*la llanta*
unleaded	*sin plomo*
waiting room	*la sala de espera*
to walk	*caminar/andar*

Accommodation

air conditioning	*el aire acondicionado*
all-inclusive	*todo incluido*
bathroom, private	*el baño privado*
bed, double/single	*la cama matrimonial/sencilla*
blankets	*las cobijas/mantas*
to clean	*limpiar*
dining room	*el comedor*
guesthouse	*la casa de huéspedes*
hotel	*el hotel*
noisy	*ruidoso*
pillows	*las almohadas*
power cut	*el apagón/corte*
restaurant	*el restaurante*
room/bedroom	*el cuarto/la habitación*
sheets	*las sábanas*
shower	*la ducha/regadera*
soap	*el jabón*
toilet	*el sanitario/excusado*
toilet paper	*el papel higiénico*
towels, clean/dirty	*las toallas limpias/sucias*
water, hot/cold	*el agua caliente/fría*

Health

aspirin	*la aspirina*
blood	*la sangre*
chemist	*la farmacia*
condoms	*los preservativos, los condones*
contact lenses	*los lentes de contacto*
contraceptives	*los anticonceptivos*
contraceptive pill	*la píldora anticonceptiva*
diarrhoea	*la diarrea*
doctor	*el médico*
fever/sweat	*la fiebre/el sudor*
pain	*el dolor*
head	*la cabeza*
period/sanitary towels	*la regla/las toallas femininas*
stomach	*el estómago*
altitude sickness	*el soroche*

Family

family	*la familia*
brother/sister	*el hermano/la hermana*
daughter/son	*la hija/el hijo*
father/mother	*el padre/la madre*
husband/wife	*el esposo (marido)/la esposa*
boyfriend/girlfriend	*el novio/la novia*
friend	*el amigo/la amiga*
married	*casado/a*
single/unmarried	*soltero/a*

Months, days and time

January	*enero*
February	*febrero*
March	*marzo*
April	*abril*
May	*mayo*
June	*junio*
July	*julio*
August	*agosto*
September	*septiembre*
October	*octubre*
November	*noviembre*
December	*diciembre*
Monday	*lunes*
Tuesday	*martes*
Wednesday	*miércoles*
Thursday	*jueves*
Friday	*viernes*
Saturday	*sábado*
Sunday	*domingo*
at one o'clock	*a la una*
at half past two	*a las dos y media*
at a quarter to three	*a cuarto para las tres/a las tres menos quince*
it's one o'clock	*es la una*
it's seven o'clock	*son las siete*
it's six twenty	*son las seis y veinte*
it's five to nine	*son cinco para las nueve/las nueve menos cinco*
in ten minutes	*en diez minutos*
five hours	*cinco horas*
does it take long?	*¿tarda mucho?*

Numbers

one	*uno/una*
two	*dos*
three	*tres*
four	*cuatro*
five	*cinco*
six	*seis*
seven	*siete*
eight	*ocho*
nine	*nueve*
ten	*diez*
eleven	*once*
twelve	*doce*
thirteen	*trece*
fourteen	*catorce*

fifteen	*quince*
sixteen	*dieciséis*
seventeen	*diecisiete*
eighteen	*dieciocho*
nineteen	*diecinueve*
twenty	*veinte*
twenty-one	*veintiuno*
thirty	*treinta*
forty	*cuarenta*
fifty	*cincuenta*
sixty	*sesenta*
seventy	*setenta*
eighty	*ochenta*
ninety	*noventa*
hundred	*cien/ciento*
thousand	*mil*

Food

avocado	*el aguacate*
baked	*al horno*
bakery	*la panadería*
banana	*el plátano*
beans	*los frijoles/las habichuelas*
beef	*la carne de res*
beef steak or pork fillet	*el bistec*
boiled rice	*el arroz blanco*
bread	*el pan*
breakfast	*el desayuno*
butter	*la mantequilla*
cake	*el pastel*
chewing gum	*el chicle*
chicken	*el pollo*
chilli pepper or green pepper	*el ají/el chile/el pimiento*
clear soup, stock	*el caldo*
cooked	*cocido*
dining room	*el comedor*
egg	*el huevo*
fish	*el pescado*
fork	*el tenedor*
fried	*frito*
garlic	*el ajo*
goat	*el chivo*
grapefruit	*la toronja/el pomelo*
grill	*la parrilla*
guava	*la guayaba*
ham	*el jamón*
hamburger	*la hamburguesa*
hot, spicy	*picante*
ice cream	*el helado*
jam	*la mermelada*
knife	*el cuchillo*
lime	*el limón*
lobster	*la langosta*
lunch	*el almuerzo/la comida*
meal	*la comida*
meat	*la carne*
minced meat	*el picadillo*
onion	*la cebolla*
orange	*la naranja*

pepper	el pimiento
pasty, turnover	la empanada/el pastelito
pork	el cerdo
potato	la papa
prawns	los camarones
raw	crudo
restaurant	el restaurante
salad	la ensalada
salt	la sal
sandwich	el bocadillo
sauce	la salsa
sausage	la longaniza/el chorizo
scrambled eggs	los huevos revueltos
seafood	los mariscos
soup	la sopa
spoon	la cuchara
squash	la calabaza
squid	los calamares
supper	la cena
sweet	dulce
to eat	comer
toasted	tostado
turkey	el pavo
vegetables	los legumbres/vegetales
without meat	sin carne
yam	el camote

Drink

beer	la cerveza
boiled	hervido/a
bottled	en botella
camomile tea	té de manzanilla
canned	en lata
coffee	el café
coffee, white	el café con leche
cold	frío
cup	la taza
drink	la bebida
drunk	borracho/a
firewater	el aguardiente
fruit milkshake	el batido/licuado
glass	el vaso
hot	caliente
ice/without ice	el hielo/sin hielo
juice	el jugo
lemonade	la limonada
milk	la leche
mint	la menta/la hierbabuena
rum	el ron
soft drink	el refresco
sugar	el azúcar
tea	el té
to drink	beber/tomar
water	el agua
water, carbonated	el agua mineral con gas
water, still mineral	el agua mineral sin gas
wine, red	el vino tinto
wine, white	el vino blanco

Index

Map index

Advertisers' index

Credits

Footprint credits

Text editor: Laura Dixon
Map editor: Sarah Sorensen
Picture editor: Claire Benison
Proofreader: Anita Sach

Publisher: Patrick Dawson
Editorial: Sophie Blacksell, Sarah Thorowgood, Claire Boobbyer, Felicity Laughton, Nicola Jones, Angus Dawson.
Cartography: Robert Lunn, Claire Benison, Kevin Feeney, Melissa Lin.
Series development Rachel Fielding
Design: Mytton Williams and Rosemary Dawson (brand)
Advertising: Debbie Wylde
Finance and administration: Sharon Hughes, Elizabeth Taylor, Lindsay Dytham

Photography credits

Front cover: Alamy
Inside: Alamy, Powerstock, Alex Robinson, Julius Honnor, Robert Harding, Travel Ink.
Back cover: Julius Honnor

Print

Manufactured in Italy by LegoPrint
Pulp from sustainable forests

Footprint feedback

We try as hard as we can to make each Footprint guide as up to date as possible but, of course, things always change. If you want to let us know about your experiences – good, bad or ugly – then don't delay, go to www.footprintbooks.com and send in your comments.

Publishing information

Footprint Bolivia
4th edition
© Footprint Handbooks Ltd
November 2004
ISBN 1 904777 24 4

CIP DATA: A catalogue record for this book is available from the British Library

® Footprint Handbooks and the Footprint mark are a registered trademark of Footprint Handbooks Ltd

Published by Footprint

6 Riverside Court
Lower Bristol Road
Bath BA2 3DZ, UK
T +44 (0)1225 469141
F +44 (0)1225 469461
discover@footprintbooks.com
www.footprintbooks.com

Distributed in the USA by

Publishers Group West

Acknowledgements

Alan Murphy

Alan Murphy would like to thank all those who helped so much in the previous edition of Bolivia: Roger Perkins and Kate Hannay, Stephen Frankham, John Biggar, Mark Kramer, Katherine Stipala of CARE International, Jean Brown, Caz Bointon and Ben Box. A special thanks to Yossi Brain, who died in 1999 while climbing in the Apolobamba range. He is sorely missed as a correspondent and a friend.

Thanks to the specialist contributors: Peter Pollard for Geology and Landscape; Nigel Dunstone for Flora and Fauna; Dr Valerie Fraser for Painting and Sculpture; Sarah Cameron for Economy; Gavin Clark for Literature; Keith Richards for Cinema; Mark Eckstein for Responsible Tourism; Dr Charlie Easmon for Health; Ashley Rawlings for motorycling; Hallam Murray for Cycling; Lucy Davies and Mo Fini for Arts and Crafts; Dan Buck for Che Guevara and Butch Cassidy and the Sundance Kid; Nigel Gallop for Music and Dance; and Tourism Concern for allowing us to adapt their Traveller's Code in 'How Big is your Footprint?'

Thanks are also due to all the travellers who emailed and wrote in with their corrections, additions and suggestions.

Julius Honnor

Thanks to an enormous number of helpful people and fellow travellers who asked good questions and gave freely of their opinions and observations. Special thanks to Roberto Prueba in tourist information in Rurrenabaque, Eduardo and Vania at Rosario, Martin Strätker at La Cupola, Marcelo Arce in many places, Gert van der Meijden at Joy Ride, Alistair and Karin at Gravity, Pete in Sorata, Alan and Laura at Footprint for encouragement and patience, Joe and Fritha for leading us through the dark, Tom and Liz and co for fantastic company and ups and downs, Jennifer and Colin for great extensive travel notes, and finally Clair, for being made redundant so that she could come with me and for being, as always, enthusiastic, supportive and wonderful.

Geoff Groesbeck

Muchísimas gracias to all the *cruzeños* who answered my innumerable questions, in particular María Isabel Rivera of La Mancomunidad; Franca Calmotti and Andreas Ohff of UPSA; René Hohenstein and Cecelia Kenning of APAC; Robert and Elva Birt of Editora Exclusiva; the wonderful Cornejo family; and especially Thomas and Denise Wallis, who kindness to me can never be repaid. Last but not least, to *la hermosa* Rose Martinez, a continual source of inspiration (although she never guessed).

The health section was written by **Dr Charlie Easmon** MBBS, MRCP, MPH, DTM&H, DOCCMed, Director of Travel Screening Services.

For a different view of Europe, take a Footprint

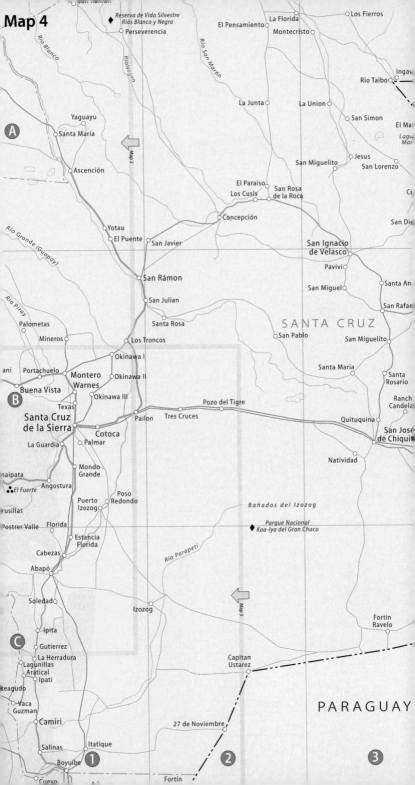

Map 4

Reserva de Vida Silvestre
Riós Blanco y Negra
Perseverencia

La Florida
El Pensamiento
Montecristo
Los Fierros

Río Blanco
Río Negro
Río San Martín

Rio Taibo
Inga

A
Yaguayu
Santa María
Ascención

La Junta
La Union
San Simon
El Ma
Lagu
Mar

San Miguelito
Jesus
San Lorenzo

Map 2

El Paraiso
Los Cusis
San Rosa
de la Roca

Río Grande (Guapay)
Yotau
El Puente
San Javier
Concepción
San Die

San Ignacio
de Velasco

Río Piray
San Rámon
San Julian
Santa Rosa

Pavivi
San Miguel
Santa An
San Rafae

Palometas
Mineros
Los Troncos
Okinawa I
Okinawa II
Santa Rosa

SANTA CRUZ
San Pablo
San Miguelito
Santa Maria

ani
Portachuelo
Montero
Warnes
Okinawa III

B
Buena Vista
Texas

Santa
Rosario
Ranch
Candela

Santa Cruz
de la Sierra
Cotoca
Palmar
Pailon
Tres Cruces
Pozo del Tigre
Quituquina
San José
de Chiqui

La Guardia
Mondo
Grande
Poso
Redondo
Natividad

naipata
El Fuerte
Angostura
Puerto
Izozog

Bañados del Izozog

rusillas
Postrer Valle
Florida
Estancia
Florida

Parque Nacional
Kaa-Iya del Gran Chaco

Cabezas
Abapó
Río Parapeti

C
Soledad
Ipita
Izozog
Map 3

Gutierrez
La Herradura
Lagunillas
Aratical
Ipati

Fortin
Ravelo

teagudo
Vaca
Guzman
Camiri

Capitan
Ustarez

PARAGUAY

Salinas
Itatique
1
27 de Noviembre
2
3

Boyuibe
Cuevo
Fortín

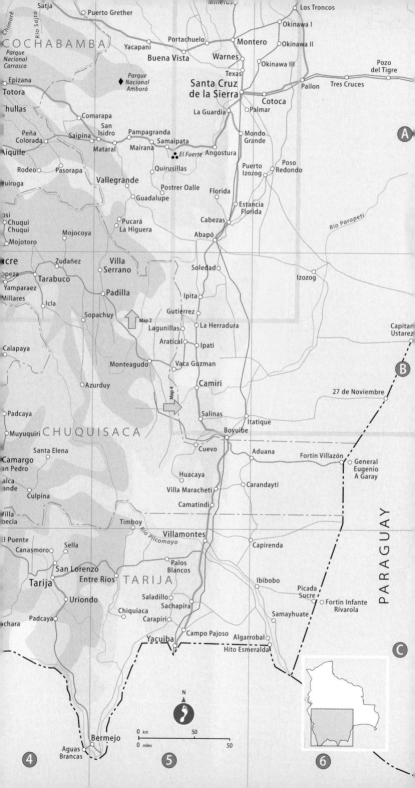

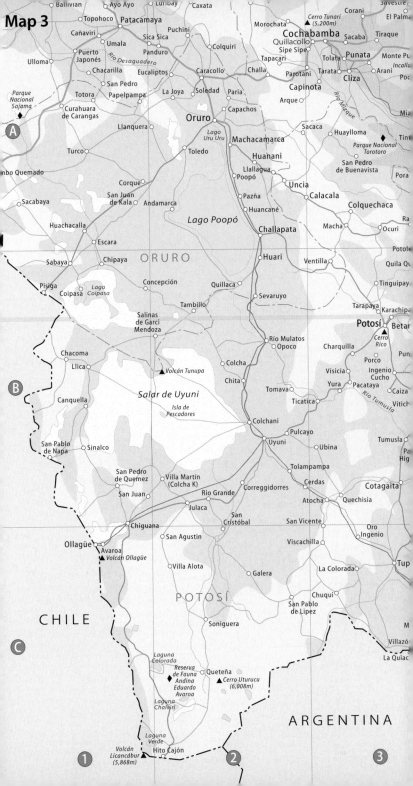

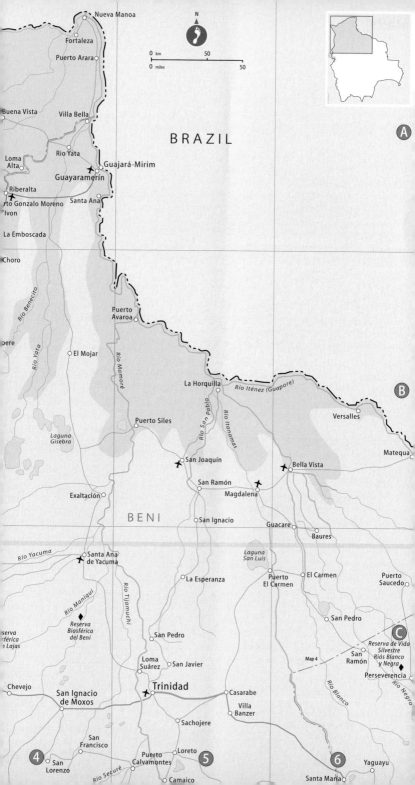

Map 1

A

Assis Brasil
Iñapari

Mukden
Cobija
Tres Estrellas
Porvenir
Fortaleza
Extrema

Libertad
San Silvestre

Chive

B

PERU

Puerto
Heath

Río Heath

Guarayos
Alto Madidi

Río Chipamanu

Santa Rosa
de Abuna
Dos Calles
Santa Estrella Nacebe
Elena Puerto Rico PANDO

Río Tahuamanu
Conquista Nueva
Río Manuripi Ethea

Río Madre de Dios Florencia

Río Manurini

Río San Matin *Río Madidi* Todos Santos

LA PAZ

Ixiamas

Map 2

Río Abuná
Río Mapirio
Río Orthón
San Pedro
Río Madre de Dios
Río B
Río

Yata

Las Palmas

Río Tuichi
Tumupasa Santa Rosa *Río Yo*

C

Puina
*Chaupi Orco
(6,044m)*
Queara
Lago Suches
Suches
Pelechuco
Antaquilla
Hichocolo
Ulla Ulla *Akamani*
Curva Hilo Hilo
Canisaya
Charazani *Iskanwaya*
Chuma Aucapata
Puerto

1

Río Amantala
*Parque
Nacional
Madidi*
Apolo
*Área Protegida
Apolobamba*
Aten
Río Atén
Río Camata
Río Llica
Consata

Río Mapiri

Mapiri

Guanay

2

Puerto
Salina
San
Buenaventura
Reyes
Rurrenabaque

Yucumo

Río Kaka
Río Alto Beni
Puerto
Linare Santa Ana

Río Tuichi

Puerto
Salina San Borja

El Po

3

Bolivia

BRAZIL

PERU

① Cobija
Riberalta
El Choro

Parque Nacional Madidi

Rurrenabaque
Mapiri
San Borja

Trinidad

④ inset
Parque Nacional Noel Kempff Mercado

Lago Titicaca
Sorata
Coroico
LA PAZ
Tihuanaco

Ascención
Concepción
Santa Ana
San Rafael

② Cochabamba
Oruro
Sajama

Parque Nacional Amboró
Samaipata
Santa Cruz de la Sierra

San José de Chiquitos
Puerto Suárez

Sucre

Potosí
Camiri

④

Salar de Uyuni
Uyuni
Chiguana
Tupiza
Tarija

③ Reserva de Fauna Andina Eduardo Avaroa

CHILE

PARAGUAY

ARGENTINA

N

0 km 100
0 miles 100

Altitude in metres
4000
3000
2000
1000
500
200
0
Neighbouring country

Paved road
Unpaved all weather road
Seasonal unpaved road, track
Railway
International border
Departmental border
Salt lake

Bolivia: regions

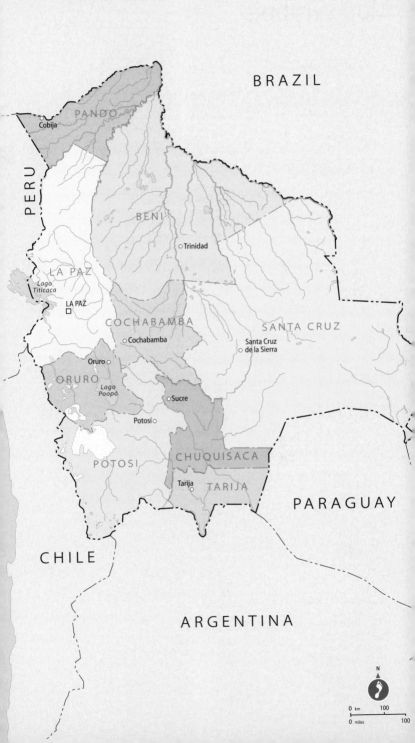

Map symbols

Administration

□ Capital city
○ Other city/town
International border
Regional border
Disputed border

Roads and travel

—— Main road (National highway)
—— Unpaved or *ripio* (gravel) road
---- 4WD track
.... Footpath
+■■ Railway with station
✈ Airport
🚌 Bus station
Ⓜ Metro station
---- Cable car
++++ Funicular
⛴ Ferry

Water features

River, canal
Lake, ocean
Seasonal marshland
Beach, sand bank
Waterfall

Topographical features

Contours (approx)
Mountain
Volcano
Mountain pass
Escarpment
Gorge
Glacier
Salt flat
Rocks

Cities and towns

Main through route
Main street
Minor street
Pedestrianized street

Ↄ Ⲥ Tunnel
→ One way street
||||||||| Steps
⩳ Bridge
▬▬▬ Fortified wall
Park, garden, stadium
● Sleeping
❶ Eating
⑪ Bars & clubs
☺ Entertainment
cp Casa particular
Building
▪ Sight
✝ Cathedral, church
☪ Chinese temple
🛕 Hindu temple
⚘ Meru
🕌 Mosque
△ Stupa
✡ Synagogue
🈺 Tourist office
🏛 Museum
✉ Post office
Ⓟ Police
Ⓢ Bank
@ Internet
♪ Telephone
🏪 Market
✚ Hospital
🅿 Parking
⛽ Petrol
⛳ Golf
Ⓐ Detail map
Ⓐ Related map

Other symbols

∴ Archaeological site
♦ National park, wildlife reserve
✿ Viewing point
▲ Campsite
⌂ Refuge, lodge
🏰 Castle
↘ Diving
🌲 Deciduous/coniferous/palm trees
🦌 Hide
🍇 Vineyard
⚗ Distillery
🚢 Shipwreck
✕ Historic battlefield

What the papers say...

"I carried the South American Handbook from Cape Horn to Cartagena and consulted it every night for two and a half months. I wouldn't do that for anything else except my hip flask."
Michael Palin, BBC Full Circle

"My favourite series is the Handbook series published by Footprint and I especially recommend the Mexico, Central and South America Handbooks."
Boston Globe

"If 'the essence of real travel' is what you have been secretly yearning for all these years, then Footprint are the guides for you."
Under 26 magazine

"Who should pack Footprint-readers who want to escape the crowd."
The Observer

"Footprint can be depended on for accurate travel information and for imparting a deep sense of respect for the lands and people they cover."
World News

"The guides for intelligent, independently-minded souls of any age or budget."
Indie Traveller

Mail order
Available worldwide in bookshops and on-line. Footprint travel guides can also be ordered directly from us in Bath, via our website www.footprintbooks.com or from the address on the imprint page of this book.

Complete title listing

Footprint publishes travel guides to over 150 destinations worldwide. Each guide is packed with practical, concise and colourful information for everybody from first-time travellers to travel aficionados. The list is growing fast and current titles are noted below.
Available from all good bookshops and online at www.footprintbooks.com

(P) denotes pocket guide

Latin America and Caribbean
Argentina
Barbados (P)
Bolivia
Brazil
Caribbean Islands
Central America & Mexico
Chile
Colombia
Costa Rica
Cuba
Cusco & the Inca Trail
Dominican Republic (P)
Ecuador & Galápagos
Guatemala
Havana (P)
Mexico
Nicaragua
Peru
Rio de Janeiro (P)
South American Handbook
St Lucia (P)
Venezuela

North America
Vancouver (P)
New York (P)
Western Canada

Africa
Cape Town (P)
East Africa
Libya
Marrakech (P)
Morocco
Namibia
South Africa
Tunisia
Uganda

Middle East
Dubai (P)
Egypt
Israel
Jordan
Syria & Lebanon

Australasia
Australia
East Coast Australia
New Zealand
Sydney (P)
West Coast Australia

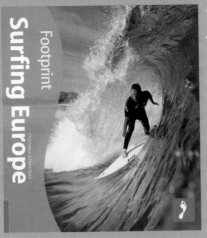